Special Edition
Using

MICROSOFT®
Office 97 with
Windows® 98

que®

Special Edition Using

MICROSOFT®
Office 97 with
Windows® 98

Ed Bott
Jim Boyce
Faithe Wempen

Special Edition Using Office 97 with Windows 98

Copyright© 1998 by Que® Corporation.

Library of Congress Catalog No.: 98-84583

ISBN: 0-7897-1661-5

First printing.

00 99 98   6 5 4 3 2 1

Interpretation of the printing code: The rightmost double-digit number is the year of the book's printing; the rightmost single-digit number, the number of the book's printing. For example, a printing code of 98-1 shows that the first printing of the book occurred in 1998.

Screen reproductions in this book were created using Collage Plus from Inner Media, Inc., Hollis, NH.

Composed in Century Old Style and ITC Franklin Gothic by Que Corporation.

EXECUTIVE EDITOR
Jim Minatel

ACQUISITIONS EDITOR
Jill Byus

MANAGING EDITOR
Thomas F. Hayes

TECHNICAL EDITOR
Vince Averello

COVER DESIGNER
Dan Armstrong

PRODUCTION TEAM
Brad Lenser
Sossity Smith

INDEXER
Cheryl Jackson

Contents at a Glance

Table of Contents

VI Outlook 98

VIII Advanced Topics

About the Authors

Faithe Wempen, M.A., operates Your Computer Friend, a computer training and trouble-shooting business in Indianapolis that specializes in helping beginning users with their PCs. Her eclectic writing credits include more than 20 computer books, including the best-selling *Microsoft Office Professional 6-in-1* and the *10 Minute Guide to Access*, plus articles, essays, poems, training manuals, and OEM documentation. Her hobbies include surfing the Internet, doing cross-stitch, being an active member of Broadway United Methodist Church in Indianapolis, and raising Shetland Sheepdogs.

Ed Bott is a best-selling author and award-winning computer journalist with more than 12 years experience in the personal computer industry. As senior contributing editor of *PC Computing* magazine, he is responsible for the magazine's extensive coverage of Windows 95/98, Windows NT, and Microsoft Office. From 1991 until 1993, he was editor of *PC Computing*, and for three years before that he was managing editor of *PC World* magazine. Ed has written eight books for Que Publishing.

Ed is a two-time winner of the Computer Press Award, most recently for PC Computing's annual edition of the Windows SuperGuide, published in 1997. Ed and co-author Woody Leonhard earned the prestigious Jesse H. Neal Award, sometimes referred to as "the Pulitzer Prize of the business press." He lives in Redmond, Washington, with his wife, Judy Merrill, and two incredibly smart and affectionate cats, Katy and Bianca.

Ty Belknap has been in the computer industry for over six years, working as a hardware technician, technical support advisor, and software support engineer. He helped launch the Windows 95 help desk for Microsoft, and vowed to "never do it again." He currently is a support engineer for a government agency in Washington State. He is spending his free time obtaining his MCSE, and currently holds MCPs in Windows 95 and Networking Essentials. Ty can be reached by e-mail at **wrldbuld@blarg.net**.

Elaine Betts, who wrote the Publisher section of this book, is a computer trainer, writer, web site designer, desktop publishing consultant, and sole proprietor of PC and MAConsultant ® in Denver Colorado. She collaborated on Que's *Word 97 Quick Reference Guide*. She also works as a product and food stylist in commercial photography and film, and is a certified English teacher. Visit her domain at **http://www.ebetts.com**.

Jim Boyce, the lead author for *Windows NT Installation and Configuration Handbook*, is a contributing editor and columnist for *WINDOWS* magazine and a regular contributor to other computer publications. He has been involved with computers since the late 1970s and has worked with computers as a user, programmer, and systems manager in a variety of capacities. He has a wide range of experience in the DOS, Windows, and UNIX environments. Jim has authored and co-authored more than two dozen books on computers and software.

Phil Callihan is the WAN Administrator at the National Center for Manufacturing Sciences (NCMS), a research and development consortium based in Ann Arbor, Michigan. Phil has six years' experience with Microsoft products and holds both the MSCE and MCT certifications from Microsoft. In addition to his employment at NCMS, he works as consultant and performs training in Microsoft Networking and Internet technologies. He is a 1993 graduate of the University of Michigan. Phil lives in Ann Arbor, Michigan with his wife Lisa and their dog Tribble. Phil can be reached on the Internet at philc@ncms.org and on his home page **http:// mis.ncms.org/philc/phil.htm**.

Read Gilgen is Director of Learning Support Services at the University of Wisconsin, Madison. He holds a Ph.D. in Latin American Literature. His professional interests include support of higher education, especially foreign language education. He has taught and written extensively on DOS, Windows, and WordPerfect since the early 1980s. He is author of Que's *Using WordPerfect for Windows Hot Tips*, contributing author to Que's *Special Edition Using WordPerfect*, and a frequent contributor to *WordPerfect for Windows* magazine.

Joe Habraken is a freelance writer and has served as an author, editor, curriculum designer, and software instructor during his career as a computer technology professional. Joe earned his MA in Communications from American University in Washington, D.C. Most recently he has written the *10 Minute Guide to Outlook 98* and *The Big Basics Book of the Internet, Second Editon*.

Curtis Knight is a Senior Quality Assurance Analyst, Technical Writer, and Technical Editor. Curtis lives in Vancouver, Washington. By day he works in Symantec Corporation's Beaverton, Oregon development site. At night he is a freelance writer and technical editor for Macmillan.

Curtis' overall computer industry experience includes MIS, Technical Support, Data Recovery, Quality Assurance, Technical Writing, and Technical Editing. Like most computer professionals, he is his family's personal computer consultant. He is currently training his 11-year-old son to take over the family consulting responsibilities.

Joe Kraynak has been writing and editing successful training manuals and computer books for over ten years. His long list of computer books include *The Complete Idiot's Guide to PCs*, *Microsoft Internet Explorer 3 Unleashed*, and *Windows 95 Cheat Sheet*. Joe has a Master's degree in English from Purdue University and a computer degree from the college of hard knocks.

George Lynch is a Microsoft Certified Professional and has written six computer books. George, Jesse, Cassill and Steve Ryan are partners in RTFM Consulting, Inc., a Microsoft Solution Provider company based in New York City that specializes in application development, training, and documentation.

Grant King is a software developer, author, and attorney who lives in Atlanta with his wife Nancy and daughter Elizabeth. He has been either the lead author or a contributing author on several books and articles relating to 32-bit Windows operating systems and software development. He also maintains *The Windows Mill*, a Web site devoted to news about Windows 95, Windows 98 and Windows NT. Grant received his B.A. from The University of the South and his J.D. from Georgia State University College of Law where he was graduated *magna cum laude*. His e-mail address is **ggking3@mindspring.com**.

Ron Person has written more than 20 books for Que Corporation, including the best-selling original editions of *Special Edition Using Microsoft Word 97* and *Special Edition Using Microsoft Excel 97*. He was lead author for the original editions of the best-selling *Special Edition Using Windows 95* and *Platinum Edition Using Windows 95*. He has an M.S. in Physics from The Ohio State University and an M.B.A. from Hardin-Simmons University. Ron was one of Microsoft's original Consulting Partners and Microsoft Solution Providers.

Patrice-Anne Rutledge is a computer consultant and author based in the San Francisco area. She writes frequently on a variety of topics including technology, business, and travel, and is the author or contributing author of 12 computer books on topics such as Microsoft Office and Microsoft FrontPage. As both an independent consultant and member of the IS team for leading international technology firms, Patrice has been involved in many aspects of computing including software development, systems analysis, and technical communications.

Liz Tasker currently works as a Senior User Interface Desginer at Hyperion Software Corporation, a company that specializes in developing client-server software applications. Her career includes twelve years in technical writing, nine years in software development, and five years in user interface design. She earned a Master of Arts degree in professional writing from Carnegie-Mellon University in 1990, and has received several awards in technical writing, including the Society of Technical Communications's International Award of Excellence in Technical Publication in 1992.

Nancy Warner is a private consultant in the computer and publishing arenas. She has written and contributed to numerous computer books, including *Platinum Edition Using Office 97*, *How to Use Access 97*, *How to Use Outlook 97*, and *How to Use Netscape Communicator*. She was graduated from Purdue University in Computer Information Systems, worked in computer and publishing positions, and is currently living in Arizona.

Introduction

What you're holding in your hands is one of the best values in computer books today. In a single volume, you'll find coverage of not only the most popular operating system in the world, but the best-selling application suite.

Windows 98 is the easiest, most powerful operating system ever. It combines the proven user-friendly interface introduced in Windows 95 with many powerful new tools designed to make Windows work seamlessly with the Internet. You'll also find new diagnostic tools, new networking enhancements, and support for dozens of the latest new technologies, including infrared systems, USB devices, and DVD drives.

Microsoft's Office application suite has a well-earned reputation as the king of the business-software industry. Word 97 includes hundreds of powerful features that enable even beginners to produce professional-quality documents. Business tools such as Excel and PowerPoint are everyday staples of office staff members all over the world, while Access provides the kind of data management power that satisfies the most demanding database programmers.

Who Should Use This Book

Anyone with at least a little bit of Windows and Office experience will feel right at home with this book. This book is not for the raw beginner learning to open menus or double-click the mouse. It doesn't explain the basics of writing a letter or entering numbers in a spreadsheet. Instead, it takes a leap into the most intriguing topics for business professionals, including how to automate tasks, use advanced productivity features, integrate Office and Windows with the Internet, and tie together applications to produce better work in less time.

How This Book is Organized

This Book contains eight parts, each dedicated to a specific application, or to special features common to several applciations. The following list presents an overview.

Part I, "Windows 98," explains the new features you'll find when upgrading from Windows 95. You'll learn about file management, adding and removing programs, customizing your desktop, and performing routine preventive maintenance on your system.

Part II, "Word 97," explains some of the most powerful and interesting features included in this top-notch word processor, including templates, styles, graphics, and tables. You'll learn how to create your own forms and use field codes, and how to prepare and perform a mail merge.

In Part III, "Excel 97," you'll learn how to work with entire sheets and workbooks, as well as named ranges. We'll delve into graph customization, forms, templates, and pivot tables. You'll even learn how to use Excel as a database.

Part IV, "PowerPoint 97," provides a whirlwind introduction to this state-of-the-art presentations program. You'll find out how to create active slides with animations, transitions, multimedia clips, and even hyperlinks for interactive Web viewing.

Part V, "Publisher 97," covers Microsoft Publisher, a desktop publishing program that comes with the Small Business Edition of Microsoft Office. You'll see how to use Publisher to create a marketing effort, complete with graphics and advanced formatting techniques.

Part VI, "Outlook 98," unveils the newest version of Microsoft's comprehensive scheduling, contact management, and e-mail utility. We'll explore configuring Outlook to replace Outlook Express as your e-mail reader, scheduling reminders of your important meetings, and managing an address book of contacts.

In Part VII, "Internet Explorer 4.0," you'll tackle the World Wide Web. You'll learn how to browse the Internet with IE4, and how to find and save information. You'll also find out about Web subscriptions and the Active Desktop, two important enhancements that come with Windows 98. We finish off the part by showing you how to create and publish your own Web pages using Office 97 and Internet Explorer.

The final part, "Advanced Topics," contains a fascinating array of chapters on some of the hottest topics in computing today. You'll find out how to ensure Internet security, how to build compound documents that employ data from multiple Office applications, how to share and secure Office data, and how to manage document version in a team computing environment.

Conventions Used In This Book

Special conventions are used to help you get the most from this book and from Windows and Office.

Various typefaces in this book identify terms and other special objects. These special typefaces include the following:

Type	Meaning
Italics	New terms or phrases when initially defined; functions and variables
<u>Underline</u>	Menu and dialog box options that appear underlined onscreen, indicating hotkeys
Boldface	Information you type

You'll find some text in all uppercase. Typically, this is used to indicate Excel objects such as functions and cell references. File names are initial-capped only as they generally appear in Windows.

Key combinations are represented with a plus sign. For example, if you should press two keys at the same time, such as Ctrl, Alt, and Delete, they appear like this: Ctrl+Alt+Delete.

If you should press keys or issue commands in succession, they are separated by commas. For example, to display the Open dialog box in a program, you might press Alt, F, O—that is, press and release Alt, press and release F, and then press and release O.

N O T E Notes such as this one offer additional information about the current topic and serve to supplement the material in the main body of the section.

T I P Tips suggest alternate methods for accomplishing a task or additional information that will help you get the most out of a feature in Office or Windows.

CAUTION

A caution such as this one points out actions that might have undesirable consequences. If we suggested you invoke the Fdisk program from a command prompt, for example, you can be sure we'd include a caution that it could wipe out all the data on your hard disk if you used it improperly.

Scattered throughout the book you'll find references to Web sites that supplement the material discussed in the chapter:

ON THE WEB

Update for home users:

http://www.microsoft.com/win98

You'll also find cross-references to other chapters along the way, or to sections in the same chapter. These point you to information that is related to or supplements the topic being discussed. The cross-reference information contains the name of the section and page number where the information appears, like this:

▶ **See** "Hacking into Secure Government Systems," **page xxx**

Windows 98

What's New in Windows 98

by Ed Bott

In this chapter

Faster, Smarter, Easier: Architectural Improvements in Windows 98

Walk up to a computer running Windows 98 and you'll be hard-pressed to distinguish between it and a PC running Windows 95 with Internet Explorer 4.0. When you work with Windows 98 for even a few minutes, though, you'll *feel* the difference.

Only three years passed between the first release of Windows 95 and the debut of Windows 98, but it might as well have been a millennium as far as personal computer users are concerned. CPUs are up to 10 times faster and cost one-third what they used to. Gigabytes of storage and gobs of RAM are commonplace. Practically everyone has e-mail. There are literally tens of thousands of applications that let you work and play on a Windows PC.

And, of course, there's the Internet. In 1995, the World Wide Web was still brand new, and the Internet was a gathering place for hard-core techies. Today, you can't pass a billboard or switch on a television without seeing a Web address, and the Internet has become the defining technology of our time.

Taken together, those two changes define Windows 98. Because Internet Explorer 4.0 is tightly integrated into Windows 98, you won't need to install any additional software to access the World Wide Web. And Windows 98 also does a superb job of getting the most out of all the new types of hardware and software that have been released since 1995. Yes, this is an upgrade to Windows 95, but the list of significant improvements seems endless:

- Windows 98 is the ultimate maintenance release: It includes more than 150 updates, bug fixes, and usability tweaks to the original Windows 95 code. These were originally included in service packs and downloadable patches from Microsoft.

- In all, you'll find drivers for more than 1200 new devices in Windows 98, and virtually all of them support Plug and Play for simplified setup. Some categories of supported hardware didn't even exist when Windows 95 first hit store shelves. Most significant of all are peripherals that use the Universal Serial Bus (USB). You can plug just about any type of device into a USB port, including mouse devices and keyboards, modems, scanners, digital cameras, speakers, telephones, and more. The technology makes your PC incredibly more flexible while doing away with the need for serial and parallel ports, IRQs, and other configuration hassles.

- Whether you upgrade an existing copy of Windows 95 or install the operating system on a new PC, you'll notice significant changes in Windows 98. The new Setup program is dramatically streamlined compared with the Windows 95 equivalent. You'll answer a few questions at the start, and then, because it's capable of restarting automatically, the setup program will run unattended.

N O T E See Appendix A, "Installing and Updating Windows 98" for detailed instructions on upgrading to Windows 98 and making sure you have the most recent version. ■

- Windows 98 is generally faster overall, although you may notice some tasks that take longer than they would on the same system running Windows 95. Startup and shutdown should go more quickly, especially on new systems. Most of the key system files, including networking components such as Windows Sockets services and TCP/IP, have also been tuned for performance. On large networks, you'll notice new options, including support for Point-to-Point Tunneling Protocol and NetWare Directory Services.

- One of the most significant weaknesses in the original retail release of Windows 95 was its dependence on the old 16-bit FAT format. That restriction becomes particularly painful when you add a hard drive greater than 2G, because FAT16 forces you to create multiple partitions that waste huge amounts of space. Microsoft fixed those problems with the introduction of the FAT32 disk format in OEM Service Release 2 of Windows 95. Windows 98 adds a major new tool that you need when upgrading: a utility that quickly converts your existing data to the new format.

- Notebook users will see improved power-management features, enhancements in the way Windows works with PC Cards, and support for the latest infrared devices.

- And if you have a dial-up Internet connection, you'll find substantial improvements in Dial-Up Networking features, including a simplified wizard for creating connections and support for multilink connections, which use two phone lines for faster data transfers.

▶ **See** "Establishing a Dial-Up Connection," **page 827**

How Windows and the Web Work Together

If you've grown accustomed to the Windows 95 interface, you'll see some changes in Windows 98. The Windows Desktop Update, first introduced with Internet Explorer 4.0 and standard in Windows 98, adds hundreds of improvements to the tools and techniques you use to manage files, folders, and programs in Windows. Most of the changes are simple refinements, but if you're willing to turn on some of the new options, you can radically change the way Windows works.

▶ **See** "Introducing the Windows Desktop Update," **page 14**

You'll notice a new Quick Launch toolbar just to the right of the Start button, for example. You can add your own shortcuts here to make it easier to get started with your favorite programs. The Start menu is also improved; most notably, you can now reorganize items on the Programs menu by dragging them directly from one place to another.

Windows 95 used the Windows Explorer for file management and a separate Internet Explorer for Web browsing. Internet Explorer brought the two Explorers into a single window, and Windows 98 incorporates that feature. If you prefer to browse files and folders using the single-click navigation techniques of Internet Explorer, you can configure Windows to work that way. And you can view any or all your folders using HTML templates, so that they look and act like Web pages.

▶ **See** "Managing Files Using Web View," **page 69**

When you use Windows 98, you'll have ready access to the Web. There's a new Favorites option on the Start menu, which lets you jump quickly to favorite Web sites. And if you turn on the Active Desktop, you can embed live HTML components (such as news or stock-quote tickers) or even entire Web pages on the Windows desktop.

▶ **See** "Web Subscriptions and the Active Desktop," **page 903**

A New Way to Explore the Internet

If you've used Netscape Navigator or previous versions of Internet Explorer, you're already familiar with the basic concepts of Web browsing. Windows 98 includes the full suite of Internet applications Microsoft introduced with Internet Explorer 4.0. There's much more than just a Web browser.

Internet Explorer 4.0: Offline Browsing and Web Subscriptions

The single biggest objection to the Internet (at least from users with ordinary dial-up connections) is that it's too slow. IE4 addresses that concern by letting you set up Web subscriptions, which you can use to download individual pages or entire Web sites at regular intervals. Then, when you tell IE4 you'd like to work offline, you can browse the stored pages without dialing up and waiting for them to download.

You'll find it easier to find information on the Internet with IE4, and its tools allow you to organize that information more intelligently, too.

▶ **See** "Web Browsing with IE 4," **page 857**

Stay in Touch with Outlook Express Mail and News

With Windows 98, Microsoft officially replaces the Windows 95-vintage Exchange Inbox with a new, Internet-standard e-mail program called Outlook Express. The new mail-client software is easy to set up, easy to use, and easy to customize. If you receive large volumes of e-mail, you'll appreciate the Inbox Assistant, which lets you define rules that the software uses to automatically manage messages for you. Outlook Express also acts as a reader for accessing Internet news servers, like those that offer support for Microsoft products.

Web Editing and Publishing Tools

Windows 98 won't let you set up a Web site that can compete with Yahoo!, but it does include basic tools you can use to create Web pages. FrontPage Express is a graphical Web-page editor that incorporates a subset of the features in Microsoft's award-winning FrontPage program.

An Operating System That Maintains Itself

Maintaining the health of your PC is like visiting the dentist—even highly motivated PC users do irksome maintenance chores less often than they should. Windows 98 can't supply extra motivation, but it does include software that automates some of the more unpleasant tasks. Most notable is the Tune-Up Wizard, which regularly scans local hard disks for errors, defragments disks, and cleans up unneeded files—all without requiring you to do any work.

And if you've ever tried to troubleshoot a hardware or software problem using Windows 95, you've experienced information overload. With Windows 98, you'll find a new System Information tool that consolidates a wealth of data—about system resources, hardware, components, and running tasks—in a single location. This well-organized window is also a launching pad for other troubleshooting tools, such as the System File Checker, which undoes the damage when a crucial file becomes corrupted, or the Registry Checker, which automatically backs up your database of system settings for quick recovery in the event of trouble. And whenever Microsoft issues a Windows patch, you can install it automatically by clicking the Windows Update icon.

▶ **See** "Maintaining and Troubleshooting Your System," **page 149**

Windows 98 at Home

If you've installed Windows 98 at home, you're probably expecting your PC to work hard and play hard. For game players, there's DirectX5 technology and MMX support, two technologies that make multimedia more appealing. The broadcast architecture components let you watch TV on your PC (if you have compatible hardware, of course).

Are you concerned about setting up a single PC that every member of the family can use? The Family Logon option lets you create custom desktops for everyone, and you can use IE4's Content Advisor to block access to Web sites that contain violence, pornography, or other undesirable material.

Windows 98 in the Office

In a corporate setting, you're most likely to be concerned with getting Windows 98 to work smoothly with an existing network. From an administrator's viewpoint, Windows 98 doesn't look dramatically different from Windows 95, although it's smoother in operation. You'll find support for many more network cards, for example, and it's easier to connect with Windows NT or NetWare networks. It's also easier to configure a TCP/IP connection (the default protocol in Windows 98) than it used to be. ●

An Overview of the Windows Interface

by Ed Bott

In this chapter

Introducing the Windows Desktop Update

When Microsoft first introduced Internet Explorer 4.0, it didn't just create a Web browser—the complete IE4 package included an optional component called the Windows Desktop Update that made radical changes in the interface that debuted in the original version of Windows 95.

With Windows 98, the Windows Desktop Update is no longer an option, but instead is an integral part of the new operating system. If you're familiar with the original Windows 95 interface and haven't previously used IE4, you'll notice the following interface changes when you install Windows 98:

- An enhanced taskbar, which includes a new Quick Launch toolbar, and changes the way taskbar buttons work.
- An enhanced Start menu, with a new menu item for Web Favorites, plus new options on the Find menu; it also gives you the capability to edit or rearrange program shortcuts directly.
- New folder and desktop options, including a choice of single-click or double-click navigation.
- Many, many small improvements to the original Windows interface, which collectively make file management more productive.
- The Web View option lets you display the contents of drives and folders as part of a customizable Web page.
- The optional Active Desktop setting lets you add Web pages and HTML components to the Windows desktop.

N O T E Because the names are so similar, it's easy to confuse the Windows Desktop Update and the Active Desktop. In fact, even some Microsoft marketing pieces use the two names interchangeably. The two are not the same, however; in fact, the Active Desktop is one small part of the Windows Desktop Update. You'll find detailed information about the Active Desktop in Chapter 43, "Web Subscriptions and the Active Desktop." ▪

Classic or Web? Choosing a Navigation Style

With the Windows Desktop Update installed, you have several important interface choices to make. To see the available options, open My Computer or an Explorer window and choose View, Folder Options. On the General tab, you'll see the dialog box shown in Figure 2.1.

Figure 2.1

Choose your interface—
the Classic Windows 95
style, one that
resembles a Web
browser, or a combina-
tion of the two.

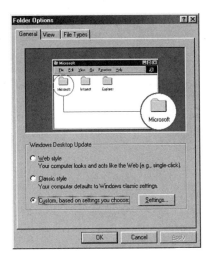

TROUBLESHOOTING

You've opened Explorer, but you can't find the Folder Options choice on the View menu. You're
probably viewing a Web page in the Explorer window, in which case the View menu offers an Internet
Options choice instead. Click in the address bar, type **C:**, and press Enter. You should now be able to
select Folder Options.

Choose one of the following three interface options:

■ Web style sets the Windows desktop and folder options to resemble your Web browser.
   Icons are underlined, like hyperlinks on a Web page. You point at icons to select them
   and click to open folders and launch programs.

▶ **See** "Using an HTML Page as Your Desktop," **page 905**

■ Classic style resembles the original Windows 95 interface. You single-click to select
   icons and double-click to open folders and launch programs.

■ Custom lets you mix and match interface options. After you choose this option, click the
   Settings button to choose from four options in the Custom Settings dialog box shown in
   Figure 2.2.

Although the Custom Settings dialog box looks daunting, it follows a simple organization. Each of the
four options includes two choices. If you choose the top item in each list, you end up with Web style;
choose the bottom option in all four cases and you end up with Classic style.

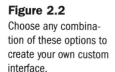

Figure 2.2
Choose any combination of these options to create your own custom interface.

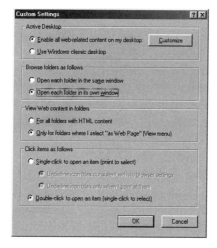

Turning on the Active Desktop

Choosing the option labeled Enable all web-related content on my desktop has the same effect as checking the Active Desktop's View As Web Page option. Clicking the Customize button has the same effect as opening the Display Properties dialog box and clicking the Web tab. Choosing Use Windows classic desktop turns off the Active Desktop.

▶ **See** "Web Subscriptions and the Active Desktop," **page 903**

Choosing a Browsing Style

In the Classic Windows interface (open each folder in its own window), the original window remains open when you display the contents of a new drive or folder; if you drill down through multiple folders and subfolders, you'll end up with a screen full of windows. Choose Open Each Folder in the Same Window to display the contents of each new drive or folder in the same window you started with, replacing the previous contents.

▶ **See** "Two Views of Windows Explorer," **page 22**

Viewing Web Content in Folders

Thanks to the Windows Desktop Update, Explorer lets you view any folder as a Web page, using a standard folder template or a custom HTML page you create. Web view adds a banner to the top left side of the folder window and an info pane below it; the file list appears on the right side of the window. Choose the top option to use Web view with all folders; the bottom option lets you selectively turn on Web view.

N O T E   For a full discussion of Web view, including details on how to create your own custom HTML folder templates, see Chapter 5, "Managing Files Using Web View." ▪

Single-Click or Double-Click?

The most important interface choice you'll make is how you use the mouse to select icons and open folders or launch programs. By default, Windows 98 takes a conservative approach, preserving the familiar double-click style introduced in the original Windows 95 interface. To change this option, choose Web style or open the Custom Settings dialog box and choose Single-click to Open an Item (point to select). The first time you choose this option, you'll see a warning dialog box like the one shown in Figure 2.3.

Part

I

Ch

2

Figure 2.3

Because the single-click interface is a radical change, Windows asks you to confirm your choice when you first select it.

Why the warning? Because when you choose the Web-style interface, you change the way Windows handles some of its most basic tasks. The following table offers a side-by-side comparison of how you deal with files and folders using the two navigation styles.

Task	Web style	Classic style
Select an icon.	Point to the icon.	Click the icon.
Open an icon.	Click the icon.	Double-click the icon.
Select a group of adjacent icons.	Point to the first icon, then hold down the Shift key and point to the last icon.	Click the first icon, then hold down the Shift key and click the last icon.
Select multiple icons.	Hold down the Ctrl key and point to individual icons.	Hold down the Ctrl key and click individual icons.
Drag and drop.	Point to an icon, press and hold down mouse button, and drag icon to new location (same as Classic style).	Point to an icon, press and hold down mouse button, and drag icon to new location.

TROUBLESHOOTING

You've chosen the single-click option, but Windows ignores you when you adjust the option to underline icons only when you point at them. When you choose the single-click option in the Custom Settings dialog box, you also have the choice to underline all icon titles, just as Internet Explorer does, or to underline icons only when you point at them. If you've selected the top choice in all four Custom options, Windows shifts your choice to Web style and ignores your underlining preferences. The only way to force Explorer to accept this change is to select the bottom (Classic) choice in one of the first three options in this dialog box.

Customizing Other Folder Options

Installing the Windows Desktop Update adds an assortment group of advanced folder options as well. To adjust these settings, choose View, Folder Options, and click the View tab; you'll see a series of items in the bottom of the dialog box, as shown in Figure 2.4.

Figure 2.4
These are the default settings for advanced folder options.

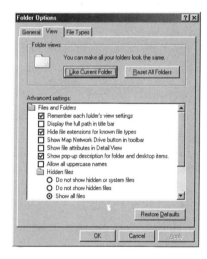

The following table lists the effect of each of these settings:

Option	Effect When Checked
Remember each folder's view settings.	Saves the icon view of folder windows; also saves size and position when using multi-window browsing option. Does not apply to two-pane Explorer windows.
Display the full path in title bar.	Shows full DOS-style path (for example, C:\Windows\System) in folder windows. Handy when comparing subfolders with identical names in different parts of Explorer tree.
Hide file extensions for known file types.	Uncheck this box to show all file extensions, even when file type is registered.
Show Map Network Drive button in toolbar.	Adds two buttons to Standard toolbar; check if you regularly assign drive letters to shared network folders.
Show file attributes in Detail View.	Adds a column at the far right of Details view.
Show pop-up description for folder and desktop items.	Displays ScreenTips when you point to My Computer and other desktop items; experienced users should uncheck this box.
Allow all-uppercase names.	Normally, Windows capitalizes only the first letter of all file names (for example, Abc); uncheck this box to allow file and folder names such as ABC.
Hidden files.	Select whether to display hidden and/or system files.

▶ **See** "Changing the Way a Folder's Contents Appear," **page 28**

Part

I

Ch

2

Managing Files with My Computer and Windows Explorer

by Ed Bott

In this chapter

Two Views of Windows Explorer

The most basic building block of Windows is the icon. Every object you work with has its own icon—files and folders, drives and network servers, programs, printers, and shortcuts to Web pages. Program icons are as distinctive as product logos, data files use standard icons that help you group related files easily, and system objects use icons that are intended to illustrate their main function. And they're all organized into folders and subfolders in a strict hierarchy.

Whenever you view or manage icons and folders, you use a program called the Windows Explorer in one of its two views. Right-click a drive or folder icon, and shortcut menus let you choose between the two faces of Explorer: Click Open, and the contents of the drive or folder you selected appear in a simple window; choose Explore, and you see a more complex view, with one pane that shows all the resources available to you and another that displays the selected folder's contents. Once they learn how Explorer works, most Windows users will incorporate both views as part of their working style.

Viewing Resources in My Computer

For a simple, uncluttered view of all the resources on your computer, find the My Computer icon on the desktop and open this window. The resulting display will look something like the one shown in Figure 3.1.

Figure 3.1
The My Computer window offers a simple way to view local resources, including drives, printers, and other hardware.

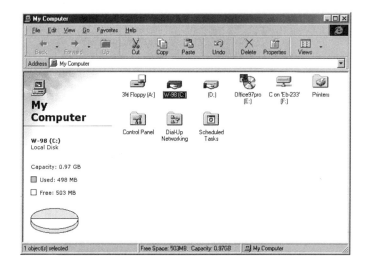

Microsoft's interface designers created My Computer as the primary file-management interface for novice users, but even Windows experts will find it ideally suited for some file management tasks. Because the My Computer window displays the amount of free disk space, for example, it's a convenient way to see at a glance how much total storage is available on your system.

T I P To see the maximum amount of information about drives in the My Computer window, choose View, Details. Click the Free Space heading to sort drives in order of available storage space.

Browsing the Contents of a Folder

Unlike the Windows Explorer, which shows you the outline-style hierarchy of all drives and folders on your system, starting with the My Computer window shows you the contents of one folder at a time. To view the contents of drives and folders from the My Computer window, open a drive icon, then a folder within that drive, then a folder within that folder. Keep drilling down in this fashion until you find the folder you're looking for.

The easiest way to go back up through the hierarchy of folders is to press the Backspace key, or to click the Up button on the Standard toolbar. (If the toolbar is hidden, choose View, Toolbars, Standard Buttons to make it visible.)

What happens to the current folder window when you open a drive or folder icon by starting with the My Computer window? If you've chosen Web style, the contents of the folder you selected replace the contents of the current window, so you're always working with a single window. If you've selected Classic style, on the other hand, the My Computer window remains open and a new drive or folder window appears. For each folder you open, you'll see a new folder window, as in Figure 3.2.

Figure 3.2
Opening a folder window shows this simple view of the folder's contents.

Up button

Using the multiple-window option results in unnecessary and confusing clutter when you delve several folders deep. But sometimes you want to open two or more windows at once so you can move or copy icons from one folder to another. Windows lets you specify whether each new

Part

I

Ch

3

folder uses the same window or opens in a separate window. To adjust the default behavior of folder windows, you must use the Custom settings in the Windows Desktop Update.

▶ **See** "Customizing Other Folder Options," **page 18**

The settings you choose in the Folder Options dialog box will determine whether new folder windows replace the current window or open a new one. You can also hold down the Ctrl key and double-click a folder or drive icon to override this default setting at any time. If you've chosen the single-window option, this procedure will open a new window; if you normally open a new window, this technique will replace the contents of the current window. Note that this option requires you to hold down Ctrl and double-click even if you've chosen the Web-style single-click option.

N O T E   When you view the contents of a floppy disk, Windows will not automatically update the display when you change disks. Likewise, if another user adds, renames, or deletes files in a shared network folder, these changes do not automatically appear in an open window on your system. Under these conditions, you need to *refresh* the display to see the most up-to-date contents. In the Windows Explorer, point to the icon for the drive or folder and click to refresh the window. You can also choose View, Refresh, or press F5. ▪

Using Windows Explorer to View Files and Folders

When you right-click a drive or folder icon and choose Explore from the shortcut menu, Windows opens the two-paned view of Explorer, with a tree-style All Folders pane on the left and a contents pane on the right. The title bar begins with the word *Exploring*, followed by the currently selected drive or folder. As the example in Figure 3.3 shows, the left pane includes every available resource, including local and network drives, system folders, and even Internet shortcuts.

 There are many ways to open the Windows Explorer. Here are some common ones—open the Start menu and choose Programs, Windows Explorer; right-click the Start button or the My Computer icon and choose Explore; type **Explorer** in the Run dialog box or at an MS-DOS Prompt; create a shortcut on the desktop or on the Quick Launch bar.

As noted earlier, the two-paned Explorer uses the same program code as the single-pane folder window, adding only the All Folders pane. When you use the Explore command to open a new window, you can show or hide this pane by choosing View, Explorer Bar, All Folders. This technique lets you quickly switch between Internet pages, folder windows, and Explorer windows. Curiously, if you start with a folder window or by opening an Internet shortcut, the All Folders pane is not available.

Figure 3.3
The Windows Explorer uses these two panes to let you quickly navigate through local, network, and Internet resources.

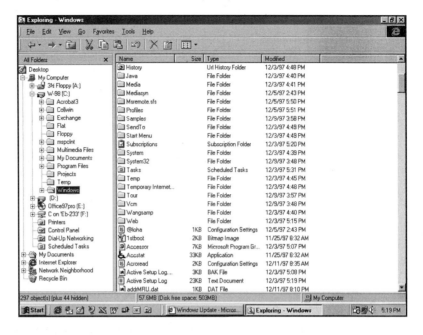

Understanding the Explorer Hierarchy

When you use the two-pane Explorer view, it's easy to see the organization of drives, folders, and system resources in the left-hand All Folders bar. If the Address bar is visible, you can see a compact version of the same tree in a folder window. Click the arrow at the right of the Address bar to see a drop-down list like the one in Figure 3.4.

Figure 3.4
The Address bar lets you jump to different drives or system folders even when the All Folders pane is hidden.

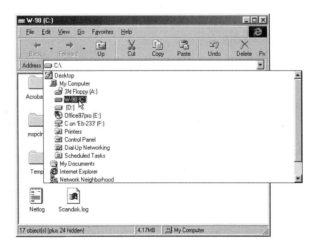

Part

I

Ch

3

If you've used MS-DOS or earlier versions of Windows, the hierarchy of a local drive is easy to understand: Each drive can contain one or more folders, starting with the root folder. Windows and Windows applications create folders to store program and data files, and you can create folders within folders to keep your files organized. In the case of data and program files, folders and subfolders are directly equivalent to MS-DOS directories and subdirectories.

But Windows also uses folders to display objects that do not correspond to directories on a hard disk. Look at the All Folders pane or the drop-down list in the Address bar and you'll see that Explorer organizes available resources using a consistent hierarchy. The Desktop icon is always at the top of the list. It includes the following objects:

- *My Computer* displays icons for all local drives, any shared network drives that have been mapped to a drive letter, and the Printers, Control Panel, Scheduled Tasks, and Dial-Up Networking folders.
- *Network Neighborhood* shows icons for all servers and workstations in your network.
- *Internet Explorer* displays shortcuts for Web pages you've added to the Active Desktop, as well as pages you've browsed recently.
- *Recycle Bin* shows files you've deleted recently.
- *My Documents* points to the folder where you store personal documents. On a single-user system, this is C:\My Documents will be default; on a system where you've set up multiple user profiles, this folder will be elsewhere.
- Any folders you create on the desktop appear at the bottom of the All Folders pane and the drop-down Address list.

 If you have set up custom profiles for individual users of your computer, you can create folders, files, and shortcuts that appear on the desktop or Start menu. You'll find the All Users folder within the Windows folder; any objects you create in the Desktop or Start Menu folders here will be visible to anyone who logs on to the computer.

Using Explorer Menus and Toolbars

When you browse files and folders using Explorer, you have access to a consistent set of menus and toolbar buttons. When you select system folders, additional menu choices and buttons appear to reflect special options available in those folders. For example, when you view the contents of the Subscriptions folder, two new toolbar buttons let you update subscriptions, while Briefcase folders add menu choices and toolbar buttons that let you synchronize files.

Navigating Through the Explorer Hierarchy

With the help of the Windows Explorer, it's easy to display the contents of any drive or folder. When you click an icon in the All Folders pane, the contents of that folder appear in the right-hand pane.

By default, each branch of the tree-style listing in the All Folders pane is collapsed when you first open the two-pane Explorer view—all you see are the top-level icons for drives and system folders. A plus sign to the left of an icon means there are additional folders beneath it; click the plus sign to expand that branch and see additional folders. When you expand the folder listing, the plus sign turns to a minus sign; click to collapse that branch again. Figure 3.5 shows a typical display, with the contents of the Accessories folder visible in the right-hand pane.

Figure 3.5
Click the plus sign to expand a branch of the tree; click the minus sign to collapse the listing again.

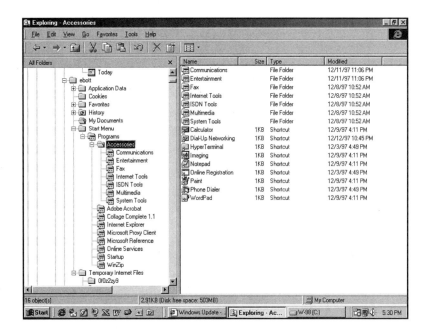

Part
I

Ch
3

TROUBLESHOOTING

You see a plus sign to the left of a drive icon, but when you click the icon, the plus sign disappears. Windows is behaving exactly as designed. When you first open the two-pane Explorer view, Windows checks the contents of all local hard drives and adds the plus sign when it detects subfolders; however, it does not automatically check for subfolders on removable drives (such as floppy disks) or network connections, because doing so might slow down the performance of your system. Instead, it places the plus sign next to each of those icons and waits until you select the icon before checking to see whether there really are any subfolders. If there are none, it removes the plus sign, as you've seen.

To display the contents of a different folder, select its icon in the All Folders pane. As you move from folder to folder, you can use the Back and Forward buttons to quickly return to folders you visited previously.

You can also use the keyboard to navigate through file and folder listings in Explorer. Here's a partial listing of useful keyboard shortcuts:

- Use the Tab key (or F6) to move from pane to pane; as you press Tab, the selection moves from the All Folders pane to the Contents pane, to the Address bar, then back to the All Folders pane, and so on.
- When the focus is in the All Folders pane, pressing the up and down arrows moves through the list of folders, without expanding collapsed branches. The contents of the selected icon automatically appear in the right-hand pane as you move through the list.
- To move to the parent of the currently selected folder, press the Backspace key.
- To expand a collapsed folder, select its icon and press the right arrow key or the plus (+) key on the numeric keypad. Use the minus (-) key on the numeric keypad to collapse a branch.
- To quickly move to the Address bar and open the drop-down list of top-level icons, press F4.
- Press the star (*) key on the numeric keypad to expand all branches of the currently selected icon.

CAUTION

Be careful when using this shortcut! Pressing the * key when the Desktop or Network Neighborhood icon is selected may result in extremely long delays as Explorer checks the contents of every available network drive.

Changing the Way a Folder's Contents Appear

Display options let you control how icons appear in an Explorer window. You can choose the size, arrangement, and order of icons, and you can also specify whether Explorer should show or hide system files. All of the options described in this section work the same in folder windows or in the right-hand contents pane of Windows Explorer.

Icons, List, or Details: Choosing a View

Windows lets you choose from four different arrangements of icons when displaying the contents of a folder. Each view has advantages and disadvantages under different circumstances. To apply a new view to the folder currently displayed, choose View, then select one of the following choices:

- *Large Icons* view uses full-sized icons (32 pixels on each side), which let you easily distinguish between different types of icons. Labels appear along the bottom of each icon. You can position icons anywhere within the folder. This view is most practical for folders that contain few icons, such as My Computer; it's an impractical choice when you want to find a small number of files in a folder that contains hundreds of icons.

- *Small Icons* view displays icons that are one-fourth the size of those in the Large Icons view (16 pixels on each side); labels appear to the right of each icon. Initially, Small Icons view arranges icons in rows from left to right, but you can move icons anywhere within the folder. This view is useful when you want to select a large number of icons in one motion.

- *List* view uses the same size icons and labels as Small Icons view. In List view, however, Windows arranges icons in columns, starting at the top left of the contents window; when the column reaches the bottom of the window, Windows starts a new column to the right. You cannot rearrange the position of icons in this view.

- Use *Details* view to see maximum information about objects in any window. From left to right, each row in this view includes the file icon, name, size, type, and the date the file was last modified. Note that these details change slightly for different types of windows; the My Computer window, for example, shows the total size and amount of free space in place of the last two columns. You cannot move or reposition icons in Details view.

TIP
The Views button on the Standard toolbar lets you cycle through all four views of the current folder. Each time you click, the view changes to the next option. Use the drop-down arrow at the right of the Views button to choose a view.

Part

I

Ch

3

Arranging File and Folder Icons

When you use either Large Icons or Small Icons view, Windows lets you move icons anywhere within the folder. You can cluster your favorite icons in one location and move the others to a far corner, for example, or just rearrange the order in which the icons appear. Two options let you control the arrangement of icons within a folder.

If you prefer to have all your icons lined up neatly at all times, choose View, Arrange Icons, Auto Arrange. A check mark appears next to this menu choice to indicate that it is in use with the current folder. You can still move icons into any order you wish, but other icons will shift position to make room for the icons you move. When you resize a folder window with this option turned on, the rows of icons will automatically reposition so that you can see them properly within the window.

If you prefer to arrange icons yourself but want them to snap to position along an imaginary grid, rearrange the icons and then choose View, Line Up Icons. This option allows you to leave empty spaces within the folder window, and if you resize the window, some icons may no longer be visible—you'll need to use the scroll bars to move them into view.

CAUTION

These icon-arranging options apply to the Windows desktop as well. Right-click any empty desktop area and choose Line Up Icons to straighten up the display of icons on the desktop. Avoid checking the Auto Arrange option on the Windows desktop, however. Most users prefer to position desktop icons in predictable

continues

continued

locations; letting Windows automatically arrange desktop icons lines them up in columns, from top to bottom and left to right, without regard for wallpaper and Active Desktop items. That can make it difficult to work with desktop icons.

Sorting Files and Folders

Windows lets you sort the contents of any folder using one of four menu choices. These options work the same in folder windows and in the contents pane of an Explorer window. To sort files within a folder, follow these steps:

1. Display the contents of the folder.

2. Choose View, Arrange Icons from the pull-down menus, or right-click in any empty space within the contents pane and choose Arrange Icons from the shortcut menu.

3. Choose one of the following options from the submenu:

    - **by Name** Sorts in ascending alphabetical order by file name, with folders grouped at the top of the list.

    - **by Type** Sorts in ascending alphabetical order by file type (note that this does not sort by file extension; Windows uses the registered name of the File Type to determine sort order).

    - **by Size** Sorts folders first in ascending alphabetical order by name, then arranges files by size, with smallest files at the top of the list.

    - **by Date** Sorts folders by date, in descending order, then sorts files the same way; in both cases, newest files appear at top of list.

By far the easiest way to sort files and folders is to switch to Details view. When you click the column headings in Details view, Windows sorts the folder's contents by the column you selected. Click again to sort in reverse order—something you cannot do in any other view.

Saving Folder Display Options

When you use the two-pane Windows Explorer, the view options you choose apply to all folders you display in the contents pane. If you choose Large Icons view for one folder, all folders will adopt that view until you choose a different view.

When you use folder windows, however, Windows lets you save separate view options for each folder. As you move from folder to folder, the view will change to reflect the settings you last used. If you prefer to set all folder windows to a single view, follow these steps:

1. Open any folder window and choose View. Select Large Icons, Small Icons, List, or Details. If you want to use Web View for all folders, choose View, as Web Page.

2. Choose View, Folder Options, and click the View tab. You'll see the dialog box shown in Figure 3.6.

Figure 3.6

Choose a view you want to use for all folder windows and apply it here.

3. In the box labeled Folder views, click the button labeled Like Current Folder.

4. When you see the confirmation dialog box, click Yes.

5. Click OK to save your changes.

Note that using this option does not save the sort order of windows, nor does it save toolbar settings.

To restore folder windows to their default view settings, choose View, Folder Options, click the View tab, and click the button labeled Reset All Folders. This will restore the My Computer, Control Panel, Fonts, and other system folders to their default Large Icons view.

Part
I

Ch
3

Displaying or Hiding Different File Types

Files and folders created under MS-DOS or Windows allow you to set four special attributes. These settings allow you to prevent inadvertent damage to important files. To see the attributes for a given file or folder, select its icon and choose Properties from the shortcut menu. Click the General tab to see the current settings for the following four attributes:

Attribute	Description
Read-only	Prevents changes to files and folders with this attribute set. Note that setting a folder's read-only attribute does not prevent changes to files in that folder.
Hidden	Prevents the display of files using Windows Explorer or MS-DOS DIR command.
Archive	If this attribute is checked, the file has been changed since it was last backed up. The MS-DOS XCOPY command and most backup programs use the Archive attributes to perform partial backups.
System	Prevents the display of files and folders required by the system.

N O T E Windows 98 sets the read-only attribute on a number of system folders, including the Windows and My Documents folders.

For the most part, Windows and Windows applications will adjust file attributes automatically. The one circumstance under which you might want to manually adjust file attributes is to set a crucial workgroup file as read-only.

CAUTION

Setting the Read-only or System attribute for an object doesn't make it impossible to delete that file or folder; it only adds a warning dialog box to the process. If the file is truly important, make sure you have a backup copy stored in a safe location.

Windows hides a tremendous number of files by default. Why? To prevent accidental changes or deletions that can cause the system to stop working properly. Look at the left-hand side of the status bar in any Explorer window to see how many hidden files are in the current folder.

If you're confident of your ability to work with hidden and system files without causing your computer to crash, adjust Explorer's options to display those files. Follow these steps:

1. Open Windows Explorer or any folder window and choose View, Folder Options.
2. Click the View tab and find the entry labeled Hidden files in the Advanced settings box.
3. Select the Show all files option, as shown in Figure 3.7.

Figure 3.7

Use this option to make hidden and system files visible.

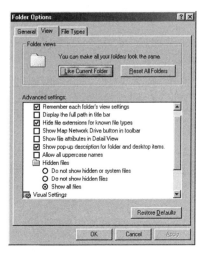

4. Click OK to save your changes and close the Folder Options dialog box.

When you choose to make hidden files visible, you'll be able to easily distinguish them in Explorer windows—they appear in Explorer as grayed-out icons. You may need to press F5 or choose View, Refresh to make these files appear.

CAUTION

There's generally a good reason why Windows sets some files as hidden or system. If you need to change that attribute temporarily (to edit MSDOS.SYS, for example) be sure to change the attribute back when you're finished.

If you use the menus or the Ctrl+A keyboard shortcut to select all files in a folder that contains hidden files, you'll see a warning message like the one in Figure 3.8. There is no way to manage hidden files from Explorer unless you make them visible.

Figure 3.8

Before you can select all the files in this folder, you must make hidden files visible.

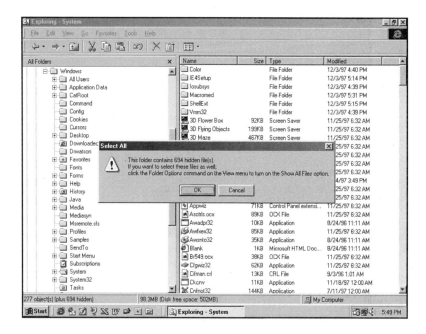

You can use Explorer to change the Read-only, Hidden, and Archive attributes of a file or folder. Right-click the icon, choose Properties, and check or uncheck the appropriate box. Explorer will not allow you to change a file's System attribute, however. If you must perform that task, open an MS-DOS Prompt window and issue the command **ATTRIB –S** *filename*. For more information about the ATTRIB command, type **ATTRIB /?** at the MS-DOS Prompt.

 Do you want to see information about file attributes every time you switch to Details view? Open Explorer and choose View, Folder Options. Click the View tab and scroll through the list of Advanced settings. Check the option labeled Show file attributes in Detail View, and click OK.

Customizing Explorer's Appearance

Like most parts of Windows, Explorer contains a wide array of customization options.

Changing the Width of Panes

To change the proportions of the two panes when using Windows Explorer, point to the vertical dividing line between the panes. When the pointer changes to a two-headed arrow, click and drag in either direction. Release the mouse button when the panes are the desired size.

Changing the Width of Columns

In Details view, Windows uses columns to display information about files, folders, and system objects. To change the width of columns, point to the dividing line between column headings. When the pointer changes to a two-headed arrow, click and drag in either direction. Double-click the dividing line to the right of a column heading to automatically resize the column to match the widest entry in the list.

TROUBLESHOOTING

One or more columns are missing when you switch to Details view. It's possible you resized a column to zero width. To restore the default column widths, click anywhere in the contents pane, then hold down the Ctrl key and press the + key on the numeric keypad.

Showing and Hiding the Status Bar

The Status Bar shows important information about the number and size of objects in the current folder, and it works the same in folder windows and in the two-pane Explorer view. To show or hide this screen element, choose View, Status Bar. A check mark next to this menu choice means the Status Bar should appear at the bottom of the window.

Showing and Hiding Toolbars

By default, the Address bar and the Standard Buttons toolbar (with text labels) appear when you open the two-pane version of Explorer. You can use both screen elements with folder windows as well. To show or hide either element, choose View, Toolbars, and check or uncheck the Standard Buttons and Address Bar menu choices.

There's no way to customize the buttons on these toolbars, but if you want maximum room to work with files and folders, you can hide the text labels on the Standard Buttons toolbar. Choose View, Toolbars, then remove the check mark from the Text Labels menu choice. The result looks like the window shown in Figure 3.9.

Figure 3.9
To conserve Explorer space, hide the text labels that normally appear under the toolbar buttons.

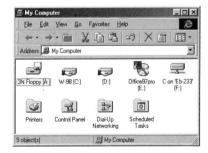

Opening Explorer at Specific Folders or Files

The full two-pane Explorer view can be overwhelming, particularly when you just want to reorganize files among a handful of subfolders in a single location. The solution is to create shortcuts for each task. It's possible to launch a copy of Explorer that opens at the location where you want to work. Even better is to restrict the display of objects in the left-hand pane so that it includes only the drives or folders with which you want to work.

If you create a shortcut with only the command **explorer**, you'll open the default two-pane Windows Explorer, with all resources visible in the All Folders pane. To reduce the clutter, you'll need to use command-line switches along with the Explorer command.

Specifically, follow the command with the /e switch to force it to open in two-pane mode (use /n to specify a single-pane windows instead). Normally, Explorer uses the Desktop as the root of the All Folders pane, but you can specify any drive or folder to fill this role. When you do, the display becomes much less confusing. Use the /root, *object* switch to restrict the scope of the All Folders pane to the object you specify. In place of the *object*, substitute the name of a network server (in UNC format), a local drive, or a folder.

N O T E   For a detailed explanation of all the options you can use when creating an Explorer shortcut, read the Microsoft Knowledge Base article "Command-Line Switches for Windows Explorer." You'll find it at

http://premium.microsoft.com/support/kb/articles/q130/5/10.asp

To open a two-pane Explorer window that includes only files and folders on drive C:, for example, follow these steps:

1. Right-click any empty desktop space and choose New, Shortcut. The Create Shortcut wizard appears.
2. In the box labeled Command line, enter the following command (the spacing and punctuation are crucial):

   explorer /e,/root,c:
3. Click Next, and name the shortcut Explore Drive C.
4. Click Finish. The shortcut appears on the desktop.
5. Open the shortcut to verify that it works. Move or copy the shortcut to another location if you want.

Managing Files and Folders

Although many Windows applications offer basic file management functions, Explorer is the tool you'll use most often to organize your files. Regardless of which view you choose, Explorer allows you to create new folders, copy and move files between folders, and delete and rename files.

Part
I

Ch
3

Selecting Files and Folders

Before you can perform any action on an object, you must first select it. The procedures for selecting files, folders, and other icons vary, depending on the folder and desktop options you've chosen. If you've chosen the Classic (double-click) interface, you click each icon to select it. If you've chosen the Web-style (single-click) interface, on the other hand, simply point at a file to select it. Objects change color to indicate that you've selected them.

▶ **See** "Customizing the Windows Desktop," **page 135**

To select multiple icons that are adjacent to one another in a folder window or on the desktop, select the first object, then hold down the Shift key and select the last object. All the icons in between the two will be selected as well.

To select multiple icons that are not adjacent to one another, select the first one, then hold down the Ctrl key and select additional objects. To deselect an icon, continue holding down the Ctrl key and select it again.

You can also use marquee selection to quickly select a group of adjacent files using the mouse. Use this technique to draw an imaginary rectangle around the group of files, as in Figure 3.10. Point to one corner of the rectangle, then hold down the left mouse button and drag the selection to the opposite corner. This technique works regardless of which icon view you've selected.

Figure 3.10

As you draw this rectangle around a group of icons, watch the dotted line. All icons within the box are selected.

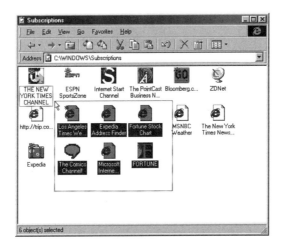

You can also select multiple icons using the keyboard. In a two-pane Explorer window, press Tab to move the focus into the right-hand contents pane, then use the arrow keys to move through the list to the first item you want to select. To select a group of adjacent icons, hold down the Shift key and use the arrow keys to move through the list. To use the keyboard to select a group of icons that are not adjacent to one another, select the first file, then hold down the Ctrl key and use the arrow keys to move through the list; press the spacebar for each file you want to select.

To quickly select all the files in a folder, choose Edit, Select All (or press Ctrl+A). To remove all current selections, click any empty space or another object in the folder window or the desktop.

 There's a lightning-fast way to select all but a few icons within a folder. This technique comes in handy when you want to archive or delete most of the files in a folder, keeping only a small number of items. Select the objects you plan to keep, then choose Edit, Invert Selection. You can now use any of the standard Windows techniques to move, copy, or delete the selected objects.

Renaming a File

To rename a file or folder, first select its icon, then use any of the following options to select the name for editing:

- Press the F2 key.
- Choose File, Rename.
- Right-click the icon and choose Rename from the shortcut menu.

When the label text is selected, type the new name. To save the name, press Enter or click any empty space on the desktop or in a folder window.

Renaming Multiple Files

There is no way to rename more than one file at a time using Explorer. To accomplish this task, you must open an MS-DOS Prompt window and use the REN (Rename) command.

To rename multiple files with long file names, use this procedure:

1. Open the Start menu and choose Programs, MS-DOS Prompt.
2. At the MS-DOS prompt, type **CD** *pathname* to switch to the directory that contains the files you want to rename. It may take several repetitions to reach the correct drive and directory.
3. Type **REN** *oldname.ext newname.ext*. If either name contains a space, enclose the name and extensions in quotation marks. Press Enter.
4. Use the ? wild card character to match any single letter in the file name; use the * wild card to substitute for any group of characters. For example, if you start with the following group of files:

    05 Sales Forecast.xls

    06 Sales Forecast.xls

    07 Sales Forecast.xls

    08 Sales Forecast.xls

    Enter this command at the MS-DOS prompt to rename them in one operation:

    REN "?? Sales*.*" "?? Mrktg*.*"

Part

I

Ch

3

The result will be four files named:

05 Mrktg Forecast.xls

06 Mrktg Forecast.xls

07 Mrktg Forecast.xls

08 Mrktg Forecast.xls

Creating New Folders

To create a new folder, follow these steps:

1. Select the icon for the drive or folder in which you plan to create the new folder.

2. Right-click the icon or any empty space in the contents pane and choose <u>N</u>ew, <u>F</u>older.

3. The new folder has a generic name; to replace it with a more meaningful name, just start typing. When you've finished, press Enter to record the new name.

▶ **See** "Working with Long Filenames," **page 61**

Moving and Copying Files and Folders

With Explorer, the easiest way to move and copy files is not always the surest. When you select one or more objects, hold down the left mouse button, and drag the objects from one location to another, the results can vary dramatically. The exact effect depends on the location and the type of file. Every time you drag and drop files using Explorer, one of three things happens:

■ When you drag an object from one location to another on the same logical volume, Explorer moves the object. On local drives, each logical volume uses the same drive letter, so dragging a group of icons from C:\Windows\Temp to the Windows desktop moves them to the new location.

■ When you drag an object from one logical volume to another, Explorer makes a copy of the file. If you drag a group of icons from C:\Data and drop them on the icon for a floppy disk (A:) or a shared network folder, Explorer leaves the original files untouched and creates copies in the new location.

■ When you drag a program file from one location to another, regardless of location, Explorer creates a shortcut, leaving the original file untouched.

There are solid logical reasons for this default behavior, but the results can be confusing for novice users. Even experienced Windows users can sometimes stumble over these rules. For example, if you drag multiple program icons from a folder onto the desktop, Explorer will create a group of shortcuts; but if you select even one icon that isn't a program, you'll get a move or a copy instead.

When dragging icons, the best way to predict what Explorer will do when you drag and drop icons is to examine the mouse pointer before you release the mouse button. If you see a plus sign just to the right of the pointer, as shown in Figure 3.11, you can expect a copy; a small arrow next to the pointer means you'll get a shortcut, and a plain pointer means you're about to move the selected objects. If the pointer you see doesn't match the result you intended, press Esc before releasing the mouse button to abort the move or copy.

Figure 3.11

The small plus sign next to the mouse pointer means you're about to make a copy of this icon.

For maximum control over the results of drag-and-drop operations, select one or more objects and hold down the right mouse button when dragging. When you release the button, Windows pops up a shortcut menu like the one in Figure 3.12. The default action appears in bold type, but you can choose any of the three actions, or cancel the whole operation, if you prefer.

Figure 3.12

When you hold down the right mouse button while dragging files, Windows lets you choose the result you prefer from this shortcut menu.

Dragging and Dropping Files Between Folders   The easiest way to move or copy files between folders is to open two folder windows and arrange them side by side. Follow this procedure to let Windows position two folder windows automatically:

1. Minimize or close all open windows. The easiest way to accomplish this task is to click the Show Desktop button on the Quick Launch toolbar.

2. Open both folder windows so that they're visible on the desktop.

3. Right-click any empty space on the taskbar and choose Tile Windows Vertically from the shortcut menu. Windows will arrange both windows so that each occupies exactly half the display.

If you inadvertently left an extra window open on the desktop before attempting this procedure, right-click an empty space on the taskbar, choose Undo Tile, and try again.

To move or copy files from one folder window to another, select the icon or icons and drag them to any empty space in the destination folder.

 To quickly copy one or more files to a floppy disk, select the icon(s) in an Explorer window, right-click, and choose Send To from the shortcut menu. Choose the floppy drive from the submenu.

Dragging and Dropping Files in Explorer View   To move or copy files using the two-pane Explorer view, follow these steps:

1. Open Windows Explorer. In the left-hand All Folders pane, select the icon for the folder that contains the files you want to move or copy.

2. In the right-hand Contents pane select the icon or icons to move or copy.

3. Hold down the right mouse button and drag the icon(s) on top of the folder icon in the left-hand pane. If the icon for the destination folder is not visible, let the mouse pointer hover over the parent icon for a second or two; the branch will expand automatically.

4. When the pointer is over the icon for the destination folder, release the mouse button.

5. Choose the appropriate action—Move, Copy, or Create Shortcut(s)—from the menu that appears.

Using Cut, Copy, and Paste   Explorer offers one final option for moving and copying files that doesn't involve dragging and dropping. Use the Windows Clipboard to cut, copy, and paste files between folders and drives, in exactly the same way you copy text and graphics between documents. These techniques work equally well in Explorer windows, folder windows, in e-mail messages, and on the Windows desktop.

To copy, move, or create shortcuts using the Clipboard, follow this procedure:

1. Select the file or files.

2. To copy a file from one folder to another, use the Copy command; to move a file, use the Cut command. Any of the following mouse or keyboard techniques will work:

   Choose Edit, Copy or Edit, Cut.

   Right-click the selected icon and choose Copy or Cut.

   Press Ctrl+C (Copy) or Ctrl+X (Cut).

   Click the Copy or Cut buttons on the Explorer toolbar.

3. Display the contents of the destination folder and use any of the following commands to complete the move or copy:

   Choose Edit, Paste.

   Right-click the folder icon or the contents pane and choose Paste.

   Right-click the folder icon or the contents pane and press Ctrl+V.

   Click the Paste button on the Explorer toolbar.

Copying Disks

It's impractical to copy an entire hard disk or CD-ROM, but it's ridiculously easy to copy a floppy disk. Windows includes a utility that handles the whole process in two passes—one for the source (original) disk, the second pass for the destination (copy) disk. To copy a floppy, make sure you have a formatted disk that's the same size as the original you plan to copy, then follow these steps:

1. Insert the original disk in the floppy drive.

2. Open the My Computer window or Windows Explorer, right-click the floppy drive icon (normally A:), and choose Copy Disk. If you have only one drive that handles the selected disk format, the same drive letter will appear in the Copy from and Copy to areas of the dialog box. If you have more than one such drive, select the destination drive in the Copy to box; if this is a different drive, insert the destination disk in that drive.

3. The Copy Disk dialog box (Figure 3.13) appears. Click <u>S</u>tart, and Windows reads the entire contents of the disk into memory.

Figure 3.13

Follow the prompts to duplicate a floppy disk.

4. If you're copying from one physical drive to another, Windows handles the operation in one pass. On most systems, where there is only a single floppy drive, you'll see a prompt when the Copy from phase is complete. Remove the original disk, insert the destination disk into the drive, and click OK.

5. Windows transfers the stored data to the destination disk; if the disk requires formatting, that will happen automatically. When the copy is completed, you'll see a message at the bottom of the Copy Disk dialog box.

6. To copy another floppy, remove the destination disk, insert another source disk, and repeat steps 3 through 5. When you've finished, click <u>C</u>lose.

CAUTION

Windows will erase a destination disk without prompting you. That can be disastrous if the destination disk contains important data. If you store important files on floppy disks, always use the write-protect tab to prevent accidental erasure.

Deleting Files and Folders

To delete one or more files or folders, select the icons and then use any of the following techniques:

- Press the Del key.
- Choose <u>F</u>ile, <u>D</u>elete from the pull-down Explorer menu.
- Right-click and choose <u>D</u>elete.
- Drag the icon(s) and drop them on the Recycle Bin icon.
- To delete files completely without using the Recycle Bin, hold down the Shift key while you press the Del key or choose <u>D</u>elete from the right-click shortcut menu.

Normally, when you delete one or more files or folders, Windows pops up a Confirm File Delete dialog box. You can turn off the dialog box that asks whether you're sure you want to send the files to the Recycle Bin; when you bypass the Recycle Bin, though, you must deal with the dialog box shown in Figure 3.14.

Figure 3.14

When you bypass the Recycle Bin, Windows forces you to deal with this dialog box.

> **CAUTION**
>
> When you delete a folder, you also delete all files and subfolders within that folder. Check the contents carefully before you trash an entire folder.

Undoing Changes

Windows allows you to undo the last three actions you perform when working with the Windows Explorer. If you inadvertently delete a file, move it to the wrong location, or make a mistake when renaming a file or folder, click the Undo button on the Standard Buttons toolbar, or press Ctrl+Z.

It's not always easy to tell exactly what Undo will accomplish, and there's no Redo option to restore your original action, either. Within an Explorer window, look at the top of the Edit menu to see what Windows can undo; likely choices include Undo Delete, Undo Move, and Undo Rename.

 Although it's not obvious, the Undo shortcuts work if you make a mistake on the Windows Desktop as well. If you inadvertently move or delete a desktop file by mistake, press Ctrl+Z immediately to recover.

Using the Recycle Bin

The Windows Recycle Bin can't prevent every file-management disaster, but it can help you recover when you inadvertently delete a crucial file. When you delete a local file using the Windows Explorer, it doesn't actually disappear; instead, the Recycle Bin intercepts it and stores it. The file remains there until you empty the Recycle Bin or it's displaced by a newer deleted file. As long as that file remains in the Recycle Bin, you can recover it intact.

> **CAUTION**
>
> The Recycle Bin is far from perfect, and every Windows user should be aware of its limitations. When you use a network connection to delete files on another computer, or when you delete files on a floppy disk or other removable media, they are not saved in the Recycle Bin. Likewise, using the DEL command from an MS-DOS Prompt removes the files permanently, without storing safe copies in the Recycle Bin. And when you overwrite a file with another file of the same name, the old file does not go into the Recycle Bin. If these limitations disturb you, check out Norton Utilities and other third-party programs, which can expand the capabilities of the Recycle Bin to cover some of these situations.

Recovering a Deleted File   To recover a deleted file, open the Recycle Bin (you'll find its icon on the desktop). Browse its contents until you find the file or files you're looking for. To return the file to its original location, right-click and choose Restore from the shortcut menu. To restore the file to an alternate location, such as the Windows desktop, drag the icon or icons to the location where you want to restore them.

Changing the Size of the Recycle Bin   By default, the Recycle Bin sets aside 10% of the space on every local hard disk for storing deleted files. If your hard disk is nearly full, that may be too much; on the other hand, if you have ample disk space, you may want to reserve more space for the Recycle Bin. On systems with more than one drive, you can choose different Recycle Bin settings for each drive.

To adjust the Recycle Bin's appetite, follow these steps:

1. Right-click the Recycle Bin icon and choose Properties from the shortcut menu. You'll see a dialog box like the one in Figure 3.15.

Figure 3.15

The default setting uses 10% of hard disk space for storing deleted files; use this dialog box to adjust this setting.

2. Each drive will have its own tab in the dialog box. Use the option at the top of the Global tab to specify whether you want to configure the drives independently or use one setting for all drives.

3. Use the slider control on the Global tab to change the percentage of disk space reserved for the Recycle Bin (adjust this setting on each of the dialog boxes for individual drives). You may choose any setting between 0% and 100%, although the most realistic settings are between 3% and 20%.

4. To stop using the Recycle Bin completely, check the box labeled Do not move files to the Recycle Bin.

5. To avoid seeing the confirmation dialog box every time you move a file to the Recycle Bin, clear the check mark from the box labeled Display delete confirmation dialog box.

6. Click OK to save your changes and close the dialog box.

Part

I

Ch

3

Emptying the Recycle Bin   Under normal circumstances, you shouldn't need to delete the Recycle Bin. When it fills up, Windows automatically deletes the oldest files to make room for new files you delete. If you run short of hard disk space—when installing a new program, for example—you may need to clear out the Recycle Bin to make room. To delete all files from the Recycle Bin, right-click its icon and choose Empty Recycle Bin.

Previewing a Document with Quick View

Even the most compulsive file-naming system can't tell you exactly what's in every file on your hard drive. Using Windows Explorer, you can examine a file's name, type, size, and the date it was last modified. But to see the contents of a file, you'll need to open it with its associated application—or use Windows' Quick View utility to peek inside.

To view the contents of a file, right-click the file and choose Quick View. When you do, you'll see a window like the one shown in Figure 3.16.

Figure 3.16

Use the Quick View utility to see the contents of a file without opening it.

Although Quick View is useful, it's far from perfect. It supports a limited number of file types, for example, and you can't copy the file's contents to the Windows Clipboard or print the file. The Quick View version included with Windows 98 lets you view simple text and graphics files and those created by some word processing programs; unlike its Windows 95 predecessor, it allows you to view files created by Office 97 applications.

N O T E   If you use Quick View regularly, consider purchasing the full commercial version from its developer, Inso Software. Quick View Plus adds support for hundreds of file types. It also allows you to copy text and graphics to the Windows Clipboard or send a file directly to a printer without having to open the application. For more details, go to

http://www.inso.com

Using Shortcuts

The files you use most often are scattered across your hard disk in a variety of folders. When you set up a new program, its files go in their own folders, and you organize data files using whatever system makes most sense—by project, date, or department, for example. If you had to root through folders and subfolders every time you wanted to open a document or launch a program, you'd hardly have any time to get work done.

So how do you maintain an orderly filing system and still keep programs and documents close at hand? The solution is to use shortcuts. As the name implies, shortcuts are pointer files that allow you to access a file without moving the file or creating a copy of it. You can create shortcuts for almost any object in Windows, including programs, data files, folders, drives, Dial-Up Networking connections, printers, and Web pages. Windows uses shortcuts extensively: Every item in the Programs folder on your Start menu is a shortcut, for example, and every time you save a Web address to your Favorites folder you create an Internet shortcut. Learning how to create and manage shortcuts is a crucial step in mastering Windows.

Part

I

Ch

3

How Shortcuts Work

Shortcuts are small files that contain all the information Windows needs to create a link to a *target file*. The shortcut uses the same icon as the target file, with one crucial difference: a small arrow in the lower right corner that identifies the icon as a shortcut rather than the original.

When you right-click a shortcut, the available menu choices are the same as if you had right-clicked the target file. Opening the shortcut has the same effect as opening the target file.

Shortcuts are a tremendous productivity aid. If you have a document file stored six subfolders deep, for example, you can create a shortcut icon and store it on the desktop, where it's always accessible. The target file remains in its original location.

You can create many shortcuts to the same file. For your favorite programs, you might create shortcuts on the desktop, on the Start menu, and on the Quick Launch bar. Each shortcut takes up a negligible amount of disk space (typically no more than 500 bytes), even if the original file occupies several megabytes of disk space.

What happens when you attempt to launch the target file using its shortcut icon? Windows is intelligent enough to re-establish the link to the target file even if you've moved or renamed the original, following these steps:

1. Windows looks at the static location (the file name and path), whether the file is stored locally or on a network.

2. If that file no longer exists, Windows checks to see whether you've renamed the file, looking in the same folder for a file with the same date and time stamp but a different name.

3. If that search fails, Windows checks to see whether you moved the file, looking in all subfolders of the target folder and then searching the entire drive. (On a network location, the search extends to the highest parent directory to which you have access

rights.) If you move the target file to a different drive, Windows can't find it and the shortcut will break.

4. If Windows can't find the target file, it will try to identify the nearest matching file, and you'll see a dialog box like the one in Figure 3.17. Confirm the choice if it's correct; otherwise, choose No, then delete the shortcut and re-create it using the correct file.

▶ **See** "Using Internet Shortcuts," **page 884**

Figure 3.17

If Windows can't locate the target file for a shortcut, it will suggest the closest matching file.

Creating a New Shortcut

The easiest way to create a new shortcut is with the help of the Create Shortcut wizard. Follow these steps:

1. Right-click an empty space on the Windows desktop and choose New, Shortcut. You'll see the dialog box shown in Figure 3.18.

Figure 3.18

Creating a new shortcut is a two-step process with this wizard.

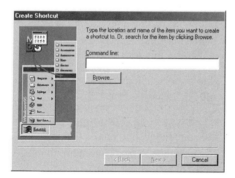

2. Click the Browse button and select the document or program file from the Browse list. To create a shortcut to a drive or folder, you must type its name directly in the box labeled Command line. Include the full path, if necessary. Click Next.

3. Give the shortcut a descriptive name and click Finish. Test the shortcut to make sure it works correctly.

You can also create a shortcut from an icon. Select the icon in an Explorer window, hold down the right mouse button, and drag the icon to the desktop or another folder. Choose Create Shortcut(s) Here from the menu that pops up.

Renaming a Shortcut

To modify the name that appears under a shortcut icon, right-click the icon and choose Rename. (This technique works with shortcuts on the Programs menu and Quick Launch folder as well.) The pointer changes to an I-beam and the entire name is selected. Begin typing to completely replace the name, or click to position the insertion point where you want to add or change text. After you edit the name, press Enter or click an empty portion of the desktop or taskbar to register the change. Note that changing the name of a shortcut does not affect the target file.

Deleting a Shortcut

To delete a shortcut, use any of the techniques described earlier in this chapter. When you delete a shortcut, you remove only the link to the target file. The target file remains intact in its original location.

Setting the Properties for a Shortcut Icon

Part

I

Ch

3

To change the appearance and behavior of a shortcut icon, right-click the shortcut icon and choose Properties. The General tab includes basic information, such as the shortcut's name and when it was created. Click the Shortcut tab to change the link between the shortcut and its target file. This dialog box, which should look like the one in Figure 3.19, lets you adjust the following properties:

- To associate a different file with the shortcut, click in the Target box and type the file name, including its full path.
- To specify a startup folder, click in the Start In edit box and enter the name of the folder, including its full path; this setting is most useful for programs.
- To define a keyboard shortcut, open the Shortcut Properties dialog box, click in the Shortcut Key edit box, and press the specific key combination you want to use. The shortcut key must consist of a letter or a number, plus any two of the following three keys: Ctrl, Alt, and Shift. (If you simply press a letter or number, Windows defaults to Ctrl+Alt+*key*.) You can also use any Function key, with or without the Ctrl, Alt, and Shift keys. You cannot use Esc, Enter, Tab, the spacebar, Print Screen, or Backspace. To clear the Shortcut Key edit box, select the box and press the spacebar.

CAUTION

Shortcut keys you create take precedence over other access keys in Windows. Be careful that you don't inadvertently redefine a system wide key combination or one that you use in other Windows applications.

- Indicate whether you want the document or application to run minimized, maximized, or in a window.
- Change the icon that appears with the shortcut.

Figure 3.19

The Shortcut Properties dialog box lets you change the target file, startup folder, shortcut key, and icon used by a shortcut.

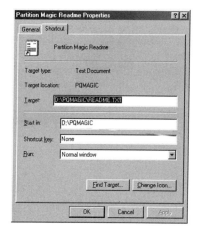

CHAPTER 4

Advanced File Management Techniques

by Ed Bott

Associating Files with Programs

When you attempt to open an icon, Windows checks the file's extension against a database of registered file types to determine what action it should take. A registered file type can have multiple actions (open and print, for example), and all such actions are available on the right-click shortcut menus; Windows uses the default action when you launch the icon. If Windows does not recognize the file type, it offers a dialog box that lets you choose which application to use with the file you've selected.

File extensions have been around since the very first version of DOS. Beginning with the first release of Windows 95, Microsoft began tracking file types as well. File types are inextricably linked to file extensions, but the relationship isn't always easy to understand. Here are the essential facts you need to know:

- File types typically have friendly names (HTML Document), while extensions are typically three or four letters (HTM or HTML).

- File types are visible in their own column when you choose Details view in the Windows Explorer; extensions for registered file types are hidden by default. You can also inspect a file's properties to see which file type is associated with it. The extension for an unregistered file type is always visible in the Explorer list.

- Every file type has an associated icon, which appears when you view files of that type in the Windows Explorer or a folder window.

- Every unique file extension is associated with one and only one file type. When you install Microsoft Word, for example, it associates the DOC extension with the Microsoft Word Document file type.

- A file type, on the other hand, can be associated with multiple extensions. The HTML Document file type works with the HTM and HTML extensions, for example, and JPEG Images can end with the extension JPE, JPEG, or JPG.

- As the previous examples illustrate, a file extension can be more than three letters long.

- Windows common dialog boxes (File Open and File Save As) include a drop-down list that lets you choose a file type; Windows adds the default extension for the file type automatically when you save a document.

- A Windows filename may contain more than one period. Windows defines the extension as all characters that appear after the last period in the filename.

Most application programs handle the details of registering file types and associations when you install them. Creating a file type manually, or editing an existing file type, is a cumbersome and difficult process best reserved for expert users as a last resort.

▶ **See** "Managing File Associations," **page 87**

TROUBLESHOOTING

Your document appears to have the correct extension, but when you try to open it, the wrong application launches. You or another user tried to add or change the file extension manually, by adding a period and the extension The associated program added its own (hidden) extension as well, resulting in a filename like Letter.doc.rtf. To see the full name, including extension, choose View, Folder Options, click the View tab, and remove the check mark next to the option labeled Hide File Extensions for Known File Types. The file extension is now visible and editable. Be sure to restore this option after you have repaired the problem file.

To see a list of all registered file types, open the Windows Explorer or any folder window (including My Computer). Choose View, Folder Options, and click the File Types tab. You'll see a list like the one in Figure 4.1.

Figure 4.1
Use this list of registered file types to see which applications are associated with different file types.

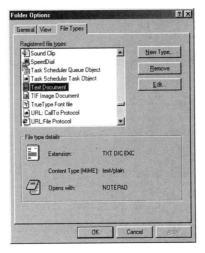

Part
I
Ch
4

The list is arranged in alphabetical order by file type. As you scroll through the list, note that the details in the dialog box change. For each entry in the list, you can view the registered file extensions, MIME details, and the name of the associated application.

CAUTION

Multipurpose Internet Mail Extensions (MIME) are the standards that define how browsers and mail software should handle file attachments. Do not adjust these settings in the File Types dialog box unless you are certain the changes will produce the correct result. Unnecessary tinkering with these settings can result in unreadable mail and Web pages.

Changing File Associations

Windows allows you to associate only one program with each action for each file type. In most cases, when two applications claim the right to edit or open a given file type, the one you installed most recently will claim that file type as its own. When a newly installed program "hijacks" a file type, you may want to restore the association with the older application. There are two ways to accomplish this goal:

- Reinstall the original program. The setup process typically edits the Windows Registry and adjusts file associations. If the setup program was written correctly, you will not lose any custom settings or data.

- Edit the file type directly, changing the associated program to the one you prefer. To do so, follow these steps:

    1. Open the Windows Explorer or any folder window (including My Computer) and choose View, Folder Options. Click the File Types tab.

    2. Select the file type you want to change and click the Edit button. The Edit File Type dialog box appears (see Figure 4.2).

Figure 4.2

Exercise caution when manually editing file types. A wrong setting in this dialog box can hinder your ability to work with common document types.

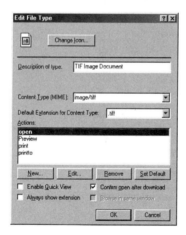

3. Select an entry from the Actions list—the default action is in bold type—and click the Edit button. The dialog box shown in Figure 4.3 appears.

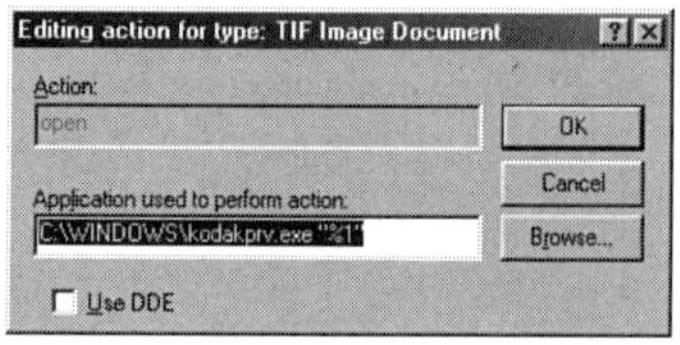

Figure 4.3

Change the program listed here to adjust how Windows works with a given file type.

CAUTION

Note that some actions require Dynamic Data Exchange (DDE), an extremely complex process that passes information between multiple programs; if you see these options listed, exit this dialog box and don't attempt to edit the action by hand.

4. Click the Browse button and find the executable (EXE) file for the program you want to use with the selected action. Click Open to insert the filename into the box labeled Application used to perform action.

5. Click OK to close the Edit Action dialog box and save your change.

6. Repeat steps 3 through 5 for other actions you want to change. When you've finished, click OK to close the Edit File Type dialog box, and click OK again to close the Folder Options dialog box.

Three options in the Edit File Type dialog box are worth noting here:

■ Choose an action and click the Set Default button to make this the default action for the file type. The previous default action will still appear as a choice on right-click shortcut menus.

■ Check the box labeled Enable Quick View to control whether you see a Quick View choice on the shortcut menu for the selected file type.

▶ **See** "Previewing a Document with Quick View," **page 44**

■ Check the box labeled Always show extension to display the file's extension in all Explorer and folder windows. This setting is useful if you regularly change the extensions of certain types of documents (such as RTF documents created by Office 97) but don't want to clutter the Explorer window with other extensions.

Part

I

Ch

4

CAUTION

It's possible to completely eliminate a file type or an action associated with this file type. Generally, however, this drastic step is not recommended. The settings for each file type take up a trivial amount of space in the Windows Registry, and removing a file type can cause installed programs to fail.

Using an Alternate Program to Open a Registered File Type

You may have several programs at your disposal to view or edit a particular type of file. For example, FrontPage Express and Microsoft Word both allow you to edit HTML files. Unfortunately, Windows forces you to associate one and only one program with the default action for each registered file type. But you can override that default decision at any time and choose which program you want to use for a given file icon. Follow these steps:

1. Select the document icon, hold down the Shift key, and right-click. The shortcut menu that appears includes a new Open with choice, not found on the default menu.

2. Choose Open with from the shortcut menu. The dialog box shown in Figure 4.4 appears.

Figure 4.4

Use this dialog box to open a document with the application of your choice instead of the default program.

3. Scroll through the list and find the program you want to use. Note that the list shows only the short names of executable files (Winword, for example) rather than the long name of the application (Microsoft Word).

4. If the program appears in the list, select its entry. If you can't find its entry, click the Other button and browse for the program's executable file, then click Open.

5. Before you click OK, note the check box labeled Always use this program to open this type of file. By default, this box is unchecked. Do **not** add a check mark unless you want to change the program associated with the Open action for this type of file.

6. Click OK to open the document.

Opening an Unrecognized File Type

When you attempt to open the icon for an unrecognized file type, Windows displays an Open With dialog box similar to the one shown in Figure 4.4. Note that there are two crucial differences between this dialog box and the one that appears when you hold down the Shift key and click a recognized file type. These changes are designed to let you quickly create a new file type for the unrecognized type:

- This Open With dialog box includes a text box at the top. Enter the name of the new file type here.

- By default, there is a check mark in the box labeled Always use this program to open this type of file. Remove this check mark if you don't want to create a new file type.

If you inadvertently create a new file type using this dialog box, it's easy to remove it. Open the Folder Options dialog box, click the File Types tab, select the newly created file type, and click the Remove button.

Finding Files

On a hard disk with a capacity measured in gigabytes, it's possible to store tens of thousands of files in hundreds or even thousands of folders. So it shouldn't be surprising when you occasionally lose track of one or more of those files. Fortunately, Windows includes a handy utility that lets you hunt down misplaced files, even if you can't remember the file's exact name. You can search for a portion of the name, or use other details, including the size and type of the file, the date it was created, or a fragment of text within the file.

Finding a File or Folder by Name

To begin searching for a file on a local disk or on a shared network drive, click the Start button and choose Find, Files or Folders. If the Windows Explorer is open, choose Tools, Find, Files or Folders. You'll see a dialog box like the one in Figure 4.5.

Figure 4.5
Use the Find utility to search for any file, anywhere on your computer or across a network.

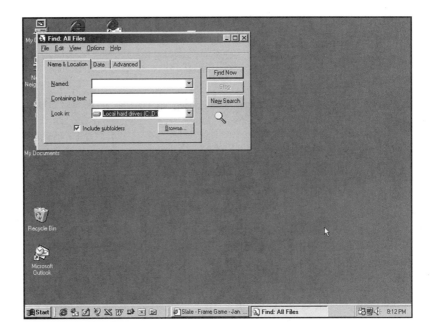

The most common type of search lets you look for a file when you remember all or part of the name.

1. Click in the box labeled Named and enter all or part of the filename. (The file extension is not necessary.)

TIP DOS-style wildcards (* and ?) are not required in the Named box, but they can be extremely useful in helping you reduce the number of matches. For example, if you enter the letter *b*, Windows will return all files that include that letter anywhere in the name. On the other hand, *b** will find only files that begin with that letter, and *b???.** will return only files that begin with the letter *b* and contain exactly four characters, not counting the extension.

2. Tell Windows which drives and folders you want to look in. If you opened Find from the Windows Explorer, the Look in box includes the name of the currently selected drive or folder; otherwise, this entry shows the location you specified when you last used Find.

Enter a folder name directly (C:\Data, for example), click the <u>B</u>rowse button to choose a folder name, or use the drop-down Explorer-style list to select any of the following default locations:

- The Windows Desktop
- The My Documents folder
- Document Folders, which includes My Documents and the Desktop
- Any local drive
- Any mapped network drive
- All local hard drives
- My Computer (searches all local hard drives as well as floppy and CD-ROM drives)

T I P You can specify multiple locations in the <u>L</u>ook in box. Enter the full path, including drive letter or UNC-style server and share name, for each location. Separate the entries in this list with semicolons.

3. To search in all subfolders of the location you selected, place a check mark in the box labeled Include <u>S</u>ubfolders.

4. Click F<u>i</u>nd Now to begin searching.

The more details you provide, the more restrictive the results will be. But don't provide too much information, or there's a good chance that you'll miss the file you're looking for, especially if the spelling of the filename is even slightly different from what you enter.

Windows compares the text you enter in the <u>N</u>amed box with the names of every file and folder in the specified location, returning a result if that string of characters appears anywhere in the filename. Entering **log** as the search parameter, for example, will turn up all files that contain the words *log, logo, catalog,* or *technology,* as in Figure 4.6. Search results appear in a pane at the bottom of the Find dialog box.

By default, the results list appears in Details view; right-click in the results pane and use the shortcut menu to change to a different view. Click column headings to sort results by name, size, type, the date the files were last modified, or the folder in which the files are stored. Click again to sort in reverse order.

T I P After you've completed a Find, look at the status bar in the bottom of the window. The message Monitoring New Items means that Windows continues to watch your actions and updates the results list automatically as you create, rename, move, and delete files that match the specified criteria.

Figure 4.6

The Find utility returns all filenames that include the characters you enter. Click any column heading to sort the results.

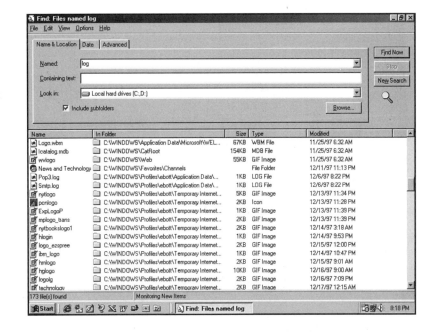

Advanced Search Techniques

The Find utility is fast and extremely effective, even when you haven't the vaguest idea of what the target file is named. Advanced options let you search using other criteria.

If you have a general idea of when you created a file or when you last edited it, click the Date tab and narrow the search by date. Spinners let you specify ranges of dates by day or month: to find all files you worked with yesterday or today, for example, click the Find all files option, choose Modified from the drop-down list, and choose the option during the previous 1 day(s). You can also specify a range of dates here, as illustrated in Figure 4.7.

Figure 4.7

Narrow down your search by entering a range of dates.

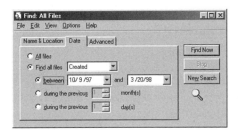

You can type dates into this dialog box, but it's far easier to use the built-in calendar controls that appear when you click drop-down arrow in date boxes, as shown in Figure 4.8. Click the month heading to produce a menu of months; click the year to reveal a spinner control that lets you quickly adjust the year.

Part

I

Ch

4

Figure 4.8

This calendar appears automatically when you click the drop-down arrow.

Click the Advanced tab to search for files by type and by size, as shown in the example in Figure 4.9. Note that this dialog box will allow you to select only registered file types. Because it requires you to enter size parameters in kilobytes, be sure to multiply by 1,000 when specifying megabytes.

Figure 4.9

This set of search criteria lets you hunt down large graphics files.

 Use the Find utility to organize and archive files. For example, you can search for all Microsoft Word files modified more than 6 months ago, then move the results to a backup location on the network. Or use advanced Find parameters to search for files larger than 1MB in size. If you leave all boxes blank and check the Include subfolders option, the resulting list will include all files on your computer, up to a maximum of 10,000. You can sort that list to find files of a certain type or size.

With the help of the Find utility, you can also search for text within files. Obviously, it won't do you much good to search for common words like "the," but if you remember a specific phrase that appears in a lost document, you can have Windows track down all files that contain that phrase. To look for a draft of your company's annual report, for example, click the Name & Location tab, and enter *annual report* in the box labeled Containing text. Click the Find Now button to begin searching. Note that text searches can take a very long time, especially on large hard disks or across a network.

 Combine settings from the Find dialog box to narrow down your search for a specific file. For example, you might order Windows to search for a Microsoft Word document that contains the phrase *annual report* and was last modified in February, 1998. With those specifics, you'll have a good chance of finding the file you're looking for, even if you can't remember what you named it.

If the search didn't find the file you were looking for, modify the criteria and click the Find Now button again. To clear all criteria and start from scratch, click the New Search button.

Managing Files from the Find Window

Because the Find dialog box is actually a specially modified version of the Windows Explorer, you can use the results pane for virtually any file management task. Right-click any icon to display shortcut menus that include file management options, or drag items from the results pane and drop them anywhere, including a folder window, the Windows Explorer, the desktop, or an e-mail message.

Use the File menu or right-click for these choices:

- Open
- Quick View
- Send To
- Cut and Copy (available only from shortcut menu)
- Create Shortcut
- Delete
- Rename
- Properties

The Find utility includes an extremely powerful feature that's so well hidden even many Windows experts don't know it exists. Select any file in the results pane and choose File, Open Containing Folder. This choice, available only from the main menu and not from the right-click shortcut menus, opens a window displaying the full contents of the folder which contains the file you selected in the Find Results pane.

Part

I

Ch

4

Saving and Reusing a Search

If you find yourself performing the same search regularly, save the search criteria as an icon so you can reuse it later. To save a search, follow these steps:

1. After you've completed your search, choose File, Save Search. You won't be prompted for a name or location; instead, Windows automatically creates a saved search icon on the desktop.

2. Close the Find window and locate the new Saved Search icon on the desktop. The icon will have a descriptive name drawn from the title bar of the search. Rename the icon, if you want. You can also copy or move the icon to any other location, including the Start menu.

3. To reuse a saved search, double-click its icon and click the Find Now button.

CAUTION

When you reuse a saved search, the results are not up-to-date. The Options menu in the Find dialog box includes a Save Results menu item, but checking this option might not have the effect you expect. Save Results keeps the search results pane open with the names of the files you found. The next time you use that saved search, the results pane will reappear, but the contents will not reflect files you've added, deleted, or renamed since the last time you used the search. To update the list, click the Find Now button.

Working with Compressed Files

File compression utilities make it possible to pack large files into small spaces. They also allow you to store large numbers of files in a single archive. Windows 98 users will typically encounter compressed files in one of two formats:

- Setup files for Windows 98 and other Microsoft products are stored in Cabinet format— you can recognize these files by the .Cab extension. Microsoft's Setup program processes cabinet files automatically, without requiring any utilities.

- The Zip compression format is a widely used standard for distributing files over the Internet. Windows does not include support for Zip files.

The Windows Explorer treat Cabinet files as though they were folders. You can open a Cabinet file, browse its contents, and copy files by simply opening a Cabinet file. Windows also includes a command-line utility that lets you pull one or more compressed files out of a cabinet. This capability is useful when Windows won't boot and you need to replace a lost or corrupted system file in order to reinstall or repair Windows. This Extract tool also lets you list the files in a cabinet, so you can determine the exact location of the file you're looking for. To see detailed instructions on this command, go to an MS-DOS prompt, type **EXTRACT /?**, and press Enter.

N O T E   Although there are many utilities that let you work with Zip files, the best by far is WinZip, from Nico Mak Computing. Download the shareware version from

http://www.winzip.com

Customizing the Send To Menu

Whenever you right-click a file or folder, one of the choices on the shortcut menu is Send To. Selecting this option opens a submenu containing destinations where you can send the selected icon with one click. The effect is just the same as if you had selected the file and dropped it directly on a shortcut. It's an extremely handy way to move files around without having to open Explorer windows.

All the entries on the Send To submenu are shortcuts stored in the \Windows\SendTo folder. When you first install Windows 98, the Send To menu includes a relatively small number of destinations: your default floppy drive, the Windows desktop, and the My Documents folder. Programs like Microsoft Outlook, Microsoft Fax, and the Web Publishing Wizard add shortcuts to this list, as does the Windows PowerToys collection.

It's simple to add new shortcuts in the Send To folder. When you do, the new shortcuts immediately show up on the Send To menu. You can add shortcuts to local or network folders, printers, applications (such as Notepad or WordPad), or drives. You can even create subfolders in the Send To folder, and then create shortcuts in that subfolder, creating cascading menus. To customize the Send To menu, follow these steps:

1. Open the Start menu, choose Run, type **sendto**, and press Enter. The \Windows\SendTo folder opens.

2. Right-click any empty space in the SendTo folder and choose New, Shortcut. Use the Shortcut wizard to create the shortcut you want to add. If you prefer, you can hold down the right mouse button and drag icons into the SendTo folder, then choose Create Shortcut(s) Here.

3. Give each shortcut a name that will be self-explanatory on the Send To menu.

4. Repeat this process for any other shortcuts you want to add.

When you're finished, select an icon, right-click, and choose Send To. You'll see an expanded menu like the one in Figure 4.10.

Figure 4.10
When you customize the Send To menu, you increase your one-click file management options.

Customizing the Send To menu can result in some unexpected side effects. If you plan to use this technique, be aware of these facts:

- All shortcuts follow the Explorer rules for moving and copying. When you "send" an icon to a shortcut on the same logical volume, you move that file; if the target is on a different drive, such as your floppy drive, you'll copy the file instead.

- You can select multiple files and then choose Send To, but the results may not be what you expect. In particular, sending multiple files to a program shortcut may not work.

- When you create a program shortcut in the SendTo folder, then use it to open a file whose name contains a space, you may see an error message or the program may open the file using its short name instead.

Working with Long Filenames

Windows allows you to create names for files and folders that are up to 255 characters long. Legal filenames may contain spaces and most special characters, including periods, commas, semicolons, parentheses, brackets ([]), and dollar signs. You are not allowed to use the following characters when naming a file or folder:

: ' " \ / * ? |

Part

I

Ch

4

How Windows Generates Short Filenames

Because Windows 98 maintains backward compatibility with older operating systems and applications, the file system automatically generates short filenames from long names you create. Although this process happens in the background, it's important to understand how the rules work.

When you save a file using Windows 98 or a 32-bit Windows application, Windows checks the filename you enter. If the name is a legal MS-DOS name, with no spaces or other forbidden characters, no more than 8 characters in the name, and no more than 3 characters in the extension, the short filename is the same as the long filename.

If the long filename contains spaces or other illegal characters or is longer than 8 characters, Windows uses the following rules to create a short filename:

1. Remove all spaces and other illegal characters, as well as all periods except the rightmost one.

2. Truncate the long filename to six characters, if necessary, and append a tilde (~) followed by a single-digit number. If this procedure duplicates an existing filename, increase the number by one: ~1, ~2, ~3, etc. If necessary, truncate the long filename to five characters, followed by a tilde and a two-digit numeric tail.

3. Truncate the file extension to the first three characters. If the long filename does not include a period, the short filename will have no extension.

4. Change all lowercase letters to capital letters.

> **CAUTION**
>
> Several books and computer magazines have published details for adjusting a Registry setting (NameNumericTail) that controls the way in which Windows automatically generates short filenames from long filenames you create. Do not make this change! The result can seriously affect the operation of some Windows accessories that depend on the Program Files folder. For more details on this problem, open **http://support.microsoft.com** and search for Knowledge Base article Q148594.

There is no way for the user to change the automatically generated short filename. To see the MS-DOS–compatible name for any file, right-click its icon, choose Properties, and click the General tab.

Using Long Filenames with Older Windows and DOS Programs

If you use 16-bit Windows programs, you will not be able to see long filenames in common dialog boxes such as File Open and File Save As. Instead, you'll see the truncated short version of all filenames. You'll see the same results if you use the old-style Windows File Manager, as in Figure 4.11.

Figure 4.11
When you view files using 16-bit Windows programs, you see only the short filenames and not their long equivalent.

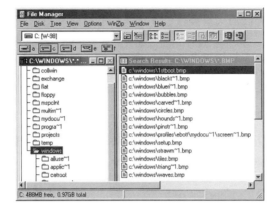

Through a process called *tunneling*, Windows allows you to preserve long filenames even when you edit them using older programs. If you create a file and give it a long name using Windows or a 32-bit Windows program, then edit it using a 16-bit program and save the file to the same short filename, Windows will preserve the long filename.

Working with Long Filenames at an MS-DOS Prompt

Part I
Ch 4

When you open an MS-DOS Prompt session within Windows 98, Windows recognizes long filenames and allows you to work with them directly. By default, directory listings display the DOS-compatible short name at left and the long name at right, as shown in Figure 4.12.

Figure 4.12
Enter DIR in an MS-DOS Prompt to see long and short filenames.

To manage files from an MS-DOS prompt, you may use either the long or short versions. If you want to display, rename, copy, or move a file using a long filename that contains one or more spaces, be sure to enclose the entire name and path in quotation marks.

Using Explorer with Shared Resources on a Network

The Windows Explorer lets you view and manage files and folders across the network, provided you have a working network connection and sufficient permissions. Use the Network Neighborhood to view all available network resources, or map shared resources to drive letters to make them easier to work with. If you know the exact name of the shared resource, you can enter it directly into any Windows common dialog box.

Using Network Neighborhood to View Shared Resources

Icons for other computers, including Windows workstations and network servers, appear in the Network Neighborhood. You'll typically see some or all of the following icon types when you open the Network Neighborhood:

- Windows workstations
- Windows NT servers
- NetWare and other servers
- Windows workgroups (which in turn contain icons for other workstations)

When you open a computer icon in Network Neighborhood, you'll see all the named shares available on that computer. These may be individual drives, folders, printers, or fax modems. Before you can browse shared files and folders or print to a shared printer, you must have permission to use that resource. To connect with a shared resource, follow these steps:

1. Open the Windows Explorer and click Network Neighborhood.

2. Click the plus sign to the left of the computer name; available shares appear in a list below the computer icon, as in Figure 4.13.

Figure 4.13
The Network Neighborhood displays all shared resources available on other workstations and servers.

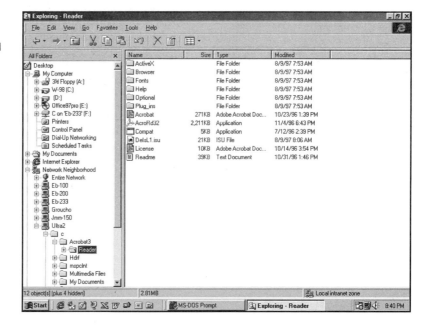

3. Select a share name from the list; its contents will appear in the right-hand pane.

4. Open a document, launch an application, or perform other file management tasks as though you were working with a local file or folder.

TROUBLESHOOTING

When you attempt to connect to a shared drive or folder on a Windows NT server, you're asked to supply a password for *servername***IPC$.** Your computer has successfully created an interprocess communication (IPC) connection with the NT resource, but your username and password are not recognized by the NT domain controller. You must log off and log on again using an account that is valid on the domain.

▶ **See** "Sharing and Securing Resources," **page 997**

Opening Shared Folders with UNC Names

In Windows programs and in the Start menu's Run dialog box, you can specify any file by entering its Universal Naming Convention (UNC) path name. To use a UNC name, you must follow this syntax:

```
\\computername\sharename\path
```

For example, if a coworker whose computer is named BillG has created a shared folder named Budget and has given you permission to access that folder, you can browse his shared files by entering \\Billg\Budget in the File Open dialog box and pressing Enter. You can also create a shortcut to a shared network drive or folder using the UNC name of the resource.

Mapping a Network Drive

Drive mapping, as the name implies, lets you assign a virtual drive letter to a shared network resource. When you map a network drive, you refer to it using the drive letter, just as though it were a local drive on your own computer.

There are two reasons why you might want to map drive letters. First, it makes working with files more convenient; instead of browsing through the Network Neighborhood, you can simply choose a drive letter from the drop-down Drives list in a common dialog box. Second, some older programs (and even some components of Windows 98) do not allow you to browse network resources directly; in these cases, the only way to access a shared file or folder is to first map it to a drive letter.

To map a shared drive or folder, follow these steps:

1. Open the Network Neighborhood in a folder window or the Windows Explorer, and open the server or workstation icon to display available shared resources on that computer.

2. Right-click the share icon and choose Map Network Drive from the shortcut menu. The dialog box shown in Figure 4.14 appears.

Figure 4.14
Mapping a shared folder
to a drive letter is the
only way to use network
resources with some
programs.

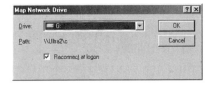

3. Select an available drive letter from the drop down Drive list.

4. If you want Windows to automatically reestablish the drive mapping every time you start your computer, check the box labeled Reconnect at logon. If you want the mapping to be temporary, clear this box.

5. Click OK to map the drive to the selected letter. The mapped drive letter will now be available in all common dialog boxes. You can also display its contents directly by typing the drive letter and a colon in the Run dialog box on the Start menu.

N O T E   All mapped drives appear in the My Computer window alongside the icons for local drives. The label for a mapped drive includes the share name, server name, and drive letter. ■

To remove a drive mapping, follow these steps:

1. Right-click the Network Neighborhood icon and choose Disconnect Network Drive. A list of mapped drives appears.

2. Choose the mapped drive from the Drive list.

3. Click OK to disconnect. You will not see a confirmation dialog before disconnecting.

Finding a Computer on Your Network

Large networks can include hundreds of computers across different domains and workgroups. On large networks, even opening the Network Neighborhood and displaying all the icons in it can take minutes. To find a specific computer without browsing through the entire network, follow these steps:

1. Click the Start button and choose Find, Computer. The Find Computer dialog box appears (see Figure 4.15).

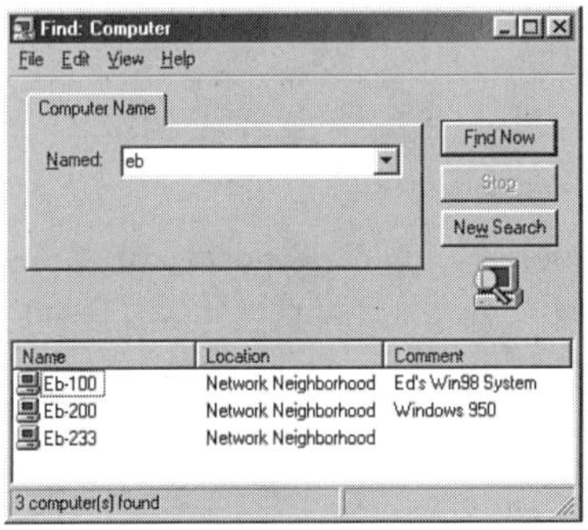

Figure 4.15
To avoid long delays
when you open the
Network Neighborhood,
search for a computer
name instead.

2. In the box labeled <u>N</u>amed, enter all or part of the computer name you're searching for.

3. Click the F<u>i</u>nd Now button. The list of matching computer names will appear in the Results pane at the bottom of the dialog box.

 Right-click a computer name and choose P<u>r</u>operties to see more information about the computer, including the name of the workgroup or domain it belongs to and the operating system it uses.

Managing Files from an MS-DOS Prompt

There are things you can do from an MS-DOS prompt that you can't do any other way, and for some people it's the most efficient way to work. Using the DIR command and MS-DOS wildcards, for example, you can quickly display a filtered list of files within a given folder and redirect the output to a text file. It's the only way to quickly rename a group of files using wildcards, and it's the fastest way to change the extension (and thus the file type) of some types of documents without having to adjust Windows Explorer preferences.

 To see command-line switches for DIR and other MS-DOS commands, type the command followed by /? at the MS-DOS prompt. If the instructions scroll off the top of the screen before you can read them, add | **MORE** to the end of the command.

Part

I

Ch

4

Starting an MS-DOS Prompt Session

To open an MS-DOS Prompt session within Windows, open the Start menu and choose <u>P</u>rograms, MS-DOS Prompt.

Note that an MS-DOS Prompt session behaves differently from the command prompt that appears when you restart your computer in MS-DOS mode. Here are some key differences:

■ The MS-DOS Prompt session allows you to work with long filenames. In MS-DOS mode, you see only the short 8.3 style names.

■ The MS-DOS Prompt session can run in a window or in full-screen mode. When you start in MS-DOS mode, on the other hand, you are limited to full-screen display.

■ All network resources are available to an MS-DOS Prompt session; accessing those resources in MS-DOS mode requires that you load real-mode network drivers.

■ You can launch any Windows or MS-DOS program or batch file from the MS-DOS Prompt window. When you restart in MS-DOS mode, you can run MS-DOS programs only.

 To switch between a windowed MS-DOS Prompt and a full-screen display, press Alt+Enter.

To close an MS-DOS Prompt window, type EXIT at the prompt and press Enter.

Using the Windows Clipboard with the MS-DOS Prompt

There's a special set of procedures for copying text to and from an MS-DOS Prompt window. These procedures are particularly useful when you need to copy a lengthy filename, complete with its full path. Follow these steps:

1. Open an MS-DOS Prompt window. If the MS-DOS Prompt session opens in full-screen mode, press Alt+Enter to force it into a window.

2. Click the control-menu icon at the far left edge of the title bar; you'll see the pull-down control menu shown in Figure 4.16.

Figure 4.16

Use this pull-down menu to cut, copy, and paste text between an MS-DOS window and the Windows Clipboard.

3. Choose the Edit command; a cascading menu will appear to the right.

4. To copy part or all of the screen, choose Mark. This switches the mouse pointer into Mark mode, which allows you to select any rectangular portion of the MS-DOS screen.

5. When you've marked the section you want to copy, press Enter. Whatever you marked is now available on the Windows Clipboard; you can paste it into the MS-DOS window or into any Windows program.

6. To paste text from the Clipboard into your MS-DOS window, position the insertion point at the right spot in your DOS screen. Click the control-menu icon on the title bar and choose Edit, Paste from the pull-down menu.

Using UNC Path Names in an MS-DOS Prompt Window

In Windows programs and in the Start menu's Run dialog box, you can specify any file by using its Universal Naming Convention (UNC) path name. In an MS-DOS Prompt window, however, UNC names are not recognized. To list or manage shared files across the network from an MS-DOS Prompt, you must first map the share to a drive letter. Use the procedures outlined earlier in this chapter.

To map a drive letter at the MS-DOS prompt, type **NET USE driveletter:** **\\servername\sharename** (substitute the appropriate drive letter, server name and share name). For more details about this command, type **NET USE /?** and press Enter. ●

CHAPTER 5

Managing Files Using Web View

by Ed Bott

In this chapter

What Is Web View?

Windows 98 incorporates a single Explorer window that lets you shift effortlessly between local files and pages on the Web. So, why not go the next step and view your files and folders as Web pages?

Ordinarily, Explorer displays files, folders, and other system objects as icons in a window. You can choose between large and small icons or arrange them in a list or in a column-oriented Details view. A separate Web view option, independent of the icon arrangement you've chosen, lets you add Web-style information panels around the display of icons.

When you turn on Web view, Explorer uses HTML templates to customize your view of files and folders. You see more information at a glance, and for a modest investment of programming time, you can even create custom views that make it easier for other users to navigate through folders. With Web view on, an ordinary folder display changes to resemble the one in Figure 5.1.

Figure 5.1
When you choose Web view, Explorer displays extra information about the current folder and files within it.

Banner —

Info panel —

File list control —

Thumbnail viewer —

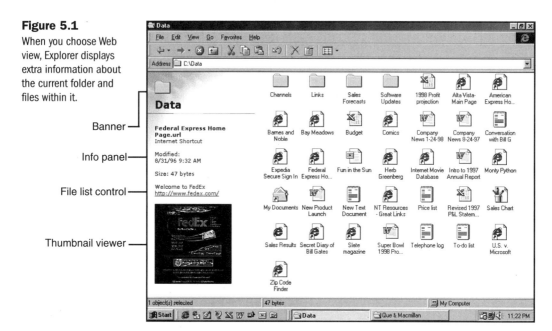

The default Web page view includes four standard elements:

- A banner identifies the title of the current folder.
- An info panel displays details about the folder and the currently selected file(s).
- Thumbnail images of certain file types appear below the contents pane, making it easier to identify the file's contents at a glance.
- The file list is contained in an ActiveX control embedded within the folder window.

Web view works in folder windows and in the contents pane of a two-pane Explorer window.

Using Web View with Folders

If you've selected Web-style navigation, Web view is turned on for all folders by default. If you've selected Classic-style navigation, Web view is disabled for all folders by default. With custom settings, you can choose whether to enable or disable Web view by default.

▶ **See** "Classic or Web? Choosing a Navigation Style," **page 14**

Regardless of the global settings, you can turn Web View on or off for any folder. The Web view menu choice is a toggle: If Web view is on, choose <u>V</u>iew, as <u>W</u>eb Page to restore the current folder window to a normal Explorer view. Setting this option for one folder window does not have any effect on other folder windows. However, if you turn on Web view using the two-pane Explorer view, your preferences apply to all folders you view in the current Explorer window.

Displaying Thumbnails and File Information

When you choose Web view and select any file, the info panel at the left side of the window displays that file's name, its file type, the date it was last modified, and its size. If you select a folder icon, the info panel shows the name only.

When you select multiple files, the details in the info panel change. You'll see a count of the number of items you've selected, as well as the total combined size of the selected files (useful if you're planning to move or copy files to another folder), and a column listing the name of each selected file, as in Figure 5.2.

Figure 5.2
When you select multiple documents in Web view, you'll see these summary details in the info pane.

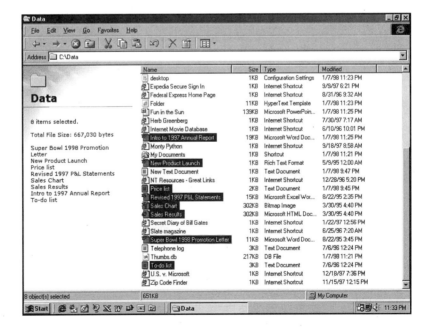

Below the info panel, the default Web view template includes a thumbnail image of certain file types. Only a handful of file formats will appear as thumbnails in Web view: Document files; Bitmap, GIF, and JPEG images; and Web pages in HTML format (if the page is stored locally or in your browser's cache). If you create a document with one of the applications in the Standard edition of Microsoft Office 97, you can see detailed information about the file, along with a thumbnail image of the document.

 TIP If you're an Office 97 user, taking advantage of Web view requires some extra effort. By default, Word and Excel files will not display thumbnail images unless you choose File, Properties, click the Summary tab, and check the box labeled Save preview picture. Likewise, the info panel will display the name of the author and other file properties, but only if you went out of your way to add that information on the Summary dialog box.

Can you turn on thumbnails for a given file type? Unfortunately, the answer is no. In theory, any application can add thumbnail support if the developer integrates its file formats with the WebViewFolderContents object; that's the ActiveX control that adds Web view capabilities to the Windows Explorer. If an application includes this feature, it should appear automatically, without requiring extra effort on your part.

TROUBLESHOOTING

You've turned on Web view, but you can't see a thumbnail view in some folders. The folder window you're using may be too small. Maximize the folder and see if thumbnails return. When you restore the drive or folder to a window, try resizing it and watch the changes in Web view as it decreases in size. The banner along the top becomes more compact, and the thumbnail viewer goes away when the window reaches a certain size.

Using Web View with System Folders

A handful of system folders use custom Web view templates. When you display the My Computer folder in Web view, for example, you'll see a display like the one in Figure 5.3.

N O T E Although it's easy to forget this fact, the Windows desktop is just another Explorer folder, minus the window borders, menus, and toolbars. When you turn on the Active Desktop and display Web content on the desktop, you're telling Windows to display the desktop folder in Web view. IE4 automatically generates a custom Web view template, Desktop.htt, every time you customize your Active Desktop settings. Although it's theoretically possible to find this template and edit it manually, this practice is not recommended. ▨

Other system folders that include custom Web view templates include Control Panel and Printers. The following table lists the built-in Web templates you'll find in a typical Windows 98 installation (all of these templates are stored in the Windows\Web folder):

Template file	Description
Controlp.htt	Displays help text in the Info panel when you select individual Control Panel icons. Includes hyperlinks to two Microsoft Web pages.
Folder.htt	The default template Windows uses when you customize Web view options for a folder. Editing this file does not change folders you have already customized.
Deskmovr.htt	Provides support for Active Desktop objects. Do not edit this file.
Mycomp.htt	Displays information about selected local and network drives in My Computer; also displays help text for system folders.
Printers.htt	Offers instructions for setting up a new printer; selecting printer icon displays the number of messages in print queue.
Safemode.htt	Contains information and troubleshooting links for resolving problems when Active Desktop crashes.
Dialup.htt	Displays information to help you use the Dial-Up Networking folder.
Nethood.htt	Provides an explanation of the contents of the Network Neighborhood.
Recycle.htt	Includes JavaScript links that let you empty the Recycle Bin or restore all its contents at once.
Schedule.htt	Explains how the Scheduled Tasks folder works.

Figure 5.3

You'll see detailed drive information when you turn on Web view in the My Computer folder.

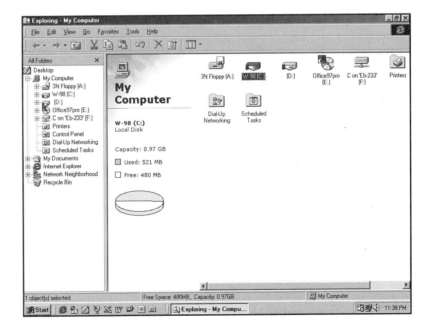

> **CAUTION**
>
> Before editing any of the default templates in the Windows\Web folder, be sure to create backup copies. This precaution will allow you to recover the original HTML files if you want to start over.

Creating Custom Web Views

There's no particular magic to Web view. When you display a folder's contents and choose View, as Web Page, you instruct Explorer to look in the current folder for two files:

- **Desktop.ini** lists shell objects that allow the folder to interpret HTML code and display files in a defined region within the folder. It also includes pointers to custom HTML templates and/or background images for the folder. If this file does not exist in the current folder, Explorer uses default settings.

- **Folder.htt** is a HyperText Template file that defines scripts, objects, and HTML code that allow files to display. If this file does not exist in the current folder, Explorer uses the default file in the Windows\Web folder. You can customize this template file, and you can use a file with a different name by specifying it in Desktop.ini.

Windows includes a wizard that lets you customize the look of a folder by editing the Web view template.

> **CAUTION**
>
> There's no way to force users to open a folder using Web view. If you've designed a custom Web page to help other users of your PC navigate in a particular folder, or to simplify file access for co-workers on a network, your work will pay off only if they choose to use Web view. If they access the custom folder using a version of Windows that does not include the Windows Desktop Update, they cannot view your changes.

Using the Web View Wizard

To customize the appearance of a folder in Web view, choose View, Customize this Folder. That action launches the wizard that appears in Figure 5.4.

As wizards go, this one is fairly crude. When you choose Create or edit an HTML document, the wizard launches Notepad and loads the HyperText Template specified in Desktop.ini. If this is the first time you've used the wizard in a given folder, it copies the Folder.htt template file from the Windows\Web folder.

After you've finished editing the file in Notepad, you can close the Customize this Folder dialog box and return to the folder to see your changes in place.

The second option lets you add a background graphic behind the file list control on the Web view folder. You can use any file in any standard graphic format, including Bitmap, JPEG, or GIF.

Figure 5.4
Use this wizard to edit
the Web view template
or add a background
graphic to a folder.

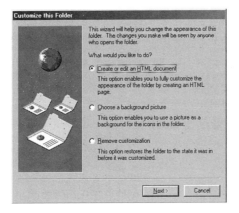

Start the Customize this Folder wizard and follow these steps:

1. Select Choose a background picture. Click the Next button.

2. The next dialog box (see Figure 5.5) displays a list of graphics files from the \Windows folder. Click the Browse button to choose a different folder, if necessary.

Figure 5.5
Choose a background
image to appear behind
the file list control in
Web view. Pick a light
image that won't
obscure icons.

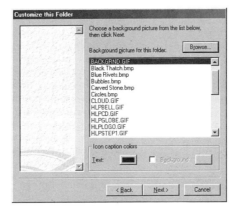

Part

I

Ch

5

3. As you click on graphics files in the list, the contents of the file appear in the preview window at the left of the dialog box. If the graphic is small, Windows tiles the image to fill the preview box.

4. After you've selected an appropriate graphic file, click the Text button to choose a contrasting color for icon labels that will appear on top of the graphic. You may also wish to check the Background box and adjust the color that appears behind the icon labels.

5. Click Next to record your changes, then click Finish to close the wizard. You may need to press F5 to refresh the folder's contents and see your changes.

T I P If you must use a graphic behind the file list control, choose a light image, preferably in a shade of gray. Dark or detailed images such as photographs can make it difficult to see icons in the file list.

Editing a HyperText Template

You'll need to be fluent in HTML, and you won't be able to fall back on the WYSIWYG editor in FrontPage Express. By default, when you choose to customize the HyperText Template file for a folder, Windows dumps you in the most rudimentary HTML editor imaginable—Notepad.

Some sections of folder.htt are strictly for Web experts; don't edit the scripts that display file information, for example, unless you're sure you know what you're doing. But even an inexperienced editor can safely add hyperlinks to the default folder template. (This procedure assumes you have used the Customize this Folder wizard to open folder.htt for editing in Notepad.)

> **N O T E**   Future updates to Windows and Internet Explorer may include more complex templates for customizing folders. In that case, you may need to adjust the instructions that follow to deal with the revised HTML code. ■

The default folder template includes a section where you can add your own hypertext links to Web pages or files. (Open Control Panel and turn on Web view to see examples of these links.) To customize this section, open folder.htt and follow these steps:

1. Choose <u>S</u>earch and enter the following text in the box labeled Fi<u>n</u>d what: A FEW LINKS OF YOUR OWN. Click the button labeled Fi<u>n</u>d Next.

2. The HTML code in this section includes two sample URLs. Replace the two sample URLs with your own link, and replace the link text (Custom Link 1 and Custom Link 2) with your own label.

3. To create additional links, copy the two lines that follow the first sample link, and paste them below the second sample. Repeat for any additional links, and customize as in step 2.

4. Delete the comment tags above and below the links to make them visible in Web view. When finished, the code should look like the sample in Figure 5.6.

Figure 5.6

Edit the HyperText Template to add links that appear in Web view. Note that links can include Web pages, folders, or file names.

```
🗋 Folder - Notepad                                          _ □ ×
File  Edit  Search  Help
<!-- HERE'S A GOOD PLACE TO ADD A FEW LINKS OF YOUR OWN -->
        <p>
        <br>
        <a href="http://www.pccomputing.com/">PC Computing</a>
        <p class=Links>
        <a href="http://www.nytimes.com/">New York Times</a>

<p>
<!-- this is the thumbnail viewer control -->
<object id=Thumbnail classid="clsid:1D2B4F40-1F10-11D1-9E88-00C0▮
```

5. Close Notepad, saving the file with the default name. Press F5 to refresh the folder view and see the links in place.

Removing Custom Web View Settings

If you've customized a folder's Web view template and you're not happy with the results, use the wizard to delete your changes and start over. The procedure is simple:

1. Choose View, Customize this Folder.
2. Select the option labeled Remove Customization and click the Next button.
3. You'll see a dialog box warning you that you're about to delete folder.htt and remove custom settings from desktop.ini. Click Next to continue.
4. Click Finish to close the wizard. You'll see the default Web view settings for the current folder.

Advanced Customization Options

There's no limit to the amount of customization that a skilled HTML author can perform. As noted earlier, you can create your own HyperText Template file, using any name. Store it in the folder you wish to customize, then open Desktop.ini and enter the name of your custom HTML file after the entry PersistentMoniker=.

 TIP Remember, both Desktop.ini and Folder.htt are hidden files. To edit either one without using the wizard, you may need to adjust Explorer's options to show hidden files.

Part
I

Ch
5

Although most users will specify an HTML file in Desktop.ini, it's also possible to call out a Web page in this file. This option is not officially supported, but it works just the same. You can point a folder to a page on the Internet or on your intranet. The effect is a bit baffling: Although the Address bar displays the name of the folder, the Explorer window shows the Web page listed in Desktop.ini.

To use the file list control in a custom Web page, open the default Folder.htt file and copy the file list code to the clipboard, then paste it in your custom HTML document. Look for this block of code:

```
<object
classid="clsid:1820FED0-473E-11D0-A96C-00C04FD705A2">
</object>
```

You may need to add a Position statement to place the control where you want it to appear on the page.

N O T E For ideas on how to create useful custom Web view pages, check out the following article on the Microsoft SiteBuilder Network:

http://www.microsoft.com/workshop/prog/ie4/folders.htm

CHAPTER 6

Installing and Managing Applications

by Bob Voss

In this chapter

Understanding How Windows Runs Applications

Windows applications fall into one of two general categories: 32-bit applications (designed for Windows NT, Windows 95, and Windows 98) and 16-bit applications (designed for Windows 3.1 and lower versions). This chapter discusses how Windows 98 runs these programs. The last part of the chapter describes how to work with DOS applications in Windows 98.

Support for 32-bit Windows Applications

Many of the benefits of using Windows 98 result from its support for 32-bit applications. Other benefits are not limited to 32-bit applications. The following list outlines the benefits of working with Windows 98:

- Support for long filenames (up to 255 characters). If adapted, 16-bit applications can use long filenames.

- More efficient memory addressing.

- Each 32-bit application runs in its own memory space, isolating other applications if an application crashes.

- Preemptive multitasking and multithreading, allowing more efficient sharing of CPU time than with cooperative multitasking.

- Greater availability of system resources, allowing you to run more applications, create more windows, use more fonts, and so on without running out of system resources.

- Support for Windows 3.1 applications. Although Windows 3.1 applications do not gain the benefits of a 32-bit application, they do benefit from the advantages Windows 98 derives from 32-bit device drivers and improved printing throughput due to multitasking at the operating system level.

- Improved support for MS-DOS applications.

▶ **See** "Working with Long Filenames," **page 61**

Support for MS-DOS and 16-bit Windows Applications

Windows 98 can run applications designed specifically for Windows 95 and Windows 98, as well as most older Windows 3.1 applications, DOS-based applications, and applications designed for Windows NT. Windows 98 does not require the traditional CONFIG.SYS, AUTOEXEC.BAT, and INI files for configuration information. However, for backward-compatibility, Windows 98 can use settings from INI files and can maintain its own versions of CONFIG.SYS and AUTOEXEC.BAT in order to support loading real-mode device drivers.

What the "Designed for Windows" Logo Really Means

The "Designed for Windows 95" logo program has evolved into the "Designed for Windows NT and Windows 98" logo program. In the early days of the Windows logo program, the requirements were relatively permissive, but the program has continually been reevaluated and revised. Microsoft has added many new requirements to better serve users who are looking for software that is designed to take full advantage of the Windows 98 and Windows NT operating environments and that is fully compatible with other Windows applications. To acquire the logo, the application must be submitted for testing by an independent, third-party testing firm (VeriTest).

The basic concept behind the logo program is to provide users with a means for selecting software that has been tested for compatibility and functionality on both the Windows 98 and Windows NT 5 platforms. The application has to conform to a series of criteria that assure that application takes full advantage of the Windows 98/Windows NT technology and that it is compatible with other Windows software. For in-depth information and specifications for the logo program and to download the "Designed for Windows Logo" handbook, visit the following Web site:

http://www.microsoft.com/windows/thirdparty/winlogo/

> **CAUTION**
>
> Beware of software that claims to "Windows compatible" and displays a logo to this effect. Be sure your applications have the genuine "Designed for Windows NT and Windows 98" logo.

Installing Windows Applications

Most Windows 98 (and Windows 95) applications are easily installed using the setup programs that come with these applications. Installing DOS-based applications is a different matter and often not as simple. This subject is covered in a later section, "Working with MS-DOS Applications."

▶ **See** "Adding and Removing Programs in the Start Menu," **page 130**

Installing Windows 95 and Windows 98 Applications

The basic technique for installing Windows 95 and Windows 98 applications consists of running the Setup (or Install) program for the application and following the prompts. The Setup program takes care of all the details of installing the application. You can start the Setup program using the Run command on the Start menu.

N O T E When you install Office 97, the Setup program runs automatically when you place the CD-ROM in the drive. This is an example of the Windows 95/98 feature called AutoPlay, which automatically launches a default program on a CD whenever it is inserted. ■

Another way to install an application is to use the Install Programs Wizard accessible via the Add/Remove Programs icon in the Control Panel. The Add/Remove Programs dialog box provides a common starting point for adding and removing Windows applications and Windows system components and accessories.

Part

I

Ch

6

To use the Install Programs Wizard to install a Windows application, follow these steps:

1. Open the Start menu and choose Settings, Control Panel.
2. In the Control Panel window, use the Add/Remove Programs icon to open the Add/Remove Programs Properties sheet shown in Figure 6.1.

Figure 6.1

The Add/Remove Programs Properties dialog box is used to add and remove applications.

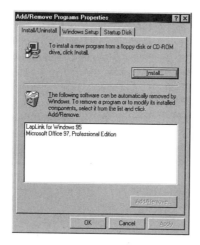

3. Choose Install to start the Install Program Wizard.
4. When the Install Program from Floppy Disk or CD-ROM dialog box appears, insert the first floppy disk or compact disc in the appropriate drive and choose Next.
5. The wizard searches the disk's root directory for an installation program (usually named SETUP.EXE or INSTALL.EXE) and displays the command line in the Run Installation Program dialog box.
6. If the wizard fails to find the setup program (perhaps because it is in a subdirectory) or you want to run a different setup program (perhaps from a network drive), you can choose Browse and select a different file in the Browse dialog box. Choose Open to insert the selected filename in the wizard.
7. After the correct command line for the setup program appears in the Run Installation Program dialog box, choose Finish to start the setup program and begin the application installation.

Installing 16-bit Windows Applications

Windows 98 features full backward-compatibility with 16-bit Windows 3.1 applications, enabling you to install and use your Windows 3.1 applications in Windows 98 without modification.

If you encounter a compatibility problem with a legacy application—an older application designed for a previous version of DOS or Windows—running in Windows 98, check with the application's developer for a patch or workaround for the problem. In some cases, perhaps the only solution is an upgrade to a new, Windows 95 or Windows 98 version of the application.

What If There's No Setup Program?

You may occasionally encounter a Windows application that does not include a setup program. Installation for small utilities, for example, usually consists of copying a couple of files to your hard disk and adding a shortcut to your Start menu to launch the application. You'll probably find instructions for installing the application in an accompanying manual or README file.

Installing 16-bit Windows Applications

You install Windows 3.1 applications in Windows 98 the same way that you do in Windows 3.1. You simply insert the first disk of the program's installation disks in your floppy disk or CD-ROM drive, run the Setup program using the Run command on the Start menu, and follow the prompts and instructions.

> **CAUTION**
>
> Save a copy of your AUTOEXEC.BAT and CONFIG.SYS files before installing any new DOS or Windows 3.x application. After you install a Windows 3.x or DOS application, it is a good idea to check your AUTOEXEC.BAT files to see if any unnecessary programs or configuration lines were added. For example, some applications add a line that loads SHARE.EXE or SMARTDRV.EXE, neither of which is needed in Windows 98. Not only do these programs waste memory, you may have problems with your system if they are loaded.

Of course, the setup program for a legacy application will be tailored to Windows 3.1 instead of Windows 98. For example, the installation program will probably offer to create Program Manager groups and update INI files. Windows 98 will intercept Program Manager updates and automatically convert them to Start menu shortcuts. Windows 98 also transfers WIN.INI and SYSTEM.INI entries into the Registry.

Organizing the Programs Menu

When you install an application, the installation process creates a new item on the Programs menu. Although this item appears automatically, you can modify it. For example, items on the Programs menu can be removed, reorganized, or renamed. While you can modify the Programs menu using the same procedure that customizes the Start menu described in Chapter 8, "Customizing the Look and Feel of Windows," you will have greater flexibility if you use the following technique to directly modify the folders and shortcuts on which the Programs menu is based.

▶ **See** "Adding and Removing Programs in the Start Menu," **page 130**

The Programs menu is a reflection of the contents of a Programs folder. You can find this folder under Windows\Start Menu if you are the only person using the computer. If the computer has multiple user profiles the appropriate Programs folder for a specific user is found under Windows\Profiles*username*\Start Menu.

Part

I

Ch

6

A simple way to make sure you are modifying the correct Program menu is to log in to Windows with the user name whose Programs menu you want to change. Right-click in the gray area of the Taskbar and choose Properties. Select the Start Menu Programs tab, then click the Advanced button. This displays an Explorer window that is restricted to the appropriate Start Menu. You can modify and reorganize the Start menu or Programs menu by modifying folders and shortcuts in this Explorer window.

To work on just the Programs menu, open and select the Programs folder in the left Explorer pane. The folder hierarchy and shortcut names you see displayed in the right pane are used to create the Programs menu. Modifying the folders and shortcut names modifies the Programs menu. Use normal Explorer techniques for modifying folders and files.

Create new submenus under the Programs menu by creating new folders in the right pane. Drag and drop program shortcuts into these folders to reorganize them. Delete folders you do not want, but make sure you first remove shortcut icons you want to retain.

Change Programs menu item names by selecting the folder or file, pressing F2, and editing or typing a new name. Reorder files and folders by renaming them. Windows sorts the folder and shortcut names in alphanumeric order to decide the order in which they display on the Programs menu. To reorganize the Programs menu, change the names to give the sort order you want. For example, if you want Microsoft Word to appear in the menu before Microsoft Excel and you want their names shortened, change the shortcut names to *1 Word* and *2 Excel*.

Working with Program Shortcuts

In Chapter 3, "Managing Files with My Computer and Windows Explorer," you learned how to create shortcuts to your files and programs. In this section, you will learn some more advanced techniques for working with shortcuts.

Starting Programs on StartUp

If there are programs that you routinely keep open because you use them throughout the day, you can have Windows 98 start these programs automatically when you start Windows. To do this, you simply create a shortcut for the program in a special folder call the StartUp folder. The StartUp folder is located in the Programs folder on the Start menu.

To create a shortcut for a program in the StartUp folder, follow these steps:

1. Open the Start menu and choose Settings and then Taskbar & Start Menu.
2. Select the Start Menu Programs tab.
3. Choose Add and then Browse.
4. Locate the program you want to add to the StartUp folder in the Browse dialog box (see Figure 6.2).

Figure 6.2
Use the Browse dialog box to locate the program you want to add to the StartUp folder.

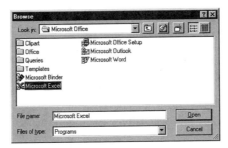

5. Select the program and choose Open (or double-click the program).

    The pathname for the selected program appears in the Command Line text box of the Create Shortcut dialog box.

6. Choose Next and select the StartUp folder in the Select Program Folder dialog box (see Figure 6.3).

Figure 6.3
Select the StartUp folder as the destination for the shortcut.

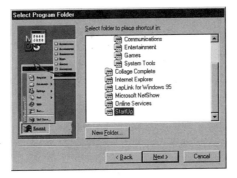

7. Type the name you want to appear in the StartUp menu in the text box and choose Finish.

8. Choose OK to close the Taskbar Properties dialog box.

Now, whenever you start up Windows, the application you added to the StartUp menu will be started automatically.

TIP You can also add documents to the StartUp menu to open them when Windows starts. For example, you might copy a shortcut to an Excel spreadsheet there, so that Excel starts and the spreadsheet opens each time you start Windows. This works because Excel data files are associated with the Excel application (see "Managing File Associations" later in this chapter for more information).

Part
I

Ch
6

Specifying How a Shortcut Starts a Program

Once you have created a shortcut for an application, you can customize the shortcut using its Properties sheet. For example, when you create a shortcut for an application in the StartUp folder, as previously described above, you can specify whether the application is started in a normal window, a maximized window, or minimized as an icon on the taskbar. You can also add command-line parameters to the command line for the application, specify a folder for the application to start in, and assign a shortcut key for starting the application from the keyboard.

To customize a shortcut, follow these steps:

1. Locate the shortcut in My Computer or Windows Explorer.
2. Right-click the shortcut and choose Properties from the shortcut menu.
3. Select the Shortcut tab (see Figure 6.4).

Figure 6.4

You can customize a shortcut using the Shortcut tab in the shortcut's property sheet.

4. To add a parameter to a command line, click in the Target text box, press End to move to the end of the command line, and enter a space. Type in the command-line parameter you want to add.

   For example, to start an application and open a document within that application, type in the path and filename for the document you want to open at the end of the application's command line, as shown in Figure 6.5.

5. Specify a folder for the application to start from in the Start In text box.

   With some applications, you need to start the application in a folder that contains files related to the application.

6. Assign a keyboard shortcut for starting the application in the Shortcut Key text box.

   Keyboard shortcuts use a combination of Ctrl+Alt+*character*. You cannot use the Esc, Enter, Tab, spacebar, Print Screen, or Backspace keys.

   Shortcut keys defined in a Windows application take precedence over shortcut keys defined for a shortcut. Be sure to use a unique keyboard shortcut.

Figure 6.5

You can add command-line parameters to the command line for an application's shortcut.

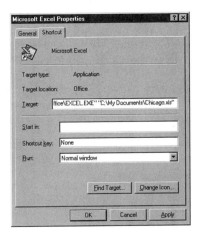

7. Specify whether you want the application to run in a normal window, a maximized window, or minimized as an icon.

8. Choose OK.

Managing File Associations

Recall that in Windows 3.x, you can associate a file extension with an application. For example, you can associate the DOC extension that Microsoft Word adds to files to Word, so that when you choose a file with the DOC extension, the file is opened in Word.

In Windows 98, you can define a *file type*, associated with a file extension, and then associate any number of *actions* with the file type. Again, using Word as an example, you can define the Microsoft Word Document file type, and then define one or more actions associated with that file type. The default action can be executed by choosing a file with the DOC extension in Windows Explorer or in a folder window or by right-clicking a DOC file and choosing the default action from the top of the shortcut menu that appears.

Other actions that you define and associate with a file type will appear in the shortcut menu when you right-click a file of that type. When Microsoft Word for Windows is installed, for example, the Print command is automatically associated with the Word Document file type, so you can right-click a Word file and choose Print from the shortcut menu. The document will be opened in Word, printed, and then closed.

How Applications Register File Types

All file types and their actions are registered in the Windows Registry. This information is stored in the HKEY_CLASSES_ROOT key of the Registry. If you are experienced in working in the Registry using REGEDIT, you can add and edit file types directly in the Registry.

Part

I

Ch

6

Registering a New File Type

Many applications automatically register a file type when you install the application. In some cases, however, you may want to register a file type for an extension that is not already associated with an application.

To register a new file type, follow these steps:

1. In the Explorer, choose View, Folder Options.

2. Click the File Types tab of the Folder Options dialog box (see Figure 6.6).

Figure 6.6

Register and modify file types on the File Types page of the Folder Options dialog box.

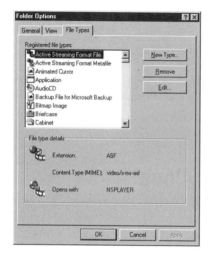

3. Choose the New Type button.

4. Enter a description of the file type in the Description of Type text box.

    This description appears in the Registered File Types list on the File Types page of the Folder Options dialog box. For example, if you want to be able to use Microsoft Word to open WordPerfect files that use the extension WPD, you could use the description WordPerfect Document, as shown in Figure 6.7.

5. Enter the file extension to be associated with this file type in the Associated Extension text box. This is the three-letter file extension associated with DOS-based files. In this example, you would enter WPD.

6. Select the type of file from the Content Type (MIME) list. This list shows all the installed applications in the registry.

7. If you want to specify an action to be performed on this file type by its associated program or if you want to add a shortcut menu item for this file type, then skip step 8 and continue with the next procedure to specify an action.

8. Click OK twice.

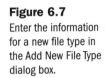

Figure 6.7

Enter the information for a new file type in the Add New File Type dialog box.

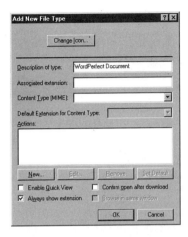

N O T E   MIME (Multipurpose Internet Mail Extensions) is a standard for defining different types of file attachments for e-mail delivered over the Internet. The goal of MIME is to allow multiple types of data, such text, video and audio files, and application files, to be gathered together in an e-mail message and transferred successfully from sender to recipient, even if they are using different e-mail applications.

You can specify the type of action which occurs on a file type when the file is chosen. The action you specify will also appear as an item on the file type's shortcut menu and on the File menu when that file is selected. This procedure begins with either the Add New File Type or Edit File Type dialog box open. To create actions for a new file type, follow the previous procedure through step 7 and then continue here. To edit an existing file type, select the file type from the Registered File Types list and click Edit.

To simultaneously specify actions for the file type and create shortcut menu items, follow this procedure:

1. Click New to add a new action to the file type in the New Action dialog box.

   The action is actually a custom command that appears on the shortcut menu when you right-click the file.

2. Type an action, for example, **Open in Word**, in the Action text box.

   What you type will appear as an item on the shortcut menu for this file type. You can type anything, but commands usually start with a verb. If you want the command to have an accelerator key, precede that letter with an ampersand (&).

3. Enter or select the application to be used to perform the action in the Application Used to Perform Action text box. If you do not know the application's path, use the Browse button to select the application.

   Some applications have command-line switches you can append to the end of the command line to control how the application behaves. See the documentation or online Help for your application to find out what command-line switches are available.

   Figure 6.8 shows the completed New Action dialog box.

Part

I

Ch

6

Figure 6.8

Designate a shortcut
menu action and the
program used to
perform that action in
the New Action dialog
box.

4. Select the Use DDE check box if the program uses DDE (dynamic data exchange) and add the DDE statements for this action. This is rarely used.

▶ **See** "Understanding DDE Statements," for more information on using DDE statements to communicate with an application.

5. Choose OK.

6. If you have more than one action listed in the Actions box, select the one you want to be the default action and choose the Set Default button.

   The default action is the one that is performed when you choose a file of this type in the Explorer or a folder window.

7. Select the appropriate check boxes for the file type.

Enable Quick View	Quick View allows you to view a file without opening it
Always Show Extension	Always displays the MS-DOS extension even when the Hide File Extension option has been chosen
Confirm Open After Download	Request confirmation before opening files after downloading them from the Internet

8. Click Close twice.

▶ **See** "Previewing a Document with Quick View," **page 44**

Understanding DDE Settings

If the application you use to create a file type and define an action uses DDE (Dynamic Data Exchange), you can use DDE statements to exercise more control over the actions carried out by the application. DDE statements are messages that are passed to the application to tell it what actions to carry out.

Figure 6.9 illustrates the use of DDE statements in the definition of the Print action for the Microsoft Excel Worksheet type. The first DDE statement in the DDE Message text box is the command passed to Microsoft Excel to specify what action should be taken when the Print command is selected from the shortcut menu for an Excel Worksheet:

```
[open("%1")][print()][close()]
```

This DDE statement tells Excel to open the selected file, print the file with the default print options, and then close the worksheet.

Figure 6.9

You can use DDE statements to control the actions associated with a registered file type.

The entry in the Application box is the string used to start a DDE exchange with the specified program. If this box is left empty, the command that appears in the Application Used to Perform Action text box is used.

The following DDE statement appears in the DDE Application Not Running box:

```
[open("%1")][print()][quit()]
```

This statement starts Excel, prints the selected file, and then exits Excel.

These two simple examples illustrate how useful the DDE statements can be. By specifying two different statements in the DDE Message and DDE Application Not Running boxes, you can control the behavior of Excel when you select the Print command from the shortcut menu. When Excel is already opened, the file you select is opened in that session of Excel (that is, another session of Excel is not started), printed, and then closed. The running session of Excel is not terminated.

When Excel is not already open, on the other hand, and you select the Print command, Excel is started, the selected file is opened and printed, and Excel is shut down.

Changing the Icon for a File Type or Other Object

You can change the icon used to designate a file type, drive, folder, and other objects on your computer. To change the icon used for a particular file type or object, follow these steps:

1. In Explorer, choose View, Folder Options.
2. Choose the File Types tab to display the File Types page of the Folder Options dialog box (refer to Figure 6.6).
3. Select the file type or other object whose icon you want to change in the Registered File Types list.
4. Choose the Edit button.
5. Choose the Change Icon button to display the Change Icon dialog box.

Part
I
Ch
6

6. Select a new icon from the <u>C</u>urrent Icon scrolling list.

The name of the file containing the icons currently shown is listed in the <u>F</u>ile Name text box. You can use the <u>B</u>rowse button to search for a new file containing different icons. Figure 6.10 shows the selection of icons in the Moricons.dll file, which is located in the Windows folder on your hard drive.

Figure 6.10
Use the Change Icon dialog box to select a new icon for a file type or other type of object.

7. Click OK and then Close two times.

Working with MS-DOS Applications

Although Windows 98 is designed to shield the user from the often-confusing world of the command line, AUTOEXEC.BAT, CONFIG.SYS, and memory-management practices, it offers surprisingly rich support for those users who still desire or need to work in the MS-DOS environment. Windows 98 offers extensive control over MS-DOS application environments, allowing you to fine-tune your MS-DOS sessions to optimize performance.

Many MS-DOS applications will run under Windows 98 without any modifications. In some cases, you will need to modify the setup for the application for it to run in Windows. For applications that won't run at all under Windows 98, a special mode helps you run them quickly and easily from within Windows, and then automatically returns you to your Windows session when you're finished.

Installing and Uninstalling MS-DOS Applications

Installing MS-DOS applications is a straightforward procedure. Simply locate and run the installation program for the application. The installation program will create a storage area for the application and copy the files to it. In addition, it will perform the additional operating system configuration chores that may be necessary for successful operation. You may have to handle some of the steps yourself. Look for the documentation for the manual program installation instructions in the program folder. Often this is a simple text file, labeled README.TXT or INSTALL.TXT.

You can also run the installation program for an MS-DOS application from the MS-DOS prompt. Running the installation program from an MS-DOS prompt is just like doing it on a machine that's running only MS-DOS. Follow these steps to begin:

1. Open a new MS-DOS session from the Start menu.

2. At the MS-DOS prompt, enter the command to start the installation program (for example, **a:\install.exe**) and press Enter.

3. When the installation program is finished, close the MS-DOS session manually or run the application if you want.

Some MS-DOS applications don't have installation programs at all. This is most common with shareware applications or small utility programs.

To install your application manually, follow these simple steps:

1. Open a new MS-DOS session from the Start menu.

2. At the MS-DOS prompt, enter the command to create a folder for your program (for example, **md c:\myprog**) and press Enter.

3. Enter the command to copy the program to the new folder, such as **xcopy a:*.* c:\myprog**. MS-DOS copies the files to the new folder.

You may need to alter the preceding routine slightly if your application comes as a compressed archive (such as a ZIP or an ARJ file). Usually, all this means is an additional step for decompression after the files are copied.

Configuring Your MS-DOS Application

Your MS-DOS applications are very likely to run fine without any reconfiguration. Preset configurations for the most popular MS-DOS applications are stored in Windows and in many cases these configurations will work perfectly. However, in those cases where your application doesn't run properly (or at all), you can modify many settings using the Properties sheet to control how your MS-DOS application runs. To display the Properties sheet, click the Properties button in the toolbar of the MS-DOS window.

General Properties   The General properties page is primarily informational, with minimal controls other than file attributes (see Figure 6.11).

The only real controls exposed in the General properties page are the file attribute settings. These are used mainly to protect documents (by setting the read-only attribute), and you shouldn't alter them unless you have a specific reason.

Program Properties   The Program properties page gives you control over the basic environment your application starts with (see Figure 6.12).

Part

I

Ch

6

Figure 6.11

The General properties page gives you most of the basic information about the file and easy access to control of the file attributes. Context-sensitive help is available at any time by using the "?" tool.

File attribute controls

Windows filename

Basic file information

File history

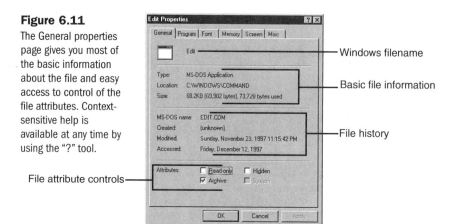

Figure 6.12

The Program properties page allows you to alter the variables used to name and start the application.

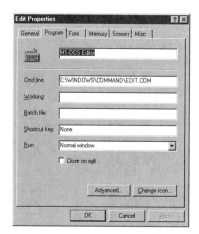

Choosing the Advanced button in the Program properties page opens the Advanced Program Settings dialog box, shown in Figure 6.13.

Figure 6.13

The Advanced Program Settings dialog box enables you to define the precise mode and environment for your MS-DOS session.

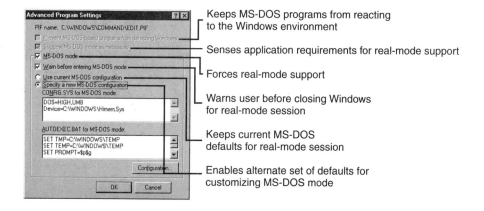

Keeps MS-DOS programs from reacting to the Windows environment

Senses application requirements for real-mode support

Forces real-mode support

Warns user before closing Windows for real-mode session

Keeps current MS-DOS defaults for real-mode session

Enables alternate set of defaults for customizing MS-DOS mode

If you need to run your application in MS-DOS mode, here's where you can enable it. You can even set up custom CONFIG.SYS and AUTOEXEC.BAT values for your session. If you click the Specify a New MS-DOS Configuration option, you can edit the special CONFIG.SYS and AUTOEXEC.BAT values right in this dialog box.

If you click the Configuration button, you see the dialog box displayed in Figure 6.14.

Figure 6.14
The Select MS-DOS Configuration Options dialog box lets you control expanded memory, disk caching, disk access, and command-line editing.

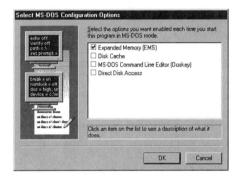

All the settings under the Advanced dialog box should be altered only if your MS-DOS application simply won't run in a standard session with the default settings. For that matter, don't even enable MS-DOS mode unless your application demands it.

▶ **See** "Using MS-DOS Mode," **page 98**

Font Properties   The Font properties page is primarily informational, with minimal controls other than file attributes (see Figure 6.15). It works just like the font list control on the MS-DOS session toolbar.

Figure 6.15
The Font properties page lets you choose the font type and size, and gives you both a window and font preview.

Part

I

Ch

6

Memory Properties   The Memory properties page makes simple work of the traditional maze of MS-DOS memory management (see Figure 6.16). With a few mouse clicks, you can configure your application memory precisely as needed.

Figure 6.16

The Memory properties page vastly simplifies this formerly arcane management issue.

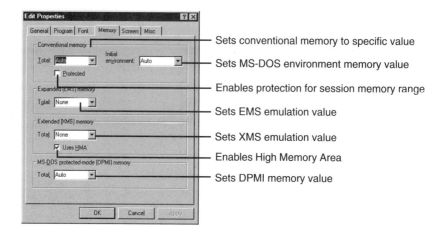

Sets conventional memory to specific value

Sets MS-DOS environment memory value

Enables protection for session memory range

Sets EMS emulation value

Sets XMS emulation value

Enables High Memory Area

Sets DPMI memory value

If your application works without altering these values, *do not change them.* If your application doesn't work with the default settings, *consult the documentation* for your application to determine what the appropriate settings are. *Then* you can alter the values in this dialog box. Proceeding in any other way, unless you have considerable experience with the techniques involved, can severely inhibit the performance of your system.

Screen Properties   The Screen properties page lets you control the appearance of the MS-DOS session (see Figure 6.17).

Figure 6.17

The Screen properties page gives you control of the size, type, and performance of the MS-DOS interface.

Choose between display modes

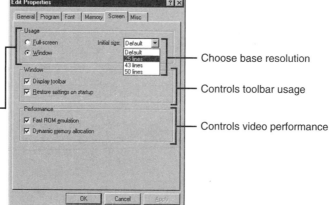

Choose base resolution

Controls toolbar usage

Controls video performance

You may find that certain MS-DOS programs (especially those running in Graphics mode) respond poorly to the video emulation used in windowed mode. If so, try defeating the performance defaults by clearing the Fast ROM Emulation and Dynamic Memory Allocation options. Fast ROM Emulation tells the Windows 98 display driver to mimic the video hardware to help display MS-DOS programs faster. Dynamic Memory Allocation releases display memory to other programs when the MS-DOS session isn't using it. If you experience strange display problems with your MS-DOS programs, try changing these settings.

Miscellaneous Properties   The Misc properties page covers the remaining configuration items that don't fit under the other categories (see Figure 6.18).

Figure 6.18

The Misc properties page controls screen saver, mouse, background operation, program termination, shortcut key, and editing options.

- The *Allo̱w Screen Saver* control lets your default Windows screen saver operate even if your MS-DOS session has the foreground.

- *Always Ṣuspend* freezes your MS-DOS application when you bring another application (either MS-DOS or Windows) to the foreground. If you have an application that must perform time-sensitive operations (such as a communications program), make sure to disable this option.

- *Idle Sensiti̱vity* tells your MS-DOS program to yield the system to other applications if it really isn't doing anything important. A word processor, for example, won't have a problem letting go of the system clock when you're not using it. A communications program, however, may need to respond quickly, so you want to set its idle sensitivity to Low.

- The *Mouse* controls enable *QuickEdit* mode (letting you mark text using just the mouse) and *E̱xclusive Mode* (the MS-DOS application has control of the mouse cursor when the application is in the foreground, even if you try to move the mouse out of the MS-DOS window).

- The *W̱arn If Still Active* item in the Termination box tells Windows to notify you before the MS-DOS session is closed. It's really best to leave this enabled, unless you are absolutely certain that the MS-DOS program will never, ever have open data files when you close it.

- The *F̱ast Pasting* setting simply tells Windows that your MS-DOS program can handle a raw data stream dump from the Windows Clipboard. Some MS-DOS programs clog at full speed, so if you paste to your MS-DOS application and you consistently lose characters, turn this one off.

- *Windows Shortcut Ḵeys* allows you to override the standard quick navigation aids built into the Windows environment, just for your MS-DOS session (some MS-DOS programs

Part

I

Ch

6

think they can get away with using the same keys, and something has to give—Windows!). By default, Windows "owns" these shortcuts, but you can lend them to your MS-DOS application by clearing them here.

Using MS-DOS Mode

Although you will be able to run most DOS applications without any difficulties from within Windows, you may run into problems with some poorly designed MS-DOS applications—some MS-DOS applications demand total control over system resources and access hardware directly.

Windows 98 accommodates a poorly behaved application to the best of its ability, via *MS-DOS mode*. This mode is the equivalent to the real mode present in earlier versions of Windows, with some improvements.

MS-DOS mode works by giving the errant MS-DOS application the entire system for the duration of the session. Windows removes itself from memory, leaving only a small "stub" loader in preparation for its return to control of your system.

Before you decide to enable MS-DOS mode for an application, try these other options:

■ Confirm that you've optimized the MS-DOS session settings for that application. Check the program's documentation for special memory requirements or other unusual needs. You may be able to adjust Windows' MS-DOS support to make the application work in a standard MS-DOS session.

■ Try running the application in full-screen mode, using the Alt+Enter key sequence.

If either of the preceding methods works, you will have a faster, more convenient alternative, allowing you the full benefit of Windows' multitasking and other features, all of which disappear during the MS-DOS mode session.

Whenever possible, Windows 98 determines that an application needs to run in MS-DOS mode and closes down all other applications and switches to this mode automatically. Unless you specify otherwise, you'll be warned when Windows is about to switch to MS-DOS mode.

In some cases, you may have to manually configure an application to run in MS-DOS mode. If you try to run such an application, you get an error message telling you that you can't run the application in Windows. If this happens, you should manually configure the application to run in MS-DOS mode, using the following steps:

1. If you haven't created a shortcut for the application, create one now. You can modify the settings of a DOS application only by using a shortcut.
2. Right-click the shortcut for the application and choose Properties.
3. Select the Program tab and choose Advanced to display the Advanced Program Settings dialog box.
4. Select the Prevent MS-DOS-based Programs from Detecting Windows option.
5. Choose OK.

Click the shortcut icon to try running the application. If the application still doesn't run, follow these steps:

1. Open the Advanced Program Settings dialog box again, as in steps 2-3 previously.
2. Select the MS-DOS Mode option.
3. Choose OK.

Try running the application again. If it still doesn't run, you have to modify the configuration for the MS-DOS mode, using the following steps:

1. Open the Advanced Program Settings dialog box.
2. Select the Specify a New MS-DOS Configuration option. The dialog box appears as in Figure 6.19.

   Selecting this option allows you to override the default settings for the MS-DOS-mode session.

Figure 6.19

Windows allows you to override the default settings for MS-DOS mode support. You can even run a special CONFIG.SYS and AUTOEXEC.BAT file for each application.

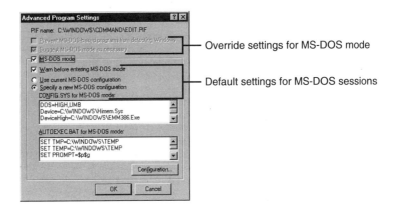

Override settings for MS-DOS mode

Default settings for MS-DOS sessions

3. Modify the lines in the CONFIG.SYS for MS-DOS Mode and AUTOEXEC.BAT for MS-DOS Mode windows as needed to allow this application to run.

   The changes you make here only affect this application. In this way, you can customize each application that must run in MS-DOS mode.

4. If necessary, choose the Configuration button and select from the options in the Select MS-DOS Configuration Options dialog box and choose OK.

   Be aware that when you choose from among the options in this dialog box, you remove the entries that already appear in the CONFIG.SYS and AUTOEXEC.BAT text boxes.

CAUTION

Use the Direct Disk Access option with great care. It is possible for an MS-DOS application to destroy long filename support when you select this option.

5. Choose OK twice to close the dialog boxes.

Part
I

Ch
6

Removing Applications

When you install a Windows application, not only do you copy the application's files into its own folder, but in most cases numerous other support files are copied into the Windows folder and the Windows Registry file is modified. For this reason, uninstalling an application can be a complex procedure. Fortunately, many application setup programs now offer an uninstall option to automate the process when you need to remove the application from your system. The Add/Remove Programs property sheet has an uninstall feature that can help with this process.

Uninstalling Applications Automatically

To uninstall an application automatically, start by opening the Control Panel and choosing the Add/Remove Programs icon to open the Add/Remove Programs Properties sheet—the same sheet you used to install the application (see Figure 6.20). Only applications that provide uninstall programs specifically designed to work with Windows 98 appear in the list of applications that Windows 98 can remove automatically.

Figure 6.20
In the Add/Remove Programs Properties sheet, you can remove applications as well as install them.

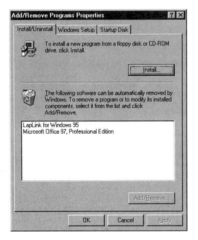

To remove an application, select it from the list of applications in the lower portion of the dialog box and choose Remove. After you confirm that you want to remove the program, Windows runs the selected application's uninstall program.

N O T E Some programs, such as Office 97, require the original CD to be in the computer while uninstalling. If you do not have the disk, the uninstallation process will abort with an error message. ▪

Removing MS-DOS Applications

If you decide to remove an MS-DOS application from your computer, follow these steps:

1. Locate the application folder in Windows Explorer or My Computer.
2. Check to make sure there are no data files in the folder (or subfolders in the folder).
3. Drag the folder to the Recycle Bin or press Del and choose Yes.

▶ **See** "Deleting Files and Folders," **page 41**

Part

I

Ch

6

CHAPTER 7

Printing

by Grant King

In this chapter

Using the Printers Folder

One of the most basic uses for a computer is to print out documents. Although as a society we are moving towards the goal of decreasing the amount of paper we generate, in many cases you will still find the need to print material from your computer to preserve it or share it with other people. Whether you need to print letters, graphs, pictures, or other such items, to do this you must install a printer on your computer and understand some of the basics of managing any printers used by your computer. This chapter shows you how to make full use of the printing features found in Windows 98.

The printer settings for your computer are stored in the Printers folder. The usual way to access the Printers folder is to click on the Start button, select Settings, and then choose Printers. This opens the Printers folder, as shown in Figure 7.1.

Figure 7.1

The Printers folder provides a central place from which to manage all your local and network printers. Note in this example that the HP LaserJet 5 is a network printer and is also shown as the default printer.

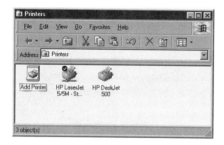

You can also access the Printers folder by any of the following methods:

- Selecting Printers from the Control Panel
- Opening My Computer and choosing Printers
- Clicking on Printers in the left pane of the Windows NT Explorer

The Printers folder contains icons for adding a printer as well as for any printers you have installed on your computer. If you have any other devices or software that use a printer driver, such as a fax modem, an icon representing the printer driver for that device also appears in this folder.

Default Printer

While you may have more than one printer installed on your computer, only one of these printers can be defined as your default printer, although you can change this default setting at any time. When a printer is set as the default printer, it is the printer that is automatically selected each time you print a document.

You can easily tell which printer is set as the default by looking at the printer icons found within the Printers folder. As you saw in Figure 7.1, the default printer has a check mark in the upper-left portion of its icon.

When you install the first printer on your computer, it is automatically installed as the default printer. Unless you change the default setting, the first printer you install on your computer remains as the default, even if you later add additional printers to the Printers folder.

If you want to select a different printer as the default, right-click on that printer's icon in the Printer Folder and choose Set as Default. The check mark moves to the selected printer's icon, and that printer is now set as the default printer.

Printer Properties

A printer's properties are the detailed settings for that particular printer. These properties are contained in the Properties page for each printer. You can access a printer's Properties page by either of the following methods from within the Printers folder:

- Right-clicking on the printer's icon and choosing Properties
- Clicking on the printer's icon with the left mouse button and then selecting Properties from the File pull-down menu

Because the Properties page for a printer is directly related to the functions exposed through the printer's driver, the Properties page looks somewhat different from printer to printer. Thus, the Properties page for your printer might appear differently than that shown in Figure 7.2.

Figure 7.2
The Properties page for a printer contains multiple tabs, each containing various options you can set for that printer.

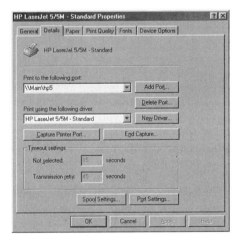

Installing a Local Printer

For installation purposes, Windows 98 distinguishes between local and network printers. A local printer is one that is physically connected to your computer via a cable, whereas a network computer is physically attached to another computer but is available for use by your computer through your network connection.

Part

I

Ch

7

Before you attempt to set up a local printer on your computer, you first need to make sure that you can connect to that printer from your computer. Some of the things you need to check are

- What port the printer needs to be plugged into
- If the printer is physically connected to the computer properly
- If the printer is turned on because otherwise, Windows 98 won't be able to detect the printer
- The exact make and model of that printer; for example, HP DeskJet 500

Plug and Play

In an effort to make it easier for you to install printers and other hardware on your computer, Microsoft has worked with hardware manufacturers to develop the Plug and Play standard. Through the use of Plug and Play support, Windows 98 can automatically detect hardware attached to your computer and install the appropriate drivers without any intervention on your part.

Assuming that your printer is Plug and Play compliant, installing your printer is as easy as turning on your attached printer and booting into Windows 98. Plug and Play can install your printer either during the Windows 98 installation process or at any time thereafter when you want to add a printer.

In either event, when Windows 98 loads, it should automatically detect that the printer has been added to your computer. It then brings up a dialog box that informs you of this fact. After Windows 98 has identified the printer, it attempts to install the correct driver for that printer. At this point, it might prompt you to insert the Windows 98 CD-ROM. After you have done that, it looks for that driver on that disk. If the driver did not come with Windows 98 or if you have an updated driver that you want to install instead, simply insert the driver disk from your hardware manufacturer into a disk drive and direct Windows 98 to that drive.

In order for this process to work properly, you have to make sure that the printer you want to add complies with the Plug and Play standard. If you are purchasing the printer in a store, look for the "Designed for Windows 98" logo on the printer box. If the box bears this logo, this indicates that the printer has undergone hardware compatibility testing to make sure that it is fully compatible with Windows 98, including Plug and Play. Because Plug and Play was also supported in Windows 95, the printer should also be fully compatible with Windows 98 if the logo indicates that the printer was designed for Windows 95.

If your printer is an older model or if it came packaged with your computer, you might not be able to tell whether it supports Plug and Play. If Windows 98 does not automatically recognize your printer, you need to manually add it to your computer configuration through the Add Printer Wizard.

Using the Add Printer Wizard

If your printer does not support Plug and Play, you can manually install the printer on your computer through the use of the Add Printer Wizard. Open the Printers folder and double-click on the Add Printer icon. After the Add Printer Wizard window appears, click on the Next button to begin using the wizard.

Select the radio button for Local Printer and click the Next button (see Figure 7.3). You are then asked to choose the manufacturer and printer model for your printer. First select the manufacturer by scrolling down to the name (or abbreviation) for your printer's manufacturer in the left window of this page of the wizard. Select that name by clicking on it, and a list of all available printers from that manufacturer appears in the right window. Select your printer's model by clicking on its name in the right window.

Figure 7.3
The Add Printer Wizard walks you through the steps needed to set up a printer on your computer.

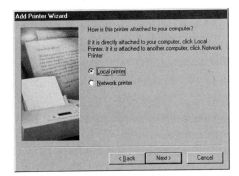

 When the Add Printer Wizard prompts you to choose a printer manufacturer and model, you can quickly skip to your hardware manufacturer's printer listings by pressing the first letter of the manufacturer's name. Thus, if you press the letter *E*, the list scrolls down and selects Epson, thereby automatically opening the available printer selections for Epson printers from which you can choose.

Unless your printer is a very recent model, it is very likely that Windows 98 already has a driver for your printer. In fact, Windows 98 includes drivers for over 1,000 different printers. However, if your printer does not appear to be among the printers listed, you need to click on the Have Disk button and insert a disk containing your printer's drivers into the floppy disk or CD-ROM drive. These drivers should have been supplied to you on disk when you bought your computer. After you indicate the drive on which Windows 98 should look, it then reads the disk you have inserted and lists any available printer drivers found on that disk. Note that the driver might be in a subdirectory on the disk, so you should check the documentation that came with your printer if you are unable to locate the driver. In the event that you are still unable to locate the driver, you need to contact the printer's manufacturer to obtain a Windows 98 driver for your printer (a Windows 95 driver should also work).

After you have selected the correct manufacturer and printer model for your printer, click on the Next button. You are then asked to choose the port on which you want to install the printer (see Figure 7.4). This is the hardware port to which you have attached the printer to your computer. In most cases, the correct port is LPT1, although you might need to check with your computer's manufacturer or the documentation that came with your computer to determine which port you should select.

Part

I

Ch

7

Figure 7.4

To install the printer correctly, you need to select the port to which your printer is attached.

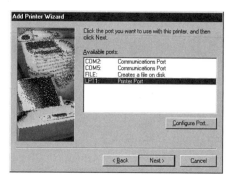

As part of the process of selecting a port, you can also configure the port, such as by having Windows 98 check the status of the port each time before it prints. If you want to change these settings, click on the Configure Port button found on this page of the Add Printer Wizard.

After selecting a port for your printer, you are then asked to choose a name for the printer (see Figure 7.5). In most cases, the default, which is usually the brand and model number, will suffice. However, if you plan to share this computer with other people on a network, you might want a more descriptive name, such as "7th Floor Laser Printer."

Figure 7.5

You need to provide a name for your printer that distinguishes it from other printers on your computer or the network.

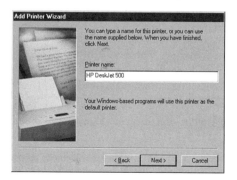

You then come to the last page of the Add Printer Wizard, where you are asked if you want to print a test page. Microsoft recommends that you print a test page when you install a printer. If you have not installed this printer on your computer before, this is a good opportunity to make sure that everything is working correctly. Simply choose the Yes radio button, which is selected by default, and a test page prints as soon as your printer has been installed.

After you click on the Finish button, Windows 98 installs and configures the printer for use on your computer. Unless the drivers for this printer have previously been added to your computer, such as if you previously installed this type of printer, a dialog box appears asking you to insert the Windows 98 CD-ROM. After you put the CD-ROM into the drive and click on the OK button, the printer driver and any other necessary files are copied to your computer. After this process has ended, an icon for your printer appears in the Printers folder. If this is the only printer installed on your computer, it is automatically selected as the default printer.

If you made it through all of these steps without incident, you are finished. Congratulations! You have just successfully installed your printer in Windows 98. If you need to install a network printer, you will find that the steps needed to make that installation are virtually the same as installing a local printer.

Setting Up a Network Printer

Setting up a network printer in Windows 98 can be as easy as connecting to a local printer, thanks in part to Microsoft's Point and Print process. This process usually allows you to automatically install the correct network printer driver without having to have the Windows 98 CD-ROM or other disk containing the printer driver. Through Point and Print, when you use the Add Printer Wizard to add a network printer, Windows 98 is often able to download the printer driver from the computer or server to which the printer is attached.

Before attempting to set up a network printer on your computer, you first need to know how to connect to the printer. Some of the information you need to know is

- The name that the printer and its attached computer or server (if applicable) uses on the network
- If the printer is set up for sharing over the network
- The exact model of that printer; for example, HP LaserJet 5

Connecting to the Network

To install a network printer on your computer, you first need to be connected to the network. If you have not already established a network connection with your computer, refer to Chapter 47, "Sharing and Securing Resources," before attempting to connect to and install a network printer. You might also need to check with your network administrator to make sure that you have been given permission to access that printer, because the printer may refuse your connection if you do not have permission.

While being connected to your network, open the Printers folder and double-click on the Add Printer icon. The Add Printer Wizard then appears. Select the radio button for Network Printer and click the Next button.

You are then asked to supply the location of the printer on the network. If you already know the name of the printer and its attached computer on the network, you can simply type it into the field on this screen, as shown in Figure 7.6. Note that you need to supply the UNC (Universal Naming Convention) path for the location of the printer, such as **\\computername\printername** where **computername** is the name of the computer to which the printer is attached, and **printername** is the name of the printer. Thus, in Figure 7.6, Main is the name of the computer on the network to which the printer hp5 is attached.

Part

I

Ch

7

Figure 7.6

You need to tell the Add Printer Wizard the location of the computer that you want to install on the network.

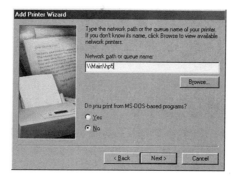

If you are not sure of the exact name of the computer and printer on the network, click on the Browse button. This brings up a separate window (see Figure 7.7) that lists all other computers on the network that have shared printers.

Figure 7.7

The Browse window allows you to select from all available shared printers on the network.

Click on the plus sign to the left of any computer listed in this window to expand the view to show all shared printers attached to that computer. Click on the OK button after you have selected the printer you want to add.

> **N O T E**   You can choose to install only a single printer each time you run the Add Printer Wizard. If you want to install more than one printer on your computer, you have to add them one at a time. After you have added the first printer, you can then add additional printers one by one. This applies to both local and network printers. ■

Before you move on to the next window in the Add Printer Wizard, be sure to check the correct radio button indicating if you want to print from MS-DOS-based programs. If you select yes and click on the Next button, the next window of the wizard requests that you capture a printer port for these MS-DOS programs. Even though this shared network printer is not physically attached to your computer, MS-DOS programs often need to believe that they are printing to a local port. By choosing a port to capture for this purpose, when MS-DOS programs attempt to print to this port, Windows 98 redirects the print job to the network printer automatically.

As with local printers, the Add Printer Wizard asks you if you want to print a test page. Select the Yes radio button if you want to see if your connection to the network printer is working properly. After you have decided if you want to print a test page, press the Finish button to install the printer on your computer.

After you have selected the network printer you want to install and have finished with the Add Printer Wizard, Windows 98 then connects to that printer to determine its exact type. After it has determined the make and model of the printer, Windows 98 then sees if you already have a correct version of that printer's driver available on your computer. If you do, the printer should install correctly, and you will be done adding this printer to your Printers folder. In most cases, however, Windows 98 either downloads the correct driver to your computer or you are prompted to insert a disk containing the driver into one of your disk drives.

To address both of these situations, we begin by looking at what happens when Windows 98 is able to download the printer driver to your computer.

 TIP Although you can use the Add Printer Wizard to add a printer to your computer, an easier way is to open Network Neighborhood and browse for the printer (you will probably first have to double-click on the icon for the computer to which the printer is attached). After you have found the printer, right-click on the printer's icon and choose Install. This opens the Add Printer Wizard but skips several windows, thus making it easier and quicker to add a network printer.

Point and Print

After you have finished using the Add Printer Wizard, Windows 98 attempts to install the printer driver from the computer to which the printer is attached (if applicable). In many cases, if the shared printer is set up correctly on the computer to which it is attached, Windows 98 can download the printer driver from that computer and install it on your computer. This feature is known as Point and Print.

Assuming that this process works correctly on your computer, you should see a dialog box telling you that Windows 98 has found the proper driver on the remote computer and is installing the driver on your computer. After this has finished, you can connect to and use that printer.

In order for the Point and Print feature to work properly, the computer to which the shared printer is attached must be running Windows 98, Windows NT Server, or be a Novell NetWare server. Note, however, that this feature does not always work properly, and as such you may still have to install the printer driver from either the Windows 98 CD-ROM or the printer driver disk supplied by your printer manufacturer.

Installing Printer Drivers from Disk

If you are unable to install the driver for your printer through the Point and Print feature described in the previous section, you will need to use the Windows 98 CD-ROM or another disk with the appropriate driver in order to provide Windows 98 with the printer driver. After Windows 98 installs the printer driver, an icon for the printer appears in your Printers folder.

Part

I

Ch

7

Printing from Applications

After you have installed one or more printers on your computer, you then can print from within any application. In Windows 98, when you print from a Windows application, you can change a number of the printer's configurations within the application itself for the print job you are processing. Windows 98 also includes a print spooler that allows you to get back to work while the operating system processes the print job in the background.

Changing Configurations

In most Windows applications, you can print the document you are working on by pressing a toolbar button or by selecting Print from the File pull-down menu. After you tell the application to print the document, you likely are presented with a window that allows you to change any needed settings for that print job. Note that although you don't always see this window when you choose a Print button on a toolbar, you should usually see a Print window if you use the pull-down menu.

Figure 7.8 shows the Print window as it appears in the WordPad application that comes with Windows 98. This window shows the relevant information on the selected printer, such as the printer's name and its current status. If you want to change from the default printer to a different printer, just choose the other printer that you want from the drop-down box next to Name. Instead of printing the entire document, you can also choose to select only one or more pages for printing by entering that information into the Print range frame.

Figure 7.8

When printing from within applications, you can change your printer settings to best match the needs of your print job.

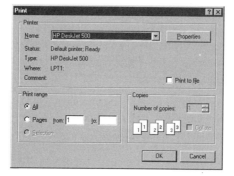

If you click the Properties button, a separate window appears that contains much of the same properties settings available for this printer in the Printers folder. From this window, you can set the printer resolution, change the paper size, alter the way the document is printed (such as from portrait to landscape), and other properties settings. After you have made any wanted changes to the printer settings, click on the OK button to return to the main Print window and print the document.

Note that the Print window includes an option to print to a file rather than to the selected printer. If you choose this option by selecting the Print to File check box, this does not save the file as a text file, but rather saves the printer output into a data file as opposed to sending it to the printer right away. Unless you want to save this raw printer data for some reason, you probably do not want to use this Print to File feature. If you want to save the file rather than print it, you should choose either $\underline{S}$ave or Save $\underline{A}$s from the $\underline{F}$ile pull-down menu.

Spooling

Windows 98 includes a 32-bit print spooler that supports preemptive multithreading and multitasking, thereby allowing you to get back to work more quickly after you initiate a print job. Before print spoolers were incorporated into the operating system, when you printed a document in an application, you often had to wait until the entire document had been printed before you could return to work in that application. However, with Windows 98, when you tell an application to print a document, the print spooler takes over and accepts the print job in place of the actual printing device to which you have directed the document.

Thus, the print spooler effectively acts as a middleman that receives the print job on behalf of the printer and temporarily stores it on your hard disk. After the application has finished sending either part or all of the print job to the spooler (depending on what print spooler options you have chosen for your printer), the application is then freed up to continue with other work, and the print spooler begins feeding the print job data to the printer in the background.

By default, the print spooler begins feeding print data to the printer after it has received the first page of data from the application. However, if you want to return control to the application more quickly, you can adjust the print spooler properties so that it does not begin printing until the entire document has been received by the spooler. To change these and other print spooler settings, you need to reconfigure the properties for each printer on which you want to make these changes. To do this, right-click on the printer's icon in the Printers folder and choose Properties. Then select the Details tab and choose the Spoo$\underline{l}$ Settings button.

In this window (see Figure 7.9), you can change the default settings by instructing Windows 98 to wait until the last page is spooled before sending the document to the printer. This shortens the time it takes to return control back to the application that is printing the document. Alternatively, if you are having printing problems and want to see if the print spooler is causing the problem, select the related radio button to have all applications print directly to the printer. However, choosing this option will probably prevent you from working in the application until the printer has finished printing the document.

Figure 7.9
You can change the Spool Settings for the print spooler on a printer if you want to return control to an application more quickly or if you need to troubleshoot printing problems.

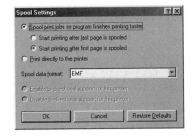

Part
I
Ch
7

In this same window, you also see that you can choose between the **EMF (enhanced metafile printing)** and RAW spool data formats. Normally you want to use the default setting for your printer to help ensure error-free printing. EMF usually returns control back to the application more quickly than using the RAW data format because the latter must be generated by the printer driver. If the default for your printer is RAW, try using EMF to speed up the printing process in your application. However, because some applications do not support EMF, if you experience problems, you should switch back to the RAW format.

After a print job has been sent to the spooler, a printer icon appears in the system tray indicating that Windows 98 is processing the print job. If you click on this icon, a window opens for that printer from which you can get additional information about the status of the print job. For more information about managing print jobs through this printer window, see the next section on managing print jobs.

Managing Print Jobs

Through the process of sending documents to your local or network printer, instances will arise when you need to cancel a print job or simply find out what other documents are waiting to be printed. If you want to view the status of a printer, you can open the printer window for that device. If you are in the process of printing a document from your computer, you can click on the printer icon in the system tray to bring up the window for that printer. You can also open that printer's window by double-clicking on its icon in the Printers folder. Note that while the former method might display only print jobs created by your computer, the latter method should display all pending print jobs, including those from any other users on your network.

When you open a printer window, all of the documents currently pending for that printer are displayed (see Figure 7.10). The pending print jobs are shown in their order in the print queue. The print job at the top of the print queue is the document currently being printed. Any documents below that are printed in descending order.

Figure 7.10

The printer window shows all print jobs currently pending on a printer and allows you to delete or pause any of your pending jobs.

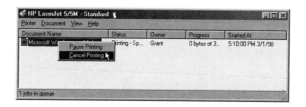

By right-clicking on any of your pending print jobs, you can choose to either pause or cancel that job. When you pause a print job, it is skipped over when its place in the queue comes up. While you can exercise control over your own documents, usually you cannot pause or cancel other people's print jobs unless you have administrative privileges on that printer.

In addition to pausing or canceling print jobs, you can elect to purge all pending documents by selecting that option from the Printer pull-down menu, subject to the security restrictions discussed earlier regarding other user's documents. You can also change any of the properties for the selected printer by choosing Properties from the Printer pull-down menu.

Special Printing Considerations

While we have already discussed most of the main printing features found in Windows 98, a number of other areas are worth considering. In this section, we look at how to print

- By dragging and dropping a file onto a printer's icon
- A file from any disk drive through the Windows Explorer
- Frames in HTML documents viewed in Internet Explorer
- From within MS-DOS applications
- Documents containing color graphics
- When your printer is unavailable
- With multiple types of paper configurations

Drag and Drop Printing

While you normally print a document from within an application in which you are working, it is also possible to print a document without being in an application. This is done by dragging and dropping the document onto a printer icon. One of the ways to do this is to create a shortcut for one or more of your installed printers on your desktop. After you have done this, you can print documents by just dragging them from the desktop or any window and dropping them onto the printer shortcut.

To create a desktop shortcut for one of your installed printers, open the Printers folder. With either your left or right mouse button, select the printer's icon from the folder and drag it to the desktop. When you release the mouse button, a shortcut for the printer is created. If you prefer not to create a desktop shortcut for the printer, you can drag and drop documents onto the printer's icon in the Printers folder.

When you drag a document onto a printer's icon and drop it, Windows 98 opens the related application, prints the document within the program, and then closes that application. Because Windows 98 looks for a program that has previously been associated with that type of file in order for it to open an application and print the document, you need to have previously installed a program on your computer that is registered for handling that file type. Thus, if you want to print a document created in Microsoft Excel, you need to have Excel loaded on your computer because Windows 98 looks for an application associated with that file extension (in this case, files having a .xls or other Excel related extension).

Part
I

Ch
7

Printing Files from Disk

In addition to printing files by dragging and dropping them onto printer icons, you can also print them directly from disk. In most cases, this is the quickest way to print a document without having to open the application yourself.

To print a file directly from disk, simply select the file from within the Windows Explorer. The file can be located on any floppy drive, hard drive, or network drive to which you have access. Right-click on the file and choose Print. The printing process is identical to that in drag and drop printing. Thus, Windows 98 opens the application associated with that type of file, prints the file within that application, and then closes the application automatically.

Printing Frames in Internet Explorer

While the print window that appears when you are printing from an application normally appears consistent from program to program, one difference occurs when you print a document from within Internet Explorer that contains multiple frames. When a Web page contains multiple frames, it means that, although it appears to be a single page, it is actually made up of multiple pages that appear within a single frameset. Each of these frames is a separate document that can be printed out through your computer.

When you print a page containing multiple frames, the print window appears with additional options not found when printing from other applications (see Figure 7.11). From this window, you can select to print the selected frame (which usually is the main, or largest, frame), to print all of the frames individually, or to print the frameset as it appears on your screen. You can also select the option to either print all linked documents, in which case Internet Explorer prints all pages for which hyperlinks appear on the page you are printing. Alternatively, you can print a table containing links for these documents.

Figure 7.11
When printing an HTML document containing multiple frames, you are provided with several options regarding which frames you want to print.

For further information on printing within Internet Explorer, see Chapter 42, "Finding, Organizing, and Saving Web-Based Information."

Printing from MS-DOS Applications

While most of the applications you run on your computer are likely written for Windows, you might have a few MS-DOS applications from which you will need to print. Windows 98 fully supports printing from MS-DOS applications, although you do not get the full benefits found in printing from Windows applications, such as EMF spooling. All print jobs created by MS-DOS applications are intercepted by the 32-bit print spooler prior to being sent to the printer, resulting in a quicker return of control back to the application.

Printing in Color

One of the problems encountered when printing color graphics is that the color displayed on your monitor might not match the color generated by the printer. To help alleviate this problem, Microsoft has included support for **Image Color Matching (ICM)** in Windows 98. While Windows 95 supports ICM 1.0, Windows 98 supports the newer ICM 2.0, which includes a number of technical improvements. The end result is a better correlation between the colors as they appear on your monitor and those generated by your color printer. Because ICM is supported on multiple platforms, the images you create in Windows 98 applications should appear virtually the same on computers that are running other ICM 2.0-compliant operating systems.

Offline Printing

If you use a laptop computer, or if your printer is only available via a network connection, you are a good candidate for using the offline printing feature found in Windows 98. With a laptop computer, there may be many times when you are not physically connected to your printer, such as when you are working on a document while on a long flight. Similarly, if you work in a networked environment, there likely will be times that you cannot print due to problems connecting to the printer over the network. As its name implies, offline printing allows you to generate print jobs when you are not connected to a printer and allows you to have them printed at a later time.

> **NOTE** Offline printing works only for portable and networked computers and also requires the use of the print spooler supplied with Windows 98. If you have configured the printer not to use print spooling, you have to enable this feature in order to put your printer into offline mode. Because offline printing is not supported for local printers, if you want to stop printing on a local printer, right-click on the printer's icon in the Printers folder and choose the Pause Printing command. ▪

To use offline printing, open the Printers folder and select the printer you want to use offline. Right-click on the printer's icon and choose Use Printer Offline, at which point a check mark appears next to this choice. Any print jobs you generate are held in the queue until you instruct Windows 98 to actually print these jobs. When you want to print out the stored jobs, right-click on the printer's icon and deselect the Use Printer Offline option.

If your laptop is configured to be used with a docking station, when you boot your computer Windows 98 automatically selects offline printing if it detects that you are not connected to the docking station. If you later boot your laptop while being docked, the offline printing feature is turned off, and any stored print jobs are sent to your printer.

Part

I

Ch

7

Managing Paper

By changing the properties for a printer, you can select the paper size, the paper tray the printer should use, and other such settings as determined by the capabilities of your printer. The properties can be changed at any time either from the Printers folder or from within any application.

To change the printer paper properties from within an application, select Print from the File pull-down menu and then click on the Properties button. You can also access these properties by right-clicking on the printer's icon in the Printers folder and choosing Properties. In either event, a properties page similar to that shown in Figure 7.12 appears (this example is from the WordPad application).

Figure 7.12

You can change a printer's paper configurations to best match the needs of the document you are printing.

After the properties page appears, click on the Paper tab. From here you can select the size of the paper on which you are printing as well as the layout of the print job; that is, landscape or portrait. If your printer has multiple trays, an envelope holder, or other paper sources, you can also change the paper source on this part of the printer's properties page. As mentioned previously, because the properties page appears differently from printer to printer, the display for your printer will likely appear somewhat differently than that shown in Figure 7.12.

Configuring a Printer for Multiple Uses

With Windows 98, you can set up multiple virtual printers, each of which points to a single physical printer. This allows you to create one configuration for high-quality graphics printing, one for landscape (as opposed to portrait) printing, or any other configurations you want. Each of these can be saved as a separate printer even though each points to a single printing device.

To have the operating system configure additional printers for this purpose, use the Add Printer Wizard to go through the same process that you used to install the printer previously, but this time give the printer a slightly different name. Thus, you might name one printer "High graphics" and another "Landscape."

When you install each of these printers, the Add Printer Wizard tells you that a driver for this type of printer is already installed on your computer. It asks whether you want to keep the existing driver or install this new one. Unless you have a version of the driver on a disk which is newer than the Windows 98 CD-ROM, elect the option to keep the existing driver.

After you have finished using the Add Printer Wizard, a new icon appears for this printer. Right-click on its icon and choose Properties. Configure the printer according to its new name. Thus, for the Landscape printer example earlier, select the option to use landscape printing rather than portrait.

After you have configured your new virtual printers, they also are available for use within your applications. Thus, when you have a print job that you want to have printed in landscape format, choose the Landscape printer rather than choosing your main printer. This gives you a quick and easy way to print in this format without having to change the printer's properties each time.

Removing Printers

Although the focus of this chapter has involved installing and managing printers, you might need to remove installed printers and related devices from your computer. For example, if you buy a new printer and give the old one away, there would probably be no reason to keep the old printer's driver installed on your computer.

To remove a printer and its related drivers from your computer, open the Printers folder. Right-click on the printer's icon and choose Delete. Windows 98 then asks you to confirm that you want to remove that printer from your computer. Click on the Yes button, and the printer is then removed from your computer.

During the process of removing the printer, a dialog box appears asking whether you also want to remove the files that were used by that printer. The files to which Windows 98 are referring are the printer's driver and any other related files needed for use by that particular printer. If you think that you might use that printer in the future, you can choose No to keep these files on your computer. By doing so, you will not need to install the files from the Windows 98 CD-ROM the next time you add the printer to your computer. Otherwise, choose Yes to remove all the files associated with this printer from your computer. After this process has completed, the printer's icon is removed from the Printers folder.

Troubleshooting Printer Problems

The Help files that come with Windows 98 include a number of Troubleshooters, which are wizard-like guides to helping you solve common print errors that might occur. If you experience a printing problem in Windows 98 and are not able to fix it on your own, you should try the Print Troubleshooter before seeking technical support.

Part

I

Ch

7

To start the Print Troubleshooter, click on the Start button and select <u>H</u>elp. After the Help window opens, double-click on the Troubleshooting book icon and then again on the Windows 98 Troubleshooters icon. This expands to show a list of Troubleshooters from which you can select. Click on Print in this listing to open the Windows 98 Print Troubleshooter in the right pane of this window, as shown in Figure 7.13.

Figure 7.13

The Print Troubleshooter can help solve many of the most common printing problems in Windows 98.

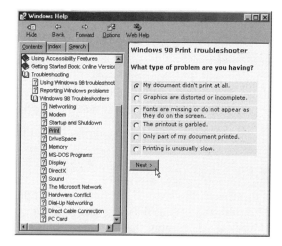

To use the Troubleshooter, select the radio button for the type of problem that is closest to that which you are experiencing. Then press the Next button and proceed through the steps that are designed to help solve your problem. If there is no Troubleshooter for your particular problem, or if the Troubleshooter does not fully solve the problem, you might need to contact either your printer manufacturer or Microsoft, such as by using the Windows Update tool located off of the Start button. ●

CHAPTER 8

Customizing the Look and Feel of Windows

by Curtis Knight

In this chapter

Establishing Custom Settings for Each User

Windows 98 enables you to create a profile for each computer user. Your user profile contains your individual customizations to Windows 98. This means that when you log onto the system, the settings you established for yourself are still there; when your coworkers log on, their settings are still there too.

 TIP As you read through this chapter, remember that where you are told to click on a file or folder and then click the OK or Open button, it is often possible to simply double-click the file or folder to finish the task.

If more than one person uses your computer, it is recommended that you set up user profiles before you begin implementing any of the customizations in this chapter. That way, when other people log on to the computer, they will be able to make their own customizations to Windows 98 without affecting each other's settings.

To establish user profiles, follow these steps:

1. Open Control Panel and activate Users. You'll see the dialog box in Figure 8.1. Click the Next button to continue.

Figure 8.1

Select Users from Control Panel and then click Next to begin setting up a new user profile.

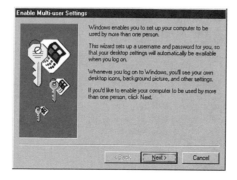

2. Type a user name in the User Name text box, and then click Next to continue.

3. Type a password into the Password text box, and press the Tab key to move the insertion point to the Confirm password text box. Retype the identical password and click Next to continue.

4. In the Personalized Items Settings dialog box, check the items you want to customize. For example, if you want a separate My Documents folder for this user, check the My Documents Folder check box. If you want this user to have his own custom Start Menu, check the Start Menu check box.

   You also need to decide whether to tell Windows 98 to create a copy of each of these items or create new ones with default settings. Creating new items for each user will save disk space if the new user doesn't make very many changes to Windows 98 settings. When you've finished making your choices, click Next to continue.

5. When the Ready to Finish dialog box displays, click Finish. Windows sets up the new user profile and prompts you to reboot the computer.

To set up more profiles, run Users from the Control Panel again, and you will be taken through the same setup routine for each new user.

Resizing the Taskbar

Occasionally you may want to resize the taskbar. If your system has enough memory to allow many applications to be open simultaneously, the taskbar can become so cluttered that the icons are too small to tell which is which. If this happens, you can resize the taskbar so you can read the icon text.

Another reason you would resize the taskbar is that with all the customization features implemented in Windows 98, the taskbar can contain numerous toolbars. Resizing the taskbar makes it easier to find the elements you need to work with.

N O T E Be careful not to add too many toolbars with lots of icons to your taskbar. If you do, you may find yourself spending more time searching your taskbar for the right icon than it would take to run the program the old-fashioned way. To gain maximum benefit from toolbars on the taskbar, use them only for programs you use frequently. ▪

To resize the taskbar follow these steps:

1. Move the mouse pointer over the inside edge of the taskbar until it becomes a double-headed arrow.
2. Drag the edge of the taskbar until it is the size you want. (It is possible to size it as large as 1/2 the screen area.)
3. Release the mouse button.

Moving the Taskbar

By default, Windows places the taskbar at the bottom of the screen. If you prefer the taskbar in a different position, you can move it to any of the four edges of the screen.

To move the taskbar, point to a blank area of it and use the left mouse button to drag it where you want it.

Using the New Taskbar Features

When you right-click on a blank area of the taskbar, a shortcut menu pops up with commands that enable you to customize it. There are also commands on the menu that help you rearrange the open windows on your desktop.

The first item on the taskbar's shortcut menu is Toolbars, which contains a menu with three options—Desktop, Quick Launch, and New Toolbar. Figure 8.2 shows the taskbar with two additional toolbars.

Figure 8.2

As you can see, the taskbar can become cluttered quickly.

The toolbars in Figure 8.2 are described as:

- *Address.* Use the Address toolbar to access files and Web pages right from the taskbar. You use this toolbar exactly as you use the one in your favorite Web browser.

- *Links.* Remember the Links toolbar right next to the Address toolbar in Internet Explorer? This is the same toolbar. You don't have to open Internet Explorer to access these links.

- *Desktop.* When you select Desktop, the Desktop toolbar is added to the taskbar. The Desktop toolbar contains all the folders, files, and shortcuts on your desktop. Use the small arrows on the left and right ends of the toolbar to scroll through the icons.

  This toolbar can be a major advantage if you normally maximize the window of the application you're currently working with, and your taskbar is set to be visible at all times. The Always on Top setting for the taskbar is covered later in this section.

- *Quick Launch.* By default, the Quick Launch toolbar appears just to the right of the start button on the taskbar. When you install Windows, Setup automatically places four useful icons in the Quick Launch toolbar: Internet Explorer, Mail, Show Desktop, and View Channels. The Quick Launch toolbar provides one-click access to your most commonly used applications.

To add your own shortcuts to the Quick Launch toolbar, drag the file or shortcut to the Quick Launch toolbar, and a shortcut is created for your application or file.

 TIP Office 97 comes with a Shortcut Bar, which is essentially a toolbar that rests at the top or side of the Windows desktop. If you have too many toolbar buttons you want to use to make it practical to set it up as a taskbar toolbar, consider creating a custom Shortcut Bar with Office 97.

Table 8.1 describes the four buttons added to Quick Launch during the Windows install.

Table 8.1   Built-in Desktop Toolbars

Toolbar Name	Description
Internet Explorer	Yep, you guessed it, this is a shortcut to Internet Explorer.
Mail	This is a shortcut to Microsoft's e-mail manager Outlook Express. Outlook Express is included with Internet Explorer 4.x.
Show Desktop	This is probably the most useful of the four buttons Windows places on the Quick Launch toolbar. If your desktop becomes cluttered with open application windows, or if your current application window is maximized and you need to get to your desktop, click the Show Desktop icon and all your windows or are automatically minimized. Click the icon again, and all your windows are restored to the previous state and position.
View Channels	When you click this button, you get a full-screen browser to view your channels. If you have not set up your Internet access, the Internet Connection Wizard will guide you through the setup.

▶ **See** "Using the Internet Connection Wizard," **page 828**

Creating Toolbars from Frequently Used Folders and Web Pages

Windows 98 provides you with an easy way to establish your custom toolbars for your most often-used files and folders: It creates a toolbar that contains shortcuts to all the files and subfolders within the folder you select.

To create a custom toolbar, follow these steps:

1. Select new toolbar from the taskbar shortcut menu.
2. The New Toolbar dialog box pops up. This dialog box provides a Windows Explorer style view of your system.
3. Navigate to the folder you want to convert to a toolbar, and click the OK button. The folder is now represented in a toolbar.

You can also create a toolbar for your favorite Web pages. To create a Web page toolbar follow these steps:

1. Point Internet Explorer to the Web page you want to display.

2. Right-click the taskbar, point to Toolbars, and select New Toolbar.

3. In the New Toolbar dialog box, scroll down to Internet Explorer, and click the plus sign to expand it.

4. Select the Web page you want, and click the OK button to create your new toolbar and close the New Toolbar dialog box. A new toolbar appears on your taskbar.

 At the taskbar's default size, you can see only one line of your Web page at a time. To see more of your Web page toolbar, you can either use the spinner buttons at the right, or resize the taskbar.

To remove a custom toolbar, right-click the taskbar or a toolbar, point to Toolbars, and click on the toolbar you want to remove.

Arranging Your Open Windows

Your taskbar's shortcut menu contains four options for rearranging the windows on your desktop. Can't make sense of what's open? Desktop too cluttered? Don't want to close any applications? No worries, this section will help you get a handle on the mess.

These options are accessed by right-clicking on the taskbar:

- *Cascade Windows.* When you select this option, all open windows are displayed in a cascading arrangement beginning in the upper left corner of the screen and going toward the lower right corner.

- *Tile Windows Horizontally.* When you select this option your windows are tiled from left to right, top to bottom in alphabetical order.

- *Tile Windows Vertically.* To arrange your windows from top to bottom, left to right in alphabetical order, select this option.

- *Minimize All Windows.* If you need to minimize all open windows, select this option. This effect is similar, but not identical to the Show Desktop button in the Quick Launch toolbar. The difference is that Show Desktop is a toggle that will restore your windows to their previous size. Minimize All Windows is not a toggle. You have to restore your windows one at a time.

- *Changing Taskbar Options.* You have several options available for giving your taskbar an attitude adjustment. These adjustments are made from the Taskbar Properties dialog box.

Right-clicking the taskbar and selecting Properties is the quickest way to access the Taskbar Properties dialog box. Figure 8.3 shows the Taskbar Properties dialog box.

Taskbar Properties can also be accessed by choosing Start, Settings, Taskbar.

Figure 8.3
Select the options you
want and click OK.

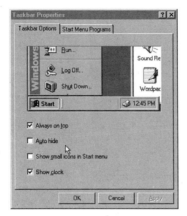

Table 8.2 describes the four options available for customizing the taskbar.

Table 8.2 Taskbar Options Tab

Check box	Description
Always on top	When you check this box your taskbar is always visible even when you maximize a window.
Auto hide	When you check this box your taskbar changes to a very thin line. To make the taskbar visible again simply point to the thin line.
Shows small icons in Start menu	If you check this box, the icons and start menu are slightly smaller and the Windows logo down the left side of the menu is removed. To see the difference watch the preview window as you check and un-checked this box.
Show Clock	Check this box to make the clock visible in the system tray, which appears to the far right of the taskbar. To remove the clock from the system tray uncheck the box.

 If you check both Always on Top and Auto Hide, you can maximize your application window and still
have easy access the taskbar anytime by pointing to the edge of the screen where your taskbar is.

Setting the Date and Time

To change the date and time on your computer follow these steps:

1. Double-click the clock in the taskbar. The Date/Time Properties dialog box appears as
shown in Figure 8.4.

Figure 8.4

Double-click the clock to bring up the Date/Time Properties dialog box.

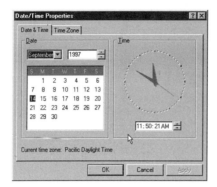

2. The dialog box is divided into two sections—date and time. To change the month, open the Month drop-down list and choose the month you want.

3. To change the year, either highlight the year in the Year text box and type the year directly or use the spinner buttons to advance one year at a time up or down.

4. Select the day of the month by clicking in the Calendar box below the month in year text boxes.

5. The time section shows an analog clock and a digital clock in a text box. The time is changed using the digital clock text box. This text box is divided into four fields—hour, min., seconds, and a.m./p.m. To change the time, place the insertion point in the field you need to change, and use the bar to the right of the text box to increment or detriment the field. You can also type directly into the fields. For instance, if the current time reads 11:00:00pm, and you need to change it to 3:00:00pm, simply use your mouse to highlight the 11 and type 3.

Changing the Time Zone

After adjusting the date and time, double check the current time zone display at the bottom of the Date & Time tab. If it displays the wrong time zone select the Time Zone tab in the Date/Time Properties dialog box.

This displays a world map and a drop-down list box from which you can select the proper time zone. To select the time zone open the Time Zone drop-down list box and choose the proper time zone from the list.

Also at the bottom of this tab is a check box titled Automatically Adjust Clock for Daylight Saving Changes. If you check this box, windows will automatically adjust for daylight savings time twice a year. If you live in an area where daylight savings time is not in use, such as Indiana, make sure this box is not checked.

When you're finished, click the OK button to close the Date/Time Properties dialog box. Your changes are applied when you click the OK button, or if you want that warm fuzzy, click apply after making your changes, then close the dialog box.

Managing Buttons on a Toolbar

Now that you've been experimenting with your taskbar, you may have too many toolbars, or one or more of them may be too big. Table 8.3 explains some taskbar management techniques.

Table 8.3   Taskbar Options Tab

Task	Description
Resizing Toolbars	When you get too many toolbars, you can't see everything. To get around this, you can resize your toolbars, shrinking those that you don't need to see and expanding the others.
	To resize a toolbar, point to the small vertical bar at the left edge of the toolbar, and drag left to expand it, right to make it smaller.
	When you resize a toolbar, the toolbar to the left of it expands or contracts automatically.
Removing Toolbars	If you got carried away with those custom toolbars and you want to get rid of some, right-click the taskbar or the title of one of the toolbars, point to Toolbars, and click the toolbar you want to remove.
Removing Buttons From Quick Launch bar	The buttons on your Quick Launch bar are just "fancy" shortcuts.
	To remove a button from the Quick Launch bar, right-click it, and choose Delete from the context menu.
Hiding Text and Titles on the Custom and Desktop Toolbars	Another way to reduce the size of your toolbars is to tell Windows not to display the text for each icon.
	To hide icon text, right-click the toolbar title, and click Show Text to remove the checkmark.
	To hide the toolbar title, right-click the toolbar title, and click Show Title to remove the checkmark.

Removing Toolbars

Figure 8.5 shows the right-click menu for a Quick Launch button.

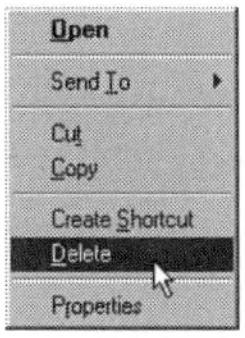

Figure 8.5

Context menu for a Quick Launch button. To remove the button, click Delete.

Adding and Removing Programs in the Start Menu

There are two ways to add items to the Start menu. If you prefer to add to the Start menu using a Wizard approach, follow these steps:

1. Right-click a blank area of the taskbar, and select Properties.
2. Select the Start Menu Programs tab.
3. Click the Add button. This starts the Create Shortcut wizard (see Figure 8.6).

Figure 8.6
Click the Add button from the Start Menu Programs tab to start the Shortcut Wizard.

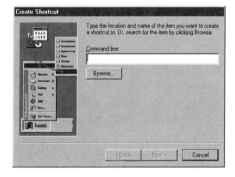

4. The first dialog box in this wizard asks for the command line of the executable file for the program. If you know the path and filename of the executable for the application, type it into the command line text box. If you don't know the path and filename, you can click the Browse button to bring up the Browse dialog box. Find the executable name and click the Open button.

   When the path and filename for the executable appear correctly in the command line text box, click the Next button.

5. The Select Program Folder dialog box appears. This is a tree-style view of your Start menu. You can select an existing folder, or you can click the New Folder button to create a new folder. If you decide to create new folder, you will see a new folder appear with the name program group (1), and folder name is highlighted in re-name mode. Type a new name for the folder and press Enter.

6. When you've selected a folder or created a new folder, click the Next button.

7. The Select a Title for the Program dialog box appears. In the Select a name for the shortcut text box, type an intuitive name for your new shortcut.

8. Click the Finish button.

9. Now check Start menu to make sure it works properly. If it does, close the Taskbar Properties dialog box with the OK button.

N O T E The Start menu is actually a folder on your hard disk, located in the Windows directory. Any files or shortcuts you place in \Windows\Start Menu\ will show up in your Start menu.

To remove a program shortcut from the Start menu, follow these steps:

1. Right-click a blank area of the taskbar, and select Properties.
2. Select the Start Menu Programs tab.
3. Click the Remove button. The Remove Shortcuts/Folders dialog box appears.
4. Navigate to the shortcut you want to remove, and click the Close button.
5. Now go to the Start menu to make sure the shortcut was removed properly. If it has been, close the Taskbar Properties dialog box with the OK button.

 T I P You can remove an entire folder from the shortcut menu by selecting the folder. When you delete a folder name, all shortcuts and some folders under that folder are removed from the Start menu.

If you prefer to create and remove folders and shortcuts for the Start menu using Windows Explorer, click the Advanced button. The Advanced button launches Explorer and takes you directly to the Start menu folder. From here, simply create new folders and shortcuts the same way you would any other folder on your hard drive.

Clearing the Documents List in the Start Menu

Windows 98 maintains a history of the documents you've accessed. You can access these documents by choosing Start, pointing to Documents, and selecting the document you need to access. Clearing the list is useful if you have accumulated several documents in your Documents history that you no longer access frequently or don't exist anymore.

To empty your Documents menu follow these steps:

1. Right-click a blank area of the taskbar, and select Properties.
2. Select the Start Menu Programs tab.
3. Click the Clear button in the Documents menu section located at the bottom of the page.

Customizing the Windows Display

Today's video cards and monitors give you a wide choice of resolutions and color schemes. This section shows you how to adjust the display to your needs.

Using Desktop Themes

One of the coolest customization features of the Microsoft Windows 95 Plus Pack now comes with Windows 98. You can use Desktop Themes to customize wallpaper, screensavers, mouse pointers (animated cursors), and many other elements of your Windows display.

Microsoft includes all the themes from the original Plus Pack as well as a few new ones, or you can create and save your own themes by either mixing existing elements, or using your own sounds, wallpaper, animated cursors, etc.

You can access Desktop Themes from the Control Panel. Select a theme from the Theme drop-down list and customize it as you wish.

Changing the Screen Resolution

Screen resolution is a measure of the density of the pixels displayed. More pixels means finer detail. One side effect of high resolution is that everything appears smaller. With higher resolution, more content will fit onscreen at once.

1. From the Display Properties dialog box shown in Figure 8.7, select the Settings tab. The top portion of this page contains one or more icons that represent your monitor(s). Multiple monitors are covered later in the chapter.

Figure 8.7

Right-click the desktop and select Properties to make changes to your display. To change screen resolution, select the Settings tab.

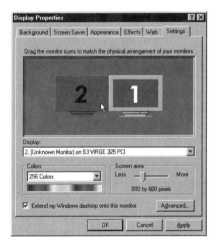

2. If you have more than one monitor attached, click the monitor you want to adjust.
3. Open the Screen Area drop-down list box, and select the resolution you want.
4. Click OK.
5. The resolution will change and you'll see a confirmation dialog box. If you're happy with the display, click the OK button within 15 seconds. If the display is unreadable, wait 15 seconds and Windows will restore the settings to the previous resolution.

Changing the Number of Colors Available to Your Monitor

The Color palette box in the Display Properties dialog box allows you to determine the number of colors your applications and Windows send to the monitor. The number of colors available depends on several factors: the quality of the video card, the quality of the video driver, and the amount of video RAM available. The combination of these factors determines the color palette and video resolution combinations you have available.

1. From the Display Properties dialog box, select the Settings tab. The top portion of this page contains one or more icons that represent your monitor(s). Multiple monitors are covered later in the chapter.

2. If you have more than one monitor attached, click the monitor you want to adjust.

3. Open the Colors drop-down list, and select the number of colors you want your applications and Windows to display.

N O T E Remember that 3D graphics require more video RAM than 2D graphics. Therefore, depending on the selected resolution, your 3D graphics may not use the number of colors you choose here. If this happens, your 3D graphics will be a bit on the ugly side until you choose a lower resolution.

Changing your resolution is covered in the preceding section.

4. If you choose a color palette too high for the resolution selected in the Screen Area section, windows will decrement the resolution to the highest resolution that can be used with the color palette you select. Experiment until you find an acceptable combination.

Changing Font Sizes

By default, Windows uses a font size of 96 dots per inch. This is referred to as Small Fonts, or Normal size. Large Fonts is 125% of Normal size, or 120 dots per inch. You can also specify a custom font size if neither of these is satisfactory.

To change your font size, follow these steps:

1. From the Display Properties dialog box, select the Settings tab. The top portion of this page contains one or more icons that represent your monitor(s). Multiple monitors are covered later in the chapter.

2. If you have more than one monitor attached, click the monitor you want to adjust.

3. Click the Advanced button. This brings up a property sheet for your video adapter.

4. On the General tab, open the Font size drop-down list box, and select Small Fonts, Large Fonts, or Other.

5. If you selected either Small or Large, click the OK button to apply the changes and close the dialog box.

6. If you want to specify a custom font size, select Other.

7. In the Custom font size dialog box, you can select from a drop-down list in the Scale fonts to be ___% of normal size drop-down list or type the scale you want directly into the box. The minimum scale is 20%. If you type something smaller into the box, Windows will change it for you to 20%.

8. The scale sample is displayed in the sample box, and states the pixels (dots) per inch. You can also drag to the scale you want by clicking anywhere within the ruler and dragging left or right to decrease/increase the font scaling.

9. When you find the scale you want, click the OK button.

10. When you finish making your adjustments click the OK button to apply the settings and close the Display Properties dialog box.

Adjusting the Refresh Rate

To adjust the refresh rate for your video adapter, follow these steps:

1. From the Display Properties dialog box, select the Settings tab. The top portion of this page contains one or more icons that represent your monitor(s). Multiple monitors are covered later in the chapter.

2. If you have more than one monitor attached, click the monitor you want to adjust.

3. Click the Advanced button. This brings up a property sheet for your video adapter.

4. At the bottom of the adapter tab is a drop-down list called Refresh Rate. Most adapters only have two settings available—Adapter and Optimal. Some will list specific refresh rates measured in Hz.

   Generally you want to set this to Optimal, especially if you're having trouble with screen flicker.

Configuring Multiple Monitors

This section shows you how to use a dual monitor setup. This text assumes a setup of two monitors and does not give details on hardware installation.

For details on changing resolution, refresh rate, and color settings for each monitor, refer to the appropriate sections earlier in this chapter.

Windows 98 supports up to eight monitors. Each must have its own PCI VGA video adapter. Your monitors are numbered from 1 through 8.

Setting up Windows to work with your monitors is very simple once you have the hardware installed. Follow these steps:

1. From the Display Properties dialog box, select the Settings tab. The top portion of this page contains one or more icons that represent your monitors. The icons are squares containing large digits representing the number of the monitor.

2. Click once on monitor number 2. In the bottom left corner of the Settings page, click the I want to use this monitor check box.

3. By default, monitor number two is assumed to be on the left side. You can move the icons around to better represent the physical setup of your monitors. If your main monitor is on the right side, simply move the icons around with the mouse until they represent the actual positioning of your two monitors. You can even arrange them in a vertical or diagonal arrangement.

4. The positioning of the icons is significant because it determines how you access each monitor.

5. Once you have the icons arranged, click OK.

That takes care of getting your second display ready to use. Now let's see how to use it.

The secondary display(s) becomes an extension of your desktop. Therefore, it does not have its own taskbar. In fact, there is nothing on the secondary display until you put something there.

Getting objects to the other monitor is very easy. All you do is drag the object to the other monitor. If your secondary monitor is to the left, just drag the object off the left side of your primary monitor. If you want to work with Netscape and Internet Explorer at the same time, drag one to the other monitor. You can even drag the taskbar over there to get it out of your way.

Customizing the Windows Desktop

You can customize your desktop so it has a look-and-feel that reflects your personality and how you work.

This section will show you how to create your own color schemes, how to put a nice nature photo on your desktop, and how to add texture to your desktop background.

Using Existing Color Schemes

1. In the Display Properties dialog box, select the Appearance tab.

2. The top half of the appearance tab shows the different elements of the Desktop, and your application windows that can be modified. This preview window shows the effect of the currently selected colors for each component or scheme.

3. To select an existing scheme, click to the right of the scheme list box, and select a scheme from the list. The effects of the scheme are displayed in the preview window.

4. If one of these schemes is suitable select it and click Apply. The new colors game will be applied immediately. If you like what you see, click the OK button to close the dialog box.

Creating Custom Color and Text Schemes

If none of these schemes is appropriate and you only want to change a few elements, follow these steps to create your own color scheme:

1. Open the Item drop-down list box, and select the element you want to change.

2. Click the Color button to display the color palette. If you see the color you want, select it. If the color you want is not there, select Other to display a larger color palette, and the custom colors dialog box. Select an existing color or create your own, and click OK.

3. When you've finished making color changes, click Apply to see what the changes will really look like. If you don't like them, switch back to the Windows standard color scheme and start over, or modify the colors you don't like. When you get the colors you want, click the OK button.

   Some elements are also sizable. If this is possible for a particular element, the Size: box will no longer be grayed.

 TIP If you find a scheme that is very close to what you want you can select that scheme, change the colors of the few items you want to change, then use the Save As button to give the new scheme the name.

4. To change the fonts, open the Font drop-down list box, and select the desired font from the drop-down list.

5. To change the font size either select from the existing lists by clicking down the Windows size text box, or highlight the contents of the size text box and type the font size directly into the box.

6. To change the color of the font, click the down arrow in the color box to display the palette, and click on the color you want to use. Click the Other button to create a custom color or select from a larger color palette.

7. Click any of the font style buttons to the right of the color palette to select or deselect font styles.

8. Once you have selected all the colors, fonts, and sizes you'll need, click the Save As button. This brings up the Save Scheme dialog box. In the Save color scheme as text box, type the name you want to give to your new color scheme and click the OK button.

Wallpapering Your Desktop with a Graphic

Would you prefer to display a graphic or even a photo on your desktop instead of that blasé background? No problem, here's how:

1. From the Display Properties dialog box, select the Background tab. The top half of this property page is a graphic representation of your monitor/desktop. When you select Wallpaper from the wallpaper list, a preview of the wallpaper is displayed there. Figure 8.8 shows the Background tab with a photo of Mount St. Helens selected as the wallpaper.

2. Scroll through the items in the Select an Internet Document (HTML) or a picture list, and click the one you want to use.

   If the graphic you want to use for your wallpaper is not visible in the Wallpaper list, click the Browse button and navigate to the location of your bitmap or HTML file. Select the file you want, and click the Open button.

Figure 8.8

Right-click the desktop and select Properties. Use the Background tab to change the wallpaper and pattern for your desktop.

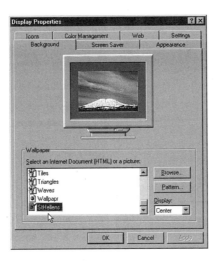

 TIP To get your own files to show up in the Wallpaper list, simply copy them to the Windows folder. The next time you go to the Display Properties dialog box, your custom wallpaper will show up in the Wallpaper list.

3. Most wallpaper bitmaps are very small bitmaps that can be tiled to create a wallpaper effect. In the lower right corner of the Background tab, you'll see the Display drop-down list. Open the List box and select either Tile or Center. If you choose Center, only one copy of the bitmap is displayed, directly in the center of your desktop. This is the recommended method for displaying photographs and HTML files.

Changing the Background Pattern

To change the background pattern:

1. Select (None) in the Wallpaper list.
2. Click the Pattern button to display the pattern dialog box.
3. Click the pattern you want to display. See the effect in the Preview window to the right of the Pattern list.
4. To modify the pattern, click the Edit pattern button. This brings up the pattern editing window, which allows you to modify the pattern to your liking. When you're finished editing the pattern, click the Change button to view the sample. If the sample is satisfactory, click Done.
5. Click OK to return to the Display Properties dialog box.
6. Click Apply to see the changes. If you like the changes, click the OK button.

Changing Desktop Icons

Want to change those system icons on the desktop? Follow these steps:

1. From the Display Properties dialog box, select the Effects tab. In the Desktop icons box you'll see the system icons that can be changed, including an option to use large icons.

2. In the Desktop icons box, select the icon you what you want to change, and click the Change Icon button. This brings up the Change Icon dialog box.

3. Locate the icon you want to use, and click on it. (Use the Browse button to look in a different DLL or EXE file if desired.) Then click OK to close the dialog box. You'll see the changes in the desktop icons box.

Icons are small images embedded inside files. Generally the icon for a particular application is embedded inside the executable file. Some of these have a DLL extension some have ICO extensions, but virtually any file can contain an icon. In fact, most Windows applications' executable files (.exe or .com) contain their own icon. This is the icon Windows uses by default.

Some .dll files and most .ico files are nothing more than a large collection of files. Shell32.dll is such a file. You can find Shell32.dll in the Windows directory. The file Windows\System\Cool.dll a;sp contains many icons you might want to use.

4. The two check boxes in the Visual settings area are pretty self explanatory. To turn the feature on, click it to place a check in the check box. To disable the feature, remove the check mark.

   - Use large icons simply displays larger versions of the all icons.
   - Show icons using all possible colors, uses the maximum number of colors in the icon, depending on what color palette you have set for your display.

Using the Screen Saver

Many of the Windows NT screen savers have been included in Windows 98. This gives you a much broader and more interesting selection of screen savers than previous versions of Windows.

Experiment with the individual setting for each screen saver, and make changes often to keep your computer a little more interesting.

Protecting Your Computer with a Screen Saver Password

If you don't want someone walking up to your computer and snooping around while you're getting coffee, follow these steps to setup password protection:

1. From the Display Properties dialog box select the Screen Saver tab.

2. Open the Screen Saver drop-down list, and select a screen saver if one isn't already selected.

3. Click the <u>P</u>assword protected check box.

4. Click the <u>C</u>hange button. This brings up the Change Password dialog box.

5. In the <u>N</u>ew Password text box, type the new password you want to use, press the Tab key to move to be Con<u>f</u>irm New Password text box. Retype your new password and click OK.

6. A dialog box appears telling you that your password has been successfully changed. Click OK. If the two passwords don't match, you'll receive a dialog box in the middle of the screen saying the passwords do not match and you must type them again.

Using Your Display's Energy-Saving Feature

The IBM XT (with the Intel 8086 processor) and its clones had a 100 watt power supply. This meant that at its peak usage it used about the same power as a 100 watt light bulb. And the monitor was a CGA that also used very little power—less than a TV set.

With all the modern computing power and high resolution video and other components now available, today's systems now use 3 to 5 times more power than they did in the '80s. In an effort to curb power waste, Energy Star standards have been developed. Energy Star includes several Environmental Protection Agency (EPA) programs that set standards for energy efficiency. These standards are implemented in most modern computer hardware and office equipment.

To take full advantage of the power saving features of your Energy Star compliant monitor, follow these steps:

From the Display Properties dialog box select the Settings tab.

You will see the property sheet for your video adapter. Select the Monitor tab. Table 8.4 describes the options on the Monitor page.

Table 8.4   Power Saving Features

Option name	Description
Monitor is Energy Star compliant	If your monitor is Energy Star compliant, check this box. It is generally pretty obvious. Most ES compliant monitors will have two power indicator lights on the front. Yellow to indicate power has been reduced, and green to indicate full power mode. Sometimes there is only one light that will change colors.
Automatically detect Plug & Play monitors	If your monitor is Plug & Play compatible, check this box. Windows will detect the power saver features of the monitor and use the appropriate software.

continues

Table 8.4   Continued

Option name	Description
Reset display on suspend/resume	Most adapters don't need to reset the display after a suspend. If your display is working properly, ignore this setting. Some monitors will flicker during a reset. If this bothers you, try unchecking this box.

Remember that you can also use your computer's CMOS settings to make your hard drive spin down when it's not in use. Refer to your BIOS manufacturer's documentation for information on adjusting these settings.

Changing the Screen Saver and its Settings

To select a new screen saver, open the Screen saver drop-down list, and select the screen saver you want. The screen saver you select will show in the Preview area.

Click the Settings button to change the behavior and appearance. The types of settings vary with each screen saver. Experiment with the different settings; you can preview settings you have selected by clicking the Preview button.

 TIP The best way to use the preview is to use the Alt+V keyboard shortcut. Often when you click the Preview button and you let go of the mouse, you move the mouse slightly. The slightest mouse movement will turn off this screen saver preview. If you use the keyboard shortcut, you won't accidentally move the mouse before you're finished previewing.

To display or own customized text, select Scrolling Marquee or 3D text from the screen saver list, and click the settings button. Type the text you want to appear on screen, and experiment with the other adjustments.

Changing the Sounds Related to Windows Events

Windows 98 associates different sounds with each event. For example, if an error occurs the default sound is a chime. You can change this so that a different sound bite is played for any particular event. In fact, you can record your own sounds if you have a microphone for your sound card. For instance, you can record a wave file that says "an error has occurred." This kind of customization is great for site impaired users.

Only sound files in the WAV format can be associated with Windows events. WAV files have the extension .WAV. In order for your own WAV files to show up in the name drop-down list box, you need to store them in media folder under your Windows folder. For example, c:\windows\media\My sound.wav.

TIP Sound America is an excellent source for WAV files on the Internet. The Sound America Web Site has literally thousands of sound files most of which are WAV format. They are free for the downloading, and most of them are less than 100k in size.

The Web site address is **http://www.soundamerica.com.**

To change the sound associated with a Windows event follow these steps.

1. From Control Panel select the sounds icon. The Sounds Properties dialog box appears (see Figure 8.9).

2. In the events box select the event you want to change the association for. If there is allowed Speaker icon the left of the sound events, then there is a sound already associated with that event. If there's no allowed Speaker icon, no sound has been associated with that.

Figure 8.9
The Sounds Properties dialog box.

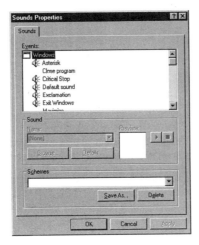

3. In the name drop-down list box, select the sound file you want to associate with this event. If you want to associate a WAV file that is not the end the media folder, click the browse button and navigate to the location of the file and select it from the Browse dialog box.

4. To preview the sound, click the right arrow to the right of the Preview icon.

TIP Windows also supplies several preset schemes that you can select from the schemes drop-down list box. Open the Schemes drop-down list to select the scheme you want to use.

5. When you finish making your Custom sound associations you can save this sound scheme with a unique name. Click the Save As button, type a name for the new sound scheme into the save this sound scheme as text box and click the OK button.

T I P One very practical use for this feature is to find or record an intuitive or unique sound to associate with New Mail Notification. This way when new Mail comes in you get something more than just a chime.

Now, when you receive a new e-mail message you will know right away, and youcan check to see if it's the important one you've been waiting all day for.

Customizing Mouse and Keyboard Settings

You can customize the behavior of mouse and keyboard to make them work exactly the way you want them.

From Control Panel select mouse. You'll see the Mouse Properties dialog box.

Table 8.5 describes the options in the tabs in the Mouse Properties dialog box.

Table 8.5   The Mouse Properties Options

Option name	Description
Button configuration	To configure your mouse for left-handed use, click the Left-handed radio button. This reverses the functionality of the left and right mouse buttons.
Double-click speed	To adjust the double-click speed, move the slider bar in the double-click speed section of the buttons tab. Double-click the Jack-in-the-box in the Test area: to test your new speed setting.

Mouse Pointers and Animated Cursors

Depending on what task you're doing, your mouse pointer changes its appearance. The normal pointer is a white Arrow pointing up slightly left. If the computer is busy, such as when it's loading an application, your mouse pointer becomes an hour glass. This indicates that no other processing can occur until the current process is finished. If a process is working in the background, the mouse pointer becomes a combination of an arrow and an hourglass.

Windows provides several other mouse pointer schemes for you to select from. To select a different scheme, click the down arrow to the right of the Scheme drop-down list. Select the pointer scheme you want to use.

The bottom half of this page shows what the mouse pointers look like. The square in the upper right corner is a preview area for the highlighted pointer. This is really only useful if it is an animated cursor (mouse pointer). For example, if you select the animated hour glasses scheme, click on the Busy cursor, then you can watch the animation in the preview box.

If you want to create your own scheme of mouse pointers, select the pointer you want to change, and click the browse button. This brings up a dialog box showing the contents of the cursors folder under Windows (c:\windows\cursors)

If you select a particular scheme but you want to use the Windows default for a few of the pointers, select the pointer you want to change and click the Use de_fault button.

When you finish creating your disk pointer scheme click the Sa_ve as button, type the new name in the Save this cursor scheme as: text box, and click the OK button.

Calibrating Mouse Movement

The Motion tab gives you the following options:

- *Pointer S_peed*. This sets the speed the pointer moves across the screen when you move the mouse. Move the slider to the left to slow down mouse movement; to the right to speed up mouse movement.

- *Pointer T_rail*. Displays pointer trails. Click the Sh_ow pointer trails check box. Adjust the length of the pointer trail with the slider bar below the check box. Kids love this feature. If you don't like the mouse trails, try not to let them find out about this one.

- *Working with the new IntelliMouse*. Microsoft has developed a great alternative to the three button mouse. Their new mouse, called the IntelliMouse, has a left and right mouse button with a small wheel/button combination between the two buttons.

To take full advantage of the wheel, your application must specifically support the mouse wheel. The wheel-button behaves differently in each application. Table 8.6 describes the functions of the wheel-button in Word 97.

Table 8.6 Functions of the IntelliMouse Wheel-button

Action	Effect
Single click	Activates a scrolling feature. The scroll box in the vertical scroll bar changes appearance, and the pointer changes to a dot with an arrow above and below it when the pointer is directly over the scroll box. If the pointer is above or below the scroll box, one of the arrows will disappear, and the page will begin to scroll in that direction. The farther the pointer is from the center of the document window, the faster the document will scroll.
Click and hold	The pointer changes to a dot with an arrow above and below. When you move the pointer up, the bottom arrow goes away and the document scrolls up. The reverse is true if you move the pointer down. A "ghost" pointer is visible at the position the pointer was in when you pressed the wheel. The farther the pointer is from the "ghost" pointer, the faster the document will scroll.

continues

Table 8.6 Continued

Action	Effect
Spin without click	If you just spin the wheel without clicking it, the document will scroll up or down three lines at a time.
Hold left button and spin	If you hold the left button down while you spin the wheel, the text is highlighted as if you were doing a drag operation with the mouse.

Making Windows Accessible for the Hearing, Sight, and Movement Impaired

The Accessibility options are indispensable for computer users with disabilities. Microsoft has done a fantastic job here. Many of these features are also useful for non-impaired users as well. Even if you don't think you need any of these features, take a glance through them, you may be surprised at what you can do!

To open the Accessibility Properties, double click Accessibility Options in Control Panel. You'll see the dialog box in Figure 8.10.

Figure 8.10.
Choose Accessibility from the Control Panel to open this box.

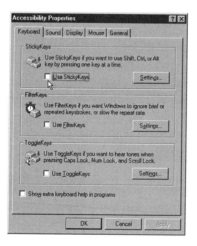

Keyboard Tab

The keyboard tab has three features:

■ StickyKeys (see Figure 8.11) makes it easier to use multiple key combinations that include the Shift, Alt, and ctrl keys. These keys are called Modifier keys. For example, Shift+F10 activates the right-click menu. When StickyKeys is enabled, you can press and release the Shift key then press and release the F10 key to get the same effect.

Figure 8.11
StickyKeys Settings
dialog box.

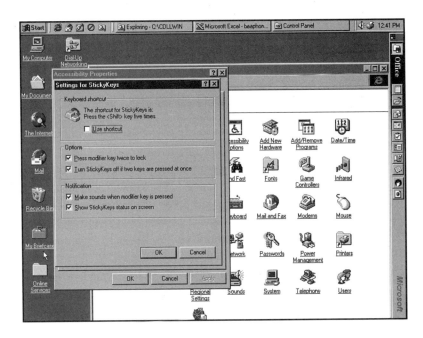

■ FilterKeys (see Figure 8.12) tells Windows to ignore repeated keystrokes.

Figure 8.12
FilterKeys Settings
dialog box.

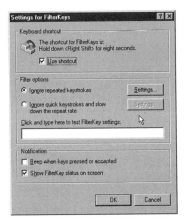

■ ToggleKeys gives audio feedback whenever Caps Lock, Num Lock, or Scroll Lock are pressed. To activate this feature, press the Num Lock key for five seconds, click the Settings button, and check the Use Shortcut box.

Sound Tab

The sound tab contains two visual feedback features—SoundSentry and ShowSounds. Sound Sentry tells windows to give visual feedback at times when normally only audio feedback would occur. The settings button allows you to select what type of visual feedback is given. ShowSounds tells your applications to give visual feedback, when they would normally only give audio feedback.

Display Tab

This feature forces your applications to use the color scheme specified in the Settings dialog box (press the settings button). In the Settings dialog box, you can check the Use shortcut box to enable the Left Alt+left Shift+Print Screen keyboard shortcut to enable the feature. In the High contrast color scheme section, you can specify what scheme to use.

MouseKeys

MouseKeys allows you to use the arrow keys and the numeric keypad keys to control your mouse pointer. Click the Settings button to fine tune the feature's behavior.

General Tab

The General tab allows you to make a few global adjustment to the Accessibility Options. Automatic Reset tells Windows to turn off all Accessibility Options after a specified time of inactivity. Notification provides two options for giving visual and audio feedback when features are turned on or off. This helps avoid accidentally toggling features on and off. SerialKey devices are used when special input devices are attached to any of the serial ports. Use the Settings button to tell Windows what port the device is plugged into.

Using the Windows "Power Toys" Collection

The Windows Power Toys is a collection of small utility programs developed for Windows 95. Some of them have been built into the new Operating System, and many of the others are still useful. For instance, the AutoPlay Extender gives you AutoPlay capabilities for CD-ROMs that don't have AutoPlay support. Cabview is a tool for viewing and extracting files from cabinet archives. An updated Cabview.dll is now included in the Windows 98 install. Installing the older version of Cabview from Power Toys is not recommended. CAB, short for cabinet, is a file archive format for distributing software, and was implemented with the original release of Windows 95. There are 13 different Power Toys and a readme.txt file is included that explains the functionality of each Power Toy.

Part

I

Ch

8

CAUTION

Remember that Microsoft does not provide support for these utilities, and they were originally designed for Windows 95. Some of them may not work properly under Windows 98.

Carefully read all documentation available before using any of the Power Toys.

N O T E   You can download the Power Toys from Microsoft's Web Site at **http://www.microsoft.com/ windows/windows95/info/powertoys.htm**

Maintaining and Troubleshooting Your System

by Ty Belknap

In this chapter

Keeping Windows 98 Up-To-Date

No software is perfect, whether it's an operating system, program, or drivers for a piece of hardware. Companies are constantly working on their products to improve performance and reliability, and the main concern today is figuring out ways to get those improvements out to people.

Microsoft has realized this concern, and has combined the use of the Internet with Windows 98 to get updates out quickly and easily, using the Windows Update Wizard.

Using the Windows Update Wizard

The Windows Update Wizard is a database of drivers, system utilities, and other software maintained by Microsoft. This gives you one convenient place on the Internet to check to see if there are Windows 98 updates available that you need for your system. This is a Microsoft site, though, and all updated drivers on the site must be approved by Microsoft, so it may not have all the drivers you are looking for.

To search for updates using the Microsoft Update Wizard:

1. Click Start, Windows Update. Internet Explorer will come up automatically and attempt to connect to Microsoft's Update Web site, as seen in Figure 9.1.

Figure 9.1

The Update Wizard and Technical Support Web sites are now combined.

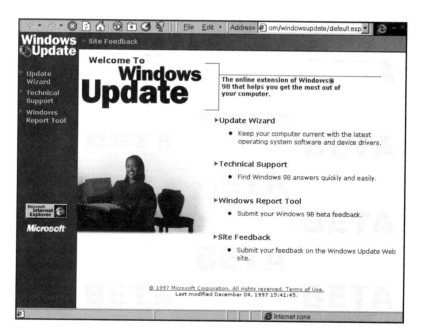

2. Click Update Wizard. A Registration Wizard will pop up if this is the first time you've used the Update Wizard, as seen in Figure 9.2. You must fill out the registration to continue. Part of the registration is uploading your configuration files to Microsoft. You can uncheck a box so this does not happen if you want to.

Figure 9.2

The Update Wizard will not start if you click No.

▶ **See** "Web Browsing with IE 4," **page 857**

3. There are two options on the Update Wizard Web page: Update and Restore. Click Update to scan the Internet for updated system files. A new Internet Explorer window will pop up, as seen in Figure 9.3. The update wizard will load necessary components into your system, then scan the database for updated drivers.

Figure 9.3

Once you click Update, a list of files available will be shown on the left side of the screen.

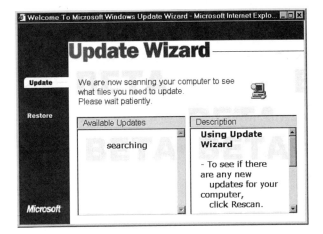

4. As updates are found, the screen will refresh with a list of files available for update. Select a file in the list on the left to see a description of the file, size, and approximate download type on the right side of the screen.

5. Click Install to install the file. Only one file can be installed at a time, and your computer may need to be restarted after a file is installed. Let the computer restart, so you know the system is working properly still, before downloading a second update.

The Update Wizard keeps track of where the new and old files are in case there's a problem. If your system crashes after installing a new file, or some functions no longer work properly, you can go back and reinstall the old files. To do this,

1. In the Update Wizard, click Restore. A new Internet Explorer window will pop up,scan your system, and give you a list of the files you have updated, as seen in Figure 9.4

Figure 9.4

The Restore option allows you to uninstall files if they cause problems.

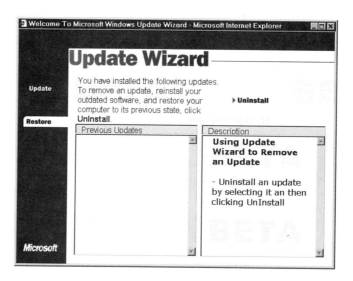

2. Select a file in the list on the left to show the description of the update.

3. To uninstall the update, click Uninstall. You may need to restart your system if prompted.

Reading Your Registration and Version Number

Your registration and version number may not seem important at first glance, but, as Microsoft updates Windows 98 with patches and service packs, knowing where this information is will be helpful.

To view your current version of Windows 98 and Internet Explorer, as well as your product ID number, right-click My Computer, then click Properties. The result is seen in Figure 9.5.

Figure 9.5

You will find the Windows and Internet Explorer version numbers under the System area. Your product ID number is the first number under the Registered To area.

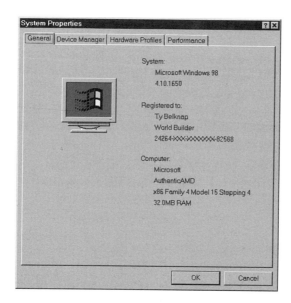

Improving Windows Performance

The performance of Windows 98 can degrade over time as programs are added and removed and updates to the system files are made.

This section describes how to use the disk Defragmenter and ScanDisk to help keep your system working at top speed. Listed below are steps on how to check your performance settings, adjust virtual memory, and track system resources. Included is a detailed explanation of what the Windows 98 Tune-Up Wizard is and how to use it to automate tasks.

Checking Performance Settings

Your computer's performance settings are vital tools in the war against problems. The main performance page can warn you about old drivers or possible viruses and gives you an easy way to check your system resources.

To check your computer's performance settings:

1. Right-click My Computer.
2. Left-click Properties to access your system settings.
3. Choose the Performance tab at the top for your performance settings, as seen in Figure 9.6.

Figure 9.6
Check the main performance page often. Problems with your computer may be seen from here.

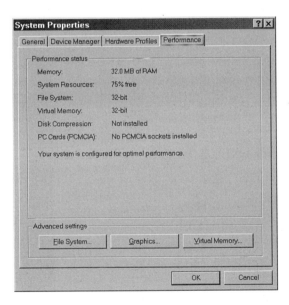

Look carefully through the main page of the Performance tab. Make sure it lists the correct amount of memory, and that the File System and Virtual Memory both say 32-bit. Incorrect amounts of RAM could show that there are bad RAM chips on your computer, or it may be that you are loading an old DOS program, like SmartDrive, in your autoexec.bat or config.sys.

CAUTION

If your File System area shows some or all of your hard drives using "MS DOS Compatibility Mode Paging," you may be using an old hard disk driver, or the *Disable all 32-bit protect-mode disk drivers* option in the Troubleshooting tab may be checked. Use the Update Manager, or contact the disk manufacturer, to see if updated drivers are available.

A virus is another potential cause of "Compatibility Mode Paging." Viruses and antivirus programs will be discussed toward the end of this chapter.

There are three advanced settings from the Performance tab: File System, Graphics, and Virtual Memory. These settings are explained as follows:

As seen in Figure 9.7, the File System has five tabs under it—Hard Disk, Floppy Disk, CD-ROM, Removable Disk, and Troubleshooting.

Figure 9.7

Hard disk properties.

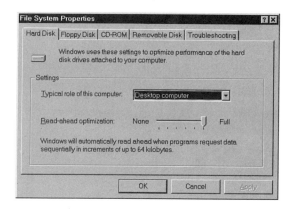

The Hard Disk tab configures the settings on how the hard disk reads files and how the VCACHE file system works. In the Settings area, you can configure:

- *Typical Role of This Computer.* The three options are Desktop Computer, Mobile or Docking System, and Network Computer. Laptop users should use the mobile or docking system. The Network Computer option could make the system run a bit faster than the Desktop Computer option, but can cause the system to hang on shutdown or restart because the file system cache was not able to completely clear itself.

- *Read-ahead Optimization.* This should be set to Full by default, and, unless your system does not shut down or restart properly, this is the best setting. If you have trouble using the normal shutdown procedures, lower this option one step at a time. It may alleviate the problem.

N O T E   VCACHE is the Windows 98 Dynamic Swap File. This file will grow and shrink in size as programs are opened and closed. The Swap File, named Win386.swp, is a hidden file on the root of your hard drive. ▨

There is only one option on the Floppy Disk tab and that is to have the computer search for new floppy drives every time the system is restarted. This is a good option for laptop users who have removable floppy drives, but desktop users can save boot time by disabling it.

The CD-ROM tab configures the read-ahead and buffer for your CD-ROM system. There are two options to configure (see Figure 9.8). They are:

■ *Supplemental Cache Size.* Set this option to Full. This is another area to lower if you are having problems shutting down or restarting your computer. If your computer hangs at shutdown, it could be because the CD-ROM cache is not flushing itself properly.

■ *Optimize Access Pattern For.* Choose the CD-ROM type you have. Raising the amount of the cache on smaller CD-ROM drives does not improve performance, and may cause problems. Anything over a Quad (4) speed CD-ROM should use the "Quad Speed or Higher" setting.

Figure 9.8
CD-ROM Properties.

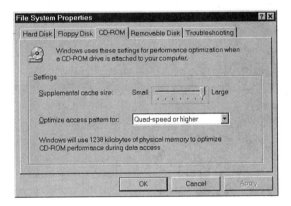

Enable Write-behind Caching on All Removable Disk Drives is the only option in the Removable Disk tab. Removable disks are drives such as Zip, Jaz, or Syquest, and this is a good option to check if you have them. Write-behind caching is enabled by default for your hard disks, though, so there is no reason to use this option if you don't have removable media.

CAUTION

If write-behind caching is used on removable disks, make sure the computer is done writing to the disk before you remove it, or some information may be lost.

The Troubleshooting tab (see Figure 9.9) is useful when working with older MS-DOS programs, specifically file utility programs like Norton Utilities that weren't made for Windows 98.

CAUTION

Windows 98 handles file systems much like Windows 95, and you can use most Windows 95 file utility programs in Windows 98. If you are using FAT 32, make sure the utility is FAT 32 compatible.

Figure 9.9

There are six items in the Troubleshooting tab. Click a check box to disable or re-enable an item.

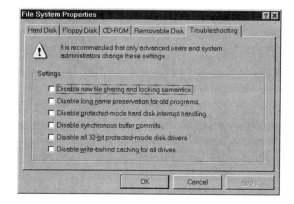

N O T E   Every time you check a box in the Troubleshooting tab, you must restart your computer.

The six items in the Troubleshooting tab are:

- *Disable New File Sharing and Locking Semantics.* Some older MS-DOS programs cannot handle the new file sharing capabilities of Windows. Check this box to disable Windows file sharing and allow older programs to work properly.

- *Disable Long Name Preservation for Old Programs.* This box is used in conjunction with the utility LFNBK (located in the \tools\apptools subdirectory of the Windows 98 CD). LFNBK allows you to backup long filenames while using older utilities, and checking this option will allow the long filenames to be unlocked so LFNBK can convert long file names to 8.3 filenames.

- *Disable Protected-mode Hard Disk Interrupt Handling.* Useful with older hard drives, this option lets the drive handle interrupt termination. This option should never be checked in computers with newer hard disk drives.

- *Disable Synchronous Buffer Commits.* This option causes a write initiation of the API buffers to the hard disk, but allows users to continue working before the write is completed. This will not gain you better performance, but may cause errors and lost data if the write is not completed. Use this option only when troubleshooting performance problems with specific programs that may require it.

- *Disable All 32-bit Protected-mode Disk Drivers.* Check this option if you feel you are having problems writing information to the hard disk, or if your computer does not start due to disk writes. This will cause "Compatibility Mode Paging" to show up in the general properties tab for all hard drives. It will also slow down your system, so only use it for troubleshooting.

■ *Disable Write-behind Caching for All Drives.* Here is another spot to check if your system does not shut down or restart correctly. It will shut off all cache options for all disk drives, including the floppy disk. It will also slow your system down, so it's not a fix, but helps in determining where the problem lies.

The Graphics button off the main Properties tab takes you to the Advanced Graphics page, as seen in Figure 9.10.

Figure 9.10
Hardware acceleration can be a double-edged sword, and is not as stable as it should be.

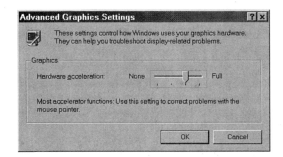

The only option is to set Hardware Acceleration. If you're upgrading from Windows 95, the upgrade should keep the same settings you had before. Hardware acceleration is usually a performance boost to computers, but using hardware acceleration can cause Fatal Exception errors. The text of Fatal Exception errors usually looks something like:

```
(filename) caused a Fatal Exception error in module (filename) at: 0128:bfff...
(more numbers)
```

The bfff series is what's important here. If the series of numbers starts with A, B or C, the error could be a video problem. The first step would be to look over the Internet or a Bulletin Board System to see if there are new drivers for your video card. If your video card has the latest drivers and you are still having problems, start lowering the Hardware acceleration one step at a time. After each restart, use your computer to see if the error comes back.

 Anytime you feel your computer is experiencing problems related to hardware, check the Microsoft Windows Update Wizard for updated drivers. An updated driver could solve the problem.

Mouse pointer problems may also be solved by lowering the accelerator option. If your mouse pointer seems jerky (and the mouse itself is not dirty), or if your pointer disappears, lower the accelerator option one or two notches and see if it goes away.

Adjusting Virtual Memory Settings

Virtual Memory is the last option in the performance tab (see Figure 9.11). Virtual memory allows Windows to load and run faster and more efficiently. If you restarted your computer, and ran System Monitor (detailed later in this chapter), you would find that Windows has about a 6MB disk cache size. This happens because Windows loads virtual drivers, video drivers, the drivers to run hard disks, and more in virtual memory. Every program that you load adds drivers and files to that virtual memory area as well.

CAUTION

Virtual memory is an integral part of Windows 98, and should never be turned off except when troubleshooting applicable problems.

Figure 9.11

Virtual Memory is the Windows 98 swap file.

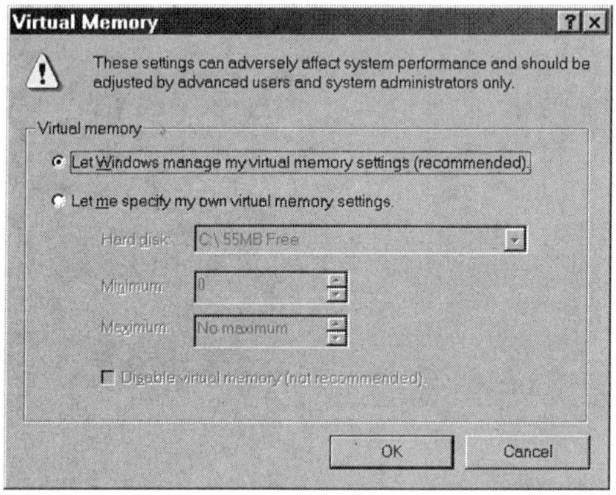

The best option is to let Windows manage your virtual memory settings. Windows 98 has a dynamic swap file that will grow and shrink in size, setting the appropriate amount determined on what you need.

Specifying your own settings can improve performance on your computer, but it imposes limitations on what Windows can swap to the file from RAM. Set the minimum and maximum size of the swap file to the same size if you decide to specify your own settings. That will make a permanent swap file on your hard disk that does not change size, so Windows doesn't have to manage the file. The more RAM you have, the smaller a swap file you need. A manually created swap file should be around 20MB if you have 32MB RAM, more if you have less RAM. The recommended minimum amount for a swap file is 12MB RAM, and that can be eaten up quickly.

There is an option to disable the swap file, but this will slow your computer down considerably. It is recommended not to disable the swap file unless you are having file-related problems.

Defragmenting Disks for Faster Access to Data

Windows 98 writes information to the hard disk drive using whatever free space there is. As programs are removed, gaps form between the files that are left on the hard disk, and those gaps get filled by new programs that get installed. This process causes fragmentation of the hard drive, and nothing can be done about it happening.

As the hard disk becomes fragmented, the computer will have to search different areas to execute programs or bring up data files. This will cause a loss of performance and can cause the computer to have problems in the normal execution of programs.

Disk Defragmenter was created to alleviate these problems. The Windows 98 Disk Defragmenter searches your hard disk for files and programs that belong together and puts them in the right spots, like organizing a filing cabinet. The new Disk Defragmenter will also watch how you use your computer and put the programs you use the most at the front of the hard disk for faster access. This is done automatically, if checked under the Settings button, so you don't have to worry about picking and choosing what programs you might use the most.

 T I P   Setting your screen saver to none before starting to defragment your hard disk will allow the process to end faster.

To begin using Disk Defragmenter;

1. Click Start, Programs, Accessories, System Tools, Disk Defragmenter. You see Figure 9.12.

Figure 9.12
Select the drive you want to defragment, then click OK to start the utility.

There are two options you can choose in the Settings box:

You can uncheck both options if you just want a quick defrag of your hard drive.

- *Rearrange Program Files so My Programs Start Faster.* This tells the utility to choose the programs you use the most and put them at the front of the hard disk drive. This causes Disk Defragmenter to run slower, but your computer could show improved performance once it's done.

- *Check the Drive for Errors.* This tests the sectors of the physical disk for problems. The utility may come back with a message to run ScanDisk if the error is something Disk Defragmenter can't handle. This causes Disk Defragmenter to run slower, but is a good option to check if you've been having system problems.

You have the option of saving your settings by clicking the Every Time I Defragment My Hard Drive button.

You also have the option of running Disk Defragmenter from the hard drive icon. To do this, select My Computer and then right-click a hard drive icon. Choose Properties, then the Tools tab at the top. You see Figure 9.13.

Figure 9.13

You do not have the option to change settings when you choose Defragment from this direction, but it is quick and will defrag the specific hard drive you choose.

The Defragmentation Status box at the bottom tells you how long it's been since your hard drive was defragmented. Select Defragment Now to start the Disk Defragmenter utility.

Using ScanDisk to Prevent and Repair Damage

ScanDisk can search all the files on your computer, as well as the physical disk(s), for errors. You will have options on how to fix any errors it finds once it is done searching.

To start ScanDisk, Click Start, Programs, Settings, System Tools, ScanDisk. You will see Figure 9.14.

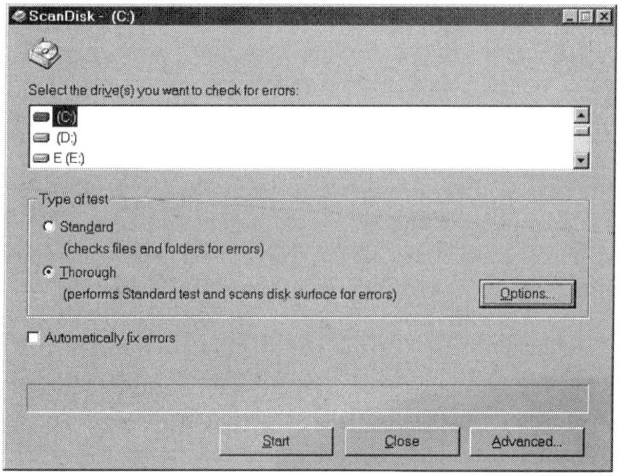

Figure 9.14

The Windows 98 version of ScanDisk is equipped to handle FAT16 and FAT32 formatted hard disks.

N O T E You can also start ScanDisk by selecting My Computer. Right-click the drive you want to scan, choose Properties, then click the Tools button at the top. Click the button labeled Check Now. ▪

There are two options to choose from in the main ScanDisk window, as well as a check box. The options are:

- ▪ *Standard.* This will check all files on your hard disk(s) for errors, and report any errors found. It will not check the physical sectors on the hard disk(s), though.

- ▪ *Thorough.* Will check all files on your hard disk(s) and do a surface scan to check the physical disk(s) for errors. If errors are found on your physical disk(s), ScanDisk will mark the affected sectors as bad and attempt to move any information found in those sectors to a good sector. If you choose the Thorough option, you can also detail what you want it to do by clicking the Options button, as seen in Figure 9.15.

Figure 9.15

Doing a Surface Scan is a good option if you have trouble installing a new program.

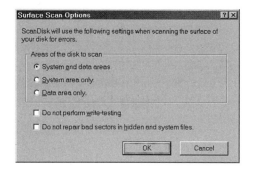

CAUTION

The files needed to run Windows reside in the system area. If your computer has a bad sector in the system area, you may not be able to restart Windows, and may have to reinstall Windows from a DOS prompt.

Toward the bottom left of the main ScanDisk window is a check box to Automatically fix errors. ScanDisk will show you each error found if this is not checked. You will then have the option to:

- ▪ *Ignore the Error and Continue.* You can ignore the error, if it's not serious, and continue scanning the rest of the disk. ScanDisk will tell you if the error is so serious that it cannot continue without fixing the error.

- ▪ *Repair the Error By.* You can repair the error and continue. ScanDisk will ask if you want to create an undo file. Always create one if you don't know what it's trying to fix. You can always delete the undo file later. The end of the sentence changes depending on what type of error was found.

- ▪ *Delete the Affected (file, folder, and so on).* ScanDisk will prompt if you want an undo file when you choose this option. It's a good idea to create an undo file, just in case.

N O T E ScanDisk automatically fixes the error and creates an undo file when you choose to automatically fix errors. ▓

The bottom of the main screen has the standard Start and Close buttons, plus an Advanced button. The options under the Advanced button are:

- *Display Summary.* You can choose to Always Display a Summary when ScanDisk is Finished, Never Display the Summary, or Only Give a Summary when Errors are Found.

- *Log File.* ScanDisk creates a log file called scandisk.log every time the utility is run. This file should be placed in the root of c:. You can choose to Replace Log, which will delete the previous log file; Append to Log, which will keep adding to the file; or Choose No Log, which will never keep a log. Having a log file is a good idea to keep track of errors. Only use Append if you want to track errors over a period of time, though.

- *Cross-Linked Files.* Cross-linked files happen when two separate files occupy the same space on a hard disk. This does not normally happen, and you may find other problems when this error comes up. The option for cross-linked files are: Delete to Remove Both Files from the Hard Disk; Make Copies to Re-copy Each File to a Different Area of the Hard Disk; and Ignore If You Want ScanDisk to Keep Searching for Other Errors Without Fixing This One. The recommended option is to make copies.

- *Lost File Fragments.* File fragments generally appear when Windows is not shut down properly. The two options are: Free to Delete the File Fragments Without Viewing Them and Convert to Files to Save Them and Look at Them Later. When you choose to Convert to files, the fragments will be saved with an extension of .CHK on the root directory of your c: drive. You can view them with Notepad or WordPad. Most often, they contain ASCII characters and can be deleted, but it's a good idea to save them if you were working on a file when Windows crashed.

- *Check Files For.* The three options are: Invalid File Names, which searches your hard disk for filenames that include invalid characters; Invalid Dates and Times, which searches for files that have improper dates or times associated with them; or Duplicate File Names, which searches for duplicate files in the same directory. This option can slow ScanDisk down while searching directories with many files. If duplicate files are found, you have the option of repairing the error (ScanDisk will rename the files so they have different names), deleting the affected files/folders, or ignoring the error and continuing.

- *Check Host Drive First.* A good option if you have a DriveSpace compressed drive. This automatically checks both drives for errors.

- *Report MS-DOS Mode Name Length Errors.* Checks for filenames that are too long for MS-DOS mode to handle.

Click OK then click Start for ScanDisk to begin after customizing the options. ScanDisk could take a long time to run (more than 30 minutes) if the Thorough option is checked, or if the hard disk is very fragmented.

Using the All-in-One Windows Tune-Up Wizard

The Windows Tune-Up Wizard is a program that automates ScanDisk and Disk Defragmenter, as well as cleaning your system of temporary files and unwanted networking components. With this wizard, you can have Windows run ScanDisk and Disk Defragmenter during times and days you are not using your system.

To run the Windows Tune-Up Wizard, Click Start, Programs, Accessories, System Tools, Windows Tune-Up. The first screen you see asks whether you want to do an Express or Custom tune-up, as seen in Figure 9.16.

Figure 9.16

Express setup is quick and easy.

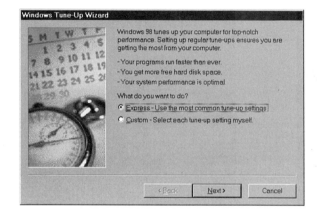

- ■ *Express Use the Most Common Tune-up Settings.* Express is a quick way to get the Tune-Up Wizard up and running. To use the Express setting, just click Next. The following screen will ask what time of day you want the wizard to run. Choose your settings, then click Next. Windows shows you what programs will be run. Click Finish and you're done.

- ■ *Custom Select Each Tune-up Setting Myself.* The custom selection allows for more flexibility, but is more difficult to set up. To use the Custom setting:

    1. Choose the Custom button, and click Next. The Wizard asks what time of day you want the programs to run. Choose the setting you want, and click Next.

    2. The Start Windows Quickly window will come up, as seen in Figure 9.17. This window shows you what programs you have opening at startup. You can make Windows 98 start faster by having no programs start automatically at startup. Click Next.

Figure 9.17

Pick your startup files carefully. They can slow down how fast Windows starts.

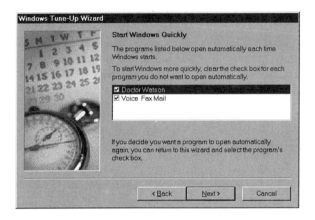

3. Scan Hard Disk for Errors. Choose the options you want, then click Next.

   Delete Unnecessary Files is a tricky option. Every time your computer shuts off, or restarts abnormally, a temporary file is created. Many newer Windows programs are created to make a temporary file in case of accidental shutdown, as well. Most of the time, these temporary files are junk and can be deleted. There may be a time that you're writing an important document, however, and your computer freezes. In that situation, a temporary file may have been created to help you get your information back. The Settings button can refine the types of files to delete, as seen in Figure 9.18.

Figure 9.18

Disk Cleanup allows you to view the files that are marked for deletion.

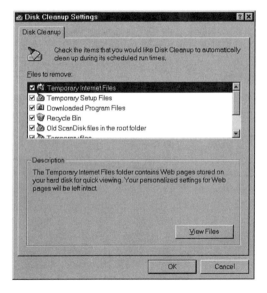

4. The last screen confirms your choices. Your computer must be on when the scheduled choices run. Verify the information and then click Finish. This will add Task Scheduler to the System Tray on the right side of your taskbar.

Keeping Track of System Resources

Throughout a normal day at the computer, you may find yourself opening and closing a few programs, jumping on the Internet for Web pages or reading email, and perhaps hiding a game in the background. Everything you do on your computer, whether it's moving the mouse around or loading the newest game, takes system resources, or memory. You can reclaim resources by closing programs, but they don't always give all the resources back. There are several easy ways to keep track of your system's resources:

■ Right-click My Computer, click Properties, and choose the Performance tab at the top right. The System Resources line will show a percentage of your free resources. Personal experience has shown that my computer becomes very slow and has a higher chance of getting errors when my system goes below 75% free resources with no programs running (using 32MB of RAM). Individual systems may vary, depending on your system and the amount of RAM you have.

■ Resource Meter is a good way to keep constant track of your system's memory. Click Start, Programs, Accessories, System Tools, and choose Resource Meter.

N O T E   Keep in mind that Resource Meter uses system resources like all other programs. ■

Resource Meter runs in the System Tray of your taskbar. Hold your mouse pointer over the icon to see the free resources you have. You can also double-click the icon to bring up a bar showing your free resources.

■ System Monitor is another utility that tracks system resources. However, because of its size and the number of options the utility has, we will be detailing System Monitor in its own section later in this chapter.

Repairing Configuration Problems

Windows 98 comes with a fantastic new utility called System Information. The System Information utility keeps track of all your computer's file versions, the resources your hardware is using, and the hardware and software components of your computer.

The Tools tab at the top of the utility also has quick access to Dr. Watson, System File Checker, Registry Checker, and more.

To access the System Information utility, click Start, Programs, Accessories, System Tools, System Information.

Gather Details with the System Information Utility

The Microsoft System Information Utility is a great tool to help with the battle against errors. It's a one-stop utility that will allow you to view the resources, system components, and the software environment on your computer. You can also run System File Checker, Registry Checker, Dr. Watson, the System Configuration Utility, and ScanDisk from here.

The main window of the System Information Utility is used to gather details about your computer, as seen in Figure 9.19. There are three main sections to this window—resources, components, and software environment.

Figure 9.19

The Microsoft System Information Utility allows you to check to make sure Windows sees all the components in your computer.

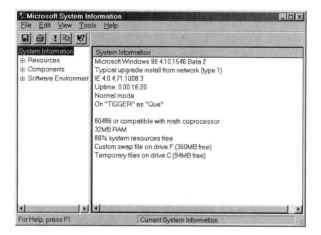

Resources is the best section to keep track of for troubleshooting purposes. The Components and Software Environment sections have good information on Registry settings and system file versions, but the Resources section will detail the majority of conflicts and settings needed to determine problems.

The Resources area in the left pane shows how the different hardware components on your computer are working together. The six areas you can view here are:

- *Conflicts/Sharing.* The utility will scan your computer for hardware conflicts and software sharing violations. The right pane will show all problems it finds.

- *DMA.* DMA (Direct Memory Access) allows hardware devices to bypass the CPU and work directly with memory. The right pane of the window will give you a list of which hardware devices are using what DMA settings. This is a great area to check when adding new hardware to your computer.

CAUTION

No two hardware devices can use the same DMA channel.

- *Forced Hardware.* Plug-and-Play devices do not always play fairly. When PnP devices conflict, you can force the hardware to use specific settings. The right window pane will show you which devices are using forced settings.

- *I/O.* I/O (Input/Output) ports are memory locations, not associated with the main memory of the computer, in which information travels between the CPU and hardware devices. Each hardware device may use several I/O ports, but no two devices can use the same I/O ports.

■ *IRQs.* When two hardware devices try to use the same IRQ, a conflict arises and neither device will work properly. This is the most common type of hardware conflict.

■ *Memory.* Details what memory address each piece of hardware uses. Again, no two devices can use the same memory address, but a single device may use several memory addresses.

Under File, you can choose to Export or Print out each section, or the entire contents of System Information Utility. It's a good idea to print out the Resources area for reference. You can use the information provided to help you easily add hardware.

Repairing Damaged System Files

System File Checker will automatically scan your computer for system files, and repair files that may be damaged or corrupt. You can access System File Checker from the Microsoft System Information Utility by clicking Tools, System File Checker. You don't have to have the Microsoft System Information Utility running, though. You can also access the System File Checker by clicking Start, Programs, Accessories, System Utilities, System File Checker.

The main screen of the System File Checker has an added bonus—a file extraction utility (see Figure 9.20).

Figure 9.20

Now there's an easy way to extract files from the CD.

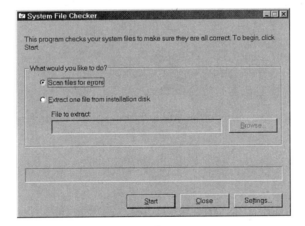

Anyone who has ever had to manually extract files out of the CAB files will love this feature. Click the Settings button at the bottom right to change the default extraction settings. To use the extractor:

1. Click the radio button to Extract One File From Installation Disk.

2. Under File to extract:, type the file name (you can also browse your hard disk to find a file that may be corrupted), and then click Start. You see Figure 9.21.

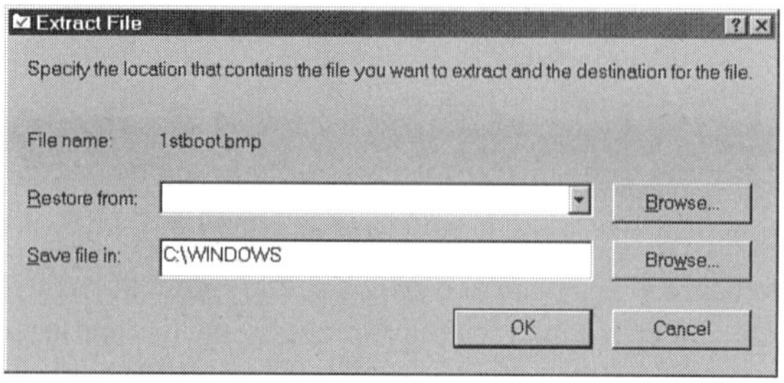

Figure 9.21

You can type the location of the source file, or click Browse to search your hard disk or the CD for where the CAB files are.

1. After you have the file location in the Restore from: area, make sure you are putting it into the correct location, then click OK.

2. Windows will come up with the option to back up the current file. This is a good idea if you are updating an older file, just in case the new file doesn't work properly. If the folder you choose does not exist, Windows will ask if you want to create it. Choose the option you want, then click OK to continue and back up the file, or skip to continue without backing up the file.

3. Windows should come back with a successful replacement message. If an error occurs, run ScanDisk to make sure there are no file problems.

Scan the Registry for Errors

Registry Checker is a simple, yet powerful, utility that is accessed from inside of the Microsoft System Information utility. To start Registry Checker, first start the Microsoft System Information utility, then:

1. Click Tools, Registry Checker.

2. Registry Checker will automatically scan the Registry for errors.

3. If errors are found, you have the option to:

4. Registry Checker will then come up with the option to back up the Registry. Having current backups of the Registry is always good in case of future problems.

Change Startup Options to Diagnose Problems

Microsoft's System Configuration Utility is the next generation in using Safe Mode to trouble-shoot problems. You have the ability to choose which parts of the startup process to use when restarting your computer.

To run System Configuration Utility, you can either click Start, Run, then type "msconfig.exe" (without the quotes) or be in the Microsoft System Information utility and click Tools, System Configuration Utility. You see Figure 9.22.

Figure 9.22
You can now choose startup options from within Windows.

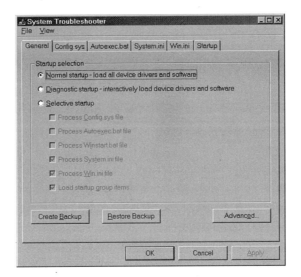

 System Configuration Utility works in Safe Mode. Use this to easily change startup troubleshooting options.

Under Startup Selection, there are three major areas; Normal Startup, Diagnostic Startup, and Selective Startup.

- *Normal Startup.* Is selected by default. It allows your computer to start as fast as possible, without loading any troubleshooting utilities.
- *Diagnostic Startup.* Brings up the Start Menu when you restart your computer. You have 30 seconds to make your choice of six options. Choose this option to go to MS-DOS mode, Safe Mode, or your previous operating system. You do not need this menu to run a Step by Step startup, because the Selective startup area of System Troubleshooter takes care of that now.
- *Selective Startup.* Allows you to choose which files to load at startup.

Selective actually has two areas within it—real mode drivers and protected mode drivers. The real mode drivers are Config.sys, Autoexec.bat, and Winstart.bat. The protected mode drivers are Win.ini, System.ini and the startup group items.

You may notice that one or more of the files are grayed out, so you can't select them. This will happen when the file is empty or missing. Most common will be the Winstart.bat, which is a real mode networking file. Windows handles all networking components in protected mode, so this file is usually not present. It is also possible to have a blank or missing Autoexec.bat or Config.sys, as well, since Windows handles most of the startup options these files used to control.

If the Autoexec.bat, Config.sys and Winstart.bat files are all grayed out, ignore troubleshooting using real mode drivers, and skip down to the section on troubleshooting protected-mode drivers.

CAUTION

Make a backup of all your files by clicking the Create Backup button at the bottom left before starting the troubleshooting process.

To troubleshoot your computer using selective startup and real mode drivers:

1. Click the Selective Startup radio button.
2. Click the box to place check marks next to Process Config.sys file, Process Autoexec.bat file, and Process Winstart.bat file (or any of the three that are not grayed out).
3. Click the box so there are no check marks next to Process System.ini file, Process Win.ini file, and Load startup group items.
4. Click OK to restart your computer.

Your system should go into a hybrid version of Safe Mode. If your system freezes or has problems, you know that the problem resides in the Autoexec.bat, Config.sys, or Winstart.bat. Go back through these steps, choosing one file at a time, until your system has the problem again. You can choose specific files from the tabs at the top of System Configuration Utility to then mark out individual lines until you've narrowed down the problem.

If you have no problems booting using real mode drivers, or you have no real mode drivers to worry about, the next step is to troubleshoot protected mode drivers.

1. Click the Selective Startup radio button.
2. Click the box to place check marks next to Process System.ini file, Process Win.ini file, and Load startup group items (startup group items may be grayed out. This is not a problem).
3. Click the box so there are no check marks next to Process Config.sys file, Process Autoexec.bat file, and Process Winstart.bat file.
4. Click OK to restart your computer.

Your computer should boot into normal mode Windows. If your system freezes or has problems, you know that the problem resides in the System.ini, Win.ini, or startup group. Go back through these steps, choosing one file at a time, until your system has the problem again. You can choose specific files from the tabs at the top of System Configuration Utility to then mark out individual lines until you've narrowed down the problem.

Track System Crashes with Dr. Watson

Windows 98 comes with a new version of Dr. Watson to help track system crashes. Dr. Watson is loaded with Windows 98, but has no associated icons. To get Dr. Watson up and running:

1. Click Start, Run
2. Type *c:\windows\drwatson.exe* (assuming Windows 98 is loaded in the windows directory of your C drive). You will see a new icon loaded in your system tray.
3. Double-click the icon. Dr. Watson opens and takes a "snapshot" of your system.

With Dr. Watson running, you can easily keep track of any errors that pop up. Dr. Watson intercepts all errors and takes a "snapshot" of what your system is doing at the time (see Figure 9.23).

Figure 9.23

The Diagnosis window of Dr. Watson will show you what program or file caused the error.

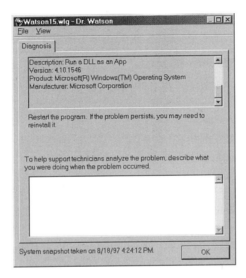

To keep track of the errors, click the white section on the bottom, and type in what you were doing at the time the error happened. Click File, Save when done to save your report. This information will be a big help if you end up calling technical support.

Troubleshooting Common Problems

Windows 98 comes with 13 troubleshooters to help with common problems. Using these troubleshooters in combination with the subjects in this chapter will give you a good basis for troubleshooting Windows 98.

The 13 troubleshooters are Networking Troubleshooter (which includes the Dial-Up Networking and Direct Cable Connection troubleshooters), Modem Troubleshooter, Startup and Shutdown Troubleshooter, Print Troubleshooter, DriveSpace Troubleshooter, Memory Troubleshooter, MS DOS Programs Troubleshooter, Display Troubleshooter, DirectX Troubleshooter, Sound Troubleshooter, The Microsoft Network Troubleshooter, Hardware Conflict Troubleshooter, and PC Card Troubleshooter. To access them, click Start, Help, Troubleshooting, Windows 98 Troubleshooters, as seen in Figure 9.24.

Each troubleshooter has options to try, and gives advice on whether you should contact technical support depending on the problem you are having. Each step is also written in plain English, so it's easy to understand what they're saying.

Figure 9.24

Each troubleshooter has a series of steps that will guide you through testing different components of your computer.

- *Networking Troubleshooter.* Whether you are hooking up a network adapter, logging on to a Microsoft or Novell network, or trying to use Network Neighborhood, this trouble-shooter has a vast array of steps that will help you figure out the problem. The LAN Troubleshooter seemed to be the most detailed of all the troubleshooting wizards. It was well done, and had a lot of good information.

- *Modem Troubleshooter.* The modem troubleshooter goes far beyond just getting your modem to work. It also helps with problems from getting the dialing properties set up right, working with communications programs and figuring out a missing dial tone, to connecting to the Internet and problems dealing with Web pages. A great tool for the Net surfer.

- *Startup and Shutdown Troubleshooter.* Startup and shutdown problems are the worst to work with. The computer is doing so many things during these times that it's almost impossible to figure out what failed. This troubleshooter details many important areas to look at when dealing with startup and shutdown problems. Use this troubleshooter in combination with the System Troubleshooter to fix the problem.

- *Print Troubleshooter.* Is an expanded Help Wizard from the Windows 95 version. It goes into greater detail on specific problems and offers a larger assortment of possible fixes.

- *DriveSpace Troubleshooter.* Is a detailed wizard on editing the ScanDisk.ini file to allow for compressed drives and unattended scanning. It mostly deals with mounting drives that are having problems, but also goes into some specific errors.

- *Memory Troubleshooter.* A basic wizard, the Memory Troubleshooter mostly deals with simple problems, like having too many applications open at one time or not enough hard disk space available. A good tool for basic memory problems, but no in-depth information on the pesky errors that pop up from time to time.

- *MS-DOS Programs Troubleshooter.* Will help you to configure MS-DOS based programs to work in the Windows 98 environment. A good tool to get MS-DOS programs to work in a window, rather than restarting in MS-DOS mode.

- *Display Troubleshooter.* Is a detailed area for display problems. This troubleshooter deals with many errors that may occur, and what you can do to alleviate them.

- *DirectX Troubleshooter.* A relatively new component to the Windows environment, it is constantly being updated and revised. This troubleshooter takes that into account.

- *Sound Troubleshooter.* Goes in-depth on configuring sound cards, figuring out sound options, and offers suggestions to fix warbling sound. Good coverage of CD audio drivers as well.

- *The Microsoft Network Troubleshooter.* This is a lightweight troubleshooter for MSN. It covers the basics to get the Internet up and running, then you can get more help from the online community.

- *Hardware Conflict Troubleshooter.* Leads you through the basics of the Windows 98 Device Manager, with explanations of the different types of conflicts and ways to resolve them.

- *PC Card Troubleshooter.* Laptop users with PC Card services will appreciate the detail this troubleshooter goes into to fix a service or card that has stopped working. This troubleshooter probably won't be used by people with desktop computers.

Protecting Your System from Viruses with McAfee VirusScan

A computer virus is a program designed to create abnormal behavior on a computer. A virus used to be defined as a "malicious" program, but some companies are finding useful purposes for programs that are basically a virus, so not all viruses are bad these days. A vast majority still are malicious, however, and some sort of antivirus program should be on every computer.

It's a common belief that viruses come from the Internet through shareware or freeware programs, or through e-mail. The first viruses created, however, came out before the government let the public have access to the Internet. Viruses came bundled with software that was bought in stores at that time. Even today, you could go to a store, pick out a program that's wrapped in plastic, and there would be a chance that a virus was on the disk.

N O T E CD-ROMs are far less susceptible to viruses, but there is still a chance of infection if the manufacturer isn't watching closely.

N O T E You cannot get a virus from reading e-mail. E-mail viruses (or, e-mail "bombs") are becoming a legend in today's world. It is impossible, however, for e-mail to be infected with a virus. This does not mean that you cannot get a virus from reading e-mail. You can receive an e-mail message with a file attached, and that file could contain a virus. Never have your e-mail program automatically open attached files. Instead, have your e-mail program save the file to a special directory; then, before you open the file, scan it with an antivirus software package.

Ch
9

There are many brands of antivirus software these days, and they all seem to do a decent job. One of the best, and most common, is the McAfee Anti-Virus program.

Once you have downloaded McAfee, just click the Setup.exe file to start the installation process.

Once installed, McAfee VirusScan pretty much runs itself, but be aware of the installation options. Figure 9.25 shows the all the options available when installing McAfee.

Figure 9.25
Choose Custom Install to be able to pick which components you want in McAfee VirusScan.

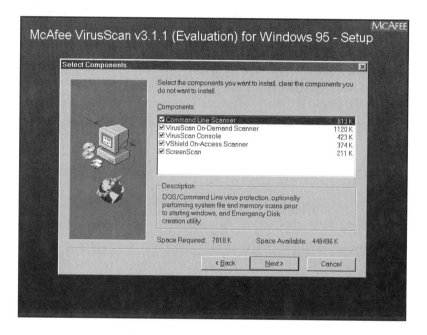

Each component can slow your computer down a bit, because McAfee searches every applicable file for possible viruses, so pick and choose which components you feel are most relevant in your situation. Here's what each component does:

- *Command Line Scanner.* Loads through the Autoexec.bat file when your computer boots. It checks all applicable files for infection. You may want to only use this component when virus security is an extremely important issue because the software loads in real mode and can take up valuable resources. This component may slow down the time it will take to boot your computer.

- *VirusScan On-Demand Scanner.* Should always be loaded. This component allows the user to scan the computer any time they want. This component also includes some added features. Since it's an on-demand utility, it doesn't slow the system down except when it's being run.

- *VirusScan Console.* Contains administrations tools. You can set up automatic scanning, and lock it so users can't shut the scanning software off.
- *Vshield On-Access Scanner.* Runs in the background of Windows 95. There is an icon in the System Tray to show you the program is running, but no other evidence is found. Vshield will scan all incoming files for viruses. This component takes very few resources, and usually makes no noticeable difference in performance.
- *ScreenScan.* Constantly scans your hard disk while your screen saver is running. The idea behind ScreenScan is sound, but the component is slow in responding when you want to access your system. Since it runs every time the screen saver is activated and is slow to stop, it can become burdensome.

Other antivirus programs also have custom controls. Choose the controls carefully so you don't lose too much performance.

Using System Monitor to Detect Bottlenecks

System Monitor is an extensive utility that will allow you to track virtually anything that accesses your CPU, hard disk, memory, and network resources. It is a great resource for determining where bottlenecks are in your computer.

The most common bottlenecks are memory (RAM) and the CPU. To track these two components using System Monitor, click Start, Programs, Accessories, System Tools, System Monitor.

The utility will come up with nothing on the screen. To add items, click Edit, Add Item and choose the item you want. To check the performance of your RAM and CPU,

1. Click Edit, Add Item.
2. Click Kernel in the left pane, then Processor Usage (%) in the right pane, and then click OK.
3. Click Edit, Add Item, then choose Memory Manager from the left pane, and Disk Cache Size from the right pane. Click OK.
4. Click Edit, Add Item, then choose Memory Manager from the left pane, and Other Memory from the right pane.
5. Click View, Line Charts. You should see something like Figure 9.26.

Ch
9

Figure 9.26

You can switch between chart, graph, and numbered list in System Monitor by clicking any of the right three icons.

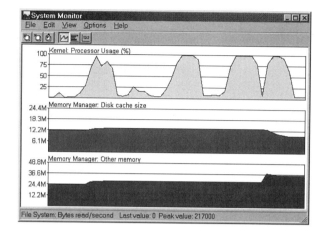

The icons in the System Monitor are:

- *Kernel: Processor Usage (%)*. Shows approximately how much time your CPU is active. The more active time, the more likely this is a bottleneck. You will notice, however, that the Usage meter hits 100% every time you open a new program.

- *Memory Manager: Disk Cache Size*. Shows how large a disk cache you have. Less memory (RAM) could mean a larger disk cache, which will make the hard disk work more. Hard disks are much slower than RAM, though, so adding RAM could be a good idea if you have a large disk cache.

- *Memory Manager: Other Memory*. Tracks all the tasks that your RAM is occupied doing. Use this chart with the Disk Cache Size chart. If you have a large disk cache size, you probably have a high amount of Other Memory as well. The two together can give you a good idea of how much memory is being swapped to the hard disk.

Word 97

CHAPTER 10

Simplifying and Automating Word Tasks

by Jim Boyce

In this chapter

Overview of New Features

Microsoft added several new features to Word in Office 97 to improve automation and ease of use. Some features are completely new, while others are enhancements to existing features. This section provides a quick overview of these features. New features that relate to other areas of Word are covered in other chapters in Part II.

Letter Wizard

The Letter Wizard in Office 97 (see Figure 10.1) has been enhanced to offer many more options for creating a letter than in the Office 95 version. The Letter Wizard can pull address information from Outlook, eliminating the need for you to enter address information manually or maintain address information in more than one location. Other options in the Letter Wizard further simplify letter creation. For example, you can choose from multiple letter types, specify mailing instructions, and define other options that determine the appearance and content of the letter.

▶ **See** "Maintaining a Contact List," **page 789**

Figure 10.1

The Letter Wizard provides several options to help you automatically create various types of letters.

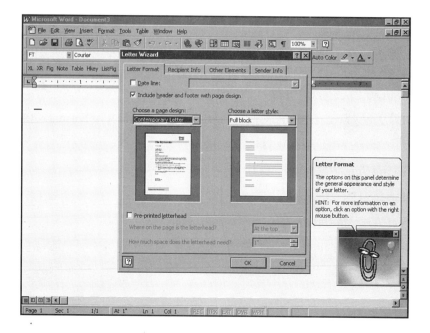

AutoSummarize

The new AutoSummarize feature in Word 97 analyzes a document to determine the key sentences and automatically creates a summary based on that analysis. AutoSummarize is helpful if you need to create an executive summary for a lengthy document. You can modify the summary as needed after Word creates it.

AutoComplete

AutoComplete is another new feature in Word. AutoComplete automatically completes text as you type. For example, if you begin to type the name of a month, Word opens a tip box near the cursor to suggest a completion for the text. Entering "Octo," for example, would cause AutoComplete to suggest the text "October." When AutoComplete displays its suggestion, just press Enter to accept the suggestion and have AutoComplete type it for you.

AutoCorrect

AutoCorrect has been enhanced in Word 97 to replace multiple words, fix common grammatical mistakes, and let you add words to the AutoCorrect dictionary with a right-click of the mouse. For example, common word pairs that are spelled correctly but are grammatically incorrect are replaced by AutoCorrect. Type "their are," for example, and AutoCorrect automatically changes it to "there are." In addition, misspelled words that are found by automatic spelling check can be easily added to AutoCorrect with a right-click of the mouse.

AutoFormat

AutoFormat has been enhanced to automatically apply a lead-in emphasis to text in bulleted lists. If the first few words in the first bullet are bold, AutoFormat will automatically apply the same formatting to subsequent lists. AutoFormat also now converts URLs (Universal Resource Locators), e-mail addresses, and UNC (Universal Naming Convention) names to live hyperlinks.

Style Preview

The Style drop-down list is enhanced to show a sample of the style's formatting, font size, and justification (see Figure 10.2). This makes it easier to choose the style you want when you are not quite sure of its name.

Figure 10.2

Style Preview shows an example of each style in the Style drop-down list.

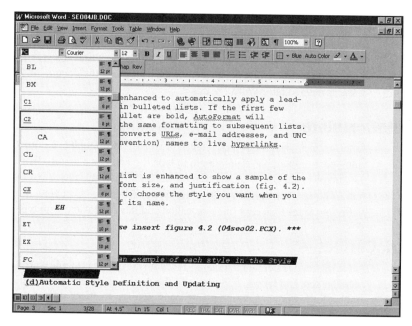

Automatic Style Definition and Updating

Another new feature in Word 97 is Automatic Style Definition. This new feature automatically creates styles based on paragraphs as you type. If you enter a one-line paragraph, center it, and apply bold to the font, for example, Word assumes you are creating a title and automatically creates a new Title style.

Automatic Style Updating has been enhanced from the previous version of Word to allow you to change a style in one location and have that change applied throughout the document.

AutoText

AutoText, which lets you add text to a document without typing it, has been enhanced to offer context-sensitive entries. This enables you to categorize AutoText entries and select from a list of entries that are relevant to the current situation.

Bullets and Numbering

Bullets and Numbering has been enhanced in several ways. Numbered lists can contain tables, nonindented paragraphs, and page breaks between numbered elements. Multilevel lists, bullets, and numbering are all integrated within a single dialog box. And Word 97 adds a new field code called NumList, which can be inserted anywhere within the text of a paragraph and used to automatically number items in the text.

Wizards

Each of the wizards in Word that help you automatically create documents and document elements have been improved to better show the process and status of the wizard. In addition, the Office Assistant offers additional levels of help after a wizard finishes.

Viewing a Document

Word provides several modes for viewing the contents of the document. These view modes make it possible for you to use different working views as you edit a document. These different types of views can make it easier to navigate in the document or see how the document will look when printed. These view modes include the following:

- *Normal*. This mode applies character and paragraph formatting but does not show the extent of the margins or how the document will appear on paper.
- *Online Layout*. This new mode improves readability by using larger fonts and shorter line lengths and by changing page length to match your monitor size.
- *Page Layout*. This mode shows the document by page, as it will appear when printed.
- *Outline*. Outline mode provides an expandable/collapsible outline view of the document based on the Heading styles.
- *Master Document*. The Master Document mode is actually a method for collaborating on documents within a workgroup.

▶ **See** "Using Master Documents," **page 1022**

To change the way the document appears, choose <u>V</u>iew followed by the desired display mode.

You also can use multiple windows to view a document. This is helpful when you need to view, for example, the first and last pages of a long document at the same time. By default, each document opens with only one window. To open another window for the document, choose <u>W</u>indow, <u>N</u>ew Window. Word opens another window containing the same document. To switch between windows, press Ctrl+F6 or select the desired window from the Window menu.

 Keep in mind that you aren't working with two copies of the document, only with two *views* of the document. Changes to the document in one window are applied in the other as well. The document name will change in the title bar of each window to reflect the same name with a different window number, such as MYDOC.DOC:2.

If you simply want to split the current window into two panes, choose <u>W</u>indow, <u>S</u>plit. Word attaches a window splitter line to the pointer. Locate the pointer where you want the window split and click the left mouse button. Word splits the window into two panes, as shown in Figure 10.3.

Figure 10.3

You can split a window to view different parts of the document in one document window.

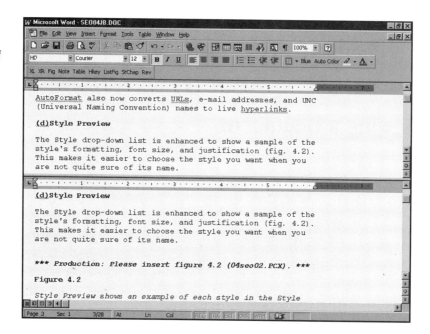

 T I P To split the window with just the mouse, point to the split box just above the up arrow at the top of the vertical scroll bar. When the cursor changes to a double horizontal line, click and drag to split the window.

To move text from one area of the document to another, select the text in one pane and then copy or cut the text to the Clipboard. Click in the other pane, locate the insertion point where you want the text inserted, and then paste it from the Clipboard. You can also move text by selecting the text and dragging it from one pane to another. To close the split, either drag the edge of the pane all the way to the top or bottom of the document window or choose <u>W</u>indow, Remove <u>S</u>plit. Or, just double-click the border between the two panes.

Using AutoCorrect, AutoComplete with AutoText, and AutoFormat

Three of the most useful features in Word for automating text entry are AutoCorrect, AutoComplete, and AutoFormat. All three speed up document creation by automatically entering text for you, either from shortcuts that you type or correcting spelling errors. With a little customization, these features can save you an enormous amount of effort in document creation. First, consider what AutoCorrect can do for you.

Using AutoCorrect

AutoCorrect is designed to automatically replace typing and spelling errors as they occur. For example, if you always type "Widnows" instead of "Windows," as I often do, AutoCorrect will correct that for you. You just have to give AutoCorrect an example of the incorrect text and the appropriate correction. AutoCorrect includes hundreds of predefined AutoCorrect entries based on the most common spelling and typographical errors. AutoCorrect will monitor for and replace these common errors automatically by default. Just type, and AutoCorrect will fix errors as you go. To configure AutoCorrect, choose Tools, AutoCorrect to display the AutoCorrect property sheet shown in Figure 10.4.

Figure 10.4
Use the AutoCorrect property sheet to control the types of errors AutoCorrect will correct.

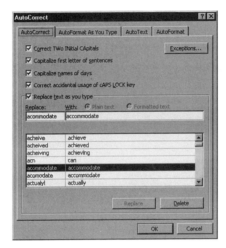

Part
II

Ch
10

The following check boxes on the AutoCorrect property page control how AutoCorrect functions:

- *Correct TWo INitial Capitals*. Enable this option to have AutoCorrect automatically replace double capitalized letters with an initial capitalization only. For example, TExas would be replaced with Texas.

TIP | Word doesn't try to correct words with just two characters, so state and other short abbreviations are not affected. You also can specify exceptions to AutoCorrect, preventing other unwanted changes.

- *Capitalize First Letter Of Sentences*. Enable this option to have AutoCorrect automatically apply capitalization to the first character in the first word of a sentence. If you fail to capitalize the word, AutoCorrect will do it for you.
- *Capitalize Names Of Days*. With this item enabled, AutoCorrect will automatically capitalize the days of the week for you.
- *Correct Accidental Usage Of cAPS LOCK Key*. Enabling this option causes AutoCorrect to detect when you are typing with the CAPS LOCK key down and automatically change the case of the text accordingly.
- *Replace Text As You Type*. Clear this check box to turn off AutoCorrect.

Customizing AutoCorrect   To add your own custom AutoCorrect entry, simply type the incorrect text in the <u>R</u>eplace text box on the AutoCorrect property sheet. Then, enter the correct text in the <u>W</u>ith text box. You also can add an entry by right-clicking an incorrect word in the document and choosing AutoCorrect. Word will suggest as many alternatives as it can, and choosing an alternative will add an entry to AutoCorrect with the selected correction.

TIP   AutoCorrect recognizes and can replace phrases as well as individual words. To add a phrase, simply treat it the same way you would a single-word AutoCorrect entry. Type the incorrect phrase in the <u>R</u>eplace text box, then type the correct phrase in the <u>W</u>ith text box. Note that the text to be replaced is limited to 31 characters.

To change an entry, type the name of the existing entry in the <u>R</u>eplace box or scroll through the list of entries and select the one to change. Enter the change in the <u>W</u>ith text box.

Applying Exceptions to AutoCorrect   You can apply several exceptions to AutoCorrect to have it ignore things it would otherwise correct. To define exceptions, click the <u>E</u>xceptions button on the AutoCorrect property page. This displays the AutoCorrect Exceptions property sheet shown in Figure 10.5.

Figure 10.5
Specify exceptions to
AutoCorrect through the
AutoCorrect Exceptions
property sheet.

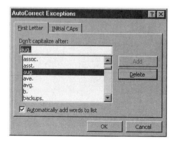

The <u>F</u>irst Letter page shown in Figure 10.5 lets you specify abbreviations after which AutoCorrect will not capitalize the first letter of the following word. If you added the text, "qty.," for example, AutoCorrect would not capitalize "of" in the sentence, "I ordered a qty. of 12 but received 2." AutoCorrect would normally attempt to capitalize "of" because it follows a period, and AutoCorrect would assume you were starting a new sentence.

You should clear the A<u>u</u>tomatically Add Words To List check box if you don't want exceptions that you allow in a document to be automatically added to the AutoCorrect exceptions list. If you make one exception in one document only, for example, leaving this option checked would cause that exception to be added to the AutoCorrect exception list. All further documents in which you typed the same text would also have the exception applied.

The <u>I</u>Nitial CAps property page (see Figure 10.6) lets you apply exceptions to the way AutoCorrect handles words with two initial capped letters. To add an entry, simply type the exception in the Don't Correct check box and click the Add button. Clear the Automatically Add Words To List check box to prevent exceptions that you make manually from being added to the list.

Figure 10.6
Use the INitial CAps property page to apply exceptions to the way AutoCorrect handles words with double initial caps.

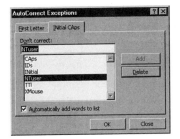

Copying AutoCorrect Entries Between Computers   Your AutoCorrect entries are stored in the *User*.acl file, where *user* is your Windows login name. This file is located in the Windows directory. If your user login name is **joeb**, for example, your AutoCorrect entries are stored in \Windows\Joeb.acl.

You might on occasion need to copy AutoCorrect entries from one computer to another to retain your settings. You might be reinstalling Office, moving your programs to another computer, or sharing your AutoCorrect entries with others.

To copy your AutoCorrect entries to another installation of Office, perform these steps (assume **joe** is the user name on the source computer and **jane** is the user name on the destination computer and that Office 97 is already installed on both computers):

1. Close Word on both computers.
2. Copy the Joe.acl file from your Windows folder to the Windows folder on the destination computer.
3. Rename the acl file according to the user name you'll be using when you log on to the destination computer to use Office. For example, rename it from Joe.acl to Jane.acl. If you are simply moving your software from one computer to another and will continue to use your same login name, do not rename the file after copying it.
4. Choose Start, Run, and enter **REGEDIT** in the Run dialog box to start the Registry Editor.
5. In the Registry Editor, open the key HKEY_CURRENT_USER\Software\Microsoft\Office\8.0\Common\AutoCorrect. Double-click the Path value and edit it to point to the acl file you renamed in step 3, such as C:\Windows\jane.acl.
6. Close the Registry Editor and start Word to verify that the AutoCorrect entries transferred properly.

Part
II

Ch
10

To share AutoCorrect entries among multiple users, place the acl file on a network server and edit each user's registry to point to the network copy of the acl file. The acl file could then have a generic name, such as Everyone.acl, and each registry would point to the same file name.

Using AutoComplete with AutoText

AutoComplete is new in Office 97 and works primarily as an extension of AutoText. When you begin to type a word that is included in the AutoText entries, a suggested completion for the text pops up near the text you're typing. Type Sept, for example, and AutoComplete suggests September as the completion. Instead of continuing to type, just press Enter. AutoComplete types the text for you. AutoComplete will automatically complete the following items:

- Current date
- Days of the week
- Month names
- AutoText entries

The first three types of entries are hard-coded into Word. You can define AutoText entries through the AutoText page of the AutoCorrect property sheet (shown earlier in Figure 10.5). See the following section for complete information on creating AutoText entries.

 The Word Help file indicates that AutoComplete will automatically complete your name, and the natural assumption is that it takes your name from the User Information page on the Options property sheet. Either the Help file is incorrect or this feature doesn't work in Word 97. The only way to insert your name is to create an AutoText entry for it, just as you would any other AutoComplete entry.

To turn off AutoComplete, choose Tools, AutoCorrect and click the AutoText tab. Then, clear the Show AutoComplete Tip For AutoText And Dates check box.

Using AutoText

AutoText provides an excellent means for automatically inserting text into a document and saving considerable document creation time. You simply define the text you use often, and Word stores it for you. You can then use AutoComplete to automatically insert the text or choose to insert the text manually using the Insert menu or the AutoText toolbar.

 To turn on or off the AutoText toolbar, right-click on any toolbar and click AutoText.

Defining AutoText Entries   To define AutoText entries, choose Insert, AutoText, AutoText to open the AutoText page of the AutoCorrect property sheet (see Figure 10.7). Or if the AutoText toolbar is being displayed, click the AutoText button in the toolbar. In the Enter AutoText Entries Here text box, type the text you want to add to the list and click Add.

Figure 10.7

You can define AutoText entries in the AutoText page, but you can't name them separately as you can using other methods for AutoText creation.

 TIP To display the AutoText toolbar, right-click any visible toolbar or the menu bar and put a check by AutoText.

If you want to include formatting in your AutoText entries, first type and format the entry in a document. Then, select the text to be included in the entry and press Alt+F3. Or, select the text and click the AutoText button or choose Insert, AutoText, and New. Either action opens the Create AutoText dialog box in which you name the entry (see Figure 10.8). The name you apply does not have to match the AutoText content in any way.

Figure 10.8

Select text and press Alt+F3 if you want to apply a name to the AutoText entry that is different from the default name.

Inserting AutoText Entries Inserting AutoText entries is easy. If AutoComplete is enabled, the text will appear near the insertion point as you begin to type it. Just press Enter when the AutoComplete tip appears to insert the text without typing all of it. To insert AutoText entries without AutoComplete, choose Insert, AutoText, AutoText. Select from the list the text you want to insert and choose Insert. If the AutoText toolbar is open, just select the text to be inserted from the drop-down list on the toolbar.

Part

II

Ch

10

If you want to insert text automatically but don't want to use AutoComplete or go through the steps necessary to insert text from the AutoText list, use AutoCorrect instead. Create AutoCorrect entries with shortcut names that, when typed, will insert other text. For example, create an AutoCorrect entry named **dun** that inserts the text **Dial-Up Networking**. Enter **dun** in the Replace text box and **Dial-Up Networking** in the With text box of the AutoCorrect property page when you create the entry. Then, just type **dun** the next time you want **Dial-Up Networking** inserted in the text. AutoCorrect will replace the text as soon as you press the spacebar after typing **dun**.

Copying AutoText Entries Between Computers   AutoText entries are stored in Normal.dot, the default Word document template. You must copy Normal.dot from one computer to another to move the AutoText entries between them. The Normal.dot file is located in the Office\Templates folder.

Using AutoFormat

AutoFormat, which has been enhanced in Office 97 with a few new features, enables you to automatically format a document either as you type or after the document is created.

Formatting as You Type   To set AutoFormat options that apply as you type, choose Tools, AutoCorrect and then click the AutoFormat As You Type tab to display the AutoFormat As You Type page (see Figure 10.9).

Figure 10.9
Word treats automatic formatting as you type and global automatic formatting separately.

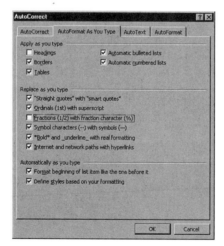

If an option is turned on (has a check by it) in the Replace As You Type section, Word will automatically make the replacement indicated beside the option. The Replace As You Type options on the AutoFormat As You Type page are generally self-explanatory. The Internet And Network Paths With Hyperlinks option controls how Word formats Internet objects such as URLs, e-mail addresses, and paths to network devices. If enabled, this option causes Word to turn these objects into hyperlinks that, when clicked, open the associated object.

Typing **http://www.microsoft.com**, for example, converts the text to a hyperlink and underlines the text to indicate that link. If you click the link, Word launches your Web browser and takes you to the Web site. Clicking an e-mail hyperlink opens your e-mail application and begins composing a new message with the hyperlinked address in the To field. Clicking a network path such as **\\server\applications** opens the selected resource on the network.

The following list summarizes the Apply As You Type options:

- *Headings*. This option causes Word to automatically apply heading styles Heading1 through Heading9 to document heads.

- *Borders*. With this option enabled, Word automatically draws lines between paragraphs. Typing three or more dashes (- - - -) inserts a thin line. Typing three or more underscore characters (____) inserts a bold line. Typing three or more equal signs (===) inserts a double line. Typing these characters within a paragraph does not result in lines being drawn.

- *Tables*. Enabling this option causes Word to automatically create a table when you type a series of plus signs and dashes: +————+——+————+. Word places column breaks at each plus sign, thus defining the width of the columns in the table. You can then click in the table to begin adding data in it.

- *Automatic Bulleted Lists*. With this option, Word automatically creates a bulleted item when you start the paragraph with an asterisk, dash, or lowercase o followed by a space or tab. When you press Enter at the end of the paragraph, Word automatically applies the bullet to the paragraph and starts another bulleted paragraph. To end bulleting, press Backspace without typing the new paragraph.

- *Automatic Numbered Lists*. Enabling this option causes Word to automatically create numbered or lettered lists. If you type at the beginning of a paragraph a letter or number followed by a period and a space or tab (**1.**), then press Enter, Word automatically numbers or letters the following paragraph in sequence.

The following options are in the Automatically As You Type group:

- *Format Beginning Of List Item Like The One Before It*. With this option enabled, Word automatically formats the remainder of a bulleted or numbered item as the first part. If the first word of a bulleted or numbered item is bold and underlined, the first word of the following bullet or numbered item will be made bold as well.

- *Define Styles Based On Your Formatting*. As you type and apply formatting to paragraphs, Word can automatically turn those combinations of character and paragraph formatting into styles. You can then use those styles to quickly format other paragraphs.

For more information on using styles, see Chapter 11, "Using Outlines, Templates, and Styles."

Formatting a Document with AutoFormat   In addition to formatting as you type, Word also can apply the AutoFormat options to a document as a whole in one operation. This is helpful if you have created or imported a document that does not contain the level of formatting you want. To apply global automatic formatting to the current document, choose Format, AutoFormat to open the AutoFormat dialog box (see Figure 10.10).

Part

II

Ch

10

Figure 10.10

You can specify the type of document on which you are working to refine the way AutoFormat treats the document.

To set options for the global AutoFormat process, click the Options button to display the AutoFormat property page (see Figure 10.11). Many of the same options you have in the AutoFormat As You Type property page appear in this page.

Figure 10.11

You can apply formatting through AutoFormat on a global basis as well as when you type text.

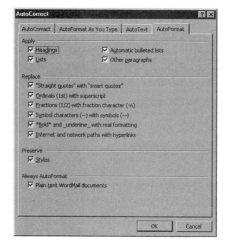

The following list explains the options included on the AutoFormat page that are not included on the AutoFormat As You Type page (discussed in the previous section):

- *Styles*. Enabling this option causes Word to retain the styles you have already applied in a document.

TIP You can control whether or not styles update on an individual basis. To do so, choose Format, Style. Select the style to change and click Modify. Clear the Automatically Update check box.

- *Plain Text WordMail Documents*. If enabled, this option causes e-mail messages in the WordMail editor to be formatted when you open the message. It does not affect documents in Word.

Using AutoSummarize

AutoSummarize, a feature new in Office 97, automatically creates a summary of the current document. AutoSummarize performs a statistical and linguistic analysis of the document to determine the most important sentences and then creates a summary based on that analysis. This is a very helpful feature for creating executive summaries of documents or in simply providing you with a working summary of a document's contents.

You configure AutoSummarize to base the summary on a percentage of the document's word count, specific number of sentences, or less than a specific number of words. Changing the percentage changes the summary and can help you fine-tune the summary. Also, you can choose from four different formats for the summary.

 T I P If you're using the Microsoft IntelliMouse, you can hold down the Shift key and move the roller to change the summary percentage.

To use AutoSummarize, choose Tools, AutoSummarize. Word performs the summary analysis and displays the AutoSummarize dialog box shown in Figure 10.12.

Figure 10.12
Word first performs the summary analysis, then lets you customize the summary.

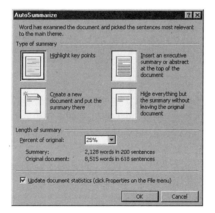

Use the controls in the AutoSummarize dialog box to configure the summary. Choose Tools, AutoSummarize to display the AutoSummarize dialog box. Choose one of the options described in the following list and then choose OK to display or create the summary. These are the options Word provides for the summary:

- *Highlight Key Points*. With this option, Word highlights the key elements of the document in yellow and displays the remainder of the document in gray. Use the small AutoSummarize dialog box that pops up to increase or decrease the word count percentage on which the summary is based.

- *Create A New Document And Put The Summary There*. This option creates a new document containing the text of the summary. This is similar to the previous option, except that the summary text is placed in a new document rather than highlighted in the current document. Use this option to create a summary that you can edit separately from the source document.

- *Insert An Executive Summary Or Abstract At The Top Of The Document*. This option creates the summary and inserts the summary as separate text at the top of the document.

- *Hide Everything But The Summary Without Leaving The Original Document*. This option summarizes the document and hides all but the summary text. It does not create separate summary text but simply turns off everything but the summary.

Two of the options create separate summary text: Create A New Document And Put The Summary There and Insert An Executive Summary Or Abstract At The Top Of The Document. If you simply want to view a summary of the document, choose one of the other two options.

Creating Simple Macros

Macros offer a method of automating both simple and complex tasks. A *macro* is a set of instructions that a program runs to automatically perform tasks. So, a macro in an Office 97 application such as Word is essentially a program. You can create the macro by manually coding it the way a programmer develops an application or use the easy method and *record* the macro.

To record a macro, you first turn on recording then perform the steps you want to automate. For example, assume you want to insert two short paragraphs with specific text and formatting. You use these two short paragraphs frequently in other documents. So, you record a macro that inserts the paragraphs for you. You name your new macro and turn on macro recording and then type and format the text for the two paragraphs. You then turn off recording. Next, you place the insertion point where you want the material inserted and run the macro. Word executes the same steps you did when you recorded the macro and essentially types and formats the information for you. Instead of spending five minutes typing and formatting the material each time you want to use it, Word does it for you in a matter of seconds.

N O T E Recording a macro actually results in a Visual Basic for Applications (VBA) program. VBA offers considerable power for creating custom applications within the Office 97 suite. Creating complex programs is very possible with VBA but goes beyond the scope of this book. This chapter provides only a brief introduction to recording simple macros. For a complete treatment of the subject, consult *Special Edition, Using Visual Basic for Applications 5.0* from Que. ▪

Recording a Macro

Recording a macro is simple. You turn on recording, perform the actions you want recorded, and then turn off recording. To begin recording a macro, choose Tools, Macro, Record New Macro. Or, click the Record Macro button on the Visual Basic toolbar. The first steps in the recording process are to give the macro a name, specify where it is to be stored, and add an optional description for it (see Figure 10.13). Use the following steps to create the macro.

Figure 10.13

You can specify the template in which the macro is stored or store it in the Normal.dot template, making it available to all documents.

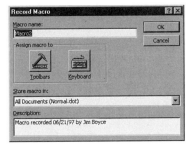

Part

II

Ch

10

1. Name your macro. Choose a name that indicates the function of the macro, such as **Insert2Paragraphs**. Note that you can't use spaces in macro names but can use any combination of letters and numbers up to 80 characters.

2. Decide where to store the macro. If you want the macro available to all documents, store it in Normal.dot. Otherwise, you can store the macro in the current document. Select your choice from the Store Macro In drop-down list.

3. Add a comment to the macro that describes its function. This description appears in the Macros dialog box to help you identify specific macros (see Figure 10.14).

Figure 10.14

The Macros dialog box lists all currently available macros and includes an optional description for each.

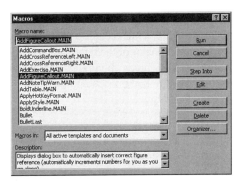

4. When you've specified the name, location, and description, you can begin recording the macro by clicking OK. You'll learn how to assign a macro to a toolbar or shortcut key later in this section.

After you click OK, a small dialog box appears containing two buttons, Stop Recording and Pause Recording. The pointer changes to include a cassette to indicate that Word is recording your actions. Perform the steps you want recorded and then click the Stop Recording button. If you need to pause recording to perform a task you don't want recorded, click the Pause Recording button. Click the button again to resume recording. When you are finished, click the Stop Recording button.

Running a Macro

If you have assigned a macro to a toolbar or keyboard shortcut, just click the toolbar button or press the key combination assigned to the macro. The macro will immediately execute.

You also can run a macro by selecting it from the Macros dialog box (refer to Figure 10.14). Choose Tools, Macro, Macros to open the Macros dialog box. Select from the list the macro you want to run and click Run. To select a macro from a specific open document or only from Normal.dot, choose the document or Normal.dot from the Macros In drop-down list. This enables you to weed out those macros you don't want to see in the list.

Editing a Macro

If you make a mistake while recording a macro, or simply decide later you would like to change part of it, you don't have to record it again. Instead, edit the macro. To do so, choose Tools, Macro, Macros or press Alt+F8 to open the Macros dialog box. Select the macro to edit and click Edit. Word opens the Visual Basic window with the macro opened for editing. Make the changes to the macro and then choose File, Close And Return To Microsoft Word, or press Alt+Q. If you are editing a macro contained in a document, the macro changes will be saved the next time you save the document. If the macro is in a template, the macro will be saved when you close the template or close Word (in the case of Normal.dot).

Using the Document Map

Word in Office 97 includes a new feature called the Document Map, which helps you quickly navigate a document. The Document Map, which consists of a new pane at the left edge of the Word workspace, gives you an outline view of the document's headings while retaining the main document window in whichever view mode you prefer. For example, you can display the full document in Normal view but have the document's outline, based on its headings, displayed in the Document Map pane (see Figure 10.15).

With the Document Map displayed, you only have to click a heading in the Document Map to jump to that point in the document. The Document Map therefore gives you the best of both worlds: quick navigation through a collapsible/expandable outline and a normal, page layout, or online view of your entire document.

To use the Document Map, choose View, Document Map. Or, click the Document Map button on the Standard toolbar. Word splits the display to show a new pane at the left side of the workspace as shown in Figure 10.15. The Document Map pane contains an outline view of the document based on its headings. To navigate through the document, just click a head in the map. Word jumps to that point in the document.

You can control the map view just as you can an outline view. Clicking the plus sign beside a head expands that head and clicking a minus sign collapses the head. You also can right-click in the map pane for a context menu that lets you select the level of detail to display in the map pane (see Figure 10.16).

Figure 10.15
The Document Map effectively combines an outline view with any other view.

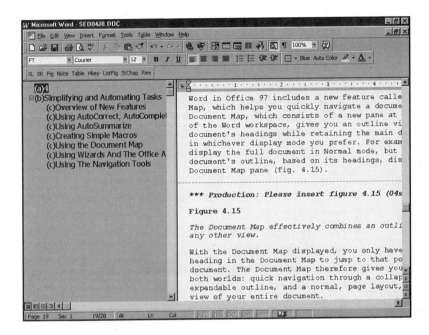

Figure 10.16
Use the context menu in the map pane to control the level of detail in the map view.

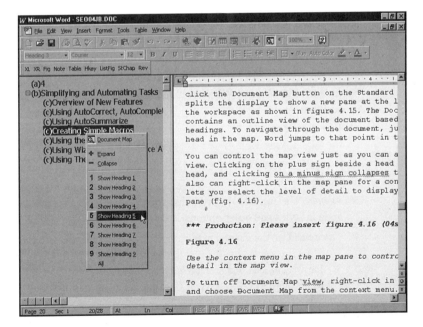

To turn off Document Map view, right-click in the map pane and choose Document Map from the context menu. Or, choose View, Document Map or click the Document Map button on the Standard toolbar.

Using Wizards and the Office Assistant

Word includes several *wizards* that automate and simplify tasks, and these wizards work in conjunction with the Office Assistant to make it easier for beginners to accomplish the task. A wizard prompts you for information and uses that information to automatically create a document or document element. For example, the Letter Wizard automates the task of creating various types of letters. You don't need to know much, if anything, about the correct structure of a letter. The Letter Wizard handles that for you.

You have the option of including specific wizards when you install Word. These wizards include the following:

- *Envelope*. The Envelope Wizard automates the process of creating and printing envelopes.
- *Letter*. The Letter Wizard offers several styles of letters from which to choose and automates letter creation.
- *Fax*. The Fax Wizard helps you create and send faxes using a variety of options and cover pages.
- *Mailing Label*. This wizard automates the creation of mailing labels. You can create individual labels or use mail merge to create labels from a mailing list.
- *Memo*. This wizard helps you create a memo using various options and styles.
- *Pleading*. The Pleading Wizard helps you create legal pleading documents for submission to a court of law.
- *Newsletter*. This wizard automates the process of laying out a newsletter, offering three different styles and several other options.
- *Résumé*. The Résumé Wizard will help you put together a professional-looking, attractive résumé.
- *Web Page*. This wizard automates the process of creating a Web page for publishing on the World Wide Web.
- *Avery*. The Avery Wizard automates the task of using and printing labels from Avery Dennison Corporation.
- *Agenda*. The Agenda Wizard helps you create agendas for meetings using various agenda styles and other options.
- *Calendar*. Use the Calendar Wizard to create and print monthly calendars.

N O T E The Avery, Agenda, and Calendar Wizards are included in the Value Pack, which is included on the Office 97 CD version only. Open the folder \Valupack\Template\Word on the CD and copy the desired template and wizard files to the Office\Templates folder. You also can download these wizards and others from the Microsoft Web site at **http://www.microsoft.com**. ■

The wizards installed with Microsoft Word appear in the New dialog box (see Figure 10.17). To run a wizard, choose File, New and click a tab on the New dialog box to choose the type of document you want to create. Search in the list of document types for a wizard icon and double-click the icon. To run the Newsletter Wizard, for example, click the Publications tab and then double-click the Newsletter Wizard icon.

Figure 10.17
Wizards are represented by a different icon from template files in the New dialog box.

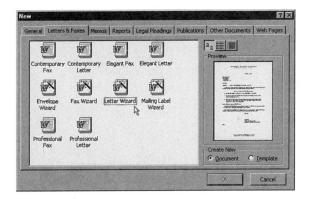

Part
II

Ch
10

Creating Documents Using Wizards

To create a document using a wizard, choose File, New. In the New dialog box, select the type of document to be created by clicking the appropriate tab. Notice that near the right side of the dialog box are two option buttons, Document and Template. To create a document, just double-click the wizard icon as soon as it appears, or verify that the Document option button is selected and click OK.

N O T E   Some wizards appear in Word's menus. You can start the Letter Wizard, for example, by choosing Tools, Letter Wizard. ▪

What happens next depends on the wizard. Figure 10.18 shows the Letter Wizard. As with other wizards, the Office Assistant pops up to help you use the wizard to complete the task. It explains the options in the wizard and gives you hints on how to proceed.

Other wizards have been completely redesigned in Office 97 to give you a better overview of the task and enable you to skip steps in the process. Figure 10.19 shows the Résumé Wizard. The left edge of the wizard's dialog box contains a flowchart you can use to skip to a specific step in the task. The flowchart also serves as a road map to the task at hand. To skip to a specific step, just click that step in the flowchart. To proceed through the wizard sequentially, click the Next button. As you can see in Figure 10.20, most of the steps include examples to show you the effect of choosing a specific option.

Figure 10.18

The Office Assistant works in conjunction with many wizards to help you through the task.

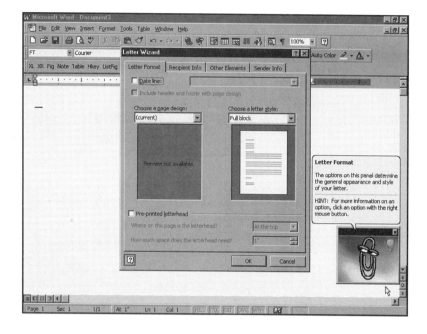

Figure 10.19

The Résumé Wizard, like many Office 97 wizards, has been enhanced to let you skip steps in the process.

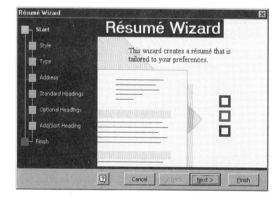

Figure 10.20

Most steps in a wizard include illustrations to help you see the effect of choosing a specific option.

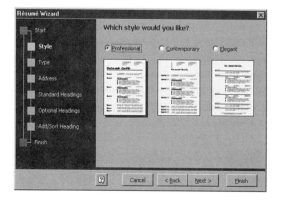

The whole purpose of a wizard is to simplify a process, so there isn't any need to explain how to use each of the wizards provided with Office 97. Through the combination of automation and hints provided by the wizard and by the Office Assistant, you should have no trouble using each of the wizards.

Creating Templates Using Wizards

In addition to creating a document from a wizard, you also can create a template. The primary difference is that the former creates a document file and the latter creates a template file. You would create a template from a wizard if you wanted to base more than one document on the outcome of the wizard. For example, you might run the Newsletter Wizard once to create a newsletter template you use each month to create that month's newsletter. The following month you would create a new document based on the template rather than running the wizard.

To create a template instead of a document file from a wizard, follow these steps:

1. Choose File, New.
2. Click the tab for the desired document type and then click the desired wizard icon once.
3. Click the Template option button and choose OK.
4. When you are finished using the wizard and the document appears, save the template file in the Office\Templates folder to make it easily accessible the next time you need it (it will appear in the New dialog box along with the others in the Templates folder).

▶ **See** "Creating and Using Templates," **page 213**

Part II Ch 10

Using the Navigation Tools

Word provides several toolbars that help you quickly access and use specific Word features. Just click the toolbar button and the associated command is executed. In addition, several new and enhanced features are provided for helping you navigate through a document. This section focuses on those features.

Navigating in Word means much more than just scrolling through a document with the PageUp and PageDown keys or the scrollbars. Word includes several features that help you browse through a document using specific criteria to determine how you move through the document. This section focuses on those features, beginning with a brief explanation of Find, Replace, and Go To.

Using Find, Replace, and Go To

The Find feature helps you locate text in the document. To use Find, choose Edit, Find or press Ctrl+F. Word displays the Find and Replace dialog box shown in Figure 10.21.

Figure 10.21

Use Find and Replace to locate specific text in the document.

To simply find some text, type the text in the Find What text box and click Find Next. To find the next occurrence of the text, click Find Next again. To apply further search criteria, click the More button to expand the dialog box as shown in Figure 10.22.

Figure 10.22

Find and Replace offers additional criteria for locating and replacing text.

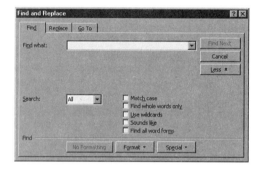

The options in the Find and Replace pages include the following:

- *Match Case*. Enabling this option causes Word to match the case of the text you type with the text in the document. **WORds** would match **WORds**, for example, but **WORDS** would not match **words**.

- *Find Whole Words Only*. Enable this option if you want the search text treated as a whole word. With this option enabled, a search for **fast** would match **fast** but not the word **faster**.

- *Use Wildcards*. Use this option to specify wildcard characters in your Find What text. For example, use **l*er** to search for **longer**, **later**, and other words that begin with l and end in er. Note that the Find Whole Words Only option becomes disabled, so a search for **l*er** would find strings in the document that began with l and ended with er, such as, "**L**ate at night is bett**er**." See the Special option described below for more information.

- *Sounds Like*. Use this option to search for text that sounds like, but is spelled differently from, the search text. A search for **best** with this option, for example, would find **best**, **based**, **beside**, and so on.

- *Find All Word Forms*. Use this option to replace all forms of a word. For example, use it to replace **fast, faster,** and **fastest** with **quick, quicker,** and **quickest**. You specify only **fast** in the Find What box, but Word actually locates the other forms of the word.

- *No Formatting*. Use this option to ignore the font, style, and other formatting characteristics of the text being located.

- *Format*. Use this drop-down list to select combinations of font, paragraph, style, and other criteria upon which to base your search.
- *Special*. Use this drop-down list to search for special document elements such as paragraph marks, tabs, fields, and so on.

The Replace page works much like the Find page except that you specify replacement text as well as the search text. You can selectively replace instances of the text or choose Replace All to replace all instances of the text. You can use all the same criteria for Replace as you can for Find.

Go To is similar to Find except that it is designed to take you to a specific point in the document based on criteria other than (and in addition to) content. To use Go To, choose Edit, Go To or press Ctrl+G. In the Go To page (see Figure 10.23), select from the Go To What list the criteria for your search. The text box on the page changes according to which criteria you select. Selecting Page from the Go To What list, for example, changes the text box as an input for the page number to go to.

Figure 10.23
Use Go To when you need to jump to a specific point in the document based on a variety of search criteria.

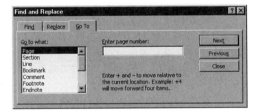

The following list explains the search criteria available from the Go To page:

- *Page*. Use this option to move by pages. Enter a specific page number or +n or -n, where n is a number, to move a certain number of pages forward or backward.
- *Section*. Documents can be divided into different sections using *section breaks*. Use this option to move to a specific section or to move a certain number of sections forward or backward.
- *Line*. Use this option to move to a specific line in the document or to move a certain number of lines forward or backward.
- *Bookmark*. You can insert named bookmarks in a document by choosing Insert, Bookmark. Use this option to jump to a specific bookmark. Bookmarks can be used to identify sections of a document by name and are often used to automatically insert text in a document.
- *Comment*. Use this option in conjunction with revision marks to jump to revisions inserted by a specific person.
- *Footnote*. Use this option to jump to a specific footnote number or a certain number of footnotes forward or backward.
- *Endnote*. Endnotes are similar to footnotes except they typically appear at the end of a document. Use this option to jump to a specific endnote or a certain number of endnotes forward or backward.

Part II
Ch 10

- *Field.* Use this option to jump to a field. Select the field type from the Enter Field Name drop-down list.

- *Table.* Use this option to jump to a specific table number or certain number of tables forward or backward in the document.

- *Graphic.* Choose this option to jump to an image by specific number or forward or backward relative to the current location.

- *Equation.* Use this option to jump to an equation in the document by specific number or relative to the current position.

- *Object.* Use this option to jump to specific types of OLE objects, such as bit maps, media clips, embedded sounds, and so on.

- *Heading.* Choose this option to jump to a specific heading number or move a certain number of headings relative to the current location.

Using the Navigation Toolbar

New in Word 97 is a navigation tool on the vertical scroll bar. The navigation tool consists of controls that work in concert with the Find and Go To features described in the previous section. You use these controls to browse through the document using many of the same search criteria described in the previous section (Page, Section, Footnote, and so on.), with the exception of the Line and Bookmark selections. Two additional items, Go To and Find, are included in the browse objects.

At the bottom of the vertical scrollbar are three buttons (see Figure 10.24) described in the following list.

Figure 10.24

The navigation tools reside at the bottom of the vertical scroll bar.

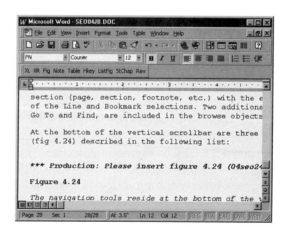

- *Previous.* Click this button to move back in the document to the previous occurrence of the selected browse object. If you're using the Find object, for example, use this button to find the previous occurrence of the word, phrase, style, and so on.

■ *Select Browse Object.* Click this button to select the type of browse object to use for navigation. Word opens a dialog box at the cursor from which you select the type of browse object.

■ *Next.* Click this button to move forward in the document to the next occurrence of the browse object.

A good example of a use for the browse tools is when you are performing a search for some specific text using the Find page of the Find and Replace dialog box. Instead of opening the dialog box each time you want to perform an additional search, you simply click the Next or Previous browse buttons to search forward or backward for the next occurrence of the text. ●

Part

II

Ch

10

Using Outlines, Templates, and Styles

by Jim Boyce

In this chapter

Overview of New Features

Word 97 includes a few new features to improve the use of styles. This section provides a brief overview of those new features. Later in this chapter you'll read about these features in detail.

Style Previews

Styles are named groups of settings that you can apply to paragraphs to quickly format text. A new feature in Word 97 is the presence of style previews. The Formatting toolbar includes a drop-down list from which you can choose a style to apply to the current paragraph. Previously, the drop-down list showed only the names of the styles. Word 97 now provides a preview of the style within the drop-down list. This preview can help you identify the style you want.

Automatic Style Definition

Word 97 makes style creation much easier by automating the process. Word automatically creates styles as you apply paragraph and character formatting. You can then use the style elsewhere in the document. Type a one-line, centered paragraph at the top of a document, for example, and Word assumes you are entering a title. Word will automatically apply a title style to the paragraph. Automatic style definition is controlled by the setting Define Styles Based On Your Formatting on the AutoFormat As You Type property page.

Automatic Style Updating

Each style has a selection of properties associated with it, including typeface, font size, character scale, indention, and much more. Word 97 adds a new property called automatic update to each style. This automatic update property enables Word to automatically update all instances where the style is used in a document when you change only one instance of the style. For example, assume you've created a heading style with 14-point font size and bold. You've marked the style for automatic updating. You create a document that uses the style in 50 locations. You then highlight all the text in the style and apply italic to it. The text in each of the other 49 locations also has italic applied to it. Thus, the style is updated throughout the document automatically.

▶ **See** "Using Word Templates," **page 216**

Creating and Using Outlines

Writing a letter is usually a simple task. Writing longer documents such as short stories, long reports, or books is a much greater challenge. Having written and contributed to more than 30 books, I can assure you that a good outline is mandatory if you hope to accomplish the task with any sort of success.

Word offers an excellent set of features for creating and using outlines to organize your documents. Outlining the document not only helps you build the structure and flow of the document but also helps you navigate through it and modify the document much more quickly. This section explains how to make the best use of the outline features in Word 97.

N O T E Styles are discussed briefly in this section of the chapter and discussed in more detail later in the section "Creating and Using Styles." If you're not familiar with styles, for now you just need to understand that a style is a set of named formatting characteristics that you can apply to a paragraph to control its appearance. You might create a style called ArialTitle, for example, with center justification, Arial typeface, and 16-point bold font. Whenever you want to use that paragraph and text formatting, you just apply the ArialTitle style and Word applies the formatting automatically. By naming styles, you make it easy to quickly apply the same style to many paragraphs within a document. ▪

Understanding Outlines in Word

An outline is really little more than a hierarchical ranking of the headings in a document. This chapter, for example, is written using several different levels of headings to help organize the material and denote the relative importance of the topics. Figure 11.1 shows an example of a chapter outline from this book.

Figure 11.1
An outline helps you organize large amounts of information into logical chunks.

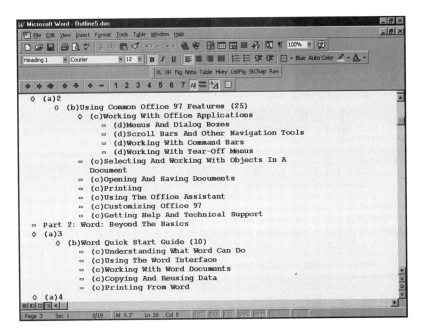

Part
II

Ch
11

Outlines in Word rely on Word's predefined heading styles. These heading styles, named Heading 1, Heading 2, and so on, each have a relative level of importance in the outline. The Heading 1 style represents the highest level in the outline. Heading 6 represents the lowest level. These different heading levels organize the structure of the document and provide a means for quickly navigating the document. Outline View, discussed in the next section, is one of the mechanisms that help you navigate through the outline.

Using Outline View

Outline View displays the document headings in a collapsible or expandable, hierarchical tree. Figure 11.1 showed a document in Outline View. To select Outline View, choose View, Outline. To switch back to Normal View, choose View, Normal (or choose a different view mode from the View menu).

Because of the different formatting characteristics associated with each heading, headings automatically indent to show their relative importance to one another. Outline View therefore gives you a hierarchical view of the document. Headings are not the only document element that appear in Outline View, however. Outline View doesn't change the structure or content of the document; it changes only your view of the document.

You can control the level of detail you view in Outline View, thereby controlling how much of the document and/or outline structure you see. When you choose Outline View, Word opens the Outlining toolbar previously shown in Figure 11.1.

1. Click the 1 in the toolbar to view only level 1 (uppermost) headings.
2. Click the 2 to view levels 1 and 2, and so on.
3. To view all of the document, including those paragraphs that have styles other than the heading styles associated with them, click All.

If you want to view only the first line of each paragraph, whether heading or otherwise, click the Show First Line Only button on the toolbar. This is helpful when you want to view the first line of the normal paragraphs within each heading but not the entire paragraph content.

When you create an outline, you'll find that each heading has its own character formatting. If you prefer not to see the character formatting, click the Show Formatting button on the Outline toolbar.

 TIP You can modify the heading styles to suit your own formatting preferences, changing typeface, font size, and other characteristics. To change a style's formatting, choose Format, Style. Select the style from the list in the Style dialog box and click Modify. For more information on using styles, see the section "Creating and Using Styles," later in this chapter.

Creating an Outline

The mechanics of creating an outline is simple—just apply to each paragraph the appropriate heading style based on the paragraph's level in the outline hierarchy. The heading will assume its correct level in the outline hierarchy. If necessary, you can change each paragraph's level in the outline. The slow method is to click in the paragraph and then choose the desired heading or other style from the style list in the Formatting toolbar. Here's the quick method: Place the insertion point in the paragraph and press Alt+Shift+Right Arrow to decrease the heading's importance (increase its indention) or press Alt+Shift+Left Arrow to increase its importance (decrease its indention).

CAUTION

Promoting and demoting existing text in an outline automatically apply the heading styles, replacing any previous style associated with the paragraph.

Because you can apply the heading styles to each paragraph at any time, you can type the entire outline and then apply the desired heading levels to it. Or, you can apply the heading levels as you go along. When you're ready to start entering normal text within a heading, just insert a paragraph after the heading and format it using the Normal style or other nonheading style as appropriate.

Using Outline Paragraph Formatting

In addition to the Heading styles, Word also includes nine outline levels that you can apply to paragraphs. These outline levels are separate from the paragraph's style. The outline levels enable Word to do a better job of integrating body text into the hierarchical structure of a document. The outline levels also give you greater flexibility in formatting and viewing the document. Normal body text does not indent within the outline structure unless you specifically apply an indent within the paragraph's formatting. The outline levels essentially perform that indention for you while maintaining the nonheading style of the paragraph and its associated character and paragraph formatting.

To apply an outline level to a paragraph, right-click the paragraph and choose Paragraph from the context menu. Or, click in the paragraph and choose Format, Paragraph to open the Paragraph property sheet shown in Figure 11.2.

Figure 11.2
Use the Paragraph property sheet to specify the outline level and other properties of the paragraph, including its formatting.

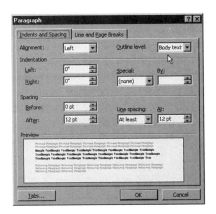

From the Outline Level drop-down list, select the outline level to apply to the paragraph. To apply no outline level to the paragraph, choose Body Text from the drop-down list.

 The outline levels provide an excellent mechanism for imposing a hierarchical outline structure to a document without affecting the appearance of the headings. The heading styles assume their associated formats in the heading. The outline levels apply the hierarchical structure without affecting the appearance of the text. Outline levels, therefore, provide an "invisible" method of outlining.

Part
II

Ch
11

The outline levels offer a means for creating your own outline heading styles without affecting or requiring that you modify the existing heading styles defined by Word. You can create your own heading styles that use the outline paragraph levels to provide outline structure while retaining the special formatting you apply through the headings' styles. You might create an entire document using outline level assignments for all paragraphs and not use the body text property for any of the document. It is irrelevant whether or not the body text is actually formatted as body text. You can apply a sufficiently low outline level (level 9, for example) to retain the text's position in the document as the lowest level in the structure but not affect appearance or printing.

Navigating with the Outline

Outlines are important for organizing the logical structure of a document, but they also play an important role in helping you navigate through a document. As explained previously in this section, the outline hierarchy is expandable or collapsible to enable you to show only the level you want to see. If you have a very long document (and thus a very long outline), you can, for example, collapse the outline to show only Heading 1 level headings. This might enable all the first-level headings to appear on the display at one time. In effect, you're seeing the entire document with everything except the first-level headings hidden.

If you need to edit text within a specific heading, just click the heading to move the insertion point, then either choose Normal view or expand the outline view to show the entire document and begin working in the selected section. When you need to move to a section elsewhere in the document, collapse the outline by clicking a lower-numbered heading level button on the Outlining toolbar, select the heading in which you want to work, and then expand the document again to begin adding or editing text.

The Document Map, explained in Chapter 10, "Simplifying and Automating Word Tasks," offers another method for viewing the structure of an outline and navigating within the document. The Document Map uses the heading levels in the document to display the Document Map view. In effect, this gives you an outline view in the Document Map pane while you retain a normal view in the document pane. This gives you the best of both worlds: an outline view for navigation and a normal view for editing. Just click in the Document Map where you want to work, and Word jumps to that point in the document.

Printing an Outline

As handy as it is to be able to view a document in Outline View, it still is sometimes helpful to have a hard copy of an outline. The hard copy is much more portable than your computer, for example.

There is nothing mysterious or difficult about printing an outline, even when the document contains plenty of other text in addition to the headings. To print an outline, just select Outline view and expand or collapse the outline to show the amount of detail you want in the printed copy. Then, choose File, Print and print the document as you would any other. Word will print the outline as it appears on your display, complete with formatting and indention, rather than the entire content of the document.

N O T E If you have configured Word to show only the first line of a paragraph in Outline view, Word prints the entire paragraph even if only one line is showing in the Outline view. ▪

TROUBLESHOOTING

When I print from Outline view, the entire document prints. How do I print only the outline? Before you print, make sure you select the desired level that includes only the information you want to appear on the printed page, such as Heading3 or Heading4. Also, make sure not to print the document from a Print Preview window. Print Preview does not properly format the document using its outline structure.

Creating and Using Templates

In Word, a template is essentially a document containing styles, macros, AutoText entries, custom toolbars, shortcut keys, and boilerplate text you use as a basis for creating other documents. It serves as a template for the creation of other documents, which is where it gets its name. Documents have a dot file extension (compared to a document file's doc extension).

You can attach one template to a document at a time, and settings and resources stored in the template are available to the document to which the template is attached. If you have multiple documents open at one time, each with its own template attached, the resources in each template are available only to the document to which it is attached.

Word includes a default global template called Normal.dot that stores resources that are available to all documents. Normal.dot, which is stored in the Templates folder, is global by design and becomes available automatically when you start Word. Because it is global, all documents have access to the resources in Normal.dot. As you begin customizing settings, you should place in Normal.dot only those resources that you want available to all documents. Create custom templates for the specific types of documents that you create.

T I P You can restore the Normal.dot template to its default state (as it was when Word was installed) by closing Word, renaming or deleting the existing Normal.dot file, then restarting Word. Word will create a default Normal.dot file in the Templates folder.

You also can create your own templates that contain resources you want made available to all documents. These are called global templates. These templates are not any different from Normal.dot or other attached templates except in the way they are loaded. Rather than being attached to a specific document, you load them manually when you need them or configure Word to load them automatically (explained later in the section "Using Global Templates").

Understanding How Word Locates Templates

Office 97 creates a specific folder structure to contain templates for the Office applications. Figure 11.3 shows the default folder structure for templates in Office 97. By default, general templates are stored in the Templates folder under the main Office folder. Other templates are stored in the subfolders within the Templates folder.

Part
II

Ch
11

Figure 11.3

Office stores all templates in a common folder structure under the primary Office folder.

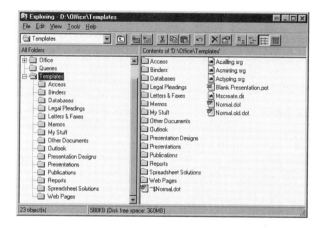

When you choose File, New, Word displays the New property sheet shown in Figure 11.4. The templates that appear in the New property sheet depend on the settings you have configured in Word for file locations (explained later in this chapter) as well as the templates stored in the specified folders.

Figure 11.4

The New property sheet lists templates and wizards you can use as a basis to create other documents.

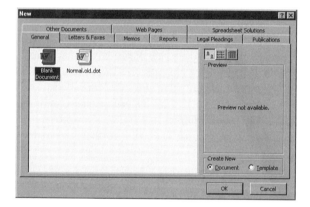

The templates stored in the Templates folder appear in the General page. Templates in the subfolders under the Templates folder appear on their own tabbed pages in the New property sheet. If you add other folders under the Templates folder, those folders will appear as additional pages in the New property sheet if the folders contain template files. Thus, you can customize the organization of your templates simply by changing the folder structure in which the templates are stored.

To specify the location in which Word looks for document templates, choose Tools, Options to display the Options property sheet and click the File Locations tab to display the File Locations page (see Figure 11.5). The User Templates setting points to the primary folder in which Word will look for templates when you choose File, New or begin the process of attaching a template to a document. The Workgroup Templates setting specifies the location of templates that are shared among a workgroup.

Figure 11.5

Use the File Locations page to specify the location of templates, your documents, and other files.

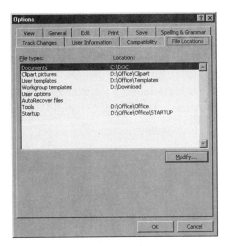

 You can place a custom Normal.dot file in the workgroup template folder on a server, making the resources available in the template available automatically to all users in the workgroup. Each user then would not have his or her own Normal.dot file.

About Wizards

In Office, wizards automate tasks, often eliminating the need for you to understand how to perform a task. The wizard prompts you for the necessary information to complete the task and then performs the task for you. Word includes several wizards for creating envelopes, letters, resumes, and other documents.

▶ **See** "Using Wizards and the Office Assistant," **page 198**

You might think that a wizard contains a lot of programming code. It does, but perhaps not in the form you think. A wizard is just a template file with a wiz file extension and all the macros, styles, and other resources necessary to automate the task for which the wizard is designed. Therefore, you can create your own wizards to automate tasks. Naturally, doing so requires an understanding of Visual Basic for Applications (VBA), the programming language used by Office 97. The point to understand, however, is that wizards are not something only a Microsoft programmer can create. Given a knowledge of VBA, you too can create complex wizards. The other point to understand is that there is no real difference between document files, templates, and wizards. The only difference is in how they are used.

N O T E Although documents, templates, and wizards are essentially the same, Word does treat them differently. You can't attach a template to another template or to a wizard, for example.

Using Word Templates

As explained earlier, Normal.dot is global by design and all its resources are available for every document. To use the resources in another template, you must either attach the template to the document or load the template globally. Attaching a template to a document makes its resources available only to that document. Loading a template globally makes its resources available to all open documents during the current Word session.

To attach a template to a document, complete the following steps:

1. Make the document active and choose Tools, Templates and Add-Ins. Word displays the Templates and Add-ins dialog box shown in Figure 11.6.

Figure 11.6

Use the Templates and Add-ins dialog box to attach a template to a document or load templates globally.

2. Click the Attach button to open the Attach Template dialog box (a standard File Open dialog box).

3. Locate and select the template and choose Open. Word returns you to the Templates and Add-ins dialog box and places the template path in the Document Template text box.

When you attach a template to a document, Word stores that association with the document. The next time you open the document, the template will still be attached and its resources available to the document.

The Automatically Update Document Styles check box on the Templates and Add-ins dialog box determines whether or not Word automatically updates the styles in the active document when you load the document. If changes have been made to styles in the template, for example, and this check box is enabled, the styles in the document will be updated automatically each time you load the document. This helps ensure that the styles in the document are always up to date and is particularly helpful when you're working as part of a workgroup.

An administrator or supervisor can modify a single shared template, and all the documents across the workgroup to which the template is attached can be updated automatically just by loading the document and saving it again.

You also can base a document on a template when you start the new document. The New dialog box (choose File, New) contains two option buttons, Document and Template, that define the type of document to create. If you choose Document, Word starts the new document based on the selected template. Choosing the <u>T</u>emplate option starts a new template based on the selected template.

Using Global Templates

A global template is one that is available to all documents during the current Word session. You might create macros that you want to use in all documents and store those in a global template. Note that a template is global only because of the way you load it—any template can be loaded globally.

To make a template global, complete the following steps:

1. Choose <u>T</u>ools, Templates and Add-<u>I</u>ns. Any templates currently loaded globally appear in the <u>G</u>lobal Templates and Add-Ins list.

2. To load a template globally, choose A<u>d</u>d. Use the resulting Add Template dialog box (a standard File Open dialog box) to locate and select the template.

3. Choose OK to place the template name in the global list.

4. Repeat the process for any other templates you want to load globally. Then in the Templates and Add-ins dialog box, click OK.

 TIP Templates consume memory and other system resources. If you are finished using a template, consider removing it from the list of global templates to free its resources for the system and other applications.

Templates that you load using this method are available throughout the current Word session. When you close Word, those global templates are closed as well and are not reloaded automatically in the next Word session. They do, however, remain in the list. All you have to do to load them is open the Templates and Add-ins dialog box and place a check mark beside the ones you want to load.

If you want one or more templates to be loaded globally and automatically as soon as you start Word, place those templates in the Startup folder. The Startup folder is located in Program Files\Microsoft Office\Office\Startup, assuming that you installed Office 97 with the default folder locations. You don't have to do anything else to have the templates load automatically—placing them in the Startup folder takes care of it.

Creating Your Own Templates

Templates are a powerful mechanism for automating document creation. So, it's likely that you'll want to create your own templates that are tailored to the type of work you do and the way you work. The following sections examine the key issues involved in creating your own templates.

To start a new template, complete the following steps:

1. Choose <u>F</u>ile, New to open the New property sheet.

2. Select the existing template on which you want to base the new template.

3. Choose the Template option button and choose OK. Word opens a new document window for the template.

4. Perform whatever customization you want, such as creating toolbars, styles, macros, shortcut key definitions, and boilerplate text. Then, save the template. Word will automatically apply a dot file extension to the file.

Using Boilerplate Text Boilerplate text is text that typically remains the same from document to document. If you compose contracts, for example, much of the language in the contract remains the same. That's boilerplate text.

Any text you put in a template carries through to the documents that are based on that template. You might create a form letter, for example, and save it as a template. When you want to write a letter based on that form letter, you just start a new document based on the form letter template. The new document will have the text included in it automatically.

When you need to define boilerplate text, just open the template you'll be using for the documents. Type and format the text, and then save the template.

Storing Resources in a Specific Template Generally, the easiest way to place resources such as custom toolbars in a specific template is to open the template, and then create the resource. In the case of custom toolbars, for example, you can store the toolbar either in Normal.dot or in the current document by selecting the desired template from the New Toolbar dialog box (see Figure 11.7). Choose Tools, Customize, Toolbars to open this property page.

Figure 11.7
When creating a toolbar, you must specify whether the toolbar will be stored in Normal.dot or the current document (or template).

The following list explains how to specify the storage location other than in Normal.dot for specific types of resources:

- *AutoText*. Open the template in which you want to store the AutoText entry. Choose Insert, AutoText, AutoText to open the AutoText page of the AutoCorrect property sheet. From the Look In drop-down list, choose the template in which you want the entries stored. Click the Enter AutoText Entries Here text box and choose Add.

■ *Macros*. Open the template in which you want the macro stored. Choose Tools, Macro, Record New Macro to open the Record Macro dialog box. From the Store Macro In drop-down list, choose the current template. Proceed with the macro recording process.

■ *Styles*. Open the document or template in which you want the style to be stored. If you want the style stored in the current document, clear the Add to Template check box in the New Style dialog box. Place a check mark in this box if you want the style stored in the template that is attached to the current document.

■ *Toolbars*. Open the template in which you want the toolbar stored. Right-click any toolbar and choose Customize or choose Tools, Customize to open the Customize property sheet. On the Toolbars page, click the New button. In the New Toolbar dialog box, select the current template.

■ *Boilerplate Text*. Open the template in which you want the text created and simply type and format the text. Save the template. Any documents you create based on the template will include all the text in the template, complete with formatting.

■ *Shortcut Keys*. Open the template in which you want the shortcut key definitions stored. Choose Tools, Customize to open the Customize property sheet. Select the Commands tab to display the Commands page. Choose the Keyboard button. Select the current template from the Save Changes In drop-down list.

The previous list is not intended as a complete explanation of how to create these types of resources. These topics are explored elsewhere in this book.

▶ **See** "AutoText," **page 182**

▶ **See** "Creating and Using Styles," **page 220**

▶ **See** "Creating Simple Macros," **page 194**

Using the Organizer

You don't have to create resources in the template where they will reside. Instead, you can use the Organizer to copy resources from one document or template to another. The section "Copying, Deleting, and Renaming Styles," later in this chapter, explains how to use the Organizer to move styles between template files. You also can use the Organizer to copy AutoText entries, toolbars, and macros from one template to another.

To open the Organizer, choose Tools, Templates and Add-Ins, and then click the Organizer button. When the Organizer appears, click the tab for the type of resource you want to copy. Figure 11.8 shows the Toolbars page as an example.

The process for copying resources is the same regardless of the type of resource. Open the two templates in the Organizer, select the source resource, and choose Copy to copy it to the other template.

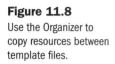

Figure 11.8
Use the Organizer to
copy resources between
template files.

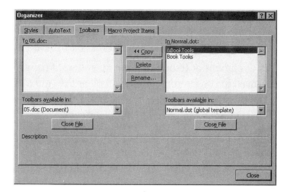

Creating and Using Styles

A style is a named set of formatting characteristics. Styles provide a means of quickly and easily applying paragraph and character formatting to text. You define the style by giving it a name and various paragraph and/or character formatting properties. Then, instead of manually applying individual formatting characteristics through the Paragraph and Font property sheets, you simply apply the style to the paragraph or text.

The paragraph or selected text automatically takes on the formatting characteristics assigned to the style. Therefore, the primary purpose of styles is to simplify and standardize formatting. Using styles in your documents can speed up document creation considerably by automating most, if not all, of your paragraph and character formatting.

Word includes several paragraph styles and a few character styles by default, but you can create any number of styles to suit your needs. In fact, you can use styles to create templates that help you quickly create specific types of documents. If you happen to be a screenwriter, for example, you could create a set of styles that set up the paragraph formats for direction, dialog, action, and so on. When you want to write a specific body of text, such as dialog, you simply apply that style to the paragraph and begin typing. Word takes care of the formatting for you.

Understanding Word Styles

Word recognizes two types of styles: paragraph and character. A paragraph style applies to an entire paragraph and encompasses all of the formatting characteristics possible that control the paragraph's appearance. The following list includes some of the common paragraph formatting characteristics:

- Line spacing
- Indention
- Tab stops
- Borders
- Font properties

Every paragraph has a style associated with it. The default paragraph style is called Normal. Character styles apply only to selections of text, rather than to entire paragraphs (although you can select all of the text in a paragraph and apply a character style to that text).

Character styles apply to individual character formatting properties such as those in the following list:

- Typeface
- Font size
- Bold
- Underline

All of the properties you can apply with the Font property sheet (by choosing Format, Font) can be applied to a character style. Unlike paragraph styles, there is no default character style. This means that characters do not have to have a character style applied to them.

Text that has no character style applied to it assumes the character formatting inherent in the paragraph style for the paragraph in which it resides. Text that has a character style applied to it assumes the character formatting inherent in the character style as well as the character formatting inherent in its paragraph style. For example, assume you apply a paragraph style that specifies the text in the paragraph be 14-point Arial bold. Then you apply to some of the text in the paragraph a character style that specifies italic. The resulting text will be 14-point Arial bold italic.

The character style takes precedence over the font characteristics specified by the paragraph style. For example, assume you have a paragraph style that specifies Arial typeface and a character style named TNR that specifies Times New Roman typeface. Any text in the paragraph with no character style will be Arial. Any text with the TNR character style will use Times New Roman.

You can create character styles that inherit the font characteristics of the paragraph style in which they are applied but which also have their own font characteristics. You might create a style that inherits the typeface of the paragraph style, for example, but which applies bold, underline, and italic to the text. If you apply the character style in two paragraphs that each use a different typeface in the paragraph style, the text in each paragraph will inherit the typeface of its paragraph style, but all of the text to which the character style is applied, regardless of which paragraph it is in, will be bold, underlined, and italic.

Applying a Style

You can apply a style to a paragraph before or after you type the text in the paragraph. The paragraph and any text in it take on the characteristics of the style as soon as you apply the style. The easiest way to apply a style is to place the insertion point in the paragraph (click anywhere in the paragraph) and select the style from the Styles drop-down list in the Formatting toolbar (see Figure 11.9). You'll notice that the list provides a preview of each style within the list, including the typeface and font characteristics. Note that paragraph styles have a small

Part
II

Ch
11

paragraph mark at the right edge of the entry in the list. The four small lines indicate the alignment of the paragraph style (left, centered, right, aligned). The number indicates the primary point size defined for text by the style.

Figure 11.9

The Styles drop-down list provides a preview of each style's major properties.

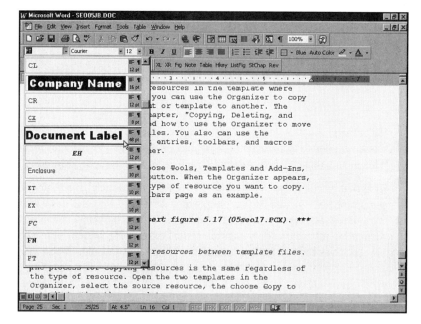

If you prefer to use the keyboard to apply styles, press Ctrl+Shift+S to highlight the current style in the Style drop-down list, and then type the name of the style to apply and press Enter. Or, press Ctrl+Shift+S and then press the up or down arrow key to scroll through the list.

 T I P Touch typists will find it easiest to use Ctrl+Shift+S to apply styles because you don't have to remove your hand from the keyboard. To quickly apply the Normal style to the current paragraph, press Ctrl+Shift+N. To activate the Font drop-down list to choose a typeface, press Ctrl+Shift+F.

You also can use the menu to apply styles:

1. Place the insertion point in the paragraph and then choose F<u>o</u>rmat, Style to open the Style dialog box (see Figure 11.10). On the left side of the dialog box, Word displays the currently defined styles.

2. Choose from the <u>L</u>ist drop-down list the types of styles to show in the list. The Styles In Use option displays all built-in styles that you have applied or modified and any styles you have defined in the active document. The User-Defined Styles option displays only those styles you have defined in the active document. The All Styles option displays all styles available to the active document.

To view the properties of an existing style, select the style from the list. The Paragraph Preview box shows a sample of the paragraph formatting for the selected style. The Character Preview box shows a sample of the character formatting for the style. The Description area provides a description of the style's properties. Select the desired style from the Styles list and click Apply.

 TIP You can assign a shortcut key to each style to help you quickly apply styles. Just place the insertion point in the paragraph and press the key combination assigned to the style. To assign a shortcut key to a style, choose Format, Style and then select the style to which you want to apply the shortcut key. Click Modify and then Shortcut Key. Word opens a Customize Keyboard dialog box in which you can assign a key combination to the style.

Creating a Style

As mentioned previously, Word includes several styles and you can modify these styles or create as many of your own as you need. Creating a style is a relatively simple process. You simply specify the name for the style and then specify the formatting characteristics of the style.

 TIP If you want to base the new style's paragraph characteristics on an existing style, first click in the existing paragraph before opening the Style dialog box. If you want the text characteristics for the style applied to a specific selection of text in the existing paragraph, highlight the text before opening the Style dialog box.

To create a style, complete the following steps:

1. Choose Format, Style. Word displays the Style dialog box shown in Figure 11.10.

Part II

Ch 11

Figure 11.10

The Style dialog box lets you view, create, and modify paragraph and character styles.

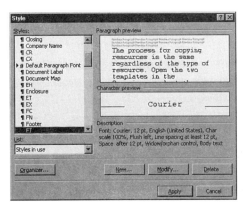

2. Then click the New button to display the New Style dialog box (see Figure 11.11). If applicable, select a style on which you want to base the new style.

Figure 11.11

Use the New Style dialog box to create your own styles.

3. In the Name text box, type the name for your new style. Style names retain their case in the list, so typing MyStyle, for example, will store the style by that name rather than all uppercase or all lowercase. The style names are not case sensitive, however. Using the previous example, you could press Ctrl+Shift+S to activate the Style drop-down list and then type mystyle or MYSTYLE to choose the style named MyStyle.

4. From the Style Type drop-down list, choose either Paragraph or Character depending on the type of style you want to create. The Based On list shows the style on which the new style will be based, which defaults to the style of the paragraph that was selected when you entered the Style dialog box.

5. From the Style For Following Paragraph drop-down list, select the style that you want applied to the paragraph immediately following the one to which the new style is applied. If you create a Figure Number style, for example, you might create a Figure Caption style for the paragraph that immediately follows. So, when you define the Figure Number style, you would select Figure Caption as the style for the following paragraph. When you press Enter at the end of the Figure Number paragraph, Word automatically applies the Figure Caption style to the next paragraph. If you don't specify a different following paragraph style, Word defaults to the same style.

6. Define the format for the paragraph and/or text. Click the Format button to open a menu from which you can select various paragraph and text style options for the paragraph. Most of the settings are self-explanatory. The following sections briefly describe those few that are not as obvious.

N O T E The following sections explain the formatting options that are less intuitively obvious. For additional explanation of other options not discussed here, use Help or the Office Assistant.

Character Spacing   The Character Spacing page on the Font property sheet (see Figure 11.12) lets you control the spacing, scale, and other font characteristics that define the size and spacing of the text. Choose the Format button and then Font from the New Style dialog box to access this sheet. The following list explains these options:

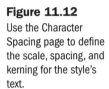

Figure 11.12

Use the Character Spacing page to define the scale, spacing, and kerning for the style's text.

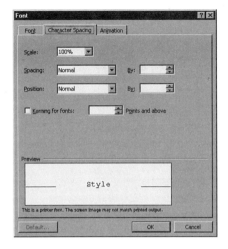

- *Scale*. This control lets you specify the scale of the text relative to a normal of 100%. Scale enables you to make the text larger or smaller, including spacing, than the default size of the typeface and font.

- *Spacing*. This option specifies the spacing between characters and can be set to normal, condensed, or expanded. The associated By control lets you specify the percentage the text is condensed or expanded. The default unit is points, but you can use other measurements by appending their units to the number (such as 3cm for centimeters).

- *Position*. Use this option to specify the position of the text relative to the baseline of the text, and the associated By control to the specify the amount above or below the baseline. The default unit is points, but you can use any unit of measure supported by Word.

- *Kerning For Fonts*. Kerning adjusts the spacing between certain pairs of characters to provide a relative even spacing between characters. The amount of spacing depends on the design of the typeface. Use the associated Points And Above control to specify the size at which Word begins kerning the text.

Paragraph   Choose Paragraph from the Format menu in the New Style dialog box to specify the indention and other characteristics of the paragraph. The following list explains some of the properties and controls on the Indents and Spacing page (see Figure 11.13):

- *Outline Level*. Using this control, specify the outline level for the paragraph. The outline level enables you to assign a hierarchical level to the paragraph to build outlines. Refer to the section "Using Outlines" earlier in this chapter for more information regarding outline levels and how they are different from Word's heading styles.

Part

II

Ch

11

Figure 11.13

Specify the general characteristics of the paragraph with the Indents and Spacing page.

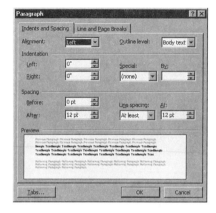

 T I P   Word uses the default measurement units specified in the General page of the Options property sheet for spacing. You can choose between inches, centimeters, picas, or points. Type a number followed by pt to specify points. Use cm for centimeters and pi for picas.

■ *Spacing*. Use these controls to specify the spacing between the current paragraph and the previous and next paragraphs. Also specify the spacing between lines in the paragraph with the Line Spacing control.

Use the Line and Page Breaks page (see Figure 11.14) to specify other general properties for the paragraph. The following list explains the options in the Line and Page Breaks page:

Figure 11.14

Specify how Word handles page breaks and other paragraph characteristics with the Line and Page Breaks page.

■ *Widow/Orphan Control*. The last line of a paragraph at the top of a page is called a widow. The first line of a paragraph at the bottom of a page by itself is called an orphan. Enable this check box to prevent Word from leaving widows and orphans with this paragraph style. Word adjusts the page breaks to move one or more lines preceding the widow to the same page as the widow or moves the orphan to the following page.

- *Keep Lines Together*. Enabling this check box prevents Word from making page breaks within a paragraph. Instead, Word moves the whole paragraph to the following page. This can result in excessive white space on the page.

- *Keep With Next*. Enabling this option prevents Word from making a page break between the current paragraph and the following paragraph.

- *Page Break Before*. Enable this option to force Word to insert a page break prior to the paragraph (always start the paragraph on a new line).

- *Suppress Line Numbers*. Enable this option to prevent Word from displaying line numbers beside the lines in the paragraph. This setting has no effect if you aren't using line numbers.

- *Don't Hyphenate*. Enable this option to prevent Word from automatically hyphenating words in the paragraph.

Adding the Style to the Current Template   The Add to Template check box on the New Style dialog box determines where Word stores the new paragraph style. If you enable this check box, Word stores the style in the template attached to the active document, which makes the style available to other documents that use the same template. If you clear this check box, Word stores the style only in the active document.

Modifying and Updating a Style

To modify a style, complete the following steps:

1. Choose Format, Style to open the Style dialog box.
2. Select the style to modify and click the Modify button. Word opens the Modify Style dialog box, which is virtually identical to the New Style dialog box.
3. Set the properties you want for the style and choose OK.

The Automatically Update check box on the New Style and Modify Style dialog boxes determines how Word handles the style globally throughout the document when you modify the style in one location. If this check box is enabled and you modify the formatting of a paragraph in the document, Word automatically applies those changes to the style and therefore to all occurrences of the style in the document.

Using the Style Area

The style of the active paragraph appears in the Style drop-down list of the Formatting toolbar, giving you a quick indication of the paragraph's current style. If you prefer, you can open the Style Area to display the style names of all paragraphs visible on the display. Figure 11.15 shows the Style Area open at the left of the document workspace.

Part
II

Ch
11

Figure 11.15

The Style Area displays the style name of each paragraph; the width of the Style Area is user-definable.

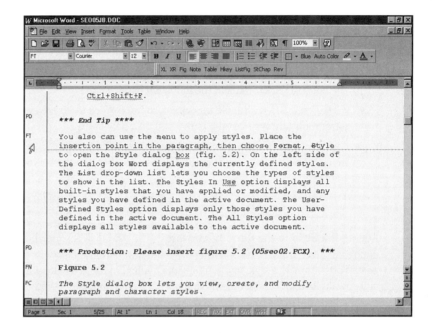

To turn on the Style Area, you simply need to allocate some space to it. To do so, choose Tools, Options. On the View page of the Options property sheet, use the Style Area Width spin control to set the width of the Style Area. To turn off the Style Area, set its width to zero.

Using the Style Gallery

The Style Gallery (see Figure 11.16) gives you a means of viewing the styles defined in all of the templates in the Templates folder and its subfolders. To open the Style Gallery, choose Format, Style Gallery.

Figure 11.16

Use the Style Gallery to preview and apply styles from other templates to the current document.

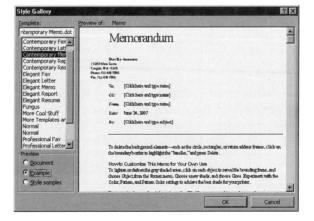

From the _Template_ list, choose the template whose styles you want to preview. From the Preview group, choose one of the following option buttons:

- ■ _Document._ Choose this option to view the active document with the styles applied from the selected template.

- ■ _Example._ Choose this option button to view a sample document that uses styles from the selected template.

- ■ _Style Samples._ Choose this option to view examples of specific styles in the selected template.

To copy the styles from a template to the active document, just double-click the template in the Template list. Word copies the styles to the active document and closes the Style Gallery. Or, select the template and choose OK. Choose Cancel to close the Style Gallery without applying any styles to the active document.

Copying, Deleting, and Renaming Styles

The Style Organizer provides a means by which you can copy, delete, and rename styles. The Style Organizer is actually a subset of the Organizer, which helps you copy objects between templates. You can use the Styles page of the Organizer to copy individual styles between documents and templates (unlike the Style Gallery, which copies all styles from the selected template to the active document). Figure 11.17 shows the Styles page of the Organizer.

Part

II

Ch

11

Figure 11.17

Use the Organizer to copy styles and other objects between documents and templates.

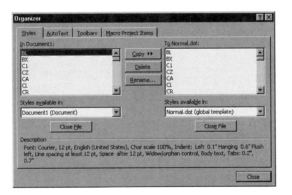

The Style Organizer displays the styles in two files at one time and enables you to copy individual styles between the two files. By default, the Style Organizer displays the active document and the default template, Normal.dot. To copy a style, select the style to be copied and click the Copy button. To delete a style, select the style and click Delete. Word will prompt you to verify the deletion. To rename a style, select the style and click Rename. To work with different files, click Close File to close the current file. Then click Open File to open a different file in the Organizer.

T I P The Organizer also lets you copy AutoText, toolbar changes, and macros between documents and templates. For more information on using AutoText, refer to Chapter 10. For more information regarding templates, see the section "Creating and Using Templates," earlier in this chapter.

CHAPTER 12

Advanced Formatting and Graphics

by Jim Boyce

In this chapter

Overview of New Features

Word 97 includes several new features and enhancements of existing features to improve document formatting, placement of graphics, and the general appearance of your documents. This section offers a brief overview of the new features and enhancements. All these topics are covered in more detail later in this chapter.

Background Picture Rendering

Word now works more like a Web browser, loading text before loading graphics. This behavior enables the document user to begin browsing through a document before it is fully loaded and also emphasizes Microsoft's shift to Internet-enabled applications and documents.

Compressed Graphics

Word reduces memory and disk-space usage by automatically compressing graphics embedded in documents. Word stores JPEG images in their native format and converts all raster image formats to a new compressed format known as Portable Network Graphic (PNG).

Online Content

The Microsoft Web site includes additional content, such as clip art and templates, that you can download and use in your documents.

Text Wrapping and Formatting

Word 97 improves character formatting by supporting 90-degree text rotation in table cells, frames, and text boxes. Word 97 also enhances text wrapping around objects by adding new wrapping styles. These new options make wrapping text around irregular-shape objects easier.

Linked Text Boxes

Linked boxes enable text to flow from one page to another with other text or objects separating the boxes. A newsletter, for example, may contain a story that starts on page 1 and continues on page 4. Linked text boxes allow the text to be continuous but to appear on the two different pages. Changes flow between the two boxes automatically.

OfficeArt

OfficeArt, a new feature in Office 97, brings to all the Office applications the drawing tools that formerly were available only in PowerPoint.

Page Borders

Word 97 enables you to add a border to each page of a document to enhance the document's appearance. In addition to new border line styles, Word includes more than 150 art styles for border art that previously were included with Microsoft Publisher.

Text Borders, Shading, and Font Effects

Word offers several new features and improvements for controlling the appearance of text. Word allows you to apply borders and shading to entire paragraphs or to any selected text within a paragraph. Word also adds several new formatting options for text to create animated special effects. You can format text with blinking, flashing, sparkling, and other special effects. You apply these animated effects as you do any other character effects: by checking the Font dialog box for them (select the text and choose Format, Font).

Using and Formatting Sections

Sections are among the primary mechanisms in Word that enable to change formatting from one part of the document to another. Sections enable you to give each section its own page formatting. You can start a new section to use different page margins or columns, for example.

▶ **See** "Using Columns," **page 247**

Using Section Breaks

You create a new section by inserting a section break between the sections. Word supports three types of section breaks:

- *Next Page*. This type of section break causes the new section to start at the beginning of the next page and is useful for elements such as new chapters, lists, and other items that you want to start on the next page.

- *Continuous*. This section break starts on the same page. You can use this type of section break to begin using a different number of columns from the preceding section.

- *Odd Page or Even Page*. These types of section breaks start the next section on the next even- or odd-numbered page.

Section breaks appear in a document as a double line with the words Section Break in the middle of the lines, followed by a notation of the type of break. You can edit a section break like other characters in a document. You delete a section mark by putting the insertion point at the beginning of the section and pressing Delete or by placing the insertion point at the end of the section break and pressing Shift+Left Arrow to highlight the section mark, then Backspace to delete it.

Section breaks contain the settings for the text that precede them. When you delete a section break, the text before the section break becomes part of the following section and takes on that section's characteristics such as margins and page number settings.

N O T E Section breaks appear in Normal view but don't appear in Page Layout or in the printed document.

Inserting Section Breaks

To insert a section break, choose Insert, Break to display the Break dialog box (see Figure 12.1). Choose the type of section break that you want, then choose OK to insert the section break.

Figure 12.1

Use the Break dialog box to insert section and column breaks.

After you insert a section break, place the insertion point in the section in which you want to change the formatting. Then choose File, Page Setup to display the Page Setup property sheet. In the Margins page, specify the margins for the section; then use the Apply To drop-down list to specify how to apply the margins. Choose This Section to apply the settings to the current section. Choose From This Point Forward to apply the margins to the current section and all sections following it. Choose Whole Document to apply the settings to the entire document.

You also can change the margins of a section with the mouse when viewing the document in Page Layout mode. The gray area in the vertical and horizontal ruler shows the current margin setting. Just click the edge of the margin and drag the mouse to change the margin. Drag the margin to the left to decrease the margin or to the right to increase the margin. As you drag the margin, a dashed vertical margin line appears on the document to serve as a guide for positioning the margin.

 In all viewing modes, you can set the left and right indents of individual paragraphs by using the horizontal ruler.

Inserting Page Breaks

Word automatically wraps text to the following page based on page margins, paragraph indents, and other criteria. You can insert a manual page break any time you want to force Word to start a new page. To insert a page break, press Ctrl+Enter. Page breaks appear as a single line in the document, with the words Page Break in the middle of the line. The breaks appear in Normal view but do not appear in Page Layout view or in the printed document. Delete page breaks the same way that you delete section breaks (described in the preceding section). You also can insert a page break from the Break dialog box (choose Insert, Break). Page Break is the default option on the Break dialog box.

Using Headers, Footers, and Page Numbers

Headers and footers appear at the top and bottom, respectively, of a document. Headers are often used for repeating the title or a document from page to page and for entering page numbers at the top of the document. Footers are often used for the same purpose, but at the bottom of a document. You have to enter the text for a header or footer only once; Word automatically repeats it from page to page. Headers and footers also are useful for placing backgrounds and watermarks on a page.

▶ **See** "Using Watermarks, Page Borders, and Textures," **page 238**

Viewing Headers and Footers

The headers and footers in a document do not appear in Normal view but do appear in Page View as dimmed text. Dimming the text helps you recognize it as header/footer text and sets it apart from the document's body text.

To view a document in Header/Footer view, choose View, Header and Footer. Word switches to Page Layout mode, dims the document's body text, and brings the header area to the foreground for editing. The program also displays the Header and Footer toolbar.

To switch to the footer, choose the Switch Between Header and Footer toolbar button or simply page down to the footer. To return to the preceding document view mode, choose Close from the Header and Footer toolbar. The other features of the Header and Footer toolbar are explained in the following sections.

Using Page Numbers

You can insert page numbers into a document manually, but you wouldn't be putting Word's power to good use. Why not have Word place, format, and increment the page numbers for you?

Inserting Page Numbers   To number a document, choose Insert, Page Numbers to display the Page Numbers dialog box. Your numbers always appear in either the header or footer.

By making choices from the Position drop-down list, specify whether you want the page numbers to appear at the top (header) or bottom (footer) of the document. Make choices from the Alignment drop-down list to specify the alignment on the page for the page numbers. The Left, Center, and Right options are relative to the page margins. The Inside and Outside options locate the page numbers relative to the document's bound edge. The Inside option places the text near the binding, and Outside places the page numbers toward the outside of the document (away from the bound edge).

Choose the Format button to open the Page Number Format dialog box. Use this dialog box to specify the number format for the page numbers, as well as other properties.

Part

II

Ch

12

From the Number F*o*rmat drop-down list, you can choose one of five options to use numbers, letters, or Roman numerals for the page numbers. If you want to include the chapter number in the page number, such as 3-1 (chapter 3, page 1), enable the Include Chapter N*u*mber check box. This option relies on the built-in heading styles in Word to indicate the start of a new chapter (or other logical document-division element). From the Chapter Starts with Style drop-down list, choose the heading style that indicates the start of the document element that you want to use as the basis for numbering the pages. Then choose from the Use S*e*parator drop-down list the character that you want Word to use as the separator between the chapter number and page number.

Next, choose how you want Word to determine the value of the first page number. If you want the page numbering to continue from the preceding section, choose *C*ontinue From Previous Section. If you want to specify your own starting letter or number, choose the Start *A*t option button; then specify the starting number or letter by using the spin control to choose a starting number or letter.

 TIP When you want to begin page numbering with a different number, letter, or format, start a new section by inserting a section break. Then use the Start *A*t option to specify a starting page number for the new section.

Removing Page Numbers   Word inserts a page number into each page when you tell it to number the document. The page numbers adjust automatically to the document as you add and remove text, so you don't have to worry about renumbering pages as you insert or delete material. You may want to remove all the page numbers to insert a different format, however, or simply not have page numbers in the document.

To remove page numbers, choose *V*iew, *H*eader and Footer. If the page numbers are in the document's footer, choose the Switch Between Header and Footer toolbar button or scroll down to the footer. Select the frame around the page number and press Del. Word deletes all the page numbers in the document.

If you want to remove the page numbers from only one area of the document, break the document into sections, placing section breaks above and below the area in which you want to remove the page numbers. Then use the method described in the preceding paragraph to remove the page numbers from the section.

Creating Headers and Footers

Headers and footers are useful for entering text and document elements other than page numbers. You may want to include a document title, your name, letterhead, graphics, or other elements at the top and bottom of a page, for example.

Creating headers and footers is easy in concept: just switch to Header and Footer view and then add the elements to the document. When you choose *V*iew, *H*eader and Footer, Word switches to Header and Footer view and then opens the Header and Footer toolbar. The header editing box, a nonprinting dashed box around the header area, appears automatically. To enter text in the header, just click the header box and start typing. Do the same to enter text in the footer.

 TIP You can use the up and down arrow keys on the keyboard to switch between the header and footer.

Using the Header and Footer Toolbar

The Header and Footer toolbar appears automatically when you enter Header/Footer view. The Header and Footer toolbar provides several controls for adding and formatting page numbers, the time, date, and other information.

The following list describes the controls in the Header and Footer toolbar:

- *Insert AutoText*. Click this button to select AutoText entries for insertion into the header or footer.
- *Insert Page Number*. This button inserts a page-number field into the header or footer. Use this control when you want to place a page number in a location within the header or footer other than where Word automatically inserts the page number (such as within some other text).
- *Insert Number of Pages*. Use this button to insert a field containing the total number of pages in the document. You can use this control in conjunction with a page-number field to add the text Page 2 of 24, for example. The number 24 is the number-of-pages field and increments automatically as more pages are added to the document.
- *Format Page Number*. Click this button to open the Page Number Format dialog box, discussed in the section "Inserting Page Numbers," earlier in this chapter.
- *Insert Date*. This control inserts a field containing the current date.
- *Insert Time*. This control inserts a field containing the current time.
- *Page Setup*. Click this button to open the Page Setup property sheet, where you can set margins and other page properties.
- *Show/Hide Document Text*. Click this button to display the document's body text on and off. Normally, the body text appears dimmed. If the page is complex, turning off the body text can speed display.
- *Same As Previous*. Use this control to automatically create a header or footer that is the same as in the preceding section of the document.
- *Switch Between Header and Footer*. Use this button to switch between the header and footer.
- *Show Previous/Show Next*. Use these controls to switch to the preceding or following header or footer, respectively.

Part
II

Ch
12

Using Graphics in Headers and Footers

You can insert graphics as well as text into a header or footer. You can insert a graphic into a header to create a letterhead, for example.

To insert the graphic, simply locate the insertion point in the header or footer at the point where you want the image to be inserted; then choose Insert, Picture. From the Picture cascade menu, choose the type of image that you want to insert; then follow Word's prompts to complete the process.

▶ **See** "Integrating Graphics," **page 242**

The header/footer box enlarges as necessary to accommodate the image. You then can resize and relocate the image as necessary to fine-tune the layout.

T I P You're not limited to inserting just text and graphics within the header or footer. Although Word automatically makes the header and footer active when you enter Header and Footer view, you can add graphics and text to the body area of the document just as easily. The elements that you insert in this way show up within the body of the document and repeat from page to page (just like headers and footers), but are dimmed. You can edit these elements by opening Header and Footer view or by double-clicking the element. The following section offers more information on inserting text and graphics into the header or footer layer of a document.

Using Watermarks, Page Borders, and Textures

Word offers several features for adding elements other than text to your documents, including background and repeating graphic elements. These elements can have a dramatic effect on the appearance of your documents. This section examines three such effects, beginning with watermarks.

Word defines a watermark as being any text or graphic that appears on top of or behind the text in a printed document. The term's origin stems from the use of special processes during paper manufacturing to add translucent designs that appear only when the paper is held up to the light. These designs are called watermarks. You can add the word Confidential to a document as a watermark, for example, or you can add the word Sold across a real estate proposal. Whatever your use of watermarks, adding them is a simple process.

Creating Watermarks

You create a watermark by inserting the watermark elements (text and/or graphics) into the Header and Footer layer of a document. When you close Header and Footer view, the watermark elements move to the background along with the header and footer elements. Generally, you want to format the watermark so that the body text does not wrap around it (as though it were truly printed on the paper before the text was added), but you can apply text wrapping around the watermark as though it were part of the main-document body. In essence, watermark elements behave just like elements in the main body of the document, but simply exist on a separate layer of the document. Like headers and footers, watermarks carry through from one page to another automatically.

 TIP To place a watermark on only one page of a document, create a new section to contain the page in which you want the watermark to appear.

To insert a watermark, first choose View, Header and Footer to open Header and Footer view; then begin inserting the elements that you want to use as the watermark. If you are inserting graphics, you can simply choose Insert, Picture and follow the same process that you use to insert graphics into the body of a document. To insert regular text as a watermark, however, you must insert the text into a text box. To insert a text box, open the Drawing toolbar by choosing View, Toolbars, Drawing. Click the Text Box button; then click and drag in the document to create the text box. Click the text box and begin typing the text.

N O T E Text boxes and frames are nearly identical in function in Word 97. Text boxes offer all the advantages of frames, plus many additional features that frames do not offer. In general, you use frames only when you need to include comments (through comment marks), footnotes or endnotes, and very few types of fields that are not supported by text boxes. Perform a search in Help on the keyword frames for more information about the difference between text boxes and frames. ■

You can rotate the text in a text box to be vertical. To do so, select the text box and choose Format, Text Direction to open the Text Direction dialog box. Select the orientation that you want for the text; then choose OK. To move the text box, just click and drag its border.

To create text that is rotated at angles other than vertical, use WordArt. Choose Insert, Picture, WordArt to open the WordArt Gallery dialog box. Text that you create with WordArt can be rotated at any angle. After you create the WordArt object, click the Free Rotate button in the WordArt toolbar to rotate the text.

Part

II

Ch

12

Controlling Watermark Transparency

Although the watermark elements appear dimmed in Word, they do not print dimmed; instead, they print at the same color depth and shading as they appear when you insert them. Typically, you want the watermark elements to be very light in shade so that they don't interfere with the visibility or readability of the main body of the document, so you often have to adjust the text and graphics to be much lighter.

To lighten text, change the text's color. Select the text and choose Format, Font. In the Font property sheet, choose from the Color drop-down list an appropriate color for the text. To adjust WordArt images, click the Format WordArt button in the WordArt toolbar. In the Colors and Lines page of the Format WordArt property sheet, use the Fill and Line controls to choose an appropriate color or shade.

Adjusting graphics for use as watermarks typically means reducing the brightness and contrast of the image. Word makes it easy to apply the right brightness and contrast by providing a special color setting for the image. After you insert the image, right-click the image and then choose Format Picture from the shortcut menu to open the Format Picture property sheet. In the Picture page, choose Watermark from the Color drop-down list. If you prefer, use the Brightness and Contrast controls to fine-tune the image's properties. When you're satisfied with the settings, choose OK to view the changes in the document.

Using Page Borders

Word 97 enables you to apply a border to the pages of a document and includes several borders among which to choose. You can apply the border to one or more sides of the page and control other options, such as the border width and distance from the edge of the page and the document text.

To add a page border, choose Format, Borders and Shading. Click the Page Border tab to display the Page Border property page.

Choose a border graphic from the Art drop-down list. Use the Width control to change the width in points of the border and graphic. Click the four buttons in the Preview area to turn on and off individual sides of the border (clicking one of these four buttons automatically selects the Custom option). When you're satisfied with the border, choose OK to apply the border to the page.

Using Page Backgrounds

Word includes several textures and other special effects that you can apply as the background for a document. These backgrounds appear in Online Layout view but do not appear in Normal or Page Layout view. Backgrounds are intended primarily for Web pages that you create with Word, but you can use borders with any documents that you view in Page Layout view.

To apply a background to a document, choose Format, Background. Choose a color from the resulting cascading menu or choose More Colors to select a custom color for the background. To apply a graphic or texture as the background instead of a color, choose Fill Effects from the menu to display the Fill Effects property sheet.

Use the Gradient page to apply a gradient fill as the background. You can choose one color, two colors, or preset color combinations. From the Shading Styles group, choose a gradient fill pattern.

The Texture page allows you to choose an image to use as a background texture. Word includes 24 sample textures among which to choose, but you can use any graphic file in a wide variety of formats supported by Word. You can download a JPEG or GIF image from the Internet, for example, or create your own to use as the background texture. Word automatically tiles the image to fill the document's background.

The Pattern page allows you to choose a two-color pattern to apply as the document's background.

The Picture property page (see Figure 12.2) allows you to choose image files to use as the background of the document. You can choose the same types of images with this option that you can in the Texture page. The difference is that the Texture option tiles the image to fill the document. The Picture option centers and scales the image to fit the document.

Figure 12.2
Use the Picture property page to choose a background image for the document.

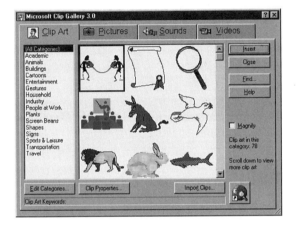

To turn off the background, choose Format, Background, No Fill.

Using Highlighting and Color

Sometimes, background fills and other special effects are just too much. In some situations, all you really need is a little highlighting or color. Word enables you to specify not only the typeface and other font characteristics of text, but also the color. In addition, you can highlight text much as you can with a highlighter pen.

Using Colored Text

In Word, Color is a property of text, just like the typeface, font size, bold, italic, and so on. To apply color to text, select the text and choose Format, Font. In the Font page of the Font property sheet, choose the color for the text from the Color drop-down list; then choose OK to apply the text. Choosing Auto sets the text to black except when the background shading is 80 percent or more, in which case the text color is white.

Part
II

Ch
12

TIP You can use the Font Color button in the Formatting toolbar to set font color. Select the text and then click the Font Color button. To choose a different color, click the small down arrow beside the Font Color button.

Highlighting Text

In addition to applying color to text, you can apply a color to the text's background. Applying a color in this way is called highlighting and is similar to highlighting text on paper with a color highlighter. To highlight text, click the Highlight button in the Formatting toolbar; then drag the mouse over the text to be highlighted. (You can select the text first, if you want.) To change the highlight color, click the small down arrow next to the Highlight button in the Formatting toolbar. To turn off highlighting, click the Highlight button again.

NOTE All that highlighting really does is apply a background color to the text. You can use highlighting in combination with font color to achieve special effects. You can use blue text with a yellow highlight, for example, to make the text really stand out. ▓

To remove highlighting from text, simply highlight it again. Word changes the background color back to its default color.

Integrating Graphics

Graphics are important parts of many types of documents. Brochures and newsletters, for example, are incomplete without graphics. Word 97 has improved its graphics support, making the process of integrating graphics into your documents easier than ever.

Office 97 supports a wide range of graphics formats, including GIF, PCX, JPG, EPS, BMP, and many, many more. Office provides support for these graphics formats through graphics converters. To view the graphics filters that are currently installed, run Office 97 Setup and choose Add/Remove Programs. Select the Converters and Filters item; then click Change Option. The installed filters have a check beside them. Place a check beside any other filters that you want to add.

In most cases, inserting graphics is just a matter of placing the insertion point where you want the image to be inserted and then choosing Insert, Picture, followed by the type of image to insert. To insert clip art, for example, choose Insert, Picture, Clip Art to display the Microsoft Clip Gallery sheet, shown in Figure 12.3. From this property sheet, you can insert any of the clip-art images, photos, sounds, and video clips that are included with Word. If you installed any of Word's graphics files when you installed Office 97, the files will be located in the Clipart folder within the main Office folder. Additional multimedia clips are available if the Office 97 CD-ROM is in the CD-ROM drive when you open this sheet.

Figure 12.3
Use the Microsoft Clip Gallery to insert multimedia clips into a document.

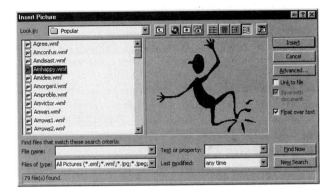

The Microsoft Clip Gallery is a utility that helps you organize multimedia clips, as well as preview and insert them. In Clip Gallery, click the tab for the type of clip that you want to insert; select the clip to insert; and then choose Insert.

N O T E Clip Gallery doesn't actually contain clips—it simply provides a means for previewing and selecting clips. The clips reside on your hard disk or Office 97 CD-ROM. You can import additional clips into Clip Gallery. Doing so only adds the preview image to Clip Gallery; it does not actually add the clip to your hard disk (if the clip is not already on the disk). You can add to Clip Gallery clips that reside on a CD-ROM or a network server, for example. ∎

You also can insert graphics from files without using the Clip Manager. To do so, choose Insert, Picture, From File. Word displays the Insert Picture dialog box, shown in Figure 12.4. Locate and select the graphics file to be inserted, set any desired options in the dialog box, and then choose Insert.

Figure 12.4
Use the Insert Picture dialog box to select and set properties for graphics files to be inserted into the document.

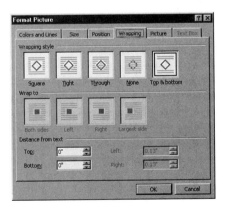

Part
II

Ch
12

The following list describes a few key controls in the Insert Picture dialog box:

- *Link to File*. Enable this check box to link the image in the document rather than embed it. The image appears in the document but does not actually reside in the document.

Instead, Word loads the image from its source file each time you load the document. Changes in the source image, therefore, automatically appear in the document the next time you open the document. To update links without reloading the document, choose <u>E</u>dit, Lin<u>k</u>s.

- *Save with Document.* This check box is enabled by default and dimmed if the Lin<u>k</u> to File check box is cleared. When enabled, this option causes Word to save the image within the document file. Saving images in the document file makes the document file much bigger, but also makes it fully portable. Other users can view the graphics if they are embedded and saved in the document file.

- *Float Over Text.* Enabling this check box causes the image to be placed in the drawing layer of the document, where it can be manipulated with various buttons in the Drawing toolbar. You can move the image in front of or behind text, for example. Clearing this check box causes the image to be placed inline (within the paragraph) and treated like text. Even if you place the image in the drawing layer, you can still wrap text around the image in a variety of ways. Generally, placing the graphic in the drawing layer offers the best flexibility in editing the image.

▶ For a detailed discussion of linking and embedding, refer to Chapter 46, "Building Compound Documents," **page 979**

N O T E　You can embed or link graphics in a document through the Clipboard. Place the graphics in the Clipboard; then choose <u>E</u>dit, Paste to embed or <u>E</u>dit, Paste <u>S</u>pecial, Paste <u>L</u>ink to link the graphics in the document. ▪

Controlling Text Wrap and Other Properties

After you insert a graphic into a document, you'll probably want to change the way that text wraps around the image or to control other properties of the image. This section explains the ways in which you can modify an image's properties after you insert it into a document.

Moving and Sizing Graphics　To move an image in the document, just click the image and drag it to its new location. You'll notice that when you place the mouse pointer on the image, the pointer changes to a four-way arrow to indicate that you can move the image. If you're moving the image a long distance in the document (from one page to another, for example), cut the image to the Clipboard and then paste it in the new location.

 T I P　Hold down the Ctrl key while dragging to copy an object. Hold down the Shift key while dragging to constrain the object's movement to horizontal and vertical movements.

Sizing images is equally easy. When you click the image, you see eight selection handles on the image, indicated by small squares on the border around the image. Click a handle and drag to resize the image. The four handles in the corner enable you to change the size of the image proportionally, and the handles on the four sides enable you to resize using only one side (stretching the image).

TIP Click the Reset Picture button in the Picture toolbar to restore an image's original settings.

Changing Text Wrapping The way that text flows around an image is called text wrapping. Word offers several options for controlling text wrapping, each of which is shown in example in the Wrapping page of the Format Picture property sheet. To display this sheet, click the image to select it and then choose Format, Picture. Alternatively, right-click the image and then choose Format Picture from the context menu. Click the Wrapping tab to display the Wrapping page. Figure 12.5 shows the Wrapping page of the Format Picture property sheet. The effects of the different wrapping options are evident in the examples.

Figure 12.5

Control the way that text flows around an image with the Wrapping property page.

In addition to selecting the wrap method, you can modify the image's wrap points—points in the image that determine how close to the image text wraps. Click the Text Wrapping button in the Picture toolbar; then choose Edit Wrap Points to display the image's wrap points. The wrap points are shown as small, solid black squares connected by dashed lines, as shown in Figure 12.6.

Figure 12.6

Wrap points enable you to control how close to an object text wraps.

Part
II

Ch
12

Click and drag existing wrap points to move them. Hold down the Ctrl key and click a wrap point to remove it. Click and drag anywhere in a dashed wrap line to create a new wrap point.

Adjusting Image Properties Word offers a few additional options for formatting images. The Image Control button in the Picture toolbar allows you to format the image as grayscale, as black and white, or as a watermark. The More Contrast and Less Contrast buttons, when clicked, adjust the contrast of the image. The More Brightness and Less Brightness buttons adjust the brightness of the image. The Set Transparent Color button allows you to click a color in the image to make it transparent (not available with all image types). The Line Style button changes the border line around the image.

You also can control an image's properties through the Format Picture property sheet. Many of the controls in the Format Picture property sheet correspond to controls in the Picture toolbar; others enable you to fine-tune the position, size, and other properties of the image. The controls in the Format Picture property sheet generally are self-explanatory.

Cropping an Image Cutting the edges off an image or trimming it to a different size is commonly known as cropping. You can crop images in Word through the Picture toolbar. After selecting the image, click the Crop button in the toolbar; then click and drag any of the resize points on the image's border. As you move the resize point, the image is cropped accordingly. Click the Crop button again to turn off cropping.

N O T E The image is not really cropped, because the cropped portion remains; it is simply hidden behind the crop lines. Think of cropping in Word as being the process of adjusting the boundary of an invisible window around the image so that you view only a portion of the image. Note that cropping an image in Word does not reduce its file size. Crop the image in a drawing program such as Photo Editor if you want to reduce the file size. ▪

Using Captions

Word uses text boxes to create captions. To insert a caption with an image, first click the image to select it; then choose Insert, Caption to display the Caption dialog box (see Figure 12.7).

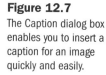

Figure 12.7
The Caption dialog box enables you to insert a caption for an image quickly and easily.

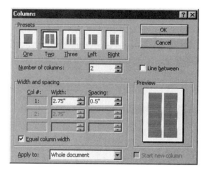

From the Label drop-down list, choose the type of caption that you want to insert. Click the New Label button to create a new type of label. In the Caption text box, modify the text for the caption as desired. Use the Position drop-down list to choose between placing the caption above or below the image. Click the Numbering button to change the type of numbering method used for the caption. When you're satisfied with the caption, choose OK to insert it into the document.

Word automatically keeps track of and numbers captions for you. If you're inserting figures into a document, for example, Word automatically labels them Figure 1, Figure 2, Figure 3, and so on.

As mentioned earlier in this section, Word inserts captions into text boxes. The text box is not directly attached to the image, however, although Word places the caption directly above or below the image as you specify. When you move the image, the caption does not automatically move with it. Therefore, you may want to group the text box and the image so that they do move together. To group these elements, click the image and hold the Shift key while clicking the caption text box. Right-click the image and then choose Grouping, Group from the context menu. After the image and the text box are grouped, they move as one. You still can edit the caption text just by clicking it, however.

Using Columns

Many types of documents use columns for formatting at least some of the text in the document. Newsletters and brochures are two common types of documents that use columns. Word offers good flexibility for the use of columns in a document. This section explains how to create and format columns.

Setting Up Columns

You can set up columns either before or after you type the text for the columns; the options available to you are the same either way. You can apply columns to an entire document or to a selection of text. To apply columns to a selection of text, you place that text in a separate section and then apply the column formatting to that section. When you select text and then apply column formatting to that selection, Word automatically creates a new section to contain the selected text. Whenever you need to use different column formats or to switch between using column and noncolumn format, just start a new section.

To apply columns to the entire document, place the insertion point at any location in the document and then choose Format, Columns to display the Columns dialog box (see Figure 12.8). To apply columns to an existing selection of text, select the text before choosing Format, Columns.

Part
II

Ch
12

Figure 12.8

Use the Columns dialog box to set column options and the extent to which the columns apply.

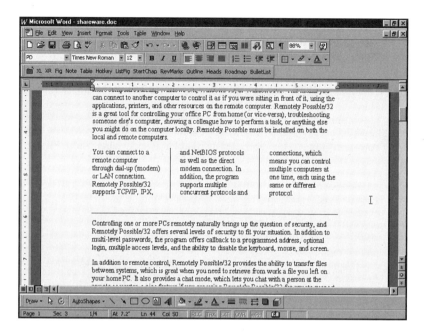

To begin using columns after a selection of text, place the insertion point after that text and start a new section by inserting a section break (choose Insert, Break). Then, with the insertion point in the new section, choose Format, Columns.

In the Columns dialog box, choose the number of columns from one of the preset options or use the Number of Columns control to specify the desired number of columns. Use the Width and Spacing controls to control the width of each column and the space between columns. Enable the Equal Column Width check box to have Word automatically size the columns equally. Clear this check box to specify different settings for each column.

Use the Apply To drop-down list to specify the extent of the document to which the columns apply. The options include:

- *Whole Document.* This option applies the column formatting to the entire document.
- *This Point Forward.* This option starts a new section and applies the column formatting to the new section.
- *This Section.* This option applies the column formatting to the section in which the insertion point is located.

Starting a New Column

Occasionally, you want to force Word to begin a new column, moving the insertion point to the top of the next column. When you choose the This Point Forward option in the Columns dialog box, the Start New Column check box becomes available. Enabling this check box causes Word to begin a new column, which moves the text following the insertion point to the top of the next column. Word begins a new column by inserting a new column break.

You also can use two easier methods to insert column breaks. Choose Insert, Break, Column Break, and OK to insert a column break, or simply press Ctrl+Shift+Enter to insert the column break.

Using Lines Between Columns

In some situations, you want to include lines between columns. You could draw the lines manually, but why not have Word do the job for you? When you place a check in the Line Between check box in the Columns dialog box, Word automatically places vertical lines between columns. To place horizontal lines between paragraphs within a column, simply apply a border to the bottom of the preceding paragraph or to the top of the following paragraph (choose Format, Borders and Shading). If you're switching from columns to noncolumn format and want a horizontal line to appear between the columns and the following text, apply a top border to the paragraph immediately following the columns. Figure 12.9 shows an example.

Figure 12.9
Apply a border to the first paragraph in the next section after columns to create a horizontal line separating the columns from the following text.

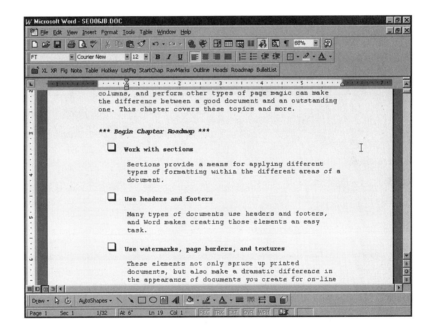

Part
II

Ch
12

T I P   When you apply a single border (one edge only) to a paragraph by clicking one of the four edge buttons on the preview area of the Borders and Shading property sheet, Word does not apply different border styles, width, or color to the border line. To apply different border properties to a single-edge border, first select the properties (color and so on) and then click the desired border button to apply the border. If you already have a border defined, select None. Then set the desired properties and click the desired edge button to turn on the border with the new properties.

Using Bullets and Numbering

Bulleted and numbered lists are common in many types of documents. Bulleted lists allow you to emphasize paragraphs by placing a graphical indicator called a bullet at the beginning of the paragraph. Figure 12.10 shows a bulleted list.

Numbered lists often are used to indicate sequential steps or processes. Figure 12.11 shows an example of a numbered list.

Both bulleted and numbered lists are commonly used throughout this book to organize steps and to draw attention to important points.

Figure 12.10
Bullets help emphasize a paragraph and often are used for such elements as checklists within a document.

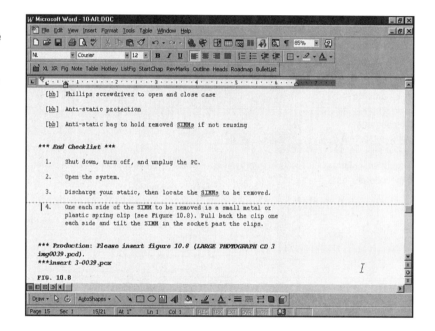

Figure 12.11
Use numbered lists to describe sequential steps or processes.

Word 97 simplifies the use of bullets and numbered lists by automating their formatting. If you apply bullet formatting to a paragraph, Word automatically applies the same bullet format to the following paragraph. When you finish adding bulleted paragraphs, you simply turn off bulleting and continue typing the next paragraph.

TIP Through AutoFormat, Word automatically converts a paragraph to bulleted format if the paragraph begins with an asterisk and a tab or space. So an easy way to start creating bulleted paragraphs is to start a new paragraph and then type an asterisk, followed by a tab or space. Type the paragraph and press Enter, and Word automatically applies bullet formatting to the paragraph.

Word also simplifies the use of numbered lists. You type a number at the beginning of the paragraph, followed by a tab or space, and then type the rest of the paragraph. When you press Enter, Word converts the paragraph to a numbered list, automatically entering the next sequential number at the beginning of the following paragraph. Note that you must enable these features on the AutoFormat Options dialog box to enable Word to perform them automatically.

You have quite a bit of control of the appearance of bulleted or numbered lists. This section of the chapter explains how to create and modify these types of document elements.

Creating a Bulleted List

As mentioned earlier in this chapter, all you have to do to start a bulleted list is type an asterisk, followed by a tab or space, and then type some additional text. Word converts the paragraph to a bulleted one when you press Enter. Alternatively, you can click the Bullets button in the Formatting toolbar to begin a bulleted list. You can format a bulleted paragraph before or after you type the text. Click the Increase Indent or Decrease Indent button in the Formatting toolbar to change the indent of the paragraph. Alternatively, right-click the paragraph and then choose either Increase Indent or Decrease Indent from the context menu.

You can use any character as the bullet character. To choose a different bullet or to modify other characteristics of the paragraph, select the paragraph and choose Format, Bullets and Numbering. Alternatively, right-click the paragraph and choose Bullets and Numbering from the context menu. Word displays the Bullets and Numbering property sheet, shown in Figure 12.12.

Part
II

Ch
12

Figure 12.12
You can use any character as the bullet, but Word provides several predefined choices.

To use a predefined bullet character, select it and choose OK. To choose a custom bullet character or to set spacing and other properties, select a predefined type and then choose Customize to display the Customize Bulleted List dialog box, shown in Figure 12.13.

Figure 12.13

You can change the bullet character, the font from which the bullet comes, and the spacing properties in the Customize Bulleted List dialog box.

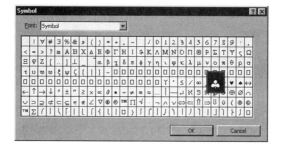

Choose the Bullet button to select a different bullet character. Word opens the Symbol dialog box, shown in Figure 12.14. Select the desired symbol and choose OK.

Figure 12.14

Choose a new bullet type from the Symbol dialog box.

Choose the Font button to open the standard Font dialog box. Select the typeface from which you want to choose a bullet character; then choose other options, such as font size and bold or italic. Choose OK when you're satisfied with the selection.

 TIP   To turn off bulleting quickly, click in the paragraph for which you want to turn off the bullet and then click the Bullets button in the Formatting toolbar.

Creating a Numbered List

Creating a numbered list is as easy as creating a bulleted list. If you begin a paragraph with a number, followed by a period and tab or space, and then type other text, Word automatically starts a numbered list when you press Enter. Type each item in the list and then press Enter after the last item. Press Backspace to remove the last number.

You also can create a numbered list through the Bullets and Numbering property sheet. Choose Format, Bullets and Numbering, or right-click the paragraph and choose Bullets and Numbering from the context menu. When the Bullets and Numbering property sheet appears, click the Numbered tab to display the Numbered property page, shown in Figure 12.14.

To choose a different starting number or to set other numbering properties, click the Customize button in the Numbered page. As you can see in Figure 12.15, you can select the number format, font, number style, starting number, and other properties for the list. Changing one item in the list changes the other items in the list automatically.

Figure 12.15

Use the Customize Numbered List dialog box to control numbered-list properties.

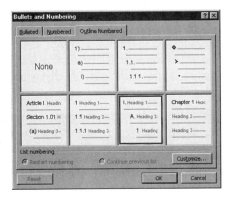

The following list explains the two options for numbering lists:

■ *Restart Numbering.* Choose this option if you want the list to begin at 1, A, or i.

■ *Continue Previous List.* Choose this option to have the list begin with the next number after the preceding bulleted item. Word takes the last number or letter from the preceding list, even if that list is separated from the current one by other text, and increments the counter to derive the new number or letter for the current list.

One of the most important advantages of using Word's automatic list numbering is that it truly is automatic. If you insert some items within the list, the numbers of following items adjust accordingly.

To turn off numbering, set the numbered list type to None.

Creating Outline Numbered Lists

An outline numbered list is similar to an outline created with Word's outlining features, except that it doesn't rely on Word's Heading styles or outline paragraph levels. The outline numbered list feature simply provides a quick way to create an outline-format numbered list.

To create an outline numbered list, choose Format, Bullets and Numbering, and click the Outline Numbered tab to display the property page shown in Figure 12.16.

Part
II

Ch
12

Figure 12.16

Use the Outline Numbered page to set the properties for an outline numbered list.

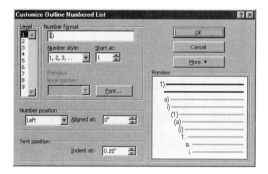

You can choose from one of the predefined styles or customize a style to suit your preferences. To customize a style, select the one that you want to customize and choose the Customize button. Word displays the Customize Outline Numbered List dialog box. Click the More button to expand the dialog box to display all items.

Choose a level from the Level list; then use the remaining controls to change that level's properties. Most of the settings in the dialog box are self-explanatory. The following list summarizes a few settings that are not self-explanatory:

- *Link Level to Style*. Choose from this drop-down list the style (if any) that you want to associate with the selected level in the outline list. Word automatically numbers with the appropriate level the paragraphs that you format with the selected style.

- *Follow Number With*. Choose from this drop-down list the character to follow the number. You can choose a tab, a space, or no character.

- *Legal Style Numbering*. Choose this item to convert numbers in the list to Arabic values (such as changing IV to 4).

- *Restart Numbering After Higher List Level*. Enabling this option causes Word to automatically start back at 1, a, or I when the selected list level follows a higher list level.

- *ListNum Field List Name*. This option allows you to use the ListNum field to insert multiple outline numbers on a single level. For more information about fields, refer to Chapter 13, "Fields, Forms, and Dynamic Content."

▶ **See** "Using Field Codes to Create Dynamic Content," **page 256**

When you're satisfied with the settings, choose OK, then OK a second time to apply the formatting. You'll find that for the most part, Word's true outlining features that rely on the Heading styles offer the most flexibility in terms of navigating and viewing the document. You can use Outline View to expand and collapse the outline to quickly view large parts of the outline and move around in it. Nevertheless, the outline numbered lists offer an excellent means of creating legal documents and other documents that rely on structured outline numbering. ●

CHAPTER 13

Fields, Forms, and Dynamic Content

by Jim Boyce

In this chapter

Using Field Codes to Create Dynamic Content

Much of the data you place in a document is static—text and graphics that do not change. However, you'll probably want to include dynamic data in your documents that changes as the document or other parameters change. For example, you might want the total editing time for the document to appear in the header or footer, along with the document author's name. Or you might want to build complex elements such as forms that automatically fill in areas of the form from information such as the date, time, or other information.

Field codes are the mechanism in Word that enable you to add that dynamic content. Field codes are particularly useful in creating document templates and forms. The field codes can automate much of the process of filling in the form or adding content to a document derived from a template. Most of Word's templates use field codes for much of their content. The following sections explain field codes and teach you to use them in your documents.

> **N O T E**   Field codes are a powerful feature for automating document content creation. A complete treatment of all of Word's 70+ fields and their options would require multiple chapters and goes beyond the scope of this book. This section of the chapter provides a solid introduction to field codes and points you in the right direction to learn more. For a detailed look at field codes, check out *Special Edition Using Microsoft Word 97*, Bestseller Edition, also from Que.

Understanding Field Codes

In Word, *field codes* are special objects you can insert into a document that act as placeholders for dynamic data—data that can change automatically. Word uses field codes to insert page numbers, for example. As new pages are added, the result of the page-number field code changes accordingly. Date and time field codes are other examples of Word field codes. These two field codes insert the current date and time into the document. If you load the document the next day and then update the field codes, you see the current date in the document again.

Word also uses field codes automatically for other features. When you create an index or table of contents in the document, for example, Word uses field codes to build those document elements.

Word supports more than 70 field codes that cover a wide range of data types. Word organizes these field codes into the following groups:

- *Date and Time.* Field codes in this group include the date when the document was created, the current date and time, the date printed, the date when the document was last saved, and total document-editing time.
- *Document Automation.* This group contains field codes for comparing values, performing conditional branching, inserting document variables, moving the insertion point, running macros, and downloading commands to a printer.
- *Document Information.* This group includes several field codes that insert information about the document. This information includes such items as author, comments, filename and size, and number of pages.

- *Equations and Formulas.* Field codes in this group enable you to insert formulas, equations, and symbols, as well as to offset the subsequent text after the field to the left, right, up, or down.

- *Index and Tables.* Use these field codes to insert tables of contents, indexes, and tables of authorities into the document. Generally, you use Word's automated features to insert these document elements instead of inserting the field codes yourself.

- *Links and References.* These field codes enable you to insert AutoText entries, hyperlinks, pictures, and other document objects.

- *Mail Merge.* Field codes in this group enable you to create mail-merge documents, which combine data documents with template documents to create individualized form letters (and other documents).

▶ **See** "Using Mail Merge," **page 304**

- *Numbering.* These field codes insert various numbering-related items into the document: bar codes, list elements, page numbers, number of times that the document has been saved, current section number, number of pages in the section, and more.

- *User Information.* These field codes insert various information from the User Information page of the Options property sheet (choose Tools, Options, User Information).

When you first insert a field code, Word calculates the result of the field code. depending on the code that is inserted. When you insert a date field, for example, Word checks the current system date, and that information appears within the document. Load the document tomorrow, and the field still shows the previous day's date. To make the field current, you must update it. Use one of the following methods to update fields:

- To update a single field, click the field and then press the F9 function key.

- To update multiple field codes, select the extent of the document that contains the field codes to be updated and then press F9.

- To update all field codes in the document, choose Edit, Select All and then press F9.

Viewing Field Codes

It's important to understand that when you insert a field code, you're not inserting the data that actually appears in the document. Instead, you're inserting a code that results in the data's being displayed. The field and the resulting displayed information are different. If you are familiar with Microsoft Excel (the spreadsheet program in Office 97), you can draw an analogy between Excel spreadsheet cells and field codes. When you enter a formula in an Excel spreadsheet cell and press Enter, you see the results of the cell, not the formula that derived the results. Field codes are the same—you see the results of the field code, not the underlying code itself.

▶ **See** Chapters 17 through 23 to learn more about Excel.

As you work with documents that contain field codes, however, you occasionally need to view the field codes rather than their results. You may want to edit the field code's option so that it displays a different result or so that the result is formatted differently, for example. You must *turn on* field codes to view them.

You can turn on field codes globally throughout the document or turn on only selected field codes. To turn on all field codes, press Alt+F9. Figure 13.1 shows a simple document containing field codes. The first two field codes are turned off, and the next two field codes are turned on.

Figure 13.1

The first two field codes in this document are turned off, and the second two are turned on.

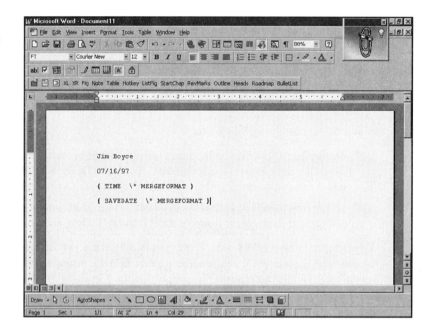

The Shift+F9 and Alt+F9 shortcuts toggle the field codes on and off. To turn off display of all field codes and view the results again, just press Alt+F9. Select individual field codes and press Shift+F9 to turn field codes off again.

Later in this chapter in the section "Formatting Field Codes," you learn about formatting field codes and using options, and understanding how to view the field codes can be important in those two tasks. Before getting into those topics, however, you need to learn how to add field codes to the document.

Inserting Field Codes

You insert field codes into a document in much the same way that you insert other document elements. To insert a field code, choose Insert, Field to display the Field dialog box (see Figure 13.2).

Figure 13.2

Insert field codes and set their options by using the Field dialog box.

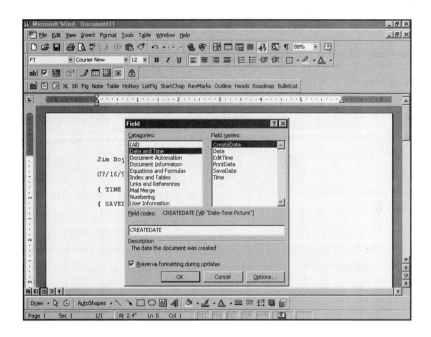

The Field dialog box groups the field codes by function in the Categories list. Select a category from the list to view the field codes in that category. The field codes appear in the Field Names list. Click (All) in the Categories list to view all the field codes, sorted alphabetically. This option is helpful when you know the field name but not the category in which it resides.

Selecting a field places the field name in the Field Codes text box of the Field dialog box. Word shows the syntax of the field in the area just above the text box, with optional parameters shown in square brackets. You then can click the Field Codes text box and add optional switches or other parameters to the field code. These parameters and switches determine how the field's contents appear in the document and differ from one field code to the next. You can insert a formula from a Word bookmark, for example. In the Field Codes text box, you add the bookmark name for the formula that you want to insert.

N O T E The Preserve Formatting During Updates check box determines how Word handles the formatting of the field-code results when the field is updated. This option is discussed in detail in "Formatting Field Codes" later in this chapter. ▪

Using field codes effectively requires that you understand the optional parameters and switches for the field code. The syntax example in the dialog box eliminates the need to memorize each field—a good thing, because each of the more than 70 field codes is different. After you select a field code from the list, click the Options button to display the Field Options dialog box (see Figure 13.3). This dialog box lists the optional switches that you can add to the field code and describes their functions. Just select the switch that you want to add and click Add to Field.

Part
II

Ch
13

Figure 13.3

Use the Field Options dialog box to view and add optional switches for each field.

An in-depth discussion of each of the field codes and their optional settings would require several chapters. See *Special Edition Using Microsoft Office 97*, Bestseller Edition, published by Que, for more information on using Word's field codes. For now, just remember these key points:

- Field codes enable you to insert dynamic data into a document.
- You can toggle field codes on or off to view either the result of the field code or the field code itself.
- Each field code can use optional switches that control its content (result) and appearance.
- Word shows a syntax example for each field code when you select the field code in the Field dialog box.
- Word uses field codes to build such elements as tables of contents, tables of authorities, and indexes.
- You must update field codes to make them show the most current information.

 If you need to include a backslash character (\) in a field code's optional information, replace single \ characters with \\. Here is an example of the INCLUDETEXT field, which includes the contents of another file—or portion thereof—in the current document:

{INCLUDETEXT "C:\\My Documents\\April\\Report"}

Exploring a Hands-On Example

In this example, you create a simple template for creating interoffice memos. Follow these steps to create the template and insert the field codes:

1. Open Word, and start a new template based on the Blank Document. To do so, choose File, New, and click the General tab on the New property sheet. Select the Blank Document icon, select the Template option button, and choose OK.
2. Choose a typeface, set the font size to 24, and type the text **Interoffice Memo**.
3. Start a new line and set the font size to 12.
4. Type **From:**, followed by a space.

5. Choose Insert, Field to display the Field dialog box and choose User Information from the Categories list.

6. Choose UserName in the Field Names list; then choose OK.

7. Start a new line and type **To:**, followed by a space.

8. Choose Insert, Field to display the Field dialog box, and choose Document Automation from the Categories list.

9. Choose MacroButton from the Field Names list.

10. In the Field Codes text box to the right of the field name, type **NoMacro "Enter recipient's name"** and choose OK.

11. Start a new line and type **Date:**, followed by a space.

12. Choose Insert, Field to display the Field dialog box, and choose Date and Time from the Categories list.

13. Choose Date from the Field Names list; then click the Options button to display the Field Options dialog box (see Figure 13.4).

Figure 13.4
The General Switches tab for the Date-Time field codes allows you to choose the format for the date.

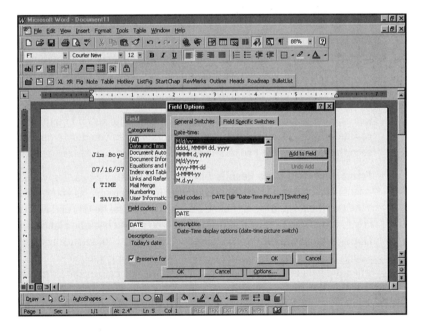

Part
II
Ch
13

14. From the Date-Time list, choose MMMM d, yyyy.

15. Click Add to Field.

16. Choose OK twice to close both dialog boxes and insert the field into the document.

17. Start a new line and type **Time:**, followed by a space.

18. Choose Insert, Field to display the Field dialog box, and choose the Date and Time category; then choose the Time field.

19. Choose Options, scroll through the list, and then choose h:mm am/pm from the Date-Time Formats list.

20. Choose Add to Field.

21. Choose OK twice to close both dialog boxes and insert the field.

22. Save the file in the Templates folder; then close the file.

Now you have a simple memo form. To test the form, choose File, New, and choose the template that you just created. Make sure that the Document option button is selected; then choose OK. Word starts a new document based on your template and automatically fills in your user name, as well as the current date and time. All you need to do is type the recipient's name in the Enter Recipient's Name box. Word replaces the field with the text that you type.

 TIP The MacroButton box is intended for running macros in the document, but you can use it to insert placeholder field codes by specifying NoMacro as the name of the macro to associate with the field. Using MacroButton with the NoMacro name is essentially like inserting an empty labeled field.

Formatting Field Codes

Just as you do with regular text, you can format field codes so that the results take on a specific typeface, font size, and other character formatting. When you update the field, the formatting can be retained or lost, depending on how you set up the field. You can format the results of field codes in either of two ways. The first way is to apply formatting directly to the results of the field code. After you insert the field code, you select its contents (results) and format its font characteristics as you would any other text. The second method of formatting field code results involves including formatting switches when you define the field code. The following sections explore these two methods.

Formatting Field Code Results Directly   As mentioned earlier, you can simply highlight the results of a field code and apply character formatting just as you would for any other text. Whether the formatting is retained the next time the field is updated depends on how you created the field. In the Field dialog box, you see a check box labeled Preserve Formatting During Updates. If this box contains a check, Word automatically appends the *MERGEFORMAT switch to the field. This option causes any formatting applied to the field results to be retained when the field is updated. Clearing this check box causes the formatting to be lost the next time that the field is updated.

 TIP Word adds the *MERGEFORMAT switch to some field codes automatically. Insert an AutoText field, for example, and Word includes the *MERGEFORMAT switch to the field, even though this switch doesn't appear in the Field dialog box when you define the field. *MERGEFORMAT is discussed in more detail in the following section.

Using Formatting Switches   You also can format the results of field codes by applying formatting switches to the field code. The following list describes general switches that you can apply to a field to control the appearance of its results:

- ■ * (Format). Use this switch to specify number formats, capitalization, and character formatting (bold, italic, and so on). Follow this switch with the formatting code, such as *Caps. This example capitalizes the first letter of each word.

- ■ \# (Numeric Picture). Use this switch to specify the characteristics (such as decimal places and currency symbols) of numeric results. Using \# $###.00, for example, formats the results as currency with two decimal places.

- ■ \@ (Date-Time Picture). Use this switch to format date and time results. Using \@MMMM, d, yyyy, for example, formats a date with the full month, the date without a leading zero, and a four-digit year, such as February 6, 1997.

- ■ \! (Lock Result). This switch prevents field codes contained in text inserted by the BOOKMARK, INCLUDETEXT, and REF field codes from being updated unless the field is first updated in its source document. Without this switch, Word updates the embedded field.

N O T E The general switches described in the preceding list cannot be applied to all field codes. For a complete list of field codes to which these switches do not apply, consult the Reference Information\Field Types and Switches section of the Word Help file. ■

Each of the general switches described in the preceding list must include additional parameters, which vary from one switch to another. The Caps parameter used in the sample Format (*) is an example of an additional parameter. For a complete list of these parameters and additional information about each switch, consult the Reference Information\Field Types and Switches section of the Word Help file.

Performing Calculations with Field Codes

In addition to pulling information from various sources—document statistics, other files, date, time, and so on—you may want to perform calculations in your documents. One method of performing calculations involves using the Formula field code. The syntax for the Formula field code is as follows:

```
{= formula [Bookmark] [\# Numeric Picture]}
```

N O T E The square brackets in the preceding syntax example indicate that the information within the brackets is optional. The brackets themselves should not be included in the formula. ■

The *formula* expression can contain a combination of numbers, bookmarks that reference numbers, other field codes that result in numbers, and numeric operators and functions. The expression also can reference values in tables and values returned by functions. The following example adds a static value to a value contained in the bookmark named "Sales," divides the number by 12, and formats the result as currency with two decimal places:

```
{= (Sales+24,389.75) / 12 \# "$#,##0.00"}
```

The `Formula` field code enables you to perform calculations on the contents of the cells in tables. As in Excel, cells are referenced by column and row. Columns are labeled with letters and rows are labeled with numbers, as in the following example:

▶ **See** "Inserting Tables," **page 284**

```
A1 B1 C1 D1
A2 B2 C2 D2

A3 B3 C3 D3
A4 B4 C4 D4
```

In Word, you reference a cell by combining the column and row with a colon. A:1, for example, references the first cell in the top-left corner of the table. When used in a formula, the cell reference is enclosed in parentheses. The following `Formula` field code sums a range of cells:

```
{=SUM(A1:A4)}
```

In this example, the field code must be located within the table, because no other information is included to identify the table itself— just the range within it. Use bookmarks to reference tables elsewhere in the document. The following example sums a range of cells in two different tables and then subtracts them:

```
{=(SUM(Sales B2:B7))-(SUM(Expense C1:C29))}
```

You also can reference an entire row or column. To reference a column, use its column letter twice, separated by a colon. The reference A:A, for example, identifies the entire column A. The reference 4:4 identifies all of row 4. You can use multiple cell references as well. The following example averages rows 2 and 4:

```
{=AVERAGE(2:2,4:4)}
```

T I P To identify a range, specify the first and last cells of the range, as in A1:F6.

In summary, you can use the `Formula` field code to perform many types of calculations. You can build a table containing sales information, for example, and summarize the table or reference the table data elsewhere in the document through calculations on the table's contents. You may need to use formulas to calculate page numbers, sections, or other items. In short, anything in Word that deals with numeric values is a good candidate for the `Formula` field code.

For a complete description of the `Formula` field-code options and the use of table cells, consult the Reference Information/Field Types and Switches/Field Codes: =(Formula) field item in the Word Help file.

T I P When you include fields in a document, you sometimes want to protect those fields from being changed or to protect an entire document from being modified. For more information on protecting fields and documents, refer to "Protecting the Document" later in this chapter.

Creating and Using Forms

Word provides several features for creating printed forms and forms to be used and filled in on-screen. You may create an invoice (see Figure 13.5) or sales form, for example, and then print it to fill in the blanks. Alternatively, you may fill in the blanks onscreen first and then print the form. In either case, Word makes creating the forms an easy task, and you end up with professional-looking forms. This section of the chapter explores features in Word for creating these forms.

Figure 13.5

Using forms can help you create attractive forms, including this company invoice.

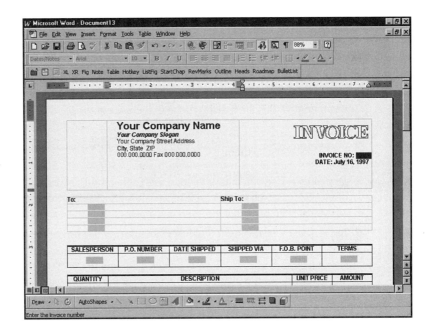

Exploring the Forms Controls

You could manually draw all the boxes and blanks in a form, and sometimes, you may need to do so, but Word provides a set of features just for creating forms. These features can considerably simplify the process of creating online forms. The first set of form controls that Word offers is located in the Forms toolbar (see Figure 13.6). Choose View, Toolbars, Forms to view the Forms toolbar.

Part

II

Ch

13

Figure 13.6

Use the Forms toolbar to create onscreen or printed forms.

The following list describes the buttons in the Forms toolbar:

- *Text Form Field*. Use this button to insert a text field in which the user enters text (on-screen) or fills in the blank in the printed document.

- *Check Box Form Field*. This button inserts a box into the document. When used on-screen, these boxes act much like Windows check boxes. Clicking one check box places an X in the box; and clicking it again removes the X.

- *Drop-Down Form Field*. Use this button to create a drop-down list from which onscreen users can make choices. This form field is not applicable to printed forms, although when printed, this form displays the first choice in the list of choices associated with the field.

- *Form Field Options*. Use this button to set the properties of individual form fields in the document.

- *Draw Table*. Use this button to open the Tables and Borders toolbar, with which you can draw custom tables and set their properties. The Tables and Borders toolbar is discussed later in this chapter.

- *Insert Table*. Use this button to insert a table that has preset properties and equal-size table fields. When you select an existing table column, this button changes to the Insert Column button, with which you can add a column to the existing table. When you click a table cell, this button changes to the Insert Rows button, with which you can insert rows in a table column.

- *Insert Frame*. Use this button to insert a frame into the document. Frames are handy for containing graphics and text, but you also can use text boxes to contain text, and text boxes offer additional features that are not provided by frames.

- *Form Field Shading*. Use this button to turn on and off shading of form fields. Shading applies to printed forms as well as onscreen forms.

- *Protect Form*. Use this button to protect the properties of the form fields from being changed. Turning on protection does not prevent data from being entered in the form fields, but simply protects the underlying form fields themselves from being modified.

Word also includes several ActiveX-based Controls that you can insert into documents. These ActiveX Controls are designed to work in conjunction with Visual Basic for Applications (VBA) to provide sophisticated programming and automation capabilities. You insert these controls by using the Control Toolbox toolbar (see Figure 13.7).

Figure 13.7

Insert ActiveX controls into a document by using the Control Toolbox toolbar.

> **TIP**
>
> Word includes several ActiveX Controls other than those shown in the Control Toolbox toolbar. These controls are provided by third-party vendors, and you typically must pay a license fee to enable and use them.

Although these ActiveX Controls are most useful in conjunction with VBA to provide document automation, you also can use them as simple form controls without any underlying VBA code. If you want a set of check boxes in a document, for example, you can insert either the Check Box Form Field from the Forms toolbar or insert the Check Box ActiveX Control from the Control Toolbox toolbar.

Creating a Form

The first steps in creating a form are sketching out what you want the form to look like and listing the information that you want it to contain. If the form will include graphics, letterhead, or other document elements, make sure that you have those elements ready, or be prepared to create them as part of the form.

Whether you are creating a printed form or a form for use onscreen, you should consider creating the form as a template. Then you can base new form documents on this template, helping ensure that your original form remains unchanged until you are ready to revise it.

▶ **See** "Creating and Using Templates," **page 213**

After you begin the new template, begin adding the static information (such as form title, letterhead, and graphics) and other elements of the form that will not change—that is, elements in the form that the form user will not modify.

When you're ready to start adding fields to the form, choose View, Toolbars, Forms to display the Forms toolbar. If you prefer to use ActiveX Controls, choose View, Toolbars, Control Toolbox. The following section explains how to use the various objects in the Forms toolbar.

Using Text Boxes and Check Boxes

Text fields and check boxes often make up the majority of the objects in a form. Use text fields when you want to create a fill-in-the-blank field in the form. Use check boxes just as you do in Windows to indicate choice of an option. If you're building an employee insurance sign-up sheet, for example, you use text fields for the employee's name, address, and other information, and use check boxes to have the employee choose a payment method or deductible option.

Part
II

Ch
13

To insert a text form field, place the insertion point where you want the field to be inserted and click the Form Field Options button in the Forms toolbar. A shaded text box appears in the document. To set the text form field's properties, double-click the field, or single-click the field and then click the Form Field Properties button in the toolbar. In either case, you see the Text Form Field Options dialog box, shown in Figure 13.8.

Figure 13.8

Use the Text Form Field Options dialog box to set the properties, such as length, of the text field.

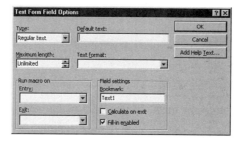

Use the Type drop-down list to choose the type of text that you want to associate with the field— regular text, numbers, a date, the current time, the current date, or a calculation. All but the current-date and current-time options enable you to specify the default value for the field. The default value appears in the form, and the user can change it. You also can use the default value to provide instructions, such as Enter your name here.

 Text fields default in width to about 3/8 inches. The field expands in size as the user types information. For printed forms, however, you probably want the text field to print at a fixed size. To expand the size of the text form field to suit the amount of space that you want in the form, use as many spaces as necessary as the default text to force the field to the desired size.

The following list describes the controls in the Text Form Field Options dialog box:

- *Type.* Choose from this drop-down list the type of text entry that you want in the field.
- *Default Text.* Type the default value for the text in this box. The default value appears in the form and is overwritten when your user enters his or her own information in the field.
- *Maximum Length.* Specify the maximum length of the field or choose Unlimited to allow the field to expand as much as needed.
- *Text Format.* Use this drop-down list to choose the format in which you want the text to appear. This drop-down list changes according to your choice in the Type drop-down list. Choose Number from the Type drop-down list, for example, and this control changes to Number Format, allowing you to choose among various numeric formatting options.
- *Entry.* Use this drop-down list to choose a macro to run when the user clicks the field.
- *Exit.* Use this drop-down list to choose a macro to run when the user exits the field by pressing the Tab key or by clicking outside the field.
- *Bookmark.* Assign a bookmark name to the field with this control.

- *Calculate on Exit*. Place a check in this box to have Word recalculate the results in the field when the user exits the field.

- *Fill-In Enabled*. Place a check in this box if you want the user to be able to fill in the blank onscreen. To prevent the field from being filled in, clear this check box.

- *Add Help Text*. Click this button to assign help messages to the field that appears in the Word status bar when the user presses F1 with the field selected. You also can define the message for a small message box that appears when the user presses F1 when the field is selected.

 To provide vertical separation between text form fields, set the paragraph properties for each line to provide additional space before or after the paragraph, or change the line spacing.

To insert a check box into the form, place the insertion point where you want the check box to appear and click the Check Box Form Field button in the Forms toolbar. Then space or tab to the right and type a name for the check box.

 Set the font size of a text form field or check box form field to control the size of the element in the form.

Using Tables in a Form

Tables sometimes are useful in forms for displaying information as well as prompting for information. How and whether you use tables in your forms depends on your needs and the contents of the forms.

To insert a table with uniform column and row arrangement, click the Insert Table button in the Forms toolbar. The control expands to allow you to choose from a 1×1 to a 4×5 table. Click the table of the size that you want. The resulting table is much like any other table that you would insert into a Word document and can be formatted as such. You can use the commands in the Table menu to modify the table.

▶ **See** "Formatting and Modifying Tables," **page 291**

To insert rows into the table, click the table where you want the rows to be inserted and then click the Insert Rows button in the Forms toolbar. To insert a column, you must first select the column where you want a new one to be inserted and then click the Insert Row button in the Forms toolbar. Notice that this button replaces the Insert Table button, as does the Insert Rows button, when you select a column or row, respectively.

If you want more control of the table's initial structure or appearance, click the Draw Table button in the Forms toolbar; then click and drag to define the overall rectangular area of the table. When you release the mouse button, the Tables and Borders toolbox appears. Use the controls in the Tables and Borders toolbox to fine-tune the appearance of your table.

▶ **See** "Inserting Tables," **page 284**

Part
II

Ch
13

After you create the structure of the table, you probably want to fill in at least some of the cells in the table. Some of the information, such as labels, is static. You may want the user to be able to fill in some of the table, however. If so, you need to add the appropriate type of text form field to each cell. Just click the cell and then click the Text Form Field button in the Forms toolbar.

 TIP   If you turn on document protection, you won't be able to modify the contents of a table. Turn off protection while you are designing the form; then turn it back on before you save it.

Using Drop-Down Form Fields

Windows (and, therefore, Windows applications) uses drop-down lists to enable you to choose among multiple options. The Forms toolbar includes a Drop-Down Form Field button that you can use to insert drop-down lists into your forms. These drop-down lists are applicable only to onscreen forms, of course.

To insert a drop-down list into a form, place the insertion point where you want the drop-down list to be inserted and then click the Drop-Down Form Field button. Word inserts a default-size drop-down list that initially looks much like a text form field, except for its greater width. Double-click the drop-down form field to open the Drop-Down Form Field Options dialog box, shown in Figure 13.9.

Figure 13.9

Add choices to the drop-down list through the Drop-Down Form Field Options dialog box.

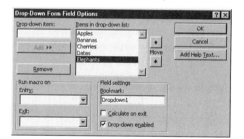

Type the first option for the list in the Drop-Down Items text box; then choose Add. Repeat this procedure to add all other options to the list. Select an item and then click the up or down arrows beside the Items In Drop-Down List area to change the order of the items in the list. Select an item and click Remove to remove it from the list.

As you can with text form fields, you can assign a macro to run when the user clicks the drop-down list or exits the list. Set these options with the Run Macro On group of controls. You also can assign a bookmark to the drop-down form field, set it to calculate on exit (applicable to formulas), and enable or disable the drop-down list. Click the Add Help Text button to add optional Help text for the status bar or F1 key, if desired. When you are satisfied with the drop-down list properties, choose OK.

Notice that the drop-down list won't actually function as a drop-down list until you turn on document protection; then it behaves just like a Windows drop-down list. Click the drop-down list and choose one of the options from the list.

Using the Form

When you finish creating the form template, save it in a folder accessible by those people who need to use it (either onscreen or to print it). As discussed in the following section, you need to make sure that you turn on protection for the document to prevent accidental changes to the form. With protection turned on, the person using the form onscreen can only fill in the blanks, check boxes, and other objects that you include in the form. With protection turned off, the user can modify any portion of the form, including deleting parts of the form.

 You can use sections in a form to segregate different sets of form fields. Then you can assign passwords to specific sections to prevent anything in those sections from being changed. The following section explains this topic.

Protecting the Document

As mentioned earlier, you need to protect forms to enable them to function properly and to prevent them from being accidentally changed by other people when they use the form. You also can protect a document in other ways. This chapter examines the methods available in Word for protecting documents. This chapter discusses how to protect a document's fields and form fields, as well as how to use passwords to protect a document. For information on using protection with revision marks and comments, see Chapter 48, "Document Collaboration."

Protecting Individual Fields

You cannot protect fields in a document per se, but you can temporarily lock them to prevent them from being updated. Nothing, however, prevents you or someone else from selecting the field and then deleting it or from overwriting its contents by clicking inside the field and typing. Locking the fields does, however, prevent the locked fields from being updated when the rest of the fields in the document are updated. To lock an individual field, click the field and press Ctrl+F11. Click a field and press Shift+Ctrl+F11 to unlock a field.

 You can protect a range of fields by using a workaround. Place the fields to be protected in their own section and then protect the section, as explained in "Protecting Sections" later in this chapter.

Protecting Forms and Form Fields

Essentially, the only time you want to turn protection off for a form is when you are designing the form. You want the form protected at all other times when the form is being used. Protecting the form prevents users from accessing or changing anything other than the contents of the form fields. In other words, all the user can do is fill in the form; the user cannot modify its structure or other content.

The easiest way to turn on form protection is to click the Protect Form button in the Forms toolbar. Alternatively, you can choose Tools, Protect Document to open the Protect Document dialog box (see Figure 13.10) and then choose the Forms button to turn on form protection. Save the document with protection turned on.

Figure 13.10

Use the Protect Document dialog box to set document protection options.

Protecting Sections

If the document contains multiple sections, you can selectively protect each section, which means that you can lock entire sections to prevent them from being changed (other than form fields in the section). If you want a user to be able to modify only part of the contents of a document, divide the document into sections and protect the desired sections.

To define protection by section, choose Tools, Protect Document to open the Protect Document dialog box. Click the Sections button to open the Section Protection dialog box (see Figure 13.11). Place a check beside each section to be protected; then choose OK. Then choose OK in the Protect Document dialog box to turn on protection.

Figure 13.11

You can protect certain areas of a document by using sections and the Section Protection dialog box.

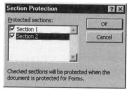

Using Passwords

You can use passwords in several ways to protect the contents of a document. These ways include the following:

- Protect a document from being opened without a password
- Protect a document from being modified without a password
- Protect a form with a password

You can protect a document with two passwords when you save the document (the first two options in the preceding list). The first password is required for opening the file. The second password is for modifying the file. If you apply both passwords, the user has to specify a password to open the file and then specify another password to modify it. Alternatively, you can use either password alone, depending on your needs.

To apply passwords to a document, open the document and choose File, Save As to open the Save As dialog box; then choose Options to display the Save property sheet, shown in Figure 13.12.

Figure 13.12
Use the Save property sheet to specify options that control how the document is saved.

In the Password to Open text box, type the password that you want to apply to the document to protect it from being opened. Only those people who have the password can open the document. The password can be up to 15 characters long and can contain any combination of letters, numbers, spaces, and symbols. Passwords are case-sensitive.

In the Password to Modify text box, type the password that you want to use to protect the document from being modified. If the user doesn't have this password, he or she cannot modify the document but can view it. Choose OK and then choose Save to save the document with the new password.

> **CAUTION**
> Don't forget the passwords that you assign to a document. If you do, you won't be able to open or modify the document.

You use a different method to protect a form from changes. With the form open, choose Tools, Protect Document to open the Protect Document dialog box (refer to Figure 13.10). Type a password in the Password text box and choose OK. Word prompts you to confirm the password by typing it again. Do so and choose OK.

With the form protected by a password, the person using the form can still enter data in the form fields. The user has to know the password to turn off protection and modify other parts of the form, however.

Creating Indexes and Tables of Contents

Word automates many tasks that would be extremely time-consuming to perform manually. These tasks include creating indexes, tables of contents (TOC), tables of figures (TOF), and tables of authorities (TOA). The following list describes these document elements:

- *Index.* An index summarizes the content of a document, listing words, phrases, and the pages on which those words and phrases appear.

- *Table of contents.* A table of contents summarizes the topics or headings in a document, and includes the page number on which each topic or heading begins.

- *Table of figures.* A table of figures summarizes the figures in a document, typically listing the figure caption and page number on which the figure is located. You also can use this feature to create a table of tables or a table of equations.

- *Table of authorities.* A table of authorities lists references to cases, statutes, rules, and so on in a legal document, and specifies the page number on which the reference appears.

The following sections explain how to create indexes, tables of contents, and tables of figures. Tables of authorities are not covered, because they apply to a smaller user segment. If you require help in creating a table of authorities, press F1 and perform a search for **table of authorities**. For additional help creating and using indexes, tables of contents, and tables of figures, refer to *Special Edition Using Microsoft Word 97*, Bestseller Edition, from Que.

Creating an Index

You can insert an index at any point in a document, but indexes typically are included at the end of the document. Word inserts the index within its own section to separate it from the rest of the document, regardless of where you locate the index within the document.

The most important aspect of creating an index is marking the index entries, which means selecting the words or phrases within the document to be included in the index. Word offers two methods for marking index entries. You can mark the entries one word or phrase at a time directly in the document, or use a *concordance file* that contains information Word uses to mark the words and phrases automatically.

To create an index by marking individual entries, begin at the top of the document and locate the first word or phrase to be included in the index. Highlight the entry, then press Shift+Alt+X or choose Insert, Index and Tables; click the Index tab; and choose Mark Entry. The Mark Index Entry dialog box appears, as shown in Figure 13.13.

Figure 13.13

Use the Mark Index Entry dialog box to mark words or phrases for inclusion in the index.

The selected word or phrase appears in the Main Entry text box automatically. Use the following controls in the Mark Index Entry dialog box to define the entry:

- *Subentry*. Use this text box to specify the text for an index subentry. The subentry text is added to the index below the Main Entry keyword or phrase, along with other subentries.
- *Cross-Reference*. Choose this option button if you want to insert a text reference, such as **See** *something else* instead of a page number.
- *Current Page*. Choose this option (the default) to have a page number inserted into the index for the selected entry.
- *Page Range and Bookmark*. Use the Page Range option button to have Word insert a range of pages rather than a single page number for the entry. The range must already be defined in the document by means of a bookmark. Choose the name of the bookmark from the Bookmark drop-down list.
- *Page Number Format*. Use these two check boxes to turn on or off boldface and italic for the page-number text for the entry.
- *Mark*. Choose this button to mark the current selection with the specified index settings.
- *Mark All*. Choose this button to mark all occurrences of the selected text in the document.

N O T E Word inserts an Index Entry (XE) field code as hidden text directly to the right of the selected word or phrase. You can view these field codes by turning on field codes. ▪

If you work with documents that contain many of the same index keywords or phrases, you can use a concordance file to significantly speed the index-marking process. A concordance file consists of two columns, one entry per line. The left column lists the text that you want to index, and the right column lists the index entries to create for the text specified in the left column. After you create the concordance file, you can use it for multiple documents as required. There is no specific command or wizard to help you create a concordance file in Word. Instead, you simply create a Word document containing a two-column table, then fill the table with the index entries.

Part

II

Ch

13

To mark a document by using a concordance file, first open the document to be indexed. Locate the insertion point where you want the index to be inserted; then choose Insert, Index and Tables, and click the Index tab to display the Index page of the Index and Tables property sheet (see Figure 13.14).

Figure 13.14

Use the Index page to specify a variety of settings that control the appearance of the index.

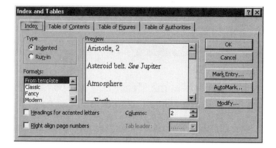

In the Index page, choose AutoMark. Word displays a standard Open dialog box. Locate and select the concordance file; then choose Open. Word searches the document for occurrences of the entries listed in the concordance file and marks them according to the right-column entries in the concordance file. Word marks only the first occurrence of the entry in each paragraph.

After the document has been marked by either of the methods described earlier in this section, you're ready to insert the index. Choose Insert, Index and Tables. Select the style of index that you want to use, using the Preview as a guide. When you're satisfied with the appearance of the index, choose OK to insert the index into the document.

As you continue to work on a document that has been indexed, the page numbers specified in the index entries are likely to become incorrect to some degree as text shifts within the document. An index is simply a table of field codes, so updating the index simply means updating the field codes. To update the index, place the insertion point anywhere in the index and press F9. Alternatively, right-click the index and then choose Update Field from the shortcut menu.

Using Word to Create a Table of Contents

Creating a table of contents requires that you perform a series of actions. These actions are summarized in the following list:

- Apply paragraph styles to the document to identify logical levels within the document. Or, you can add Table Entry (TC) field codes as hidden text in the document to identify index items.
- Specify the style of table you want to use.
- Specify settings that control the appearance of the TOC.
- Insert the TOC.

To create a table of contents, you first apply paragraph styles to your document. Although you can create your own styles, probably the easiest method for you at first is to rely on the styles that are included with your default template.

TIP You can build a TOC by adding Table Entry (TC) field codes as hidden text at the end of each TOC entry throughout the document. Using styles is by far the easiest method, however, and is the one explained in this chapter. Notice that you also can build a TOC by using a combination of styles and TC field codes.

If the document is long enough to include a TOC, you are likely to have used outlining with the document. Assume that you've created a document and applied the predefined Heading 1, Heading 2, and Heading 3 styles to the appropriate headings in the document. The paragraphs with the Heading 1 style appear leftmost in the TOC, with the Heading 2 and Heading 3 headings being indented to the second and third stops in the TOC, respectively.

N O T E If you haven't used the Heading styles in the document, assign a style to each of the heads in the document that you want to be included in the TOC. Use a different style for each level of the document. All chapter titles, for example, have the same style; section heads all use their own style; and so on.

To insert the TOC in Word, locate the insertion point where you want the TOC to be inserted; then choose Insert, Index and Tables, and click the Table of Contents tab (refer to Figure 13.14). From the Formats list, choose the style of TOC that you want. Word applies paragraph and font formatting to the TOC table according to your choice. If you want Word to use the default paragraph style in your document for the TOC, choose the From Template option.

Next, use the four controls at the bottom of the Index and Tables dialog box to specify options for the TOC. Enable the Show Page Numbers check box if you want the page number to be listed for each heading. Enable the Right Align Page Numbers check box to have the page numbers aligned at the right edge of the TOC. Use the Show Levels spin control to choose how many levels to include in the TOC. Finally, if the TOC style that you chose supports tab leaders, choose the desired tab leader from the Tab Leader drop-down list. The tab leader is the character, if any, that separates the page numbers from the heading.

Next, click the Options button to display the Table of Contents Options dialog box (see Figure 13.15). Make sure that the Styles check box is enabled; then scroll through the available styles list to locate the Heading 1 style. You find that Word has already assigned the appropriate TOC level to the style. If you're basing your TOC on other styles, locate the styles and assign to them the appropriate level by clicking the TOC Level text box next to the style and then typing the level number (1, 2, 3, and so on). When you've set all the necessary style levels, choose OK. Then choose OK in the Index and Tables dialog box to insert the TOC into the document.

Part

II

Ch

13

Figure 13.15

Set up the styles to be used for the TOC by using the Table of Contents Options dialog box.

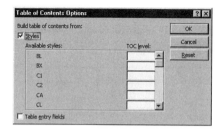

Most likely, your document won't remain static after you insert the TOC; page numbers may change, new headings come and old headings go, or you may just change a few words here or there. So understanding how to update the TOC is important. To do so, right-click the TOC table and then choose Update Field from the context menu to open the Update Table of Contents dialog box. You can choose to update just the page numbers or update the entire TOC. Choose the desired option in the dialog box; then click OK.

Creating a Table of Figures

If your document contains several figures, you may want to include a table of figures (TOF) that lists the figures. You include a TOF in much the same way that you insert a TOC. As for a TOC, an easy way to mark the figure entries is to use a style. If you inserted captions for each figure, however, you can use the caption as the tag by which the TOF is defined. You can use Table Entry (TC) field codes as hidden text with each figure reference, but using the styles or caption method is much easier.

If you plan to use captions as the basis for the TOF, first insert a caption for each equation, figure, or table. If you are using styles as the basis for defining the TOF, apply the desired style to each figure caption.

To insert the TOF, locate the insertion point where you want the TOF to be located. Then choose Insert, Index and Tables, and click the Table of Figures tab to display the Table of Figures property page.

The following list describes the controls in the Tables and Figures page:

- *Caption Label*. Use this list to specify the type of caption element to use to define the TOF.

- *Formats*. Choose the overall style of the table from this list.

- *Show Page Numbers*. Place a check in this check box if you want each table entry to list the page number of the associated figure.

- *Right Align Page Numbers*. Place a check in this check box to force the page numbers to the right margin of the document. When this option is enabled, the Tab Leader control becomes available.

- *Include Label and Number*. Use this control to turn on or off the inclusion of the selected caption label in the entry.

■ *Tab Leader.* Use this drop-down list to choose the type of separator to place between the entry and its page number. This item is enabled only when Right Align Page Numbers is checked.

If you are using styles or field codes to define the TOF, choose the Options button to open the Table of Figures Options dialog box. Click the Style check box; then choose the style associated with the figure caption or other document element that you want to be included in the TOF entry. Alternatively, click the Table Entry Fields check box and choose the appropriate table identifier. Choose OK when you finish setting options.

When you are satisfied with your TOF settings, choose OK. Word inserts the TOF as a table of field codes. ●

Part

II

Ch

13

CHAPTER 14

Using Tables

by Jim Boyce

In this chapter

Overview of New Features

Word 97 includes only a few new features relating to tables, but those few features offer considerable power. The following sections provide a brief overview of these new features.

Drawing a Table

In previous versions of Word, as in Word 97, you can quickly create a table by specifying the number of columns and rows for the table. Word creates the table with the same number of cells in each row. That is, the cells in each column are equally distributed (see Figure 14.1).

Figure 14.1

A typical table created by Word's predefined table styles results in equally-spaced rows and columns.

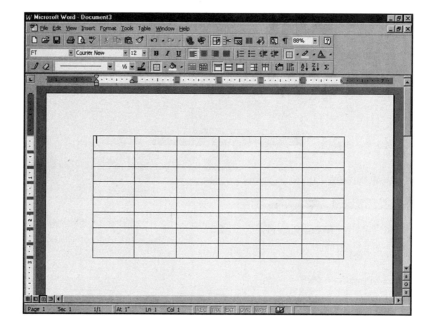

You can modify this type of table quite easily to change row and column spacing and consolidate cells, but Word 97 offers a new feature that lets you draw the table. You define the rectangular area for the overall table size, then begin drawing the row and column lines at any point desired in the table (see Figure 14.2). This new feature makes it easy to create custom table layouts.

Figure 14.2

Quickly create custom table layouts using Word 97's new feature for drawing a table right in the document.

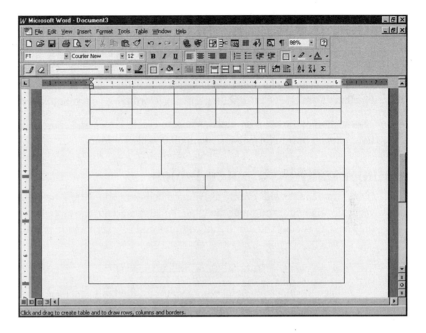

Tables and Borders Made Easier

Another change in the way Word handles tables is the integration of table and border commands in one toolbar called the Tables and Borders toolbar. Adding these border commands to the toolbar makes it easier to change table border styles and sizes.

Merging Cells Vertically

Previous versions of Word allowed you to merge cells horizontally in a table. Word 97 also offers the ability to merge cells vertically in a table. You can merge cells using commands in the Table menu or by simply erasing the line that separates the two cells with the new Eraser tool in the Tables and Borders toolbox.

▶ **See** "Splitting and Merging Cells," **page 293**

Vertical Text Alignment and Orientation

You can easily align the text in a table cell at the top, center, or bottom of the cell. Word 97 also lets you rotate the text vertically in the cell. You can adjust the alignment of the vertical text just as you can the horizontal text.

▶ **See** "Changing Text Orientation and Alignment," **page 292**

Resizing and Alignment

Word 97 now lets you change the height or width of rows and columns by simply dragging the row and column borders. You also can easily align rows and columns to distribute them evenly within the table.

Part
II

Ch
14

Inserting Tables

Tables in Word consist of rows and columns of cells in which you can enter text, formulas, and graphics. You can use tables to create a grid of images or even arrange side-by-side paragraphs. You can perform calculations not only within cells, but perform summation and other functions from one cell to another, making Word tables act much like a spreadsheet.

This section of the chapter explains how to create tables and enter data into them. Later sections explain how to format and manipulate table contents.

Creating Evenly-Distributed Tables

If you want a table with evenly-distributed cells—one in which the cells are horizontally and vertically aligned throughout the table, Word can create the table for you automatically. You only have to specify the number of columns and rows to include in the table. Word does the rest.

To create an evenly-distributed table, follow these steps:

1. Place the insertion point where you want the table inserted.

2. Choose Table, Insert Table to open the Insert Table dialog box (see Figure 14.3). Or, click the Insert Table button on the Standard toolbar.

Figure 14.3

Quickly create evenly-distributed tables using the Insert Table dialog box.

3. Use the Number of Columns and Number of Rows controls to specify the number of columns and rows in the table.

4. If you want the columns equally spaced, choose Auto from the Column Width control. Or, type or select the column width from this same control.

5. Choose OK to insert the table in the document.

After the table appears in the document, you can click in individual cells to begin entering data in the cells.

▶ **See** "Adding Data to the Table," **page 287**

Using the Table Drawing Tool

While the Insert Table dialog box offers a very quick way to create simple, evenly-distributed tables, you might need to create a more complex table. For example, you might need to structure the table cells to place a varying number of cells in each column. Word 97 includes a new feature that lets you draw a table one cell at a time.

Use the following steps to draw a complex, custom table in a Word document:

1. Choose Table, Draw Table. Word switches to Page Layout view and displays the Tables and Borders toolbar. The pointer changes to a pencil pointer.

2. Click and drag in the document to define the overall size of the table (see Figure 14.4).

Figure 14.4

Draw the outline of the table first.

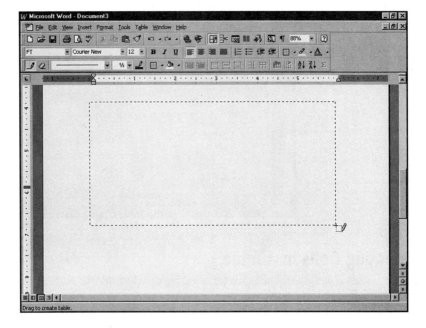

3. Use the pencil pointer to draw initial column and row lines (see Figure 14.5).

4. To remove lines, click the Eraser button on the Tables and Borders toolbox, then drag the resulting eraser pointer over the line to be erased.

5. Click outside the table to exit the Table Editor mode.

At this point, you have a simple, custom table. You'll learn how to format the table and change its appearance later in the section "Formatting and Modifying Tables." Before learning how to insert data in a table, you must first learn how to select cells.

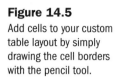

Figure 14.5
Add cells to your custom table layout by simply drawing the cell borders with the pencil tool.

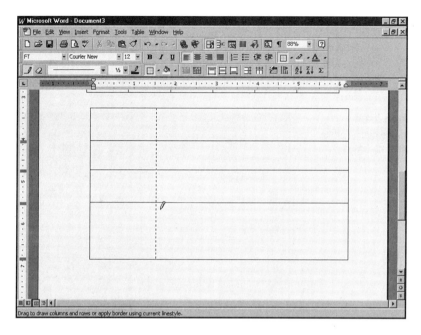

Selecting Cells in a Table

Word offers several methods for selecting cells individually and as a group. Use the following methods to select cells:

- *Select a cell.* Place the arrow cursor just inside the left edge of the cell and click.
- *Select a row.* Click to the left of the row.
- *Select a column.* Click the column's top gridline or border. The pointer will change to a vertical arrow when it is in the correct position to select a column.
- *Select multiple cells, rows, or columns.* Click the first cell and drag to the last cell of the desired selection. Or, click in the first cell, hold down the Shift key, and click in the last cell of your selection.
- *Select text in the next cell.* Press the Tab key or simply select the text using the pointer. You can use the arrow keys to move between cells.
- *Select text in the previous cell.* Press Shift+Tab or select the text using the pointer.
- *Select the entire table.* Click the table and press Alt+5 (use the 5 character on the numeric keyboard with NumLock turned off).

N O T E You can select a row or column by placing the cursor in a cell, then choosing Table, Select Row or Select Column. Select the entire table by choosing Table, Select Table.

Adding Data to the Table

Adding data to a table is easy. In most cases, you simply click in the cell in which you want the data, then start typing. Word automatically wraps the text within the cell as you type. If necessary, Word also automatically increases the row height to accommodate all of the text within the cell.

 T I P Word automatically changes the row height across the table when the amount of text in a particular cell requires more vertical space. You can't prevent the other cells in the row from also changing, but you can erase the row lines and draw them back in at the previous spacing.

You can format the text in a table cell in the same way you format text outside a table. Either set your formatting options before you begin typing, or select the text afterwards and apply formatting (bold, italic, and so on) to the text.

You can insert graphics in a table cell almost as easily as text. Essentially, you click in the cell and insert the graphic. However, you can't use Insert, Picture to insert the image. Instead, use the following method to insert an image in a table cell:

1. Click in the cell.
2. Choose Insert, Object to open the Object dialog box (see Figure 14.6).

Figure 14.6

Insert graphics or other OLE objects in a table using the Object dialog box.

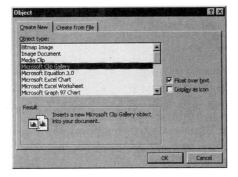

3. Scroll through the object list to find the type of object you want to insert (such as Microsoft Clip Gallery).
4. Clear the Float Over Text check box.
5. Choose OK.
6. Depending on the type of object selected, you might see an application, an Open dialog box to select a file, or in the case of Microsoft Clip Gallery, the Clip Gallery itself.
7. Select the image or file to insert, then choose OK or Insert depending on what is offered in the application or dialog box.

Part

II

Ch

14

Depending on the size of the table cell and the image, the image may not fit inside the cell. If not, a right and/or bottom portion of the image might extend behind the next cell to the right or below the current cell. You can click the image and drag its resize handles to make it fit in the cell. Or, simply adjust the cell size as necessary. Click the cell's border and drag it to the desired size to resize the cell. To resize the height of a cell, you must resize the entire row. First select the row by moving the pointer to the left margin of the row until the pointer changes to point to the right, then click to select the row. After selecting the row, choose Table, Cell Height and Width. In the Cell Height and Width dialog box, specify the desired cell height and choose OK.

Importing Data from a Database

You don't need to create a table first to insert data from a database into the table. Instead, you can let Word create the table for you automatically. That way you don't have to worry about getting the number of columns or rows set beforehand.

To insert a database as a table, use the following steps:

1. Choose View, Toolbars, Database to open the Database toolbar.
2. Place the insertion point in the document where you want the table to be inserted.
3. Click the Insert Database button on the Database toolbar to display the Database dialog box (see Figure 14.7).

Figure 14.7
Use the Database dialog box to begin the process of selecting the data to be inserted.

4. Choose the Get Data button.
5. Use the resulting Open Data Source file dialog box to locate and select the database you want to open. Choose MS Access Databases from the Files of Type drop-down list to view available Access databases. After you select the database, choose Open.

    Microsoft Access starts and displays a Microsoft Access dialog box similar to the one shown in Figure 14.8.
6. Select the desired table from the list and click OK.
7. Word returns to the Database dialog box. Choose the Query Options button to display the Query Options dialog box.
8. Click the Select Fields tab to display the Select Fields property page (see Figure 14.9).
9. Select the fields you want included from the database into the table, then choose OK.

Figure 14.8
Choose the table(s) from which to bring the data.

Figure 14.9
Use the Select Fields page to choose the data to include from the database into the table.

10. Choose Insert Data. Word prompts you to select which records to insert (see Figure 14.10).

Figure 14.10
You can insert a range of records or all records in the database.

11. Choose All if you want all the records in the table, or specify the beginning and ending record numbers.

12. If you want to be able to update the table records later, place a check in the Insert Data As Field check box. With this option selected, Word will insert the data in the table using field codes that can be updated later if the source data changes.

13. Choose OK to insert the table.

In step 12, you had the option of inserting the data using field codes. If you want to be able to update the data in the table from the database later if or when the database changes, insert the records using field codes. When you need to update the table, simply update the fields in the document. Word will retrieve the data from Access.

▶ **See** "Using Lists and Databases," **page 433**

Part
II
Ch
14

Finding Specific Records   If you have a long, complex table, it can be time-consuming to search through the table manually to find a specific record, particularly if the table is not sorted by the field in which you are searching. Word provides a search feature to help you quickly search through the table. Open the Database toolbar, then click the Find Record button. Word opens a dialog box in which you specify the search text and field in which you want to search (see Figure 14.11). Fill in the dialog box according to your search needs and choose Find First. The dialog box stays visible after the first record matching the search criteria is found. Choose Find Next to search for the next occurrence of the data.

Figure 14.11

Specify the search text and the field in which to search to locate specific records.

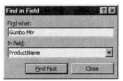

Using a Data Form   Although you can add new entries simply by adding new rows and typing the data in the cells, it often is easier to use a data entry form, particularly if the table contains several columns. To add, modify, and delete records from a table using a data form, first click in the table. Then on the Database toolbar click the Data Form button. Word displays a Data Form dialog box similar to the one shown in Figure 14.12.

Figure 14.12

A data form makes it easier to add records to a large table.

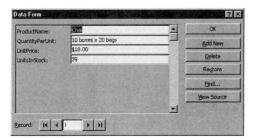

You can use the data form to browse the records in the table or modify the table. Click the Add New button to clear the form to add a new record. Fill in the data form and choose OK if this is the only record you want to add. Otherwise, choose Add New again and repeat the process for additional records. Note that the records won't appear in the table until you click OK in the Data Form dialog box. Use the Delete and Restore buttons, respectively, to delete records and restore a record's original values. Use Find to locate records. Use View Source to open the source table.

Converting Existing Text to a Table

If you have a document containing tabular data created without using tables, you can easily convert that text to a table. Word does all the hard work for you. To convert text to a table, first select all of the text to be converted. Then choose Table, Convert Text to Table. Word displays the Convert Text to Table dialog box shown in Figure 14.13.

Figure 14.13

Specify the character that Word should use to locate the separator between table fields.

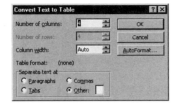

Word will determine the number of columns and rows required automatically, but you can change the number of columns if needed, as well as the column width. The key factor you must specify is the character Word will use when determining how to separate the text into different table columns. You can choose from Paragraph, Tab, Comma, or specify a different character using the Other option button. If the text uses tabs to separate columns of text, for example, choose the Tab option button. Then choose OK to convert the text to a table.

 Errors that occur while converting text to tables usually are caused by extra separator characters within the text. Be sure to use unique separator characters when creating or editing text that will be converted to a table or database format.

Formatting and Modifying Tables

Creating a table usually involves more than just defining the number of rows and columns and filling in the data. You'll probably want to use Word's formatting options to add borders, shading, and other formatting characteristics to the table. You also might want to make content changes to the table. This section focuses on Word features that enable you to format and modify tables.

AutoFormatting Tables

You can apply table formatting manually to achieve a custom look for a table, but Word offers a feature that can automatically format the table, saving you a lot of time and work. You can use the AutoFormat feature when you insert the table or afterwards. To use AutoFormat during table creation, set the row and column options in the Insert Table dialog box (choose Table, Insert Table), then click the AutoFormat button to display the Table AutoFormat dialog box (see Figure 14.14).

Word provides several predefined formatting schemes in the Formats list. Choose a scheme to view it in the Preview box. Use the check boxes in the dialog box to turn on and off various formatting aspects (the options are self-explanatory). Choose OK to return to the Insert Table dialog box, then choose OK to insert the table with the specified formatting options.

To use automatic formatting to format an existing table, right-click the table and choose Table AutoFormat, or choose Table, AutoFormat from Word's menu. Word will open the Table AutoFormat dialog box with which you can specify formatting options.

Part
II

Ch
14

Figure 14.14
Use the Table
AutoFormat dialog box
to set formatting options
for the table.

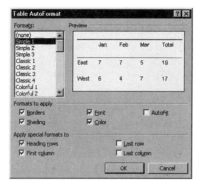

Working with Borders

Word automatically places a single-line, thin border around a table and draws similar lines to separate the table cells from one another. You can apply a different border to the table and selectively turn off border lines around each cell (or change their line characteristics).

To change border properties, choose View, Toolbars, Tables and Borders to turn on the Tables and Borders toolbar. If you want to change the border around a cell or group of cells, click in the cell or select the group. Choose the line style and weight you want from the Line Style and Line Weight controls on the toolbar. Then click the small arrow beside the Border button on the toolbar, and choose the border style for the selection. To apply a border to the whole table, select the whole table by choosing Table, Select Table, then choose the border style using the Outside Border button.

You also can draw individual border lines. To do so, first select the line style and weight for the line, then click the Draw Table button. Draw the border lines by clicking and dragging over the existing border and cell lines. Click the Eraser button and drag over lines to erase them.

Numbering Cells in a Table

Word makes it easy to number the cells in a table. To number the first cell in each row, select the first column in the table and then click the Numbering button on the Formatting toolbar. Or, select the column and choose Format, Bullets and Numbering, then select the type of numbering method and choose OK. If you want to number the cells in a row instead of a column, choose the row to be numbered.

If you want to number a selection of table cells rather than a whole column, select the range of cells. Then click the Numbering button on the Formatting toolbar.

Changing Text Orientation and Alignment

Word places text in the table horizontally by default. This is the orientation you'll probably use most often. In some cases, however, you might want to align the text vertically in one or more cells. You might also want to change the alignment of text in the cell to the left, center, or right (vertical text), or top, middle, or bottom (horizontal text).

To align text, click in the cell or select the range of cells to change. On the Tables and Borders toolbar, click the Align Top, Center Vertically, or Align Bottom toolbar buttons. Note that when you click in a cell containing vertical text, these buttons change to Align Left, Center Horizontally, and Center Right to reflect the alignment choices for vertical text.

To change the orientation of text, click in the cell or select a range of cells and click the Change Text Direction button on the Tables and Borders toolbar. This button acts a toggle, changing the text from horizontal to vertical left and vertical right.

Splitting and Merging Cells

Sometimes you might want to merge cells together or split a cell into multiple cells. To merge cells into a single cell, first select the cells to be merged. Then on the Tables and Borders toolbar, click the Merge Cells button. Or choose Table, Merge Cells. Word will automatically merge the cells.

To split cells, first click in a cell to select it or select a range of cells. Then on the Tables and Borders toolbar, click the Split Cells button. Or choose Table, Split Cells from the menu. Word displays the Split Cells dialog box shown in Figure 14.15.

Figure 14.15
Use the Split Cells dialog box to split one or more cells into additional cells.

Use the Number of Rows and Number of Columns controls to specify the number of rows and columns to create. Place a check in the Merge Cells Before Split check box if you want Word to merge together a selected range of cells before splitting them into the specified number of cells. Choose OK when you're ready to split the cells.

Controlling Tables Across Multiple Pages

Word offers a few handy options for controlling the way long tables flow onto multiple pages. The following sections describe those options.

Repeat Column Headings Across Pages   If you use column headings in a lengthy table, you probably want them to appear in the first row on each page of the table. All you have to do is specify the row to use as the table headings and Word takes care of the rest. Any changes you make to the headings are applied on each page.

To apply the headings, first select the row you want to use as the column headings. Then choose Table, Headings. Word automatically applies the headings to each page of the table.

Controlling Breaks Across Pages   Word determines where a table will break to the next page. You can, however, force the table to break at a specific location. Just click in any cell of the row you want placed on the next page, then press Ctrl+Enter. Word will move the row and its following rows to the next page. To prevent a row from breaking to the next page, choose Table, Cell Height and Width to open the Cell Height and Width dialog box (see Figure 14.16). Clear the Allow Row to Break Across Pages check box, then choose OK.

> **CAUTION**
>
> Inserting a table break causes headers on subsequent pages to be lost. You can insert a separate header table in Header/Footer view to compensate for the lost headers.

Figure 14.16

Use the Cell Height and Width dialog box to prevent rows from breaking across pages and to set column and row width and height.

Sorting

The ability to sort a table is particularly useful when you have imported data into a large table. If the original data was not sorted, or you want to use a different sort method, Word will take care of the task for you.

You can sort using a single set of criteria or multiple criteria. You need only select one column to perform the sort on the whole table. For example, if the table contains a list of first and last names for a group of people, you need only select the last-name column to sort the table. Word will keep the correct first names associated with the last names, because it sorts the rows, not the individual cells in the rows.

The options available to you when you sort a table depend on how much of the table you select. If you want the most options for sorting the table, just click in a cell to select the table. If you want to sort using a specific column only, select the column. Then, choose Table, Sort to open the Sort dialog box (see Figure 14.17).

Figure 14.17

Use the Sort dialog box to specify options when sorting a table.

If you did not select a column prior to opening the Sort dialog box, the Sort By drop-down list will include all of the columns in the table, allowing you to select any column as the sort key. If you selected a column prior to opening the Sort dialog box, that column will be the only one listed in the drop-down list. Select the column on which you want the sort operation to be based, choose Ascending or Descending according to your desired outcome, then choose OK.

You also can sort the table based on multiple criteria. Assume, for example, that your table contains an address list with first and last names in separate columns with other address information in other columns. Also assume that you want to sort the table by last name, but also want the first names to be in order within each last-name group. Bob Johnson, for example, should come before Karen Johnson.

To sort using multiple criteria, click in the table and then choose Table, Sort. In the Sort dialog box, select from the Sort By drop-down list the column you want to use as the primary criteria. Choose from the Then By list the criteria for the secondary sort operation. For example, you might select Last Name as the primary criteria and First Name as the secondary criteria. Choose OK to sort the table.

You can set two options when sorting a table. Choose Options on the Sort dialog box to view the Sort Options dialog box (see Figure 14.18). To make the sort case sensitive, choose the Case Sensitive option button. You can specify the language Word will use for the sort operation by selecting the language from the Sorting Language drop-down list.

 TIP The Separate Fields At section of the Sort Options dialog box is applicable only to sorting data in delimited text.

Figure 14.18
Choose a language and specify whether the sort is case sensitive using the Sort Options dialog box.

Using Formulas

In addition to placing text and graphics in a table, you also can use formulas to perform calculations. The calculations are not limited to the cell in which the formula is contained, but instead can reference other cells in the table or data marked in the document with a bookmark. Word uses field codes to create the formulas. This section of the chapter explains how to use formulas, beginning with an overview of cell referencing.

▶ **See** "Using Field Codes to Create Dynamic Content," **page 256**

Part
II

Ch
14

Understanding Cell References

In Word, you reference a cell by combining the column and row with a colon, with A:1, for example, referencing the first cell in the upper-left corner of the table. When used in a formula, the cell reference is enclosed in parentheses. The following Formula field code sums a range of cells (note that you do not type the brackets {}, but instead Word inserts these for you automatically):

`{=SUM(A1:A4)}`

N O T E   Field codes are turned off by default. You can turn on field codes by choosing Tools, Options, and checking the Field Codes option on the View property page. ■

In this example, the field code must be located within the table because no other information is included to identify the table itself, but just the range within it. Use bookmarks to reference tables elsewhere in the document. The following example sums a range of cells in two different tables, then subtracts them:

`{=(SUM(Sales B2:B7))-(SUM(Expense C1:C29))}`

You also can reference an entire row or column. To reference a column, use its column letter twice, separated by a colon. The reference A:A, for example, identifies the entire column A. The reference 4:4 would identify all of row 4. You can use multiple cell references, as well. The following example averages rows 2 and 4:

`{=AVERAGE(2:2,4:4)}`

Defining Formulas

You can insert a formula in a table cell by simply inserting a field code in the cell, but Word offers a slightly easier method. Click in the cell in which you want the formula placed, then choose Table, Formula to display the Formula dialog box (see Figure 14.19).

Figure 14.19

Use the Formula dialog box to insert a formula in a table cell.

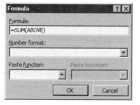

Type the desired formula in the Formula text box. If you aren't sure which functions you can use in your formulas, click the Paste Function drop-down list to view a list of available functions.

From the Number Format drop-down list, choose the format you want to apply to the results of the calculation. If you have bookmarks defined in the document, you can use them in calculations as well. The Paste Bookmark drop-down list contains all of the bookmarks defined in the document. When you're ready to apply the formula to the cell, choose OK.

▶ **See** "Performing Calculations with Field Codes," **page 263**

Creating a Chart from a Table

You can easily create a chart in Word using a table as the basis for the chart. To create the chart, first select the cells in the table that you want included in the chart. If the entire table contains chart information, click in the chart and then choose Table, Select Table to select the entire table. If you want the chart to have axis labels, make sure the table has column and row labels and include those in the selection.

After you have selected the chart or range of cells, choose Insert, Object. In the Object property sheet (see Figure 14.20) select Microsoft Graph 97 Chart from the Create New list. Make sure you place a check in the Float Over Text check box, and then choose OK. Word uses the data in the table as the basis for the chart, placing the chart in the document.

 TIP For better control over the placement of the chart in the document after you insert the chart, make sure the Float Over Text check box is selected. If this check box is cleared, Word inserts the chart in the document directly after the table and you'll have less flexibility in moving the chart on the page.

If the table includes column headings, those column headings appear as the X-axis labels for the chart. Row column headings, if any, are used as the chart legend. Figure 14.20 shows a simple chart created from a table in Word.

Figure 14.20

Word can quickly create 3-D charts from the data in a table.

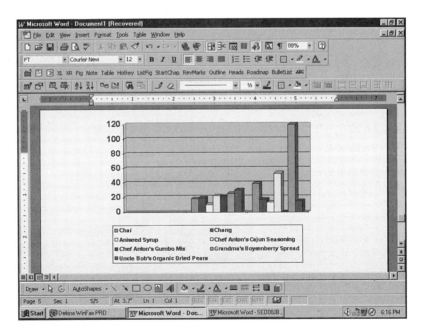

You can drag the chart on the page to relocate it as necessary. You also can change the content of the chart without changing the table data from which it was created. Double-click the chart to edit it. The Standard toolbar and menus change in Word as Microsoft Chart 97 becomes active. To change values in the chart, choose View, Datasheet. Word displays a data sheet similar to the one shown in Figure 14.21. As you can see, the datasheet is a simple spreadsheet. Use it to change the labels and other values on which the chart is based.

Figure 14.21
You can edit the contents of the chart using a data sheet that functions much like Excel.

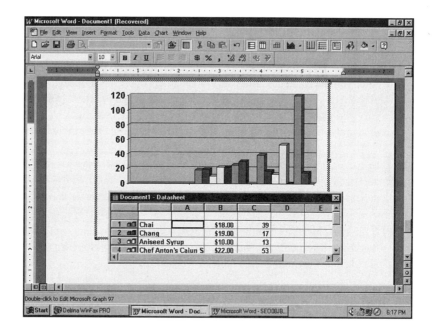

To change the chart type, choose Chart, Chart Type to display the Chart Type property sheet shown in Figure 14.22. Choose a chart type and click OK.

Figure 14.22
You can choose from many different types of charts to change the chart's appearance.

To control other chart options, choose Chart, Chart Options to display the Chart Options property sheet shown in Figure 14.23. The options on each of the tabbed property pages are generally self-explanatory.

▶ **See** "Advanced Formatting and Charting," **page 411**

Figure 14.23

You can control a wide variety of options to fine-tune the appearance and content of the chart.

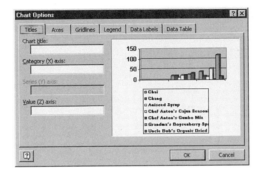

CHAPTER 15

Merging Documents

by Jim Boyce

In this chapter

Overview of New Features

Word 97 offers a few new features to make merging documents even easier. This section of the chapter provides a brief overview of these new features and enhancements.

Envelope and Label Wizards

Previous versions of Word enabled you to create envelopes and labels through commands in the Tools menu. Word 97 provides a new Label Wizard to step you through the process of creating labels. Word also provides an Envelope Wizard to help you set up and print envelopes. You get to these wizards just as you do to any new document—by choosing File, New.

Creating Custom Labels

You can create custom labels and save them by name for use later as the basis for other labels. The custom labels appear in the same list as Word's predefined labels (see Figure 15.1). In addition, Word 6.0 did not offer the capability to change the page size for a page of labels. Word 97 adds this capability, giving you even better control of size and placement of labels.

Figure 15.1

Word 97 enables you to create and save custom label definitions, and you can use existing label definitions as the basis for your custom labels.

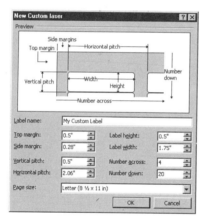

Merging Outlook and Word

Because integration is a theme throughout Office 97, you should expect to see integration between Outlook—the messaging and Personal Information Manager (PIM) included with Office 97—and Word. Word enables you to use the Outlook Contacts and Personal Address Book to import addresses and other information for addressing letters and creating mail-merge documents.

▶ **See** "Maintaining a Contact List," **page 789**

Merging Documents

In its simplest form, *merging* means bringing information from another application and incorporating that information into a Word document.

One form of document merging is bringing one document, or a portion thereof, into another document. You can achieve this in a few ways, depending on the type of document from which you are merging data and on whether you want to import the entire document. The following section briefly explains how to copy only part of a Word document to another.

Copying Between Word Documents

You can copy a portion of one Word document to another through the Clipboard. To do so, follow these steps:

1. Open the source document and the destination document.
2. In the destination document, locate the insertion point where you want the other data to be inserted.
3. Press Ctrl+F6 to switch to the source document.
4. Select the information that you want to place in the other document.
5. Choose Edit, Copy (or press Ctrl+C) to copy the data to the Clipboard.
6. Press Ctrl+F6 to switch to the destination document.
7. Choose Edit, Paste (or press Ctrl+V) to copy the data into the document from the Clipboard.

Instead of copying the data into the destination document, you can link the data. Rather than placing the data in the destination document, linking places a reference to the data in the document instead. As the source document changes, the link in the destination document also changes, showing you the most up-to-date copy of the data. Use these steps to link data:

1. Open the source document and the destination document.
2. In the destination document, locate the insertion point where you want the other data to be inserted.
3. Press Ctrl+F6 to switch to the source document.
4. Select the information that you want to place in the other document.
5. Choose Edit, Copy (or press Ctrl+C) to copy the data to the Clipboard.
6. Press Ctrl+F6 to switch to the destination document.
7. Choose Edit, Paste Special to view the Paste Special dialog box (see Figure 15.2).
8. Choose the Paste Link option button.
9. Choose Formatted Text (RTF) from the As list; then choose OK.

Word inserts the data as the result of a field code. To update the data in the destination document after the source document changes, just update the field code. To do so, click the field code and press F9. Select the entire document and press F9 to update all fields in the document.

Figure 15.2

Use the Paste Special dialog box to link data into Word.

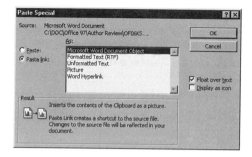

▶ **See** "Using Field Codes to Create Dynamic Content," **page 256**

N O T E   You can insert the text into the destination document as unformatted text by choosing the Unformatted Text option from the As list. To retain character and table formatting, make sure to choose the Formatted Text (RTF) option. You also can use the Microsoft Word Document Object to insert the data and retain its formatting. Using this option causes Word to insert the data in a format that enables you to double-click the data to edit it. This option is helpful for inserting or linking large bodies of text into the document. ■

Through Word 97's new support for hyperlinks, you also can insert links to a portion of a document. Choose the Word HyperLink option in the Paste Special dialog box to insert a link to the data. Or, choose Edit, Paste as Hyperlink.

Inserting One Word Document into Another

Sometimes, you want to insert or link an entire document into another. The process is simple. Follow these steps:

1. Open the destination document and place the insertion point where you want the other document to be inserted.

2. Choose Insert, File to display the Insert File dialog box (a standard Word Open dialog box).

3. Locate and select the file that you want to insert.

4. If you want to link the file instead of inserting it, place a check in the Link to File check box.

5. Choose OK to insert or link the selected document into the current document.

▶ **See** "Using Master Documents," **page 1022**

Using Mail Merge

The term *mail merge* typically is used to describe the process of merging some form of address database with a form letter to create a group of individualized letters. You may want to send out a promotional offer, for example, but personalize each letter with the recipient's name, address, and other personal information. Mail merge allows you to do just that.

Although mail merge is designed to help you create these personalized form letters, you can use mail merge to merge any kind of data with any other kind of document to individualize the documents. This chapter explains how to use the mail-merge features in Word to merge data from Word, Access, and Outlook into a Word document.

Mail merge in Word consists of a few common steps, regardless of what type of data source you use. When the process is complete, you have a single document containing all the personalized documents and can print all the documents in a single operation. Alternatively, you can print individual documents in the set by printing only those pages or sections of the document that are relevant.

The following list summarizes the steps involved in performing a mail-merge operation:

- *Create the main document.* The first step is creating the main document that is used as the basis for your personalized documents. In the case of a form letter, for example, you first create the form letter.

- *Create the data source.* The next step is creating the external data source from which the names, addresses, or other information will come. You may already have this step completed if you are bringing information from Outlook or an Access database (if you've already created the address book or database, for example).

- *Define merge fields in the main document.* Next, you define merge fields in the main document. These fields tell Word where to insert specific data items from the data source. In a form letter, for example, you define merge fields for the first name, last name, address, and other information that appears in the address and salutation of the letter.

- *Merge the data with the main document.* When the main document and data source are ready, you can merge the two. The result is a single document containing all the personalized documents, with page breaks separating one document from another.

- *Print the document.* Because all the personalized documents are placed in a single document file, you can print all the documents in one operation just as you would any other type of document. Alternatively, you can select individual pages or sections for printing.

Types of Documents You Can Create

The main document in a mail-merge operation is the one that contains the boilerplate text and graphics, which are the same in all the resulting documents. In the case of a form letter, for example, the form letter itself is the main document. You then personalize the main document by using information from the data source, which may be another Word document, an Excel document, an Access database, or your Outlook contact list.

Word helps you create four types of main documents for a mail merge:

- *Form letter.* When you opt to create a form letter, Word merges the main document and the data source to create a single document that contains all the personalized letters, with each letter in its own section. You then can modify each section separately, if you want, and print an individual letter simply by printing only its section. Print the entire document to print all the letters.

- *Envelopes*. Word automates the process of creating envelopes, enabling you to specify the envelope type, print options, and other variables. The resulting merged document contains all the envelopes, each in its own section.

- *Labels*. Word allows you to specify the type of label (size, number per page, and so on) and then creates a main document consisting of a page of labels. Each label cell contains the fields necessary to insert the address information that you specify. The resulting merged document contains multiple pages of labels, all in one section.

- *Catalog*. A catalog is much like a form letter, with one major exception: The resulting merged document contains all the data in one section, rather than individual sections. In other words, you create a single document from the data source, rather than one document per record. You can use this option to create membership lists, for example.

Using Different Data Sources

Word enables you to use several sources for mail-merge data. The following sections provide an overview of using Word, Access and Outlook as data sources.

Using Word as a Data Source   To use a Word document as the source for the data that gets merged into another document, set up the Word source document by using columns, with each column representing a specific field (last name, first name, address, and so on). Each row represents a record. In the case of addresses, for example, each row represents all the information for one person's address. Figure 15.3 shows an example of a Word table used to store addresses.

Figure 15.3

Use tables to simplify the process of creating mail-merge source documents in Word.

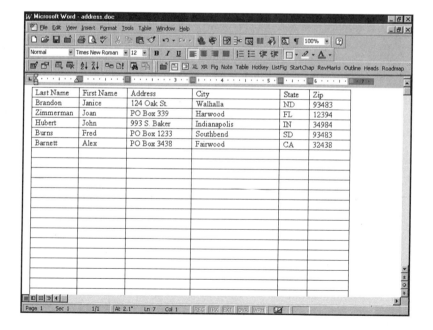

Last Name	First Name	Address	City	State	Zip
Brandon	Janice	124 Oak St.	Walhalla	ND	93483
Zimmerman	Joan	PO Box 339	Harwood	FL	12394
Hubert	John	993 S. Baker	Indianapolis	IN	34984
Burns	Fred	PO Box 1233	Southbend	SD	93483
Barnett	Alex	PO Box 3438	Fairwood	CA	32438

You can set up the Word source document by using tabs to separate the fields, but you also can use a table. Because Word offers several features for editing and sorting tables, you should consider using a table whenever you want to create a mail-merge source document in Word.

Using Access as a Data Source   You can use Microsoft Query, dBASE, FoxPro, and Access databases as a source of mail-merge data.

Before you can use Access as a data source, you have to create a database that contains the information you want to import. You may have a product database that you want to use to generate a promotional flier, for example. Each record in the database may have a field called Sale, which specifies whether the item is on sale at the current time, and another field called SalePrice, which specifies the sale price. You could then perform a mail merge and import information from only the records that were currently on sale to generate your sales flier.

When you import data from Access, you open the Access data table from which you want the data to come and then specify which record fields to merge into the document.

▶ **See** "Using Lists and Databases," **page 433**

Using Outlook or Exchange as a Data Source   You can use Outlook as a data source to import contact information, such as names, address, and phone numbers. To use Outlook as the data source, you first must enter the contact information in Outlook. If you are using Outlook to maintain your contact addresses, the work of creating the addresses is already done.

If you are using Exchange (Windows Messaging) as your e-mail program, you can import source data from your Personal Address Book. The process is virtually the same as for importing data from Outlook, so this chapter focuses on using Outlook.

Creating a Form Letter

You probably are familiar with form letters. Sweepstakes letters are a good example of form letters. These letters are mailed out to millions of people and contain the same information except for the address, salutation, and occasionally a few other details in the letter.

Creating a form letter by using Word is a relatively simple process. The first step is writing the body of the letter, containing all the text and graphics that you want to be included in every letter. Then you insert merge fields into the letter. These merge fields include the name and address for the address section of the letter, the addressee's name in the salutation, and sometimes other information that changes from one letter to another. When you merge the documents, Word fills in each merge field, using data from the data source to create personalized letters.

Follow these steps to create and mail-merge a form letter in Word:

1. Begin a new document, and type the body of the letter and all other text and graphics that you want to be included in each letter (see Figure 15.4).

Figure 15.4

The main document includes all the text that you want to be printed in each letter.

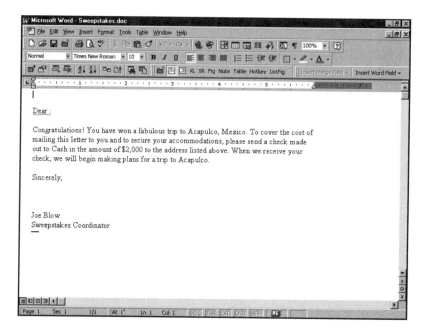

2. Create the data source, if it does not already exist. This means creating a Word or Excel document, Access database, Outlook contact list, or other data-source document supported by Word.

3. With the main document open, choose Tools, Mail Merge to open the Mail Merge Helper dialog box (see Figure 15.5).

Figure 15.5

The Mail Merge Helper dialog box steps you through the process of creating a mail-merge document.

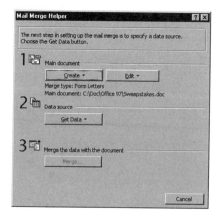

4. Choose Create, Form Letters. A simple dialog box with two options appears.

5. In this example, you have already opened the main document, so choose Active Window. If you want to start a new document to be the main document, choose New Main Document and type the letter's body text.

Part

II

Ch

15

6. Choose Get Data; then choose from the drop-down list the source for the data that you will be importing into Word (see Figure 15.6).

You can create a new data source, open an existing source, specify header options, or use an address book. This example uses Outlook, so choose Use Address Book.

Figure 15.6

Specify whether you want to create a data-source document or work with an existing data source.

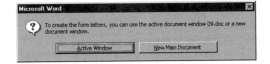

Word displays the Use Address Book dialog box (see Figure 15.7).

Figure 15.7

Choose the address book that you want to use as the source for the merged data.

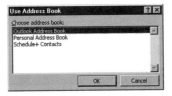

7. Choose the address book you want to use; then choose OK.

8. If you don't already have merge fields inserted into the main document, Word detects that fact and prompts you with a dialog box, asking you to edit the document to add the fields. The only option in the dialog box is Edit Main Document, so make that choice. Word switches to the main document and opens the Mail Merge toolbar.

9. Place the insertion point in the document where you want to insert the first field.

Place the insertion point where you want the address field to be located, for example.

10. From the Merge Field drop-down menu, choose the field that you want to insert.

To create the address, for example, choose First_Name, press the space bar, and open the drop-down list again to choose Last_Name. Press Enter and then choose Postal_Address from the Merge Field list.

11. Repeat step 10, inserting all the desired fields into the document. Figure 15.8 shows an address block defined with merge fields.

12. Choose Tools, Mail Merge to open the Mail Merge Helper dialog box.

13. Choose Merge. Word displays the Merge dialog box, shown in Figure 15.9.

Figure 15.8

This form letter contains an address block that will be filled in when the document is merged.

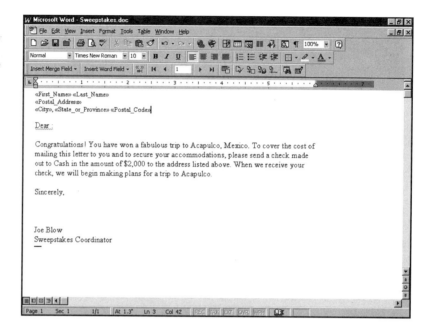

Figure 15.9

Use the Merge dialog box to specify options before performing the mail-merge operation.

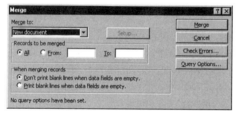

14. Specify the desired options (explained in the following bulleted list).

15. Choose <u>M</u>erge to merge the source data with the main document and create the new merged documents.

The following list explains the options in the Merge dialog box:

- *Merge To.* Use this drop-down list to choose New Document, Printer, or Electronic Mail, depending on what you want to do with the resulting merged document. Choose New Document if you want to save the merged document for editing. If you don't want to save the document, choose Printer to print it or Electronic Mail to send it to other people through your e-mail program.

- *Records to be Merged.* Use the controls in this group to specify which records (all or a range) to include in the merge.

- *When Merging Records*. The two options in this group determine whether Word ignores empty data fields. If you have some addresses with two lines and others with just one, for example, the records with only one address line include a blank second address-line field. You probably want Word to ignore the blank fields in most cases, which prevents those fields from being merged.

- *Check Errors*. Choose this button to configure the way that Word handles any errors that occur during the merge operation.

- *Query Options*. Choose this button to specify how Word filters the incoming data.

To specify how Word handles errors during the merge operation, click the Check Errors button to display the Checking and Reporting Errors dialog box (see Figure 15.10).

Figure 15.10

You can specify how Word handles any errors that occur during the merge operation.

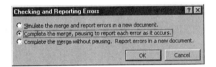

The following list explains the options in the Checking and Reporting Errors dialog box:

- *Simulate the Merge and Report Errors in a New Document*. Choose this option to test for errors before actually merging the documents. Word creates a new document containing a list of errors generated during the merge operation.

- *Complete the Merge, Pausing to Report Each Error As It Occurs*. Choose this option (the default) to have Word complete the merge operation and report any errors as they occur.

- *Complete the Merge Without Pausing. Report Errors in a New Document*. Choose this option to have Word perform the merge without pausing to report errors. Word creates a new document to contain the list of errors.

You can refine the way Word processes the incoming data by specifying query options. To do so, choose the Query Options button in the Merge dialog box to display the Query Options property sheet (see Figure 15.11).

Figure 15.11

You can use the Query Options property sheet to set query filters and other options that control the way that Word merges the documents.

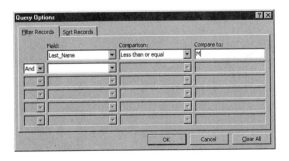

The Filters page, shown in Figure 15.11, enables you to filter out certain records based on criteria that you specify. You may want to merge only the records with last names ranging from A through M, for example. Choose Last_Name from the Field drop-down list, choose Less Than or Equal from the Comparison drop-down list, and then type M in the Compare To text box. You can specify multiple criteria by setting additional filters.

> **TIP** For more help with filters, press F1 to open the Office Assistant search dialog box and perform a search using **filters** as the keyword.

The Sort Records page of the Query Options property sheet (see Figure 15.12) allows you to sort the data as it is coming in to be merged. You may want to merge the document so that the letters are sorted by postal code for quicker mail processing, for example. From the Sort By drop-down list, choose the field on which to base the sort operation. Then specify either Ascending or Descending. You can specify multiple sort criteria by using the Then By and Then By drop-down lists.

Figure 15.12

Use the Sort Records page to sort the records before merging the document.

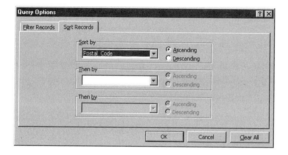

When you're satisfied with the filter and sort options, choose OK. Choose Merge in the Merge dialog box to merge the documents and create your personalized form letters.

Although this example uses Outlook as the source, the process of importing data from other sources (such as Access) is essentially the same. After you select the source document (and, in the case of Access, the desired data table), Word checks the selected source for all the available fields. These fields then become available from the Insert Merge Field drop-down list in the Mail Merge toolbar.

Creating Mailing Labels

The process of creating mailing labels is only slightly different from that of merging a form letter. One primary difference is that you must specify the size and type of label to use. The other difference is that instead of multiple documents separated by sections, Word creates multiple pages of labels, one record per label.

To create mailing labels, first make sure that you have created the address information on which the labels will be based. Then follow these steps:

1. Choose <u>T</u>ools, Mail Me<u>r</u>ge in Word to display the Mail Merge Helper dialog box.

2. Choose <u>C</u>reate, <u>M</u>ailing Labels on the Mail Merge Helper dialog box. Word prompts you to choose between the current document or creating a new main document.

3. Choose <u>A</u>ctive Window to create the labels in the active window, or choose <u>N</u>ew Main Document to start a new document for the labels.

4. Choose <u>G</u>et Data, and choose the desired source for the address data from the drop-down list.

    After you choose the data source, Word prompts you to set up the main document.

5. Click <u>S</u>etup to open the Label Options dialog box (see Figure 15.13).

Figure 15.13
Choose predefined labels or define your own by using the Label Options dialog box.

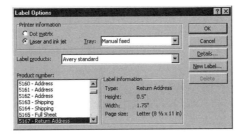

6. Click the <u>D</u>etails button to view the details for the label (see Figure 15.14).

7. If you want to create a new label, choose the <u>N</u>ew Label button. The resulting dialog box is essentially the same as the one shown in Figure 15.14.

Figure 15.14
You can view and change individual settings for the label to fine-tune it to your needs.

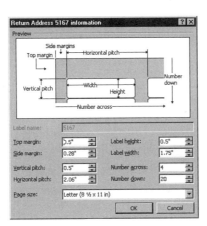

8. After you specify the label parameters, choose OK in the Label Options dialog box. Word opens the Create Labels dialog box, shown in Figure 15.15.

Part

II

Ch

15

Figure 15.15
Use the Create Labels dialog box to insert fields into the label.

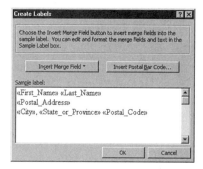

9. Choose the Insert Merge Field button to open a menu of available fields.
10. Select the field that you want to insert into the label.
11. Repeat Steps 9 and 10 to insert all the desired fields; then choose OK.
12. If you want to include a delivery bar code in the label, click the Insert Postal Bar Code button to display the Insert Postal Bar Code dialog box, shown in Figure 15.16.

Figure 15.16
You can insert delivery bar codes into your mail-merge labels and envelopes.

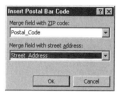

13. From the Merge Field with ZIP Code drop-down list, choose the field in the source data that contains the ZIP or postal code from which the delivery bar code should be generated.
14. From the Merge Field with Street Address drop-down list, choose the field in the source data that contains the street address; alternatively, leave this option blank.
15. Choose OK. Word creates a page of labels containing the necessary merge fields (see Figure 15.17).
16. Set any desired filter options (explained in the preceding section).
17. Choose Merge to open the Merge dialog box.
18. Set any other desired options.
19. Choose Merge to merge the data.

Figure 15.17

Word creates a page of labels that contain the specified merge fields.

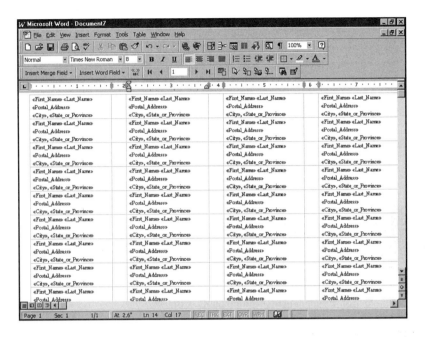

 TROUBLESHOOTING

The lines of each label are too far apart. How do I set the spacing between lines? Word uses the paragraph settings from the paragraph in which the insertion point is located when you start the process of creating the labels. So between steps 4 and 5 of the preceding example, set the paragraph-formatting options accordingly. You also can set the formatting after you create the labels, but setting it beforehand is easier, because you have only one paragraph to set.

Creating Envelopes

You create envelopes in much the same way that you create a mailing list. The only real difference is that you specify the type of envelope to use, rather than the type of label. To create mail-merge envelopes, choose Tools, Mail Merge to display the Mail Merge Helper dialog box. Choose Create, Envelopes. Use the process described in the preceding section for creating mail labels, except that in step 6, you specify the envelope settings rather than label settings. The remainder of the process is essentially the same.

Creating a Catalog

Unlike a form letter that, when merged, results in multiple documents with each document in its own section, a catalog results in a single document within one section. In a form letter, the data records are merged one to a document; in a catalog, all data records are merged into the same document. The catalog mail-merge option is useful for creating mailing lists, membership lists, product lists, and any other type of list in which you want to import data from another source into a single document.

The primary thing to remember when you are creating a catalog is that any boilerplate text that you type in the document is duplicated within the document for each record. You probably want to perform the merge first to insert the list and then edit the document to add any other text or graphics to it.

Using Other Field Codes

You may have noticed that the Mail Merge toolbar includes a menu labeled Insert Word Field. You can use this menu to insert various other Word field codes, to customize the outcome of the merge process. For additional information regarding the use of field codes, refer to Chapter 13, "Fields, Forms, and Dynamic Content."

▶ **See** "Using Field Codes to Create Dynamic Content," **page 256**

CHAPTER 16

Customizing Word

by Jim Boyce

In this chapter

Setting View Options

Word enables you to set a variety of options that determine the types of document elements that Word displays, which nonprinting characters to show, and which Word interface elements to show. To set these options, choose Tools, Options and then click the View tab to display the View page of the Options property sheet, shown in Figure 16.1. Note that the options that appear in the View property page vary slightly according to the type of document view you are using (Normal, Page Layout, and so on). All of the available commands for all modes are described later in this section.

Figure 16.1

Use the View page to control the document elements and interface components that Word displays.

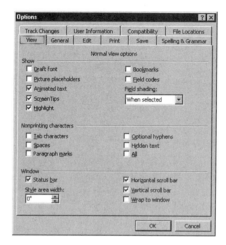

The controls in the Show group specify whether Word displays certain document elements. These controls enable you to turn on and off the display of these elements. The following list describes all the controls that can appear in the Show group:

- *Draft Font*. This check box causes Word to display most formatted text as underlined or bold, with graphics shown as empty boxes. Use this option to speed up display updating with heavily formatted documents.

- *Drawings*. This check box determines whether Word displays objects that you draw in a document by using the Drawing toolbar. You can clear this check box to hide drawing objects and improve the speed at which you scroll through documents that contain many drawings. Place a check in this box to have Word display the drawing objects.

- *Object Anchors*. Object anchors lock objects, such as pictures, to a paragraph. Anchors are represented in the document by small anchor icons. To view these anchors, place a check in this check box. Clear this check box to hide the anchors. You also can view anchors by clicking the Show/Hide button in the Standard toolbar.

- *Text Boundaries*. When this option is selected (checked), Word displays dotted lines to indicate page margins, text-column boundaries, and objects. You can think of these lines as being layout lines that help you view the boundaries of these objects. Clear this check box to turn off text boundary lines.

- *Picture Placeholders*. Documents that contain several pictures can display slowly on some computers. Place a check in this box to display a box in place of the image. The box acts as a placeholder for the image.

- *Animated Text*. When this box is checked, Word displays animated text, according to its animation formatting. Blinking text, for example, blinks onscreen. Clear this check box if you want to see how animated text appears when printed.

- *Screen Tips*. This setting applies to documents that have been edited with revision marks. If this option is turned on and you allow the mouse pointer to hover over a comment reference mark or text that has been modified by revision marks, Word will display a pop-up box containing the reviewer's comments.

- *Highlight*. You can highlight text in a document, changing the background color of the text. Changing this color is similar to highlighting text on a printed page by using a highlighter pen. Place a check in this box to view highlighting, and clear the box to turn off display of highlighting. Turning off display of highlighting does not remove the highlighting from the text.

- *Bookmarks*. Place a check in this box to have Word display bookmarks in the document. Bookmarks are displayed inside brackets [ ]. These bookmark indicators appear in the document but do not print, even when this option is turned on.

- *Field Codes*. Enable this check box to turn on the display of field codes, and clear the check box to hide field codes. You can achieve the same result by pressing Alt+F9.

- *Field Shading*. This drop-down list determines how Word shades field-code results. The default, when selected, causes Word to shade a field onscreen only when you place the insertion point inside the field. Choose Always if you want the field-code results to be shaded even when they are not selected. Choose Never if you don't want the field-code results to be shaded.

Word uses several nonprinting characters to represent characters in the document that do not print. An example is the paragraph mark that you insert at the end of a paragraph when you press Enter. Sometimes, you must view these nonprinting characters to help you format a document or determine why a document is not formatting the way that you expect it to.

The following list describes the check boxes in the Nonprinting Characters group of the View property page:

- *Tab Characters*. Tabs normally display as white space in the document. Place a check in this box if you want to view the tab character, which appears as a right arrow.

- *Spaces*. Spaces normally appear in a document as white space. Place a check in this box to view spaces as dots.

- *Paragraph Marks*. Placing a check in this box causes Word to display a special character to indicate the new line character (which you insert by pressing Shift+Enter) and paragraph marks (which you insert by pressing Enter).

- *Optional Hyphens*. Word can automatically hyphenate a document to break words at the end of lines, which is particularly useful in paragraphs that use justified alignment. You also can insert optional hyphens by pressing Ctrl+hyphen (-). These hyphens, which are hidden text, break the word only if it falls at the end of a line. Place a check in this box if you want Word to display the optional hyphen characters instead of hiding them.

- *Hidden Text.* You can format text in a document as hidden text. Hidden text normally does not appear in a document (thus, its name). Place a check in this box to view hidden text as dotted-underline text.

- *All.* Place a check in this box to turn on the display of all hidden and nonprinting characters. You also can click the Show/Hide button in the Standard toolbar to display all hidden and nonprinting characters.

The Window control group provides several controls that you can use to define the way the elements that appear as part of the Word document interface. These options vary slightly depending on the view mode you are using. The following list describes all options that can appear in the Window group:

- *Status bar.* Place a check in this box to turn on the Word status bar that provides page, section, line, column, and other information at the bottom of the Word document area.

- *Style area width.* Use this control to specify the width of a scrap area at the left edge of the display to show the name of the style assigned to each paragraph.

- *Vertical ruler.* Place a check in this box to turn on a vertical ruler for the document area.

- *Horizontal scroll bar.* Place a check in this box to turn on a horizontal scroll bar for the document area.

- *Vertical scroll bar.* Place a check in this box to turn on a vertical scroll bar for the document area.

- *Wrap to window.* Place a check in this box to have the text wrap to the width of the window in Online Layout mode.

- *Enlarge fonts less than.* Use this control to have Word automatically enlarge in the document any text with a font size smaller than the specified size. This control appears only in Online Layout mode.

Setting General Options

Word offers several settings that allow you to control a variety of general options that determine how Word functions. To view and change these settings, choose Tools, Options and click the General property page of the Options property sheet (see Figure 16.2).

The following list describes the settings in the General Options property page:

- *Background Repagination.* With this option checked, Word automatically repaginates the document as you work. Generally, background repagination does not affect performance, except on slow computers with large documents. This setting does not affect repagination in Page Layout view, and this control is dimmed when in Page Layout view.

- *Help for WordPerfect Users.* When this option is checked, Word displays instructions or demonstrates an example of performing a task in Word when you press a WordPerfect for DOS key combination.

Figure 16.2

The General property page contains several controls that specify a variety of general settings to control the way that Word functions.

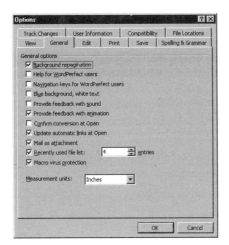

- *Navigation Keys for WordPerfect Users.* Placing a check in this check box causes Word to change the behavior of the PgUp, PgDn, Home, End, and Esc keys to match the behavior of these keys in WordPerfect.

- *Blue Background, White Text.* Choose this option if you want Word to display the document using white text on a blue background rather than black text on a white background. The white-on-blue option resembles the standard WordPerfect for DOS screen colors.

- *Provide Feedback with Sound.* Word can emphasize certain events, such as the completion of a task, by playing a sound. If your computer contains a sound card, placing a check in this box turns on those sound notifications. You can set individual sounds through the Sounds object in the Control Panel.

- *Provide Feedback with Animation.* With this option checked, Word animates the mouse pointer and other Word interface elements to indicate when tasks are being performed (such as printing and saving a document). Clear this check box to turn off animation.

- *Confirm Conversion at Open.* Word can automatically detect document types and convert them to Word format when you attempt to open a file that is not a Word document. Enable this check box if you want Word to choose a converter automatically. Clear this check box if you want Word to prompt you to choose a converter.

- *Update Automatic Links at Open.* With this check box selected, Word automatically attempts to update all links in a document when you open the document. Clear this check box if you don't want Word to update the links automatically. You then can direct Word to update the links whenever you desire.

- *Mail As Attachment.* When this option is checked and you choose File, Send To, Mail Recipient, Word attaches the current document to the resulting e-mail message as an attachment. Clear this check box if you want Word to insert the current document into the message as text instead.

- *Recently Used File List /Entries.* Place a check in the Recently Used File List to have Word list the most recently used (MRU) document files in the File menu. Use the

Entries spin control to specify the number of MRU documents to appear in the menu (1 to 9).

■ *Macro Virus Protection*. Word documents can contain macros, customized toolbars, menus, and shortcuts. Macros can be designed to run automatically when the document opens, which means that macros can act as viruses, performing unwanted actions on your computer and files. Place a check in this check box if you want Word to warn you when you open a document that contains macros or other custom elements. You then have the option of opening the document without loading the macros.

■ *Measurement Units*. Use this control to specify the default unit of measure. Choose inches, centimeters, points, or picas.

Setting Editing Options

You can set several options that control the way that Word handles text selection, text insertion, graphics editing, and other common document editing tasks. To set these options, choose Tools, Options and then click the Edit tab to display the Edit property page, shown in Figure 16.3.

Figure 16.3
Use the Edit page to specify how Word handles common document-editing tasks.

The following list explains the options in the Edit property page:

■ *Typing Replaces Selection*. If you select text and begin typing, the new text that you type replaces the selected text. If you want the new text to be inserted in front of the selected text, clear this check box.

■ *Drag-and-Drop Text Editing*. With this option selected, you can select text and move it around in the document by using the mouse. If you have a problem accidentally moving text when you select it, clear this check box to turn off this feature.

■ *When Selecting, Automatically Select Entire Word*. With this option checked, Word automatically selects the entire word when you select (with the mouse) a portion of the word, the following space, and part of the next word. Turning on this feature makes selecting text a little easier, particularly when the text is located at the left edge of the document.

■ *Use the INS Key for Paste.* This option is off by default; turning it on causes Word to paste from the Clipboard when you press the Ins key.

■ *Overtype Mode.* When overtype mode is turned on, new text that you type replaces the text to the right of the insertion point. You can turn this feature on and off by double-clicking the OVR button in the status bar.

■ *Use Smart Cut and Paste.* With this item selected, Word removes extra spaces when you delete text and adds spaces when you insert text from the Clipboard. Clear this check box to prevent Word from adding or removing spaces during a cut or paste operation.

■ *Tabs and Backspace Set Left Indent.* When this option is turned on, you can place the insertion point at the beginning of an indented paragraph and press Tab to increase the indent or press Backspace to decrease the indent. With this option turned off, these keys act as Tab and Backspace.

■ *Allow Accented Uppercase in French.* This option applies to text that you format as French (set the language property of the text to French). With the option selected, the Word spell checker prompts you to suggest accent marks for uppercase letters. Clear this check box if you don't want Word to suggest accent marks.

■ *Picture Editor.* Use this drop-down list to choose Microsoft Photo Editor or Microsoft Word as the application to use when you double-click an image to edit it.

Setting Print Options

The Print page of the Options property sheet (see Figure 16.4) allows you to specify settings that control the way that Word prints documents. To display this page, choose Tools, Options and click the Print tab.

Figure 16.4

Set printing options with the Print property page.

The Print options are separated into four groups. The Printing Options group allows you to specify several options that control the way that Word prints. These options are explained in the following list:

- *Draft Output.* Some printers support a special draft mode that doesn't print some document-formatting characteristics, to provide faster printing. Choose this option if you want to print in draft mode.

- *Update Fields.* Choose this option if you want Word to update field codes in the document automatically before printing the document.

- *Update Links.* Choose this option if you want Word to automatically update all links in the document before printing the document.

- *Allow A4/Letter Paper Resizing.* Place a check in this box if you want Word to automatically reformat documents formatted for A4 to letter, and vice versa, when the document is printed. This option affects only the formatting in the printed page, not the formatting in the document.

- *Background Printing.* With this option (the default) selected, Word prints documents in the background, enabling you to continue working on the document while it prints. Background printing uses additional memory and can slow the print process. For fastest printing when you don't need to continue working on the document, clear this check box.

- *Print PostScript over Text.* This setting applies only to Word for Macintosh documents. Choose this setting to print Word for Macintosh files that contain watermarks or other PostScript code.

- *Reverse Print Order.* Choose this option if you want Word to print the document beginning with the last page and working to the first page.

The settings in the Include with Document group of the Print property page allow you to control which document elements print and which do not. Generally, you want to print text and graphics and to omit hidden text and other support elements. Being able to print these normally hidden objects is necessary sometimes. The following list explains the elements that you can turn on or off for printing through the Include with Document group:

- *Document Properties.* Choose this check box to include the author's name, document-editing time, file size, filename, title, and other information from the Summary page of the document's properties (choose File, Properties to view document properties). Word prints the information on a separate sheet at the end of the print job.

- *Field Codes.* Choose this option if you want Word to print field codes instead of field-code results.

- *Comments.* Choose this option to print comments that have been inserted into the document through revision marks. Word prints the comments beginning with a new page at the end of the document.

- *Hidden Text.* Choose this option if you want hidden text in the document to be printed. Hidden text appears on the screen with a dotted underline, but this underline is omitted from the printed text.

■ *Drawing Objects.* Choose this option to have Word print drawing objects (objects that you insert by using the drawing tools in the Drawing toolbar). Word prints an empty box as a placeholder for each drawing object.

The Print Data Only for Forms option in the Print page allows you to control the way that Word prints forms that you created using form fields. With this option selected, Word prints the data entered in the form fields but does not print the rest of the form. This option is handy for extracting the form data from the form.

 TIP Turn on this option and print to a text file to extract data from a form to a text file.

The Default Tray drop-down list allows you to specify which printer tray to use by default.

Setting File Open and Save Options

The Save property page (see Figure 16.5) contains settings that allow you to specify the way that Word handles saving a document. You also can specify how Word is to handle automatic features related to saving documents, such as automatically saving a document after a certain period.

Figure 16.5
Use the Save page to define how Word handles document-saving tasks.

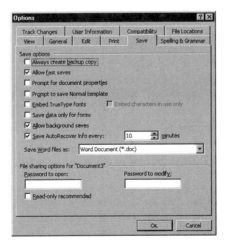

The following list describes the controls in the Save property page:

■ *Always Create Backup Copy.* Place a check in this box to have Word make a backup copy of the current document file before saving the changes from the current editing session. Word names the backup file *DOC.BAK*, in which *DOC* is the name of the current file. If you open BARNEY.DOC, for example, and then make changes and save the file, Word renames BARNEY.DOC as BARNEY.BAK and saves the changes in BARNEY.DOC. You can restore the preceding file by opening BARNEY.BAK and saving it as a document file (or simply renaming the .BAK file as a .DOC file).

■ *Allow Fast Saves.* With this check box selected, Word saves only changes in the document file, rather than resaving the entire file. Turning on this option can reduce save time when you are working on a large document. You should turn off this feature and perform a full save when you finish working on the document, however. Unless you are working with a large document, leave this option turned off to ensure that Word saves the entire file each time you save.

■ *Prompt for Document Properties.* Enable this check box if you want Word to prompt you to fill in the document properties (author, title, and so on) each time you save the document.

■ *Prompt to Save Normal Template.* With this option selected, Word asks you when you exit Word whether you want it to save in NORMAL.DOT the default font, menu, toolbar, and other settings modified in the current session. If you clear this check box, Word saves these changes to NORMAL.DOT without prompting you.

■ *Embed TrueType Fonts.* Choose this option if you want Word to store in the document file any TrueType fonts used in the document. This option enables other people to view the document with those fonts, even if they don't have the fonts on their systems. Embedding TrueType fonts in a document increases the size of the document file.

■ *Save Data Only for Forms.* With this option checked, Word saves only the data from an on-screen form, placing the data in a tab-delimited text file.

■ *Allow Background Saves.* Choose this option to allow Word to save a document in the background while you continue to work on the document. Generally, this option has a noticeable effect only when you work with large documents.

■ *Save AutoRecover Info Every xx.* Place a check in this box to allow Word to automatically save the document to a special backup file. If the system or Word hangs, you can restart Word and have it automatically recover the document at the point of the last AutoRecover save.

■ *Save Word Files As.* Use this drop-down list to specify the file format Word that uses as the default file type for saving new documents.

■ *Password to Open.* Use this box to specify a password that a person must specify to open the file.

■ *Password to Modify.* Use this box to specify a password that a person must specify to modify the file.

■ *Read-only Recommended.* Place a check in this box to have Word suggest to anyone who opens the file that it be opened in read-only mode. If the person answers affirmatively, Word opens the document in read-only mode, preventing changes in the document.

Setting Spelling and Grammar Options

Word includes the capability to check the spelling and grammar in a document. The settings in the Spelling & Grammar property page (see Figure 16.6) determine how Word performs these spelling and grammar checks.

Figure 16.6

You can configure Word's capability to check the spelling and grammar in a document.

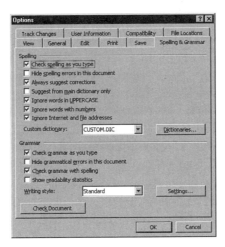

The following list describes the settings in the Spelling & Grammar property page that control Word's spell-checking features:

- *Check Spelling as You Type.* Enable this check box if you want Word to check your spelling as you type, underlining questionable words in red.

- *Hide Spelling Errors in This Document.* Choose this option to have Word ignore spelling errors in the current document.

- *Always Suggest Corrections.* If selected, this option causes Word to automatically display a list of suggested alternatives to misspelled words when Word performs a spell check. This setting does not apply to Word's Check Spelling As You Type option.

- *Suggest from Main Dictionary Only.* Choose this option to have Word suggest spelling alternatives only from the main dictionary. Clear this check box to have Word suggest spelling alternatives from all dictionaries.

- *Ignore Words in UPPERCASE.* Choose this option to have Word ignore words in upper-case when it performs a spelling check.

- *Ignore Words with Numbers.* Choose this option to have Word ignore words that contain numbers when it performs a spelling check.

- *Ignore Internet and File Addresses.* This option, when selected, causes Word to ignore Internet URLs, e-mail addresses, and file path names when it performs a spelling check.

- *Custom Dictionary.* Use this drop-down list to choose the current custom dictionary. When you direct Word to add a word to the dictionary during a spell check, Word adds it to the dictionary selected by this option.

- *Dictionaries.* Click this button to add, remove, or modify custom dictionaries. Use custom dictionaries to contain words that are not included in Word's default dictionary.

The settings in the Grammar group specify the way that Word handles grammar checking. The following list describes the settings in this group:

- *Check Grammar as You Type.* This option, when selected, causes Word to check for grammatical errors as you type. Grammatical errors are underlined with a wavy green line.

- *Hide Grammatical Errors in This Document.* Choose this option to have Word ignore grammatical errors in the current document.

- *Check Grammar with Spelling.* Place a check in this box to have Word check grammar whenever you perform a spell check on the document.

- *Show Readability Statistics.* Readability statistics indicate the reading-difficulty level of a document. Choose this option if you want Word to display readability statistics after it completes a grammar check.

- *Writing Style.* Use this drop-down list to indicate the writing style of the current document. Changing the style changes the way that Word checks the grammar of the document and reports readability level.

- *Settings.* Click this button to display the Grammar Settings dialog box (see Figure 16.7). The controls in the Grammar Settings dialog box enable you to specify the types of things that Word looks for during a grammar check.

Figure 16.7

Use the Grammar Settings options to specify which items Word checks during a grammar check.

Setting Options for Tracking Revisions

Word enables you to track revisions in a document, and also maintains information about which changes were made and by whom. Revisions are useful when more than one person works on a document or when you must submit a document for review to someone else. Changes made by each person reviewing the document appear as underlined text in a specific color. You can specify the colors used by Word to indicate revisions, as well as font characteristics and other revision settings, through the Track Changes property page of the Options property sheet (see Figure 16.8).

The following list explains the settings in the Track Changes property page:

- *Inserted Text.* Use the two controls in this group to specify the color and font formatting that Word uses to indicate new text inserted into the document when revision marks are turned on. If you choose By Author, Word assigns a unique color to the first eight people who review the document.

Figure 16.8

Use the Track Changes page to specify how Word is to handle revision marks.

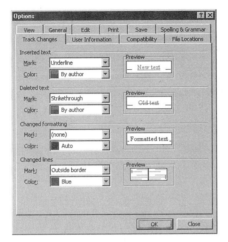

- *Deleted Text.* Use these two settings to specify how Word should mark text for deletion during document review.

- *Changed Formatting.* By default, Word does not mark formatting changes during document review. Use these two controls to specify a desired formatting mark and color to apply to text when a user changes the formatting.

- *Changed Lines.* Word automatically marks paragraphs with a line at the left margin to indicate those that contain changes. This option makes it easier to locate changes, particularly those that are relatively insignificant and could be hard to find (a change in one character, for example). The Color setting specifies the color of the line. Use the Mark drop-down list to specify a different location for the change mark. Notice that this setting does not affect Normal view, in which Word always places the revision indicator at the left border.

Setting User Information Options

The User Information page of the Options property sheet (see Figure 16.9) enables you to enter your name, initials, and mailing address.

These settings are used throughout Word for various purposes, as indicated in the following list:

- *Name.* Word uses this name as the author in the document's properties (choose File, Properties to view document properties), in letters and envelopes, and when you insert revisions or comments into a document.

- *Initials.* Word uses these initials for letter and memo elements, as well as for comment marks.

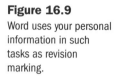

Figure 16.9

Word uses your personal information in such tasks as revision marking.

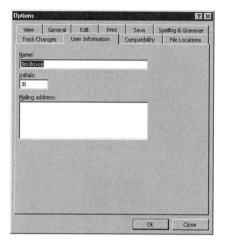

■ *Mailing Address.* Word uses this information as the default mailing address when you create an envelope or letter.

▶ **See** Chapter 48, "Document Collaboration," for information about revisions and comments, **page 1021**

Setting Compatibility Options

Word has evolved considerably since its introduction in the late 1970s. The program's file formats have evolved as well to incorporate new features and support other hardware platforms, such as the Macintosh. Word 97 provides full backward compatibility with previous versions of Word. You can save a file by using a specific Word document format, but you can specify the parameters for each of the document file types to fine-tune compatibility between users.

The settings in the Compatibility property page (see Figure 16.10) enable you to specify settings for each of Word's native document file formats. To specify settings, choose a file format from the Recommended Options For drop-down list; then enable and disable check boxes in the Options group as desired.

If your system does not contain fonts that are specified in the current document, you can click the Font Substitution button to select which fonts on your system are used to represent the unavailable fonts.

Setting File Location Options

By default, Word looks in its own folders for its support files— templates, clip art, and so on. The program looks in the My Documents folder (which it creates during installation) for documents. If you are using a different folder to contain your document files, templates, or other files, or want to specify a different startup folder for automatically loaded templates, do so through the File Locations property page of the Options property sheet (see Figure 16.11).

Figure 16.10

Use the Compatibility property page to fine-tune compatibility settings for other Word file formats.

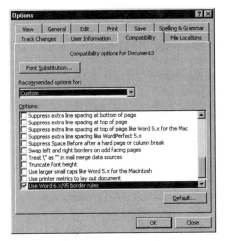

Figure 16.11

Specify your own locations for document files, templates, and other Word files by using the File Locations page.

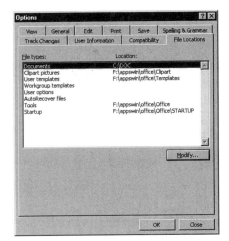

To change a folder setting, just double-click the item in the list or select the item and choose Modify. Word opens a standard browse dialog box that you can use to locate the desired folder.

TIP The Startup folder specifies the folder in which Word looks for templates and add-ins to load automatically as soon as Word starts. To make templates and the macros and other custom elements contained in the templates available to all documents, place the templates in the Startup folder. Notice that this folder is the Startup folder specified in the File Locations page in Word, not the Startup folder for Windows 98.

Using Word Startup Switches

Word supports several command-line switches that control the way that Word starts. You can use some of these switches to make Word perform actions automatically at startup. Word supports the following command-line switches:

- **/a.** The /a switch directs Word to not load add-ins and global templates, including NORMAL.DOT, at startup. Use this switch when you want to start a clean copy of Word or when you suspect that something in an add-in or the global templates is causing a problem in Word. If Word functions properly after you start it with the /a switch, a problem exists with one of the add-ins or global templates. Close Word, rename NORMAL.DOT to NORMAL.OLD.DOT, and restart Word normally. If Word starts and functions normally, your NORMAL.DOT file contained an error.

- **/l addinpath.** Use this switch to load a specific add-in when you start Word. Replace *addinpath* with the path to the add-in file.

- **/m macroname.** Use this switch to run a specific macro when Word starts. Use the /m switch by itself without a macro name to prevent Word from running any macros at startup. Using /m by itself is a good method for preventing a macro virus from executing when you load a document that you suspect contains one.

- **/n.** The /n switch directs Word to start without opening a new document. Use this switch if you want Word to start with no document window.

- **/t document.** Use the /t switch to direct Word to load a document as a template. Specify the document name in place of *document* after the /t switch.

You can use several methods to start Word with command-line switches. The first method is to start Word from a command prompt and include the switches in the command line that you use to start Word. To do so, open a command prompt window by choosing Start, Programs, MS-DOS prompt. When the DOS window opens, use the DOS CD command to change to the drive and folder containing the Winword executable file (Winword.exe). Typically, Winword.exe is located in *OFFICEHOME*\OFFICE\\, in which *OFFICEHOME* is the primary folder in which you installed Word. So if you installed Office to C:\PROGRAM FILES\OFFICE97, WINWORD.EXE is located in C:\PROGRAM FILES\OFFICE97\OFFICE. The following example starts Word without opening a new document window:

```
Winword.exe /n
```

The second way to start Word with a switch is to create a shortcut to Word and specify the switch in the command line of the shortcut. Follow these steps to create such a shortcut:

1. Right-click the desktop or the folder of your choice and then choose New, Shortcut to start the Create Shortcut Wizard.

2. In the Command Line text box, type (in quotes) the path to WINWORD.EXE, followed by a space, and include the desired switch at the end of the command line (example: "C:\Program Files\Office97\Office\Winword.exe" /n). See Figure 16.12 for an example.

3. Click the Next button to view the next page of the Wizard.

Figure 16.12

Use the Create Shortcut Wizard to create a shortcut that starts Word with a specific switch.

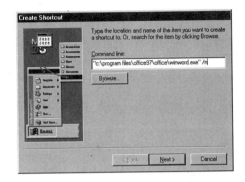

4. Type a name for your shortcut.

This name appears below the shortcut's icon.

5. Click Finish.

You can create as many shortcuts to Word as you want, each with its own command line and optional switches. If you prefer to have only one shortcut, simply edit the shortcut to change the command line as needed. To edit a shortcut, right-click the shortcut's icon and then choose Properties from the shortcut menu. Click the Shortcut tab to display the Shortcut property. Modify the command line in the Target text box; then choose OK. ●

Excel 97

CHAPTER 17

Excel Workbooks, Worksheets, and Ranges

by Patrice-Anne Rutledge

In this chapter

Working with Multiple Workbooks and Worksheets

In Excel, you can easily modify your workbooks and worksheets with special features that simplify the tasks of editing, copying, moving, inserting, and deleting.

Editing Worksheets

Excel provides two ways to edit cell contents you've previously entered. You can select the cell and edit the contents in the formula bar, or you can double-click the cell and edit the contents directly in the cell. Excel refers to this second option as *in-cell editing*. To be sure that in-cell editing is active, choose Tools, Options and verify that the Edit Directly in Cell check box is checked on the Edit tab.

Clearing Cell Contents   To clear cell contents, select the cell or range of cells and choose Edit, Clear to display a shortcut menu. From this menu you can choose from the following options, each clearing your cell contents in a different way:

- *All*. Clears everything including contents, formatting, and cell notes.
- *Formats*. Clears only cell formatting, not the contents.
- *Contents*. Clears the contents but leaves cell formatting.
- *Comments*. Clears comments only.

TIP As a shortcut, select the data you want to clear, right-click the mouse, and choose Clear Contents from the shortcut menu. This performs the same function as choosing Edit, Clear, Contents.

TIP To spell-check only a specific worksheet range, select it before clicking the Spelling button.

Checking Worksheet Spelling   An important part of editing any worksheet is to verify that the spelling is correct. Excel's spelling feature checks worksheets, macros, and charts for errors. To check the spelling in more than one worksheet, select the tab of each sheet you want to check by pressing and holding down the Ctrl key and clicking the tabs of the sheets you want to include.

TIP If Excel finds no spelling errors, it displays a dialog box telling you that the spell-check is complete for the entire sheet.

N O T E   The Spelling feature in Excel works almost identically to the one in Word, so if you learn to use one, you can easily pick up the other, too.

To start checking spelling, follow these steps:

1. Click the Spelling button on the Standard toolbar or choose Tools, Spelling.
2. When Excel encounters an error, the Spelling dialog box displays, shown in Figure 17.1.

Figure 17.1

Excel provides many different spell-check options.

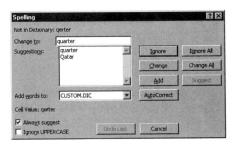

3. The misspelled word is highlighted in the Not in Dictionary field and potential suggested spellings, if any, display in the Change To box.

TIP To add the selected word to the custom dictionary, click the Add button.

4. Choose one of the suggestions or enter the correct spelling in the edit box and click the Change button to change this instance of the word or Change All to change all instances of the misspelled word.

Excel also offers several other options with the following buttons:

- *Ignore*. Ignores the suggested change and continues checking the spelling.
- *Ignore All*. Ignores all occurrences of the suggested change and continues checking the spelling.
- *Add*. Adds the word to the custom dictionary as it is currently spelled.
- *Suggest*. Offers additional suggestions related to the current selection in the Suggestions list.
- *AutoCorrect*. Add the misspelled word and its correction to the AutoCorrect list.

5. When Excel completes checking spelling, it displays a message box telling you so. Click OK to return to the worksheet.

Viewing Workbooks and Worksheets

Excel 97 offers many different ways you can view a worksheet once you've created it. With large worksheets, you can create frozen column and row headings that display as you scroll through your data. You can also split the worksheet to view different parts at the same time. Excel also provides the ability to hide specific rows, columns, and worksheets to make working with your data easier. Finally, you can also view multiple workbooks and worksheets at the same time.

Viewing Row and Column Labels   With long worksheets you'll often lose sight of your column labels as you scroll down your list of data. Scrolling to the right can make the row labels disappear. To avoid this problem, you can "freeze" the label row and column.

To freeze only the horizontal pane (row labels), choose the row immediately underneath the one you want to freeze. For example, to freeze only the first row, you would select row 2.

Choose <u>W</u>indow, <u>F</u>reeze Panes. Now when you scroll down, this first row is frozen. Figure 17.2 shows an example of a frozen row.

Figure 17.2

Freezing panes makes it easier to identify column and row headers.

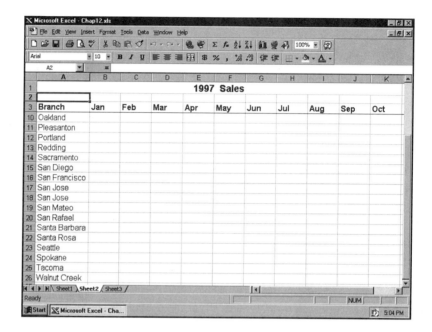

To freeze only the vertical pane (column labels), choose the column immediately to the right of the column you want to freeze. Choose <u>W</u>indow, <u>F</u>reeze Panes to freeze it.

To freeze both the horizontal and vertical panes, select the cell immediately beneath and to the right of where you want to freeze the pane. For example, to freeze row 1 and column A, you would select cell B2. Choose <u>W</u>indow, <u>F</u>reeze Panes to freeze.

 TIP   To unfreeze all panes, choose <u>W</u>indow, Un<u>f</u>reeze Panes.

N O T E   Frozen panes don't display when you print a worksheet. For example, if you freeze the first row in what will print as a multiple page document, the frozen row won't print as a column heading after the first page. To print column headings, choose <u>F</u>ile, Page Set<u>u</u>p to open the Page Setup dialog box. In the Print Titles group box on the Sheet tab, enter the <u>R</u>ows to Repeat at Top and <u>C</u>olumns to Repeat at Left. ▪

Viewing Two Parts of a Worksheet Simultaneously   You can view two parts of the same worksheet simultaneously. For example, you may want to view the top five rows and bottom five rows of a 50-row worksheet at the same time. To do this, you'll use the split boxes you find at the top of the vertical scroll bar or at the right of the horizontal scroll bar. Figure 17.3 illustrates an example of using split boxes.

TIP To remove these splits, drag the split bar back to the top or right of the worksheet window.

Figure 17.3
Use split boxes to split your worksheet display.

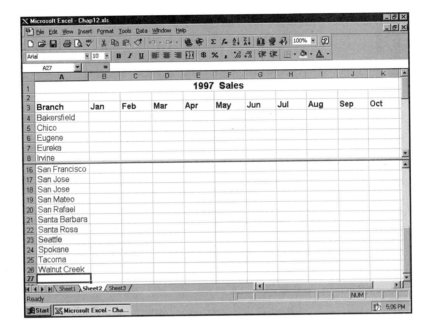

Point to the split box and drag the mouse to the location where you want to place the split. To display the top and bottom five rows in your worksheet, you would drag the vertical split box to just below row 5. Then you could scroll in the lower pane to the last five worksheet rows.

Enlarging or Reducing Worksheet View   To enlarge or reduce the view of your current worksheet, select an appropriate zoom percentage from the Zoom drop-down list. To enlarge the view of the selected cells only, choose Selection from the drop-down list.

 TIP In addition to the predetermined zoom percentages in the Zoom drop-down list on the Standard toolbar, you can also manually enter your own zoom percentage in this box. Excel supports zooms from 10 to 400 percent.

Hiding Worksheets, Columns, and Rows   In Excel, you can hide worksheets, columns, and rows from view. This is useful if you temporarily want to work only with specific data and prefer to only view that data.

To hide a worksheet from view, select the Worksheet tab and choose Format, Sheet, Hide. Excel removes the worksheet from view, but doesn't delete it. To view the worksheet again, choose Format, Sheet, Unhide to open the Unhide dialog box, shown in Figure 17.4.

Part
III

Ch
17

Figure 17.4

Choose the worksheet to unhide in the Unhide dialog box.

Select the sheet you want to unhide in the Unhide Sheet list and click OK.

To hide rows, select the row or rows you want to hide and choose Format, Row, Hide. To restore these rows, select the rows that surround the hidden rows and choose Format, Row, Unhide. The hidden rows display again. Figure 17.5 shows a worksheet with rows 4, 7, and 10 hidden.

Figure 17.5

Rows 4, 7, and 10 are hidden.

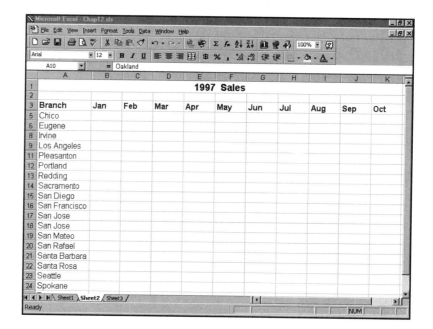

To hide columns, choose the column or columns to hide and select Format, Column, Hide. Similarly, to restore select the columns that surround the hidden columns and choose Format, Column, Unhide.

Creating a Custom View   If you've made numerous customizations to worksheets that you want to save in your workbook before exiting—such as hidden rows and columns, print settings, and filters—you can create a custom view. To do so, follow these steps:

1. Choose View, Custom Views to open the Custom Views dialog box, shown in Figure 17.6.

Figure 17.6

You can create custom views in Excel.

2. Click the Add button to open the Add View dialog box, which Figure 17.7 illustrates.

Figure 17.7

Specify what you want to include in your custom view.

3. Enter the Name of the view and then decide whether you want to include either or both of the Include in View options:

- *Print Settings.* Saves the currently selected print settings with the view.
- *Hidden Rows, Columns, and Filter Settings.* Saves the formatting of currently hidden rows and columns as well as any filters you've applied.

4. Click Close to return to your current worksheet.

To display a custom view, choose View, Custom Views. In the Custom Views dialog box select the view you want to display and click the Show button.

To delete a view, select a view in this same dialog box and click the Delete button. A message box confirms that you want to delete. Click Yes.

Viewing Multiple Worksheets and Workbooks   At times you may want to work with multiple worksheets or workbooks simultaneously.

CAUTION

Be careful about viewing too many workbooks or worksheets at once. Too much clutter can make your screen unreadable.

To view multiple workbooks, follow these steps:

1. Open all the workbooks you want to view.

2. Choose Window, Arrange to open the Arrange Windows dialog box, illustrated in Figure 17.8.

3. Decide how you want to arrange your window. Excel offers four views:

- *Tiled.* Divides the window into tiled squares. For example, four open workbooks would display in two rows with two columns.

Figure 17.8

Excel offers four view styles—tiled, horizontal, vertical, and cascade.

- *Horizontal*. Displays workbooks in horizontal rows.
- *Vertical*. Displays workbooks in vertical columns.
- *Cascade*. Layers the workbooks in overlapping rows.

4. Click OK to apply the view. Figure 17.9 illustrates a tiled view for three different workbooks.

Figure 17.9

Viewing multiple workbooks and worksheets is easy.

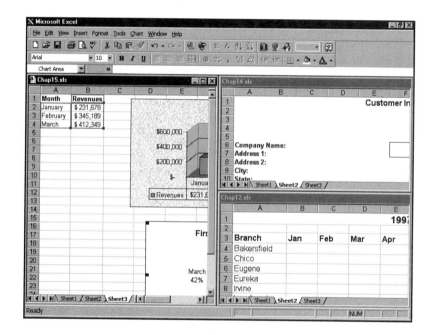

TIP To display only one worksheet again, click the Maximize button of the worksheet you want to view.

To view multiple worksheets in the same workbook, follow these steps:

1. Open the workbook that contains the worksheet you want to view.
2. Choose Window, New Window. In the window that opens, click the tab of each worksheet you want to view.
3. Choose Window, Arrange to open the Arrange Windows dialog box.
4. Choose from the four options for arranging your worksheets—Tiled, Horizontal, Vertical, or Cascade.

5. Check the Windows of Active Workbook check box to be sure that you view only the currently selected workbook.

6. Click OK to apply the view.

The selected worksheets are arranged according to the option you chose. To change the arrangement you selected, simply apply a new arrangement. To view only one worksheet, maximize the worksheet you want to view.

Selecting and Using Ranges

In Excel 97 you can select entire worksheets or portions of worksheets including columns, rows, and ranges. To select an entire worksheet, click the rectangle that is diagonally to the left of cell A1.

Part
III

Ch
17

 T I P Excel highlights the column and row headings of selected cells in bold text to help you easily identify selected cells and ranges.

You can also select specific rows and columns. To do so, click the row or column header. Row and column headers are the gray cells that border the active worksheet and use letters of the alphabet to represent columns and numbers to represent rows. To select nonadjacent rows and columns, press and hold down the Ctrl key as you make your selections.

Selecting Ranges

In Excel, you'll often want to group cells into ranges of data. You can select ranges with either the mouse or keyboard. To select a range of data with the mouse, select the upper-left cell in your range and drag the mouse to the lower-right cell in the range.

To select a range with the keyboard, go to the cell in the upper-left corner of the range. Press and hold down the Shift key and use the arrow keys to select the range.

Selecting Multiple Ranges

You can select more than one range of cells at a time using either the mouse or the keyboard. To use the mouse to select a multiple range of cells, click the first cell you want to include and drag the mouse over the entire range of cells. Press the Ctrl key and, while holding it down, select the other ranges in the same way. Figure 17.10 shows a worksheet with multiple ranges selected.

To select multiple ranges with the keyboard, follow these steps:

1. Press and hold down the Shift key and use the arrow keys to select your first range.

2. Press Shift+F8. The ADD indicator appears at the right of the status bar, letting you know that you can add additional ranges.

3. Go to the upper-left cell of the next range you want to select.

Figure 17.10
You can select multiple ranges of data in Excel.

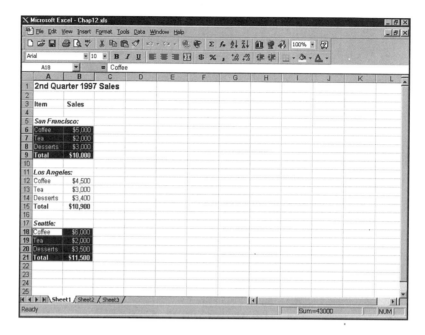

4. Press Shift and the arrow keys to select this next range. ADD disappears from the status bar, the long horizontal bar at the bottom of the screen directly above the taskbar.

5. To add additional ranges, continue to repeat steps 2 through 4.

Naming Ranges

You'll often want to name individual cells or ranges of cells for easier identification. Range names make it easier to understand how a worksheet is organized. They also are useful for referring to specific cells in a formula and for moving quickly to a specific worksheet location.

> **CAUTION**
>
> Be sure that your range name starts with either a letter or underline and doesn't include any spaces. The remaining characters can be letters, numbers, periods, or underlines. Excel won't accept a range name that doesn't follow these standards.

To create a range name, follow these steps:

1. Select the individual cell or range you want to name.

2. Click in the Name box on the left side of the formula bar.

3. Enter the name you want to give to the range.

4. Press Enter to save the range name.

TIP You can also create a range name by choosing Insert, Name, Define to open the Define Name dialog box. Enter the range name in the Names in Workbook box, click the Add button and then select OK to exit.

Figure 17.11 illustrates an example naming an individual cell as Jun97_Sales.

Figure 17.11

It's easy to name a cell or range using the name box in the formula bar.

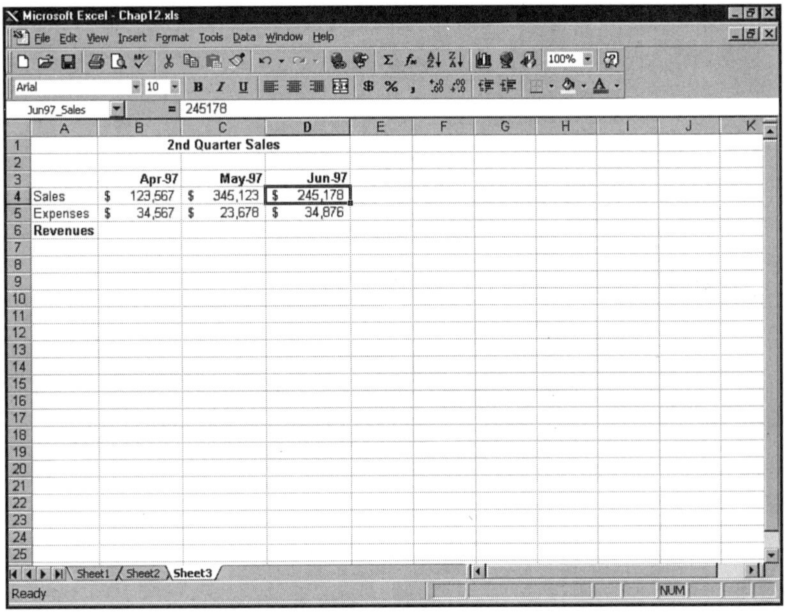

Using Range Names in Formulas

Once you've created a range name, you can refer to it as you would a cell reference in a formula. For example, if you've named your sales and expense totals for June 1997 as Jun97_Sales and Jun97_Expenses, you could enter the following formula in the formula bar to determine total revenues for June 1997: =Jun97_Sales-Jun97_Expenses. Figure 17.12 illustrates this formula.

▶ **See** "Working with Formulas," **page 362**

If you've created long or detailed range names, you can also enter them into formulas by using the Paste Name dialog box. To do so, follow these steps:

1. Select the cell in which you want to place your result, then enter = in the formula bar.
2. Choose Insert, Name, Paste to open the Paste Name dialog box, shown in Figure 17.13.
3. Choose the range name you want to insert from the Paste Name drop-down list.
4. Click OK to return to the formula bar.

Figure 17.12
Naming a cell or range
makes creating formulas
easier.

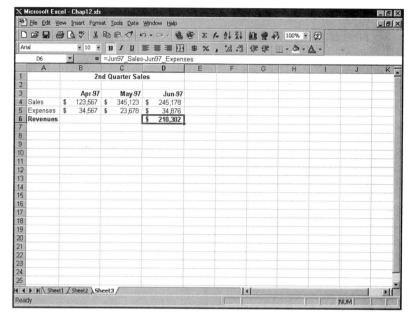

Figure 17.13
Use the Paste Name
dialog box to insert a
range name into a
formula.

5. Continue entering the formula, returning to the Paste Name dialog box whenever you need to select a range name.

Deleting Range Names

To delete a range name, follow these steps:

1. Choose Insert, Name, Define to open the Define Name dialog box, shown in Figure 17.14.

Figure 17.14
You can delete
unwanted range names.

2. Select the range name to delete from the Names in <u>W</u>orkbook drop-down list.

3. Click the <u>D</u>elete button.

Filling a Range

You can, of course, manually fill a range with data or apply specific formats to it, but Excel offers two features to automate these common tasks.

Filling a Range with AutoFill

Excel's AutoFill feature lets you easily copy cell data to adjacent cells. In general, Excel copies the data exactly as it is in the original cells, but for series such as dates and numbers, Excel extends the data. For example, you could enter Jan and Feb in cells and use AutoFill to extend the remaining months. If you wanted to enter the numbers 1 through 100 in a column, you could enter the first two numbers and let AutoFill take care of the rest.

 You can also combine text and numbers with AutoFill. For example, you could use AutoFill to extend Quarter 1 to Quarter 2, Quarter 3, etc.

To use AutoFill, follow these steps:

1. Select the cells you want to copy or extend.

2. Position the mouse pointer on the handle in the lower-right of the selected area. A large plus sign appears.

3. Drag the handle to the last cell you want to fill or extend and release the mouse.

CAUTION

Be sure to drag the AutoFill handle in the lower-right corner rather than the edge of the cell, which moves data. When the AutoFill handle is active, you'll see a plus sign (+) next to it.

 Holding down the Ctrl key reverses the fill effect from standard to series and vice versa. For example, in general, extending cells containing the numbers 1, 2, and 3 would extend the number series to include 4, 5, 6, etc. Pressing Ctrl enables you to simply repeat the content of the existing cells again.

Figure 17.15 illustrates the use of AutoFill.

Filling Range Formats with the Format Painter

Format Painter is an Excel feature that lets you copy the formatting of a particular range of cells, but not the data itself. This is particularly useful if you've done extensive cell formatting and don't want to repeat the same steps again. To use Format Painter, follow these steps:

Part
III

Ch
17

Figure 17.15
With the AutoFill feature, you can automatically extend a series of data.

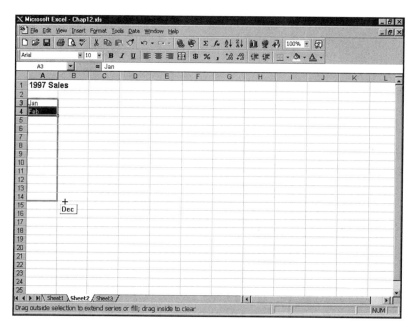

 T I P To copy formatting to more than one additional location, double-click the Format Painter button. It remains active and continues to apply formats until you click it again.

1. Select the cells from which you want to copy the format.
2. Click the Format Painter button on the Standard toolbar. The area you've selected is surrounded by a flashing marquee.
3. Select the cells to which you want to apply the formatting and release the mouse button.

Figure 17.16 illustrates the process of using the Format Painter. The new cells take on the styles of the cells in the marquee. For example, bolding, italics, text style, and size are all copied with the Format Painter.

▶ **See** Chapter 20, "Advanced Formatting and Charting in Excel," **page 411**

Moving, Copying, Inserting, and Deleting Ranges

Excel provides several options for manipulating ranges of data including techniques for moving, copying, inserting, and deleting.

Copying Worksheets and Worksheet Ranges

Excel makes it easy to copy worksheets and worksheet ranges. To copy an entire worksheet, follow these steps:

1. Select the sheet tab of the worksheet you want to copy.

Figure 17.16
Apply formatting options using the Format Painter.

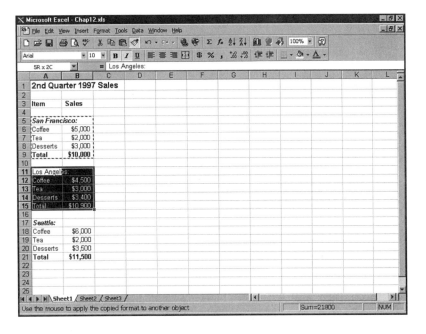

2. Right-click the mouse and choose <u>M</u>ove or Copy from the shortcut menu. The Move or Copy dialog box appears, shown in Figure 17.17.

Figure 17.17
Select the Create a Copy check box to copy the worksheet.

3. Select the workbook to which you want to copy the worksheet from the <u>T</u>o Book drop-down list. Or, select (new book) to place the worksheet in a new workbook.

 You can copy a worksheet only to an open workbook. Only open workbooks display in the <u>T</u>o Book drop-down list.

4. Indicate where to place the worksheet from the <u>B</u>efore Sheet scroll list. You can place this worksheet before any of the listed worksheets, or you can choose to move it to the end.

5. Be sure to select the <u>C</u>reate a Copy check box. If you don't, you'll move your workbook rather than copy it.

Part
III

Ch
17

6. Click OK to copy the sheet. Excel places a (2) after the original worksheet name. For example, if you copied a worksheet named Budget, Excel would name the copy Budget (2).

In addition to copying worksheets, you may also want to copy worksheet data. The four ways to copy data and formatting in Excel are included in the following list:

- Use the drag-and-drop method
- Copy and paste
- Use the AutoFill Method
- Use the Format Painter

Copying with Drag-and-Drop   To copy using the drag-and-drop method, follow these steps:

1. Select the range of cells you want to copy.
2. Place the mouse pointer on the edge of the selected data. When the pointer changes from a large white plus sign to an arrow, press the Ctrl key. A small plus sign appears next to the mouse pointer.
3. Drag the selected cells to the new location and release the mouse.

 T I P   If drag-and-drop won't work, choose Tools, Options and verify that the Allow Cell Drag and Drop check box on the Edit tab is checked.

Figure 17.18 illustrates the process of copying using drag-and-drop.

Figure 17.18
You can see an outline of your data as you drag and drop it.

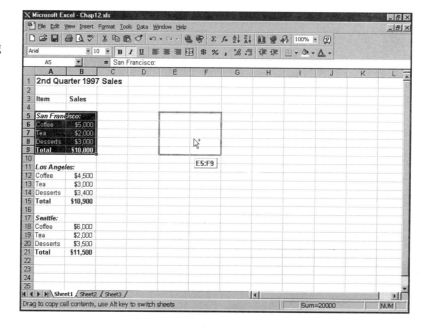

Copying with Copy and Paste   To use the copy and paste method to copy worksheet data, follow these steps:

 T I P   You can also press Ctrl+C to copy and Ctrl+V to paste.

 T I P   If you make a mistake when copying data, choose Edit, Undo Paste or press Ctrl+Z. You can undo up to the last 16 actions.

N O T E   Excel provides a way for you to copy only certain characters within a cell rather than the entire contents. To do so, double-click the cell, choose the characters you want to copy either in the cell or in the formula bar, and then use the copy and paste method. ▪

1. Select the range of cells you want to copy.

T I P   You can also right-click the mouse and choose Copy from the shortcut menu.

2. Choose Edit, Copy. A flashing marquee surrounds the data you want to copy.
3. Select the cell in which you want to place the data you're copying. If you're copying a range of cells, select the upper-left cell in the new location range.

T I P   You can also right-click the mouse and choose Paste from the shortcut menu.

N O T E   The marquee surrounding the data to copy remains until you press **Enter** or **Esc**. This allows you to continue copying the same data to multiple locations. ▪

4. Choose Edit, Paste to paste the data in the new location.

Figure 17.19 demonstrates using copy and paste.

Moving Worksheets and Worksheet Ranges

Moving worksheets and range data in Excel is similar to copying. To move a worksheet, follow these steps:

1. Select the sheet tab of the worksheet you want to move.
2. Right-click the mouse and choose Move or Copy from the shortcut menu. Figure 17.20 illustrates the Move or Copy dialog box which appears.

Part

III

Ch

17

Figure 17.19
Copying and pasting
data is simple in Excel.

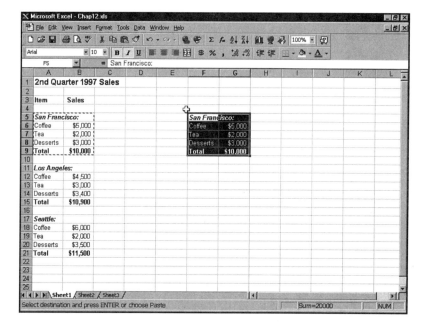

Figure 17.20
You can move a
worksheet within the
same worksheet or to a
new workbook using the
Move or Copy dialog
box.

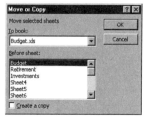

 T I P You can move a worksheet only to an open workbook. Only open workbooks display in the To Book
drop-down list.

CAUTION

Don't select the Create a Copy check box. If you do, you'll copy your worksheet, not move it.

---

3. Select the workbook to which you want to move the selected worksheet from the To
   Book drop-down list. Or, select (new book) from the To Book drop-down list to place the
   worksheet in a new workbook. The existing workbook is the default.

4. Indicate where to place the worksheet from the Before Sheet scroll list. You can place
   this worksheet before any of the listed worksheets, or you can choose to move it to the
   end by selecting the (move to end) option in the Before Sheet scroll list.

5. Click OK to move the sheet. The sheet tab order changes based on your move.

In Excel, you can move worksheet data in two ways. You can move it using the drag-and-drop method, or you can cut and paste.

Moving with Drag-and-Drop   To move worksheet data using the drag-and-drop method, follow these steps:

1. Select the data you want to move.

2. Place the mouse pointer on the edge of the selected data; an arrow appears.

3. Drag the selected cells to the new location and release the mouse.

Figure 17.21 illustrates how to use drag-and-drop to move data.

Figure 17.21

An arrow appears when you're ready to drag-and-drop.

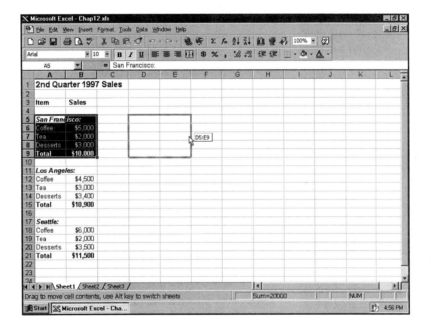

Part

III

Ch

17

Moving with Cut and Paste   To use the cut and paste method to move worksheet data, follow these steps:

1. Select the cells you want to move.

T I P   You can also press Ctrl+X to cut and Ctrl+V to paste.

T I P   If you make a mistake when moving data, choose Edit, Undo Paste.

You can also right-click the mouse and choose Cut from the shortcut menu.

2. Choose Edit, Cut. A flashing marquee surrounds the data you want to move.

3. Select the cell to which you want to move the data. If you're copying a range of cells, select the upper-left cell in the new location range.

4. Choose Edit, Paste to paste the data in the new location. The data no longer remains in its original location; it's removed.

Inserting Worksheets, Columns, and Rows

To insert a new worksheet into a workbook, select Insert, Worksheet. Excel inserts a new sheet before the currently selected worksheet and automatically names it. For example, if you already have three worksheets in a workbook, Excel would name the new sheet Sheet 4 regardless of its position in the workbook.

CAUTION

If you don't select a sheet tab before right-clicking the mouse, the shortcut menu that displays will apply to inserting rows and columns rather than the worksheet itself.

You can also add a new worksheet by selecting a sheet tab, right-clicking the mouse, and choosing Insert from the shortcut menu. The Insert dialog box appears.

Select the Worksheet icon on the General tab and click OK. Depending on the installation options you chose and the templates you've created, your Insert dialog box may vary from the one illustrated in Figure 17.10.

You can also insert new columns, rows, and cells in Excel. This ability is useful when you've already created a worksheet and decide to add additional data.

Inserting Columns   To insert a new column, select the column that occupies the location where you want to add the column. Choose Insert, Columns to insert the new column, which appears to the left of the currently selected column. You can also select the column header, right-click the mouse, and choose Insert from the shortcut menu.

 To insert more than one column at a time, select the number of columns you want to insert before choosing Insert from the menu. For example, if you want to insert three columns before Column C, you would select Columns C, D, and E and then choose Insert, Columns.

Inserting Rows   To insert a new row, select the row above which you want to add the row. Choose Insert, Rows to insert the new row. You can also select the row header, right-click the mouse, and choose Insert from the shortcut menu.

 T I P   To insert more than one row, select the number of rows you want to add before proceeding with insertion.

Inserting Cells   To insert new cells in a worksheet, select the cell or cell range where you want to insert and choose Insert, Cells. The Insert dialog box appears, illustrated in Figure 17.22.

 T I P   You can also insert a new cell by selecting where you want to insert, right-clicking the mouse, and choosing Insert from the shortcut menu to open the Insert dialog box.

This dialog box gives you the following options for inserting new cells:

Figure 17.22
Excel provides several options for inserting data.

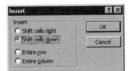

- ■ *Shift Cells Right*. Inserts new cells to the left of the selection.
- ■ *Shift Cells Down*. Inserts news cells above the selection.
- ■ *Entire Row*. Inserts a new row.
- ■ *Entire Column*. Inserts a new column.

Deleting Worksheets, Columns, and Rows

At times, you'll want to delete the worksheets and data in your Excel workbooks. You may have made a mistake, the data is no longer needed or valid, or you simply want to reorganize how you've presented your data.

CAUTION
Choosing Edit, Delete only deletes rows, columns, and data, not the entire sheet.

Deleting Worksheets To delete a worksheet from a workbook, select the worksheet tab and choose <u>E</u>dit, De<u>l</u>ete Sheet. Figure 17.23 displays the warning box that appears.

Figure 17.23

A warning box appears when you delete a worksheet.

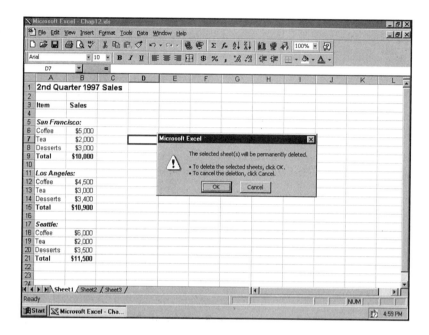

Click OK to continue with the deletion or Cancel to cancel it.

Deleting Columns To delete a column, select the column header of the column or columns you want to delete and choose <u>E</u>dit, <u>D</u>elete. The remaining columns move to the left. You can also select the column header, right-click the mouse, and choose <u>D</u>elete from the shortcut menu.

Deleting Rows To delete rows, choose the row header of the row or rows you want to delete and choose <u>E</u>dit, <u>D</u>elete. The remaining rows move up. You can also select the row header, right-click the mouse, and choose <u>D</u>elete from the shortcut menu.

Deleting Ranges To delete specific cells from a worksheet, select the cells and choose <u>E</u>dit, <u>D</u>elete. This opens the Delete dialog box, illustrated in Figure 17.24.

T I P You can also delete cells by selecting them, right-clicking the mouse, and choosing <u>D</u>elete from the shortcut menu to open the Delete dialog box.

Figure 17.24
There are several
deletion options for
deleting worksheet
cells.

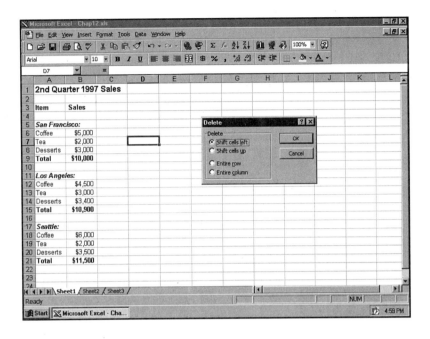

This dialog box gives you the following deletion options:

- *Shift Cells Left*. Moves existing cells to the left of the deleted cells.
- *Shift Cells Up*. Moves existing cells up.
- *Entire Row*. Deletes the selected row or rows.
- *Entire Column*. Deletes the selected column or columns.

Using Reference Operators

In Excel, you'll want to be able to combine ranges of cells for use in calculations and formulas. *Reference operators* let you determine how to group cells or ranges in these calculations.

▶ **See** "Using Range Names," **page 377**

Table 17.1 lists the references operators you can use.

Table 17.1   Reference Operators

Operator	Description
: (colon)	Defines a range, encompassing all cells between and including the two referenced cells
, (comma)	Defines a union, combining multiple references into one
single space	Defines an intersection, which calculates one result for cells included in both references

Part

III

Ch

17

For example, SUM(B12:B15) would sum the range of cells between B12 and B15—B12, B13, B14, and B15. SUM(B12:B15,C5) would sum all the cells between and including B12 and B15 as well as cell C5.

Intersections are a bit more complicated. SUM(A1:A5 A4:A9) would find the cells included in both references (A4 and A5) and sum only those two cells. ●

CHAPTER 18

Formulas and Functions

by Joe Habraken

In this chapter

Overview of New Features

Excel 97 provides a number of new features that make working with formulas and functions a very straightforward process. These enhancements include

- **Formula Palette**. This new tool provides you with help in editing formulas that contain an Excel function. Select the cell that holds the formula and then click on the Edit Formula button on the Excel Formula Bar. The Formula Palette will appear detailing the type of function you are using and the cell ranges involved. Use the Palette to edit the cell ranges or get additional help from the Office Assistant.

- **Paste function**. With the help of the Office Assistant, you can enter a text description of the type of function you want to use to return a calculation and Excel will suggest the formula that you should use in Excel's Paste function dialog box. Open the Paste function dialog box and then click the Office Assistant button for help.

- **Range Finder**. When you edit a formula or function in Excel, the cells and ranges associated with the formula or function will be highlighted.

- **Natural-language formulas**. You can use your column and row headings to designate cells in a formula. For instance, a cell could be designated by East Total, where East would be the Row heading and Total would be the column title for the total value that was entered for the East region.

Two other improvements found in Excel 97 aren't directly related to formulas and functions but may also help you design fool-proof calculations in your worksheets. Data validation allows you to specify what type of data goes in a particular cell, such as text, whole numbers, or dates. Placing restrictions on cell data entry can assure that your formulas will return correct values. The Auditing Toolbar also provides a Circle Invalid Data button that will find any invalid data entered in your spreadsheet cells.

Taking advantage of these improvements requires a basic understanding of how formulas and functions do their jobs in an Excel worksheet. Formulas in particular can be tricky because you must design them yourself.

Working with Formulas

A **formula** is an expression or equation that you design to perform calculations in your Excel worksheets. You can use your formulas to add, subtract, multiply, and divide the numerical values that you place in the worksheet cells. You can also design formulas that will complete more complex calculations. In many cases, however, you will find that Excel provides a built-in function that will handle more difficult calculations like mortgage payments, or conditional statements, or complex statistics like a linear trend.

A good rule to follow is to create your own formulas only when Excel does not provide a function that will do the same job. You can usually limit your formula writing to include simple math like subtraction, multiplication, and division.

The real beauty of Excel formulas is the fact that you can design them so that they do their calculations on the contents of cells. You do this by specifying the cell address in the formula. That way you can change the values in the cells that are involved in the formula without needing to edit the formula.

Some people use this technique for "what if" analysis. For instance, you can set up an Excel spreadsheet using the PMT function that can show you the monthly payment for a car at different car prices and loan interest rates. In effect, you are saying What if the car is 20,000 and the interest rate is 8 percent? Can I afford the calculated monthly payment? Each time you type a different interest rate into the interest rate cell or a different car price in the price cell, you are analyzing the potential monthly payment; each set of values returns a different payment amount. You are using "what if."

The formulas that you enter into your worksheets will consist of cell references and the appropriate operators. When you enter a formula into a spreadsheet, it must always start with an equal sign (=). This tells Excel that the information in the cell is an equation and will return a value. The most commonly used operators are shown here:

Operator	Performs	Examples
+	Addition	=A1+B1
–	Subtraction	=A1–B1
*	Multiplication	=A1*C12
/	Division	=A1/B3
	Exponentiation	=A^12

Part III
Ch 18

You can also combine operations in one formula using parentheses such as (A1+B1)/C1. These compound formulas can be a little trickier than a straightforward addition or subtraction formula.

▶ **See** "Understanding and Controlling Operator Precedence," **page 365**

You can enter your formulas into your worksheet two different ways: You can enter the formula including the cell references via the keyboard; or, you can use the mouse to point to the cells that will be involved in the formula.

For instance, you may have a worksheet that contains two columns of numerical data (see Figure 18.1). One column holds the total sales (in dollars) achieved for the year by each of your regional salespersons. The second column contains the commission percentage that you pay each person (the commission is different for each employee because commission is based on the number of years of employment with the company). With Excel, it is easy to calculate the actual dollar amount of the commissions that you will have to pay out to each person.

The formula will be

total sales×commission percentage = commission amount

Figure 18.1

This spreadsheet requires a simple multiplication formula to return the dollar amount of the commission that will be paid to each of the sales staff.

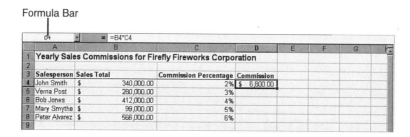

To type the multiplication formula into the worksheet:

1. Click the cell where you want to place the formula (D4).

2. Type the formula—in this case, **=B4*C4**.

3. Press Enter to enter the formula in the cell. The actual value that the formula calculates will appear in the cell. The formula itself will appear on the Formula Bar as shown in Figure 18.2.

 TIP The numeric keypad on your keyboard provides you with the easiest access to the math operators that you will use in your formulas (*, +, /, and so on). Make sure that your Num Lock is on before you try to use the keypad.

Formula Bar

Figure 18.2

The formula multiplies the total sales by the commission percentage and calculates the commission amount.

You can also create your formula using the point-and-click method to identify the cells that you want to include in the expression. We'll use the spreadsheet shown in Figure 18.2 for this example:

1. Click the cell where you want to place the formula (D5).

2. Type = (equal sign).

3. Click the first cell you want to appear in the expression (B5), then type * (multiplication sign).

4. Click the second cell you want to appear in the expression (C5). Then click the Enter icon on the Formula Bar. The formula will be placed in the cell and display the result of the calculation.

 TIP Using the point method to select the cells that will appear in a specific formula can help cut down on incorrect cell references and typographical errors in your formulas.

You can also use the methods described previously to create addition, subtraction, and division formulas. All you have to do is make sure that you reference the correct cells and use the appropriate operator.

You will find that you need to create your own formulas for many simple situations such as subtraction, multiplication and division. For more complex equations you will want to use one of Excel's built-in functions.

▶ **See** "Understanding and Using Functions," **page 366**

Understanding and Controlling Operator Precedence

Designing your own formulas requires that you understand the natural order of math calculations or operator precedence. Order of precedence is a set of rules for carrying out calculations, meaning that certain operations must be carried out before others. Excel follows the order-of-precedence rules and they are especially important for formulas that contain more than one operator.

For instance, in the formula A2+B2*C2, the multiplication sign takes precedence over the addition sign. This means that B2 will be multiplied by C2 and then A2 will be added to their product. The order of precedence operations is the following:

Order	Operator	Symbol in Excel
1	Exponent	
2	Multiplication	*
	Division	/
3	Addition	+
	Subtraction	−

So, in the formula A2*B2 + C23, the first operation calculated will be C2 raised to the third power, the second will be A2*B2, and the third will be the product of the multiplication cells A2 and B2 added to the exponentiation of C2.

When a formula contains more than one operator of the same type or precedence value, Excel computes the result from left to right. In the formula A2*A3/A4 the multiplication and division operators have the same precedence value. So Excel will multiply A2 by A3 and then divide their result by A4.

You can control operator precedence in your formulas using parentheses. Operations enclosed in parentheses take precedence over operations that are not. In the formula (A1+A2)*B2, the parenthetical calculation takes precedence over the multiplication operator. So, A1 and A2 will be added and their sum will then be multiplied by B2.

 TIP A good way to test your understanding of the order of precedence is to create several formulas on paper that use numerical values rather than cell references. For instance, 5*5+2 will return the result 27, while the formula 5*(5+2) returns the result 35.

Part
III

Ch
18

Keeping the rules of operator precedence in mind when working in Excel will help you design formulas that do not return unexpected or unusual results. Remember that you can use the parentheses to change the natural order of calculations in any formula that you create.

Understanding and Using Functions

Functions are the ready-made formulas that are built into Microsoft Excel. Excel functions exist for almost every type of calculation; there are financial functions, statistical functions, logical functions—even database functions.

Functions can do everything from add a range of numbers, to count the number of entries in the range, to provide you with a conditional statement that can return an either/or result depending on the particular value in each cell of the range.

A function consists of two parts: the name of the function and the range of cells that you want the function to act upon. For instance, the function =AVERAGE(B4:B8) will give the average of the cells in the range B4 to B8.

 TIP Functions are built to calculate simple and complex equations. It is a good idea to use functions whenever you can; you can count on a function returning the correct answer, while formulas that you design yourself can potentially be incorrect.

The following table gives you a list of a number of the Excel function categories, example functions from the category, and the purpose of the function.

Category	Function	Purpose
Financial	PMT	Calculates loan payments.
	PV	Calculates current value of an investment.
Date and Time	NOW	Returns the current date.
	WEEKDAY	Identifies a text day entry by a number 1–7.
Math and Trig	COS	Calculates the cosine of an angle.
	EVEN	Rounds a number to the nearest integer.
Statistical	AVERAGE	Calculates the average for a range of cells.
	COUNT	Counts the number of cells with entries in a particular range.
Database	DMIN	Returns the smallest number in a column of cells.
	DMAX	Returns the largest number in a column of cells.
Logical	IF	Returns a true or false answer to a conditional statement.

Obviously, the category or categories of functions that you use most often will depend on the type of worksheets you develop. If you are involved in a tree population study in the Amazon rainforest, you would probably use a number of the statistical functions. If most of your spreadsheets are used to track loans and investments, you will use the financial functions.

Commonly Used Functions

You will find that while Excel offers a great number of functions for your use, you will probably end up using only a small number of those available. The most commonly used Excel function is the SUM function; this function adds a specified range of cells:

```
=SUM(cell range)
```

Other commonly used functions are described here:

Function	Example	Description
AVERAGE	=AVERAGE(**cell range**)	Calculates the statistical mean or average for the range of numbers.
COUNT	=COUNT(**cell range**)	Counts all the cells in a specified range.
MAX	=MAX(**cell range**)	Returns the maximum (largest) value in the specified range of cells.
MIN	=MIN(**cell range**)	Returns the minimum (smallest) value in the specified range of cells.
PMT	=PMT(**interest rate cell, # of payments cell, loan value cell**)	Calculates the periodic payment of a loan with a fixed term and a fixed interest rate.
IF	=IF(**logical test, true value, false value**)	Evaluates a conditional statement to either true or false. Being equal to or less than a certain number (<=50) may be the conditional statement and the actual value returned to the cell will depend on the True/ False values you specify.
COUNTIF	COUNTIF(**range, criteria**)	Counts the cells in a range that meet the function criteria. For instance, you could establish the criteria as <5000. The function will then return a count of only the cells in the designated range that have a value of less than 5000.

continues

Part

III

Ch

18

Function	Example	Description
HLOOKUP	HLOOKUP(lookup_value, table_array,row_index_num, range_lookup)	Enables you to look up information in a data table based on a row of values in the worksheet. A lookup value could be the total sales for a particular region. This value is then cross-referenced in the designated lookup table (the table array and row index number). The value found in the lookup table is returned to the cell holding the HLOOKUP function.
VLOOKUP	VLOOKUP(lookup_value, table_array,row_index_num, range_lookup)	Enables you to look up information in a data table based on a column of values in the worksheet. VLOOKUP functions the same as HLOOKUP and will return a value from a lookup table based on a lookup value (a particular cell in the spreadsheet).
COUNTA	=COUNTA(**cell range**)	Counts all the cells in a range that hold data, including numerical and text entries. COUNTA differs from COUNT in that COUNT only counts the cells in a range holding numerical information.
HYPERLINK	HYPERLINK(link_location)	Specifies the location and filename of an object linked to a particular cell in an Excel worksheet. The hyperlink can consist of a Microsoft Word document, another Excel spreadsheet, or any OLE-compliant object.
ROUND	=COUNTA(**cell range**)	Counts all the cells in a range that holds data, including numerical and text entries. COUNTA differs from COUNT in that COUNT only counts the cells in a range holding numerical information.

Function	Example	Description
NOW	=NOW	Returns the numeric value of the current date. Each day is assigned a number with January 1, 1900 serving as the start point. This numeric system of returning the date allows you to use dates in formulas. To format the NOW numerical value, use the Date format.
RANK	=RANK(number,ref,order)	Assigns a ranking number to the value in a particular cell based on the other values in the range of cells (ref) specified. The order can be set at descending by placing a zero in the order position of the function. To set the order to ascending, use the number 1.
ROUND	=ROUND(number,num_digits)	Rounds a value to a particular number of digits. For instance, ROUND would take the value 2.16 and round it to 2.2 if the number of digits (num digits) specified in the function is set to 1, meaning you want to round the number to the first decimal place.

Part

III

Ch

18

When you enter functions into an Excel worksheet, you can type the function into a cell, specifying the function name and the range of cells you want the function to act upon, or you can use function entry tools like AutoSum and Paste function. Both of these features are available as buttons on Excel's standard toolbar.

 TIP If you want a truly exhaustive list of Excel functions, refer to Que's *Special Edition Using Microsoft Excel 97, Bestseller Edition*.

Using AutoSum

SUM is definitely the most-used Excel function. Cognizant of this fact, Microsoft has placed a button on the Excel Standard toolbar called AutoSum.

AutoSum is particularly useful in that it will try and anticipate the range of cells that you want to add. Use the AutoSum in a cell at the bottom of a column of cells you want to add, and AutoSum automatically selects the cells above it for inclusion in the SUM range. AutoSum will also select the range of cells to add when you use it to place the SUM formula to the right of a row of cells.

To total a range of numbers using AutoSum:

1. Click the cell where you want to place the SUM function.

2. Click the AutoSum button. The SUM function will be entered in the cell, and a possible range of cells to be totaled will be designated by a marquee box as shown in Figure 18.3.

AutoSum button

Figure 18.3

The AutoSum button provides you with a quick way to add a range of numbers in your worksheet.

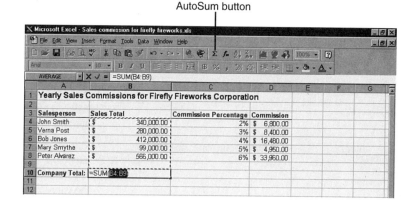

3. If the cell range selected by AutoSum is the correct range, press Enter to complete the formula. If the cell range is incorrect, use the mouse to select the correct range of cells, then press Enter to place the function in the current cell. A completed SUM function is shown in Figure 18.4.

4. If you want to edit the range in the function, select the cell holding the function. Use the mouse to select the new cell range, then click the Enter icon on the Formula Bar, or press Enter.

The result of the formula or function appears in the cell, and the formula or function appears on the Formula Bar. You can edit any formula or function by double-clicking in the cell and editing the equation in the cell, or by clicking in the Formula Bar and editing the equation there.

Figure 18.4

The completed SUM function returns the total in the cell and shows as a formula on the Formula Bar.

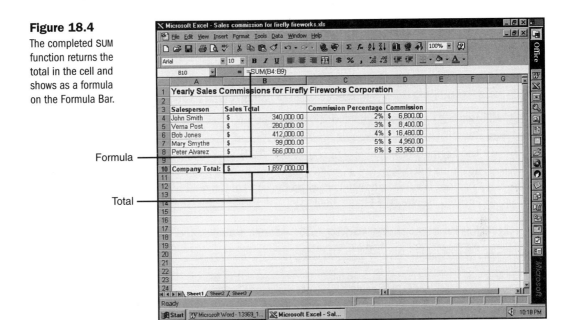

Formula —

Total —

Entering Functions Using Paste Function

Excel gives you access to a very large number of functions. The easiest way to insert these functions into your worksheets is via the Paste function button on the Standard toolbar. Once the function itself is inserted into a particular cell, it is up to you to provide the cell addresses that the function will act upon.

To insert a function into your worksheet:

1. Click the cell you want to place the function in, and then click Paste function. The Paste Function dialog box appears as shown in Figure 18.5.

2. The Paste Function dialog box is divided into two panes. Click the Category pane to view the functions in each category, which appear in the Name pane.

Figure 18.5

The Paste Function dialog box allows you to view and select functions by category.

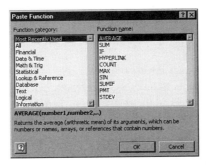

Part

III

Ch

18

TIP Excel keeps track of your most recently used functions. Click Most Recently Used in the Category pane and then select the function you want to use from the Name pane.

3. When you've found the function that you want to use, select it in the Name pane. A short description of the function appears at the bottom of the Paste Function dialog box.

4. To paste the selected function into the worksheet, click OK. The function will be pasted into the cell and the Formula Palette appears.

   The Formula Palette shows the range of cells that the function selected for use (not all functions will designate a possible range) and provides you with information on the function. The function result based on the current range of cells is also listed in the Formula Palette (see Figure 18.6).

TIP The Formula Palette also provides a function button at the top of the dialog box that you can use to change the currently selected function.

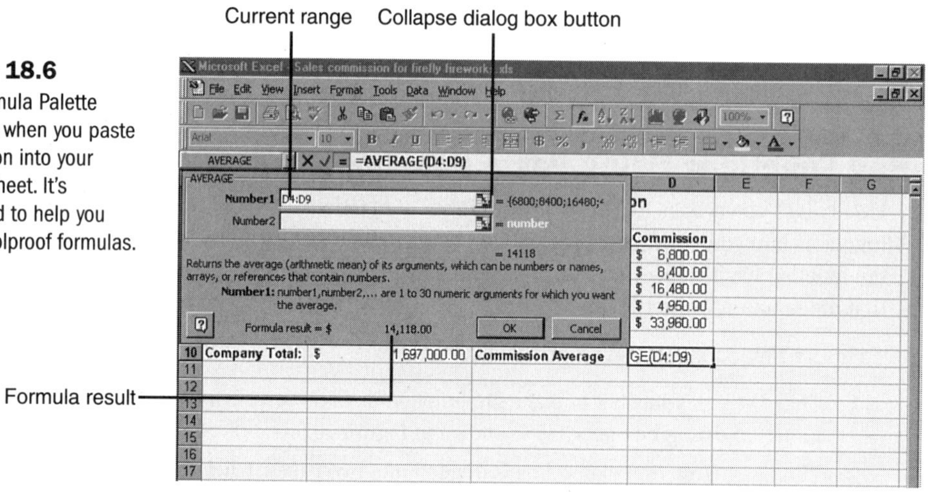

Current range   Collapse dialog box button

Figure 18.6
The Formula Palette appears when you paste a function into your spreadsheet. It's designed to help you build foolproof formulas.

Formula result

5. To change the current range, click the Collapse dialog box button next to the range box. The Formula Palette will collapse, allowing you to see your worksheet. Select the appropriate range of cells for the function, then press Enter or click the Enter button on the Formula Bar.

6. The Formula Palette reappears, showing the newly selected range and the new result of the function based on the range. If the range is correct, click the OK button. The function is inserted into the cell and the result is returned.

Getting Help with a Function

To get help with a function, follow these steps:

1. If you need more help with a particular function when you are in the Paste Function dialog box, click the Office Assistant button in the Paste Function dialog box. The Office Assistant appears, as shown in Figure 18.7.

2. In the Office Assistant's balloon, click Help with this Feature. For help specific to the currently selected function, click Help with Selected Function in the balloon.

3. The Excel Help system opens a page with specific help on the selected function. When you're finished with the Help page, close it and return to the Excel window, where you can paste the selected function into your worksheet.

Figure 18.7

Use the Office Assistant to get more information about the Paste function feature or for specific functions.

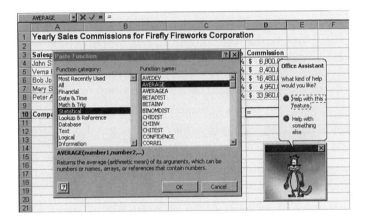

Part

III

Ch

18

N O T E You can also insert functions via the Insert menu. Choose Insert, Function.

Copying and Moving Formulas and Functions

You can copy and move formulas and functions in your Excel worksheets using several different tools such as the Edit menu, various toolbar buttons, and the Excel Fill handle. Because many of your worksheets are designed to give you comparative data on sales figures, or stock performances, or population growth over time, being able to copy formulas and functions can save you time typing or inserting the same formula or function over and over again.

For instance, the worksheet shown in Figure 18.8 details the sales performance of a particular company's sales force. The worksheet also computes the commission that each sales representative will receive for the year. While the sales total and commission rate (a percentage) are different for each salesperson, the formula that you use to compute their commission will be the same.

Figure 18.8

The formula used to compute the commission for each of the sales people will be the same.

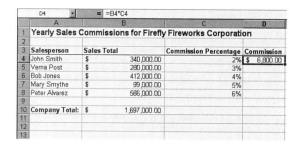

The only difference in the formula is that John Smith's commission is computed by =B4*B4, and Verna Post's is computed by =B5*B5. The formula is exactly the same—only the cell references differ.

Excel allows you to copy the formula from D4 (John's commission) to D5 (Verna's commission) and still get the correct answer because of the way Excel sees the formula. Excel sees the formula as, "Multiply the two cells that are to the left of this formula." So when you copy the formula to other cells where you want to compute the same type of answer, Excel adjusts the cell references in the formula to take into account the formula's new location.

The ability of Excel to change the cell addresses in a formula when you copy it is called **relative cell referencing**. Excel adjusts the cell references depending on where you copy the formula.

The easiest way to copy a formula that will adjust to its new location because of relative cell referencing is to use the Fill handle:

1. Click the cell that holds the formula or function you want to copy. In the lower right-hand corner of the cell box, a small black handle will appear. This is the Fill handle.
2. Drag the Fill handle to select the cells to which you want to copy the formula as shown in Figure 18.9.
3. When you release the mouse button, the formula or function will be pasted into the selected cells and the cells will be highlighted. Click in any cell to deselect the cells.

Figure 18.9

Drag the Fill handle to select the cells to which you want to copy the formula.

	A	B	C	D
1	Yearly Sales Commissions for Firefly Fireworks Corporation			
2				
3	Salesperson	Sales Total	Commission Percentage	Commission
4	John Smith	$ 340,000.00	2%	$ 6,800.00
5	Verna Post	$ 280,000.00	3%	
6	Bob Jones	$ 412,000.00	4%	
7	Mary Smythe	$ 99,000.00	5%	
8	Peter Alvarez	$ 566,000.00	6%	
9				
10	Company Total:	$ 1,697,000.00		
11				

You will notice that when you click the cells to which you pasted the formula, Excel has adjusted the cell references so that the formula returns the correct answer. The Fill handle works very well for copying formulas across columns or down rows that hold similar data.

In some worksheets, you will design formulas or use functions where you do not want all of the cells referenced in the formula to adjust to their new location. In fact, if the cell reference does change, your formula or function will no longer return the correct answer. To keep a cell address from changing as you copy the formula to a new location, you must make the cell address an **absolute reference**. This tells Excel not to use relative referencing on that particular cell address in the formula.

A good example of absolute referencing would be a worksheet where you are calculating your sales force's yearly commission and all the commissions are figured using just one percentage rate (cell B12) as shown in Figure 18.10. The formula used to compute the total commission would be =B4*$B$12. The absolute referenced cell is designated by typing a $ in front of the column designation and a $ in front of the row designation.

N O T E When you place a cell address in a formula or function, you can make it an absolute reference by pressing the F4 function key. Excel will place the $ sign before the column and row designations.

Once you've correctly entered the formula using the absolute reference, you can use the Fill handle to copy the formula to other cells as detailed earlier in this section.

CAUTION

A value contained in a single cell that is referenced in a formula or function that you copy to multiple locations on the spreadsheet must be designated as an absolute reference. Otherwise, the copied formula will adjust to its new location and incorrectly reference a cell other than the cell you specified in the original formula or function.

T I P Financial functions such as PMT will require you to use absolute referencing if you want to calculate payments for a particular loan amount at different interest rates. Because the loan amount does not change, the cell holding this information must be an absolute reference.

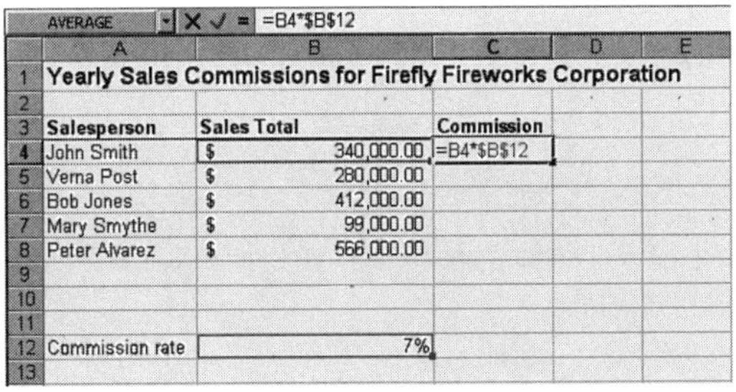

Figure 18.10
To copy some formulas and functions, you must make sure that you've designated which cell addresses in the formula should be absolute references.

Copying and Pasting a Formula

You can also use the copy and paste commands to copy a formula or function to another location or locations. To copy a formula from one cell to another:

1. Click the cell that holds the formula or function you want to copy. Click the Copy button on the Standard toolbar.

2. A selection marquee will appear around the cell as shown in Figure 18.11. Click in the cell that you want to copy the formula to and click the Paste button.

3. To copy the formula to several cells, select the cells and then click Paste. When you are finished pasting, press the Esc key to remove the selection marquee from the copied cell.

Figure 18.11

A selection marquee will appear around cells that you copy.

Yearly Sales Commissions for Firefly Fireworks Corporation				
Salesperson	Sales Total		Commission	
John Smith	$	340,000.00	$ 23,800.00	——— Selected cell
Verna Post	$	280,000.00		
Bob Jones	$	412,000.00		
Mary Smythe	$	99,000.00		
Peter Alvarez	$	566,000.00		

 TIP   Use Ctrl+C to copy a cell's contents and Ctrl+V to paste the contents into another cell(s).

Moving a Formula or Function

You can also move a formula or function from one cell to another in Excel. This is particularly useful if you've inadvertently placed a formula in the wrong cell. Moving a formula or function does not change the cell references in the formula; they remain the same as when you input them during the creation of the formula. You will remember that the Fill handle and the copy command change the cell references in the formula to relate to their new location.

Moving a formula or function in Excel is mouse work. To move a formula or function:

1. Click on the cell that holds the formula or function you want to move.

2. Place the mouse pointer on any of the selected cell's border. The mouse pointer will become an arrow.

CAUTION

Do not inadvertently drag the Fill handle of the formula cell you want to move. This will copy the formula to the new location instead of moving it.

3. Drag the formula cell to the new location and then release the mouse. The formula or function has been moved.

To move a formula or function from one worksheet to another in a workbook, hold down the Alt key when dragging the formula. You access the other worksheets by dragging the formula onto the appropriate worksheet tab.

 To move a formula or function via the keyboard, press Ctrl+X to cut the cell contents and Ctrl+V to paste it into another cell.

Using Range Names

Range names can be used to specify a range of cells in an Excel formula or function. You've already worked with range names in Chapter 13. Naming a range of cells is just a matter of selecting the cell range and then choosing Insert, Name to create the range's name.

▶ **See** "Naming Ranges," **page 346**

Using range names in your formulas not only saves you time as you design your formulas, but it will also help make sure that you designated the correct range in your formula or function.

Part III

Ch 18

TIP You will find that you will use Range names more often in Excel functions, which usually act on a number of cells to return an answer.

To use a range name in a function:

1. Click the cell that will hold the function. Click the Paste button. Select the function in the Paste Function dialog box and then click OK.

2. The Formula Palette will appear, and the range in its range box will be selected. To designate a range name as the range in the function, choose Insert, Name, Paste. The Paste Name dialog box appears as shown in Figure 18.12.

3. Select the range name you want to use in the function and then click OK in the Paste Name dialog box. The range name appears in the Formula Palette.

4. To complete the function, click OK in the Formula Palette. The completed function will return the appropriate answer in the designated cell.

To use a range name in a formula:

1. Click the cell that will hold the formula. Begin your formula with =.

2. When you are ready to designate a cell range for the formula to act upon, choose Insert, Name, Paste. The Paste Name dialog box appears.

3. Select the range name you want to use in the formula and then click OK. The range name will be placed in the formula; add the appropriate operators or other cell addresses or range names and then press Enter to complete the formula.

Figure 18.12

The Paste Name dialog box lists all the range names that you have defined for the current workbook.

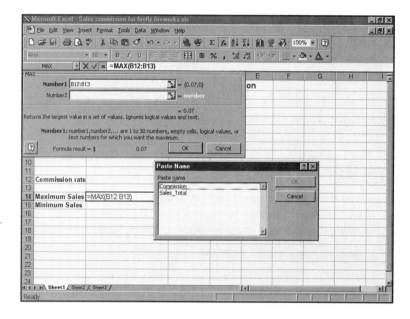

Using Arrays

An **array formula** is a single formula that can produce multiple results. An array formula does this by operating on a group of cells containing arguments or values and returning the answers to the equation to another group of cells.

For instance, you may want to create one formula to compute the payment that you would make on a new car at different interest rates. One array formula (using Excel's PMT function) could be created to show the payments at different interest rates; the array formula would do this by referencing an **array constant**, which is the group of cells that hold the different interest rates that the PMT function would use in its calculations.

Cells that share an array formula are called an **array range**. In Figure 18.13, the array range is the cells where the various payments on the car based on the different interest rates appear.

Array formulas can be very useful in that you only have to design one formula or set up one function to get multiple results. This can cut down on the need to troubleshoot multiple formulas later.

To create an array formula using an Excel function:

1. Select the array range (the cells that will hold the array formula) as shown in Figure 18.14.

2. Use the Paste Insert button to open the Paste Function dialog box. Select the function you want to use and then click OK.

Array formula   Array range

Figure 18.13

The Paste Name dialog box lists all the range names that you have defined for the current workbook.

Array constant —

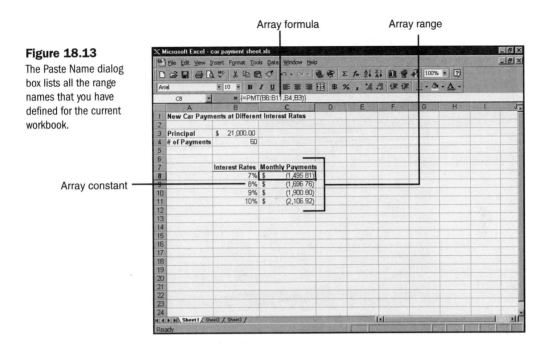

Figure 18.14

Select the cells (the array range) in which you want to place the array formula.

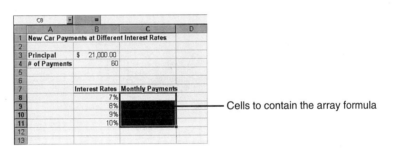

Cells to contain the array formula

3. The Formula Palette will open, displaying the various ranges that must be entered to complete the formula. To specify the array constant, select the range of cells that hold the constant values as shown in Figure 18.15.

4. Enter any other cell addresses or ranges required by the Excel function in the Formula Palette and then click OK to close the Formula Palette. The array formula will only appear in the first cell of the array range.

5. To complete the array formula, click in the Formula Bar next to the right of the formula. Press Ctrl+Shift+Enter. The array formula appears in all the cells of the array range as shown in Figure 18.16. Click in any worksheet cell to deselect the array range.

You will notice that an array formula has braces around it. This signifies the fact that it is a formula that is shared by an array range of cells.

Figure 18.15

The array constant is the range of cells that hold the constant values you will use in the array formula.

Constant values ——

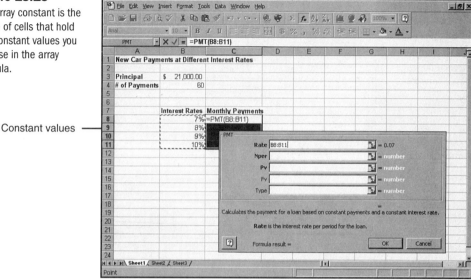

Figure 18.16

The array formula appears in each of the cells in the array range.

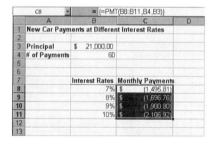

You can also use array formulas when you must create a formula from scratch, such as a simple formula for multiplication or division.

1. Select the cells in the array range.

2. Type = to begin the formula. Enter operators and cell addresses as you would for any other formula.

3. When you need to enter the array constant range, select the range with the mouse.

4. When you've complete the array formula, press Ctrl+Shift+Enter. The array formula appears in the cells of the array range. Click anywhere in the worksheet to deselect the array range.

You can create array formulas from any formulas that you normally design, or from any of Excel's functions. You can even create compound array formulas where the constant range of the array formula consists of the return from another formula or Excel function.

Using Links

Excel provides you with the ability to link to data that resides outside of the current worksheet. This data can be on another worksheet in the current workbook or in an entirely different workbook. Links can also be made to external data on company intranets or even the Internet.

▶ **See** "Workbooks, Worksheets, and Ranges," **page 337**

You can use links to pull data into a worksheet so you don't have to re-enter the information. Using links in your worksheets can be particularly useful when you are building formulas and functions that summarize information contained on other worksheets or in other workbooks.

For instance, a company may have used a different worksheet each quarter to track its profits and losses. This means that four spreadsheets would be created for each year, one every three months.

Using links, you can pull data from the four quarterly reports and use them in formulas and functions on an end-of-year summary worksheet. You can use linked data as values in cells or place the link directly into a formula.

To create a link to external data:

1. Select the cell where you will place the linked data.
2. Type = to begin the link. If the data is on another worksheet in the same workbook, click the tab for that sheet or open the other workbook. Click the cell to which you want to link.
3. Press Enter. You will be returned to the worksheet and cell that holds the new link. The cell will show the data from the link as shown in Figure 18.17.

Part
III

Ch
18

Figure 18.17
Linked data will appear in the cell as data, while appearing as a link formula in the Formula Bar.

Linked formula —

Linked data —

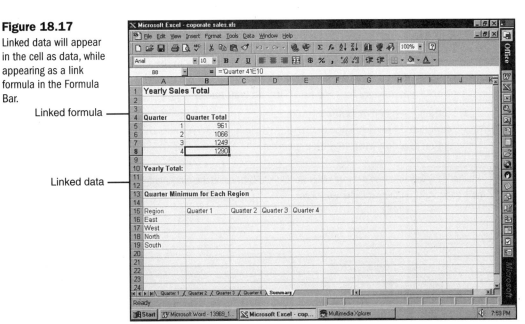

The great thing about linked data is that if you change the data in the cell to which you have linked, the link will update itself the next time you open the workbook containing the link.

The real power of links is unleashed when you use them in your formulas and functions. Data from several different worksheets or workbooks can conceivably be included in the same formula or function.

Placing a link in a formula is very similar to placing a link in a cell.

1. Begin the formula with =. To insert a link, go to the worksheet that holds the data, select the cell(s), and then return to the worksheet that holds the formula you are building.

2. Place the appropriate operator or operators in the formula. If you need to add another link, go to the worksheet holding the information that you want to link to the formula and select the appropriate cell or cells.

 Use the worksheet tabs to move from worksheet to worksheet within a workbook. If you need to switch to another open workbook, open the <u>W</u>indow menu and select the appropriate workbook file.

3. When you complete the formula, press Enter. The result of the formula appears in the formula cell. If you want to view the links in the formula, you can view them in the Formula Bar.

Links can also be used in Excel functions. To place a link in a function:

1. Use the Paste Insert button to open the Paste function dialog box. Select the function you want to use and then click OK.

2. The Formula Palette opens, displaying the various ranges that must be entered to complete the formula. To use a link for one of the function ranges, go to the worksheet that holds the cell or cell range for the link.

3. The Formula Palette will accompany you to the worksheet. Select the cell or cells for the link as shown in Figure 18.18. The cell range appears in the Formula Palette. If you need to enter more cell addresses or ranges to complete the function, return to the worksheet where you are building the function and continue.

4. If the linked cell or range completes the function, click OK in the Formula Palette. The completed function appears in your worksheet and returns the appropriate answer. The actual function with the link appears in the Formula Bar (see Figure 18.19).

 Another easy way to link to data on other worksheets is by using the range names that you created for cells and ranges on the particular worksheet.

Figure 18.18

The Formula Palette will be available in the worksheet you want to use for the function link; select the cell(s) for the link.

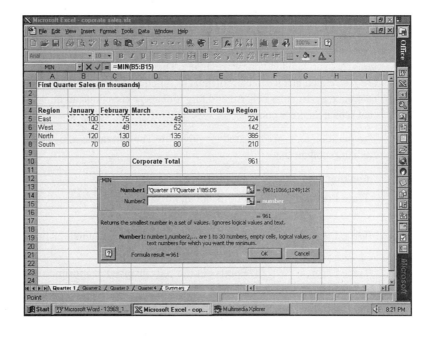

Figure 18.19

The completed function will contain the link to the external data.

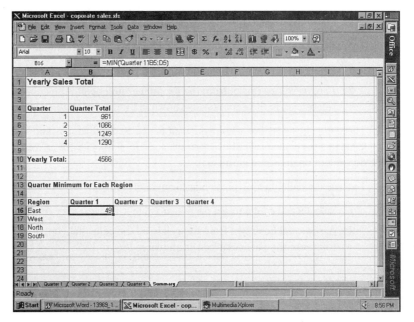

Auditing Formulas and Functions

Excel also provides you with a set of tools to check the soundness of the formulas and functions that you build in your worksheets. These auditing tools allow you to trace the cells that are referenced in a particular formula or function, or trace all the formulas or functions that reference a particular cell. An auditing tool also exists that can be used to trace formulas that return an error code.

The Auditing tools are reached by either the Tools menu and the Auditing command or the Auditing toolbar:

Auditing Tool	Purpose
Trace Precedents	Points out all the cells that are referenced in the selected formula or function.
Trace Dependents	Points out all the formulas or functions that reference the value in the currently selected cell.
Trace Error	Points out the cells involved in a formula or function that returns an error message.
Remove All Arrows	Clears the arrows and lines drawn by the tracing tools.

Cells referenced in a particular formula or function are called **precedents**. Tracing precedents enables you to see exactly which cells and ranges are involved in a particular formula.

To trace the precedents for a formula or a function in a worksheet:

1. Select the formula or function. Choose Tools, Auditing, Trace Precedents.
2. Arrows will be drawn from the formula or function to the cells and cell ranges that are referenced in the equation, as shown in Figure 18.20.

There may be occasions when you want to see all the formulas and/or functions that use a value in a particular cell. These formula and function cells are called **dependents**; they are dependent on the value in the cell.

To trace dependents for a particular formula or function:

1. Select a cell containing a particular value. Choose Tools, Auditing, Trace Dependents.
2. Arrows will be drawn from the cell to all the cells that contain formulas or functions that reference the particular cell as shown in Figure 18.21.

Figure 18.20

The Auditing feature can locate the precedents for a particular formula or function.

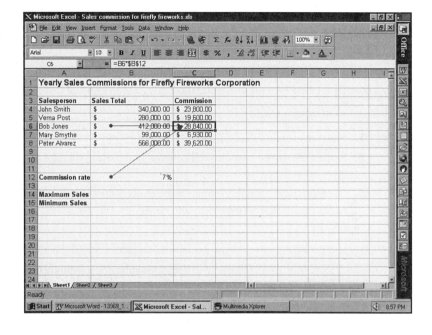

Figure 18.21

The Auditing feature can locate the formula or function dependents for a particular cell.

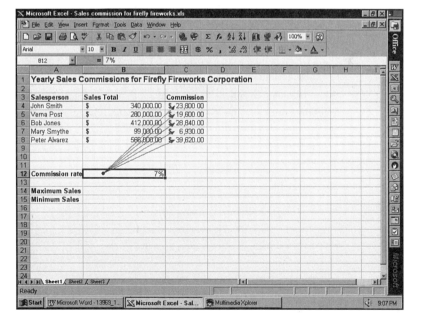

Part
III

Ch
18

You can also trace the cells involved in a formula or function that returns an error message. An **error message** means that the formula could not return an appropriate answer using the cells or cell ranges referenced in the formula.

An example would be the #DIV/0! error message. This error message appears when you inadvertently create a formula in which you divide a value by a cell that currently has no value (0).

To trace an error message:

1. Select a formula cell containing an error message. Choose Tools, Auditing, Trace Error.
2. Arrows are drawn from the cell containing the error-yielding formula to all the cells involved in the formula.
3. Once you have used the Auditor to trace precedents, dependents, or errors, you can easily remove the arrows from the worksheet. Choose Tools, Auditing, Remove All Arrows.

Excel also provides tools that you can use in conjunction with the auditing tools. Whenever you double-click a formula to edit it, the Range Finder feature highlights all the cells and cell ranges involved in the particular formula. This is not unlike tracing precedents via the Auditor.

Another feature that can help you troubleshoot your formulas and functions is Excel's ability to display the **formulas** in your worksheet rather than the **results**. To display the formulas in your worksheet:

1. Choose Tools Options, and then click the View tab. To display formulas in cells, select the Formulas check box.
2. Click OK to return to the worksheet. Cells containing formulas will display the actual formulas and functions.
3. When you want to return the worksheet to Normal and view the results of formulas and functions, return to the View tab and clear the Formulas check box.

CHAPTER 19

Using Outlines, Templates, and Forms in Excel

by Patrice-Anne Rutledge

In this chapter

Using Outlines

Excel 97 enables you to create outlines that group data automatically based on summary formulas or manually based on your exact specifications. Creating an outline is a good idea if you have a long list that contains numerous subtotals. By creating an outline, you can more easily view summary information or specific sections of data.

> **N O T E**   Another way to summarize a long list of data is to create a PivotTable. A PivotTable is an interactive report that summarizes and analyzes data. To create a PivotTable from your list, select it and choose Data, PivotTable Report. ▓

▶ **See** "Creating Pivot Tables," **page 454**

You can also create an outline automatically by using Excel's subtotal feature. This feature creates subtotals and an outline at the same time. To use it, select the data you want to subtotal and choose Data, Subtotals to open the Subtotal dialog box. Note that you must sort your data before subtotaling.

▶ **See** "Creating List Subtotals," **page 447**

Once you've created an outline, Excel makes it easy to display the outlined data as a chart. To do this, select the data you want to chart and click the Chart Wizard button on the Standard toolbar to open the Chart Wizard dialog box.

▶ **See** "Creating Charts with the Chart Wizard," **page 421**

Creating an Automatic Outline

Excel 97 creates an automatic outline if your list data includes cells with summarized information. For example, if cells A1 through A3 include numeric data and cell A4 includes a formula such as =SUM(A1:A3), Excel will automatically outline the data. Figure 19.1 displays an Excel list in a format that will accept automatic outlining.

> **CAUTION**
>
> If the data you want to outline isn't in the proper format, you'll receive an error message. Either reformat the Excel list to include summarized cells or manually create an outline.

To have Excel create an automatic outline, follow these steps:

1. Position the cell pointer in the list you want to outline.
2. Choose Data, Group and Outline, Auto Outline.
3. Excel automatically applies an outline based on the summarized cells you created. Figure 19.2 displays an outline of the list data illustrated in Figure 19.1.

Use the Hide Detail Level and Show Detail Level buttons to hide and display the detail in an outline.

Figure 19.1

List data must be in a summarized format to use Excel 97's Outline feature.

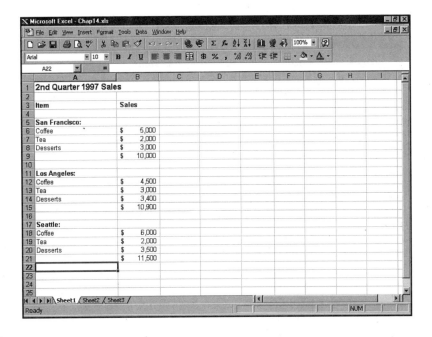

Figure 19.2

Click the Hide Detail Level button to hide summary detail.

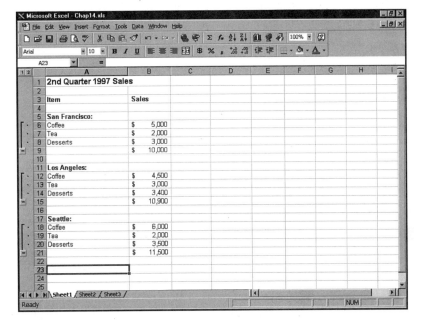

Part

III

Ch

19

Creating a Manual Outline

If you can't create an automatic outline because of the way your list is designed, or you want control over how you create the outline, you can outline your data manually. You might also want to use manual outlining to outline the content of a workbook or report, for example, that doesn't include summarized numeric data.

To manually create an outline, follow these steps:

1. Select the rows you want to group in an outline. Do not include the row that contains the summary formula.

2. Choose Data, Group and Outline, Group to group the selected items.

3. The Group dialog box appears, as shown in Figure 19.3.

Figure 19.3

In the Group dialog box you can group by either rows or columns.

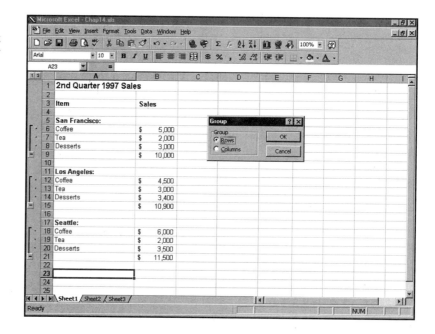

4. Choose to group either by Rows or Columns and then click OK to return to the worksheet.

T I P   If you've made a mistake or no longer need to view grouped data, you can remove a grouping. To do so, select the data you grouped and choose Data, Group and Outline, Ungroup.

Modifying an Outline

If you want to display your data in outline format but don't want to show the outline buttons, you can hide them. Choose Tools, Options and select the View tab. Figure 19.4 displays this tab.

Clear the check from the Outline Symbols check box and click OK. Your summarized outline format remains, but the outline button symbols no longer display.

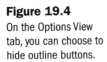

Figure 19.4
On the Options View
tab, you can choose to
hide outline buttons.

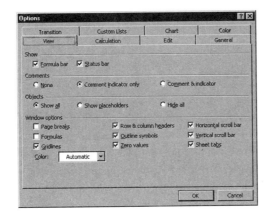

Removing an Outline

To remove an outline, choose <u>D</u>ata, <u>G</u>roup and Outline, <u>C</u>lear Outline. Excel removes the outline and outline buttons.

Protecting Documents and Data

Excel 97 includes several tools for protecting your data from other users' changes as well as
from macro viruses. Before working with templates and forms, it's a good idea to understand
how Excel's security features work.

▶ **See** "Sharing Office Documents," **page 1010**

Protecting Worksheets

You can protect individual worksheets in Excel 97. To do so, follow these steps:

1. Select the worksheet you want to protect and choose <u>T</u>ools, <u>P</u>rotection, <u>P</u>rotect Sheet to
   open the Protect Sheet dialog box, shown in Figure 19.5.

Figure 19.5
You can protect
worksheet content,
objects, and scenarios.

Part
III

Ch

19

2. Choose to protect any or all of the following worksheet elements:

N O T E   You can unlock specific cells in a worksheet you're going to protect to allow users access only to those specific cells. For example, in a form you could allow access only to data entry cells. To do this, select the cells you want to unlock, right-click the mouse, and choose Format Cells from the submenu to open the Format Cells dialog box. In the Protection tab, clear the Locked check box.

- *Contents*. Protects locked cell contents, formulas and cells you've hidden, and chart elements.
- *Objects*. Protects graphic objects, maps, charts, and comments.
- *Scenarios*. Protects scenarios, used for generating different answers for what-if analysis.

▶ **See** "Evaluating What-if Scenarios," **page 498**

CAUTION

Remember that passwords are case sensitive. If you enter a password for a protected worksheet and it doesn't work, try entering the password again with the exact case for each character. If you forget your password, there is no way to recover it, so be very careful about storing passwords for essential documents in a safe place.

---

3. You can enter an optional Password if you want to require users to enter a password to have access to the worksheet.

4. Click OK to return to the worksheet. If you chose to require a password, the Confirm Password dialog box, shown in Figure 19.6, asks you to Reenter password to proceed.

   To hide the contents of certain cells before protecting a worksheet, select those cells, right-click the mouse, and choose Format Cells. On the Protection tab of the Format Cells dialog box, click the Hidden check box.

Figure 19.6

Reenter your password to confirm it.

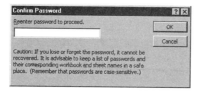

5. Enter the password again and click OK.

CAUTION

You'll receive an error message if you try to run a macro that changes cell contents on a protected worksheet.

To unprotect a worksheet, choose Tools, Protection, Unprotect Sheet. If you required a password for this worksheet, the Unprotect Sheet dialog box displays, shown in Figure 19.7.

Figure 19.7
You have to enter a password to unprotect a sheet you've password protected.

Enter the Password and click OK to unprotect.

Protecting Workbooks

In addition to protecting individual worksheets, you can also protect entire workbooks. Protecting a workbook is different from protecting a worksheet. Excel lets you protect either the workbook structure, the workbook windows, or both.

Protecting the structure of a workbook prevents users from adding, deleting, or changing worksheets; creating macros; displaying PivotTable source data; creating a summary report with the Scenario Manager; or using Analysis ToolPak tools. Protecting the workbook windows prevents users from resizing, moving, or closing windows.

To protect a workbook, follow these steps:

1. Select the workbook you want to protect and choose Tools, Protection, Protect Workbook to open the Protect Workbook dialog box, shown in Figure 19.8.

Figure 19.8
Excel lets you protect the structure and windows in a workbook.

Part
III

Ch
19

2. Choose to protect either or both of the following workbook elements:
   - *Structure.* Protects worksheets. Users can't add, delete, hide, move, copy, or rename worksheets.
   - *Windows.* Protects windows. Users can't move, resize, or close windows.

3. You can enter an optional Password if you want to require users to enter a password to have access to the workbook.

4. Click OK to finish. If you chose to require a password, the Confirm Password dialog box asks you to Reenter password to proceed.

5. Enter the password again and click OK.

To unprotect a workbook, choose Tools, Protection, Unprotect Workbook. If you required a password for this workbook, the Unprotect Workbook dialog box displays. Enter the Password and click OK to unprotect.

 T I P You can also protect shared workbooks. To use this feature, select Tools, Protection, Protect and Share Workbook to open the Protect Shared Workbook dialog box.

▶ **See** "Collaborating in Excel," **page 1032**

Protecting from Macro Viruses

A *macro* is a series of commands that allow you to automatically perform specific tasks in Excel. A macro virus is a type of computer virus that's stored in a workbook or template macro and can cause damage to your data when you open the workbook or template. By disabling unknown macros, you can avoid infection.

To activate the macro virus protection feature, choose Tools, Options and select the General tab on the Options dialog box. Figure 19.9 illustrates this tab.

Figure 19.9
The General tab includes an option for macro virus protection.

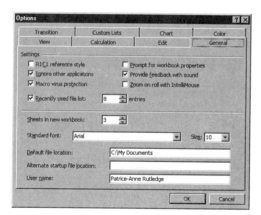

Select the Macro Virus Protection check box to enable detection. When you open a workbook, Excel displays a warning dialog box if it contains any macros. Figure 19.10 displays this warning.

Figure 19.10
Excel displays a warning if you open a worksheet that contains macros.

You can choose from the following options:

- *Disable Macros*. Opens workbooks and deactivates all macros. No macros in this workbook will run.
- *Enable Macros*. Opens workbooks and activates all macros.
- *Do Not Open*. Closes both warning and workbook.

If you don't want Excel to tell you when macros are present in a workbook, clear the check from the Macro Virus Protection check box.

TROUBLESHOOTING

My worksheet macros won't work. If you activated macro virus protection and chose the Disable Macros option in the warning dialog box that displays when you open a worksheet, your worksheet macros won't function. If you're sure that these macros are virus-free, you can reopen the worksheet, choosing the Enable Macros option.

Using Templates

In Excel, a *template* is a saved workbook that you can use as the basis for other similar workbooks. At the most basic level you can create an Excel worksheet or workbook, save it as a template, and then reuse it as the basis for other like documents.

You can also use Excel's built-in templates to create sophisticated worksheets for invoices, purchase orders, and expense statements. In addition, Excel lets you create form templates to use for data entry that you link to a database—in either Excel or another application, such as Access—for analysis and reporting.

Creating a Template

Creating a template is a good idea for worksheet and workbook types that you routinely use. For example, let's say that every quarter you create a detailed sales report. You've applied a lot of special formatting that you don't want to redo every time. You can save a formatted workbook as a template and then reuse it.

TIP You can also reuse a worksheet by simply saving it with another name and replacing the contents.

Excel templates store the following settings: cell and worksheet formatting, cell styles, page formats, print areas, headers, row and column labels, data, formulas, graphic objects, macros, hyperlinks, custom toolbars, ActiveX controls, worksheet and workbook protection, calculation options, and window display options.

To create a template based on an existing worksheet or workbook, follow these steps:

1. Open the worksheet or workbook you want to save as a template.
2. Choose <u>F</u>ile, Save <u>A</u>s to open the Save As dialog box, shown in Figure 19.11.

Figure 19.11

Save your worksheet as a template in the Save As dialog box.

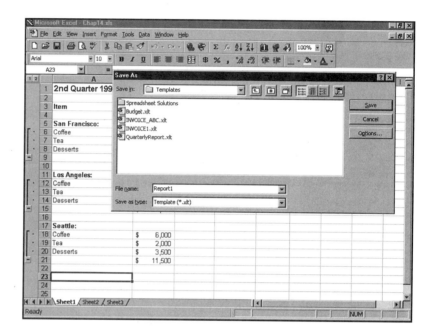

3. Be sure the Save <u>I</u>n drop-down list points to the Templates folder.

 T I P   *.xlt is the file extension for Excel templates.

4. Enter the File <u>N</u>ame and choose Template(*.xlt) as the Save as <u>T</u>ype.
5. Click the <u>S</u>ave button to return to the worksheet.

To use the template, choose <u>F</u>ile, <u>N</u>ew to open the New dialog box, illustrated in Figure 19.12.

Select the new template and click OK to open a new document based on this template.

Using Excel's Built-in Templates

Excel 97 includes several built-in templates that you can use to create common business forms such as invoices, purchase orders, and expense statements. To use one of the templates as a basis for your own worksheet, follow these steps:

1. Choose <u>F</u>ile, <u>N</u>ew to open the New dialog box. Figure 19.13 illustrates the second tab, Spreadsheet Solutions.

Figure 19.12
You can open the template you've saved in the New dialog box.

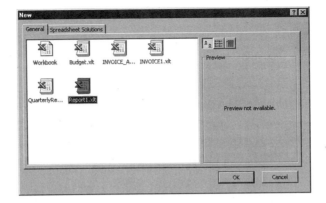

Figure 19.13
Excel includes three built-in templates for invoices, expense reports, and purchase orders.

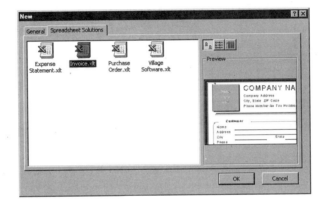

Part
III

Ch
19

2. In this example, you'll choose the Invoice template, Invoice.xlt, to create an invoice form. Click OK to open the template.

▶ **See** "Protecting Documents and Data," **page 391**

3. A warning box appears, telling you that the template you're about to open contains macros. Figure 19.14 displays this dialog box.

Figure 19.14
Excel warns you that the template contains macros.

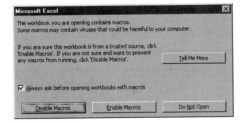

CAUTION

Enabling a macro that contains a virus can damage your Excel files. By installing virus scanning software on your computer, you can be sure that any file you're opening is free of viruses.

4. Click the Enable Macros button to continue.

5. A ready-made invoice form displays, as shown in Figure 19.15.

Figure 19.15
You can modify this invoice form to suit your needs.

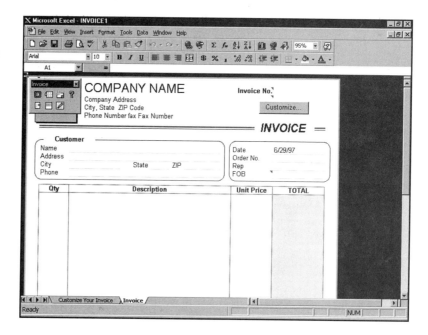

6. To customize the invoice, click the Customize Your Invoice worksheet tab. Figure 19.16 displays this tab.

7. Enter your company's name, address, and other information in this worksheet.

8. When you've completed your customizations, you can lock in your changes and save the template with another name. To do this, click the Lock/Save Sheet button to open the Lock/Save Sheet dialog box, illustrated in Figure 19.17.

9. You can choose to Lock But Don't Save or to Lock and Save Template. In this case, select Lock and Save Template and click OK.

10. The Save Template dialog box appears, shown in Figure 19.18. Enter the new File Name of your template and click OK.

TIP To make additional customizations, click the Customize button in the upper-right corner of the invoice.

Figure 19.16

Enter your company's own information on the Customize Your Invoice worksheet tab.

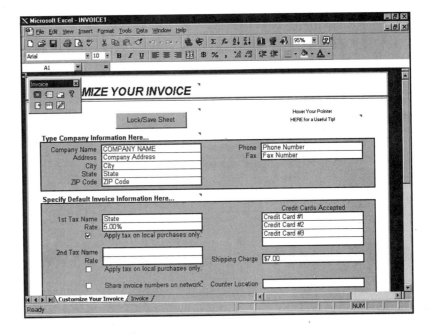

Figure 19.17

You can lock and save changes you've made to the template.

Figure 19.18

Save your new template for later use.

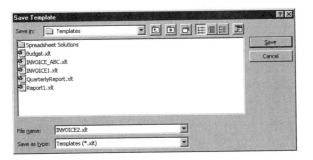

11. Excel saves the template and returns to the Invoice worksheet tab.

To use the new template you've saved, choose File, New and open it from the New dialog box.

Using the Template Wizard

Excel 97 includes a feature called the Template Wizard with Data Tracking, which enables you to link specific worksheet cells to database fields. The invoice template you just used to create your own invoice has already been linked to an Excel database named Invdb.xls. Figure 19.19 illustrates this worksheet.

Figure 19.19
You'll use the Invoice database to store your data.

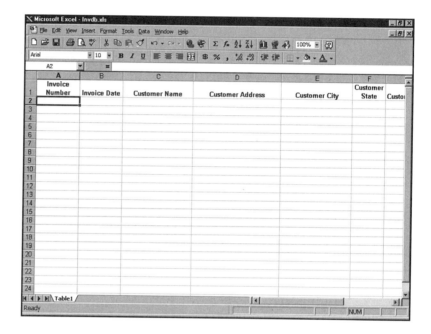

Invdb.xls includes the following fields which have been linked directly to cells in the Invoice template:

- Invoice Number
- Invoice Date
- Customer Name
- Customer Address
- Customer City
- Customer State
- Customer ZIP
- Customer Phone
- Total Invoice
- Rep

N O T E   You can also store your data in applications other than Excel. For example, you could enter the data in your Excel form and store it in Access or FoxPro. ▓

The Invoice form provides an easy way to enter this information and also provides a well-designed document to send to customers. For data tracking and analysis, the database is a more suitable format. Using the Template Wizard with Data Tracking, you can enter the information once and use it in both ways.

To get a clearer understanding of how this works, let's look at how the Template Wizard was set up to work with the Invoice form and database.

To do so, follow these steps:

1. Choose Data, Template Wizard to open the Template Wizard, shown in Figure 19.20.

Figure 19.20

The Template Wizard offers step-by-step guidance.

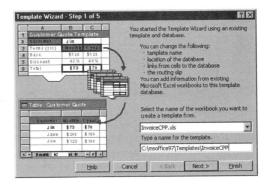

2. In step 1 of the Wizard, you select the name of the workbook that is the basis for the template and then assign a name to the template. Click Next to continue.

3. Figure 19.21 illustrates step 2. In this step, you enter the name and location of the database in which to store your data. In this case, you've elected to store your data in the invdb.xls database.

Figure 19.21

Enter information about the database in which you'll store data.

Part

III

Ch

19

4. Next, continue to step 3, illustrated in Figure 19.22. In this step, you determine which cells to store in which database fields.

5. First, choose the worksheet from which to select cells in the Sheet drop-down list.

TIP   Before you link worksheet cells to database fields, it's a good idea to create a paper map of how you want to link this data, particularly if your template is complex.

Figure 19.22

Step 3 lets you link cells to field names.

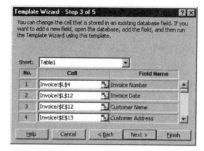

T I P   Use the Cell Reference button to return to the worksheet to select the cells to link.

---

6. For each cell that you select, enter a corresponding database field name. In this example, you'll see that ten worksheet cells have been linked to database field names. Remember that when you initially set up linked fields, you enter field names in the Field Names edit boxes; here they appear dimmed.

T I P   In order to add information from other workbooks, you must have organized your data in exactly the same way as in the existing template. Otherwise, the data won't match up properly.

---

7. Step 4, shown in Figure 19.23, asks if you want to include information from existing Microsoft workbooks to your database. If you answer No, Skip it, step 5 displays when you click the Next button.

Figure 19.23

You can include data from an existing worksheet in your database.

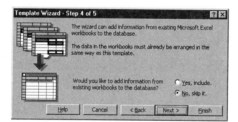

8. If you answer Yes, Include, a revised step 4 displays when you click the Next button. Figure 19.24 illustrates this revised step 4.

9. Click the Select button to open the Select Files to Convert dialog box, shown in Figure 19.25.

T I P   You can also Delete and Preview the workbook you've selected.

Figure 19.24
You can select, delete, and preview other worksheets.

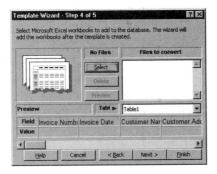

Figure 19.25
Choose the file you want to convert.

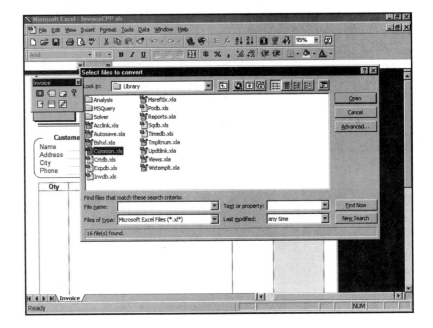

10. Choose the file you want to add to the database and click Open to return to the Template Wizard.

▶ **See** Chapter 33, "Using Message Providers," **page 731**

11. Figure 19.26 displays step 5 of the Template Wizard. In this step, you can choose Add Routing Slip to send a message to others via electronic mail each time you create a new workbook based on this template.

12. Click Finish to return to the worksheet. The Invoice form is set up to enter data in the Invoice database.

As you enter data in the Invoice form, you can click the Capture Data in a Database button on the Invoice toolbar to save data in the database. Figure 19.27 illustrates the Create and Interact with Database dialog box.

Figure 19.26

You can send notices via e-mail when you create a new workbook based on this template.

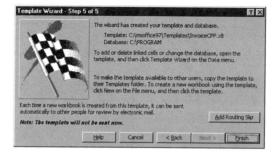

Figure 19.27

You'll update your database with new information you enter on your form.

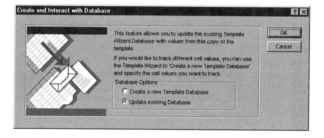

Select the Update Existing Database option button and click OK. The Template File - Save to Database dialog box appears, shown in Figure 19.28.

Figure 19.28

Create a new record in the database you've specified.

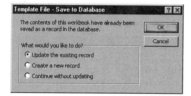

Indicate that you want to Create a New Record and click OK. Excel copies the data you entered on the Invoice form to the Invoice database.

TROUBLESHOOTING

The New dialog box doesn't display a template I created. You must place templates in the Templates subfolder in the folder in which you installed Office 97. Alternatively, you can place templates in the Alternate Startup File Location you specified in the Options dialog box General tab.

I can't find the Expense Statement, Purchase Order, or Invoice templates in the New dialog box. You need to reinstall Office 97, adding the Expense Report Template, Invoice Template, and Purchase Order Template in the Excel, Spreadsheet Templates window.

The Template Wizard doesn't work. Reinstall Office 97, adding the Template Wizard with Data Tracking option in the Excel, Add-ins window.

Creating Forms in Excel

In Excel 97 you can create forms to automate and standardize many data entry tasks. You can create online forms that are meant to collect and analyze data in Excel, forms designed to be printed, and forms to collect information from a Web site. You can also create your own forms for other users to use as a template.

 TIP To create an Excel form to use on the Web, choose Tools, Wizard, Web Form to open the Web Form Wizard.

 TIP Use the built-in Excel form templates as examples when creating your own forms. You'll find these templates by choosing File, New and selecting the Spreadsheet Solutions tab.

To create a simple form template that tracks customer information, follow these steps:

1. Click the New button on the Standard toolbar to create a new worksheet.
2. Enter your form title, such as Customer Information.
3. Next, create a list of fields you want users to enter. Figure 19.29 displays your form so far.

Figure 19.29
Creating forms is simple in Excel.

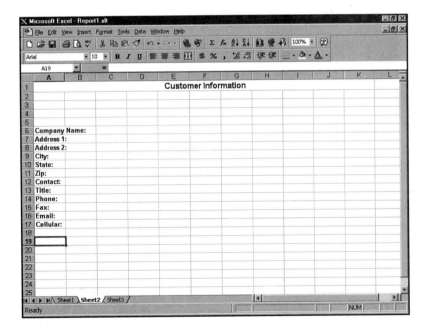

Part
III

Ch
19

4. To make it easier for users to tab through the fields they need to enter in your form, you can unlock only those cells in which users are to make entries, and protect the rest of the worksheet. In this step, select the cells you want to unlock.

▶ **See** "Protecting Documents and Data," **page 391**

5. Choose Format, Cells to open the Format Cells dialog box. Figure 19.30 displays the Protection tab.

Figure 19.30

Unlock cells on the Protection tab.

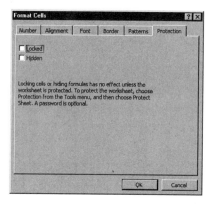

6. Clear the check mark by the Locked check box and click OK to return to the worksheet.

7. Choose Tools, Protection, Protect Sheet to open the Protect Sheet dialog box, shown in Figure 19.31.

Figure 19.31

You can protect worksheet data in Excel.

8. Specify whether you want to protect for Contents, Objects, and/or Scenarios.

▶ **See** "Protecting Worksheets," **page 391**

9. Enter an optional Password, if you want to password protect your worksheet, and click OK.

10. If you selected to use a password, the Confirm Password dialog box opens. Reenter the password and click OK to return to the worksheet.

CAUTION

Remember that if you password protect a worksheet, you'll have to enter this password whenever you open it in the future.

Users now tab only from one data entry field to another, rather than to the next cell.

11. To hide the gridlines on your form, choose Tools, Options to open the Options dialog box. On the View tab, clear the check mark by the Gridlines check box. Figure 19.32 displays this dialog box. Your cells remain, but you now have a blank background.

Figure 19.32
Removing gridlines creates a blank form background.

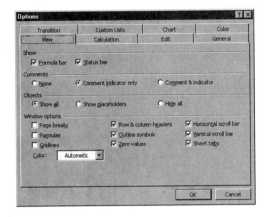

12. To save your file as a template, choose File, Save As to open the Save As dialog box.

13. Enter your template name in the File Name box and choose Template (*.xlt) in the Save As Type box.

When you want to use this template, choose File, New and select this template in the New dialog box.

Using the Form Toolbar

You can add controls to your forms to automate or simplify tasks. Check boxes, drop-down lists, and option buttons are all examples of controls. In Excel 97 you can use the Form toolbar to add controls to forms. These controls are similar to the controls that you use in Access to create a form.

Another way to create a drop-down list of possible options in Excel is by using the data validation feature.

N O T E Data validation has other uses beyond simply creating a list of possible data choices. Using this feature you can also validate and limit numeric entries as well as date and time formatting. Open the Data Validation dialog box by choosing Data, Validation.

Table 19.1 displays the buttons you'll find on the Form toolbar.

Part
III

Ch
19

Table 19.1   Buttons on the Form Toolbar

Button	Description
	Label
	Edit Box
	Group Box
	Button
	Check Box
	Option Button
	List Box
	Combo Box
	Combination List-Edit
	Combination Drop-Down Edit
	Scroll Bar
	Spinner
	Control Properties
	Edit Code
	Toggle Grid
	Run Dialog

These buttons enable you to place controls on your forms that you'll use to perform tasks or run macros. Look at Excel's built-in form templates for examples of how to use controls on a form. For instance, choose File, New and open the Purchase Order template from the New dialog box. Figure 19.33 displays this template.

Figure 19.33
You can add buttons, group boxes, and option buttons to a form.

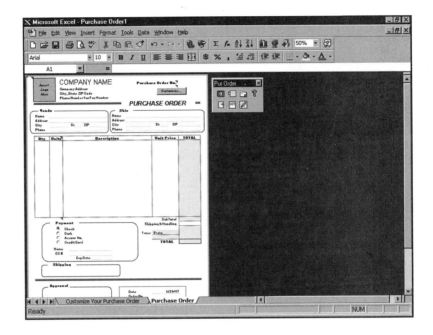

This form includes many form controls including buttons, option buttons, and group boxes.

Adding a Control to a Form

To add a basic control to a form, follow these steps:

1. Choose View, Toolbars, Forms to open the Forms toolbar if it isn't already open.

2. Select the button of the control you want to add. For example, to add a list box to your form, select the List Box button and then drag the mouse across the worksheet area in which you want to place it. Figure 19.34 illustrates the empty list box.

3. Select the list box, right-click, and choose Format Control from the submenu. Figure 19.35 displays the Control tab on the Format Control dialog box.

N O T E You must create a list of possible values in an Excel worksheet before you format the control. If this data is on the same form or worksheet, you can hide it from view later by selecting it, opening the Format Cells dialog box, and choosing Hidden on the Protection tab.

4. In the Input Range, enter the cell range that contains the values you want to include in the drop-down list. You can click the Cell Reference button to return to the worksheet to select this data.

5. If you want to return a value representing the selected drop-down list item, enter the cell in which to place this value in the Cell Link field.

Part
III

Ch
19

Figure 19.34

Users can choose from several predefined options in a list box.

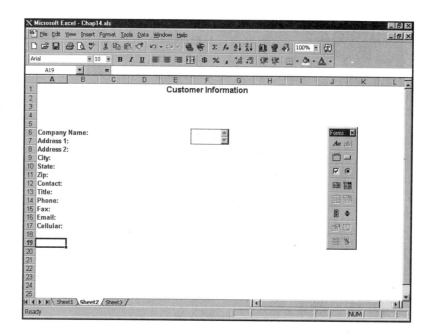

Figure 19.35

The Format Control dialog box lets you set parameters for your form control.

6. Next, determine your selection type—Single, Multi, or Extend—depending on whether you want to be able to select one or more than one item in the list.

7. Finally, you can apply 3D Shading to this list box if you want.

8. Click OK to return to the worksheet.

Users can now choose from the designated values in the list box when they use your form. You can continue adding form controls until you've completed the form. ●

CHAPTER 20

Advanced Formatting and Charting in Excel

by Patrice-Anne Rutledge

In this chapter

Overview of New Features

Excel 97 includes numerous new formatting and charting features that both simplify procedures and enhance the appearance of charts and worksheets. These features include:

- *Conditional formatting.* Excel 97 includes a new feature that allows you to apply specific formatting to the contents of cells under certain conditions.

- *Rotated text.* You can rotate text within cells by using this new feature.

- *Merge cells.* By merging the contents of one or more cells, you can create one cell.

- *Chart Wizard enhancements.* Excel 97 consolidates all charting options into one wizard, including the capability to select subtypes and preview the chart in step 1.

- *Chart menu.* This new menu consolidates many common chart-formatting options, including the capability to modify the chart type, location, and source data.

- *Chart toolbar enhancements.* The toolbar includes new features that automate chart modifications.

- *New chart types.* New types include bubble, pie of pie, and bar of pie, as well as three 3-D shapes: pyramid, cone, and cylinder.

- *Chart Tips.* When the mouse pointer hovers over a particular element, a Chart Tip tells you the name of the chart element, as well as its value.

- *Single-click selection.* Rather than having to double-click a chart to activate it and then click the selection that you want to modify, you can now simply select a chart element with a single click.

- *Time-scale chart axes.* Excel 97 includes special formatting options for charts based on a time scale such as month, day, or year.

- *Chart data tables.* You can combine a graphical representation of data as well as the data itself in a single chart.

- *Additional graphical enhancements.* Now you're able to add pictures, textures, and gradient fills to your Excel 97 charts.

Formatting Numbers, Dates, and Times

To apply numeric formatting options, select the cell or range of cells that you want to format
and then click the appropriate button(s) described in Table 20.1.

Table 20.1 Numeric Formatting Buttons

Button	Description
$	Currency Style
%	Percent Style

Button	Description
	Comma Style
	Increase Decimal
	Decrease Decimal

To display revenue data as a currency amount with no decimal places, for example, first select the Currency Style button and then click the Decrease Decimal button twice.

TIP You can also open the Format Cells dialog box by right-clicking the data you want to format and choosing _F_ormat Cells from the shortcut menu.

For more complex numeric formatting, choose F_o_rmat, C_e_lls to open the Format Cells dialog box (see Figure 20.1).

Figure 20.1

When you choose they type of format to apply, the options on the right side of the screen change. If you choose the Currency _C_ategory, for example, you can determine the number of decimal places, the current Symbol, and the Negative Numbers format.

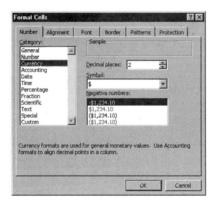

Excel also recognizes common date and time formats, and converts them to the current default format when you enter data. If your default date format is 9/1/97, for example, the entries 9-1-97, 9/1/1997, or 9/01/97 would all be converted to 9/1/97. From the Format Cells dialog box, select either Date or Time in the _C_ategory list, then choose from among the default _T_ypes listed.

Part
III

Ch
20

Creating a Custom Numeric Format

If you need a numeric format that Excel 97 doesn't include, you can create it yourself by using a custom format. To do so, choose the Custom _C_ategory in the Number tab of the Format Cells dialog box. Enter the custom format codes in the _T_ype text box, using the samples in the drop-down list as a starting point.

If you want to create a custom date or time format, for example, you can use date and time format codes to design a format that is specific to your needs. Table 20.2 lists these codes.

Table 20.2   Date and Time Format Codes

Code	Description
m	Month as a number with no leading zero
mm	Month as a number with leading zero
mmm	Month as a three-letter abbreviation
mmmm	Month as a full name
d	Day of week with no leading zero
dd	Day of week with leading zero
ddd	Day of week as a three-letter abbreviation
dddd	Day of week as a full name
yy	Year as a two-digit number
yyyy	Year as a four-digit number
h	Hour with no leading zero
hh	Hour with leading zero
m	Minute with no leading zero
mm	Minute with leading zero
AM/PM	AM or PM indicator

Using these format codes, you can enter **d-mmm-yy h:mm** to represent 30-Aug-97 0:00, for example.

Formatting Alignment

From the Formatting toolbar, you can right-align, left-align, or center your text. For other kinds of alignment, select the cells to format and then choose Format, Cells to open the Format Cells dialog box. Figure 20.2 displays the Alignment tab of this dialog box.

TIP To center your text across columns, select the cells that you want to center and then click the Merge and Center button on the Formatting toolbar.

TIP To activate the Indent scroll box, choose Left (Indent). You can then specify an exact amount of indentation.

Figure 20.2

You can change the alignment of data in the Alignment tab of the Format Cells dialog box.

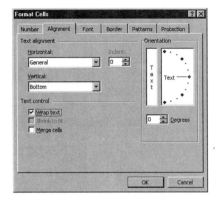

From the drop-down lists, you can choose the Horizontal and Vertical text alignment that you prefer.

The Alignment tab offers several options for controlling text:

- *Wrap Text*. Wraps the text within a single cell, adjusting row height accordingly.
- *Shrink to Fit*. Shrinks the text to fit the size of the existing cell.
- *Merge Cells*. Creates one cell by merging the contents of one or more cells.
- *Rotate Text*. Rotates text from 90 to –90 degrees.

Figure 20.3 illustrates each of these options.

Figure 20.3

In Excel 97, you can wrap text, shrink text to fit, merge cells, or rotate text in a worksheet.

Wrapped text ⎯

Shrink-to-fit text ⎯

Merged cells ⎯

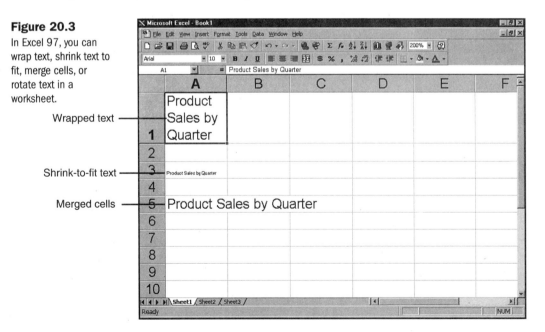

Part
III

Ch
20

N O T E In the Orientation group box of the Alignment tab, you can choose either vertical or horizontal orientation. If you choose vertical orientation, you also must choose a specific vertical alignment (Top, Center, Bottom, or Justify) from the Vertical drop-down list. ▪

Customizing Fonts

The Formatting toolbar contains several options for customizing the fonts in your worksheet. Table 20.3 illustrates these options.

Table 20.3   Font Formatting Buttons

Button	Description	Enables You To:
Arial	Font	Choose a new font from the drop-down list.
10	Font Size	Choose a new font size—from 8 to 72—from the drop-down list.
B	Bold	Bold the selected text.
I	Italic	Italicize the selected text.
U	Underline	Underline the selected text.
A	Font Color	Choose a font color from the palette that displays.

If you require more flexibility than the Formatting toolbar offers, you can select the text that you want to format and choose Format, Cells to open the Format Cells dialog box. The Font tab, displayed in Figure 20.4, provides additional options for underlining and other effects, such as strikethrough, superscript, and subscript.

Applying a Border and Pattern

Borders serve as visual separators between worksheet areas and can also enhance the appearance of printed reports.

T I P A shortcut for applying borders is selecting the cell or range that you want to format and then clicking the arrow next to the Borders button to display the Borders palette.

Figure 20.4
The Font tab includes several advanced formatting options including effects such as strikethrough, superscript, and subscript.

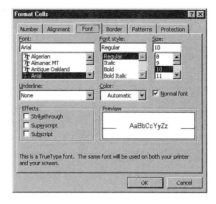

To apply a border, select the Border tab of the Format Cells dialog box, illustrated in Figure 20.5. You can open this dialog box by choosing Format, Cells.

Figure 20.5
In the Format Cells dialog box, select a border to add to a cell.

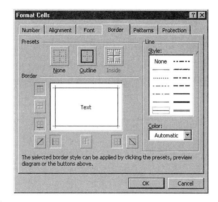

The simplest way to apply a border is to use one of the preset borders:

- *None*. No border—choose to remove an existing border.
- *Outline*. Border around the outside edge of the selected cells.
- *Inside*. Border on the inside grid of the selected cells.

The preview area displays what the border will look like.

You can also design your own border with the border buttons that appear in the bottom half of the dialog box. These buttons give you the option to create top, bottom, left, right, or diagonal borders.

You can enhance your worksheet even more with patterns and colors. The Patterns tab of the Format Cells dialog box allows you choose among a variety of colors and patterns (see Figure 20.6).

Figure 20.6

Apply patterns and colors to a cell with the Format Cells dialog box.

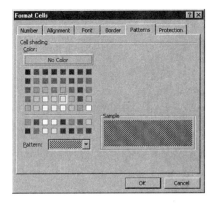

Choose a Color from the selection of available colors. Click the arrow next to the Pattern box to display the Pattern palette. The Sample box displays the effects of your selected color and pattern.

Using Automatic Formatting

Using Excel's AutoFormat feature enables you to choose among predesigned templates that include preformatted numbers, cell alignments, column widths, row heights, fonts, borders, and other options.

To use AutoFormat, follow these steps:

1. Select the range that you want to format.

2. Choose Format, AutoFormat. The AutoFormat dialog box appears, as shown in Figure 20.7.

Figure 20.7

The AutoFormat dialog box displays preformatted templates.

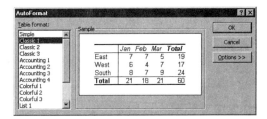

3. Select one of the format types in the Table Format list box. You can view the selected format in the Sample box.

4. Choose OK to apply the format.

Using Conditional Formatting

Excel 97 includes a new feature called *conditional formatting*, which allows you to apply specific formatting to the contents of cells under certain conditions. Excel automatically applies the format that you specify (such as a certain color) to the cell if a condition is true. You can use conditional formatting to highlight values that you want to track or the result of a formula. You can display a cell in red if it contains a negative number, for example.

To use conditional formatting, follow these steps:

1. Choose Format, Conditional Formatting to open the Conditional Formatting dialog box, shown in Figure 20.8.

Figure 20.8

Using Excel 97's conditional formatting feature, you can specify the conditions under which to apply a particular format.

2. From the Condition 1 drop-down list, choose either Cell Value Is or Formula Is, depending on whether you want to track a cell value or formula.

3. If you choose to track a cell value, select a condition from the second drop-down list.

4. Enter the conditional data in the adjacent text box, or click the Cell Reference button to return to the worksheet to select the appropriate cell.

   You must enter data in two text boxes if you choose a condition that evaluates between two values. In this example, you want to apply formatting if the cell content is greater than 0.

5. Click the Format button to open the Format Cells dialog box.

6. Select the desired formatting options and click OK to return to the preceding dialog box. In this case, you want to set the color to red.

7. To include additional conditions, click the Add button, which adds Condition 2 below Condition 1 in the dialog box.

8. When you finish, click OK to return to your worksheet.

When you enter data that matches one of your conditions, Excel formats that data as you specify. A negative amount in the cell that you just formatted displays in red, for example; a positive amount displays in the default color.

To delete a condition, follow these steps:

1. Choose the Delete button in the Conditional Formatting dialog box, which opens the Delete Conditional Format dialog box, shown in Figure 20.9.

Part
III

Ch
20

Figure 20.9

Deleting conditional
formatting is simple in
Excel 97.

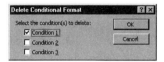

2. Select the condition that you want to delete and click OK to return to the Conditional Formatting dialog box.

3. When you finish, click OK to return to your worksheet.

Turning Data into Charts

When you finish entering and analyzing data in a worksheet, you may want to represent this data visually in a chart. Excel 97 offers a variety of chart types that you can easily create with its Chart Wizard. Table 20.4 lists these chart types.

Table 20.4   Chart Wizard Chart Types

Chart Type	Description
Column	Compares a set of values across categories in vertical columns.
Cylinder	Creates a column chart with a cylindrical shape.
Cone	Creates a column chart with a cone shape.
Pyramid	Creates a column chart with a pyramid shape.
Bar	Compares a set of values across categories in horizontal bars.
Line	Displays a line with a marker at each data value.
Pie	Displays the amount contributing to a total as a numeric value or percentage.
Doughnut	Functions as a pie chart, but can contain multiple series of data.
(XY) Scatter	Compares pairs of values with scatter marks.
Bubble	Similar to a scatter chart, but compares three sets of values.
Area	Displays a contribution trend for each value.
Radar	Creates markers at each data point.
Surface	Creates a 3-D surface showing value trends.
Stock	Displays three sets of values as stock high, low, and close.

TIP   Cylinder, cone, and pyramid charts are new variations of a column chart and provide an enhanced way to depict column data.

Choosing the right chart type is an essential first step in creating a meaningful chart, because all other chart formats and options depend on this selection. Suppose that you want to graphically represent your company's revenue over the past three months. A column, bar, or line chart is a good choice for this kind of data. Figure 20.10 illustrates the same information displayed in these three kinds of charts.

Figure 20.10

In Excel charts, the x axis is the category axis and the y axis is the value axis. In the column chart, the category axis is horizontal and the value axis is vertical. In the bar chart, the opposite is true.

Data that charts are created from

Column chart

Bar chart

Line chart

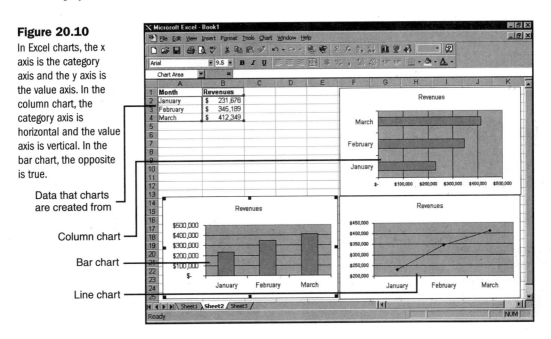

A pie chart is a good way to represent separate values that make up a whole. Figure 20.11 illustrates a sample pie chart.

Creating Charts with the Chart Wizard

Using Excel's automated Chart Wizard, you can quickly and easily create sophisticated charts from your existing worksheet data. To create a chart by using the Chart Wizard, follow these steps:

1. Select the data to be included in the chart (including column and row labels).
2. Click the Chart Wizard button in the Standard toolbar to open the wizard. Figure 20.12 displays step 1 of the wizard.

TIP You can include nonadjacent data ranges in your chart by holding down the Ctrl key as you select additional ranges.

Part
III

Ch
20

Figure 20.11

A pie chart can represent percentages of a whole.

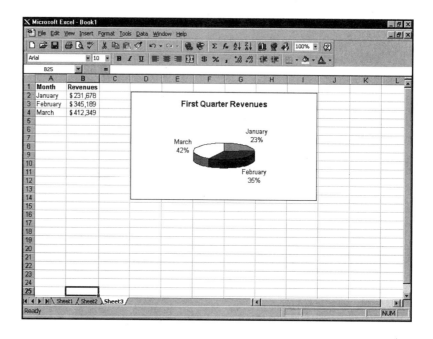

Figure 20.12

You can choose from among 14 chart types in step 1 of the Chart Wizard.

 TIP For additional chart-type choices, look at the Custom Types tab in step 1 of the Chart Wizard.

The Standard Types tab includes a list of 14 chart types, each with a number of chart subtypes that appear on the left side of the dialog box.

TIP After you identify a potential chart type and subtype, click the Press and Hold to View Sample button, which displays a larger sample of this chart type on the left side of the dialog box.

3. Click Next to continue to the second Chart Wizard step, in which you select source data. Figure 20.15 illustrates this dialog box.

4. Determine whether to display your data in Rows or Columns.

The preview box illustrates how each option would appear in a chart.

Figure 20.13

The range of cells that you initially selected appears in the Data Range box. You can change this range, if you prefer.

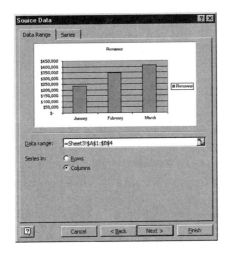

N O T E In Excel, a *data series* is the set of data that a chart element (such as a column, bar, or pie slice) graphically represents. You can have multiple data series. The Series tab of the Source Data dialog box provides more options for determining the data series in your chart. ▪

5. Click Next to continue. The third step of the wizard includes six tabs, each of which offers a different charting option for determining titles, axes, gridlines, legends, and data labels.

6. In the Titles tab, specify a Chart Title, which centers across the top of a chart. Figure 20.14 displays this tab.

The other tabs in step 3 allow for the following:

- *Axes.* In this tab, you determine whether to display the Category (x) axis, the Value (Y) axis, or both axes.
- If you decide to display a category (x) axis, you then need to choose among the following formatting options: automatic, category, or time-scale.
- *Gridlines.* In this tab, you can choose to display or hide the gridlines in your chart (which can make your chart easier to read). You can add major or minor gridlines to either the category (x) axis or the value (y) axis. The default for most charts is to include major gridlines for the value (y) axis.
- *Legend.* In this tab, you can specify whether to show a legend in your chart. (A *legend* associates descriptive text with the colors or patterns of data in your chart.) You can place your legend at the bottom, corner, top, right, or left of your chart.

Part
III

Ch
20

- *Data Labels.* Often, you want to display a descriptive label next to its graphical representation in a chart. You can do this in the Data Labels tab, shown in Figure 20.15.

Figure 20.14

You can also specify the Category (X) Axis label and a Value (Y) Axis label. If available, you can also specify Second-Category (x) and Second Value (y) axes.

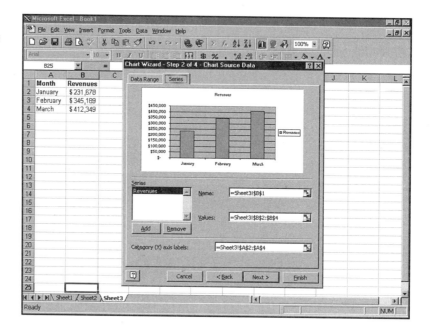

Figure 20.15

Using the Data Labels tab, you can choose to display actual monetary amounts in a chart, rather than just display them visually.

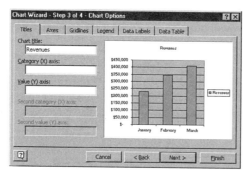

- *Data Table.* Finally, you have the option of displaying a data table below your chart. A *data table* includes the actual data that you're representing graphically, in a format similar to the original data range in your worksheet. Figure 20.16 shows the Data Table tab.

7. Click Next to continue to step 4 of the Chart Wizard (see Figure 20.17), where you determine the location of your chart—either as a New Sheet or as an Object in an Existing Sheet.

Figure 20.16
A data table displays detailed data in your chart.

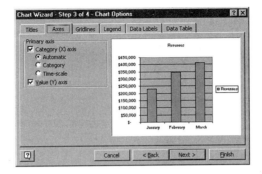

Figure 20.17
You can place your chart in the same worksheet or a different one.

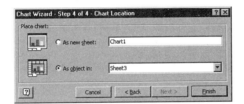

8. Finally, at the end of step 4, click the Finish button to complete your chart.

 To deactivate Chart Tips, choose Tools, Options and then deselect the Show Names and Show Values check boxes in the Chart tab of the Options dialog box.

To identify each section of your new chart, hover the mouse pointer over the particular section to allow the Chart Tips feature tell you the name of the chart element, as well as its value.

Modifying Charts

After you create a basic chart, you'll probably want to modify it in some way. The easiest way to modify a chart is to use the buttons in the Chart toolbar, which appears after you create your chart. Table 20.4 describes the buttons in this toolbar.

NOTE Not every toolbar button is available at all times. Angle Text Upward and Angle Text Downward, for example, are active only when you are choosing a text field. ■

Part
III

Ch
20

Table 20.4   Chart Toolbar

Button	Name	Description
Chart Area ▼	Chart Objects	Lists available chart objects.

continues

Table 20.4 Continued

Button	Name	Description
	Format	Opens Format dialog box, which contains available formatting options.
	Chart Type	Displays the Chart Type palette, in which you can change the chart type.
	Legend	Activates and deactivates the chart legend.
	Data Table	Activates and deactivates the chart data table.
	By Row	Displays the data by row.
	By Column	Displays the data by column.
	Angle Text Downward	Rotates selected text down.
	Angle Text Upward	Rotates selected text up.

T I P Right-clicking a chart produces a shortcut menu that lists many of these same options.

The Chart menu also includes many options for modifying a chart after you create it. From this menu, you can modify the chart type, source data, location, and other options.

Modifying the Chart Type

To modify the chart type, click the arrow to the right of the Chart Type button in the Chart toolbar. A chart palette (see Figure 20.18) displays the available types of charts. Select the new chart type, and the chart updates automatically.

Moving a Chart

To move an existing chart, click inside it to activate it and then drag it to a new location in the worksheet.

Figure 20.18

Choose a new chart type from the palette.

TIP To copy the chart rather than cut it, choose Edit, Copy or press Ctrl+C.

To move a chart to another worksheet in your workbook, select it and then choose Edit, Cut. Move to the new worksheet and choose Edit, Paste to paste the chart to the new location.

Resizing a Chart

To resize an existing chart, follow these steps:

1. Select the chart by clicking it.
2. Position the mouse pointer over a chart handle until the mouse pointer becomes a double arrow.

TIP To maintain proportions while resizing, hold down the Shift key.

3. Drag the chart handle to increase or decrease the chart to the desired size.

Formatting Charts

To perform basic formatting of your chart, choose the chart area that you want to format from the Chart Objects drop-down list in the Chart toolbar. Then click the Format button to open the Format dialog box. The complete names of the Format button and the Format dialog box change, depending on the chart object that is currently selected. If you selected the Chart Title object, for example, the button and dialog box are named Format Chart Title. The tabs of the Format dialog box also vary, depending on the selected chart object.

Suppose that you want to format the font of the chart title—a common formatting task. To do so, select Chart Title as your chart object and then click the Format Chart Title button to open the Format Chart Title dialog box, shown in Figure 20.19.

This dialog box has three tabs: Pattern, Font, and Alignment. In the Font tab, you can make any necessary font changes.

Part

III

Ch

20

Figure 20.19
You can format the pattern, font, and alignment of your chart title.

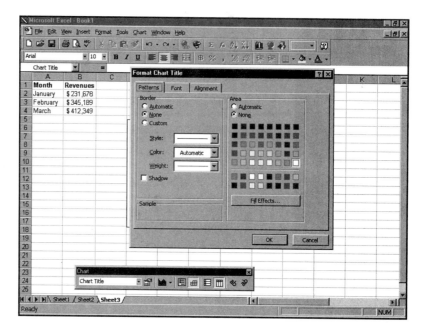

Enhancing Charts

After you create a chart and make basic modifications in it, you may want to make further enhancements to improve its aesthetic appearance. Here are some suggestions:

- Change the gradient, texture, or pattern of your chart's background by selecting it and then clicking the Fill Color button in the Formatting toolbar. From the Fill Color palette, select Fill Effects to open the Fill Effects dialog box, shown in Figure 20.20.

Figure 20.20
In the Fill Effects dialog box, you can change a gradient, texture, or pattern.

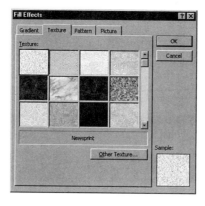

You can choose among a variety of fill options in the Gradient, Texture, Pattern, and Picture tabs. Figure 20.21 shows a sample chart that uses the Newsprint texture.

Figure 20.21

Applying a textured background to a chart can enhance its appearance.

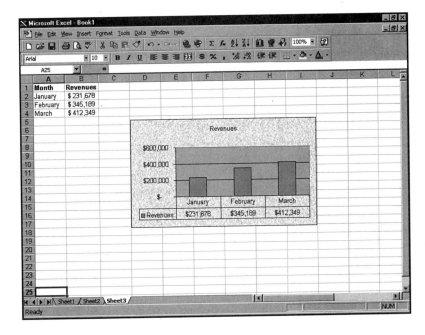

- Incorporate WordArt into your charts by choosing Insert, Picture, WordArt to open the WordArt Gallery, where you can choose among many WordArt styles.
- Rotate a text element by selecting it and then clicking the Angle Text Downward or Angle Text Upward button in the Chart toolbar.

CAUTION
Be sure to make enough room for this rotated text; otherwise, it can overlap other chart elements.

If you selected a 3-D chart subtype, Excel 97 provides additional formatting options. To work with these additional options, choose Chart, 3-D View to display the 3-D View dialog box (see Figure 20.22).

Figure 20.22

You can adjust a chart's elevation, rotation, or perspective in the 3-D View dialog box.

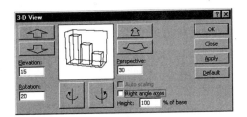

To remove all customizations that you made in the 3-D options, click the Default button.

Part
III

Ch
20

You can change the Elevation—the level at which you view the chart—either manually by entering a value in the text box, or by clicking the elevation control to increase or decrease the value incrementally.

In addition, you can adjust the Rotation of the 3-D chart—its angle—in the same way. Either enter a manual rotation level in the text box or adjust by using the rotation controls.

N O T E The perspective option doesn't appear if you selected the Right Angle Axes check box in the 3-D View dialog box.

The Perspective feature allows you to set depth. Again, enter the level manually or use the controls. Check the Right Angle Axes box to remove perspective from the chart.

Enter Height as a percentage of the base. If you select Auto Scaling, Height defaults to 100 percent.

Saving Customized Chart Formats

After you make extensive customizations in a chart, you may want to reuse the format. To create a custom chart format, follow these steps:

1. Select the chart that you want to use as a custom format.

2. Choose Chart, Chart Type to open the Chart Type dialog box, shown in Figure 20.23.

Figure 20.23
Add a user-defined chart type in the Chart Type dialog box.

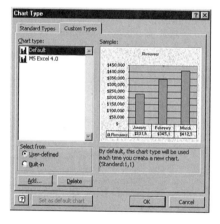

3. Select User-Defined in the Custom Types tab. A list of user-defined chart types appears, and the Add button is activated.

T I P Click the Delete button to delete a user-defined chart.

4. Click the Add button to open the Add Custom Chart Type dialog box, shown in Figure 20.24.

Figure 20.24

You can enter a name and description of your custom chart.

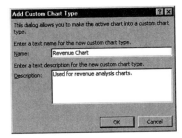

5. Enter a Name and Description for this custom chart type.

6. Click OK.

The user-defined custom chart is now available for selection the next time you create a new chart. ●

CHAPTER 21

Using Lists and Databases

In this chapter

Overview of New Features

Excel 97 includes a few new features that further automate list and database entry:

- *Data validation*. To ease entry and help avoid entry errors, data validation lets you specify entry parameters by field.

- *Custom data entry messages*. In Excel 97 you can customize input and error messages when using data validation.

Understanding Lists and Databases

In Excel 97, a *list* is a series of rows in a worksheet containing similar data. A worksheet with client names and addresses, a series of stock performance data, or a project to-do list are all examples of lists. In each case the columns contain similar information based on each column label. Figure 21.1 shows two list examples.

Figure 21.1

In Excel 97, a list contains a series of rows with like data.

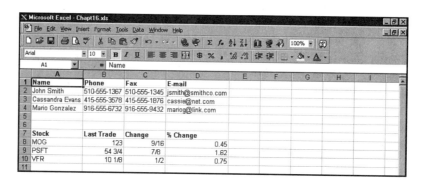

Excel automatically considers any data in a list format to be a database and enables you to find, sort, or total this data—common database functions. When using a list as a database, each *column* is a database field that determines the type of information required for data entry. Excel considers the column label to be a field name and each *row* to be a database record.

Designing and Creating a List

You can create a basic list in any Excel worksheet. To create a list, enter the column labels in the first row. For example, let's say that you want to create a project to-do list for a design firm. You want to include the following columns:

- Project
- Customer
- Estimated Revenue
- Due Date
- Designer
- Estimated Hours

TIP You can use formatting features such as bolding, italics, or cell borders to differentiate parts of your list.

CAUTION
Be sure that your worksheet doesn't include other data in the area beneath your new list. If the list grows, it may collide with the data you've entered below it.

You'll enter the data for each individual project in a separate row. Because Excel considers all consecutive rows to be part of the same list, avoid blank rows between sections or between the column labels and the list data. Figure 21.2 illustrates the first few rows of this project list.

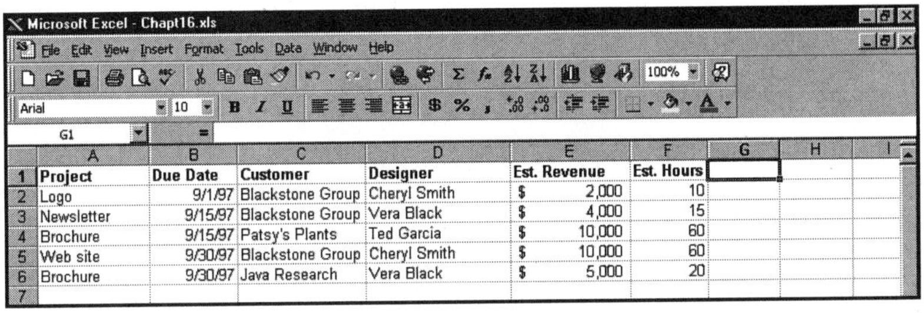

Figure 21.2
Organize list data in columns.

	Project	Due Date	Customer	Designer	Est. Revenue	Est. Hours
1	Project	Due Date	Customer	Designer	Est. Revenue	Est. Hours
2	Logo	9/1/97	Blackstone Group	Cheryl Smith	$ 2,000	10
3	Newsletter	9/15/97	Blackstone Group	Vera Black	$ 4,000	15
4	Brochure	9/15/97	Patsy's Plants	Ted Garcia	$ 10,000	60
5	Web site	9/30/97	Blackstone Group	Cheryl Smith	$ 10,000	60
6	Brochure	9/30/97	Java Research	Vera Black	$ 5,000	20
7						

Entering List Data

Once you've created an Excel list, you can continue entering data in the worksheet, or you can create a data form to simplify your data entry tasks. A *data form* displays field names in a database format and allows you to enter information in text boxes. In a data form, you can add, modify, find, and delete records.

▶ **See** "Using Templates," **page 395**

NOTE If more than one user is going to enter data in your Excel database, the Template Wizard with Data Tracking can make this easier. To open this wizard, choose Data, Template Wizard and follow the prompts that appear for each step. ■

Entering Data with the Data Form

A data form uses the column labels from your list as text box labels and enables you to quickly add new data records.

To enter data using the data form, follow these steps:

1. Position the cell pointer in any cell in your list.

CAUTION

Before choosing <u>D</u>ata, F<u>o</u>rm, you must first select any cell within the list you want to modify; otherwise Excel displays an error message stating that no list was found.

2. Choose <u>D</u>ata, F<u>o</u>rm. Figure 21.3 displays the Data Form dialog box.

Figure 21.3
A data form can simplify data entry tasks.

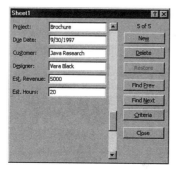

3. Click the Ne<u>w</u> button to add a new row or record to the list. Excel displays a new blank record.

N O T E   If you make a mistake and want to erase your current entry, click the <u>R</u>estore button on the data form to remove the entry from the form. You must click <u>R</u>estore before pressing Enter to avoid saving the record.

T I P   Press Tab to move forward to the next text box. Press Shift+Tab to move to the previous text box.

4. Enter your data in each text box.
5. Press Enter to save the record and display another blank record once you've completed entering data.
6. Click the C<u>l</u>ose button to return to the worksheet.

Using Data Validation

Using Excel 97's data validation feature, you can specify the exact information you can enter in your list, reducing the chance for data entry errors. For example, you can limit entries to a select list of choices, ensure that a user enters a valid date in a date column, and prevent numeric entries outside set parameters you've specified.

CAUTION

Any data validation you set doesn't apply to entries you make using the data form.

CAUTION

You can't set data validation options if you're currently entering data or if you've applied protection to your worksheet; the Validation option on the Data menu appears dimmed. Complete your data entry and unprotect your worksheet by choosing Tools, Protection, Unprotect Sheet and then try to access the Validation menu again.

To set data validation criteria, select the column whose data entry you want to validate and choose Data, Validation to open the Data Validation dialog box. To validate the data only in part of a column, select the specific cells you want to validate rather than the entire column. Figure 21.4 displays this dialog box.

 TIP To remove data validation criteria, select the column from which you want to remove validation and choose Data, Validation to open the Data Validation dialog box. Then click the Clear All button in the Data Validation dialog box. To remove data validation from the entire worksheet, select the worksheet and then click Clear All.

Figure 21.4

Set parameters for data entry in the Data Validation dialog box.

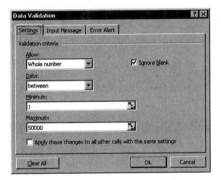

You can choose to Allow the following criteria:

- Any value
- Decimal
- Date
- Text length
- Whole number
- List
- Time
- Custom

Note that the default selection in Allow depends on the data in the column that you're validating.

Validating Numeric, Date, and Time Entries   If you choose Whole Number, Decimal, a numeric, Date, or Time as the Allow criteria, you have the following Data operator options:

- Between
- Equal to
- Not between
- Not equal to

Part
III

Ch
21

- Greater than
- Greater than or equal to
- Less than
- Less than or equal to

You'll enter Minimum and Maximum values for numeric values, or start and end parameters for date and time. Click the Cell Reference button, located to the right of the Minimum and Maximum fields, to return to the worksheet to select these values.

For example, in the project list you might want to specify that a user must enter a date between the current date and **1/1/99** for the project due date. You could also specify that the estimated project cost must be at least $1 and no more than $100,000 to help avoid data entry errors. If you enter an invalid value, Excel displays an error message, shown in Figure 21.5.

Figure 21.5

An error message appears telling you that you've entered invalid data.

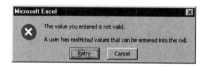

Validating List Data   To create a drop-down list of values from which a user must choose, first select the entire column that you want to validate. Next, choose the List as Your Allow option in the Data Validation dialog box, and then enter your Source list. By clicking the Cell Reference button, you can return to your worksheet and select your list of valid values. For example, if the only project types you'll want to enter are those that currently exist in your list, you can select those options. Then when you enter your next value in the Project column, a drop-down list displays the values from which you can choose, shown in Figure 21.6.

CAUTION

Only choose a validation list when you don't want to enter any data other than the list values. Otherwise, it's better not to use data validation and let Excel's AutoComplete feature finish your entries after you type in the first few characters of a value you've previously entered.

Figure 21.6

Choose from the list of valid values.

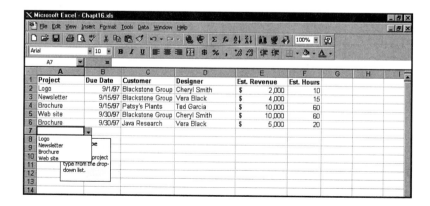

Specifying Input and Error Messages   To specify an input message to display when a user makes an entry in a column you've validated, go to the Input Message tab in the Data Validation dialog box. Figure 21.7 illustrates this tab.

> ### CAUTION
> Be sure you select an entire column to validate rather than just one cell in the column or Excel may not display an error message when users enter invalid data. If you select only a specific cell, Excel applies data validation only to that cell.

Figure 21.7
You can specify the exact input message you want the user to see.

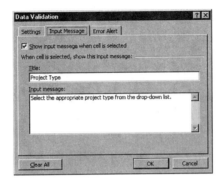

Select the Show Input Message When Cell Is Selected check box. Enter your desired Title and Input Message. Click OK to return to the worksheet. Figure 21.8 illustrates how this message displays when you enter a value.

Figure 21.8
When users enter data, they'll see the input message you've created for that field.

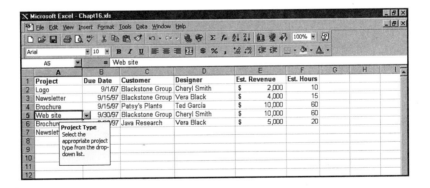

To display a custom error message when a user enters invalid data, choose the Error Alert tab. Figure 21.9 illustrates this tab.

Part
III

Ch
21

Figure 21.9
Specify a custom error
message on the Error
Alert tab.

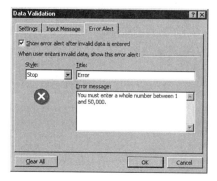

Select the Show Error Alert After Invalid Data Is Entered check box. Select an error alert
Style: Stop, Warning, or Information. Then enter your Title and Error Message. Click OK to
return to the worksheet. Figure 21.10 shows a sample custom error message.

Figure 21.10
When a user enters an
invalid value, Excel
displays the custom
error alert you've
created.

TROUBLESHOOTING

After I choose Data, Form, Excel displays an error message stating that no list was found. Before
choosing Data, Form, you must first select any cell within the list you want to modify.

I set data validation parameters, but didn't receive an error message when I entered invalid data.
Be sure you selected an entire column to validate rather than just one cell in the column. If you only
select a specific cell, Excel only applies data validation to that cell.

The Validation option on the Data menu appears dimmed. You can't set data validation options if
you're currently entering data or if you've applied protection to your worksheet. Complete your data
entry and unprotect your worksheet by choosing Tools, Protection, Unprotect Sheet and then try to
access the Validation menu again.

Modifying Records

Once you've entered data in your list, either directly on the worksheet or using the data form,
you'll probably want to modify the list data in some way. You can use the data form to display,
delete, edit, and search for specific records. You can also choose Data, Subtotals to use the
subtotal feature to create subtotals based on your list data.

Displaying and Finding Records

In Excel 97, you can use the data form to locate and display records in your list. Position the cell pointer in a cell in your list and choose Data, Form. Table 21.1 lists the navigational commands for locating data in a data form.

 TIP You also can use the scroll bar to view each record in your list.

Table 21.1   Data Form Navigational Commands

Command	Result
Find Next button	Displays next record
Find Prev button	Displays previous record
Page Up	Displays first record
Page Down	Displays blank record

 TIP You can use multiple criteria when searching for records. Just enter the criteria values in the appropriate text boxes.

When searching for data, you can specify a single criterion or multiple criteria. Entering multiple criteria creates an AND condition. You can't use the data form to search using an OR condition. In addition to searching for exact matches, you can use a number of comparison operators in your search criteria. Table 21.2 illustrates the available search comparison operators.

 TIP You can also use the ? wildcard to search for any single character or the * wildcard to search for any group of characters. For example, news* would locate newsletter, newsletters, newspaper, and so on.

 TIP To search for blank column fields, enter the = in the text box of the field you want to search. Don't include any other characters in the box, only the = with no additional criteria.

Table 21.2   Comparison Operators

Button	Description
=	Equals
>	Greater than
<	Less than

Part
III

Ch
21

continues

Table 21.2 Continued	
Button	**Description**
>=	Greater than or equal to
<=	Less than or equal to
<>	Not equal to

For example, to locate projects with an estimated revenue greater than $5,000, you would enter >**5000** in the Est. Revenue text box. To find all records for Newsletter projects, enter **Newsletter** as your Project criterion.

To locate records in a data form, follow these steps:

1. Select a cell in the list.
2. Choose Data, Form.
3. Click the Criteria button.
4. Enter the search criteria in the text box of the field you want to search, illustrated in Figure 21.11.

Figure 21.11
In this example, the search criterion is an Estimated Revenue amount greater than 5000.

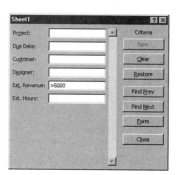

5. Click the Find Next button to locate the next match. Excel emits a beep if no matches exist.
6. Select the Close button to return to the worksheet.

Editing Records

Once you've located the record you want to edit, make any desired changes and either Close the data form or move to a new record to save the changes. You can also edit the data in a list directly in the worksheet as you would any other data.

Deleting Records

In the data form, you can also delete records from your list. You can only delete one record at a time using the data form, not multiple records.

To delete a record from the data form, follow these steps:

1. Position the cell pointer in any cell in your list.

2. Choose Data, Form to open the data form.

3. Click the Find Next button to locate the record you want to delete.

4. Click the Delete button to delete the record.

   Excel displays a warning box, illustrated in Figure 21.12, to verify that you really want to delete the record.

Figure 21.12

A message box appears reminding you that the record will be permanently deleted.

5. Click OK to delete the record; click Cancel to cancel the deletion.

6. Select the Close button to return to your worksheet.

Sorting and Filtering Lists

Excel enables you to both sort and filter your list data based on a number of criteria. You can sort by up to three fields and apply sophisticated filtering options to locate very specific list information.

Sorting List Data

In Excel 97, you'll sort based on the column fields you created in your list. The fastest way to quickly sort a list is to select the column by which you want to sort and then click the Sort Ascending or the Sort Descending button on the toolbar.

 T I P   To sort only selected records in a list, highlight the records you want to sort and then apply sorting.

CAUTION

If you don't select the entire list (for example, you select only a few cells in a column), Excel displays a Sort Warning dialog box asking if you want to only sort the selection you've made or if you want to expand the selection to include the entire list. It's important to avoid sorting only certain columns in a list while excluding others. Excel doesn't sort columns that aren't selected and the result can be mismatched data across rows.

To sort a list by more than one field, follow these steps:

1. Position the cell pointer in the list you want to sort.

2. Choose Data, Sort. Figure 21.13 displays the Sort dialog box.

Part
III

Ch
21

Figure 21.13
You can sort based on
up to three different
fields.

 To undo a sort you applied by mistake, choose Edit, Undo Sort to redisplay the original order. You must choose this command immediately after performing the sort and before performing another action.

3. At the bottom of the Sort dialog box, indicate whether your list has a Header Row or No Header Row in the My List Has section. If you have a header row, you don't want Excel to think this row is part of your data and sort it.

4. In the Sort By drop-down list choose the name of the column field by which you want to sort. You can sort in either Ascending or Descending order.

5. To sort records using additional fields, select additional sort fields in the two following Then By drop-down lists. You can sort by up to three fields.

6. Click OK to apply the sort. Figure 21.14 illustrates the result of sorting by project.

Figure 21.14
The worksheet data is
now ordered based on
specifications to sort by
Designer.

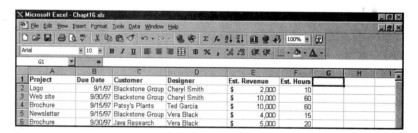

Setting Sort Orientation Normally, you'll want to sort your list data from top to bottom. Occasionally, however, you may want to sort data from left to right. To do so, select the Options button on the Sort dialog box to open the Sort Options dialog box, shown in Figure 21.15.

Figure 21.15
Set sort orientation in
the Sort Options dialog
box.

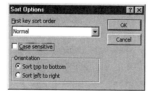

In the Orientation group box, select Sort Left to Right to change the sort orientation.

Sorting Days and Months   To customize the format of days of the week or months, choose Tools, Options and select the Custom Lists tab. If none of the existing lists are formatted the way you prefer, choose New List under Custom Lists, enter the new list items in the List Entries box and click the Add button to add your new list.

When you sort a text field, Excel sorts in alphabetical order. If your field is a day of the week or a month, this produces undesirable results. To sort dates appropriately, click the Options button on the Sort dialog box to access the Sort Options dialog box. From the First Key Sort Order drop-down list, illustrated in Figure 21.16, select the date order in which you want to sort.

Figure 21.16
You can sort days of the week and months in chronological order.

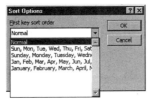

Filtering List Data

When you want to view only a portion of the data in a list, you can apply filters to hide the selected data that is outside of the selected filter parameters. Excel 97 doesn't delete this data; it just prevents you from viewing it until you remove the filter.

In Excel, you can use the AutoFilter feature to apply a basic filter or create a custom filter to match specific criteria.

Using AutoFilter   To filter a list using AutoFilter, follow these steps:

TIP   Once you've applied filters, to remove AutoFilter filters, choose Data, Filter, AutoFilter again.

1. Select a cell in the list you want to filter.
2. Choose Data, Filter, AutoFilter. You'll see drop-down lists next to each column heading, shown in Figure 21.17.

Figure 21.17
Excel displays drop-down arrows next to each column heading.

Part
III

Ch
21

3. Click the drop-down list in the column that you want to filter. For every column, you can choose to filter on a unique item in the column; display all items, the top ten items in the list, blank items, or nonblank items; or create a custom filter. Figure 21.18 displays this drop-down list.

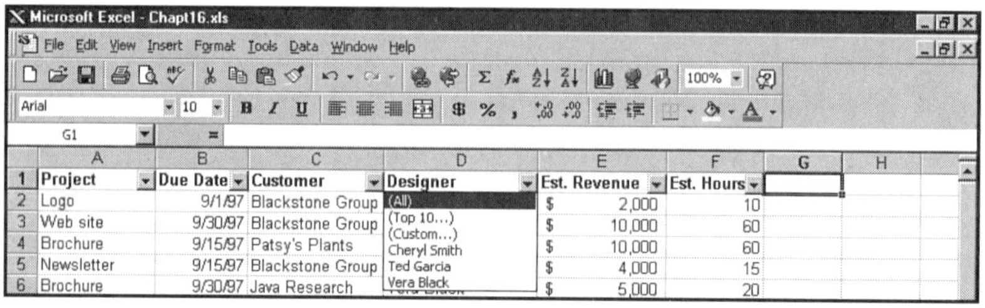

Figure 21.18

You can choose the item to display from the drop-down list.

4. Select the item you want to display. If you select Top Ten, the Top 10 AutoFilter dialog box displays, as shown in Figure 21.19.

Figure 21.19

You can filter based on the top or bottom items.

Choose whether to display the Top or Bottom Items or Percents and then indicate the quantity to display. Click OK to return to the worksheet.

5. Repeat the previous two steps for each additional column you want to filter.

 To remove a filter from a specific column, select All from the drop-down list of that column.

Excel displays the records that match your filter criteria and hides all other records.

Creating a Custom AutoFilter

If you want to apply specific criteria to your filter, you can create a custom AutoFilter. To do so, follow these steps:

N O T E   For even more sophisticated filtering capabilities, you can use Excel's Advanced Filter feature, which lets you filter based on calculated criteria and apply detailed AND and OR criteria. Choose Data, Filter, Advanced Filter to access this feature. ■

1. Select a cell in the list you want to filter.
2. Choose Data, Filter, AutoFilter.
3. Select the drop-down arrow in the column you want to filter and choose Custom from the list. Figure 21.20 displays the Custom AutoFilter dialog box that opens.

Figure 21.20

The Custom AutoFilter dialog box lets you create a custom filter.

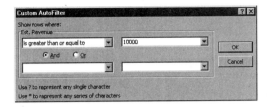

4. The first drop-down list includes all available comparison operators from which you can choose. Select the appropriate operator.

5. In the second drop-down list, select the data you want to compare.

 TIP You can also enter specific criteria in this text box using wildcard characters rather than selecting an item from the list. The ? wildcard searches for any single character; the * wildcard searches for any group of characters.

6. To include a second set of criteria, choose And to indicate that the records must meet both sets of criteria. Choose Or to indicate that the records need only match either set of criteria. Select the second set of criteria as described in steps 4 and 5.

7. Choose OK to return to the worksheet. Excel applies the filter and displays the records that match the criteria you entered. Figure 21.21 illustrates the filtered list.

Figure 21.21

Excel displays the filtered list of Revenue greater than or equal to 10,000.

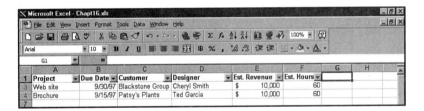

Subtotaling List Data

When you sort data in a list, Excel enables you to summarize the data with subtotals. When you summarize a list, Excel calculates subtotals based on subsets of the data and also calculates a grand total.

Creating List Subtotals

To create list subtotals, follow these steps:

1. Sort your list data in the order in which you want to create subtotals. For example, if you want to create subtotals based on the amount of revenue generated by each designer, first sort your list by designer.

▶ See "Sorting List Data," **page 443**

Part
III

Ch
21

2. Select a cell in the list you want to subtotal.

3. Choose Data, Subtotals. The Subtotal dialog box opens as illustrated in Figure 21.22.

Figure 21.22

Use the Subtotal dialog box to create data subtotals.

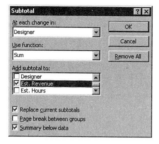

4. Specify the field by which to subtotal from the At Each Change In drop-down list.

5. From the Use Function drop-down list, select Sum to create subtotals. You can also select average, count, and other summary functions.

6. In the Add Subtotal To box, choose the data to subtotal. For example, if you want to subtotal all estimated revenues, select the Est. Revenue check box.

7. Select any of the following options if you want to apply them: Replace Current Subtotals, Page Breaks Between Groups, or Summary Below Data.

8. Click OK to create the subtotals and return to your worksheet, illustrated in Figure 21.23.

Figure 21.23

The worksheet now displays subtotal lines for each Designer's Estimated Revenue.

Level 1, 2, 3 buttons

Hide Detail Level button

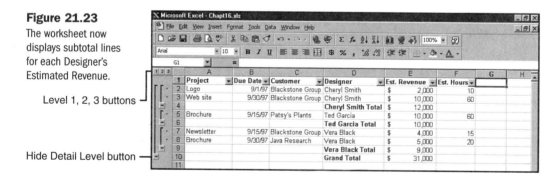

Controlling Data Display in a Subtotaled List

Excel displays subtotaled data in Outline view. Using this view, you have control over the amount of data you want to display. For example, you can display only the data subtotals and grand totals or all the detail data as well.

To display only the subtotal, select the Hide Detail Level button for that subtotal. Excel hides the detail and displays only the summary data, illustrated in Figure 21.24.

▶ **See** "Using Outlines," **page 388**

Figure 21.24

The Hide Detail Level button lets you hide subtotal detail.

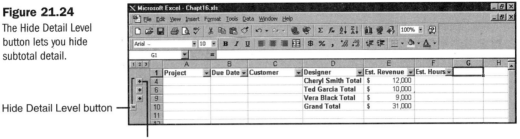

Hide Detail Level button ⎯

Show Detail Level button

To restore the data detail, select the Show Detail Level button. Excel displays the full detail again.

Removing Subtotals from a List

To remove list subtotals, select a cell in the subtotaled list and choose Data, Subtotals to open the Subtotal dialog box again. Click the Remove All button to restore the original list.

TROUBLESHOOTING

After sorting the database, Excel sorts the column titles along with the data in the list. To prevent the column titles from sorting with the rest of the list, choose Header Row in the My List Has section of the Sort dialog box.

Excel created a subtotal for each entry in my list rather than by group. You must sort on the field on which you want to subtotal first. To do so, choose Data, Sort.

CHAPTER 22

Using Pivot Tables

by Patrice-Anne Rutledge

In this chapter

Overview of New Features

Excel 97 provides a number of new features that make Pivot Tables a more powerful data analysis tool. These features include the following enhancements:

- Persistent formatting. This option lets you apply formatting such as bolding or color enhancements that the Pivot Table maintains when you refresh data.
- Page field layout options. You can now place multiple page fields in either columns or rows in a Pivot Table.
- PivotTable selection. Using the Pivot Table selection feature, you can select only specific PivotTable data for formatting or analysis.
- Dates displayed in order. Excel 97 displays dates in the appropriate order rather than alphabetically.
- Enhanced PivotTable options. Step 4 of the PivotTable Wizard includes an Options button that opens a detailed PivotTable Options dialog box for advanced users.
- AutoShow and AutoSort capabilities. Excel 97 includes options for sorting Pivot Table data as well as filtering the top and bottom data-field entries.
- Calculated fields and items. You can create formulas using Pivot Table data and store them as calculated fields and items.
- External data access improvements. Excel 97 offers server-based page fields to enhance memory and performance when accessing large amounts of external data.

Understanding Pivot Tables

A Pivot Table is an interactive report that summarizes and analyzes data in an Excel worksheet or an external database. Using Pivot Tables, you can quickly and easily analyze data in a variety of ways without creating a new report each time. A Pivot Table cross-tabulates data in columns and rows with the option to filter and sort the display data as well as to expand on its detail.

The layout of a Pivot Table includes four main areas:

- Row. Displays the field items in a row.
- Column. Displays the field items in a column.
- Data. Summarizes a field by row, column, and page.
- Page. Allows you to filter Pivot Table data.

You can create a Pivot Table from four different types of sources:

- An existing Excel database or list
- An external data source, such as an Access database
- Multiple consolidation ranges
- Another Pivot Table

Before creating a Pivot Table, particularly if you're new to the idea of Pivot Tables, it helps to create a diagram of what you want your Pivot Table to look like and what you want it to summarize. This makes it easier to determine what fields to place in the row, column, page, or data areas.

Figure 22.1 illustrates an Excel list and its accompanying Pivot Table. The list includes four columns—the name of a salesperson, the product that salesperson sold, the month the salesperson sold the product, and the product sales amount. In the Pivot Table you've summarized and totaled this data.

Part
III

Ch
22

Figure 22.1

A Pivot Table can summarize and analyze the data in an Excel list.

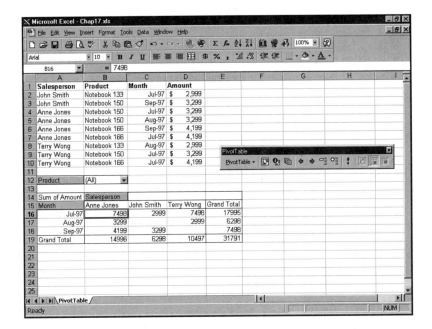

In this example, you've placed the Month field as a Pivot Table row, the Salesperson field as a column, the Amount as your summarized data, and the Product as the page field on which you can filter. With the page field, you're able to adjust the contents of the Pivot Table based on product. You can display the data for all products combined or for a single product. To display a single product, click the arrow next to the page field and select that product.

You could also switch the row and column fields by switching Month and Salesperson. The amount in the cell that intersects between these two fields will remain the same. If you want to filter based on Salesperson or Month, you could move either of these to the page field and move the existing page field, Product, to a row or column. Pivot Tables are extremely flexible and allow you to view data in many ways.

Creating Pivot Tables

Excel's PivotTable Wizard simplifies Pivot Table design. The PivotTable Wizard guides you through the four steps of creating a Pivot Table. Depending on your choice of data source in step 1, the second step differs as it assists you in selecting this data source. The following example shows you how to create the Pivot Table illustrated in Figure 22.1, which uses an existing Excel list as its data source.

To create a Pivot Table from an Excel list or database, follow these steps:

1. Select the data you want to analyze in the PivotTable.

2. Choose Data, PivotTable Report to open step 1 of the PivotTable Wizard, shown in Figure 22.2.

Figure 22.2

In step 1 of the PivotTable Wizard, you can specify what kind of source data to use.

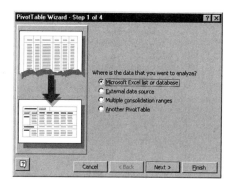

3. Indicate that you want to analyze data in a Microsoft Excel list or database.

4. Click Next to continue to step 2, shown in Figure 22.3.

Figure 22.3

In the PivotTable Wizard's step 2, you'll select the data range to include in the Pivot Table.

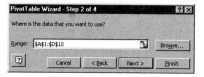

 TIP Excel automatically selects the data range for you if you position the cell pointer in your list before activating the PivotTable Wizard.

5. The cell references of the data you previously selected appear in the Range edit box. You can change this data by selecting the Cell Reference button, to the right of the Range edit box, to return to your worksheet.

CAUTION

If you didn't select your column headings when you created your Pivot Table, they won't display in step 3. You won't see field names, just row data. Go back to step 2 and include these headings in your data range. Otherwise, Excel recognizes the first row of data as your field button names.

6. Continue to step 3 of the wizard, illustrated in Figure 22.4, by clicking the Next button.

Figure 22.4

You can define your Pivot Table layout in step 3.

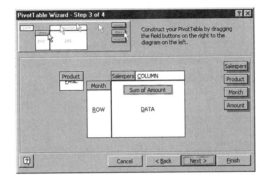

TIP Double-click a field button to customize it. The PivotTable Field dialog box opens in which you can specify subtotal, formatting, sort, display, and page field options.

7. Drag the field buttons on the right of the dialog box to the appropriate location on the diagram. In this example, you want to place the Month field as a Row, the Salesperson field as a Column, the Product field as the Page, and the Amount field as your summarized Data.

8. Click the Next button to go to step 4, shown in Figure 22.5.

Figure 22.5

You can place your Pivot Table in a new or existing worksheet.

9. Determine whether you want to place your Pivot Table in a New worksheet or an Existing worksheet. If you choose to place it in an existing worksheet, you can specify its exact location by clicking the Cell Reference button to return to the worksheet.

10. To set advanced PivotTable options, click the <u>O</u>ptions button to open the PivotTable Options dialog box.

▶ **See** "Setting Advanced Pivot Table Options," **page 460**

11. Click the <u>F</u>inish button to complete and create your Pivot Table.

Creating a Pivot Table from Another Pivot Table

To create a new Pivot Table from an existing Pivot Table, choose the <u>A</u>nother PivotTable option in step 1 of the PivotTable Wizard. Step 2 then differs from the previous example. Figure 22.6 illustrates step 2 based on this selection.

Figure 22.6

You can create a new PivotTable from the data in an existing PivotTable.

In step 2, indicate <u>W</u>hich PivotTable contains the data you want to use. Click Next to continue to steps 3 and 4.

Creating a Pivot Table from Multiple Consolidation Ranges

You can create a single Pivot Table from multiple ranges or worksheets. To do so, follow these steps as you complete Step 1 of the PivotTable Wizard.

1. Select the Multiple <u>C</u>onsolidation ranges option in step 1 of the PivotTable Wizard. Step 2a then displays, as illustrated in Figure 22.7.

Figure 22.7

Excel 97 will create a single page field for you or you can create your own.

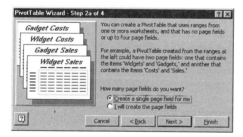

2. When creating a Pivot Table from multiple ranges you can include from zero to four page fields. In step 2a, you can choose one of the following options:

   - Create a Single Page Field for Me.
   - I Will Create the Page Fields

3. Depending on your selection here, step 2b varies. If you chose to have Excel create a single page field, step 2b displays as illustrated in Figure 22.8.

Figure 22.8

Select the ranges to include in step 2b.

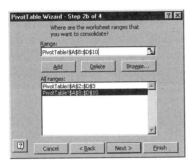

TIP To delete a range you've chosen, select it and click the Delete button.

To choose each range to consolidate, enter it in the Range edit box and click the Add button to move it to the All Ranges box. You can use the Cell Reference button to return to a worksheet for selection.

If you chose to create your own page fields, step 2b displays as illustrated in Figure 22.9.

Figure 22.9

You can set up to four page fields when you consolidate multiple ranges.

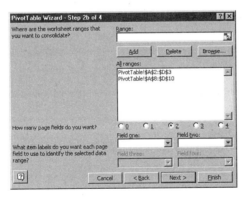

Step 2b expands to include options for selecting page fields. First, determine the number of page fields you want—from zero to four.

4. The Field One, Field Two, Field Three, and Field Four drop-down lists display based on the corresponding number of page fields you selected. For example, if you chose to display only two page fields (2), Excel 97 would activate only Field One and Field Two. If you chose to display four page fields, Excel would activate all four drop-down lists. Enter or select the item label you want to associate with each data range in the Field drop-down lists.

5. Click Next to continue to steps 3 and 4, which are identical to the instructions in the "Creating Pivot Tables" section earlier in this chapter.

Creating a Pivot Table from an External Data Source

In many cases, you'll use an application such as Microsoft Access to track and store large amounts of data. You can then use the quantitative power of Excel to analyze this data in a Pivot Table. For example, if you have an order-entry database in Access, you can use a Pivot Table to analyze sales by customer, employee, data, or geographic area.

To create a Pivot Table from an external data source, such as an Access database, follow these steps as you complete step 1 of the PivotTable Wizard.

CAUTION

Be sure that you've installed Microsoft Query with Excel 97 before trying to create a Pivot Table from an external data source or you'll receive an error message. To install this feature, return to Microsoft Office 97 Setup and choose the Data Access, Microsoft Query Option.

1. Select the External Data Source option in step 1 of the PivotTable Wizard. Figure 22.10 illustrates step 2 of the wizard based on this data-source selection.

Figure 22.10

Excel 97 lets you create a Pivot Table from an external data source.

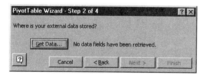

2. Click the Get Data button to open the Choose Data Source dialog box, shown in Figure 22.11.

Figure 22.11

Specify your external data source in the Choose Data Source dialog box.

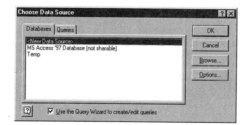

 You can also select queries you've already created as your data source. You'll find these in the Queries tab of the Choose Data Source dialog box.

3. In this example, you'll choose MS Access '97 Database on the Databases tab and click OK to continue.

4. The Select Database dialog box opens, as illustrated in Figure 22.12.

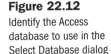

Figure 22.12
Identify the Access database to use in the Select Database dialog box.

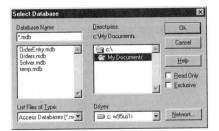

5. Select the Database Name and click OK.

N O T E Microsoft Query, with its Query Wizard, is an optional feature for Excel 97. Using the Query Wizard enables you to select specific information from external data sources to use in Excel.

6. The Query Wizard opens. Use the wizard to select the Access database data you want to include in your Pivot Table.

7. Once you finish your query and click the Finish button in the PivotTable Wizard, you'll return to step 2.

8. Continue with steps 3 and 4 of the wizard. Excel 97 connects to your data source and completes your Pivot Table.

Excel 97 includes several new options for improving memory performance when accessing large external databases. To set these options, select the Pivot Table, click the Pivot Table Field button on the Pivot Table toolbar to open the PivotTable Field dialog box, and click the Advanced button.

The PivotTable Field Advanced Options dialog box includes the following Page Field options:

■ Retrieve external data for all page field items (faster performance). Speeds up data retrieval by accessing all items at once.

■ Query external data source as you select each page field item (requires less memory). Retrieves the data for each page field item as it's displayed. Excel requires less memory to do this.

■ Disable pivoting of this field (recommended). If you move a page field to a different part of the Pivot Table and you've chosen to query the external data source as you select each page field, the data for all items is instead retrieved at once. This requires more memory and slows down performance. Checking this option helps you avoid this problem.

Setting Advanced Pivot Table Options

To specify additional Pivot Table options, click the Options button on step 4 of the PivotTable Wizard. Or, right-click a finished Pivot Table and choose Options from the shortcut menu. Figure 22.13 illustrates the PivotTable Options dialog box.

Figure 22.13

You'll set advanced options in the PivotTable Options dialog box.

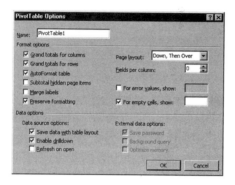

The PivotTable Options dialog box includes a variety of formatting options you can set:

- Grand Totals for Columns. Calculates and displays column item grand totals.
- Grand Totals for Rows. Calculates and displays row item grand totals.
- AutoFormat Table. Applies the default AutoFormat formatting to the Pivot Table.
- Subtotal Hidden Page Items. Includes page field items you hid in the PivotTable Field dialog box in Pivot Table subtotals.
- Merge Labels. Merges cells in all Pivot Table outer row and column labels.
- Preserve Formatting. If you select this option, you'll preserve any formatting you made if you refresh your data. If you don't select this option, your Pivot Table reverts back to its original unformatted version.
- Page Layout. You can display page fields in a single column (Down, Then Over) or across columns (Over, Then Down).
- Fields Per Column. Determines the number of page fields you want to include in a Pivot Table row or column.
- For Error Values, Show. You can indicate the value to display for errors, such as #.
- For Empty Cells, Show. You can indicate the value to display for empty cells, such as 0.

The PivotTable Options dialog box also includes several data source options:

- Save Data with Table Layout. Saves a copy of the external data on which you based the Pivot Table. You'll want to select this option if you plan to customize your Pivot Table later, otherwise you'll have to refresh your data to perform any additional customizations or analysis.

■ Enable <u>D</u>rilldown. Drilldown enables you to display the source data a particular cell summarizes when you double-click it.

■ <u>R</u>efresh On Open. Refreshes data automatically when you open the Pivot Table.

If you've accessed an external data source, you can also set the following options in this dialog box:

■ <u>S</u>ave password. Saves the password used to access an external data source as part of the query. Then you won't need to enter the password again when you refresh your Pivot Table.

■ <u>B</u>ackground query. Runs the query in the background so that you can continue working in Excel. Useful for complex queries that take a long time.

■ <u>O</u>ptimize memory. Optimizes Pivot Table memory performance. Useful when creating a Pivot Table from an external database and the system tells you it doesn't have enough memory.

Formatting Pivot Tables

Once you've created your Pivot Table, you'll probably want to customize its format.

 To preserve the formatting you apply to Pivot Tables once you refresh them, select the <u>P</u>reserve Formatting option in the Pivot Table Options dialog box. Also be sure to enable selection, by right-clicking the mouse on the PivotTable and choosing <u>S</u>elect, <u>E</u>nable Selection from the menu.

 If the PivotTable toolbar doesn't display, choose <u>V</u>iew, <u>T</u>oolbars and select PivotTable from the submenu.

The PivotTable toolbar provides several ways to easily format and modify your Pivot Table. Table 22.1 lists the PivotTable toolbar buttons and their use.

Table 22.1 PivotTable Toolbar Buttons

Name	Description
PivotTable	Displays a submenu with the most common PivotTable options.
PivotTable Wizard	Opens the PivotTable Wizard.
PivotTable Field	Opens the PivotTable Field dialog box for the field selected.

continues

Table 22.1   Continued

Name	Description
Show Pages	Opens the Show Pages dialog box in which you can choose to Show all pages of any of the page fields you specified in Step 3 of the PivotTable Wizard.
Ungroup	Ungroups PivotTable items you grouped.
Group	Groups selected PivotTable items.
Hide Detail	Hides PivotTable details.
Show Detail	Displays PivotTable details.
Refresh Data	Refreshes PivotTable based on current source data.
Select Label	Using the selection feature, selects specific field labels.
Select Data	Using the selection feature, selects specific data.
Select Label and Data	Using the selection feature, selects both labels and data.

In Excel 97, you'll use the PivotTable toolbar buttons as well as other features to format the overall appearance of a Pivot Table, its text, and numeric data.

Changing the Appearance of a Pivot Table

To easily change the overall appearance of your Pivot Table, place the cell pointer in the Pivot Table and then choose Format, AutoFormat from the Excel menu. This opens the AutoFormat dialog box, as shown in Figure 22.14.

Figure 22.14
Use the AutoFormat feature to apply a variety of predesigned styles to your Pivot Table.

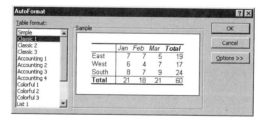

Choose a new format from the Table Format list and then click OK to return to the worksheet.

TIP If you don't want autoformatting to apply to all areas of your Pivot Table, click the Options button on the AutoFormat dialog box to expand it. You can then specify exactly which formats to apply.

Formatting Numeric Data

To format the numbers in the Pivot Table data area, select a cell in the data area and click the PivotTable Field button on the PivotTable toolbar. Figure 22.15 displays the PivotTable Field dialog box.

Figure 22.15
The PivotTable Field dialog box offers a multitude of options for formatting numeric data.

▶ **See** "Formatting Numbers, Dates, and Times," **page 412**

TIP You can also right-click and select Field from the submenu to open the PivotTable Field dialog box.

In this dialog box, you can Summarize in the following ways:

- Sum. Sums the values (default setting)
- Count. Counts the number of instances the item occurs
- Average. Averages the values
- Max. Displays the maximum value
- Min. Displays the minimum value
- Product. Displays the product of the values
- Count Nums. Counts the number of rows that include numeric data
- StdDev. Estimates the standard deviation
- StdDevp. Displays the standard deviation
- Var. Estimates the variance
- Varp. Displays the variance

As an example, let's say that instead of showing the total amount of sales for each salesperson in the Pivot Table, you now want to display the number of products each salesperson sold. By changing the summarization option to Count, your Pivot Table automatically reflects this. Figure 22.16 illustrates this change.

Figure 22.16

You can apply several different numeric summary options, including Count.

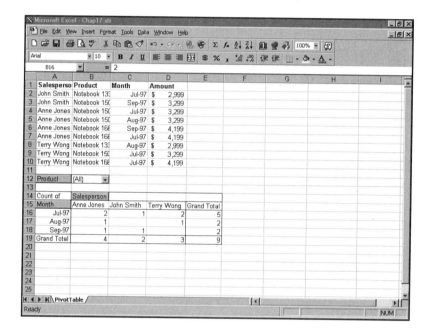

Click the Options button to expand the dialog box, providing more choices. You can choose to show your data in the following ways:

- Normal. Displays default format
- Difference from. Displays data as the difference from a selected base field and item
- % of. Displays data as a percentage of the value for a selected base field and item
- % Difference From. Displays data as a percentage difference from a selected base field and item
- Running Total in. Displays successive items as a running total based on the selected base field
- % of Row. Displays data as a percentage of the row total
- % of column. Displays data as a percentage of the column total
- % of total. Displays data as a percentage of the grand total of all PivotTable data
- Index. Displays data using the following formula: ((value in cell) × (grand total of grand totals)) / ((grand row total) × (grand column total))

If you choose Difference from, % of, or % Difference from, you'll activate the Base Field and Base Item fields. Depending on which base field you select, the Base Item drop-down list includes the option of comparing the base field to a specific field item, the previous item, or the next item.

TIP Click the Number button to open the Format Cells Number tab, in which you can set other numeric formatting options.

NOTE In addition to formatting numeric data in a Pivot Table, you can also create calculated fields and items in a Pivot Table by defining formulas using existing Pivot Table data. For example, you could create a new field called Quota Percentage, which compares a salesperson's sales totals for a period of time as a percentage of the required sales quota. To create calculated fields and items, select PivotTable, Formulas, Calculated Field or Calculated Item from the PivotTable toolbar.

Formatting Pivot Table Fields

You can also easily format Pivot Table text fields, including options on how to display and sort field data.

To format a PivotTable field, select a designated field such as Salesperson, and click the PivotTable Field button on the PivotTable toolbar. Figure 22.17 displays the PivotTable Field dialog box.

Figure 22.17
You can also format text fields in the PivotTable Field dialog box.

NOTE In addition, you can set subtotal options in the PivotTable Field dialog box. For more information on setting summarization options, see the "Formatting Numeric Data" section earlier in this chapter.

In this dialog box, you can change the orientation for the selected field Name by Row, Column, or Page.

If you want to hide specific items and not display them in the Pivot Table, select those items in the Hide Items list.

Select Show Items with No Data if you want to display empty data cells.

Setting AutoSort Options   Click the Advanced button to open the PivotTable Field Advanced Options dialog box, shown in Figure 22.18.

Figure 22.18

You can set AutoSort and AutoShow options in Pivot Tables.

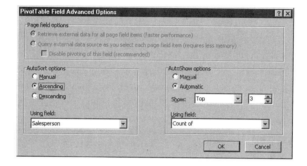

N O T E   Excel 97 displays dates in chronological order, rather than alphabetical order. ▪

In this dialog box, you can set automatic sorting and display options. You can sort on the selected field in Manual (default), Ascending, or Descending order. If you choose to sort in ascending or descending order, Excel activates the Using Field drop-down list, from which you can choose the field to sort.

Setting AutoShow Options   Use the AutoShow feature to display only a certain number of entries for the selected field. To use this feature, select the Automatic option button and then specify whether you want to Show the Top or Bottom entries. Next, indicate the number of entries you want to display. Select the field on which to base this display in the Using Field drop-down list. For example, if you had twenty salespeople, you could display only the top three by total sales in a Pivot Table and then quickly change this to show only the bottom three.

Formatting Selected Pivot Table Data

Excel 97 includes a new feature that lets you format items or fields based on data, labels, or both data and labels.

 You can also use the selection feature to select data for formulas.

To enable PivotTable selection, first select the Pivot Table you want to format. Then choose PivotTable, Select from the PivotTable toolbar. From the Select submenu, choose the Enable Selection option. Selecting the data you want to format activates the following toolbar buttons: Select Label, Select Data, and Select Label and Data.

For example, if you want to bold all the Month item labels, you would select the Month field button. This highlights all the Month item labels. To include the data as well, click the Select Label and Data button on the PivotTable toolbar. To select only the data, click the Select Data button. Once you've made your selection, click the Bold button on the Formatting toolbar. Figure 22.19 illustrates the effect of bolding all the Month labels using this technique.

Figure 22.19
Data selection enables you to format only specific PivotTable data, such as all the month labels in this figure.

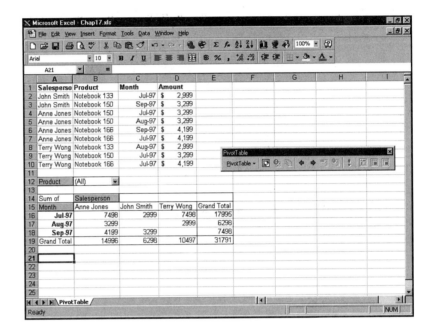

To highlight all data for "Jul 97" in red, select that row and apply the appropriate color format with the Font Color button.

You can also apply any other formatting option to specific data using the selection feature. Set selection options from the shortcut menu that displays when you choose PivotTable, Select from the PivotTable toolbar.

Modifying Pivot Tables

Once you've created a Pivot Table, you can easily modify both its source data and its layout. If you change the data source, an Excel list for example, you can select the Pivot Table and click the Refresh Data button on the PivotTable toolbar. Excel immediately updates the Pivot Table with the new information.

Rearranging a Pivot Table

Drag the Field buttons to a new column or row location to rearrange the Pivot Table. For example, let's say you want to rearrange the Pivot Table in Figure 22.19 to move the page field

Product to the row level. To do so, select the Product field button and drag it next to the Month row field button. The Pivot Table automatically rearranges, as illustrated in Figure 22.20.

Figure 22.20

You can quickly modify Pivot Table columns and rows by dragging field buttons to a new location.

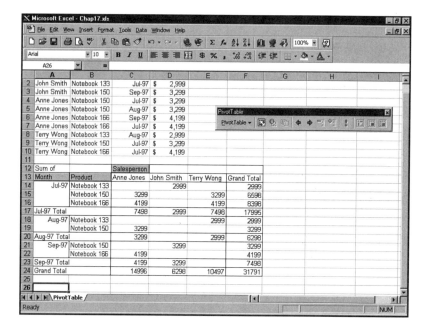

To do more complex rearrangements, you can select the Pivot Table and click the PivotTable Wizard button on the toolbar to reopen the PivotTable Wizard. From the PivotTable Wizard, you can make more extensive modifications.

Adding or Removing Fields

To add or remove a Pivot Table field, select the Pivot Table and click the PivotTable Wizard button on the PivotTable toolbar. Step 3 of the wizard displays. You can drag new fields to the Pivot Table layout diagram or drag existing fields off the layout and back to the field button list on the right side of the dialog box.

TROUBLESHOOTING

I lost my formatting when I refreshed data. To preserve the formatting you apply to Pivot Tables once you refresh them, select the Preserve Formatting option in the PivotTable Options dialog box. Also be sure to enable selection by right-clicking the mouse and choosing Select, Enable Selection from the menu.

I made a mistake in formatting or modifying my PivotTable, and my data is gone. In many cases, you can undo your modification by choosing Edit, Undo. If this command isn't available, return to the PivotTable Wizard to recreate your Pivot Table based on your original specifications.

Analyzing Spreadsheet Data

by George T. Lynch

Overview of New Features

Excel 97 has a number of interesting new features that enhance the model-building power of Excel.

Excel and the Web

Web Query enables you to retrieve data from the Internet into a spreadsheet. Several sample queries are included with Excel 97 to demonstrate the power of this new feature. Using these sample Web Queries, you can perform the following tasks:

- Retrieve stock price information directly into a spreadsheet cell from a stock information service on the Internet.
- Retrieve timely information directly into your spreadsheet to update a portfolio model with current pricing information.
- Create your own Web Queries, which can function on a local-area network to update your spreadsheets from databases within your company.

Excel is also "Web Aware" in other ways. It contains the following tools:

- A Web toolbar
- Web based help extensions (links to Microsoft's Web site at points relevant to Excel users)
- A Hyperlink button to enable you to insert references to files on the World Wide Web
- A local Web server (intranet) or a file on a local or network file service

You can also use the enhanced Save <u>A</u>s feature to publish your worksheet as an HTML page for viewing with a browser like Microsoft Internet Explorer. You can even use Excel itself to browse the Internet.

Multiple Level Undo

Excel now provides a multiple level undo so you can step back through changes you have made. You can undo up to the last 16 actions you have taken. Remember, though, that some actions cannot be undone (for example, deleting a sheet from the workbook).

Dialog Boxes

Some dialog boxes have been enhanced to include a collapse feature. This enables you to minimize the dialog box to make it easier to find a range on the spreadsheet. (To see an example, choose <u>F</u>ile, Page Set<u>u</u>p. In the Page Setup dialog box, select the Sheet tab. Note the buttons at the end of the Print Area and the Print Title boxes. If you click one of those buttons, the Page Setup dialog box collapses.)

Formula Enhancements

Excel 97 contains several new and exciting improvements for working with formulas. What follows is a description of some of the most interesting new features:

- The new Formula AutoCorrect automatically fixes 15 of the most common formula entry errors. You have the option of accepting or rejecting any change that Excel proposes.

- Excel now automatically uses column and row headings (that are part of the table) as substitutes for cell references in Natural Language formulas. This can reduce common errors and simplify entry and readability of formulas.

- When you edit a formula cell by pressing F2 (or double-clicking on the formula cell), Excel displays color-coded frames and text in the formula to aid in identifying the cells, which are used as inputs. This new feature is called the Range Finder.

> **N O T E**   The Range Finder feature is available only if you enable the Edit Directly in Cell option. To do this, select Tools, Options, then click the Edit tab and enable the Edit Directly in Cell option.
>
> Some experienced Excel users have preferred to disable this option in previous versions. The reason is that when this option is disabled and you double-click a formula cell, Excel will select all the precedent cells (cells that contribute to the formula). Some users find that to be a better auditing tool.
>
> Disabling the Edit Directly in Cell option still holds one advantage over the new Range Finder—Range Finder only indicates precedent cells on the same worksheet as the formula cell, whereas using the double-click method selects precedent cells from other worksheets.
>
> As you can see, each option has its own advantages.

- An enhanced Formula Palette incorporates features of the Function wizard and the formula bar into a single more intuitive tool. The Formula Palette appears automatically when you activate the formula bar.

- Excel 97 has enhanced tools for tracking and eliminating unnecessary circular references. A warning appears when a formula is entered, which causes a cell to refer directly or indirectly to itself and the Circular Reference toolbar opens automatically. The Circular Reference toolbar contains a Navigate Circular Reference list box, and a Trace Dependents and Trace Precedents tool to help locate cells which are part of a circular reference.

▶ **See** "Formulas and Functions," **page 361**

A Few Definitions

Before we begin looking at Excel's analysis tools, it might be helpful if we review a few definitions that we will be using in this chapter (see Table 23.1).

Table 23.1 Definitions

This Term	Means
Function	A built-in calculation that comes with Excel 97. Functions take *Arguments*, which are specific values that you need to enter in a specific order for the function to work properly. (Excel's Function Wizard guides you through entering arguments for functions.)
Argument	Most functions in Excel require numbers or values in order to return an accurate answer. These are called arguments. Arguments must be entered in a specific order for the function to work correctly. Some functions have both required arguments (which you must enter) and optional arguments (which you can enter to modify the way the particular function works).
Formula	A calculation that you create to resolve a problem. You can create complex formulas that contain several functions.
Absolute/Relative References	Excel uses relative references when you first create a formula. A relative reference tells Excel the location of the referenced cell (for example, the referenced cell is two columns to the left and one row up) instead of using a cell address. Thus, when you copy a formula that uses relative references, the formula will change the referenced cells according to where you paste the copied formula. An absolute reference, on the other hand, refers to a specific cell address, regardless of where you copy the formula. Absolute addresses show dollar signs (for example, $A$1, $C$225). You can mix absolute and relative references (for example, $A1, A$1, A1, $A$1).
Syntax	This term relates to the order of a function's arguments.

Building and Using Data Tables

Data tables allow you to calculate many values within a function by varying one or two of the function's arguments. Excel expects data tables to be organized in a specific layout. You need to understand how Excel expects data tables to be constructed in order to create meaningful data tables of your own.

Purpose of Data Tables

Data tables provide a method for creating a set of similar or related formulas arranged in a rectangular array. They are generally used as part of a larger model. There are two types of data tables: one variable and two variable.

A one variable data table enables you to change the values for a single argument within a function and calculate answers for all the values. For example, you could calculate the monthly payments on a loan for a number of different interest rates in a one variable data table. (To do this, you would need to know the total amount of the loan, the interest rate and the number of payments to be made. Then you can use the PMT function (this function calculates payments based on amount, rate and number of payments) to calculate the monthly payment. You could then set up a one variable data table, listing different interest rates and calculate the monthly payments on each interest rate.)

A two variable data table enables you to change the values for two arguments within a function. The table lists the different arguments and the results of each. For example, you could calculate the monthly payments on a loan for both different interest rates and different periods of time for repaying the loan.

Data Dialog Box

When you create a data table, whether one or two variable, you need to use the Table dialog box (see Figure 23.1).

You need to first construct your data table before opening the Table dialog box. Once you have your data table, select the appropriate table range and select Data, Table. In a one variable table, you need to enter either the column or row input cell, while in a two variable table, you need to enter both the column and row input cells.

▶ **See** "Selecting and Using Ranges," **page 345**

Figure 23.1
This figure shows the
Table dialog box.

Excel uses the cells you enter to calculate the variables you list in your data table. You need to be sure you enter the correct cells to insure correct calculations. This may seem a little confusing now, but the following examples should make it clear.

Data Table Layout

When you create a data table, whether one variable or two variables, you need to pay attention to the layout of the table itself. Your data table will not return accurate calculations unless it is laid out exactly the way Excel expects.

A one variable data table can be constructed down a column or across a row. The next three examples illustrate a one variable data table using a column to list the variables (see Figures 23.2, 23.3, and 23.4).

Figure 23.2

This example lists interest rates from 6.00 percent to 8.25 percent in a one variable data table. The rates are in a single column. Note that cell E4 contains a function (the NPV function, which is explained in The One Variable Data Table, below).

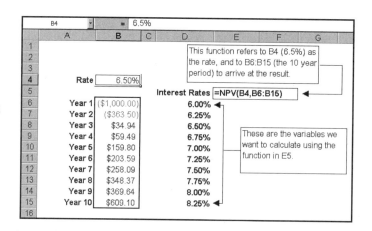

Figure 23.3

This example shows how to select the entire data table. Note particularly that you need to select all the cells that comprise the data table, including the cell that contains the function and the blank cell to its left, and the blank cells under the function and to the right of the rates.

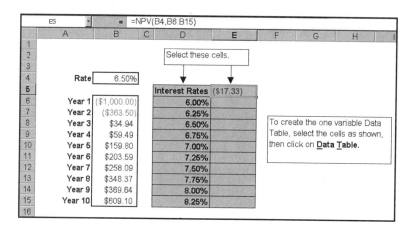

Figure 23.4

This example shows the Table dialog box.

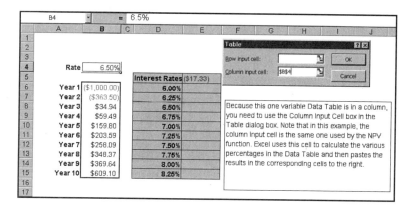

You first select the table (refer to Figure 23.3), then select Data, Table. Note that you would use the Column Input Cell box because this table was constructed down a column. You can also create a one variable data table that uses a row rather than a column to list the variable data (see Figure 23.5). In this case, you type the cell reference for the input cell in the Row Input Cell text box in the Data dialog box. This is illustrated more completely in the following section about two variable data tables.

Figure 23.5
This example shows a one variable data table constructed along a row rather than down a column. Note that the formula here is in cell D4, one cell below and to the left of the first cell of the interest rates.

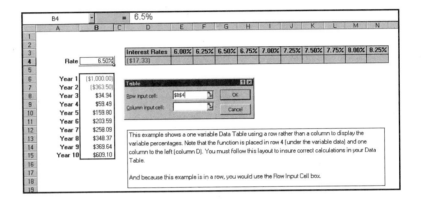

Two variable data tables use both rows and columns to list the two variables. You need to be sure you enter the correct cells in the Data dialog box in order to ensure correct calculations.

The One Variable Data Table

The one variable data table is a useful and efficient method of entering and managing a group of related formulas. This type of data table enables you to vary one of the arguments of a function so you can compare the results quickly. So, for example, you could see how different interest rates could affect your repayments on a loan.

We will use the NPV function as an example. This is the Net Present Value function which calculates the net present value of an investment (a number by which different cash flows from investments can be compared). It takes two arguments, the "discount" or interest rate, and the list of payments, positive (income) and negative (payments), which represent the stream of cash flows from the investment.

The syntax of the NPV function is: NPV(rate,value1,value2,...). The value arguments represent the list of payments. You can enter up to 29 values.

Setting Up the Table   Begin by preparing a spreadsheet as shown in Figure 23.6, with the cash flows from five alternative investments listed in columns C5:C14 through G5:G14.

Figure 23.6

This is an example of the projected cash flows for five different investments. You can calculate the Net Present Value (NPV) for each of these cash flows, assuming the projected interest rate is the same for each investment, in order to compare the investments.

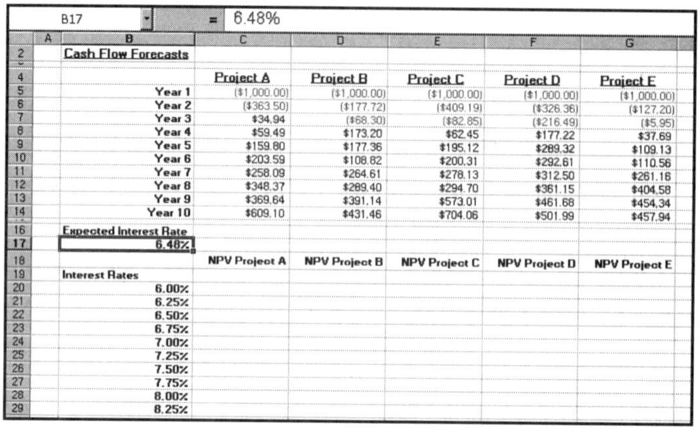

	B17		=	6.48%			
	A	B	C	D	E	F	G
2		Cash Flow Forecasts					
4			Project A	Project B	Project C	Project D	Project E
5		Year 1	($1,000.00)	($1,000.00)	($1,000.00)	($1,000.00)	($1,000.00)
6		Year 2	($363.50)	($177.72)	($409.19)	($326.36)	($127.20)
7		Year 3	$34.94	($68.30)	($82.85)	($216.49)	($5.95)
8		Year 4	$59.49	$173.20	$62.45	$177.22	$37.69
9		Year 5	$159.80	$177.36	$195.12	$289.32	$109.13
10		Year 6	$203.59	$108.82	$200.31	$292.61	$110.56
11		Year 7	$258.09	$264.61	$278.13	$312.50	$261.16
12		Year 8	$348.37	$289.40	$294.70	$361.15	$404.58
13		Year 9	$369.64	$391.14	$573.01	$461.68	$454.34
14		Year 10	$609.10	$431.46	$704.06	$501.99	$457.94
16		Expected Interest Rate					
17		6.48%					
18			NPV Project A	NPV Project B	NPV Project C	NPV Project D	NPV Project E
19		Interest Rates					
20		6.00%					
21		6.25%					
22		6.50%					
23		6.75%					
24		7.00%					
25		7.25%					
26		7.50%					
27		7.75%					
28		8.00%					
29		8.25%					

Preparing the Table

Preparing the Table   The cash flows all begin with a value of -$1000, indicating that all investments require an initial outlay of $1000. All five cash flows are initially negative in the first couple of periods before becoming positive.

This is typical of investment projects that initially require money to be spent and then eventually begin to generate money as they grow. The NPV function provides a way of comparing these streams of income and expense over time and determining which is the most profitable.

The way the NPV function reduces a stream of payments to a single number is by combining the present value of each payment (or expense). The present value of an expense or payment is determined by the interest rate. Future payments and expenses are reduced or "discounted" based on interest or "discount" rate.

Using this example (see Figure 23.6), in cell B17 enter the Expected Interest Rate, which is 6.48 percent. This is the value you will use to calculate the NPV for the five Projects. In the range B20:B29, enter a range of alternative interest rates, from 6.00 through 8.25 percent. You will use this column of alternative rates to calculate a table of NPV values for each of the five Projects.

Figure 23.7

This example shows how you could begin creating individual formulas to calculate the NPV for each project and for each projected interest rate.

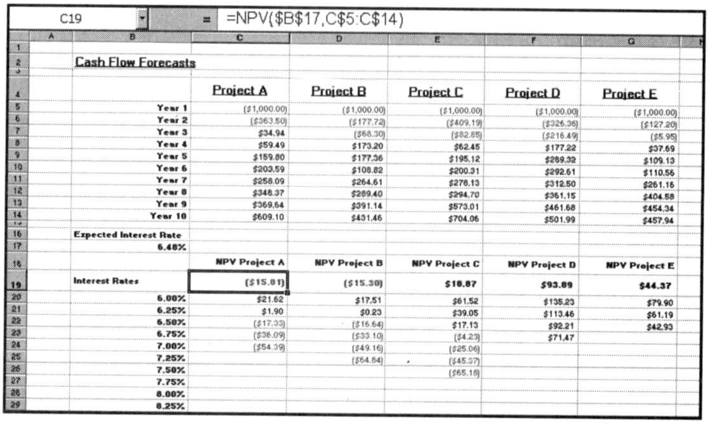

	C19		=	=NPV($B$17,C$5:C$14)			
	A	B	C	D	E	F	G
2		Cash Flow Forecasts					
4			Project A	Project B	Project C	Project D	Project E
5		Year 1	($1,000.00)	($1,000.00)	($1,000.00)	($1,000.00)	($1,000.00)
6		Year 2	($363.50)	($177.72)	($409.19)	($326.36)	($127.20)
7		Year 3	$34.94	($68.30)	($82.85)	($216.49)	($5.95)
8		Year 4	$59.49	$173.20	$62.45	$177.22	$37.69
9		Year 5	$159.80	$177.36	$195.12	$289.32	$109.13
10		Year 6	$203.59	$108.82	$200.31	$292.61	$110.56
11		Year 7	$258.09	$264.61	$278.13	$312.50	$261.16
12		Year 8	$348.37	$289.40	$294.70	$361.15	$404.58
13		Year 9	$369.64	$391.14	$573.01	$461.68	$454.34
14		Year 10	$609.10	$431.46	$704.06	$501.99	$457.94
16		Expected Interest Rate					
17		6.48%					
18			NPV Project A	NPV Project B	NPV Project C	NPV Project D	NPV Project E
19		Interest Rates	($15.81)	($15.38)	$18.87	$93.89	$44.37
20		6.00%	$21.62	$17.51	$61.52	$135.23	$79.90
21		6.25%	$1.90	$0.23	$39.05	$113.46	$61.19
22		6.50%	($17.33)	($15.64)	$17.13	$92.21	$42.93
23		6.75%	($36.09)	($33.10)	($4.23)	$71.47	
24		7.00%	($54.39)	($49.16)	($25.06)		
25		7.25%		($64.64)	($45.37)		
26		7.50%			($65.16)		
27		7.75%					
28		8.00%					
29		8.25%					

Setting Up the Data Table   You could create a block of formulas manually by entering a formula in each cell in the range C20:G29 (see Figure 23.7). In C20 you would enter the formula =**NPV(B20, C5:C14)** and then in D20 you would enter =**NPV(B20, D5:D14)** and so on (see Figure 23.8).

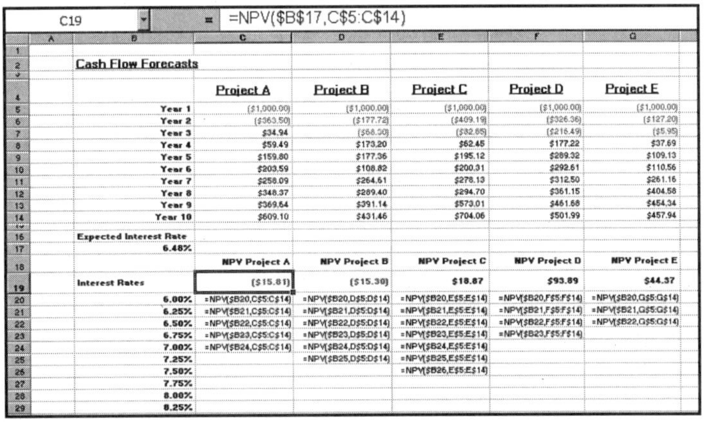

Figure 23.8

This example shows the same approach as does Figure 23.7, except here you can see the formula in each cell rather than the result.

	C19	▼	=	=NPV($B$17,C$5:C$14)		
	B	**C**	**D**	**E**	**F**	**G**
2	**Cash Flow Forecasts**					
4		**Project A**	**Project B**	**Project C**	**Project D**	**Project E**
5	Year 1	($1,000.00)	($1,000.00)	($1,000.00)	($1,000.00)	($1,000.00)
6	Year 2	($363.50)	($177.72)	($409.19)	($326.36)	($127.20)
7	Year 3	$34.94	($68.30)	($32.95)	($216.49)	($5.95)
8	Year 4	$59.49	$173.20	$62.45	$177.22	$37.69
9	Year 5	$159.80	$177.36	$195.12	$289.32	$109.13
10	Year 6	$203.59	$108.82	$200.31	$292.61	$110.56
11	Year 7	$258.09	$264.51	$278.13	$312.50	$261.16
12	Year 8	$348.37	$289.40	$294.70	$361.15	$404.58
13	Year 9	$369.64	$391.14	$573.01	$461.58	$454.34
14	Year 10	$609.10	$431.46	$704.06	$501.99	$457.94
16	**Expected Interest Rate**					
17	6.48%					
18		**NPV Project A**	**NPV Project B**	**NPV Project C**	**NPV Project D**	**NPV Project E**
19	Interest Rates	($15.81)	($15.36)	$18.87	$93.89	$44.37
20	6.00%	=NPV($B20,C$5:C$14)	=NPV($B20,D$5:D$14)	=NPV($B20,E$5:E$14)	=NPV($B20,F$5:F$14)	=NPV($B20,G$5:G$14)
21	6.25%	=NPV($B21,C$5:C$14)	=NPV($B21,D$5:D$14)	=NPV($B21,E$5:E$14)	=NPV($B21,F$5:F$14)	=NPV($B21,G$5:G$14)
22	6.50%	=NPV($B22,C$5:C$14)	=NPV($B22,D$5:D$14)	=NPV($B22,E$5:E$14)	=NPV($B22,F$5:F$14)	=NPV($B22,G$5:G$14)
23	6.75%	=NPV($B23,C$5:C$14)	=NPV($B23,D$5:D$14)	=NPV($B23,E$5:E$14)	=NPV($B23,F$5:F$14)	
24	7.00%	=NPV($B24,C$5:C$14)	=NPV($B24,D$5:D$14)	=NPV($B24,E$5:E$14)		
25	7.25%		=NPV($B25,D$5:D$14)	=NPV($B25,E$5:E$14)		
26	7.50%			=NPV($B26,E$5:E$14)		
27	7.75%					
28	8.00%					
29	8.25%					

Part III

Ch 23

This would be tedious, time-consuming, and could lead to many errors, which might be difficult to track down. It would also be inefficient in terms of the time required to recalculate your spreadsheet, because Excel has to calculate each formula individually. The one variable data table is a better way to accomplish this task.

Entering the Table Formula   To create the one variable data table to calculate the NPV values for your projects based on the range of alternative discount rates you have specified, begin by entering the reference formulas in cells C19 through G19.

In cell C19, enter =**NPV($B$17, C5:C14).** Then Click the button in the lower-right corner of cell C19 (your pointer should change to a crosshair) and drag it to G19 to fill the formula across the range C19:G19.

▶ **See** "Filling a Range," **page 349**

N O T E $B$17 is an absolute reference to cell B17, required for the Formula Drag in the next step to work correctly. You can make a relative reference absolute by selecting the reference in the formula bar and pressing F4. If you repeatedly press F4, you will see that it is a four-way toggle (A1, $A$1, A$1, $A1).

Also, if you don't see the small button on the lower-right corner of a selected cell, select Tools, Options, and then select the Edit tab and put a check mark next to Cell Drag and Drop. This option enables you to use the Fill handle, so you can simply grab the handle and use it to fill in formulas and other items across or down a range of cells.

Alternatively you could enter **=NPV(B17, D5:D14)** in D19, **=NPV(B17,E5:E14)** in E19, and so on to G19. This approach eliminates the need to create an absolute reference, but it is a little less elegant in that you need to enter the NPV function five times instead of once.

Next, select the range B19:G29, and select Data, Table to open the Table dialog box (see Figure 23.9).

Figure 23.9

This is an example of the Table dialog box.

Click in the Column Input Cell edit box, and then either type **B17** or click the spreadsheet cell B17. Click the OK button and the table will fill in as shown in Figure 23.10.

Figure 23.10

Completed one variable data table.

	B	C	D	E	F	G	H
		C20		{=TABLE(,B17)}			
1							
2	Cash Flow Forecasts						
4		Project A	Project B	Project C	Project D	Project E	
5	Year 1	($1,000.00)	($1,000.00)	($1,000.00)	($1,000.00)	($1,000.00)	
6	Year 2	($363.50)	($177.72)	($409.19)	($326.36)	($127.20)	
7	Year 3	$34.94	($68.30)	($82.85)	($216.49)	($5.95)	
8	Year 4	$59.49	$173.20	$62.45	$177.22	$37.69	
9	Year 5	$159.80	$177.36	$195.12	$289.32	$109.13	
10	Year 6	$203.59	$108.82	$200.31	$292.61	$110.56	
11	Year 7	$258.09	$264.61	$278.13	$312.50	$261.16	
12	Year 8	$348.37	$289.40	$294.70	$361.15	$404.58	
13	Year 9	$369.64	$391.14	$573.01	$461.68	$454.34	
14	Year 10	$609.10	$431.46	$704.06	$501.99	$457.94	
16	Expected Interest Rate						
17	6.48%						
18		NPV Project A	NPV Project B	NPV Project C	NPV Project D	NPV Project E	
19	Interest Rates	($15.81)	($15.30)	$18.87	$93.89	$44.37	
20	6.00%	$21.62	$17.51	$61.52	$135.23	$79.90	
21	6.25%	$1.90	$0.23	$39.05	$113.46	$61.19	
22	6.50%	($17.33)	($16.64)	$17.13	$92.21	$42.93	
23	6.75%	($36.09)	($33.10)	($4.23)	$71.47	$25.11	
24	7.00%	($54.39)	($49.16)	($25.06)	$51.22	$7.73	
25	7.25%	($72.24)	($64.84)	($45.37)	$31.45	($9.24)	
26	7.50%	($89.65)	($80.14)	($65.18)	$12.15	($25.78)	
27	7.75%	($106.63)	($95.08)	($84.49)	($6.69)	($41.93)	
28	8.00%	($123.19)	($109.66)	($103.31)	($25.09)	($57.69)	
29	8.25%	($139.35)	($123.89)	($121.67)	($43.05)	($73.07)	

The value of a data table is its use within a larger model. In our example we have entered constant values in each cell indicating payment or expense expected for each project in each year. In a real model these values would be calculated based on a number of different conditions.

The Two Variable Data Table

A two variable data table enables you to vary two arguments of a function. You could, for example, create a two variable data table that shows you what your monthly payments would be for different interest rates over different amounts of time.

For this example you will use the DB function. The DB function in Excel calculates the cost of depreciation on an asset for a given period based on an initial value and a final or "salvage" value, using the Fixed-Declining Balance method of calculating the depreciation. See Table 23.2 for an explanation of the arguments for the DB function.

Table 23.2 DB Function Arguments

This Argument	Means
Cost	The initial value of the asset.
Salvage	The final value of the asset (for example, the amount for which it could be sold after it had been used for the period specified by the `Life` argument).
Life	Represents the useful lifetime of the asset.
Period	Used to specify for which year in the asset's useful lifetime the depreciation cost is being calculated.
Month	(optional) Indicates that the depreciation cost is to be calculated for a specific month of the year.

▶ **See** "Understanding and Using Functions," **page 366**

Setting Up the Inputs   In cell B2, enter the initial value of the asset, $1000. In cell B3, enter the final salvage value of the asset, $100. In cell B4, enter the expected life of the asset in years, 10. In cell B5, enter the number 1 to indicate the year in the life of the asset for which you want to calculate the depreciation cost. In cell E4, enter the formula =**DB(B2,B3,B4,B5)** and press Enter. The result displayed in cell E4 should be $206.00 (see Figure 23.11).

The depreciation formula can only return the depreciation cost for a single year (or month) in the life of an asset. In a financial model, which spans several historical and forecast years, the cost of depreciation for assets would be needed for each year and for each asset.

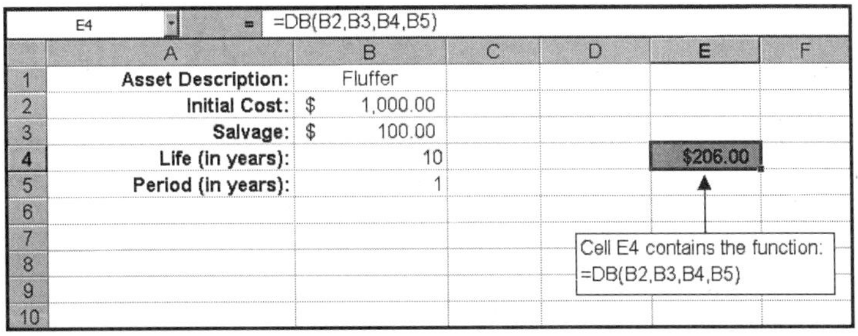

Figure 23.11

This is an example of the DB function. Note that the inputs are entered in their own cells (B2:B5), and that the DB function refers to those cells. That way, if you decide to change one of the input figures, the function will recalculate automatically.

You could enter the formula separately for each period as described previously, or you could use a single input table to calculate the depreciation for the entire life of the asset. You might have many assets with many initial costs, purchased at different times (therefore at different periods in their useful life). You could set up separate tables for each or you could use a two variable data table for efficiency (see Figure 23.12).

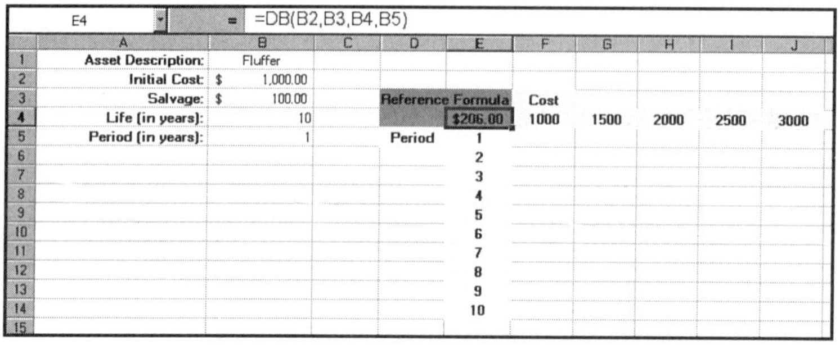

Figure 23.12

This is one example of a two variable data table. Here the period is varied from one to ten years in Column E, while the initial cost is varied from $1,000 to $3,000 in row 4. Now we can create a table that will calculate all the values based on these varied inputs.

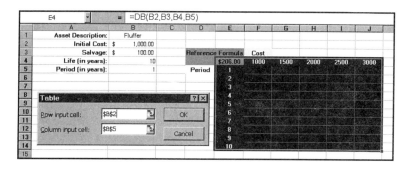

In cells E5 through E14, enter the numbers **1** through **10** for the number of years in the life of the asset. These values will be used as the Period variable in the DB formula for the table.

In cells F4 through J4, enter the values **1000, 1500, 2000, 2500,** and **3000**. These values will be used as the Cost variable in the DB formula for the table.

With the mouse, select the area for the table E4:J14, which is bordered on the top by the Cost values and on the left by the Period values. The DB formula is in the upper-left corner of the table area, which is how Excel chooses the formula to use for the two-way table. You need to construct your two variable data table in this manner for it to return accurate calculations.

Select Data, Table to open the data table dialog box. The data table dialog box contains two input text boxes: the Row Input Cell box and the Column Input Cell box. For a two-input table, both of these boxes will be filled in. Click in the Row Input Cell box and then click cell B2. Then click in the Column Input Cell box on the dialog box and click cell B5 (see Figure 23.13); then click the OK button.

Figure 23.13

This example shows the data table area selected and the Data dialog box with the appropriate cell entries. Note that the Row Input Cell is B2. This is because you varied the initial cost along a row.

The table will fill in with values (see Figure 23.4). Each cell in the table indicates the depreciation cost for an asset, with the initial cost indicated by the value at the top of the column; the period in the asset's life cycle is indicated by the number at the left side of the table.

Figure 23.14

This is an example of the completed two variable data table.

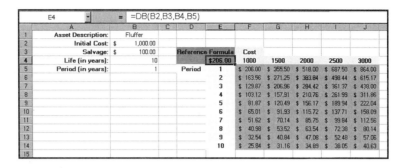

You can check the calculation by entering the DB function in cell D17, for example: **=DB(2000, 100, 10, 7)**. Compare the value in cell D17 to the value in cell H11. They should both read $85.75. Now change the formula in cell D17 to read **=DB(J5, 100, 10, E9)**. The value should match the value in cell J9, $222.04.

This check formula does the same substitution that the data table does. You could duplicate the calculation done by the two-way table by setting up an area with formulas referring to the top row of each column for the Cost parameter and the left column of each row for the Period parameter.

This would require entering the formula in each cell in the table, which would be tedious and could lead to errors that would be difficult to find. The resulting set of formulas would slow down calculation of your spreadsheet because Excel calculates data tables more efficiently than a group of formulas entered separately in adjacent cells.

Deeper Inside Two Variable Data Tables   The data table dialog box labels are somewhat cryptic and are the causes of most of the confusion people have with data tables. The data table is based on a formula in the Reference Formula cell, which is the top-left corner cell of the data table area you select. The formula in this cell must use at least two arguments, and the two arguments that you want to substitute must be entered into the formula as cell references.

The top row of the table to the right of the Reference Formula cell must have values, which will be substituted in the formula for one of the arguments. You can choose to set up the table with either of the arguments on the top row and the other in the left column. In the previous example (see Figure 23.14), you could have used "Period" across the top row and "Cost" down the left column, or you could have substituted for another argument, say Salvage instead of Cost. The order of the arguments in the function in the Reference Formula cell is not related to the way you set up your table. What is important is that you select the appropriate cells when setting the Row Input and Column Input in the data table dialog box.

The first argument in the function is substituted in each cell with the value in the top row of the column, and the fourth argument is substituted in each cell with the value in the left column of the table. When you set up the data table you arranged the Cost values on the top row of the table and the Periods down the left column (see Figure 23.14).

Part
III

Ch
23

Because Cost is in the top row of the table area, you selected the cell that the table reference formula (the DB function in cell E4) uses for its Cost argument (cell B2) as the Row Input Cell. The Period values are in the left column of the table area, so you selected the cell that the table reference formula uses for the Period argument (cell B5) as the Column Input Cell. (See Figure 23.13 to see the Table dialog box.)

The values substituted for the Period argument are listed in the left column of the table. In the data table dialog box, select the cell used by the Reference Formula cell for the Period parameter (cell B5) as the Column Input Cell.

The values substituted for the Cost parameter are listed in the top row of the table. Therefore, in the data table dialog box, you select the cell used by the Reference Formula cell for the Cost parameter (cell B2) as the Row Input Cell.

Remember that the Row Input Cell means the cell used by the Reference Formula for that argument (the top row of the table), and Column Input Cell means the cell used by the Reference Formula for that argument (the left column of the table).

Using Goal Seek

Goal Seek is a quick and easy approach to arriving at a desired result by changing the value of another cell. The purpose of Goal Seek is to find a desired value for a cell that contains a formula.

Using Goal Seek in a Worksheet

Although the Goal Seek feature can be used with a chart (see the following section), it is most commonly used in a worksheet. One way to see how Goal Seek can be used in a worksheet is to use a financial function such as the Rate function.

The Rate function calculates the interest rate per period of an annuity. The Rate function can take up to five parameters: Nper, Pmt, PV, FV, Type, and Guess, as shown in Table 23.3.

Table 23.3   Rate Function Arguments

This Argument	Means
Nper	The number of periods in the life of the annuity (required).
Pmt	The value of the payments from the annuity each period (required).
FV	The future value (required).
Type	Indicates whether payments are made at the end of the period (if Type=0 or is omitted) or at the end (if Type=1) (optional).
Guess	Used to help the function determine the correct value (optional).

Figure 23.15

Rate function example.

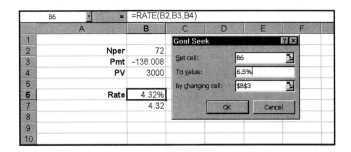

	A	B	C	D
1				
2	Nper	72		
3	Pmt	-136.008		
4	PV	3000		
5				
6	Rate	4.32%		
7		4.32		
8				
9				

B6 = =RATE(B2,B3,B4)

Using the example shown in Figure 23.15, you would enter the number of periods—in this case, 72—into cell B2. In cell B3, enter the amount of the periodic payments from the annuity, -136 (negative to indicate payment). In cell B4, enter the present value of the annuity, **4,000**. In cell B6, enter the rate formula **=RATE(B2,B3,B4)**. The value displayed should be approximately 4.32 percent.

Suppose that you want to find the payments, which would cause the rate of the annuity to equal 6.50 percent. You could begin trying different values manually, changing cell B3 until cell B6 shows the desired value. It would probably take quite some time to reach the correct value. Instead you could use Goal Seek to find this payment level very quickly.

To use Goal Seek, select Tools, Goal Seek from the menu bar. The Goal Seek dialog box opens and prompts you to enter the information required to find the payment (see Figure 23.16). Click in the Set Cell text box and click the worksheet in cell B6. Then click in the To Value text box and type **6.5%**. Then click in the By Changing Cell text box and click cell B3. Click OK and Excel will quickly display the dialog box indicating that a solution was found. You can click OK and the change will be saved to cell B3, or if the value is not correct, you can click Cancel and revert to the previous value.

Figure 23.16

This is one example of the Goal Seek dialog box and how to use it.

B6 = =RATE(B2,B3,B4)

	A	B	C	D	E	F
1			Goal Seek			? ×
2	Nper	72	Set cell:	B6		
3	Pmt	-136.008				
4	PV	3000	To value:	6.5%		
5			By changing cell:	$B$3		
6	Rate	4.32%				
7		4.32		OK	Cancel	
8						
9						
10						

If you have problems finding a solution with Goal Seek, you can create a custom formula that contains a different but related value. In this example, the value of the rate you are trying to find is a fairly small number. You could put a formula in cell B7: **=100*B6**. Then you could use the Goal Seek dialog box to set B7 to value 6.5 by changing cell B3.

Using Goal Seek in a Chart

Another way of using the Goal Seek tool is to invoke it automatically when working with a chart. Given a chart like the one in Figure 23.17, you can select a data point and drag it to a desired level (see Figure 23.18).

Figure 23.17

This shows a sample chart embedded on a worksheet. Note the data to the left of the chart. These data are not numbers that were typed in. Rather, they are the results of formulas.

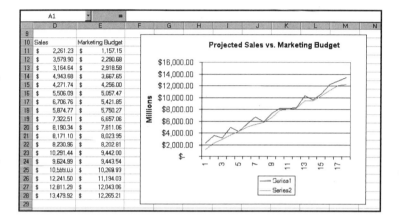

Figure 23.18

This example shows the effect of selecting a specific data point on one of the lines and dragging that data point to a different value.

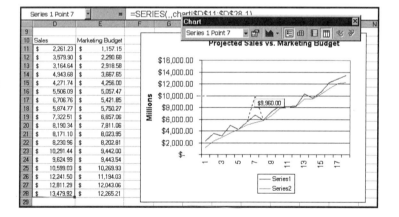

This causes the Goal Seek dialog box to open and prompt you for the cell to change to cause the change (see Figure 23.19), which you indicated by moving the data point on the graph.

N O T E You should note that charts that are created from numbers that are typed into cells will not use the Goal Seek feature when you drag a data point on the chart. In this case, Excel will just change the underlying number.

The Goal Seek feature can be used only on charts where the underlying numbers on the worksheet are the results of formulas. When you change a data point on a chart like this, Excel displays the Goal Seek dialog box so you can indicate where you want the change in the underlying data to occur. ▨

Figure 23.19

This example shows the Goal Seek dialog box, which Excel displays automatically as a result of changing the data point.

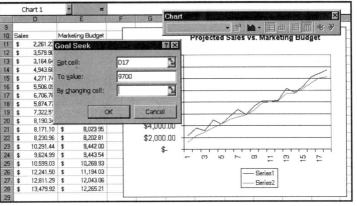

There may be no way to achieve the result you have requested, in which case Goal Seek will indicate that a solution may not have been found. If the value displayed is "good enough," you can accept the change; otherwise, you can revert to the original value by canceling the dialog box.

▶ **See** "Modifying Charts," **page 425**

Using Solver

The Solver utility is similar to the Goal Seek tool, except that the features and flexibility it offers are much greater. The types of problems Solver can be used to solve are very diverse. You could use Solver in the same way as the Goal Seek tool, to set a single cell to a particular value, or to a maximum or minimum value. However, Solver can modify many more cells in attempting to find the desired solution. Solver can be required to find a solution that meets criteria you specify. For instance, a particular input cell may be required to be greater than 0, or the solution could require an integer value.

For example, the Solver tool can be used to model complex problems in engineering, economics, or finance. It can also be used to find solutions for optimal distributions of goods among warehouses or to schedule employees to minimize expenses while making sure that all work shifts have minimum required staff.

Loading Solver

You need to be sure that the Solver is available to you when you want it. To do this, select the Tools menu and look for the Solver command. If it is not there, you will first need to use the Add-Ins command.

To load the Solver add-in, select Tools, Add-Ins. Scroll through the list of add-ins to Solver Add-In and click the check box. If the Solver add-in doesn't appear in the list, you will have to browse for it. If it was not installed during your Office 97 installation process, you may have to install it separately.

After the Solver add-in is loaded Solver appears on the Tools menu. Select Tools, Solver to open the Solver tool.

Setting Up a Sample Problem

To demonstrate the Solver tool you can use this simple example. Given a fixed budget of $1,000, you want to find an optimal mix of commodities that could be purchased at given costs. To set up the problem, enter the values as shown in Figure 23.20.

Figure 23.20

This example shows a list of commodities, their individual costs, and the overall budget.

	E9		=	=SUM(E3:E6)	
	A	B	C	D	E	F
1						
2			Unit Cost	Units	Total Cost	
3		Car	220	0	0	
4		Telephone	35	0	0	
5		Food	29	0	0	
6		Clothes	104	0	0	
7						
8						
9		Budget	1000		0	
10						
11						
12		Constraints				
13		None				
14						

Using Figure 23.20 as an example, you would enter =**D3*C3** into cell E3. In cell E4 enter = **D4*C4** and so on through cell E6. The range D3:D6 represents the number of units purchased of each commodity, and the range E3:E6 represents the total amount spent on each commodity. In cell E9, enter the formula =**SUM(E3:E6)**, to represent the total amount spent on all commodities.

You can enter different values in the range D3:D6 to indicate different mixtures of the commodities purchased. The problem is to figure out how to spend the entire budget but no more.

Figure 23.21

The Solver Parameters dialog box.

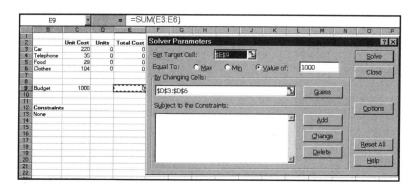

The Solver dialog box (see Figure 23.21) prompts for several parameters, which you can set. The most important is the Target Cell, which is the cell that contains the formula for which you want to find a particular value.

N O T E The Target Cell must be a single cell on the current sheet. ▪

You can click in the Set Target cell text box and then click the cell that contains the formula. In this case, that is E9. The next choice is whether Solver is to find a particular value or find a minimum or maximum for the model. For this example, in the Equal To options, click the Value Of button and enter **1,000** in the box (see Figure 23.21).

N O T E All Precedents of the Target cell must be on the same sheet as the Target cell. ▪

Next, you need to specify the cells that are to be changed in order to set cell E9 to a value of 1000. Click in the By Changing Cells text box and type **D3:D6**, or select the range D3:D6 on the spreadsheet.

CAUTION

Solver will overwrite a cell formula with a constant value if the cell is one of the "Changing Cells" you specify. You can lose your formulas if you are not careful.

Having entered the minimum information necessary you can now click the Solve button (in the upper right part of the dialog box). Solver now displays the solution shown in Figure 23.22.

Figure 23.22

A solver solution.

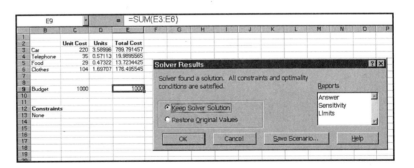

Solver displays a dialog box indicating that a solution has been found and offers several choices. You can choose to keep the values Solver found (they are displayed in the cells D3:D6). Or you can choose to restore the original values in the cells. You can create a *scenario* with the values Solver has found by clicking the Save Scenario button, after which you will be prompted for a scenario name.

▶ **See** "Evaluating What-if Scenarios?," **page 498**

Part
III

Ch
23

Solver also offers a list of three reports, which it can generate and add to the current workbook. The three reports are called Answer, Sensitivity, and Limits. You can select any combination of these from the list and click OK to generate the reports. Each report you select inserts a new worksheet in the workbook with an appropriate sheet name.

The Solver Reports give detailed technical information about the solution that was found including the final value, the input values, and the constraints applied on the solution. In the first case, you did not apply any constraints, and as a result, the values found may not represent realistic choices. You can refine the Solver solution by adding constraints.

Adding Constraints

The process of using the Solver tool is often iterative. That is, the best solution to the original problem may not be found in a single attempt. Observing the results of our first attempt to find an optimal mix of commodities, notice that the values suggested are not integral values. It may be that you can't have fractional values for the commodities purchased, so add constraints to the Solver dialog box.

The values you originally entered are remembered by Solver, so you only need to modify the settings you have already created. Select Tools, Solver to open the Solver dialog box, and in the Subject to the Constraints section, click the Add button (see Figure 23.23).

Figure 23.23

This is an example of the Add Constraint dialog box.

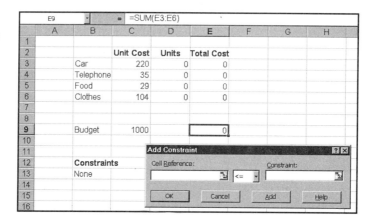

The Add Constraint dialog box opens and prompts you to enter the Cell reference and the condition which must hold. In this case, select the range D3:D6 in which the Units for each commodity are entered. In the middle list box, change the operator from "<=" to "**int**". This will also change the constraint box to "integer" (see Figure 23.24). Click the OK button to save the constraint and return to the Solver dialog box. The Subject to Constraints list should now include the item $D$3:$D$6 = integer (see Figure 23.25).

Figure 23.24

This is an example of the Add Constraint dialog box after a constraint has been added.

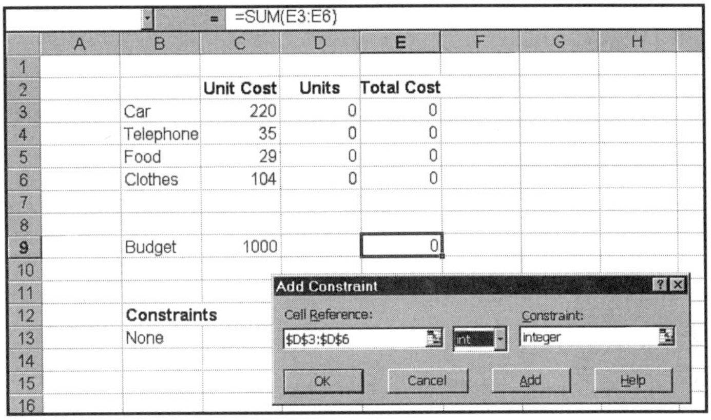

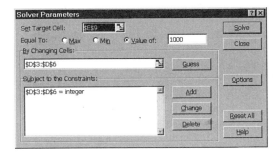

Figure 23.25

This example shows the Solver Parameters dialog box with added constraints. Each time you need to add a constraint, you need to use the Add Constraints dialog box.

If you choose the Solve button now the Solver will determine a combination of goods that can be purchased at the stated prices so that the total equals $1000 and all of the units are whole numbers (see Figure 23.26).

Figure 23.26

This shows Solver's resolution of the problem after having added the constraints.

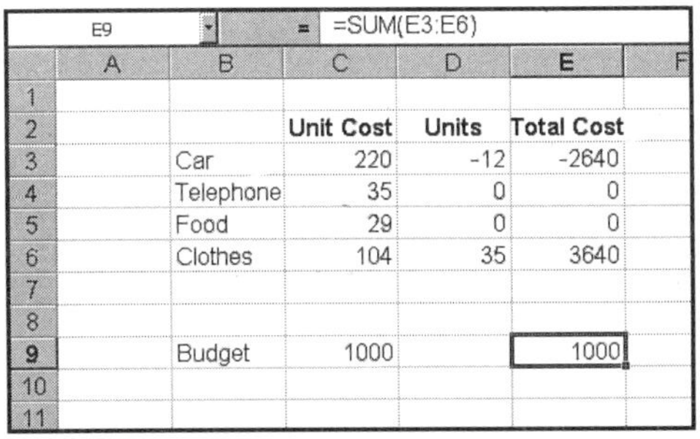

The results are not perfect, however, because the value Solver chose for Car is a negative number. This would violate the sense of the problem, so we need to add further conditions to the Solver Constraints. To do so, follow these steps:

1. Select Tools, Solver to open the Solver dialog box again and click the Add button to open the Add Constraints dialog box.

2. In the Cell Reference text box, select cells D3:D6.

3. Change the <= sign to >=.

4. In the Constraint text box type 0 and click OK.

A list of constraints is displayed (see Figure 23.27). The list indicates that the solution Solver can reach is now limited to non-negative, integer units. If you click the Solve button, Solver recalculates and finds a new combination subject to the conditions you have specified (see Figure 23.28).

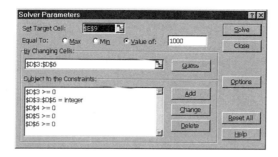

Figure 23.27

This is an example of the Solver Parameters dialog box showing the new constraints.

Figure 23.28

This example shows the new results that Solver came up with based on the new constraints you added.

	A	B	C	D	E	F
					=SUM(E3:E6)	
1						
2			Unit Cost	Units	Total Cost	
3		Car	220	2	440	
4		Telephone	35	16	560	
5		Food	29	0	0	
6		Clothes	104	0	0	
7						
8						
9		Budget	1000		1000	
10						

You can continue to refine the model, adding, changing, or deleting constraints as appropriate. For the final step you will add a set of minimum values for each of the units, to insure that the solution not only satisfies the budget constraint of $1,000 but also satisfies requirements of the uses of the commodities in the model.

To perform the final step in this example, look at Figure 23.29 and note the values entered in cells B17:C21. Enter these values in your worksheet. You are preparing to tell Solver to use these values when calculating the problem.

Figure 23.29

This example shows several new constraints in cells B17:C21. You can enter these in your worksheet and then add them to Solver from the worksheet.

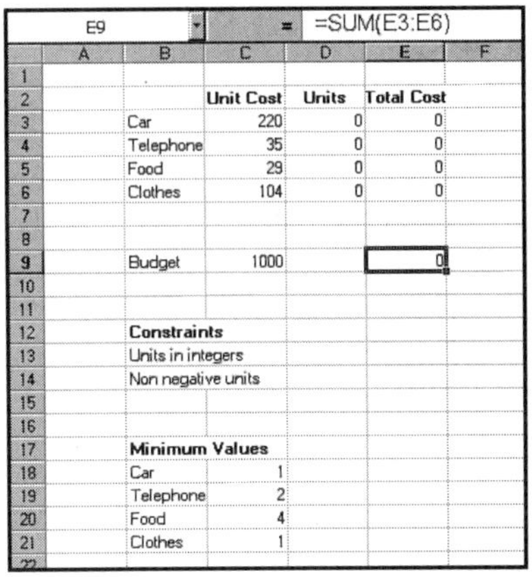

	E9			=	=SUM(E3:E6)	
	A	B	C	D	E	F
1						
2			Unit Cost	Units	Total Cost	
3		Car	220	0	0	
4		Telephone	35	0	0	
5		Food	29	0	0	
6		Clothes	104	0	0	
7						
8						
9		Budget	1000		0	
10						
11						
12		Constraints				
13		Units in integers				
14		Non negative units				
15						
16						
17		Minimum Values				
18		Car	1			
19		Telephone	2			
20		Food	4			
21		Clothes	1			
22						

To add the minimums as constraints to the Solver, follow these steps:

1. Select Tools, Solver to open the Solver dialog box again and click the Add button to open the Add Constraints dialog box.

2. In the Cell Reference box, click in cell D3.

3. Change the operator box to >=.

4. Click in the Constraints box and click cell C18.

5. Click Add to save the constraint condition and add another.

6. Repeat the process for cells D4:D6. Be sure to select the correct constraint cell for each commodity.

7. Click OK on the last constraint (D6 >= C21) instead of Add.

The Subject to the Constraints list displays the conditions you have set. You can scroll through the list to verify that all constraints are present and correct. If you click the Solve button, Solver will search for a new solution using the new constraints (see Figure 23.30).

Figure 23.30

This example shows that Solver reached a new solution based on the latest set of constraints.

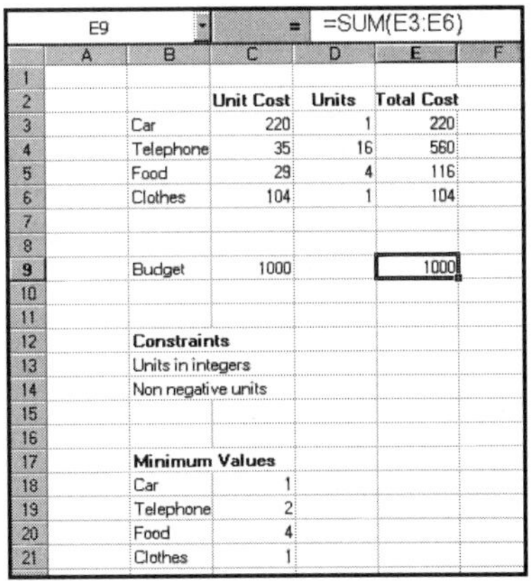

	E9			=	=SUM(E3:E6)	
	A	B	C	D	E	F
1						
2			Unit Cost	Units	Total Cost	
3		Car	220	1	220	
4		Telephone	35	16	560	
5		Food	29	4	116	
6		Clothes	104	1	104	
7						
8						
9		Budget	1000		1000	
10						
11						
12		Constraints				
13		Units in integers				
14		Non negative units				
15						
16						
17		Minimum Values				
18		Car	1			
19		Telephone	2			
20		Food	4			
21		Clothes	1			

You can continue to add or modify conditions as necessary. You can also add formulas to the model, which may simplify the way you specify certain types of constraints.

As you work with Solver you will find that a combination of constraints set in Solver and formulas on the worksheet that calculate comparisons, differences, and sums of other inputs allow the greatest flexibility in modeling a problem and satisfying complex sets of conditions. As the model gets more complex, calculation may slow down, and it will be even slower if you do not model some constraints as formulas to keep the list of Solver constraints to a minimum.

Setting Solver Options

Solver enables you to control the way that it works through the Solver Options dialog box. To open this dialog box, select Tools, Solver and when the Solver dialog box is displayed, click the Options button (see Figure 23.31).

Once you open the Solver Options dialog box, you can modify the settings to affect the way Solver works. See Table 23.4 for an explanation of the Solver options.

Figure 23.31

This example shows the Solver Options dialog box.

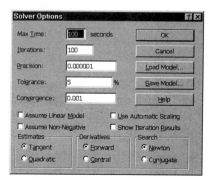

Table 23.4   Solver Options

This Option	Means
Max Time	You can specify that Solver should not continue to search for a solution to the problem forever by entering the number of seconds allowed for calculation in the Max Time text box. If Solver has not found a solution within the specified time, it will halt and display a message that it could not find a feasible solution. You can keep or discard the value reached within the allowed time.

Part III
Ch
23

Iterations

In the Iterations text box, you can specify that Solver should stop searching for a solution after recalculating the changing cells in the worksheet any number of times (100 is the default). If a solution has not been found, Solver notifies you with a Show Trial Solution dialog box that offers the options of Saving a Scenario with the Current Values, Continuing to Search for the Solution, or Canceling the Search. If you continue, solver will ignore the Iterations value as it continues to search for the solution.

Precision

The Precision value is used to control how Solver evaluates the conditions you have set. It is used to determine whether the value in a constraint cell satisfies the condition of the constraint, being equal to, less than, or greater than a value. The value must be between 0 and 1. Larger values speed up searches at the risk of increasing errors in the constraints.

Tolerance

The Tolerance Value is used only in problems involving integer solutions. It is the percentage by which the target cell can vary from the true optimal value (possibly a non-integer) and still be considered acceptable. The default is 5 percent.

Convergence

Convergence is used by Solver to determine when a solution has been reached in a nonlinear model. When the ratio of the previously calculated value of the target cell to the currently calculated value is less than the convergence value for 5 iterations, Solver stops searching, whether it has found a solution or not. The value must be between 0 and 1 (default 0.001) and smaller values will require longer search times.

Linear Model

If the problem you are modeling is linear, you can speed calculation by setting the Assume Linear Model option. The simple model, used in this chapter, is a linear model and could safely use this option. If you set this option on a nonlinear model, Solver will not calculate correctly and probably will not reach the correct solution.

continues

Table 23.4   Continued

This Option	Means
Assume Non-negative	The Assume Non-Negative option forces Solver to treat all changing cells as if they have a constraint to be greater than or equal to 0. You can reduce the number of constraints by selecting the Assume Non-Negative option. This should only be set when all or most of the adjustable cells in the model are non-negative because Solver will ignore possible negative values for those variables that are allowed to be less than 0.
Use Automatic Scaling	The Use Automatic Scaling option is useful when you have a model in which the target cell and the changing cells contain values that differ greatly in size. Using this option allows Solver to adjust for these large variations automatically. Choose this option if Solver is not able to find a solution for a problem with these conditions.
Show Iteration	Show Iteration Result causes Solver to pause after each iteration and display the currently calculated value. This can be useful in troubleshooting a problem for which Solver doesn't reach a solution, or in seeing the way Solver reaches a particular solution. This option slows calculation dramatically because you will be prompted to continue at each step. Calculation will not continue until you have clicked the Continue button. You can also stop calculation at any iteration and save a scenario.
Estimates/Derivative/Search	The Estimates, Derivative, and Search method options are advanced features that control the way Solver attempts to find a solution. The explanation of these methods is beyond the scope of this chapter. You can try different methods if Solver is having difficulty finding a solution, or if you want to try to speed up the search. The defaults are Tangent Estimates, Forward Derivatives, and Newton Search.

From the Solver Options dialog box, you can also choose to Save and Load the constraints and conditions you have specified. You only need to save the model if you will be evaluating multiple sets of constraints.

To save the current set of constraints, for example, click the Save Model button. You need to choose a range of cells large enough to contain all the formulas in the Solver constraints, so click cell I2 and click OK. Solver starts in the specified cell and fills formulas down as needed. If you select more than one cell, you must select a range large enough to hold all the formulas. If you select a range that is too small, Solver prompts you with the number of cells necessary to save the current set of constraints.

CAUTION

Solver will overwrite any cells in the range you specify or from the cell you specify to the end of the range necessary to store the constraint formulas.

You can choose to load the set of constraints by clicking the Load Model button and selecting the entire range of saved formulas (I2:I13) and clicking OK (see Figure 23.32).

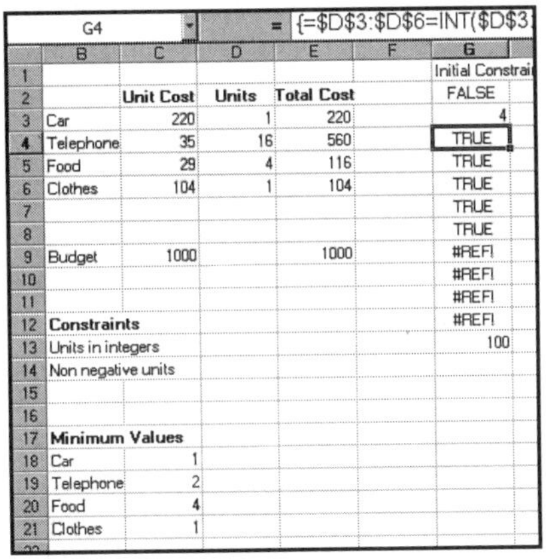

Figure 23.32

This is an example of a worksheet displaying a list of constraints.

	G4		= {=$D$3:$D$6=INT($D$3}			
	B	C	D	E	F	G
1						Initial Constrai
2		Unit Cost	Units	Total Cost		FALSE
3	Car	220	1	220		4
4	Telephone	35	16	560		TRUE
5	Food	29	4	116		TRUE
6	Clothes	104	1	104		TRUE
7						TRUE
8						TRUE
9	Budget	1000		1000		#REF!
10						#REF!
11						#REF!
12	Constraints					#REF!
13	Units in integers					100
14	Non negative units					
15						
16						
17	Minimum Values					
18	Car	1				
19	Telephone	2				
20	Food	4				
21	Clothes	1				

N O T E The Save Model feature enables you to store many different sets of constraints for the same problem. If you use the Save Model feature often, you will find that naming the range of cells that contains a set of constraints as well as labeling them in a cell will make them much simpler to manage and maintain. To label the set of constraints in this example, go to cell I1 and type Initial Constraints. Then select the range I1:I13 and choose Insert / Name / Create and choose Create Names in Top Row (the default) and click OK. Now you can load the set of constraints by entering the name **Initial_Constraints** in the Load Model dialog box instead of selecting the range.

Circular References and Iteration

A circular reference is created when a formula in a cell refers directly or indirectly to the cell in which it is contained. The simplest example of a circular reference is a cell that refers to itself. If the cell B2 contains the formula: =B2, this is known as a circular reference. An example of several cells that form a circular reference is shown in Figure 23.33.

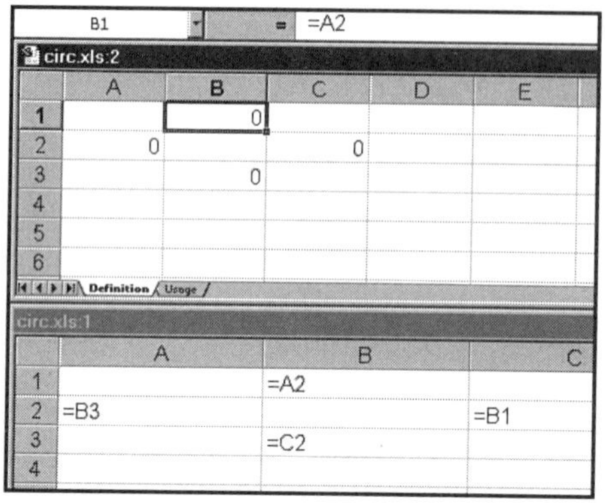

Figure 23.33

Two views of a worksheet containing circular references. (One view shows formulas; the other view shows results.)

Excel will warn you when you enter a circular formula and provides a toolbar for tracking down circularity in a worksheet. Circular references can be a big problem when they occur unintentionally because Excel can't fully complete calculating all the formulas in the worksheet.

Circular references are not always a problem, however, and some problems require circular references in order to model them correctly. A system of simultaneous equations, such as those that commonly occur in engineering models, or a complex iterated function in economics are examples of problems that require circular references. These types of problems also require special calculation methods to solve them.

A simple example of a system of simultaneous equations is shown in order to illustrate the problem. This example uses a pair of equations to solve the following:

$$X = 9 + Y / 7$$
$$Y = 1 + 2 * X$$

You can put these formulas directly into Excel as shown in Figure 23.34:

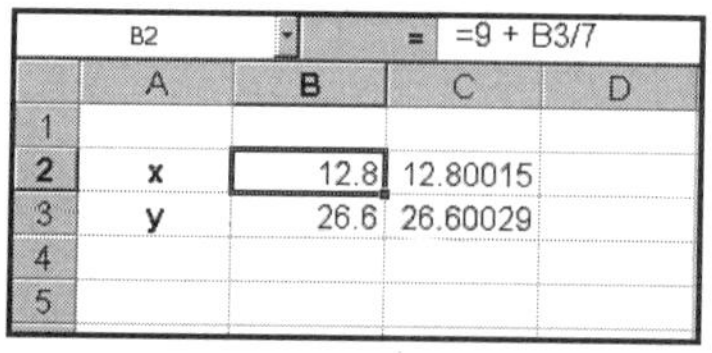

Figure 23.34

This is an example of a pair of sample equations.

In cell B2 enter **=9 + B3/7** and in cell B3 enter **=1 + 2* B2**. If you do not have the Iteration option checked (in the under the Calculation tab), Excel will warn you of the circular dependency you have just entered. This is useful for avoiding accidental circularity, but you have the choice of dismissing the dialog box and continuing to work with the circular formulas without being reminded again.

In order to calculate values for these cells Excel must calculate repeatedly until it gets close to the correct value. To allow this, you must turn on Iteration by selecting Tools, Options and clicking the Calculation tab (see Figure 23.35). The values in the Maximum Iterations text box and Maximum Change text box can be left at the default values of 100 and .001 for this example (see Figure 23.35). With these settings Excel will quickly display the values for X and Y.

In B2 the value 12.8 will be displayed, while in cell B3, the value 26.6 will be displayed. To see what is going on, change the Maximum Iterations value from 100 to 1. This causes Excel to stop calculating after a single attempt to calculate the cells. Select cell B2 and re-enter the formula **=9+B3/7** and press Enter. The value displayed will not equal 12.8 and cell B3 will not equal 26.6. Repeatedly pressing F9 will show the values used in the intermediate calculation or "iteration" of the calculation procedure.

At each stage of the calculation process, Excel uses the value of the referenced cells in a formula as if they were constant values. Excel calculates the value of B2 and treats B3 as if it were a constant value. Then Excel calculates the value of B3, treating B2 as if it were a constant.

After B3 has been calculated, B2 would normally be recalculated (because a cell it is dependent on has changed value), but you set iterations to 1, effectively telling Excel to stop at this point. Pressing F9 tells Excel to recalculate the worksheet again, and the values in B2 and B3 will change again. When Iteration is on, Excel will recalculate repeatedly until either it has recalculated the worksheet the number of times specified in the Maximum Iterations box (default 100), or until all the values being calculated change by an amount less than the amount specified in the Maximum Change box. (the default is 0.001.)

Figure 23.35

This shows the Tools Options dialog box with the Calculate tab selected. Note the default values for Maximum Iteration and Maximum Change.

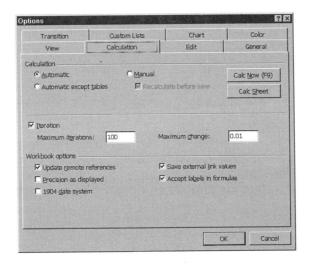

Not all equations like this will reach a final value. If you change the formula in B2 to =2+B3^2, and the formula in B3 to =SQRT(2+B2), the values will never reach a stable value for the two equations. In this case the values will continue to grow without bound, but in other cases the problem may not be as obvious. The values in a set of cells with circular references could bounce up and down erratically without ever settling down to the "true" value. This is another reason to be careful with circular references and be sure you understand the process you are attempting to model.

Evaluating What-if Scenarios

One of the most common uses of spreadsheets is for what-if analysis. You can create a model of a problem in Excel by preparing a spreadsheet with formulas that calculate results based on *input* cells. When you change the values of the input cells to reflect different conditions for the model and recalculate, you are performing a what-if analysis. You can use this analysis to see the values that the model produces under different conditions, or scenarios.

The Scenario Manager is a tool for manipulating worksheets for what-if analysis. Typically, there are multiple cells that change with each set of conditions. Using Scenario Manager you can do the following:

■ select up to 32 cells per scenario to define as changing cells

■ specify values for each of those cells

■ save the entire set of cells and values with a descriptive name

■ reload the values from a saved scenario to set the values of the changing cells to a known value

To illustrate the use of the Scenario Manager, you can use the sample worksheet shown in Figure 23.36.

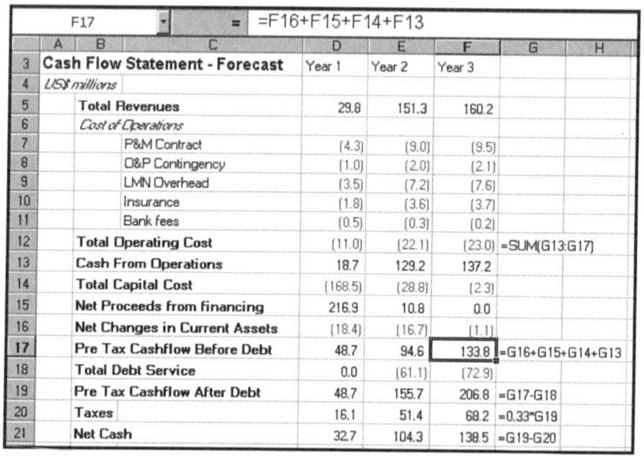

Figure 23.36

This worksheet shows a simple model that might require what-if analysis.

	F17		=	=F16+F15+F14+F13				
	A	B	C	D	E	F	G	H
3	Cash Flow Statement - Forecast			Year 1	Year 2	Year 3		
4	US$ millions							
5		Total Revenues		29.8	151.3	160.2		
6		Cost of Operations						
7			P&M Contract	(4.3)	(9.0)	(9.5)		
8			O&P Contingency	(1.0)	(2.0)	(2.1)		
9			LMN Overhead	(3.5)	(7.2)	(7.6)		
10			Insurance	(1.8)	(3.6)	(3.7)		
11			Bank fees	(0.5)	(0.3)	(0.2)		
12		Total Operating Cost		(11.0)	(22.1)	(23.0)	=SUM(G13:G17)	
13		Cash From Operations		18.7	129.2	137.2		
14		Total Capital Cost		(168.5)	(28.8)	(2.3)		
15		Net Proceeds from financing		216.9	10.8	0.0		
16		Net Changes in Current Assets		(18.4)	(16.7)	(1.1)		
17		Pre Tax Cashflow Before Debt		48.7	94.6	133.8	=G16+G15+G14+G13	
18		Total Debt Service		0.0	(61.1)	(72.9)		
19		Pre Tax Cashflow After Debt		48.7	155.7	206.8	=G17-G18	
20		Taxes		16.1	51.4	68.2	=0.33*G19	
21		Net Cash		32.7	104.3	138.5	=G19-G20	

The sample worksheet shows a simplified and abbreviated Cash Flow statement. Column G displays sample formulas for the rows that are not constant values.

The range D7:F11 represents the detailed information of the Operating Costs for this fictional company. Because this is a forecast of future events, the Operating Costs aren't known in advance. For this reason, a great deal of effort can go into creating complicated models to predict these and other forecast values. Even so, predictions can be high or low, and scenarios can be useful for investigating the effect on the company under different conditions.

For this example, you can use a simplified version of this analysis. To begin, you need to create a scenario from the values, which we have initially entered in the spreadsheet. To do this, select the range D7:F11 and choose <u>T</u>ools, Sc<u>e</u>narios to open the Scenario dialog box (see Figure 23.37).

Figure 23.37

This example shows the Scenario dialog box.

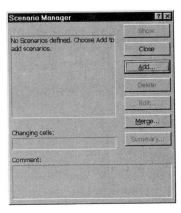

Click the Add button in the Scenario Manager dialog box to open the Add Scenario dialog box (see Figure 23.38).

Figure 23.38

This example shows the Add Scenario dialog box.

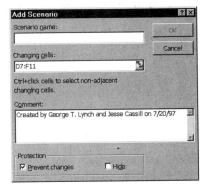

Adding a Base Case Scenario

The Add Scenario dialog box prompts you for a name for the Scenario. In the Scenario Name text box, type **Base Case**. The range of Changing Cells is D7:F11; it was previously selected. You could add other cells as necessary, but in this case there is no need.

In the Comment text box enter a descriptive comment that will be useful in distinguishing this scenario from others you might create. Enter: **This scenario contains the values for Cost of Operations which represents the most likely case given status quo** and click the OK box to save the scenario.

The Scenario Manager then prompts you with a list of the Changing Cells and the values to be saved for this scenario. You can keep the values listed by just clicking the OK button. The Base

Case scenario is now saved and appears in the Scenario Manager list. Close the Scenario Manager dialog box and return to the spreadsheet (see Figure 23.39).

Figure 23.39

This sample worksheet shows a base case Scenario. Note the values in cells D7:F11.

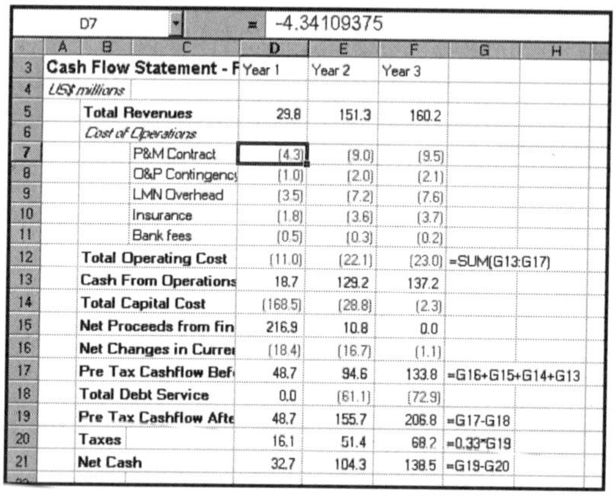

With only a single Scenario defined you can do what-if analysis by editing the values in any or all of the changing cells in the range D7:F11. You can then reset all of the values to the Base Case by selecting Tools, Scenarios, and then selecting the Base Case Scenario in the scenario list, and clicking the Show button. All the values you stored will be pasted back into the range and your spreadsheet will be back to the initial state you saved.

Adding a Worst Case Scenario

The real value of the Scenario Manager, however, is in storing many scenarios. Now you will create a Worst Case Scenario.

Begin by changing the values in the range D7:F11.

1. In cell C1 enter the value **1.3**.

2. Right-click C1 and select Copy from the shortcut menu.

3. Select the range D7:F11. Right-click the selected range and select Paste Special from the short-cut menu.

4. Choose the Multiply option from the Paste Special dialog box and click OK. This increases the values in the range by 30 percent.

Because these are costs, this represents a situation of higher expense, which represents a Worst Case Scenario. Now we need to add this scenario to the Scenario Manager.

Select the range D7:F11 and select Tools, Scenarios from the menu to open the Scenario Manager dialog box. Click the Add button in the Scenario Manager to open the Add Scenario dialog box and enter **Worst Case** for the Scenario name. Enter a comment, such as **This scenario includes a 30% increase in Operating Costs**. Click OK to save the scenario and return to the Scenario Manager dialog box. The Worst Case scenario should appear below the Base Case in the scenario list. Click Close to close the Scenario Manager dialog box. Your sample worksheet should now show the values that represent a worst case scenario (see Figure 23.40).

Figure 23.40

This sample worksheet shows a worst case scenario. Note the values in cells D7:F11.

	D7	= -5.643421875					
	A	B	C	D	E	F	G	H
2								
3	**Cash Flow Statement - Forecast**			Year 1	Year 2	Year 3		
4	*US$ millions*							
5		Total Revenues		29.8	151.3	160.2		
6		*Cost of Operations*						
7			P&M Contract	(5.6)	(11.7)	(12.3)		
8			O&P Contingency	(1.3)	(2.6)	(2.7)		
9			LMN Overhead	(4.5)	(9.4)	(9.8)		
10			Insurance	(2.3)	(4.7)	(4.8)		
11			Bank fees	(0.6)	(0.4)	(0.2)		
12		**Total Operating Cost**		(14.3)	(28.7)	(29.9)	=SUM(G13:G17)	
13		**Cash From Operations**		18.7	129.2	137.2		
14		**Total Capital Cost**		(168.5)	(28.8)	(2.3)		
15		**Net Proceeds from financing**		216.9	10.8	0.0		
16		**Net Changes in Current Assets**		(18.4)	(16.7)	(1.1)		
17		**Pre Tax Cashflow Before Debt**		48.7	94.6	133.8	=G16+G15+G14+G13	
18		**Total Debt Service**		0.0	(61.1)	(72.9)		
19		**Pre Tax Cashflow After Debt**		48.7	155.7	206.8	=G17-G18	
20		**Taxes**		16.1	51.4	68.2	=0.33*G19	
21		**Net Cash**		32.7	104.3	138.5	=G19-G20	

Adding a Best Case Scenario

Now that you have a base case scenario and a worst case scenario, you can add a best case scenario. In this example, that would mean a scenario where the operating costs are lower.

Follow these steps to add a Best Case Scenario:

1. Select Tools, Scenario to open the Scenario Manager dialog box.
2. Click the Base Case scenario and click the Show button to reset the Operating Cost items in the range D7:F11 to the original values. Then click Close to close the dialog box.
3. In cell C1 enter the value **0.8**.
4. Right-click C1 and select Copy from the shortcut menu.
5. Select the range D7:F11. Right-click the selected range and select Paste Special from the shortcut menu.
6. Choose the Multiply option from the Paste Special dialog box and click OK. This will decrease the values in the range by 20 percent.

Because the costs are lower, these values will represent a best case scenario.

Now create another scenario following the steps just described. Name this scenario the **Best Case** and enter a description, such as **This scenario represents a 20% decrease in Operating Costs**. When you close the Scenario Manager dialog box, your worksheet should show the values that represent the best case scenario (see Figure 23.41).

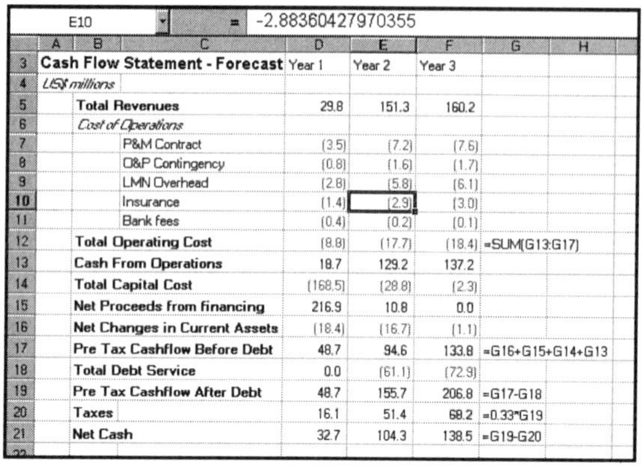

Figure 23.41

This sample worksheet shows a best case scenario.

	E10		=	-2.88360427970355			

	A B	C	D	E	F	G	H
3	Cash Flow Statement - Forecast		Year I	Year 2	Year 3		
4	US$ millions						
5	Total Revenues		29.8	151.3	160.2		
6	Cost of Operations						
7	P&M Contract		(3.5)	(7.2)	(7.6)		
8	O&P Contingency		(0.8)	(1.6)	(1.7)		
9	LMN Overhead		(2.8)	(5.8)	(6.1)		
10	Insurance		(1.4)	(2.9)	(3.0)		
11	Bank fees		(0.4)	(0.2)	(0.1)		
12	Total Operating Cost		(8.9)	(17.7)	(18.4)	=SUM(G13:G17)	
13	Cash From Operations		18.7	129.2	137.2		
14	Total Capital Cost		(168.5)	(28.8)	(2.3)		
15	Net Proceeds from financing		216.9	10.8	0.0		
16	Net Changes in Current Assets		(18.4)	(16.7)	(1.1)		
17	Pre Tax Cashflow Before Debt		48.7	94.6	133.8	=G16+G15+G14+G13	
18	Total Debt Service		0.0	(61.1)	(72.9)		
19	Pre Tax Cashflow After Debt		48.7	155.7	206.8	=G17-G18	
20	Taxes		16.1	51.4	68.2	=0.33*G19	
21	Net Cash		32.7	104.3	138.5	=G19-G20	

You now have created three scenarios for Operating Costs in this simple model. You can quickly replace an entire group of cells with values that represent different assumptions about the future.

In a real model, you might want to create multiple scenarios for Revenues, and a separate set for Expenses. You could then show a best case Revenue scenario with a worst case Expense scenario, for example. You can mix and match scenarios to explore different possibilities.

CAUTION

Remember that a scenario stores information for each cell you specify, so if two scenarios store different values for the same cell, the last scenario you show will set the value for that cell. This could lead to results that are inconsistent with the assumptions you are trying to model.

Merging Scenarios

If you have created scenarios in the past that will exactly fit a current model, you can merge them into the current worksheet. You will find, however, that if the models aren't identical, merging an existing set of scenarios may not give you the results you want.

To merge scenarios, you need to have at least two workbooks open: one that contains the existing scenarios and the one in which you want to create scenarios.

If it isn't open already, open the workbook that contains the existing scenarios. Make the current workbook (the one in which you want to create scenarios) active. (You can do this by clicking on the Window menu and selecting the appropriate workbook from the list at the bottom of the pull-down menu.) Then, with the current workbook active, select Tools, Scenarios and click the Merge button. This opens the Merge Scenarios dialog box (see Figure 23.42).

Figure 23.42

This example shows the Merge Scenarios dialog box.

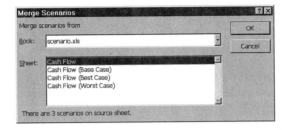

Select the worksheet that contains the scenarios you want to merge and click the OK button. The scenarios will be merged into the current workbook.

Scenario Summaries

After you've created your scenarios, you can create summaries of the different scenarios on additional worksheets. To do this, select Tools, Scenarios to open the Scenario Manager dialog box. Click the Summary button to open the Scenario Summary dialog box (see Figure 23.43). The Scenario Summary offers two options:

- Scenario Summary
- Scenario PivotTable

Figure 23.43

This example shows the Scenario Summary dialog box. Note that you can create either a Scenario Summary or a Scenario PivotTable from here.

Use Scenario Summary to create a new worksheet that displays the changing cells and their results. It is best to select this option when your scenarios have only one set of changing cells.

If your scenarios have more than one set of changing cells and more than one user creates scenarios, you can create a Scenario PivotTable instead. This will give you the ability to obtain an instant what-if analysis of the existing scenarios. The Scenario Manager creates a new worksheet with a pivot table containing the scenarios on the active sheet.

Scenarios Notes

Scenarios are stored in the worksheet and can contain cells only in one worksheet. You can create scenarios on each sheet in a workbook, but you must activate the worksheet in order to change the scenario for that worksheet. Scenarios are limited to 32 changing cells.

Printing Scenarios

There are a couple of methods you can use to print scenarios. Perhaps the simplest is to create a Scenario Summary sheet (see the previous section on Scenario Summaries), define the print area, and print the summary.

One other method you can use is the Report Manager. You can store as many scenarios as you create and print them using the Report Manager.

To do this, select View, Report Manager to open the Report Manager dialog box. Click the Add button to open the Add Report dialog box. Here is where you add your scenarios to the Report Manager.

1. Type a name for the report in the Report Name text box.
2. In the Section to Add portion of the dialog box, click the down arrow to the right of the Sheet list box. This will display a list of the sheet names in the workbook. Select the sheet that contains the scenarios you want to add to the report.
3. Click the down arrow to the right of the Scenario list box. This will display a list of the scenarios you have defined on that worksheet. Select one of the scenarios by clicking once on it.
4. Click the Add button to add that scenario to the Sections in this Report text box at the bottom.
5. Repeat steps 3 and 4 until you have added all the scenarios you want to this report.
6. Click OK to close the Add Report dialog box and return to the Report Manager. Note that now all the options are available.
7. Repeat steps 1 through 6 to create new reports.
8. To print a report, select it in the Report Manager and click the Print button.

NOTE When you use the Report Manager to print scenarios, you cannot use print preview to see what will print. You should use print preview before you add the scenario to the Report Manager to see how it will print. Make any necessary modifications before adding the scenario to the Report Manager.

PowerPoint 97

CHAPTER 24

PowerPoint Quick Start Guide

by Reed Gilgen

In this chapter

Understanding What PowerPoint Can Do

PowerPoint is a tool that extends your ability to communicate. The better you know how to use PowerPoint, the more likely you are to be successful in making effective presentations.

Communicating Ideas More Effectively

A PowerPoint presentation is similar to a Word outline in that it reduces your subject to the bare essentials. As a result, you must focus more on the structure of the presentation including

- What is the main purpose of the presentation?
- Who is my audience?
- What do I want them to know?
- What do I want them to do?

Once you understand what you are trying to communicate, you then proceed to present information in a concise, easy-to-understand way. For example, rather than listing all fifteen reasons your client should buy your product, you might focus instead on the top three or four reasons.

Finally, once you have determined the content of your presentation, you then begin to format the presentation in such a way that audiences will want to listen. PowerPoint enables you to add the following:

- Color-coordinated backgrounds that match the tone and purpose of your presentation
- Consistent font styles so that the audience gets the message without being distracted by the presentation of the text
- Animated slide elements that wake up the audience, or that highlight important points
- Multimedia objects such as graphics, sound, or video to increase audience attention and understanding

Your PowerPoint presentation is more likely to be successful if you focus first on the content and organization of your presentation and then add a design and other formatting.

What Skills Do You Bring to PowerPoint?

PowerPoint is just a tool that extends your ability to communicate. If you were applying for a job as a PowerPoint presentation designer, you might see the following job description:

PowerPoint Designer Wanted. Must know subject thoroughly. Must understand intended audiences. Must have experience communicating subject to intended audience. A sense of graphic design helpful but not required.

You can do this! You are the expert and PowerPoint is there to help. After you create your first presentation, you'll be amazed at how easy it is to add a professional look to what you present.

What Kinds of Presentations Can I Create?

PowerPoint enables you to create anything from one-page presentations, such as posters, to multipage slideshows. However, PowerPoint is not a genuine graphics design program; other programs do a better job of designing and editing graphic objects. PowerPoint's real strength lies in being able to put together various textual and graphical elements to create superior slideshows.

Single-page presentations include posters, flyers, signs, or advertising layouts.

Slideshow applications are much more extensive, including the following:

- Presentations designed for face-to-face contact, such as board meetings, classroom training, or sales contacts
- Unattended presentations, such as an information kiosk or a Web-based presentation

How Do I Make the Presentation?

All presentations can be printed or presented electronically. For example, you probably will want to print, duplicate, and distribute flyers, posters, and signs.

However, you have several options for distributing or showing your PowerPoint presentation:

- If you have a computer and a data projector or data display panel, you can run your PowerPoint presentation from the computer. This gives you a great deal of flexibility to make last-minute changes to your presentation and also to adjust the rate of presentation to match your audience. Increasingly, businesses and educational institutions own this type of display equipment and make it available if you need it for your presentation to them.
- Using the Pack-and-Go feature, you can prepare a slideshow that you can take with you on the road, or that you can send to anyone. You, or someone else, can even play the show on a computer that doesn't have PowerPoint installed.
  - ▶ **See** "Using the Pack and Go Wizard," **page 600**
- You can print your PowerPoint slides onto overhead transparencies or convert them to 35mm slides for traditional overhead or slide presentations.
- You can print PowerPoint slides in handout format, complete with slides and speaker notes, or in outline format.
- You can publish your slideshow to the World Wide Web. PowerPoint enables you to export your slides, including graphics, to an HTML format that you can use on any Web server, thus making your slideshow available to the whole world.

Working with the PowerPoint Interface

The PowerPoint interface is much like any other Windows program, so if you are familiar with other Windows programs, you should have no problem using PowerPoint.

Starting PowerPoint for the First Time

If you performed a typical installation of the Office 97 suite, you will find two buttons on your Start Menu—New Office Document and Open Office Document. If you click New Office Document, you see the dialog box shown in Figure 24.1. Three of the ten tabs pertain to PowerPoint documents:

Figure 24.1

To create a new PowerPoint document, choose New Document from the Windows 98 Start menu, and choose the type of presentation you want to create.

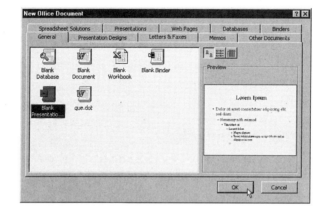

- *General.* Double-click the Blank Presentation icon to start a new, blank presentation.
- *Presentations Designs.* Click a design to preview it, then double-click a design to start a new presentation using that design. You create the content.
- *Presentations.* Click a presentation template to preview it, then double-click a template to create a new presentation based on typical predefined slides. PowerPoint suggests the content and presentation structure.

Looking Over the PowerPoint Screen

Assuming you choose a Blank Presentation, PowerPoint starts and asks you what type of layout you want. For now, just click OK. You then see the screen shown in Figure 24.2. The PowerPoint screen includes typical Windows elements such as a menu, several toolbars, an editing screen where you create and modify your slides, and a status bar that shows information about your slideshow.

Figure 24.2

The PowerPoint screen offers many tools for working on your presentation.

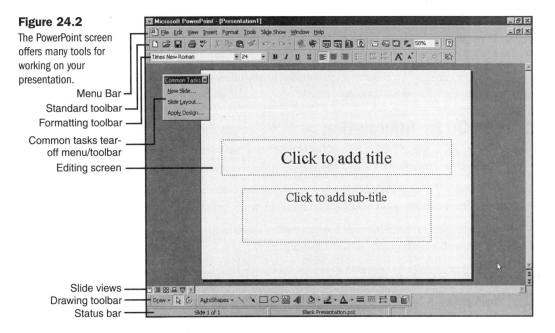

Menu Bar
Standard toolbar
Formatting toolbar
Common tasks tear-off menu/toolbar
Editing screen
Slide views
Drawing toolbar
Status bar

Understanding PowerPoint's Default Toolbars and Buttons A default PowerPoint screen includes the following toolbars:

- *Standard toolbar.* This contains buttons common to all Office 97 programs, such as Open, Save, Print, and so on. The right side of this toolbar offers buttons commonly used in PowerPoint, for example, New Slide. Point at a button to see a ToolTip describing that button.

- *Formatting toolbar.* Font and alignment buttons are the most common buttons on this toolbar. These buttons are also common to all Office 97 programs.

- *Drawing toolbar.* This contains aids to adding graphic elements to your slides and is located at the bottom of the editing area.

- *Common tasks.* By default, this toolbar displays as a floating palette. As with all toolbars, you can drag the title bar of this toolbar to any side of the screen and display it as a toolbar.

One important bar that isn't a typical toolbar is the row of Views buttons displayed to the left of the horizontal scroll bar at the bottom of the screen. Clicking one of these buttons displays your slides in outline, slide, slide sorter, or notes views. The last button plays the current slide as a slideshow.

Adding/Removing Toolbars   Typical of all Office 97 applications, you can add or remove PowerPoint toolbars by right-clicking the toolbar and selecting or deselecting toolbars from the list.

You also can drag a toolbar from its location to any other side of the screen or into the editing area to display it as a floating tool palette.

Where to Go for Information

PowerPoint's online help is invaluable as you begin working with the program, and even after you become a seasoned PowerPoint user.

The core of PowerPoint's help is the Office Assistant, which, depending on how you have it set up, offers suggestions or asks you questions to better help you.

PowerPoint also offers indexed help, as well as a link to the Microsoft Web site where you can receive updates and other helpful information.

Hidden in an unlikely spot is the very useful PowerPoint Central. Choose Tools, PowerPoint Central, and PowerPoint runs a slideshow that offers ideas, tips, and access to additional resources that help you create the best slideshows possible. For example, PowerPoint Central includes "The 'Four P's' for Better Presenting," a tutorial from the Dale Carnegie Training Institute. If it has been some time since you accessed PowerPoint Central, PowerPoint offers to connect you to the Microsoft Web site to update PowerPoint Central with new information and additional resources.

Working with PowerPoint Documents

If you normally create only word processing documents, working with PowerPoint documents may take some getting used to. Before launching your first project, take some time to become familiar with the various elements of a PowerPoint presentation.

Understanding Slide Layers

Each PowerPoint slide consists of three basic layers:

- The *design* layer is also the *master slide* level that provides the *background* graphics, color scheme, text fonts, and location of slide elements for your slides. The design layer is the same for all slides in a presentation, thus providing a consistent look.
- The *layout* layer is based on the type of slide you are creating, such as title, bullet, chart, table, or blank slides. The layout determines where various slide elements are located. Layout elements can be modified or ignored on any individual slide.
- The *slide* layer is where you add your own *content*. Each slide's content is unique, so text or graphics added to the slide appear only on that slide.

Although you can modify the design, or master layer, at first you should just use the formats provided by PowerPoint and focus on the content, or slide layer. As you become more experienced, you can begin making modifications to the background layers or even create your own.

N O T E One option for starting a presentation is to use the AutoContent Wizard. However, if you understand how a PowerPoint presentation is built, you will be able to take better advantage of the AutoContent Wizard. ▨

▶ **See** "Using the AutoContent Wizard," **page 531**

Choosing an Initial Layout

When you first start PowerPoint, you can choose a blank presentation, start with a design, or use one of PowerPoint's templates. If you start with a blank presentation, PowerPoint asks you first what layout you want to use (see Figure 24.3).

Figure 24.3

Choose a layout for your slide from the Slide Layout dialog box.

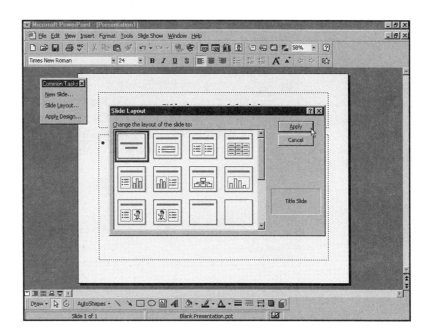

Generally, your first slide will be a title slide. If you are creating something other than a slideshow, such as a poster or flyer, you may wish to choose some other layout, such as blank slide.

N O T E You can choose from 12 layouts, including title, bulleted list, and blank (the most commonly used), and several combinations of charts, text, and clip art. ▨

You can change the layout by choosing Format, Slide Layout, or click Slide Layout on the Common Tasks tool palette. Choose a different layout style by clicking it to select it and then clicking the Apply button.

Choosing an Initial Design

If you start with a blank slide, regardless of the layer you choose, you still need to choose some sort of background or design layer.

To choose a background layer, choose Format, Apply Design, or click Apply Design on the Common Tasks tool palette. PowerPoint displays the Apply Design dialog box shown in Figure 24.4. Click a design file on the list at the left, and PowerPoint previews it for you on the right. When you find just the design you want, click the Apply button. If the design you choose isn't quite what you had hoped for, repeat this process until you find what you need.

Figure 24.4

Choose a master background design from the Apply Design dialog box.

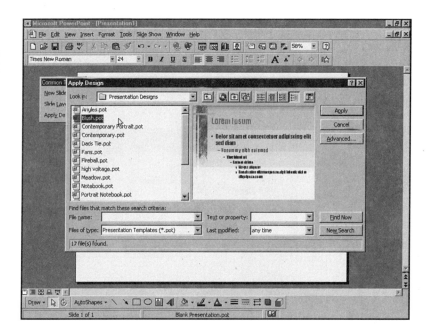

N O T E Although you can change the design layer of a slide at any time, doing so may affect the position of text or graphics you have already created. If you don't like the result, you can change the design layer back to your original selection. You can also reposition graphics, or reposition or edit text to match better the new design layer.

Adding and Editing Text

Once you have chosen your design and layout layers (see Figure 24.5), you can begin adding your own text and other objects to your slides.

Figure 24.5
Use the Slide View to modify elements of your slide after applying a design and layout.

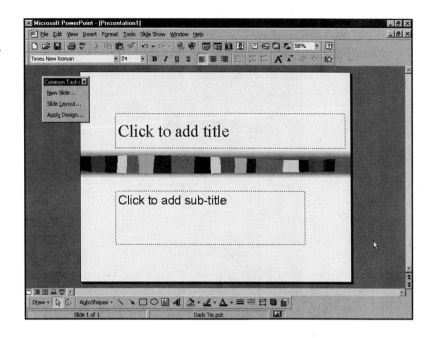

Part
IV

Ch
24

To edit a title slide, for example, click the title box. The title box prompt disappears and a blinking insertion point appears. At this point, you can use most of your typical word processing editing procedures, such as typing, deleting, selecting, changing font or other attributes, and so on. Remember also that you can use Edit, Undo if you don't like the results.

Click the mouse anywhere on the slide to deselect the text box you have just created. To return to a box to edit its content, simply click that box. To add text to another text box, for example, the sub-title, simply click the box and enter text.

▶ **See** "Editing Outline Text," **page 527**

Using PowerPoint Views

The basic element of a slideshow is the slide. However, to give you a better sense of what your slideshow looks like, PowerPoint offers several different *views* of your presentation. Each view is accessed by choosing View, and then by choosing the type of view you want. You also can click a view button on the View bar (to the left of the horizontal scroll bar).

The following list shows the five views and their purposes:

■ *Slide.* The basic editing view is the Slide view (refer to Figure 24.5). Here you edit slide objects such as text or graphics. Note the two buttons at the bottom of the vertical scrollbar. Click these to go to the preceding or next slide.

■ *Outline.* The structure of your slide presentation is similar to an outline (see Figure 24.6). The slide's title is a main outline heading, and bulleted text items are outline subheadings. You can use this view to create the entire slideshow, switching to the Slide view later to modify specific slide objects.

NOTE Even in this view, PowerPoint displays a Preview box so you can see the general look of the slide you are creating in Outline view. ■

Figure 24.6

The Outline view enables you to focus on the structure and content of your slideshow.

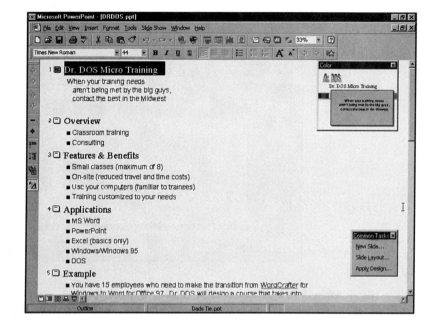

■ *Slide Sorter.* The slide sorter displays miniature versions of your slides, enabling you to see the general organization of your slideshow (see Figure 24.7). In this view you can quickly change the order of your slides, or modify slide transitions—the way PowerPoint changes from one slide to the next.

▶ **See** "Advanced Techniques and Graphics," **page 553**

■ *Notes Page.* You prepare speaker notes to help you remember what to say during your presentation. If you do create speaker notes, you can view them along with the slide in the Notes Page view (see Figure 24.8). To go to a different slide, click the Previous Slide or Next Slide buttons.

▶ **See** "Creating a Slide Show and Making the Presentation," **page 577**

■ *Slide Show.* When you play your slideshow, the slides fill the entire screen. The Slideshow view enables you to see what the slides will look like when played. To exit the Slide Show view, press the Escape key.

Figure 24.7
The Slide Sorter view gives you an overall view of your slideshow.

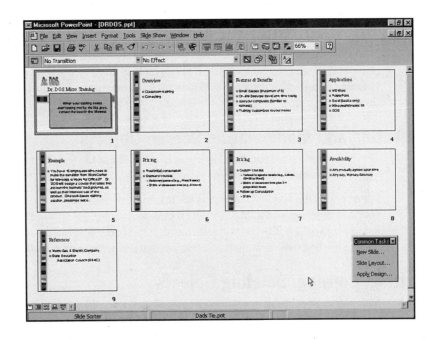

Figure 24.8
View speaker notes along with the slide in the Notes Page view.

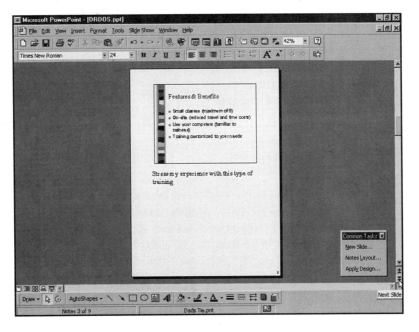

Copying and Reusing Data

PowerPoint uses all of the same Windows procedures you use in Word and other Windows programs, to select and manipulate text or graphics images, or to cut, copy and paste material. Learning to take advantage of the Windows environment can help make creating PowerPoint presentations easier and faster.

Selecting and Manipulating Screen Objects

Text and graphics are contained inside boxes, and these boxes with their content become slide *objects*. Each object can be moved or resized.

For example, the box that surrounds the text in a title slide can be sized or moved to make your text fit where you want it. Use the mouse to drag the sizing handles to reshape the text box. To move the entire box without changing its shape, position the mouse pointer on any edge of the box until it changes to a four-headed arrow, then drag the box to a new location.

Cutting, Copying, Deleting Objects

Slide objects can be cut or copied, and pasted onto any other slide. To select an object, click the edge of the object box. Then choose Edit, Copy (or Cut), or use any other Windows method for copying (or cutting). Windows places a copy of the object in the Windows clipboard.

To delete an object, first select it then press Delete. If you delete a text box, PowerPoint deletes only the contents of the box, replacing the text with a prompt for new text, for example, "Click to add title" (refer to Figure 24.5). If you really don't want text in the box, you can ignore the prompts because they do not display when you play the slideshow, nor do they print.

Using Paste Versus Paste Special

When you choose Edit, Paste, PowerPoint retrieves a copy of the object from the Windows clipboard and places it on the screen. You then can drag the object (drag the edge of the object) to the desired location.

Some objects, especially graphic images, have special characteristics that you may want to maintain. For example, if you use a chart that was produced in Excel, you may want to maintain the ability to update the chart should the underlying data be changed. In such cases you copy the chart as you normally do while in Excel. However, to paste it in PowerPoint, you choose Edit, Paste Special. In the Paste Special dialog box (see Figure 24.9), you choose Paste link to paste a copy of the chart while maintaining its link with the spreadsheet from which it came.

Figure 24.9
Use the Paste Special option to maintain links between graphic objects and the programs that created them.

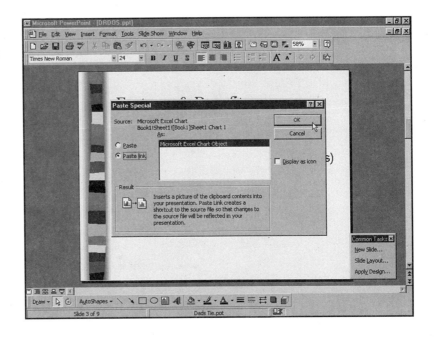

Printing from PowerPoint

Whether you need a backup copy for your own records or you want to provide handouts for your audience, chances are that at some point you'll need to print your slideshow.

▶ **See** "Printing a Slide Show," **page 601**

Previewing Documents

There is no separate print preview. Instead, the slideshow itself is the preview. However, you can see what your slide will look like when printed in black and white.

Choose View, Black and White, or click the Black and White (B&W) View button on the toolbar. This view removes the background layer and converts color elements to shades of gray. For reference, PowerPoint also displays a color version in a separate small window (see Figure 24.10).

Part
IV

Ch
24

Figure 24.10

Preview how your slide will print by using the Black and White view.

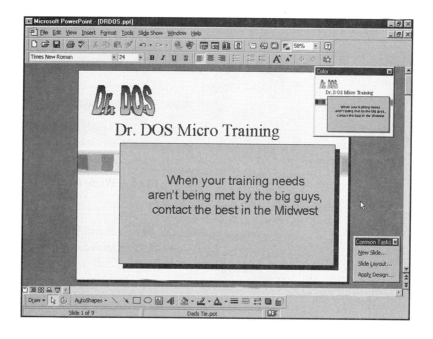

Default Printing

To print your slides, choose File, Print, or press Ctrl+P. The Print dialog box appears (see Figure 24.11). By default, PowerPoint prints one copy of each of your slides in black and white. Choose OK to print using these default settings.

Figure 24.11

Choose Print dialog box options to print your slideshow.

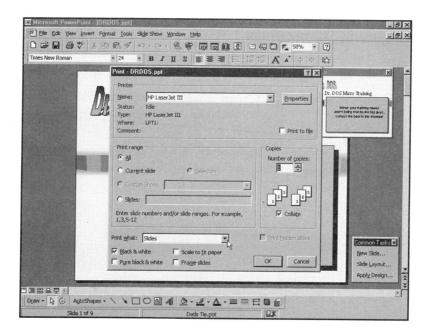

Choosing Printing Options

In the Print dialog box, you can specify the printer you are printing to, the number of copies you need, and which slides you want to print.

Using the Print what drop-down menu, you can also choose to print full slides, handouts (with 2, 3, or 6 slides per page), notes pages (one slide per page along with speaker notes), or the outline view of the slideshow.

If you have a color printer and want to print your slides in color, uncheck the Black & White box. Doing this prints the background layer of your slides.

Finally, you can adjust the slide to print Pure Black & White (no gray shades), Scale to Fit Paper, or you can add a thin frame line to Frame slides.

> **N O T E**   If you uncheck the Black & White box when using a black-and-white printer, the back-ground prints in shades of gray. However, if your printer doesn't have enough memory, PowerPoint may not be able to print the entire slide. The background may also obscure text or other images when printed this way.

Part
IV

Ch
24

CHAPTER 25

Building PowerPoint Presentations

by Read Gilgen

In this chapter

Using Outlines to Plan and Organize a Presentation

No amount of pizzazz can compensate for a poorly organized presentation. Your job is to make it easier for audiences to grasp concepts, understand processes, or to see how pieces of information fit together.

An outline is an excellent tool to help you organize your thoughts and to give structure to your PowerPoint presentation. If you can clearly see your presentation's structure, it's quite likely your audience will too.

Starting PowerPoint in Outline View

As you learned in Chapter 24, you can start PowerPoint in several different ways. If you don't want to be distracted by fancy layouts or designs, your best option is to begin with a blank presentation screen in Outline view. Follow these steps:

1. From the Windows 98 Start menu, click New Office Document to display the New Office Document dialog box.

2. Choose the General tab and double-click the Blank Presentation file. PowerPoint starts, and the New Slide dialog box appears.

N O T E   Alternatively, you can start PowerPoint from the Start menu by choosing Programs and
then Microsoft PowerPoint. From the opening dialog box, choose Blank presentation and
click OK. ▓

3. Since you're just getting started, click OK to accept the Title Slide layout.

4. Finally, switch to the Outline view by choosing View, Outline or click the Outline View button on the View menu. PowerPoint displays the Outline View screen (see Figure 25.1).

 T I P   In Outline view, the Common Tasks tool palette can be in the way. Drag the tool palette (click and drag its title bar) to the lower-right of the screen to uncover the outline editing screen. If the Common Tasks tool palette is not visible, choose View, Toolbars, Common Tasks.

Figure 25.1

The Outline view helps you organize your presentation without being distracted by layouts and designs.

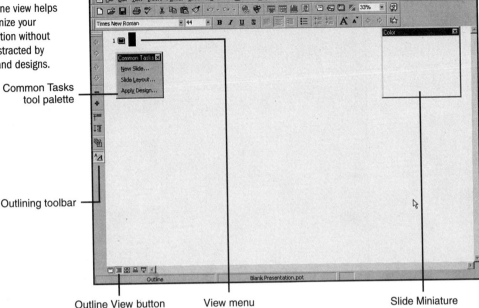

Common Tasks tool palette

Outlining toolbar

Outline View button   View menu   Slide Miniature

Creating Outline Text

An outline helps you to organize your presentation into major sections or headings, along with subsections or subheadings. Once you see the overall structure of your slideshow, you then can fill in the details and work on polishing the slides themselves.

Let's suppose you're creating a brief presentation to show clients what your company is all about. Since your first slide is a title slide, you'll probably want to use your company name as the title, and some sort of motto as the subtitle.

To enter outline text, follow these steps:

1. Begin by typing the title, for example **The Company Store.** Notice that what you type also appears in the Slide Miniature box. When you have typed the title, press the Enter key. PowerPoint adds a new slide.

2. Press the Tab key to *demote* slide 2 so it becomes the subtitle for slide 1. Type the subtitle, for example, "We Sell Only the Best."

3. Now when you press Enter, PowerPoint remains at the subtitle level. Press Shift+Tab to *promote* the subtitle to become the title for a new slide (see Figure 25.2).

Figure 25.2

Promote and Demote outline levels to create slides with subtitles or bulleted lists.

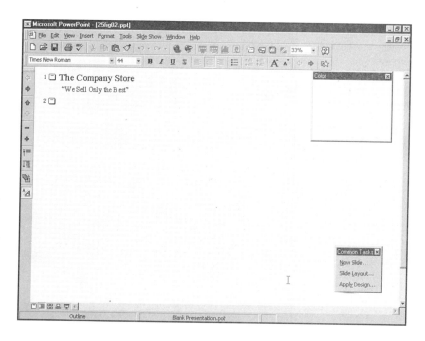

Setting Outline Levels

Although promoting and demoting sounds rather complicated, it's really not. In a typical outline you have major headings, along with various levels of subheadings. All of this helps you to clearly see the organization of your material.

Suppose your second slide is a bulleted list showing what your company is all about. Begin by typing the major heading for slide 2, for example, "The Company Store ...". Then press Enter.

To add bulleted subheadings (there is no subtitle on a bulleted slide), you can press the Tab key or you can click the Demote button on the Outlining toolbar to establish that the next lines you type are at the second outline level. As you type each item, simply press Enter to add a new item at the same subheading level. (See Figure 25.3 for sample text.)

N O T E   Only titles, subtitles, and bulleted text items appear in the Outline view. You must switch to the Slide, Slide Sorter, or Slide Show views to see other objects such as charts, graphics, or text objects. ▓

PowerPoint's promote and demote options are shown in the following list:

   Demote. Press Tab or click the Demote button on the Outlining toolbar. This moves the insertion point to the right and creates a subheading to the current outline level.

   Promote. Press Shift+Tab or click the Promote button. This moves the insertion point to the left and returns to the next higher subheading, or to the slide title.

   Move Up. Click the Move Up button to switch the order of the current outline item with the one that precedes it. The item maintains its subheading status.

■ *Move Down.* Click the Move Down button to switch the order of the current outline item with the one that follows it.

Figure 25.3

The complete outline for a presentation includes only essential text.

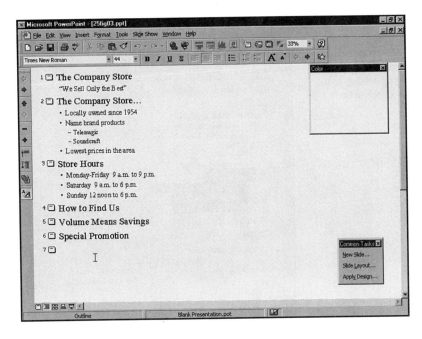

Finally, to get a better overview of your outline, you can use the following options:

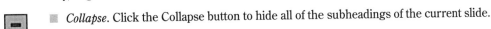 ■ *Collapse.* Click the Collapse button to hide all of the subheadings of the current slide.

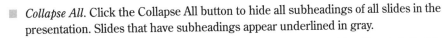 ■ *Expand.* Click the expand button to display all of the subheadings of the current slide.

■ *Collapse All.* Click the Collapse All button to hide all subheadings of all slides in the presentation. Slides that have subheadings appear underlined in gray.

■ *Expand All.* Click the Expand All button to display all of the subheadings of all of the slides in the presentation.

To add a new slide, promote a blank line until a slide and number appear. Alternatively, you can click New Slide on the Common Tasks tool palette and choose the slide layout you want for the next slide.

Editing Outline Text

Editing text in the outline view is simple. Click the text area you want to edit and use typical word processing editing procedures including backspace, delete, or cut and paste.

To change a subheading level, click anywhere on the subheading text and use promote or demote.

Part

IV

Ch

25

If you want to change the order of a slide, click the slide icon in the Outline view and drag it to its new location. The pointer changes to a four-headed arrow and a thin horizontal line indicates the new position of the slide (see Figure 25.4).

Figure 25.4

Change the slide order in a presentation by dragging the slide to a new location in Outline view.

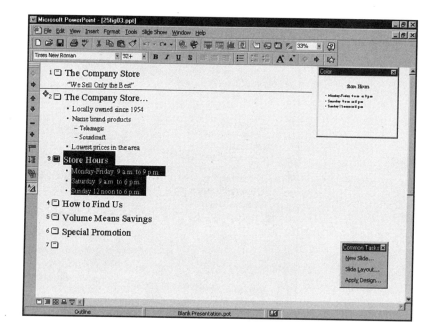

CAUTION

Creating a presentation requires a lot of thought and effort. Be sure to save your presentation early and then save it often as you build your presentation. Reward your creativity by not losing your work!

Importing Outline Text from Word

The Outline view helps you visualize and organize your presentation. However, you may already have material organized in a Word document that uses headings and subheadings. If so, you can import that material directly into the PowerPoint Outline view by following these steps:

1. In Microsoft Word, make sure the Word document uses outline headings and that you have saved the outline.

2. In Word, choose File, Send to, Microsoft PowerPoint. Word starts PowerPoint and transfers the data to PowerPoint.

3. Check the outline in PowerPoint. If the Word headings have been prepared properly, all first-level headings become slide titles, second-level items become subtitles or bullet items, and so on.

4. In PowerPoint, edit the text as necessary, promoting or demoting items as needed.

CAUTION

Don't forget to save your PowerPoint presentation or modifications to the imported outline will be lost.

Applying a Slide Layout

When you complete your presentation outline, you're ready to add the appropriate layouts and design to fit the material you're presenting.

The first slide you create in Outline view is, by default, a title slide. Subsequent slides, by default, are bulleted list slides.

In the sample slideshow (refer to Figure 25.3), the last four slides are neither standard title nor bulleted list slides. For example, the "How to Find Us" slide will include a title, no subtitle, and a graphic map and text to give directions. Thus, each slide must have its own layout. To change the layouts for the last four slides, follow these steps:

1. Click the slide 4 icon. PowerPoint highlights the slide title.

2. Click Slide Layout on the Common Tasks tool palette. Alternatively, you can choose Format, Slide Layout from the menu bar. PowerPoint displays the Slide Layout dialog box and highlights the Bulleted List layout since that is the default slide layout (see Figure 25.5).

Figure 25.5

Change the layout of a slide in the Slide Layout dialog box.

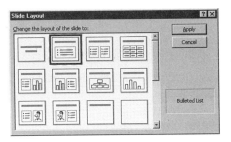

3. Click the slide layout you want to change to, for example, Title Only (the third slide layout on the bottom row).

4. Click Apply to change the layout of the currently selected slide. Although it may appear that nothing has happened, when you view your slide you will note the layout change.

5. Repeat steps 1–4 to change slide 5 to the Chart layout.

6. Repeat steps 1–4 to change slide 6 to the Title Only layout.

7. Repeat steps 1–4 to change slide 7 to the Blank layout.

 Use the scroll bar to see all 24 layouts. These include everything from blank slides to combinations of titles, subtitles, bullets, data and organization charts, clip art images, and media clips.

Applying a Slide Design

Now that you've prepared the content and selected appropriate layouts for each slide, you're ready to choose a slide design. PowerPoint offers several predefined slide designs that coordinate text, layout, graphic objects, and colors to provide a consistent look throughout your entire presentation.

To choose a design, follow these steps:

1. Click Apply Design on the Common Tasks tool palette. Alternatively, you can choose Format, Apply Design from the menu bar. PowerPoint displays the Apply Design dialog box (see Figure 25.6).

Figure 25.6

Choose a master design for your presentation from the Apply Design dialog box.

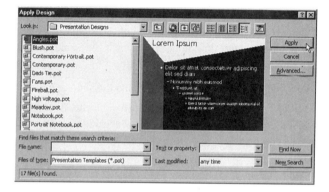

2. Browse the list of design files and click one to see what it looks like in the Preview Box at the right side of the dialog box.

3. When you find a design you like, choose Apply. PowerPoint applies the design to each and every slide in your presentation.

> **N O T E**   PowerPoint normally opens the Presentation Designs folder on your hard drive. More designs can be found in the Presentations folder. Click the Up One Level button, then choose the Presentations folder. ▨

Viewing the Presentation from the Outline View

After you apply a design to your slides, PowerPoint displays the currently selected slide from the outline in the Color View miniature view (see Figure 25.7). To view a different slide, simply click that slide in the outline.

However, what looks good in miniature may not look so good in a full sized view. To change the view of your presentation, choose View from the menu and then choose one of five views: Slide, Outline, Slide Sorter, Notes Page, and Slideshow.

▶ **See** "Using PowerPoint Views," **page 515**

Figure 25.7
The Color View window enables you to see the currently selected outline slide in miniature.

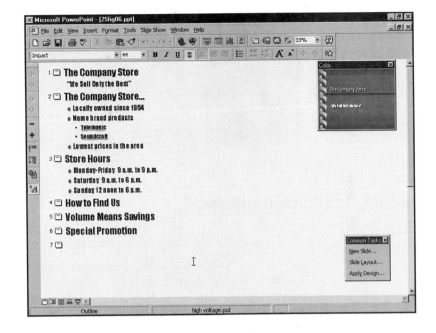

Using the AutoContent Wizard

If you're not feeling particularly well organized or creative, PowerPoint's AutoContent Wizard can help guide you through the required steps to a successful presentation. It asks you what kind of presentation you are making, suggests what you need to include, and then provides you with a predefined design and style template.

Starting the AutoContent Wizard

Earlier you learned how to start PowerPoint by choosing New Office Document from the Start menu. You also can start PowerPoint by clicking the Start button, choosing Programs, and then choosing Microsoft PowerPoint. When you use this method, PowerPoint starts and presents you with the PowerPoint dialog box containing the choices shown in Figure 25.8. Choose the AutoContent Wizard to assist you in putting together your slideshow and click OK. PowerPoint displays the AutoContent Wizard dialog box shown in Figure 25.9.

Figure 25.8
When you start PowerPoint, you can choose how you want to create your new presentation.

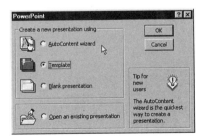

Figure 25.9
The AutoContent Wizard helps you get started with your presentation.

Providing Initial Information

The AutoContent Wizard first asks you basic questions about your presentation. Each time you click Next, you provide additional bits of information, such as the following:

- *Presentation type.* PowerPoint offers several presentation categories and topics. For example, you might choose a presentation that helps you recommend a corporate strategy. You could even choose one of the Carnegie Coaches to learn or teach others specific human relations skills, such as how to introduce a meeting or thank a speaker. (See Table 25.1 for a list of PowerPoint's predefined presentation types.)

- *Output options.* Do you plan to make this presentation yourself, in a meeting, using handouts? Or do you plan to place the presentation by itself on the Internet, or in a kiosk-style setting?

- *Presentation style.* If you are making the presentation yourself, will you use a computer to make an on-screen presentation, or will you rely on black and white or color overheads or 35mm slides? Will you print handouts?

- *Presentation options.* If you choose to make the presentation yourself, PowerPoint asks you to provide information for the title slide. If the presentation is to be an Internet or kiosk presentation, you can specify copyright information, your e-mail address, or when the presentation was last updated.

Table 25.1   PowerPoint's Predefined Presentations

Category	Presentation Type
General	Recommending a Strategy
	Generic
Corporate	Company Meeting
	Financial Overview
Projects	Status
	Project Overview
Operations/HR	Information Kiosk
	Organization Overview

Category	Presentation Type
Sales/Marketing	Marketing Plan
	Product/Services Overview
Personal	Announcement/Flyer
	Personal Home Page
Carnegie Coach	Facilitating a Meeting
	Introducing a Speaker
	Managing HR's Changing Role
	Motivating a Team
	Presentation Guidelines
	Presenting a Technical Report
	Selling Your Ideas
	Thanking a Speaker

N O T E You do not need to click Next, nor do you have to complete each of the questions in order. Simply click directly on the box to the left of any of the questions and click Finish when you are ready to view the slideshow. ■

After you complete the information for these initial questions, choose Finish. PowerPoint generates a slideshow for you and takes you directly to the Outline view (see Figure 25.10).

Figure 25.10
The AutoContent Wizard creates a complete slideshow that you edit to fit your needs.

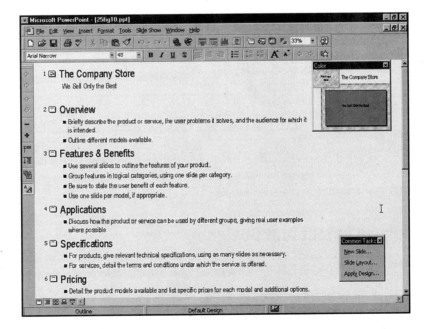

Editing Suggested Content

Suppose, for example, you choose to create a Sales Marketing Plan (refer to Figure 25.10). PowerPoint can suggest the organization and format, but you must now provide the information you will present.

Begin by clicking each slide and changing the data to fit your corporation. The miniature slide preview box shows you what each slide looks like, but for now, focus on the content of each slide.

Finally, switch to the Slide view by choosing View, Slide, or click the Slide view button on the View menu. Beginning with the title slide, change slide elements as necessary (see Figure 25.11). For example, you can move text boxes or other objects to make them fit more neatly on the screen.

Figure 25.11
Switch to the Slide view to make sure all slide elements look the way you want them to.

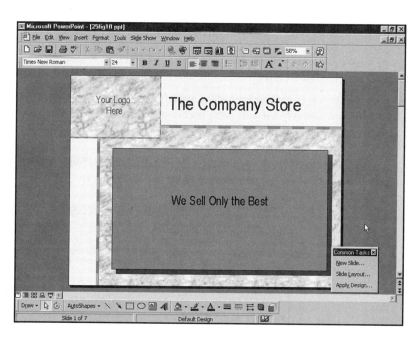

N O T E Some presentations contain more complex slide objects, such as clip art images or embedded Word tables or Excel charts. See "Creating Static Presentations" on page 540 for information on changing these objects. ▨

Applying Layout and Design

Although PowerPoint suggests the layout and design for each type of presentation, you can change these to match your sense of what will appeal to your audience.

For example, if you intend to add a clip art image to one of your bulleted slides, you would follow these steps:

1. Switch to the slide you want to change, for example to slide 5, which contains a bulleted list.

2. Choose Format, Slide Layout from the menu, or choose Slide Layout from the Common Tasks tool palette. PowerPoint displays the dialog box shown in Figure 25.12.

Figure 25.12

The Slide Layout dialog box enables you to choose a different layout for each slide.

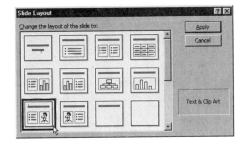

3. Select the layout you want, such as Clip Art and Text or Text and Clip Art.

4. Choose Apply. PowerPoint changes the slide layout as shown in Figure 25.13.

Figure 25.13

Layouts can include text, bullets, and even clip art images.

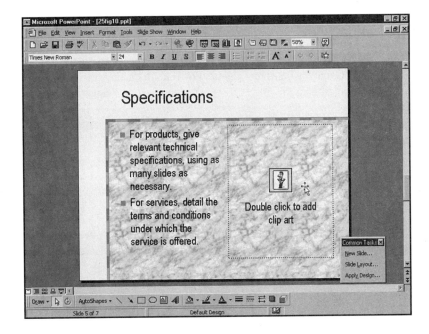

Part
IV

Ch
25

5. As prompted, double-click the Clip Art box. PowerPoint presents a gallery of clip art images (see Figure 25.14).

N O T E If you did not install the entire clip art gallery on your computer, and if the Office 97 CD-ROM is not in your CD drive, PowerPoint notifies you that you can obtain additional clip art from the CD-ROM. Otherwise, PowerPoint simply shows all the available clip art. ▪

Figure 25.14

Microsoft's Clip Gallery offers you hundreds of clip art images for your presentations.

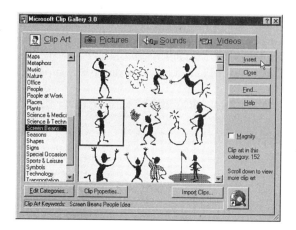

6. Select a clip art category and image and choose Insert.

7. Position the clip art image where you want it on the slide.

▶ **See** "Creating Static Presentations," **page 540**

You also can change the overall background and design of your slideshow by following these steps:

1. Choose Format, Apply Design from the menu, or choose Apply Design from the Common Tasks tool palette. PowerPoint displays the Apply Design dialog box shown in Figure 25.15.

Figure 25.15

Choose just the design you want in the Apply Design dialog box.

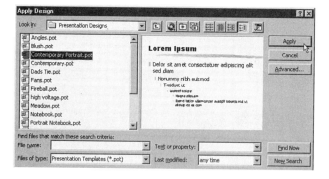

2. Click a design. In the design list at the left of the dialog box, PowerPoint displays that design, with sample text, in the preview box.

3. Choose the design you want and then choose Apply. PowerPoint changes the design of all the slides in your presentation.

Having changed the design, you should also review your slides to make sure the title and other slide objects are positioned appropriately. For example, in Figure 25.16, changing the design resulted in a larger font, which caused the title to wrap in the text box. If necessary, resize or reposition slide objects until the slide appears the way you want it.

Figure 25.16
Changing a slide design may also force you to make additional changes to your slides.

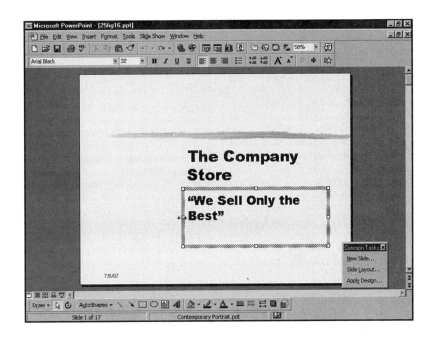

Using Templates

Templates are nothing more than predefined layouts and designs for your presentation to which you add your own material. You've already been using templates in this chapter, although we haven't referred to them as such. For example, the AutoContent Wizard uses templates, and you added both layout and design templates to the slideshow you created from the Outline view.

Selecting a Template

If you start PowerPoint from the Start Menu, you can choose to begin with a blank presentation, use the AutoContent Wizard, or use a template (refer to Figure 25.8). If you are already in PowerPoint, simply choose File, New and the New Presentation dialog box appears (see Figure 25.17).

Figure 25.17

Choose a template from the New Presentation dialog box to begin your presentation with a predefined layout or design.

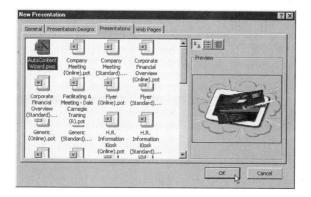

If you start PowerPoint from the New Office Document option on the Start Menu, you have the same PowerPoint options, plus other options related to Word and Excel.

Finally, if PowerPoint is already running, you can choose File, New and the New Presentation dialog box appears (refer to Figure 25.17)

PowerPoint's templates fall into four general categories:

■ *Blank presentations.* When you use this template, nothing is provided. You have to create the content and add layouts and designs of your choosing.

■ *Presentation Designs.* These templates provide color schemes, font designs, and background graphics. While these provide a consistent look to your presentation, you must determine the entire content and which layouts to use.

■ *Presentations.* These are complete templates that include the design as well as suggested layouts, along with suggested content. These are the same templates used by the AutoContent Wizard.

■ *Web Pages.* These templates can be used when developing a World Wide Web page.

Providing Template Information

If you use any of the Presentations templates, you must add basic template information yourself. You also have to know which template is designed for which application. For example, the Marketing Plan (Online) is designed to be used on the Web and already includes buttons and links that connect from one slide to another.

Generally, if you plan to use a Presentation template, you're better off using the AutoContent Wizard to help you choose the right template and fill in basic template information.

On the other hand, if all you want is a design template, select a design from the list of templates and choose OK. Before you can begin, PowerPoint requires you to select the layout for the first slide. Select a layout, for example, the Title layout, and choose OK. PowerPoint displays the first slide with blank text objects (see Figure 25.18).

Figure 25.18

A template contains blank objects that you fill in.

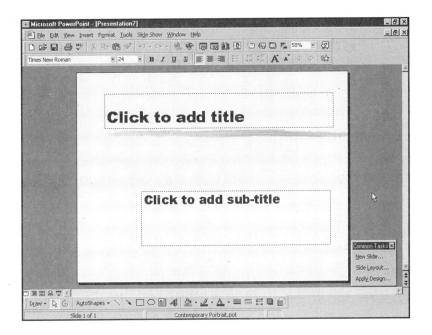

Changing Template Objects

Changing template objects is really quite simple. For example, to add title text to your title slide, just click the Click To Add Title box, and PowerPoint displays a text editing box (see Figure 25.19). Type the text you want. You may need to adjust the size or position of the template object (for example, the text box). However, usually you should try to make your additions match the suggested size and location of the original template objects.

Part

IV

Ch

25

Figure 25.19
Click a blank object and then type the text you want to insert.

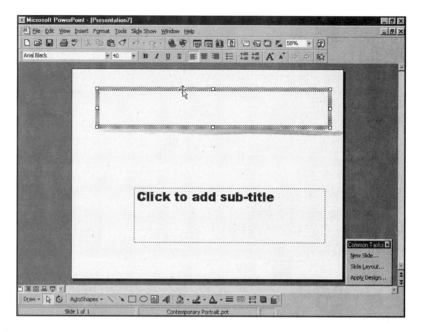

Creating Static Presentations

Whether you create a flyer based on the Flyer template, create a sign from a Blank template, or simply wish to enhance or modify any slide, you need to know how to add elements or *objects*, such as text boxes, graphic images, tables, or charts.

Adding Text Objects

Text boxes are perhaps the most common of all slide objects. Although most templates have ample text objects, you can add more. For this exercise (and all others in this section), after having started PowerPoint, choose File, New, choose the General tab, then choose the Blank Presentation template, and select the Blank layout.

To add a text object, follow these steps:

1. Choose Insert, Text Box.
2. Position the mouse pointer where you want to begin your text box and click. PowerPoint displays a text editing box.
3. Type the text you want, for example, "Sale Today!" (see Figure 25.20).

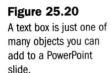

Figure 25.20

A text box is just one of many objects you can add to a PowerPoint slide.

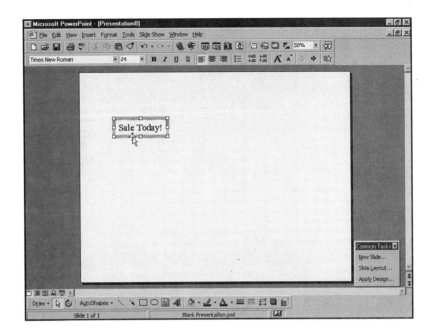

To edit the content of text boxes, simply click the text box. You can then edit the text, or select text within the box and choose Format, Font to change the font or the size, style, or color of the font.

To change the size of a text box, click and drag any of the sizing handles (the eight hollow boxes around the edge of the text box). Text size does not change, but where it wraps within the box does change depending on the size of the box.

To move a text box, you must position the mouse pointer on one of the box edges so that the mouse pointer changes to a four-headed arrow (refer to Figure 25.20). Then click and drag the box to its new location.

 TIP If you accidentally resize the box instead of moving it, just choose Edit, Undo and try again, being careful not to drag a sizing handle.

You can further modify text boxes in many creatively different ways. For example, suppose you want your text to appear in a shaded box, at a 45 degree angle, and in a larger and different font (see Figure 25.21). You would follow these steps:

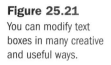

Figure 25.21

You can modify text boxes in many creative and useful ways.

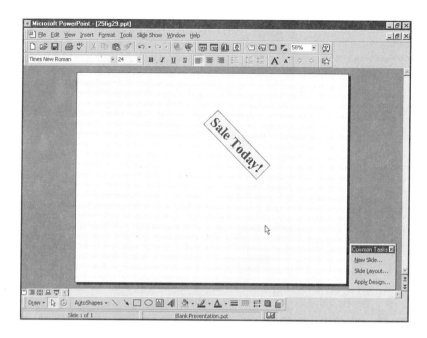

1. Click the text box and choose Format, Text Box. Alternatively, you can right-click the text box and choose Format Text Box from the menu. PowerPoint displays the Format Text Box dialog box (see Figure 25.22).

Figure 25.22

The Format Text box dialog box lets you change fill colors, line styles, and more.

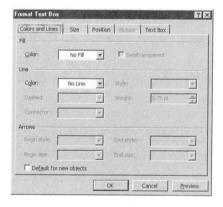

2. Click the Colors and Lines tab if it isn't already selected. Then choose Color or click the drop-down menu for the Fill Color (see Figure 25.23). Here you can simply choose a fill color you like, for example, yellow.

Figure 25.23

Fill styles include colors, patterns, and special effects.

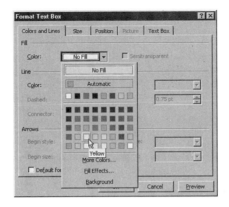

3. Objects are stacked on top of each other, with the most recently created objects on top. If you want objects from the back to appear through the fill color you have chosen for your text box, choose Semitransparent.

TIP You can add special gradient color effects, or add textures, patterns or pictures as fill backgrounds to your text box, by choosing Fill Effects from the drop-down menu. Don't be afraid to explore PowerPoint's many formatting options.

Part
IV

Ch
25

4. Choose the Line Color, Style, Weight (thickness), and Dashed (whether the line is solid, dashed, or dotted). For example, change the line color to Automatic, which gives you a single, solid black line around the text box.

5. Click the Size tab to display the information shown in Figure 25.24. Change Rotation to 45 degrees.

Figure 25.24

You can rotate text boxes as needed.

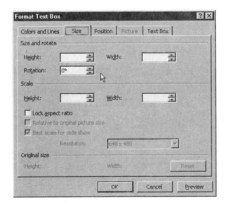

6. Click the Text Box tab and change the box's Internal margins, if necessary (see Figure 25.25). For example, since you are using a filled background, you may want more space between the text and the edges of the box.

Figure 25.25

Change the box's internal margins for more space between the box edge and the text.

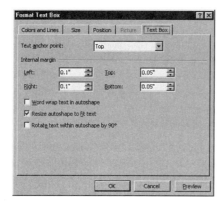

7. If you want to make your changes apply to all new text boxes, on the Colors and Lines tab choose Default for new objects.

8. Choose OK to apply the changes to your text box.

Adding Clip Art Objects

Well chosen graphic images can enhance your presentation in ways that words alone cannot. PowerPoint comes with several standard clip art images, as well as many more on the Office 97 CD-ROM. In addition, you can insert graphic files from other sources, such as scanned images or PowerPoint's own AutoShapes and Draw features. You can even connect to the Web for more clip art images.

To add a clip art image, choose Insert, Picture, Clip Art, or click the Insert Clip Art button on the toolbar. PowerPoint displays the Microsoft Clip Gallery (see Figure 25.26). Click the category you want, find and select the image you want, and choose Insert (see Figure 25.27).

Figure 25.26

Insert clip art images from the Microsoft Clip Gallery.

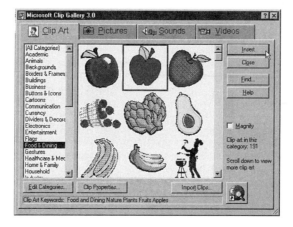

Figure 25.27

Clip art images appear in boxes that you can size and move.

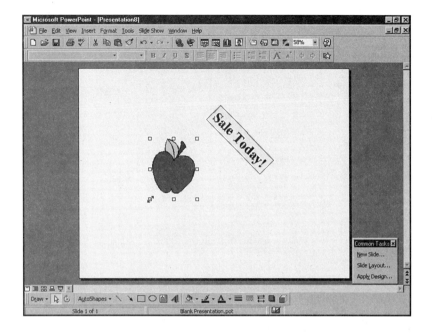

You manipulate clip art images the same way you size and move text boxes, although there are some differences. For example, dragging the sizing handles to change the size of the image box also changes the size of the image inside the box. For example, if you drag a side handle, you stretch the image horizontally. Dragging a corner handle changes the size proportionally. Also, you can click anywhere on the image and drag it to a new location.

To change the format of a clip art image, choose Format, Picture. PowerPoint displays the Format Picture dialog box (see Figure 25.28). The fill and line options are the same as for text boxes.

▶ **See** "Adding Text Objects," **page 540**

Figure 25.28

Modify an image using the Format Picture dialog box.

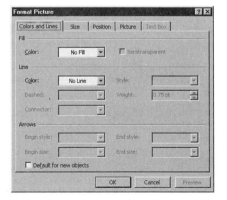

Click the Picture tab to display options used exclusively with clip art images (see Figure 25.29). Here you can adjust the following:

Figure 25.29

Crop an image's edges or change its colors.

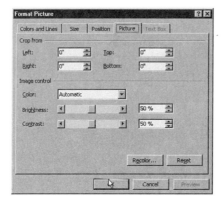

🔲 *Crop from.* Move the box edges in from the left, right, top, or bottom to hide part of the image.

 If you want more space between the edge of the image and the box, set the cropping to a negative number. For example, a cropping measurement of -0.1 inch places an extra .1 inch between the edge of the box and the image.

🔲 *Color.* When set to Automatic, the image displays in its original colors. You can also choose Grayscale (shades of gray), Black and White (no gray), or Watermark (lightly shaded, with greater brightness and less contrast).

🔲 *Brightness.* If the image is too dark or too light, you can adjust its brightness.

🔲 *Contrast.* If you increase or decrease the brightness, you may also need to adjust the contrast so the image doesn't look washed out.

🔲 *Recolor.* This option enables you to exchange one color in an image for another. For example, you could change the red car to a yellow one by substituting yellow for red.

🔲 *Preview.* As you make changes, you can preview those changes before actually applying them to the image. You may have to drag the Format Picture dialog box out of the way to see the preview.

🔲 *Reset.* Choose this option if you don't like how you've changed the settings and you want to start over again.

Adding Draw Objects

You can add graphic shapes to your presentations by using Office 97's Draw features. Many of these features can be accessed from the Insert, Picture menu. However, it is much quicker and easier to use the Drawing toolbar, which normally is displayed toward the bottom of the PowerPoint editing screen. If it's not displayed, choose View, Toolbars, and choose the Drawing toolbar.

Table 25.2 describes each of the Drawing toolbar buttons and their functions. In addition to creating graphic objects, you also can modify them using the Drawing toolbar.

Table 25.2   The Drawing Toolbar Options

Tool	Tool Name	Description
Draw ▾	Draw	This pop-up menu gives you options to group or ungroup objects, to change their order in the stack of objects, to rotate or flip an object, and so on.
▨	Select Objects	Before you can make changes to an object, you must select it. When an object displays sizing handles it has been selected.
◷	Free Rotate	Use this option to drag a corner sizing handle and rotate the object.
AutoShapes ▾	AutoShapes	This tool allows you to add many predefined shapes, including basic shapes, flow chart symbols, block arrows, stars and banners, and callouts.
╲	Lines	This is for straight lines only. For multisegment or curved lines, use the AutoShape menu.
↘	Arrows	This is a single-line, straight arrow, with the arrow-head appearing at the end of the line as you draw it.
▢	Rectangles	This shape can be square or rectangle, filled with a solid color.
◯	Ovals	This shape can be a circle or oval, filled with a solid color.
▤	Text Box	This tool creates a box into which you type text.
4	WordArt	With this tool you can add shapes and color schemes to words or phrases.
⬦ ▾	Fill Color	This button fills the selected object with the color displayed on the button. Click the drop-down menu to the right of the button to choose a different color.
✎ ▾	Line Color	This button changes the line around the object to the selected color. Click the drop-down menu to the right of the button to choose a different color.
A ▾	Text Color	This tool changes the color of the text in the selected text box to the color displayed on the button. Click the drop-down menu to the right of the button to choose a different color.

continues

Part
IV

Ch
25

Table 25.2   Continued

Tool	Tool Name	Description
	Line Style	Use this tool to select the thickness and style of the line surrounding an object.
	Dash Style	Use this tool to choose whether a line is solid, dotted, or dashed.
	Arrow Style	This button allows you to add arrow heads or tails to lines.
	Shadow	Add a background shadow to the object with this tool.
	3-D	Use this tool to add a three-dimensional look to the object.

TIP   The Drawing toolbar is available in all Office 97 programs. What you learn here can be used also in Word documents, for example.

To insert a graphic shape, choose the shape type and click and drag on your screen to get the location and the size image you want.

You can modify the shape of any of these graphics by right-clicking the object and choosing the Format option from the menu. For example, right-click a WordArt image and choose Format WordArt from the menu. The options you see are similar to those you learned when working with clip art and text boxes.

▶ **See** "Adding Text Objects," **page 540**

▶ **See** "Adding Clip Art Objects," **page 544**

In addition, from the Drawing toolbar you can modify specific image features directly, without going first to a formatting dialog box. For example, you first select an object by clicking it, then you can change the line style or color, the fill color, and so on.

Let's try something practical using these tools. Suppose you want to create a "No Smoking" sign (see Figure 25.30). Follow these steps:

1. Create the International "No" symbol by choosing AutoShapes from the Drawing toolbar Choose Basic Shapes and then select the "No" symbol.

2. Move the mouse pointer to the editing screen and click and drag the mouse pointer to create the size symbol you want.

Figure 25.30

Create signs like this one using PowerPoint's drawing tools.

Part
IV
Ch
25

TIP To drag an autoshape proportionally, hold down the shift key while dragging.

3. With the shape selected, click the Fill Color menu (the arrow just to the right of the Fill Color button) and choose a different color, for example, red.

4. Finally, click the Shadow settings button and from the dialog box choose a shadow you like, for example, lower left.

5. Choose the Text Box button and click the editing screen to insert a text box.

6. From the Formatting toolbar, choose Center and change the Font Size to, for example, 60 points.

7. Type "No," press Enter twice and then type "Smoking."

8. Click the Free Rotate button on the Drawing toolbar and drag the corner rotate handle on the text box until it aligns as shown in Figure 25.31.

9. Click the Shadow settings button on the Drawing toolbar and choose the same shadow you did for the graphic image, for example, lower left.

You've barely scratched the surface when it comes to creating and manipulating graphic images. Explore and play with other images and settings until you're able to get exactly the images you want in your PowerPoint presentations.

Importing Data from Word

You're probably already used to moving text from one Office 97 program to another. For example, in Word you simply select the text you want to copy and choose Edit, Copy. Then move to PowerPoint, position the insertion point in a text box, and choose Edit, Paste.

Copying Word objects such as tables, however, isn't quite that simple. The reason is that the size of objects in a PowerPoint slide are considerably larger than those same objects in a Word document.

The key, then, is to create the object in Word at roughly the same size that you expect it to appear in PowerPoint. For example, if you create a table, make the font size about 36 points. Also, add lines (thicker than usual) and any other formatting features such as fills *before* copying the table to PowerPoint.

After creating and copying the table, you have two options for pasting the table in PowerPoint:

- Paste, by choosing Edit, Paste.
- Paste Special, by choosing Edit, Paste Special. You then can choose Paste Link and paste a Microsoft Word Document Object. This method has the advantage of linking the original table with the PowerPoint copy so that changes in the Word table automatically appear in the PowerPoint table.

 If your table contains relatively little data, you should consider creating the table directly in PowerPoint. Choose Insert, Picture, Microsoft Word Table and then follow the same procedures you use when creating a Microsoft Word table (see Chapter 14, "Using Tables," for more information on how to create and format tables.)

Importing Data from Excel

You also can insert worksheets or charts created in Excel into your PowerPoint presentations. Once again, the key to successfully moving data or charts from Excel to PowerPoint is to first create the data carefully and completely in Excel.

To move data from Excel to PowerPoint, first select the cells you wish to copy from Excel and choose Edit, Copy. Switch to PowerPoint and choose Edit, Paste, or choose Edit, Paste Special if you want to create an active link between the Excel worksheet and the PowerPoint copy.

The same procedure works for charts created in Excel.

Generally the size of worksheets and charts you can see on an Excel screen is similar to the same objects in a PowerPoint presentation. Thus you don't need to take unusual steps to create larger data cells or charts before copying them to PowerPoint.

Finally, you can import an entire Excel worksheet to a PowerPoint screen (see Figure 25.32). Make sure you save your Excel worksheet, then in PowerPoint choose Insert, Object, Create From File. Supply the filename of the worksheet and choose OK. PowerPoint imports the data, along with any special formatting and charts or graphics you added.

Figure 25.31

You can link Excel worksheets to your PowerPoint presentations.

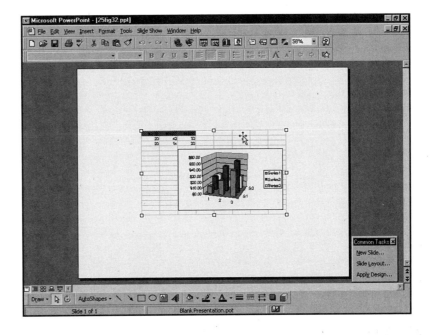

CAUTION

When you insert an Excel file into PowerPoint, the entire active area of the worksheet is inserted. Thus, you want to be sure that the worksheet contains relatively few columns and rows, or the data will appear very small.

CHAPTER 26

Advanced Techniques and Graphics

by Read Gilgen

In this chapter

Using Slide Transitions

In an old-fashioned slideshow, moving from one slide to another created a brief flash and a noise from the slide projector. Computer slideshows, on the other hand, are quick and noiseless. PowerPoint enables you to use special transition effects so that your audience clearly sees that you are changing from one slide to the next.

Choosing a Slide Transition

Suppose you are continuing work on "The Company Store" slideshow that you began in Chapter 25, "Building PowerPoint Presentations." In PowerPoint, open that slideshow, or any other you want to work on. In Outline view, your slideshow appears as shown in Figure 26.1.

Figure 26.1

The overall structure and major headings of your presentation are best seen in the Outline view.

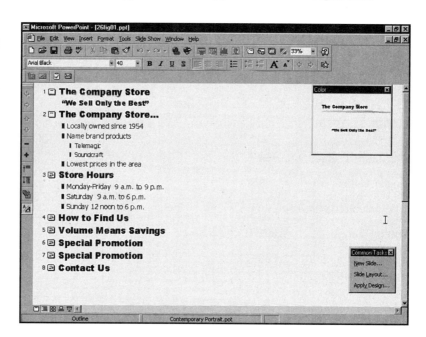

You can choose a slide transition while in any view, but for this exercise, switch to Slide Sorter view by choosing View, Slide Sorter, or click the Slide Sorter View button on the View menu. PowerPoint displays the slideshow as seen in Figure 26.2.

Figure 26.2

You can see the overall layout of your slideshow in the Slide Sorter view.

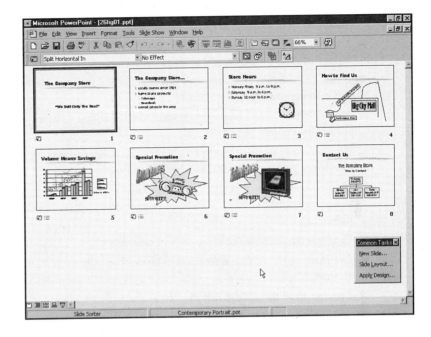

To add a slide transition to the currently selected slide, complete the following steps:

1. Choose Slide Show, Slide Transition. PowerPoint displays the Slide Transition dialog box shown in Figure 26.3.

Figure 26.3

The Slide Transition dialog box helps you determine how your presentation moves from one slide to the next.

2. Choose the transition you want by clicking the Effect drop-down menu.
3. Choose other effects, such as transition speed, method for advancing the slide, and sound.
4. Choose Apply to add the transition to your slide.

 T I P You can preview the effect of your transition by choosing Effect or by clicking the preview box at the upper-left corner of the dialog box. PowerPoint displays the transition from a dog to a key, or vice versa.

You can choose from the following transition effects:

- *No Transition.* The slideshow simply moves from one slide to the next, like an old-fashioned slide projector.

- *Blinds (Horizontal, Vertical).* This effect looks like venetian blinds, closing on one slide and opening to another.

- *Box (In, Out).* Here a box shape grows from the center outward, or from the edges toward the center.

- *Checkerboard (Across, Down).* This transition causes the new slide to appear in small, checkerboard-like squares that grow in the direction selected.

- *Cover (Down, Right, Left, Up, Left-Down, Left-Up, Right-Down, Right-Up).* This transition looks like a window shade, with the new slide on it, being drawn in the selected direction.

- *Cut.* This transition is the same as No Transition.

- *Cut Through Black.* This effect cuts to black, then cuts from black to the next slide. However, the transition is so quick that it appears the same as Cut, or No Transition.

- *Dissolve.* Here the slide slowly dissolves, gradually revealing the next slide.

- *Fade Through Black.* This effect causes the slide to fade to black, then the second slide gradually appears.

- *Random Bars* (Horizontal, Vertical). In this transition, the second slide begins to appear in randomly placed bars of varying widths. At first, the bars look like a bar code.

- *Split (Horizontal In, Horizontal Out, Vertical In, Vertical Out).* With the split in effect, the first slide seems to shrink from the outside edge to the center. With the split out effect, the second slide grows from the center to the edge.

- *Strips (Left-Down, Left-Up, Right-Down, Right-Up).* This transition is like a typical wipe, but diagonal. The second slide replaces the first slide with a jagged line of strips, from one corner to another.

- *Uncover (Down, Right, Left, Up, Left-Down, Left-Up, Right-Down, Right-Up).* This effect is the opposite of the Cover transition. Here, it's as if the window shade, with a slide on it, is being opened to reveal a slide behind it.

- *Wipe (Down, Left, Right, Up).* A wipe looks as if the first slide is being erased to reveal the second slide.

- *Random Transition.* PowerPoint selects the transition, randomly. If you want to control the effect of your transitions, this is not a good choice.

Additionally, you can choose these options:

- *Speed.* You can choose a Fast, Medium, or Slow transition.

- *Advance.* The default is to require you to click the mouse or press a key to advance a slide. However, you can let PowerPoint advance your slides Automatically after a specified number of seconds.

■ *Application*. You can apply the slide transition to the current slide only, or you can Apply to All slides in your presentation. If you choose to apply the transition to all slides, you still can change the transition for any single slide in your presentation by selecting the slide, choosing a transition, and choosing Apply.

> **CAUTION**
>
> Transitions are fun and easy to use, but too many different transitions can distract the viewer. Pick one transition and stick with it, except when you feel that a particular slide would benefit from something different.

■ *Sound*. You can specify a .WAV file to play as background music for your slide. You can even have it "loop" (repeat) until you play another sound. For more information on adding sounds to your presentation, see "Adding Sound," later in this chapter.

N O T E　PowerPoint slide background sounds start over at each slide transition and stop playing when another sound is introduced. ■

Checking Transitions in Slide Sort View

You can easily view how your transitions look while in the Slide Sorter View. Beneath each slide, PowerPoint displays tiny icons that represent special effects that you add to your slides. Click the icon that looks like a screen with an arrow (refer to Figure 26.2). PowerPoint shows the transition each time you click, briefly displaying the preceding slide and making the transition to the current slide.

Using Preset Animations

PowerPoint enables you to add movement to otherwise static slides, thus adding appeal to your presentation. Although animations can get complex, PowerPoint offers several preset animations that are quick and easy to use, and that make you look like a professional.

Creating Animation Objects

The content of each slide consists of several *objects* that appear on top of a design. These objects include text objects (titles, subtitles, bullets, or text boxes), graphic images, and even multimedia objects (sound or video.)

▶ **See** "Creating Static Presentations," **page 540**

Adding a Preset Animation

N O T E　You can edit objects only in the Slide View. Therefore, before adding animations, switch to Slide View. ■

Part
IV

Ch
26

Suppose you want to make the title of your second slide look *and* sound as if it is being typed, one character at a time.

To add a preset animation to an object, while in the Slide View follow these steps:

1. Click the object you want to animate.

2. Choose Slide Show, Preset Animation. PowerPoint displays a menu with the choices shown in Figure 26.4.

Figure 26.4

PowerPoint offers easy-to-use animation effects right from the menu.

3. Choose the animation you want—for example, Typewriter.

Although PowerPoint does not appear to do anything, it has quietly added the animation and sound effect you requested. PowerPoint also has determined that the animation will occur only after you click the mouse (or press a key) while playing the slide.

To view the animation, choose View, Slide Show; or simply click the Slide Show button on the View menu. The slide appears but does not display the title. Click the slide or press any key and PowerPoint displays the title one character at a time, while making a typewriter sound.

N O T E All references in this chapter to playing multimedia clips (sound or video) assume you have the necessary hardware and software installed on your computer. If you don't, you see the animation motion, but do not hear the sound effect.

Using Animated Bullets

One of the most common uses for animation is to animate bulleted text objects. Adding animation to a bullet causes each bulleted item to appear on the screen one at a time.

Suppose, for example, you want the bullets on your second slide to appear as if painted from left to right. Complete the following steps:

1. Click the bullet text you want to animate.

2. Choose Slide Show, Preset Animation. Refer to Figure 26.4 for the possible choices.

3. Choose the animation you want—for example, Wipe Right.

PowerPoint adds the Wipe Right animation effect you requested. This particular effect does not have sound associated with it. PowerPoint also has determined that each first-level bulleted item will appear along with its subgroups only after you click the mouse (or press a key) while playing the slide.

Adding Customized Animation Effects

Using preset animation may be adequate for most presentations, but you can also customize your animation for clever and very interesting effects.

N O T E Adding animation effects is a creative, artistic endeavor. Don't be afraid to explore and try out various animation until you get just the effect you want. ▪

Suppose you want to animate the three objects you find on your third slide (see Figure 26.5). In Slide view, with none of the objects selected, choose Slide Show, Custom Animation. PowerPoint displays the dialog box shown in Figure 26.6.

Figure 26.5
You can customize animation for slide objects such as title, bullet list, and graphic image.

Figure 26.6
Custom animation enables you to animate any or all of the objects on a slide.

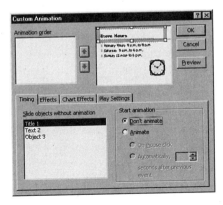

Part
IV

Ch

26

Setting an Object's Animation Timing

There are three objects in the sample slide: the Title, the Bullet List, and a graphic image. None of these objects is currently animated. Click Title 1 in the Slide Objects Without Animation box to select it. PowerPoint highlights the title in the preview box at the top-right of the Custom Animation dialog box with what looks like an edit box. This also brings up the Start animation buttons.

To animate the title, first click Animate. PowerPoint places the Title Object in the Animation Order box and shows the Animate options. By default, during a slideshow, you must click the mouse on a slide or press any key to start the animation. If you choose Automatically, you can specify that the animation take place automatically after any number of seconds.

Adding Special Effects

Adding animation to an object does nothing more than cause it to appear on the screen, either after a mouse click or automatically after a specified number of seconds. You can make the animation much more interesting by adding special effects to change the way the object enters the screen.

Click the Effects tab and PowerPoint changes the dialog box, as shown in Figure 26.7.

Figure 26.7
The Effects tab provides many special effects that you can add to slide objects.

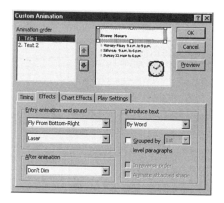

Suppose you want the title to fly in from the bottom-right, one word at a time, making a laser sound as it does. Complete the following steps:

1. Click the Entry animation and sound drop-down menu and choose (from over 50 effects) the animation effect you want—for example, Fly From Bottom-Right. PowerPoint starts the other dialog controls.

2. Click the sound drop-down menu and choose Laser from the list.

3. Click the Introduce text drop-down menu and choose By Word.

4. Click the Preview button to view and hear the animation effect.

Other options shown in this tab of the dialog box are usually used for bulleted text objects. To change the animation for the bulleted list in the sample slide, first click the Timing tab (refer to Figure 26.6). Then click the Text 2 object to add it to the Animation Order list. Click Animate and click the Effects tab (refer to Figure 26.7).

Some of your options for animating the bulleted text items are included in the following list:

- *Entry Animation and Sound*. Choose the animation (for example, Fly From Bottom-Right), but unless you want to distract your audience, you may want to leave the sound setting at [No Sound].

- *Introduce Text*. For example, if you choose All at Once, whole lines of bulleted text will appear instead of one word at a time.

- *Grouped By*. Unless you specify otherwise, first-level bullets appear accompanied by their subheadings. If you want subheadings to appear by themselves, click the level at which they should do so, for example, 2nd. If you want the entire bulleted list to appear at once, clear the Grouped by box.

- *In Reverse Order*. You can have the bulleted items appear last item first, as in a Top 10 Countdown list.

- *After Animation*. You can specify that each bullet, after entering the screen, change color, hide, or hide after the next mouse click. If you are lecturing while displaying the slide, this option enables you to make the current bullet distinguishable from the bullets you have already presented.

N O T E To animate just a single object on a slide, click the object to select it before choosing Custom Animation. This takes you directly to the Effects tab of the Custom Animation dialog box. Selecting an effect for the object automatically adds the object to the Animation Order box and turns on animation in the Timing tab of the dialog box. ■

Part IV

Ch 26

Setting Order of Appearance

Although you have three objects on your slide, you added animation to only two of them. The third, the graphic image, simply appears along with the slide.

The two animated objects appear on the screen in the same order you added animation to them. If you want to change the order in which they appear, simply click the item you want to change in the Animation Order box (refer to Figure 26.6) and then click the up or down arrow.

Figure 26.8 shows a slide that, when played, appears to display an animated map that leads, street by street, to the Company Store. To create that effect, each street in the map, beginning at the right, is added one at a time, using the Wipe Left animation effect.

Figure 26.8

Using animation effects, you can make a map appear to lead to your store.

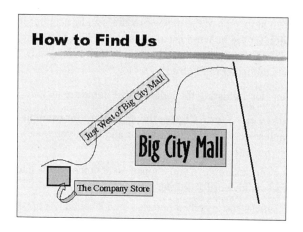

Chart Effects

You can add data charts to the slide's animation order, but the animation effects you use are different from those used for text and graphics. Consider, for example, the slide shown in Figure 26.9.

Figure 26.9

Even charts like this one can benefit from animation effects.

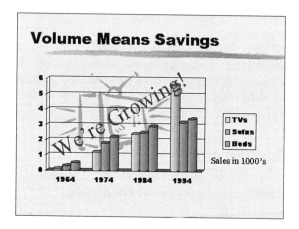

To add animation to the data chart, first click the chart to select it and then choose Slide Show, Custom Animation, or right-click the data chart and choose Custom Animation from the menu. PowerPoint displays the Custom Animation dialog box with the Chart Effects tab selected (see Figure 26.10).

Figure 26.10

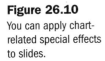

You can apply chart-related special effects to slides.

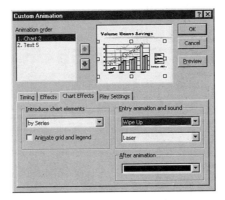

Begin by selecting the Entry animation and sound effect, if any, you want for your data chart. For example, if you want to make the bars in the chart appear to be growing, choose the Wipe Up effect.

Having added animation to your chart, you can now specify how the various elements of the chart are introduced by choosing one of the options listed below:

- *All at Once*. All of the bars of the chart appear at the same time, using the animation effect you selected.
- *By Series*. In the sample chart, all of the bars representing TVs would appear at the same time, followed by the sofa bars, and then the bed bars.
- *By Category*. In the sample chart, all of the bars for 1964 would appear, followed by the 1974 bars, and so on.
- *By Element in Series*. In the sample chart, the TV bar for 1964 would appear first, then the TV bar for 1974, and so on. After all the TV bars appear, then the Sofa bar for 1964 appears, and so on.
- *By Element in Category*. In the sample chart, each bar for 1964 appears in sequence, followed by each bar for 1974 and so on.

You also can choose to Animate the grid and legend. Otherwise, those elements appear immediately before the appearance of the data chart bars.

Finally, you can choose how the chart will appear when the next animated object appears. For example, suppose you want to add text that says, "We're growing!" You can make the data chart dim (change to a single color) as the text appears on the screen (see Figure 26.11). Choose After Animation and then choose the color the chart will change to, for example, black. You also can choose to hide the chart after it is animated or to hide it at the next mouse click.

Part

IV

Ch

26

Figure 26.11
The Dim feature enables you to change the color or hide an object after it is displayed.

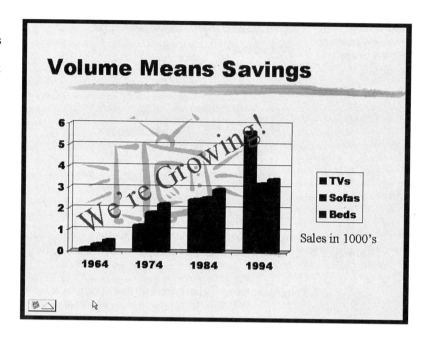

Play Settings

The options found in the Play settings tab of the Custom Animation dialog box apply to multimedia clips such as sound or video.

Some of these options are explained in the following list (see Figure 26.12):

Figure 26.12
Multimedia clips have extra animation options that determine how they play in a presentation.

- *Play Using Animation Order.* If this box is not checked, the media object is not played.
- *Pause Slide Show.* If you do choose to animate the media object, you can pause the slideshow while it plays.

- *Continue Slide Show.* If the media clip is particularly long, and you allow the slideshow to continue, you may need to stop the media clip before it is finished playing.
- *After Current Slide.* The media clip stops playing as soon as you move to the next slide.
- *After Slides.* This option specifies the number of slides that must play before the media clip stops playing.

You also can choose the More options button, and PowerPoint displays the Play Options dialog box shown in Figure 26.13. Here you can choose from the following options:

Figure 26.13

Control how a media clip is played during a presentation.

- *Loop Until Stopped.* The media plays over and over until it is stopped by another media action.
- *Rewind Movie When Done Playing.* The video clip can stop and continue to display the last frame, or it can rewind and display the first frame as a static image.

If the media being played is an audio CD, you can specify the track or tracks to play and the precise starting and ending time for the audio selection.

▶ **See** "Adding Multimedia," **page 569**

Part
IV

Ch
26

Creating Actions

Besides making objects dance on your screen or making noise, you also can make them do practical things, such as jumping to another slide, navigating to a Web site, or starting another program.

Selecting an Action Object

Actions can be attached to nearly any object, including graphic images, text boxes, or entire bulleted lists or organization charts.

However, you cannot attach an action to just a portion of an object. For example, in the organization chart shown in Figure 26.14, you can attach an action to the entire organization chart but not to individual names in that chart.

Figure 26.14

You can create action links to any area of your slide, including each person in an organization chart.

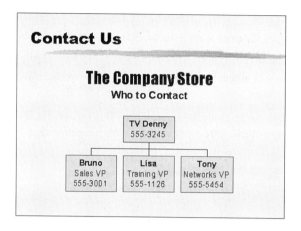

The way around this limitation is to create "dummy" objects that can't be seen when playing the slideshow but that will allow action to occur when you click them. In the sample slide, complete these steps to create a clickable object:

1. Choose the Rectangle tool from the Drawing toolbar.

2. Drag from one corner of an organization chart box name to the opposite corner and release the mouse button. PowerPoint creates a filled rectangle that covers the organization chart box (see Figure 26.15).

Figure 26.15

"Dummy" objects, even when hidden, can serve as action links.

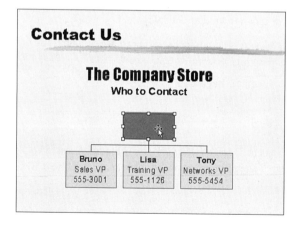

3. Choose Format, AutoShape, or right-click the rectangle and choose Format AutoShape from the menu.

4. Click the Colors and Lines tab.

5. Choose Fill Color and select No Fill.

6. Choose Line Color and select No Line.

7. Choose OK to add the invisible rectangle to the slide.

8. Repeat steps 1-7 for each action area of the object.

PowerPoint hides the rectangle and its border line but does display the sizing handles for the rectangle. If you click anywhere else, PowerPoint deselects the rectangle. To select the rectangle again, you must click the mouse pointer right on the edge of the box.

 You can also select an invisible object by choosing the Select Objects tool from the Drawing tool bar, and dragging an area that includes the object. When you release the mouse button, PowerPoint displays the object's sizing handles.

Adding a Link to a Web Site

With the box selected, you now can attach an action to it. For example, to link the Company Store's owner to his Web page on the company's Web site, follow these steps:

1. Choose Slide Show, Action Settings, or right-click the rectangle and choose Action Settings from the menu. PowerPoint displays the Action Settings dialog box (see Figure 26.16).

Figure 26.16
Action links can take you to slides, to the Web, and more.

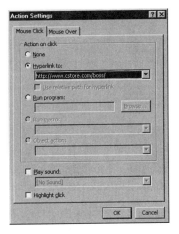

2. Choose Hyperlink to.
3. In the Hyperlink to. edit box, type the full URL of the Web site, for example http://www.cstore.com/boss/.
4. If you want, you can choose Play Sound and specify a .WAV file to play when this object's action is chosen.

You also can tell PowerPoint to highlight the object when you click it. However, because the sample rectangle is invisible, this setting will have no effect.

Using Other Actions

Several of the actions PowerPoint offers are included in the following list:

- *Hyperlink.* This enables you to jump to the previous, next, first, last, or any slide. You also can jump to an URL (Web site), to another PowerPoint slideshow, to a file, or to a Custom Show (a subset of the current show).

- *Use Relative Path for Hyperlink.* This option is grayed out if the link requires a full path name (for example, http://..., and so on) or if the selected object image is saved with the slideshow. For details, see "relative links in hyperlink addresses" in PowerPoint's Help, Contents and Index.

- *Run Program.* Clicking an action object can launch another program, such as Notepad, the Calculator, a game, a statistics program, and so on.

- *Run Macro.* Plays a macro you create for use in the slideshow. If you have not created a macro, this option is grayed out.

- *Object Action.* If you select an embedded, editable object, such as the organization chart, you can edit the object while playing the slideshow. For example, you could replace a clip art image, edit a data chart, or play a media clip.

- *Play Sound.* You can play a .WAV sound file, in addition to any other action you have chosen.

- *Highlight Click.* Choose this option if you want to highlight an action object after you click it.

Using Mouse Over to Start an Action

By default, PowerPoint requires you to click the object during a slideshow to make the action take place, for example, to go to a Web site. But you also can make an action take place by merely passing the mouse pointer over it. For example, to add a sound effect to the VP for Training box, complete these steps:

1. Select the rectangle that covers the organization chart box. This is the action object.
2. Choose Slide Show, Action Settings, or right-click the rectangle and choose Action Settings from the menu. PowerPoint displays the Action Settings dialog box.
3. Click the Mouse Over tab. PowerPoint displays the same information as shown in Figure 26.16.
4. Choose Play Sound.
5. From the Play Sound drop-down menu, choose the sound effect you wish to play, for example, Camera.
6. Click OK.

CAUTION

Passing a mouse over an object is the easiest way to start an action. Unfortunately, it can be too easy. Reserve the Mouse Over feature for actions that are quick, such as a sound effect. Use the Mouse Click option for actions that should be chosen deliberately, such as jumping to a Web site or to another slide.

Adding Multimedia

PowerPoint keeps up with today's powerful computers by enabling you to include sound and video clips in your presentation. The combination of graphics, text, sound, and video constitutes a multimedia presentation.

Deciding to Use Multimedia

Before integrating media clips into your presentation, you should consider whether you really need them. Do the clips add to the understanding of the presentation's content? Do they add necessary pizzazz that holds your audience's attention? Or are they merely window dressing that could just as easily be left out?

Make sure the need justifies the effort required to add multimedia effects.

Finding Media Clips

The simplest of multimedia effects are text and the clip art image. As you learned in Chapter 25, Office 97 comes with an extensive clip art gallery.

However, when you use the gallery, you'll notice that there are other media types as well. The collection that is installed on your computer is quite limited, but if you leave the CD-ROM in your CD drive, you have access to thousands of clips. These include the following types of images and sounds:

- _Clip Art._ The gallery contains 3,184 clip art images, grouped from academic to weather categories.
- _Pictures._ PowerPoint includes 144 photo-quality pictures.
- _Sounds._ Twenty-nine sounds are available for your use.
- _Videos._ You can choose from 21 sample videos, most of which last only 3–4 seconds.

In addition, there are many other media clips you can find on the Internet, in other programs, or from commercial sources. You can even create your own media clips.

▶ **See** "Adding Clip Art Objects," **page 544**

▶ **See** "Adding Sound," **page 570**

Part

IV

Ch

26

> **CAUTION**
>
> While copying images and media clips from the Web is technically easy to do, you will usually be in violation of copyright laws if you take images from a public site without permission. Although many people do not know it, you cannot reuse photographs, clip art, or media clips that you find in public sources without the permission of the creator.
>
> Be sure to e-mail the administrator of the site where you find clip art and ask his or her permission prior to using images you find.

Choosing the PowerPoint Player (Clip) or the Media Player

You can insert PowerPoint media clips in two ways. One method uses the Windows 98 Media Player, whereas the other uses the PowerPoint Player.

The PowerPoint Player is internal to the PowerPoint program and generally does a better job of playing clips. However, it is limited to starting, pausing, or resuming a sound or video. You can insert media clips most easily from the Office 97 CD-ROM using the PowerPoint Player by choosing Insert, Movies and Sounds and selecting the appropriate media type.

The Windows 98 Media Player can handle the same kinds of clips but is an external program that doesn't always work as well as the PowerPoint player. However, it does enable you to start, stop, pause, fast forward, and rewind your clip. To insert media clips using the Media Player, choose Insert, Object and then choose the media file you want to play.

Generally, you should use the PowerPoint player. However, if you can't insert a media clip any other way, use the Media Player. The following sections assume you are using the PowerPoint Player.

CAUTION

Be aware that a bug in PowerPoint sometimes causes PowerPoint to stop working if both sound and video players are being used to play objects on the same PowerPoint slide. Be sure to test your slides thoroughly and, if necessary, use only one player or the other on any given slide.

Adding Sound

You have already learned how to associate sounds with animated objects as well as action objects. However, you also can insert sounds by themselves as objects.

Suppose, for example, you want to insert a sound clip into a PowerPoint presentation from the Clip Gallery. Complete these steps:

1. Choose Insert, Movies and Sounds, Sound from Gallery. PowerPoint displays the dialog box shown in Figure 26.17.

CAUTION

If you choose a sound (or other media clip) from the Office 97 CD, PowerPoint will look for that sound on the CD when you play your slideshow. To ensure that all of your media clips are available when you make your presentation, you should copy them to the same folder on your computer where you save your PowerPoint presentation.

2. Select the sound clip you want.
3. Choose Play to preview the sound.
4. Choose Insert to place the sound in your presentation. PowerPoint displays a small audio speaker icon.

Figure 26.17
The Microsoft Clip Gallery 3.0 provides clip art, photographs, sound clips, and video clips.

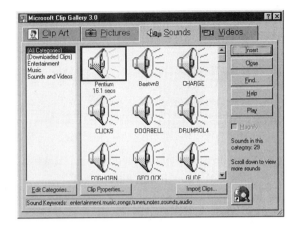

5. Drag the icon to the location on the slide where you want it and size it as desired (see Figure 26.18).

Figure 26.18
Clicking on a speaker icon plays a sound.

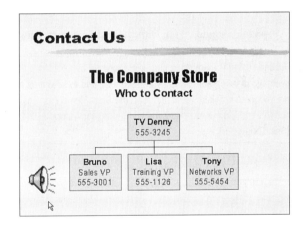

To play the sound clip while running your slide show, simply click the speaker icon.

You also can change a few of the special effects for the sound icon. For example, you can add animation effects or change the play action to Mouse Over, and so on.

Recording and Editing Sound Clips

If you have a microphone attached to your computer's sound board, you also can record your own clips to add to your presentation.

Suppose, for example, you want to include the Company Store's sales manager telling people to "Save 50% on boomboxes and TVs !" Complete these steps:

1. Prepare your "script" and make sure your microphone is properly connected.

Part IV
Ch
26

2. Choose Insert, Movies and Sound, Record Sound. PowerPoint displays the Record Sound dialog box shown in Figure 26.19.

Figure 26.19

Record your own sounds in PowerPoint.

3. Type a description for the sound you are about to record, for example, "Special Deal."
4. Click the Record button (the button with the red dot).
5. Speak into the microphone.
6. Click the Stop button (the button with the square black box).
7. Click the Play button (the one with the triangle) to hear the recording.

N O T E   If you don't like the recording and want to do it over again, you must Cancel and start over. Otherwise, what you record a second time is added to the first recording. ■

8. Click OK to insert the sound, along with the sound icon, in your presentation.

T I P   You can also record sounds using the Sound Recorder that comes with Windows 98. The Sound Recorder has the advantage of being able to edit your recording and to save it as a separate .WAV file. If you have the Sound Recorder installed, you'll find it on the Start Menu, Programs, Accessories, Entertainment. If you don't find it there, you must install it from your Windows 98 CD-ROM with Add/ Remove Programs. (See Chapter 6.)

The sound clip is saved with your presentation, and therefore it can be used anywhere that you need a sound in your current slideshow only. For example, if you want to hear the sound when you click a photograph of the sales manager, complete these steps:

1. Select the photo object and choose Slide Show, Action Settings, or right-click the photo object and choose Actions Settings. PowerPoint displays the Actions Settings dialog box (refer to Figure 26.16).
2. Check the Play Sound check box.
3. Click the Play Sound drop-down menu and from the list choose the sound you just recorded.
4. Click OK.

Now when you play the slideshow, clicking the photo object plays the sound you recorded.

Suppose you have a 2-minute recording of music, but you want only about a 10-second introduction to your slideshow. PowerPoint does not have the capability to edit an audio clip, but the Sound Recorder that comes with Windows 98 does.

You can open the sound clip in the Sound Recorder, edit it as desired, and then save the resulting clip with a new name.

N O T E If you see a green and black waveform box in the Sound Recorder, you can edit the sound. However, some of the .WAV files that come with the Office 97 Clip Gallery must be converted to an editable file format before you can edit them. To do this in the Sound Recorder, open the .WAV file and choose File, Properties. Then choose Convert now and click OK twice. ▪

Using Audio CDs

In addition to sound clips, you can add audio tracks, or just parts of audio tracks from audio CDs. Unlike sound clip files, you cannot associate CD tracks to animated objects or to slide transitions. Instead, you must insert a CD track as an object and then tell PowerPoint how to play it.

To insert a CD track into your presentation, complete these steps:

1. Make sure the CD you want to use has been placed in the CD-ROM drive.

CAUTION

If you play a CD track during your slideshow, make sure nothing else is demanding use of the CD-ROM drive. For example, if the Windows 98 CD Player is running, even if it is stopped or paused, PowerPoint cannot access the CD at the same time.

2. Choose Insert, Movies and Sounds, Play CD Audio Track. PowerPoint displays the Play Options dialog box (see Figure 26.20), which indicates how many tracks the CD contains and the CD's total playing time.

Part
IV

Ch
26

Figure 26.20

Play audio CD tracks, or just portions of a track.

3. Specify the track number you want to start with and the one you want to end with. If you want to play just one track, the number should be the same in both the Start Track and the End Track boxes.

4. If you want to play just a portion of a track, indicate the Start At and the End At times.

T I P   PowerPoint does not offer any way to preview the CD track to determine exactly where you want to begin or end a track. However, you can use the CD player that comes with Windows 98 to play the CD and to note the beginning and ending times you want. Be sure to close the CD player before returning to PowerPoint.

5. If you want the track to play continuously until you stop it, check the <u>L</u>oop Until Stopped box.

6. Click OK to insert the CD audio track as an icon in your presentation.

To enable the CD track to be played, you must use Custom Animation to include the track and to specify how it is to be played.

▶ **See** "Adding Customized Animation Effects," **page 559**

Adding Video

The "multi" part of multimedia is particularly evident when you use video clips in your presentation. A video segment can add significant impact if used appropriately.

> **CAUTION**
>
> Most video clips are recorded to play back in a small window on the screen. A short segment, for example, three to four seconds, even when played in a small window, can require a huge amount of disk space. Before committing resources to a video clip, make sure you really need it.

Unless you have the facilities for converting video into a digital format, you must use clips already prepared by others. In addition to the 21 video clips that come with Office 97, you can find others on the Web. Remember, however, that copyright restrictions often apply to multimedia material you find on the Internet.

Suppose you want to add impact to the slide that shows your TVs on sale (see Figure 26.21). You can use the Cost Cutting video clip that comes with Office 97.

Figure 26.21
Carefully chosen video clips, such as this cost-cutting video, can add impact to your presentation.

To add a video clip, complete these steps:

1. Choose Insert, Movies and Sounds, Movie from Gallery. PowerPoint displays the videos in the Clip Gallery (see Figure 26.22).

Figure 26.22
The Clip Gallery provides 21 video clips.

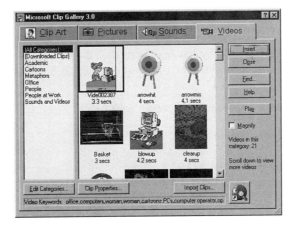

2. Select the video clip you want to use and, if you want, choose Play to preview it.
3. Choose Insert to place a copy of the video clip in your presentation.
4. Select the video object and move it or resize it as needed.
5. Choose Edit, Movie Object, or right-click the object and choose Edit Movie Object from the menu. PowerPoint displays the Play Options dialog box (see Figure 26.23).

Figure 26.23
Control how you want to play a video clip.

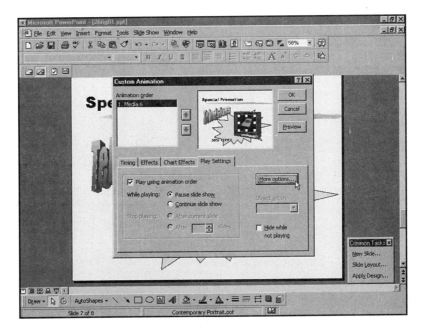

6. If you want the video to continue repeating itself until you stop it, choose Loop Until Stopped.

7. If you want the movie to display the first frame after it plays, choose Rewind Movie When Done Playing. However, if you want the movie to display the ending frame—for example, the dollar bills cut in half, leave this box unchecked.

8. Click OK to return to PowerPoint.

You can preview the video clip by double-clicking it on the screen. However, to enable the video clip to be played during a presentation, you must use Custom Animation to include the clip and to specify how it is to be played.

▶ **See** "Adding Customized Animation Effects," **page 559**

CAUTION

If you choose a video clip from the Office 97 CD, PowerPoint will look for the video clip on the CD when you play your slideshow. To ensure that all of your media clips are available when you make your presentation, you should copy them to the same folder on your computer where you save your PowerPoint presentation.

CHAPTER 27

Creating a Slide Show and Making the Presentation

by Read Gilgen

In this chapter

Creating the Slide Show

In preceding chapters you learned how to create slides, add transitions, and organize your slides into a complete presentation. PowerPoint offers yet more tools to help you complete the preparations for your slide show.

Creating and Using Comments

As you create your slides, you may find that you're missing a bit of needed information, or you're not quite sure whether to include a particular item.

If you were creating such a presentation on paper, quite likely you'd use a sticky note to remind yourself to resolve the problem before finalizing the project. To avoid interrupting your train of thought, or putting a damper on your creative process, you can use the PowerPoint Comments feature to make notes for yourself.

Suppose, for example, that you're preparing a presentation for your employer about the Company Store, and you can't remember the Sunday hours. To create a comment on the store hours slide, you follow these steps:

1. Go to the slide where you want to create a comment—for example, the store hours slide.

2. Choose Insert, Comment; alternatively, if the Reviewing taskbar is displayed, click the Insert Comment button. PowerPoint displays a yellow-shaded text box and the name of the person adding the comments (see Figure 27.1).

Figure 27.1
Use the Comment feature to add notes to yourself or others during the review of your presentation.

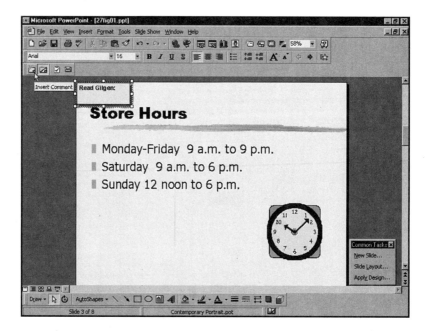

3. Type your comments in the comment box.

4. Position and size the comment box the same way you do any text box.

5. Click outside of the comment box to deselect it.

By default, PowerPoint displays any comments that have been added to a slide. If you want to hide the comments, choose <u>V</u>iew, <u>C</u>omments and the comment boxes disappear.

> **CAUTION**
>
> If you don't hide your comments, they appear during your presentation and print out on your handouts.

Creating Speaker Notes

If you're making your presentation in person, you may need help remembering what to say during each slide. That's where Speaker Notes come in handy.

To add Speaker Notes to your presentation, follow these steps:

1. Go to the first slide.

2. Choose <u>V</u>iew, <u>N</u>otes Page; or click the Notes Page View button on the View menu. PowerPoint displays your slides as shown in Figure 27.2.

Figure 27.2

View your speaker notes in the Notes Page view.

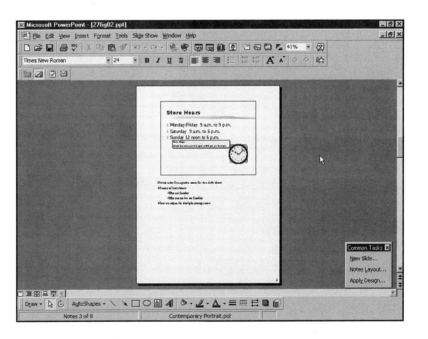

Part

IV

Ch

27

3. Choose <u>V</u>iew, <u>Z</u>oom; or click the Zoom button and choose a larger zoom size—for example, 100%. PowerPoint now displays the Notes text box in a size you can read.

4. Type your notes in whatever manner they work best for you. For example, if you work best from detailed outlines, click the Bullets button on the Formatting toolbar.

T I P Although it's tempting to prepare everything you plan to say ahead of time, presentations that the viewer must read word for word tend to be very boring. If you can, learn to make a presentation from an outline to maintain a measure of spontaneity.

Generally you print your speaker notes rather than view them during your presentation. If you choose Format, Notes Layout you can choose to display just the slide, just the notes, or both (see Figure 27.3). The other options under the Format menu (Notes Color Scheme and Notes Background have no effect either during the slide presentation or on your printed speaker notes.

Figure 27.3

You can view your speaker notes and slides together as you review your presentation.

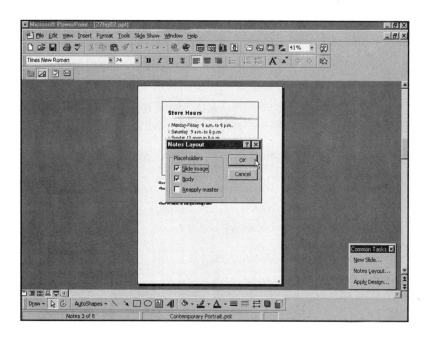

Setting Up the Show

Before presenting the slide show for the first time, you need to set up how you want the show to run. Choose Slide Show, Set Up Show to display the dialog box shown in Figure 27.4. You can choose three basic approaches to your slide presentation:

■ *Presented by a Speaker (Full-Screen)*. If you plan to show the presentation using a computer and a data projector, this option enables you to use the full screen to do so.

■ *Browsed by an Individual (Window)*. Choose this option if you want viewers to control the slide show. During the presentation the viewer sees a browser-like interface (see Figure 27.5).

Figure 27.4
Use the Set Up Show screen to specify how you will show your presentation.

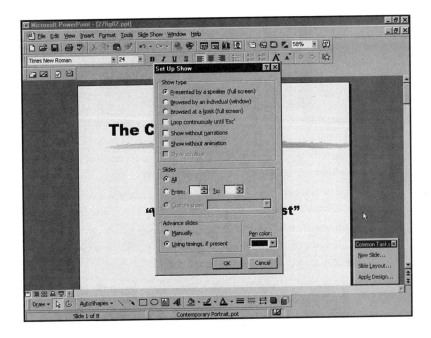

Figure 27.5
You can show your presentation using a browser-like interface.

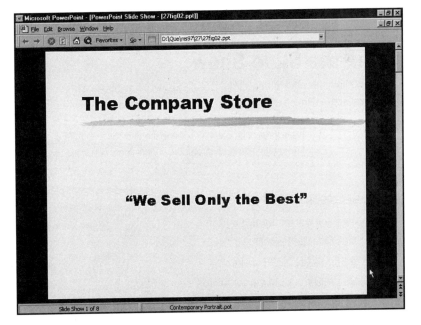

Part
IV

Ch
27

■ *Browsed at a Kiosk (Full-Screen).* Choose this option if you intend to leave the show running on its own and if you don't want viewers to control the show with a mouse or the keyboard.

Each of the previous approaches is affected by other settings you make in this dialog box and elsewhere. For example, an unattended (kiosk) presentation requires automatic timings for each slide since the viewer cannot advance the slide manually.

Other options in the Set Up Show dialog box include:

- *Loop Continuously Until ESC*. Checking this option means the show will repeat itself until someone presses the Esc key. A kiosk-type presentation assumes the slide show will loop.
- *Show Without Narrations*. Use this option if you're at a trade show and you don't want to bother the people in the booth next to you.
- *Show Without Animation*. If you get an audience that reacts adversely to busy multimedia screens, choose this option to display only the completed slides.
- *Choose Which Slides to Display by Choosing All, or Specifying the Starting and Ending, From and To Slide Numbers*. You also can choose a Custom show if any are defined.

▶ **See** "Creating Custom Shows," **page 588**

- *Advance the Slides Manually (Requiring a Keystroke or Mouse Click), or by Using Timings, If Present*. Advancing a slide manually suppresses, but does not delete, any automatic timing you may have set for a slide transition. It does not affect object animation within a slide.
- *Choose the Pen Color You Will Use When Highlighting Your Slide During a Presentation.*

Playing the Slide Show

To play your slide show, choose Slide Show, View Show. This starts the presentation with the first slide, using the settings you chose in the preceding section.

NOTE Choosing View, Slide Show, or clicking the Slide Show button on the View menu displays the presentation, beginning with the current slide, not at the beginning of the slide show. ■

To advance to the next slide you can:

- Click the left mouse button
- Press the Page Down key
- Press the N (Next) key
- Press the right cursor or down cursor keys
- Press the spacebar

When you press any of these keys, PowerPoint makes the next transition, whether it is to advance to a new slide, or to activate an animation sequence.

To back up to the previous slide, you can:

- Press the Page Up key
- Press the P (Previous) key
- Press the left cursor or up cursor keys
- Press the Backspace key

There are so many slide control options, you may find it difficult to remember them all. To get a quick list of options, press F1 (Help) at any time during the slide show. PowerPoint displays the dialog box shown in Figure 27.6.

Figure 27.6
Press F1 to get a list of slide control options while showing your presentation.

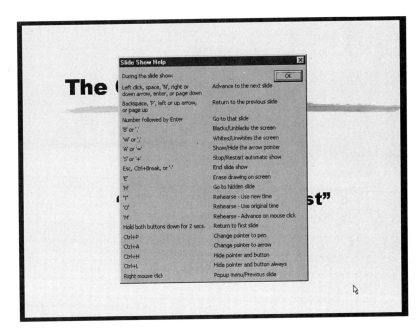

You can also access many of the slide control options by clicking the right mouse button. PowerPoint displays the shortcut menu shown in Figure 27.7. From this menu you click the left mouse button to choose any of the options shown.

 TIP Clicking the small button at the lower left of the screen also displays the slide controls shortcut menu.

The first group of menu options (Next, Previous, and Go) change slides. Choose Go to jump directly to any slide in the presentation.

Using the Screen Pen

By default, PowerPoint displays a pointer. You can use the pointer to direct the audience to notice specific parts of your slide. However, the pointer is easy to lose track of, especially when used with a data display.

Part
IV

Ch
27

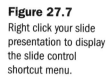

Figure 27.7
Right click your slide
presentation to display
the slide control
shortcut menu.

Instead of relying on the pointer, use the Pen option, which enables you to draw on the slide show screen much as you would with a marking pen.

To use the screen pen, follow these steps:

1. Right-click the screen to display the slide controls menu (refer to Figure 27.7).
2. Choose Pen. PowerPoint displays a pointer shaped like a pencil.
3. Click and drag on the screen to draw a freehand line.
4. Right click and choose Arrow from the menu to turn off the pen.

Using the pen to highlight areas of your screen takes some getting used to. However, with a little practice you can learn to make a point by drawing on the screen.

By default, PowerPoint uses a color that complements the screen design you have chosen. If you want to change the color of the pen, right click the screen and choose Pointer Options, Pen Color.

Using a Black Screen

During your presentation you may want to conduct a discussion without the distraction of a slide behind you. If you know when these discussions will occur, you can add blank slides at the appropriate places in your slide show.

However, if you encounter an unplanned need for a blank slide, you can right click the screen and choose Screen, Black Screen. To display the current slide again, choose Screen, Unblack Screen.

TIP Instead of using the mouse, you can simply press the B key to black the screen, and press B again to display the slide.

Using Speaker Notes

Earlier you learned how to create speaker notes. During a slide show you can refer to these notes, or even add to them. To view the speaker notes, simply access the shortcut menu (right click the screen) and choose Speaker Notes to open the Speaker Notes dialog box.

All formatting, such as bulleted lists, is lost in this view. Likewise, if you add text, you are limited to adding plain text without formatting.

Using the Meeting Minder

The Meeting Minder is a handy tool for taking minutes and recording assignments made during a presentation. You can even prepare assignments ahead of time.

Suppose you are making a presentation to your sales staff, and you want to note that everyone agreed to increase sales by 100 percent. Further, Karen agreed to publish a daily bar chart showing progress toward this goal. To write Meeting Minutes and to create Action Items, follow these steps:

1. Right click the screen and choose Meeting Minder from the Menu. PowerPoint displays the Meeting Minder dialog box.
2. On the Meeting Minutes tab, enter any notes you want to record, for example, "Everyone agreed to increase sales by 100 percent."
3. Click the Action Items tab to see the Action Items page.
4. Type a Description of the action item, for example, **Prepare bar chart to track sales increases**. Your description can be much longer than the space you see on the screen.
5. Type the name of the person to whom the task is assigned in the Assigned To box.
6. Modify the due date, if appropriate.
7. Choose Add to add this particular action item to the list of items created for this presentation.

As you add action items, PowerPoint builds a final slide that appears at the end of the show, summarizing action items noted during the presentation.

Also, after you complete the presentation, you can then Export the minutes and the action items to Word.

▶ **See** "Using Other Output Methods," **page 602**

Timing Your Presentation

Every speaker lives in fear that his or her presentation will be too long or too short. Good timing is essential if you don't want a lot of "dead time" by ending too early, or if you don't want to rush and skip over important material because you're taking too long. PowerPoint can help.

Part

IV

Ch

27

Rehearsing Timings

You can rehearse your presentation using the Rehearsal feature. Choose Slide Show, Rehearse Timings and PowerPoint starts your slide show and displays the Rehearsal dialog box.

The overall length of your presentation is displayed at the upper left, while the length of the current slide is shown at the right. You can use the following options:

- *Pause.* Click the pause button to suspend the timing. Click it again to resume the timing.
- *Repeat.* If you want to time the current slide over again, click repeat to reset the timing for the current slide to zero.
- *Advance.* When you're ready to advance to the next slide, click the Advance button and PowerPoint records the time and moves on.

N O T E The Advance button moves to the next animated object, and not necessarily to the next slide. The timing you see indicates the elapsed time since the last animated object or slide. ■

As you rehearse each slide, repeating as necessary, you gradually gain confidence in your delivery and the amount of time it takes you to present the material. When you complete the slide show, PowerPoint tells you the total elapsed time and asks if you want to save the timings. If you do, the timings are added to each slide as timed transitions.

PowerPoint also asks if you want to review the timings in the Slide Sorter View. If you do, you see the actual elapsed time recorded beneath each slide.

Finally, when you play the show, the slides and animated objects change automatically based on your rehearsed timings.

Using the Slide Meter

If you have set automatic or rehearsed timings for your slides, you can use the PowerPoint Slide Meter to gauge how closely you're staying with the targeted time. To turn on the Slide Meter, while playing the slide show, right-click the slide and choose Slide Meter from the menu. PowerPoint displays the Slide Meter.

More likely than not you'll use the Slide Meter only for rehearsal, since you don't really want to distract your audience with an on-screen meter. Besides being a distraction, the Slide Meter could curb spontaneous discussion. For example, if you rehearsed and set the transition time for a slide at 25 seconds, but someone asks a question, you could quickly get far behind.

If you use the Slide Meter during the slide show, and also want to allow for audience participation, you can pause the show, and the meter, by right-clicking the slide and choosing Screen, Pause from the menu. To resume the slide show, and also set the meter in motion again, right-click the slide and choose Screen, Resume.

Using a Recorded Narration

Another method for timing your show, but also for enabling the show to run by itself, is to record a narration. Then when you play the slide show, slides advance in synch with your narration.

Recording the Narration

To record a narration, your computer must have a microphone connected to its sound board. Then, follow these steps:

1. Prepare and rehearse your narrative script before attempting to record it.
2. Choose Slide Show, Record Narration. PowerPoint displays the Record Narration dialog box.
3. Adjust the recording Settings if needed. By default PowerPoint records at a medium ("radio") quality. The dialog box shows you how many minutes you can record based on the space on your hard disk and the quality of the recording.
4. Choose Link narrations in if you want to keep the recorded material in a separate .WAV file. If you don't check this box, the narration is embedded in your presentation, thus making the presentation file considerably larger.

N O T E If you link your narrations to a file, the resulting .WAV file is placed in the same folder as your slide show. Remember that if you move the slide show file elsewhere, you must also move the .WAV file that accompanies it.

5. Choose OK and PowerPoint begins to play the slide show beginning with the first slide.
6. Record your narration, advancing through the slide show as you normally do.
7. At the conclusion of the slide show, tell PowerPoint whether to save the narration timings with the slide show.
8. Also indicate whether to view the slides and their timings in the Slide Sorter View.

Playing the Recorded Narration

Playing a slide show along with its recorded narration is easy. Simply choose Slide Show, View Show. PowerPoint presents the slides along with the narration, and also advances the slides at the same pace you did when you recorded the narration.

If you want the slide show to play over and over again, choose Slide Show, Set Up Show and select the Loop Continuously Until 'ESC' box.

N O T E The narration is a .WAV sound file. Because PowerPoint can play only one .WAV file at a time, other .WAV files you may have included in your presentation (such as sound effects) will not play if you use recorded narration.

Part

IV

Ch

27

CAUTION

Removing a narration from your slide show can be a rather tedious process unless you use Undo right away. To remove narration from your slides later you must remove the media object (a speaker icon) from each slide that contains a narration.

Creating Custom Shows

If you repeat your presentation often, you may find that sometimes you have to modify it to better suit your audience. In some cases you need to remove slides, but for other situations you must put them back in.

PowerPoint enables you to create one single slide show, and to hide, expand, or summarize slides as needed. You also can create custom slide show lists so that you don't have to set up individualized presentations each time you need them.

Hiding Slides

When you hide a slide, you simply prevent it from being shown during the slide show. However, the slide remains part of the total presentation file. To hide a slide, follow these steps:

1. Switch to Slide Sorter view. Although you can perform these steps in any view, the Slide Sorter View helps you see the overall presentation, thus enabling you to choose the proper slides to hide.
2. Click the slide you want to hide.
3. Choose Slide Show, Hide Slide; or click the Hide Slide button on the Slide Sorter toolbar. In Slide Sorter view, beneath the selected slide, PowerPoint displays a page icon with a line through it.

To unhide a slide, repeat the preceding steps.

Expanding Bullet Slides

For some of your audiences, you may want to expand on the information presented in a bullet slide. Or, you might want to create a table of contents slide, and use its bulleted items as titles for the next several slides.

To expand a bulleted list, simply go to the slide you want to expand and choose Tools, Expand Slide. PowerPoint leaves the original bulleted slide intact, but inserts a new slide for each bulleted item from the original.

You then can hide the original, or you can add objects to the expanded slides. If you don't want the expanded slides to display, you can hide them as well.

NOTE You can't unexpand a slide but it's relatively easy in Slide Sorter view to delete the expanded slides. Hold down the Shift key and click each of the slides you want to delete. Then release the Shift key and press Delete. ▪

Creating an Agenda Slide

If you want to create a summary slide— one that lists several slide titles in one bulleted list— follow these steps:

1. Switch to Slide Sorter view. (This procedure does not work in other views.)
2. Select the titles of the slides you want to include in the summary slide.
3. On the Slide Sorter toolbar, click the Summary Slide button.

PowerPoint creates a Summary Slide, with a bulleted list of the selected slide titles, and inserts the slide immediately preceding the first of the slides you selected. You then can edit or enhance the summary slide, or you can drag the slide to any position you want.

Inserting Slides from Other Shows

Another way to customize your slide show is to insert slides from another show. Suppose, for example, you want to create an agenda for a meeting and you want to discuss slides from last month's Board of Directors meeting.

After starting a new show and selecting the design you want, follow these steps to insert slides from another show.

1. Choose Insert, Slides from Files. PowerPoint displays the Slide Finder dialog box (see Figure 27.8).

Figure 27.8
You can insert slides directly from previously created slide shows.

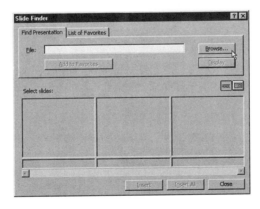

2. Type the File Name of the slide show that contains slides you want to use, or Browse to find the file.
3. Choose Display to view a thumbnail sketch of all of the slides in the show.

4. Select the slides you want to include and choose <u>I</u>nsert. If you want to use all of the slides, choose In<u>s</u>ert All.

5. If you want to include slides from other shows, repeat steps 1–4. Otherwise, choose Close to return to your slide show.

If you are creating an agenda—and the inserted slides contain titles that serve as agenda items—you can create a summary slide as described in the preceding section.

Saving and Using Custom Shows

Another method for creating a custom show is to make a custom slide list based on the current slide show and save the list for when you need it. Suppose, for example, you want to create a presentation for the company's board of directors, changing the order of some slides and leaving others out altogether.

To create and save a custom show, follow these steps:

1. Choose Sli<u>d</u>e Show, <u>C</u>ustom Shows. PowerPoint displays the Custom Shows dialog box.

2. Choose <u>N</u>ew. PowerPoint displays the Define Custom Show dialog box (see Figure 27.9).

Figure 27.9

Create custom slide lists using the Custom Show feature.

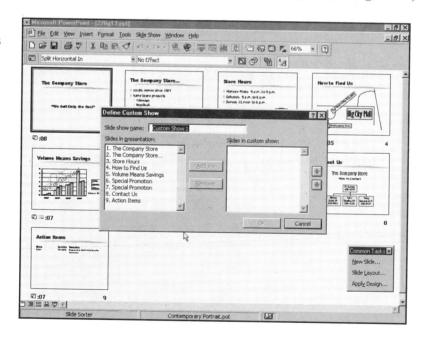

3. Type the name of your custom show in the Slide show <u>n</u>ame box—for example, **Board of Directors**.

4. Click the first slide you want to use to select it.

5. Choose <u>A</u>dd to copy the slide from the left column to the right column.

6. Repeat steps 4 and 5 until your slide list is complete.

7. To remove a slide from the Slides in Custom Show column, select the slide and choose Remove.

8. To change the order of a slide, click the slide to select it and click the up or down arrows to move the slide up or down in the list.

9. Choose OK to save the custom show list. In the Custom Shows dialog box (see Figure 27.10) PowerPoint adds the custom show to any others you have created.

Figure 27.10
Save your tailor-made presentations to use at any time.

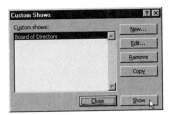

10. Choose Close to close the Custom Show dialog box.

To play a custom show, simply choose Slide Show, Custom Shows, then select the show you want to play and choose Show.

Using Branching

When you present a slide show, typically you move sequentially from one slide to the next. PowerPoint also enables you to branch, which means to jump from one slide to another, out of sequence.

Designing a Branched Slide Show

Using a branched presentation requires careful planning. The easy part is setting up links to jump from one slide to another. But if you're not careful, you can create a maze from your slide show so that you get sidetracked or even lost altogether.

The key to a well organized, branched presentation, is to create a home slide which becomes the reference point for the entire slide show. You branch out from the home slide, and then always provide for yourself a way to get back to the home slide.

An example would be an agenda slide where you might not want or need to discuss each agenda item in sequence. You would create a link from the agenda slide to the first slide for a given agenda item. At the last of the slides for an agenda item, you create a link to return to the agenda slide.

Before you begin creating branched links, stop and sketch out an actual diagram of what you want to do. Then creating the branched presentation will be relatively simple and you won't leave out important links.

Part
IV

Ch
27

TIP If you print an outline view of your presentation, you can use the printout to draw and redraw your planned links, until you're sure the branching roadmap is complete. See "Printing a Slide Show" later in this chapter for information on printing various views of your presentation.

Adding Action Settings to Slide Objects

You can link any object on your slide to any other slide in your presentation. Whatever object you link, however, should clearly suggest where that link leads. On an agenda slide, for example, you might link bulleted items to slides that illustrate or explain the agenda item in greater detail.

Suppose, for example, you want to link the bulleted items shown in Figure 27.11. Follow these steps:

Figure 27.11

Bulleted lists make great presentation agendas.

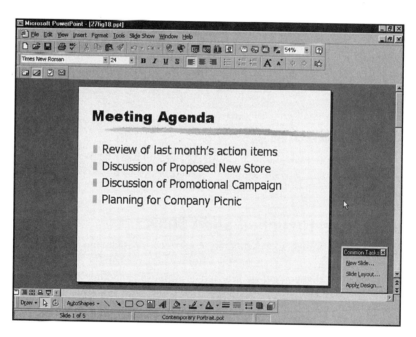

1. Go to the agenda slide and switch to Slide view.
2. Click the bulleted slide list.
3. Select the bulleted item you want to link.
4. Choose Slide Show, Action Settings. PowerPoint displays the Action Settings dialog box.
5. Choose Hyperlink To, and click the Hyperlink To drop-down list (see Figure 27.12).
6. Select Slide and PowerPoint displays the Hyperlink to Slide dialog box (see Figure 27.13).

Figure 27.12

You can branch to many different locations inside or outside of your presentation.

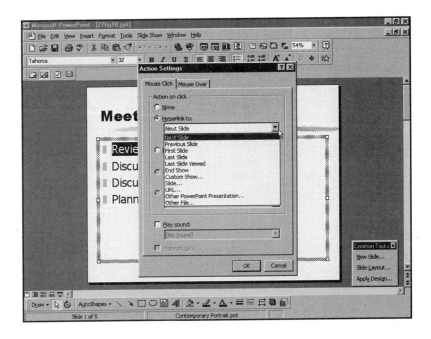

Figure 27.13

A hyperlink enables you to quickly jump from one slide to another.

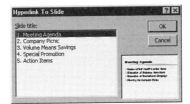

7. Select the target slide you want to link to, and choose OK.

8. Choose OK again to return to your slide. PowerPoint adds the action link, and also highlights the bulleted item (see Figure 27.14).

When you play the slide show, you simply click the highlighted bulleted item to jump to the target slide.

TIP If you don't like the look of the highlighted item, you can create an invisible "dummy" object over the bulleted item, and link that object to the target slide.

▶ **See** "Selecting an Action Object" in Chapter 26 for information on creating invisible action objects, **page 565**

Adding Action Buttons

Getting to the target slide is easy because the home slide contains a reference to it. However, the target slide might not contain anything that remotely suggests returning to the home slide.

Part
IV

Ch

27

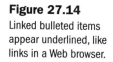

Figure 27.14
Linked bulleted items appear underlined, like links in a Web browser.

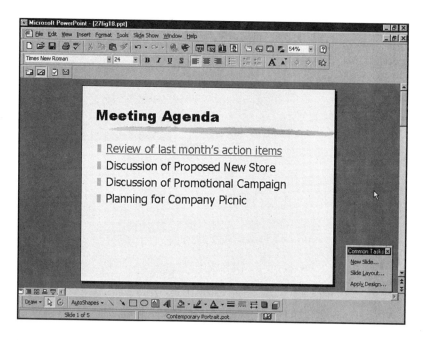

A common method for providing linking clues is the action button, often an arrow or some other visual indicator that tells you where you'll go if you click it. For example, suppose you want to add an action button that links the Action Items list to the home slide. Follow these steps:

1. Go to the slide where you want to create the link, for example, the Action Items list.

2. Choose Slide Show, Action Buttons, and from the menu list shown in Figure 27.15, choose the button you want to insert, for example the Home button. PowerPoint displays a cross-hairs mouse pointer in the slide editing area.

3. Drag the mouse pointer to create a button. PowerPoint then displays the Action Settings dialog box (see Figure 27.16).

4. Click the Hyperlink To drop-down list, and choose the slide you want to jump to.

5. Choose OK to return to your slide. PowerPoint displays a button similar to the one shown in Figure 27.17.

6. Drag the sizing handles to size the button.

7. Drag the button to the location you want it to appear.

8. Drag the yellow diamond near the button to increase or decrease the three-dimensional effect of the button.

Now when you play the slide show, you click the Home button to return to the home slide.

Figure 27.17
You can size or move a button, and even increase or decrease its three-dimensional look.

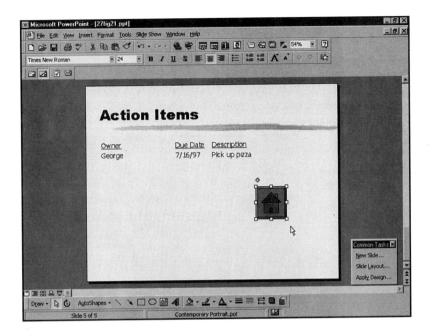

After connecting the computers (see your local computer support person for details on connecting two computers using a serial cable), choose Slide Show, View on Two Screens. PowerPoint displays the dialog box shown in Figure 27.18.

Figure 27.18
You can view your presentation simultaneously on the screens of two interconnected computers.

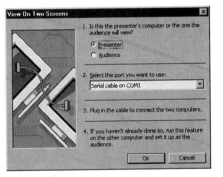

Part
IV
Ch
27

Follow the directions in the dialog box for each of the two connected computers. Then, on the Presenter's computer, run the slide show.

Conferencing with Others Over the Network

If you want to connect several computers, you can use the Presentation Conference feature. For example, you want an entire training classroom to see on their screens the slide show you are presenting. Or perhaps you want to conduct a conference among several colleagues from around the country.

The key requirement for conferencing is that each computer must be connected by a local area network, or by the Internet.

To set up a Presentation Conference, follow these steps if you are an audience member:

1. Choose Tools, Presentation Conference. PowerPoint displays the Presentation Conference Wizard (see Figure 27.19). Choose Next to advance to each of the following steps.

Figure 27.19

The Presentation Conference Wizard helps you set up a conference of online audience members.

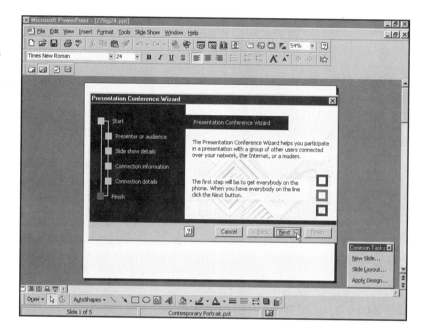

2. Indicate that you are the Audience.
3. You are prompted for the connection type. If you are connected to a local server (Windows NT, NetWare, Windows for Workgroups), you should specify Local Area Network. If you are connecting through the Internet, even if you're also connected to a Local Area Network, choose Dial-in to Internet.
4. Note the name of your computer, which the presenter must know in order to include you in the conference. If you are connecting over the Internet, this name takes the form of an IP number, a network address that consists of four sets of numbers separated by periods. If the connection is via a Local Area Network, the name will be something more recognizable, such as George or Mary.
5. Choose Finish to set yourself up as a member of the conference. Then wait for the presenter to begin the slide show.

If you are the presenter, you follow slightly different steps:

1. Choose Tools, Presentation Conference. PowerPoint displays the Presentation Conference Wizard (refer Figure 27.19). Choose Next to advance to each the following steps.

2. Indicate that you are the Presenter.

3. PowerPoint indicates what slide show setup is currently set. To change the setup, choose Cancel and go to Slide Show, Set Up Show and change the slide show settings. Otherwise continue to the next step.

4. If you are connecting through a modem to an Internet service provider, you must now connect with that service. When you are connected, or if you already are connected to the Internet through a local network, choose Next.

5. Type each participant's Computer name or Internet address (IP number), choosing Add for each person you add.

N O T E The wizard may not report correctly to audience members what their network address is. If conferencing does not work for an audience member, ask her to run WINIPCFG.EXE which reports her correct IP number and other information about her network connection. ▪

6. When the conference list is complete, assure that all conference participants have clicked Finish. Then choose Finish yourself to establish the connections and begin the slide show.

Once the show is running, you control how the presentation advances. You also can use the Meeting Minder or your speaker notes without the audience seeing them. See Figure 27.20 to see the presenter's view of the conference.

Figure 27.20

As the presenter in an on-line conference, you have complete access to speaker notes, the Meeting Minder, and so on.

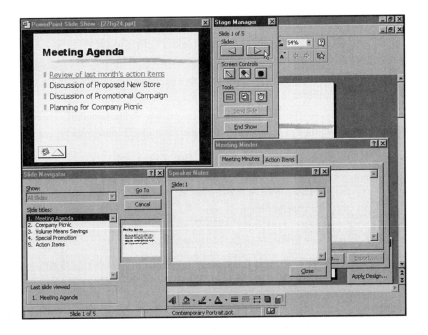

Part

IV

Ch

27

Using the Pack and Go Wizard

Not always do you have the luxury of making your presentation using your own computer. If you want to transport your presentation to be used on another computer, you should ask these questions:

- Does the other computer use Windows 95/98, Windows NT, or an older version of Windows?
- Does the other computer have Office 97 and PowerPoint installed on it?
- What resolution does the other computer's display use?

If the answers to all of the above match your computer's setup exactly, you are very lucky. You can simply copy your show to a floppy disk and run it on the other computer.

If the answers don't match, in many cases you still can take your show with you and play it on the other computer by using the Pack and Go feature.

To prepare your presentation to play on the other computer, follow these steps:

1. Choose File, Pack and Go. PowerPoint displays the Pack and Go Wizard. Each time you choose Next, you advance to the next item on the wizard's list.
2. In the Pick Files to Pack, indicate whether you want to include the active (open) presentation, or specify another file to pack. You can pack more than one file.
3. Choose the destination. Typically you save the packaged file to a floppy disk, but you can also specify a local hard drive, a network drive, or some other location.
4. Under links, choose Include Linked Files if you want to make sure sounds and other clips get packed with the show.
5. If you want to ensure that fonts display properly, whether they're installed on the other computer of not, choose Embed TrueType fonts.
6. If the remote computer does have PowerPoint installed, you need not install the viewer. Usually it's best to include the viewer, just in case, by choosing Viewer for Windows 95/98 or NT.

N O T E   If you intend to play the show on a computer running Windows 3.1, you will need to make a separate viewer disk and follow other special instructions. Click the Help button on the Pack and Go Wizard for details.

7. Choose Finish to pack the show.

If you choose to include the viewer and prepare the show for Windows 95/98 or NT, PowerPoint creates a file with a name that ends in .PPZ. In addition, PowerPoint also places the setup file PNGSETUP.EXE on the destination disk.

To play the show on another computer, copy the two files to the other computer's hard disk, then from the Start menu, choose Run and run the PNGSETUP program, which unpacks, then plays your PowerPoint presentation as it would on your own computer, complete with transitions, sounds, and so on. If you included more than one slide show, upon completion of the first, the second begins, followed by the third, and so on.

Printing a Slide Show

You've just dazzled your audience with an entertaining and motivating presentation. Now you want them to walk away with something that keeps the presentation fresh in their minds.

PowerPoint enables you to print your presentation in a variety of formats.

Printing Handouts

To print a presentation, simply choose File, Print; or press Ctrl+P. PowerPoint displays the Print dialog box (see Figure 27.21). In addition to typical print options, such as destination printer or number of copies, you have the following options:

Figure 27.21
PowerPoint helps you print your presentation in many different formats.

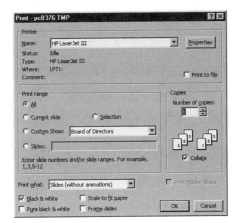

- *All.* Print all of the slides in the presentation.
- *Current.* Print just the currently displayed slide.
- *Selection.* If you are in Slide Sorter view and have one or more slides selected, this option prints just the selected slides.
- *Custom Show.* If you have defined custom shows, you can choose to print only the slides for a given show.
- *Slides.* Specify by slide number the slides you want to print.

You also can specify just what you want to print from your slides. For example, from the Print what drop-down list you can choose:

- *Slides (without animations).* This is the default printout choice.
- *Slides (with animations).* Print a slide's hidden action objects.
- *Handouts.* You can print summary pages, with 2, 3, or 6 slides per page.

Part
IV

Ch
27

■ *Notes Pages*. Print speaker notes for yourself, or even as handouts for your audience.

■ *Outline View*. Print the outline as a summary for yourself or for your audience.

Finally, you can fine tune the output as well:

■ *Black & White*. Optimizes the output of color slides to a black and white printer, or prints in black and white shades on a color printer.

■ *Pure Black & White*. Prints only black and white, with no gray shading.

■ *Scale To Fit Paper*. Adjusts the size of the image to fit your paper, but does not change the shape of the actual presentation slides.

■ *Frame Slides*. If you are in Slide view, this option prints a frame border around the slide.

Printing Overhead Transparencies

You can also print your slides to overhead transparencies in case you don't have a working display computer where you will be making your presentation. You can print them in black and white or in color, depending on the printer and the overhead film you have available.

For example, you can purchase special overhead film that you can use in your laser printer. Choose the best black and white option, and print directly on the overhead film. You can also print overheads using ink jet printers. However, ink jet printers require a special, more expensive film that allows the ink to dry without smearing.

> **CAUTION**
> Don't try to use your laser printer to print on regular transparency film. The heat from the laser printer's fuser roller will melt the film, and can cause serious damage to your laser printer.

In any case, it's not a bad idea to have a set of overhead transparencies as an emergency back up to your computer presentation.

Using Other Output Methods

In addition to printing in PowerPoint, you also can print some of your presentation in Word, publish your slide show to the Web, or send your slides to a slide service to be converted to 35mm slides.

Exporting to Word

To create specially formatted notes or handouts, you can send your presentation to Microsoft Word. Choose File, Send to, Microsoft Word and PowerPoint displays the Write-Up dialog box (see Figure 27.22). Printout options include:

■ Print notes along with the slides, either to the right or below.

■ Print blank lines for audience note taking, either to the right or below the slides.

Figure 27.22
You can create special speaker or audience notes by sending your slide presentation to Microsoft Word.

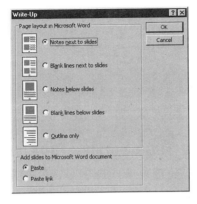

■ Print only the presentation's outline.

You also can export minutes and action items created with the Meeting Minder. Simply choose Tools, Meeting Minder, and in the Meeting Minder dialog box choose Export. Output options include:

■ Post action items to Microsoft Outlook

■ Send meeting minutes and action items to Microsoft Word

If you choose to send the information to Word, you get the document shown in Figure 27.23.

Figure 27.23
Export Meeting Minder information to Microsoft Word for a summary of minutes and action items.

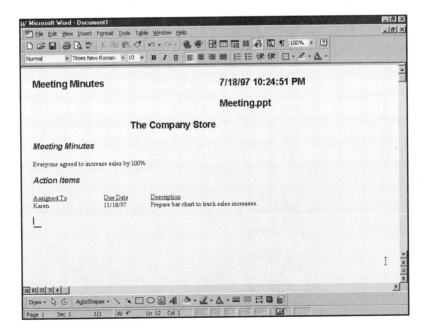

Part
IV
Ch
27

NOTE   Your audience also can take with them the entire presentation, including graphics, media clips, and interactive links. In addition, you can save some natural resources by not providing them with paper printouts.

You accomplish this amazing feat by publishing your presentation to the World Wide Web. You then provide your audience with a Web address (URL), and they use their favorite browser to play your slide show on their own computer.

Exporting a Presentation to a Slide Service Bureau

If you're taking your slide show someplace where they don't even have computers (there are such places still), you can convert your presentation into 35mm slides or crystal clear color overheads.

Some slide service bureaus can take your PowerPoint file and do the rest of the work for you. Often you can send your file by e-mail and within a matter of days (or hours) you receive a package of slides in the mail.

PowerPoint also includes a special wizard that can help you prepare and submit your presentation to Genegraphics, a service bureau that can produce slides, overheads, and full-color handouts. To use this service, you must first install the Genegraphics wizard by performing a custom install of Office 97, and choosing Genegraphics from the PowerPoint options.

To use the Genegraphics wizard, simply choose File, Send to, Genegraphics. You then can choose the exact type of output you need and how quickly you need to have it. You can even contact Genegraphics 24 hours a day, seven days a week. For current information on Genegraphics, visit their Web site at **http://www.genegraphics.com**. ●

P A R T

V

Publisher 97

CHAPTER 28

Using Publisher to Market Your Business

by Elaine Betts

In this chapter

Publisher as a Marketing Tool

In 1794, Benjamin Franklin said, "Build a better mousetrap and the world will beat a path to your door." Two centuries ago that may have worked, but today it's not enough. Today you'd better support good products and services with good marketing. Publisher is a page layout design program with tools to create all your printed and electronic marketing media: fliers, brochures, catalogs, business cards, letterhead, signage, mailers, newsletters, and Web pages. You can even create banners, shelf tags, price tags, gift certificates, ad layouts, and promotional give-aways.

If you're somewhat baffled by the term "page layout program," think of a publication as a wall with many frames. You can fill the frames with a variety of contents, some with text, some with graphics. Unlike Word, you cannot type directly into the document—you must have a frame to hold each element of your design. Frames can hold text, your logo, drawings, and photographs.

To maintain consistency of design in your marketing materials, you should create a pleasing arrangement of frames. You may choose to use the PageWizard, which we'll talk about later in this chapter, to establish your designs because PageWizard simplifies and speeds up production. If you are artistic or already have a company look, you can design your own layouts. No matter which you choose to do, remember that a good design conveys who you are and it sells.

Visit these Web sites to learn more about desktop publishing:

> **http://www.pocketgofer.w1.com/desktop.htm**
>
> **http://desktoppublishing.com/tips.html**

Planning a Publication

You can create an entire suite of marketing materials with Publisher. If you don't already have a "corporate identity," here's your chance to develop one and use it throughout all your marketing and business operations materials. You can have business cards, letterhead and envelopes, brochures, signage, table tents, business forms, even a Web page, all with distinctive design that conveys the tone of your business. Whether your business is button-down collar, blue ink conservative, or blue jeans and sunglasses casual, consistent design within each of your publications reinforces your business image and promotes customer recognition. What you do, your logo, and your target market dictate the look and content of your publications and only you can determine that. You will, however, discover that as you become more familiar with Publisher, you will want and can produce more and more materials.

You should consider a series of questions before you get down to actually working with your publication. This is true if you choose to start a publication from the PageWizard or from a blank document to create your own layout.

- What kind of document do you want? A single or multiple page publication? For example, a folded brochure or a newsletter with varying numbers of pages?

- What size will the final publication be? Do you want it portrait (tall) or landscape (wide)? Do you want each page printed on a separate sheet? Single-sided or double-sided? Folded or bound?

- Will it be in color or black and white? If it is to be color, will it be spot color, those pre-mixed inks based on a color matching system such as Pantone, or the more pricey Cyan, Magenta, Yellow, and Black (CMYK) separated colors?

- What size and kind of paper will you print on? The paper is determined by your decisions about size, orientation, color or black and white, and, of course, your budget.

- How many copies do you plan to produce at one print run? Whereas this may seem like the cart before the horse, this decision has a profound effect on all your other decisions.

- What method of outputting your publication do you plan to use? A print house that produces volumes of copies and has sophisticated printing presses? A color or black and white copy machine? Your desktop printer? Huge numbers of copies are less costly when you use a service bureau or print house. A smaller number of copies may be more economical to produce in your own office.

When all these concerns are resolved, it's time to start using Publisher.

Introduction to Publisher

If you have just installed Publisher and are opening it for the very first time, you see the Introduction to Publisher screen (see Figure 28.1). This is a series of concise and informative screens covering the principles of page layout and the tools available in Publisher.

There are unique terms used in Publisher, for instance, the things you produce in Publisher are called "publications," not documents. The content of publications, each body of text or graphic, is held in a container called a "frame."

▶ **See** "Creating Frames for Content in a Publication," **page 622**

Although it may not be immediately evident, every publication has, by default, two layers: a Background and a Foreground layer. You perform most of your design tasks on the Foreground layer, but a few things require switching to the Background layer.

If you prefer to bypass the Introduction for now, click the Cancel button. You can reopen the Introduction at any time by choosing Help, Introduction to Publisher.

Thereafter, each time you open Publisher, the PageWizard appears. It has icons representing a variety of publication templates. Before working on a specific publication, it helps to familiarize yourself with the Publisher window. Click the Cancel button at the lower right of the PageWizard window to close it. A blank publication is displayed in the Publisher window (see Figure 28.2).

Part V
Ch 28

Figure 28.1

Tour through the Introduction screens for a brief look at Publisher's tools and techniques.

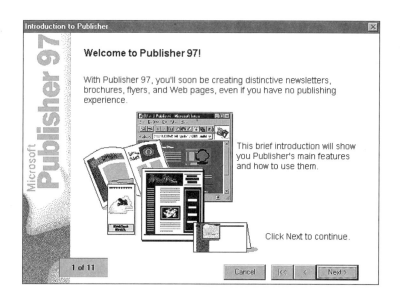

Figure 28.2

This blank publication is the surface on which you create and position frames to hold text and graphic objects.

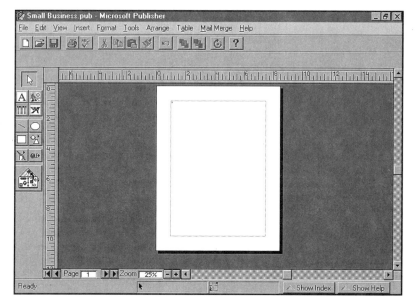

NOTE You can have only one publication open at a time but you might want to work on two publications simultaneously. You can. Simply open a second copy of Publisher using the Start button in the Windows taskbar. In the second copy of Publisher, open the other publication you want to use. With resized windows, you can see both publications at once and compare, Copy and Paste between them. ■

Button	Name	Task
	Undo/Redo	Toggles between reversing and reapplying your last action.
	Bring to Front	Elevates an item to the topmost position in a tack of multiple layers.
	Send to Back	Places an item at the bottom of a stack of multiple layers.
	Rotate	Rotates a page element.
	Help	Opens the Help files.

Moving Around in a Publication

Working in a page layout publication is a bit different from working in most other kinds of documents. You are constantly moving from one place on the page to another, zooming in for a closer look, making adjustments and zooming out to assess the overall effect. A little tweak here, a little tweak there, and so it goes.

If you've used Word, you're probably familiar with the Page Up and Page Down keys. Unlike Word, however, in Publisher these keys move only up or down in a single publication page—the one you are viewing onscreen. If you are working on a multiple page publication, you can move from page to page using the Status Line tools. Each of the tools available in Publisher Status Line is described in Table 28.3.

You can view two pages, side-by-side if you choose View, Two Page Spread.

Table 28.3   The Status Line

Button	Name	Function
	First page	Moves to the first page of your publication.
	Previous Page	Moves to the page before the page currently onscreen.
Page 1	Change Page	Opens the Go To Page dialog where you enter the page number of the page you want to view.
	Next Page	Moves to the page following the page currently onscreen.
	Last Page	Moves to the final page of your publication.

Part

V

Ch

28

If you click the Last Page button while viewing the final page of your publication, Publisher offers to insert another page. If your click was just a mistake, you can decline the offer by clicking the Cancel button in the dialog box.

Button	Name	Function
Zoom 33%	Select Zoom Mode	Allows you to choose up to 400% or Full Page, which fits the entire page into the size of your window.
[−]	Zoom Out	Reduces the percentage of your view to show more of the page onscreen. Repeated clicks shrink the view further.
[+]	Zoom In	Increases the percentage of your view to scrutinize details. Repeated clicks further increase the magnification.

 Use the F9 key to toggle between your current percentage view and 100%. This is especially helpful when you are working at a very large magnification making highly refined adjustments and want to see the effect of your adjustments at actual size.

Button	Name	Function
[◄]	Left Horizontal Scroll Bar Arrow	Slides the view of your page to the left.
[►]	Right Horizontal Scroll Bar Arrow	Slides the view of your page to the right.
[▲]	Up Vertical Scroll Bar Arrow	Slides the view of your page toward the top of the window.
[▼]	Down Vertical Scroll Bar Arrow	Slides the view of your page toward the bottom of the window.

 You can also scroll your publication page by positioning the pointer on the little box in either Scroll Bar, depressing the mouse and dragging the box.

Now that you've reviewed these tools, you need to learn only two more basic skills before actually getting down to creating a publication. Both of them require navigational skill.

N O T E   If you have an IntelliMouse, you can use the Wheel button to zoom in and out. For example, if you roll the Wheel button up, the zoom percentage changes from 33% to 50% to 66%. When you roll the button down, the magnification decreases.   ▣

Creating Publications

When you start a publication, you have some idea of the sort of publication you want. It may be a promotional postcard, a brochure, a company newsletter, a Web site, or any of the many other creative possibilities Publisher can produce. There are two approaches to beginning a publication, using the PageWizard, or starting with a Blank Publication.

Using the PageWizard

Are you feeling a bit tentative about creating a publication? Do you have an idea of what you want to create but are unsure of where to begin? If time is staring you in the face and demanding output NOW, then PageWizard is for you. It's also a perfect place to start learning the program.

PageWizard is a collection of predesigned templates for producing just about any marketing material a small business could ever need. It also has business forms, labels for everything from bulk mailings to audio and video cassettes, résumé designs, and origami and paper airplanes for those days when the pressure of juggling the demands of owning your own business seem overwhelming. Just touring through the array of available templates is a source of inspiration.

PageWizard opens automatically each time you start Publisher. If you already have the program open and running, you can access PageWizard by choosing File, Create New Publication.

If it's not already showing, click the PageWizard tab at the top of the window to access the display of generic template icons (see Figure 28.4). Select any one that you want to use and click the OK button near the bottom of the screen.

For discussion purposes, let's look at Business Forms. After you click OK, your decision making is narrowed in the next screen which has a list of more specific kinds of business forms. Click the kind of form you want to create. We'll use the Invoice. As you click through the PageWizard, you make choices, such as the one shown in Figure 28.5.

Click the Next button to move to the next screen and select from a series of predesigned Invoice forms. In many instances, more choices are available than can be shown in one screen; so, if the word "More" appears by the arrows at the right of the screen, and they become active, click the arrows to see the rest of the choices. As you see in Figure 28.6, there are many styles to choose from.

Part
V

Ch
28

Figure 28.4

Each of these icons leads you to a variety of designs targeted to your specific needs and to the tone of your business.

Figure 28.5

Your choice of form type here dictates the design options available in following screens.

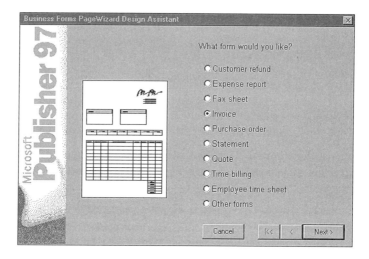

The next screen offers additional elements you can apply to the basic design. If you opt for a picture, Publisher inserts a placeholder graphic that you can replace later with something you prefer, perhaps your logo. As you see in Figure 28.7, you can also choose to add your Company initials, or have no graphic element at all.

Figure 28.6

Many styles are available to suit the tone of almost any business, from conservative to contemporary to retro.

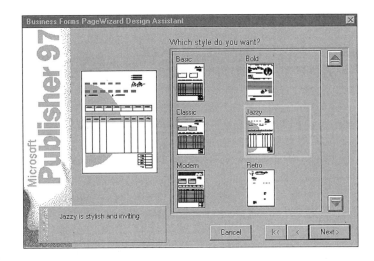

Figure 28.7

As you click one of these choices, a brief description of the result appears below the list of choices.

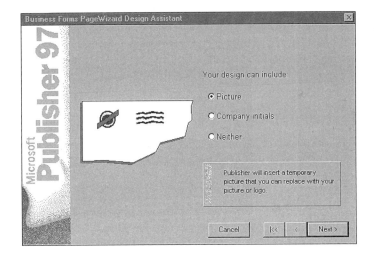

Now that you've decided on the overall look of your invoice, you can select the page orientation for your design, vertical (Portrait) or horizontal (Landscape), in the next screen. After that, it's time to decide whether you want your company name and address automatically entered on the invoice. If you choose "Yes," select the address type and enter the specific information in the text boxes in the next screen (see Figure 28.8). You don't need to enter this information for later PageWizards. Publisher remembers and automatically re-enters this information in other template designs you use.

Part
V

Ch
28

Figure 28.8

You can leave lines blank in the address text box.

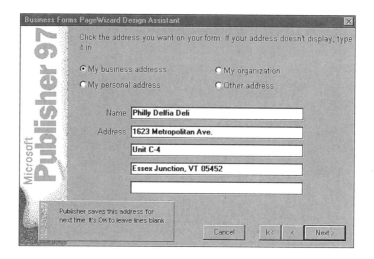

Each template has different options specific to the template you are using. In the invoice form, you can request to include a remittance stub in your design (or not to have one), to create a space for customer ID and other business-related numbers, if you use them. If your company is international, you can even design your invoice to use language conventions other than English.

TROUBLESHOOTING

I forgot to add something I wanted on one of the screens. How hard is it to fix this? If you make a mistake, or want to review your choices before finishing the PageWizard screens, use the buttons at the bottom of each screen to navigate forward and backward through the screens, making changes.

Finally, click the Create It! button. After a moment during which all the choices you've made are assembled, the PageWizard Design Assistant window opens (see Figure 28.9).

TROUBLESHOOTING

I accidentally chose the wrong kind of publication in the PageWizard. Am I stuck with it? No. You can stop the development process in PageWizard at any time. Click the Cancel button at the bottom of any screen. If, by chance, you have gone through all the screens, and clicked the Finish button, you can start a new publication, and not save the one you decided against. Presuming you haven't saved it, Publisher will ask if you want to save it before starting a new publication. Just say no.

It's a good idea to click "Yes" in response to Design Assistant's query, "Do you want step-by-step help for adding your own text and pictures?" Publisher Help files open to the right of your publication (see Figure 28.10). You can perform any of the instructions with the Help files open, so, go ahead, click a topic and learn about specific tasks.

Figure 28.9
Design Assistant opens to further simplify setting up print options and to open Publisher Help files that assist you in completing your invoice publication.

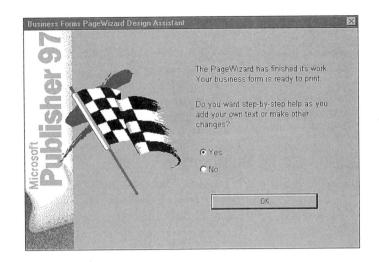

Figure 28.10
Like a Web page hyperlink, when you have clicked on a topic, the arrow to the left of the clicked topic changes color to indicate you've read that information.

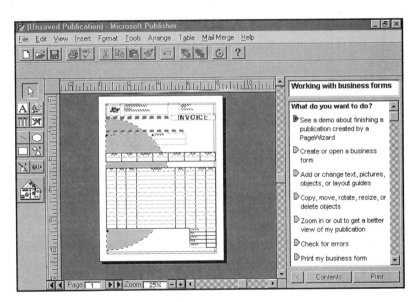

If you don't want the Help files open right now, click the Hide Help button in the Status Bar to close it. You can always reopen this file by clicking the Show Index or Show Help button.

This is but a brief glimpse at Help available in Publisher 97. The folks at Microsoft suspect that most people don't read their documentation, so they provide a wealth of onscreen help files. So much, in fact, that a full chapter about Help appears later in this book.

Part
V

Ch
28

TROUBLESHOOTING

After I finished creating a PageWizard publication, I find I don't want some of the things that Publisher put in it. Can I change these? Indeed, you can. Because everything in a publication is held inside a frame, click on the frame you want removed or changed. You can either delete a frame, or edit the contents of any frame on any page of your publication, at any time that suits you.

Starting with a Blank Publication

If you're a little intimidated by the idea of designing your own publications, you can always use the PageWizard as the foundation for your publications, then make the publication "your own" by revising it to suit your design preferences and particular needs. Selecting and replacing predesigned elements is a breeze, because every component on a page is held in a frame.

▶ **See** "Working with Frames," **page 622**

If you're artistically inclined and adventurous, you can also start from scratch and build your own publications. Who knows better than you what you need and like?

▶ **See** "Planning a Publication," **page 608**

It never hurts to make a rough paper-and-pencil sketch of your page design before you begin. Planning your publication *is* necessary because you need to be prepared to make some choices as soon as you start to design your own materials.

If you are just starting up Publisher, the first thing you see is the Microsoft Publisher 97 tabbed dialog box. If you already have Publisher open, choose File, Create New Publication to access this screen (see Figure 28.11).

Figure 28.11
Ten suggested formats are offered as well as a custom page option for beginning with a blank page.

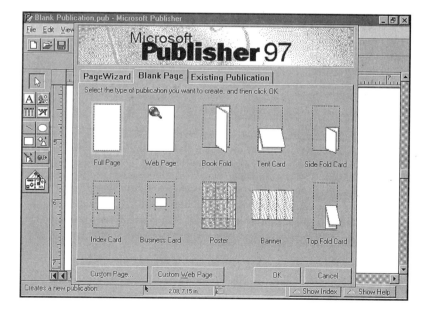

Follow these steps to begin creating your own publication:

1. If it is not on top of the stack of tabs, click the Blank Page tab.
2. Make a selection from among the publication types by clicking the appropriate icon, or the Custom Page button at the bottom of the dialog box.

If you choose a custom page, the next step is to click your choices in the Page Setup dialog box (see Figure 28.12). If, as you work on your publication, you want to change the choices you made in this dialog box, you can re-access the dialog box by choosing File, Page Setup.

Figure 28.12
You will use this dialog box often if you produce newsletters, brochures, and flyers.

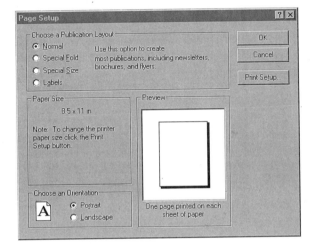

3. Choose among the options for Page Layout and Orientation by clicking the option buttons next to your choice. A preview of the selected options appears in the Preview box at the right side of the dialog box.
4. Set your printing options. This is very important because it can affect the final output. If you are planning to send your work out to be printed, choose File, Outside Print Setup, to choose a composition printer, then choose File, Print Setup to establish your Proof Print Setup.

▶ **See** "Outputting Publisher Publications," **page 628**

N O T E The term "composition printer" refers to the printing device used by a professional print house. You need only be concerned with this if you are planning to have your publication printed professionally. That being the case, as you work with your publication, you will make a surprising number of test prints on your desktop printer. Your desktop printer is the "proof printer." ■

CAUTION
Setting your printer at the beginning of your design process is critical because a change of printer setup can cause unexpected adjustments to your publication layout.

5. When all your decisions are made, choose OK to close the dialog box and display your blank page in the Publisher window.

TROUBLESHOOTING

What do I do if I want to change my Proof Printer? This is easy, and has no effect on your Outside Print Setup. Just return to the Print Setup dialog box, using the File, Print Setup. Select a different printer listed in the Name drop-down menu there, and choose OK.

My print house just called and gave me a quote on full color printing. I had no idea! Can I change my publication to black and white, or to spot color? Sure. Choose File, Outside Print Setup. If you want Black, White, and Shades of Gray, click that radio button. If you've decided to use Spot Color, you'll also need to choose the one (or two) colors you want to use. These are under Select Spot Colors in the Outside Print Setup dialog box.

Creating Frames for Content in a Publication

Whether you begin a publication using the PageWizard or start with a Blank Page publication, you're going to be working with frames and their contents. You may decide to add elements to a publication created with the PageWizard. That means adding frames, because everything in a publication is contained within a frame. You're going to fill each frame with either text or a graphic.

Working with Frames

Frames are what allow you to create an arrangement of text and graphics that look completely different from word processing documents.

A few things don't require you to draw a frame first and then fill it. Things you draw using the Publisher toolbar line tool, oval tool, box tool, and custom shapes tool have a frame after they are created, although the surrounding frame is not apparent until the object is selected. The eight handles that appear on the perimeter of a drawn object you click indicate the frame boundaries.

Each inserted object, as opposed to a drawn object, is inserted in your publication with its own frame, and can be moved or resized the same as all frames.

▶ **See** "Inserting a Frame," **page 623**

Because you'll be using the Publisher toolbar to work with frames, let's take a look at those buttons and what they do. The toolbar appears to the left of the publication window, and Table 28.4 describes the buttons.

Table 28.4 The Publisher Toolbar

Button	Name	Function
	Pointer	Moves frames or drawn objects. Click this button to reactivate the Pointer tool after using one of the other tools.
	Picture	Creates a graphic frame.
	Text Frame	Creates a text frame.
	Table Frame	Creates a table frame.
	WordArt	Creates a frame and opens the helper application, WordArt.
	Line	Creates lines.
	Oval	Creates ovals and circles.
	Box	Creates rectangles.
	Custom Shapes	Accesses a display of shapes to draw. Click a shape to select the one you want to draw.
	PageWizards	Provides access to the Design Assistant in order to create a few of the commonly used publications: Calendar, Ad, Coupon, and Logo.
	Insert Object	Creates a frame that holds any of a vast array of objects including an icon representing linked or embedded objects.
	Design Gallery	Accesses a huge collection of predesigned graphic elements.

TIP To create perfectly symmetrical circles and squares, hold down the Shift key while dragging the Oval or Box tool with your mouse pointer.

Inserting a Frame   When you use the Insert Object tool in the Publisher toolbar, or make a selection from the Insert menu, you do not need to create a frame first. The frame for inserted objects, Clip Art, and Picture files is automatically generated when the item is imported. Importing or creating text, tables, or graphics within Publisher, however, is a different matter. For these page elements, you must create frames using the appropriate tool and then fill the frame.

You can create an empty frame in two ways, with a click, or by dragging the size you want.

■ *Click.* In the Publisher toolbar, select the specific frame creation tool for the contents you want inside the frame, text, picture, or table. Click the page where you want to position the frame. A perfectly square frame is created. As you move the mouse along the perimeter of the frame, the shape of the cursor changes. In some positions, it is a Move pointer, and in others, the Resize pointer (see Figure 28.13).

Figure 28.13

The Move pointer lets you reposition the frame.

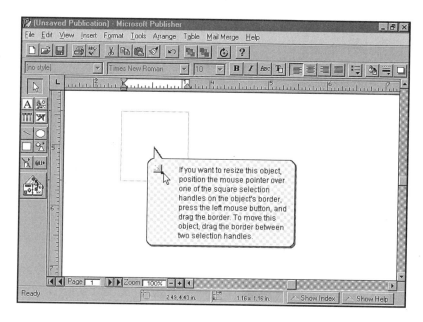

■ *Drag.* Select the specific frame creation tool for the contents you want inside the frame, text, picture, or table. Position the mouse pointer on the page (now in the shape of a crosshair) at the place where you want a frame. Hold down the mouse button, and drag diagonally to create the frame. Release the mouse button when you have the size frame you want.

You can resize any frame using one of the eight handles that appear on the perimeter of a selected frame. To select a frame, click it with the Pointer tool. You can reposition a frame using the Move pointer (refer to Figure 28.13), or resize it with the Resize pointer that appears when your Pointer is over a handle.

Resizing or Reposition a Frame   To maintain the proportions of a frame you are resizing using a corner handle, press the Shift key before you click the mouse on the frame's corner handle and continue holding down the Shift key until you have dragged the frame to the size you want. Release the mouse button first, then the Shift key.

To resize a frame from the center, press the Control key before you click the mouse button and continue holding it as you drag any handle. Release the mouse button first, then the Control key. The frame is resized, but the center of the frame remains in its original position.

If you press both Shift and Control before dragging, you maintain the frame's proportions and resize it from the center.

TROUBLESHOOTING

If I resize a frame and don't like its new size, how do I go back to the way it was? The all powerful Undo button in the Standard toolbar saves the day, *if* you use it immediately after resizing. Publisher has only one level of Undo!

When I resized a frame holding a graphic, the picture was distorted. How did this happen? Chances are, you resized using a side handle rather than a corner handle. If resizing was your last action, you can use Undo to restore the frame to its original proportions, then try again. Remember, you can only Undo your most recent action.

Sometimes you decide that you don't want a frame that you've created. If the frame is still empty and not selected, click it and use the Delete or Backspace key to remove it. If you have already filled the frame, click the frame to select it, then click the Cut button in the Standard toolbar.

If you want to move a frame, move the Pointer tool to an edge of the frame (*not* a handle), click and drag the frame to a new position. The pointer changes to a little moving van when the Pointer is in position for dragging a frame (see Figure 28.14). Release the mouse button when the frame is in the position you want.

Figure 28.14
Repositioning with the Move pointer does not affect the size of the frame.

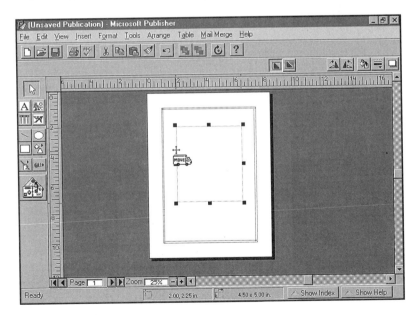

You can rotate any frame. Click the frame to select it, hold down the Alt key, and position the pointer over one of the corner handles. Click the left mouse button and continue holding down the mouse button until two arrows circle the handle, then drag either clockwise or counterclockwise. When you achieve the rotation you want, release the mouse button.

Using Grids, Guides, and Rulers for Positioning

Marketing materials need to be as polished and professional as possible because they represent you and your business. The alignment and spatial relationship between frames is one of the things you can do to assure that your publications don't look haphazard. Use nonprinting grids, guide lines, and the rulers as positioning helpers.

Grids appear in the same place on every page in a publication. This maintains consistent placement of elements in the publication. Guides are used on specific pages to position frames. The rulers allow you to position guides by the numbers.

You can temporarily hide grids and guides by choosing View, Hide Boundaries, and Guides. To hide rulers, choose View, Toolbars and Rulers and click the check mark next to Rulers. To again display grids, guides or rulers, repeat the above process.

 To simplify your designing chores, and assure that things on your pages align properly, you can create what amounts to a magnetic field for Guides. This causes frames you are moving to pop into an exact position established by Guides. Choose Tools, Snap to Guidelines. If you no longer need or want the magnetic assistance, return to the Tools menu, and deselect Snap to Guidelines.

Surrounding the print area, all pages in a publication have a nonprinting double line (one pink, one blue). These are the Margin Guides and are placed according to choices you make in the Page Setup dialog box that was covered earlier in this chapter that covers "Starting with a Blank Publication."

▶ **See** also "Outputting Publisher Publications," **page 628**

Grids

Grids are especially useful in multi-page publications. They help you maintain consistent placement of elements on each page. Unlike guides, grids appear on every page of your layout. You can have horizontal or vertical grid lines, or both. The spacing of grid lines is consistent, like graph paper.

To set up grids, choose Arrange, Layout Guides. A dialog box appears and you set the Margin and Grid Guides. Margin and Grid Guides reside on the bottom layer of every publication and define the print area of your pages. You can establish any number of Grid Guides for columns and/or rows (see Figure 28.15).

Figure 28.15
In the Preview and on your publication, Margin Guides are pink and Grid Guides are blue. These colored lines do not print.

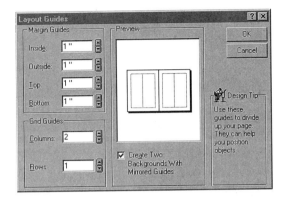

 To adjust the placement of grids, choose View, Go to Background. This instructs Publisher that you want to adjust the grid line. Hold down the Shift key and position the pointer on a grid line you want to move. When the pointer changes to the Adjust cursor, drag the grid line to a new position.

To return to working on frames in your page layout, choose View, Go to Foreground.

Guides

You can also use nonprinting guides to help you accurately position frames on publication pages. Publisher's rulers have a hidden supply of guide lines. To use a ruler guide, position the pointer on either the horizontal or vertical ruler, hold down the Shift key and drag a guideline from the ruler to the place you want it.

 As you drag out a guide, notice the dotted red line that runs across the screen and into the ruler. The ruler has a black line in it that indicates the guide's position. You can drag a guide and watch the ruler to accurately place your guidelines.

Removing or Repositioning Guides   To remove or reposition a guide, move the pointer over the guide line, hold down the mouse button until the cursor becomes a two-headed arrow, the Adjust cursor. Continue holding the mouse button and drag to reposition the guide, or drag it back into its "home ruler" for use later.

Rulers

Rulers usually reside on the left and top perimeters of the publication area in the Publisher Window, but they don't have to stay there. You can move either ruler into the publication area for a positioning reference closer to where you are working in a publication page. Move the pointer to the edge of a ruler. When the shape changes to a double-headed arrow, press and hold down the mouse button and drag the ruler onto the publication page. Release the mouse button when you have it where you want it. Moving the rulers does *not* reset the zero point to a different spot on your page. Zero is always the uppermost, left corner of the page.

If you prefer, you can move both rulers at once. Position the pointer at the intersection of the rulers in the upper, left corner of the publication area. Position the pointer at the intersection of vertical and horizontal rulers, hold down the mouse button, and drag both rulers into position simultaneously.

To return the rulers to their home position or reposition them, repeat this process.

N O T E   If you reposition rulers in one view magnification, say 25%, and then change magnification, the rulers remain in the same position relative to the screen, not the page. ▨

Outputting Publisher Publications

The whole reason for creating publications is to communicate with your customers, clients, or colleagues. There are several ways to get your message to your audience. Some publications may be delivered electronically. Most publications you create will be printed, either in-house, at a service bureau, or outsourced to a print house. You can establish a method for outputting at the initial stage of creating a publication, or after the job is completed.

N O T E   Publisher does not have a page preview command because the reason for Publisher's existence is to design how pages look when you are finished. What you see onscreen is what you get for final output. ▨

Sending a Publication via E-mail

One of the ways to deliver your marketing materials electronically is via e-mail. Naturally, you must have a modem and either an Internet account, or one of the online services, such as Microsoft Network, CompuServe, or America Online.

When you're all set up with Internet access, it remains only to choose File, Send, and select the information service you want to use to deliver your publication. (See Figure 28.16.)

Figure 28.16
Before you can send a publication via e-mail, you need to tell Publisher which of your information services to use.

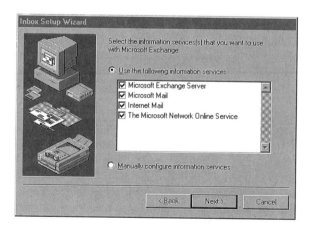

When you select your information service, you activate the Inbox Setup Wizard. Click through the screens, making the appropriate choices or entering text where required, and click the Finish button.

An icon of your publication is displayed in the New Message window of Microsoft Exchange, and your ready to send it to any or all of the clients in your Address Book.

▶ **See** "Establishing a Dial-Up Connection," **page 827**

▶ **See** "Delivering a Publication via E-mail," **page 703**

▶ **See** "Composing E-mail," **page 740**

Outputting a Web Site Publication

There is no marketing medium hotter than the Word Wide Web. It's cost effective and simple to accomplish in Publisher. ISPs (Internet Service Providers), the folks who store your Web Site and make it accessible to Web surfers, typically charge a very reasonable monthly fee to host multiple page sites. Some ISPs even offer single page sites for free to people who pay for and use their other services, such as e-mail. The search robots that locate and catalogue Web Sites, such as Yahoo! and AltaVista, charge nothing at all to list your site in their databases. Matter of fact, they locate you within the first week that you upload your files.

If you haven't used a site that catalogues other Web sites, point your browser to:

http://www.Yahoo.com or **http://www.altavista.com**

These sites offer complete instructions online for locating just about anything or anybody on the Web.

You have several options for creating a publication destined for the Web. You can start from the PageWizard, and create a Web Site. You can begin with a Web Page found among the Blank Page templates, or you can convert an existing publication by choosing File, Create Web Site from Current Publication.

▶ **See** "Using the PageWizard," **page 615**

▶ **See** "Starting with a Blank Publication," **page 620**

▶ **See** "Converting a Publication to a Web Site," **page 703**

Printing the Publication

If you want to use the printer on your desktop, but have created a publication larger than your printer is capable of handling, you can tile the printing process and assemble the tiles after printing.

N O T E If you have a spiffy, color printer in your office, be sure you read and understand all the documentation before depending on it to produce the results you want. Color is the bugaboo of all publications. Each device, your monitor, and the printer, must be calibrated to produce publications that look as close to alike as possible, onscreen and on paper. Check your mail order software catalogs for calibration software; or, the current computer magazines may have ads or articles about calibration. ▪

Part

V

Ch

28

Printer Resolution

With the exception of impact printers, all printing devices, whether a desktop printer or a fancy web press, use dots of ink to print. The greater the number of ink dots per inch, the smaller the dots. The smaller the dots, the more detailed the print. Resolution is measured in dots per inch (dpi). Highly refined publications, such as art books, are printed at 12000 dpi and up! That's why they cost so much. Publisher supports full-color printing up to 600 dpi, grayscale (varying amounts of black ink), and black and white.

Don't be surprised if the proof prints or final output prints made on your desktop printer are less refined than output from a professional print house. You probably are using a much lower resolution and that makes your publication look a little fuzzy.

Using an Outside Print Service

Many of the publications you create will be printed on a standard size paper, then cut to the dimensions you specified as you created the publication. These, obviously, need to be sent out to a print house. Very large pages, such as posters, need that professional touch, too.

Publications you plan to send out can be set up for particular printing devices after the file arrives at the print house or service bureau, but you may find that fonts and margins do some odd transformations.

The very best advice in the publication world is to *call your printer sales representative before you begin a publication.* These folks can help you make the right decisions and avert costly delays, to say nothing of the money you have to spend to get the printer to set things up. They often can direct you to the proper printer driver you need for their printing devices. Some even sell, rather reasonably, color matching kits to assure you get what you had in mind when you created your publication.

One handy feature in Publisher that can smooth the printing process is a checklist that guides you toward successful output from your print house. It helps you with some questions that should be asked of the printer, and specific concerns that should be resolved before you cast your publication to the winds of Fate. The Outside Printing Checklist is available in the final screen of the Outside Print Setup dialog box.

 Many service bureaus, such as Kinko's Copies, have excellent color copy machines. If budget is a concern, investigate their printing and duplicating options. They also have a few bindings you may want to use for multi-page publications.

Printing an Information Sheet

Finally, give those folks all the help you can. When you choose File, Print InfoSheet, you produce a hard copy of specifications that, quite possibly, only printers understand. Font usage information, information about the colors used in the publication, resolution settings, what proof printer you used, and other invaluable information are on this page. *Don't send out a publication file for printing without this.*

TROUBLESHOOTING

Why do my publications look awful when I print them? About a zillion reasons can cause this to happen, but a most helpful section of the Publisher Help files is available that may resolve the problem. You can tap into this information bank every time you print by choosing Tools, Options and then click to put a check mark next to Print with Print Troubleshooter. The Help file opens every time you initiate a print command.

CHAPTER 29

Formatting Publisher Pages and Text

by Elaine Betts

In this chapter

Using Special Papers

Using special papers is a simple and effective way to customize the look of your publications. A "special" paper may mean printing your publication on a patterned paper, folding your publication in a particular way, or using a non-standard size of paper stock, such as an envelope, labels, a poster or a banner.

> **CAUTION**
>
> You need to determine your output device before deciding on the kind of special paper you want to use. Printing capabilities always depend on the device you are using to do the printing.

Your desktop printer has certain mechanical limitations, such as paper size and margin minimums. Some things you want to accomplish may not be possible, such as printing a band that runs off the edge of the paper. Although you can print an extra large publication on standard size paper by tiling it so that only a portion of the whole prints on a single sheet of paper, you will have to do some additional cutting and pasting to assemble the printed tiles. If you want a publication smaller than the paper your printer can accommodate, you'll need to trim off the excess paper from each copy you print.

If you plan to use an outside printer, there are very few limitations on paper size and graphic techniques, other than your budget, of course. Print houses can easily trim down a small publication or print a large publication on large paper stock. Remember, it is always best to speak with those who will be doing your outside print job *before* you begin creating a publication, to be certain they can accommodate your design wishes.

Choosing a Special Fold

Some special folds require that you set up your pages in Landscape (wide) orientation, others require Portrait (tall) orientation. To choose a special fold:

1. As you begin a new publication using File, Create New Publication, and click the Blank Page tab, you see every paper size option available in Publisher, including a Custom Page option you can fold any way you like (see Figure 29.1). Click one of the predesigned options.

2. Next, click the Custom Page button and you have some additional decisions to make (see Figure 29.2). Each set of choices displays a preview in the right side of the Page Setup dialog box.

3. Notice also the button for Print Setup. Click it to select a printer if your computer has more than one printer driver installed (see Figure 29.3).

TROUBLESHOOTING

What if I chose the wrong fold? Choose File, Page Setup to re-open the series of dialog boxes that let you set Special Folds.

What if I forgot to set the publication orientation? Again, Choose File, Page Setup to click the Portrait or Landscape option button.

I forgot to set the print orientation. Now what? This time, choose File, Print Setup and click the Portrait or Landscape option button, although you may discover that Publisher already set it correctly for you.

Figure 29.1
You can choose from four predesigned options for folded paper publications and a Custom Page for creating folds not shown, such as a three fold brochure.

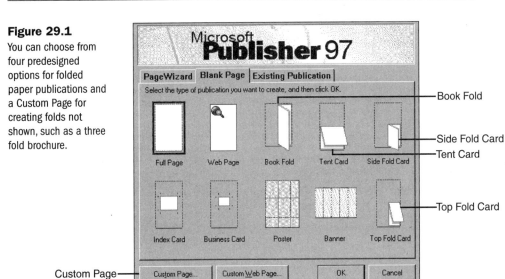

Book Fold

Side Fold Card

Tent Card

Top Fold Card

Custom Page

Figure 29.2
You need to select the layout, size, and orientation for your publication.

Publication Layout

Publication Size

Portrait/Landscape

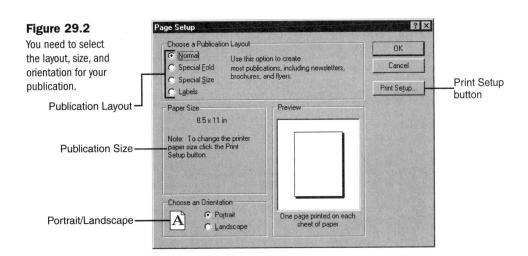

Print Setup button

Creating a Custom Fold

In your overall marketing plan, you may decide to create a publication that is uniquely folded, a tri-fold brochure, a mailer, or a menu. How do you start?

Figure 29.3

If your printer can handle unusual sizes of paper, select User-Defined in the Print Setup Dialog box.

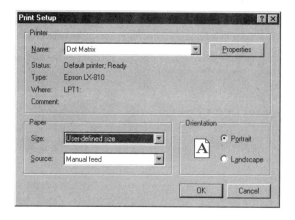

1. Click the Custom Page button at the bottom of the Blank Page dialog box.

2. Click the Special Size option button in the Page Setup dialog box. If you want, you can change the paper size under Choose a Publication Size, and establish the design orientation as Landscape or Portrait. Be sure to check the print orientation in the Print Setup, as well.

3. To define where you want special Custom Folds to be, choose View, Go to Background. (When you are in the Background layer, you can redefine the predefined page margins.)

N O T E   Working in the Background layer to establish Custom Folds means two things: you can't accidentally move the positions of the fold lines while designing other components of your publication, and you need to return to the Background layer if you want to remove these fold lines before final output. ▧

4. Choose Arrange, Layout Guides, and set Margin Guides to zero or any other dimension you prefer. (If you plan to output on your desktop printer, remember, you need enough margin for the paper to feed through the printer.) Leave the Grid Guides set to at least 1 for Columns and Rows.

5. Use ruler guides in the Background layer of your publication to indicate fold lines parallel to the rulers, or draw lines or a box to establish custom folds if you plan to use a folding pattern that is not parallel to the rulers (see Figure 29.4).

▶ **See** "Using the Standard Toolbar Buttons," **page 612**

▶ **See** "Adding and Formatting Objects," **page 669**

▶ **See** "Choosing a Special Size Paper," **page 637**

▶ **See** "Drawing Shapes," **page 671**

▶ **See** "Rotating Objects," **page 683**

▶ **See** "Working in the Background Layer," **page 639**

Figure 29.4

In this example of Custom Folds, we have set up a square publication with corner folds. It uses a Special Size paper, with a light colored border, applied to a square box that is rotated 45 degrees.

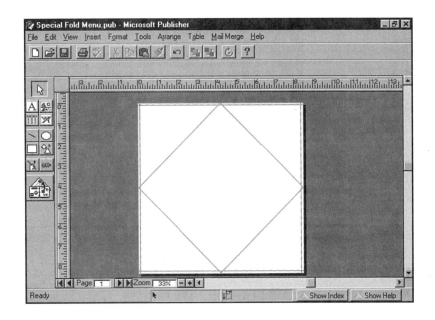

Choosing a Special Size Paper

Posters, banners, business cards, index cards, envelopes, and some custom publications you design, need to be printed on a special size paper or printed on standard stock and cut to size (see Figure 29.5).

Figure 29.5

As you see, there is also an option for defining a Blank Page publication as a Web Page, an Index Card, Business Card, Poster, or Banner.

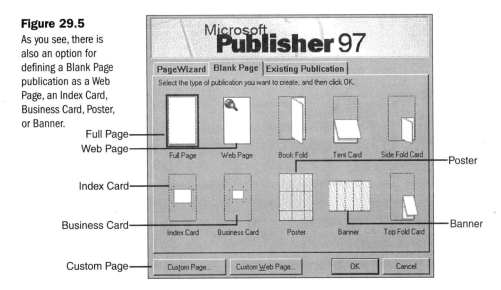

Because Web Pages are viewed on computer monitors, naturally, the size of the publication is different from paper based publications.

▶ **See** "Choosing a Special Fold," **page 634**

▶ **See** "Creating a Custom Fold," **page 635**

▶ **See** "Converting a Publication to a Web Site," **page 703**

If want to print on a nonstandard size paper stock, you can select User-defined paper in the Print Setup dialog box. When you return to the Page Setup dialog box, Printer Sheet Size appears in the box below Choose a Publication Size. Enter the dimensions of the paper (see Figure 29.6).

Figure 29.6

With the Special Size option selected, you need to enter the width and height of the paper as well as the orientation.

Special Size

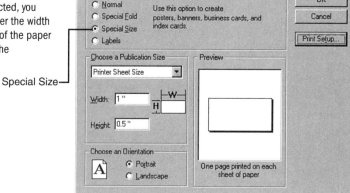

 TIP   Save a tree! Check with your outside printer representative to see what specific size paper stock your Special Size publication requires. Often you can save money by adjusting your publication ever so slightly to use paper stock more efficiently.

Creating Labels

Although the option to create labels does *not* appear in the Blank Page dialog box, it does appear if you click the Custom Page button at the bottom of the Labels dialog box. This opens the Page Setup dialog box. Click the Labels option button and scroll through the labels available in Publisher (see Figure 29.7).

In the Help file that opens at the right of your new label, Click Label or Set of Labels to read tips for completing your job, depending upon whether you plan to print your own labels or are sending them out to be printed.

TROUBLESHOOTING

What do I do if I chose the wrong label? If you accidentally select the wrong kind of label or the wrong size, choose File, Page Setup to re-open the list of labels. Click the one you want and choose OK.

Figure 29.7
The collection listed under Choose a Label is broad enough to satisfy the needs of any small business.

Labels—

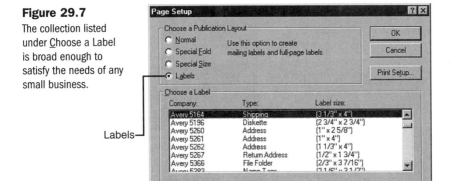

Using Design Assistant to Create Envelopes

The Design Assistant, a component of the Page Wizard, is probably the quickest and easiest way to develop your envelope design. Choose File, Create New Publication, and, in the PageWizard tab, select the Envelope icon. Follow the step-by-step instructions, making your envelope choices.

▶ **See** "Using the PageWizard," **page 615**

Designing Envelopes from Scratch

Starting an envelope publication from ground zero is a little different from starting other kinds of blank publications. Begin by choosing File, Create New Publication, and canceling the PageWizard dialog box. This leaves a blank page on-screen. Now, follow these steps:

1. Choose File, Print Setup. Click the Properties button at the top right of the Print Setup dialog box.

2. In the Properties dialog box, be sure you are looking at the Paper tab at the top of the dialog box. If not, click it. Scroll through the Paper Size options until you find the size envelope you want (see Figure 29.8).

3. When you locate and click the icon of the envelope you want, choose OK to close the Properties dialog box, and then choose OK to close the Print Setups dialog box.

▶ **See** "Creating Frames for Content in a Publication," **page 622**
▶ **See** "Changing Page Margins," **page 641**

Working in the Background Layer

In the Background, you establish the foundation for consistency of design and the overall look of your publication. In the Foreground, you add content to the publication, articles in a newsletter, or fresh copy in an ad.

Figure 29.8

Click an envelope icon and look beside the words "Paper Size" for the description and dimensions of that envelope. You are now ready to adjust the page margins and add frames with text and elements.

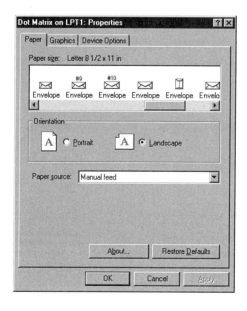

Text that identifies the volume and number of a catalog, page numbers, a watermark, graphics, or other page components you want standardized throughout a publication, are created on the Background layer. You can also use the Background layer for a design enhancement that appears beneath all the frames on the Foreground layer; for instance, a watermark on stationery. When you place text or graphics on the Background layer, you can't inadvertently move or delete them as you work on other elements in the Foreground.

Typically, in Blank Page publications, you design a Background before adding text and graphics to the Foreground. If you opt for a publication with facing pages, such as a catalog, you need to design two Backgrounds—one for the left pages and one for the right pages.

▶ **See** "Creating a Two-Page Spread," **page 643**

TIP   You can suppress the display and printout of all or some the background elements on any page in a publication. You may want to do this on certain pages in publications that have multiple pages. Be sure the page you want to have no background elements is in view on-screen. Choose View, Ignore Background.

Getting to the Background

To get to the Background of your publication, choose View, Go to Background. To exit the Background, choose View, Go to Foreground. Simple as that.

N O T E   When you are working in the Background layer, many commands in the menus are dimmed, such as Insert, Page. To activate these dimmed commands, you must return to the Foreground layer. Choose View, Go to Foreground. ■

TROUBLESHOOTING

What's this? As I am working on my publication, everything I worked so hard to place in the Foreground disappears when I go to the Background. Fear not. That's the way things are supposed to be, and that's why it's a good idea to create the Background elements before the Foreground. The Background shows only those things you want to use as foundational design elements. As soon as you G̲o to the Foreground, everything shows.

Changing Page Margins

Publisher defaults all new publications to a 1-inch margin on every edge. Especially on smaller publications, you will want to adjust these page margins. Choose V̲iew, G̲o to Background. When you are in the Background layer, choose A̲rrange, L̲ayout Guides, and set Margin Guides to any other dimension you prefer. Leave the Grid Guides set to at least 1 for C̲olumns and R̲ows. To return to the Foreground layer and complete your design, choose V̲iew, G̲o to Foreground.

If your publication is to be printed professionally, you can set margins as small as zero. You can even design graphics to run off the edges of your pages, then the print house will use a paper larger than your publication measures and trim it to size. If you are using a desktop printer, the minimum margins are determined by your printer's specifications. Check its documentation to be certain you have sufficient margin allowance to feed the paper through the printer.

TROUBLESHOOTING

I reset the margins of my publication, but when I printed it, some of my page elements near the edges of the paper were cut off. Every printing device has a certain print area beyond which it cannot print. It's a mechanical limitation, not some evil scheme designed to frustrate you. You probably placed page elements beyond to scope of your printer's abilities. Try moving the truncated elements farther away from the edges of your publication. Most printers can print everything that is at least half an inch in from the edge of the paper.

Setting a Background Grid

The Background Grid Guides are a framework for frames. The grid is a series of squares that help you align frames. Grid Guides are nonprinting lines that you use to consistently and accurately position elements on your pages.

Choose V̲iew, G̲o to Background. When you are in the Background layer, choose A̲rrange, L̲ayout Guides, and set Margin Guides to any other dimension you prefer. Leave the Grid Guides set to at least 1 for C̲olumns and R̲ows. To return to the Foreground layer and complete your design, choose V̲iew, G̲o to Foreground.

T I P Layout Guides have a "come hither" characteristic called "snap to." Choose Tools, Snap to Guides. Page elements that you move close to a Layout Guide line automatically snuggle right up to the line. In this same menu, you can also activate Snap to Ruler Marks, aka: Ruler Guides, and even create a magnetic field around Objects on a page that causes other objects to snap to them if you choose Tools, Snap to Objects.

Hiding and Showing Boundaries and Guides   Page layout designing succeeds or fails, in large measure, based upon the accuracy of positioning things on your pages. Guides help you succeed, but they also tend to clutter the pages with lines, lines, lines. After setting your Guides, you can alleviate the visual distraction by temporarily hiding them. Out of sight does not mean out of commission, though. Hidden Guides still retain their magnetic fields.

▶ **See** "Using Grids, Guides, and Rulers for Positioning," **page 626**

To hide or reveal Guides, choose View, Hide/Show Boundaries and Guides. The command toggles between Hide and Show.

Inserting Page Numbers

In multipage publications with more than four pages, page numbers are a must. You can place page numbers on the Foreground, but tucking them away on the Background layer is a better idea so they can't be inadvertently moved or deleted.

In publications that do not have facing pages, you can place page numbers anywhere on the page that pleases you. Choose View, Go to Background, and create a small text frame. With the cursor inside this text frame, choose Insert, Page Numbers. Publisher enters a code symbol, #, that automatically sequences page numbers for you, even if you shuffle the pages in your publication. Use the Move tool on the Publisher toolbar to reposition the frame to fit your overall design.

▶ **See** "Creating Frames for Content in a Publication," **page 622**

> **CAUTION**
>
> Do *not* type in the # symbol. This produces only page after page with a #. You *must* use the Insert menu command, Page Numbers, to get sequencing numbers.

In facing page designs, conventions dictate where page numbers appear. You don't put page numbers in the gutter, the inside margin where the two pages meet. You also must place frames with page numbering code on *both* the left and right Backgrounds. You can create the first page numbering frame, then Copy and Paste it on the other Background page. This assures that both page numbers look the same. Use Ruler Guides to be certain that both page numbers are located in the same horizontal plane on both pages. If you prefer page numbers along the outside margin of pages, top or bottom, remember to reverse the position of your page number frame.

▶ **See** "Using Grids, Guides, and Rulers for Positioning," **page 626**

T I P You can add words in front of or after the page number code symbol, #. Position the cursor and type what you want, such as, **Page #**, or **page # of 24**. Remember to put a space between the symbol Publisher inserts and the words you type.

Using a Background Graphic

Any graphic object can be placed on the Background layer, whether you are creating a multipage publication or a single page flyer. You can create an elegant (or whimsical) watermark on a stationery layout, for instance, by placing a subtly colored graphic on the Background. Your company logo can easily be incorporated into any page layout design, but if you want the logo or any graphic element to appear in exactly the same position on multiple pages, it's wise to place it on the Background layer.

To insert a graphic on the Background, choose View, Go to Background, then choose Insert and select the particular kind of graphic element you want, Picture File, ClipArt, or other Object.

▶ **See** "Adding and Formatting Objects," **page 669**

Creating a Two Page Spread

The term "spread" in publishing means two or more pages side by side. For the sake of discussion, let's assume you are starting with a Blank Page publication and have set up the page size. Now you want a two page spread. This typically involves some work in the Background layer, designing left and right page elements.

▶ **See** "Starting with a Blank Publication," **page 620**

▶ **See** "Using Special Papers," **page 634**

To define your publication as a two page spread, choose Arrange, Layout Guides. Click the check box below the Preview area to Create Two Backgrounds with Mirrored Guides (see Figure 29.9).

Figure 29.9
In addition to establishing page Margin and Grid Guides, you define a publication as a two page spread in this dialog box.

Mirrored Guides ———

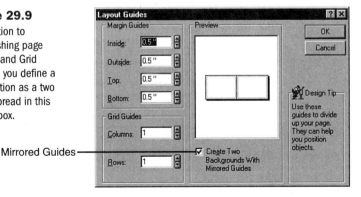

After you define a publication as a two page spread, the Background layer shows facing pages and the two icons in the Status line at the lower-left of the publication window indicating Left and Right pages (see Figure 29.10).

Figure 29.10

Design a different look for each of the facing pages using Background elements that appear consistently on every left or every right page.

Left and Right Pages

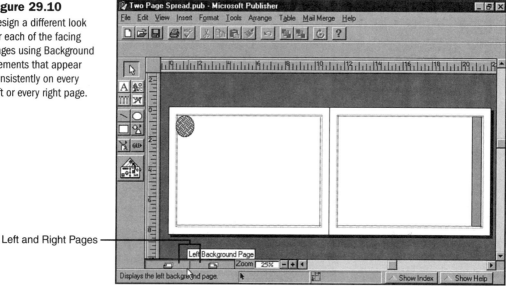

Creating Booklets

Use Publisher Booklets to create multipage publications such as catalogs, a portfolio of services you offer, a mini-annual report, business plans, any publication you want to print on both sides of standard letter paper stock. You also can fold and staple, or bind these Booklets.

You print these publications as two sided, and have different left page and right page elements on the Background layer. For example: the left pages may have a header with the volume number of the publication, and the right pages may have the name of the publication as the header.

To set up a folded Booklet, follow these steps:

1. Choose File, Page Setup and click the Special Fold option button under Choose a Publication Layout.

2. Be absolutely *sure* that Book Fold is selected from the drop-down menu under Choose a Special Fold!

    This is the way that Publisher determines the print order of folded page publications.

3. For a folded publication that measures 5.5 inches wide by 8.5 inches tall, click the Landscape orientation option button. This also sets your Print Setup to Landscape output. Choose OK to close the Page Setup dialog box.

A Publisher query appears asking if you want to add three more pages to your publication. Because a folded Booklet design prints two pages on each side of a single sheet of letter sized paper, you probably do want those added pages. Choose <u>Y</u>es. If you'd rather wait, choose <u>N</u>o.

▶ **See** "Adding or Deleting Pages," **page 648**

Now you are ready to work in the Background, adjusting Margin Guides and adding master elements, such as volume and page numbers.

▶ **See** "Inserting Page Numbers," **page 642**

▶ **See** "Changing Page Margins," **page 641**

> **CAUTION**
>
> The total number of pages in your folded publication *must* be a multiple of four; that is, 4, 8, 12, and so on, because each single sheet of $8^1/_2$-by-11-inch paper actually holds four $5^1/_2$-by-$8^1/_2$-inch pages, two on each side.

A Booklet is designed and laid out the way it is read, that is, pages are sequential. When it's time to print your folded Booklet, however, the pages do *not* print sequentially, but you needn't be concerned. Because you chose Book Fold in the Page Setup dialog box, Publisher understands what order to print the pages. The last two pages are printed on the back of the first two pages, and so on through your entire set of pages.

TROUBLESHOOTING

Why did my folded page publication print out pages that aren't in sequence after I collate and fold the pages? You probably forgot to select Book Fold in the Page Setup dialog box. All is not lost. Go back and reset your Page Setup and try another test print.

Formatting Pages

If you've ever used Word and tried to make a nice, straight border that encloses everything on a page of paragraphs with varied margins, you know that you can't. Although Word has some powerful page layout capabilities, it is, after all, a word processor. Publisher, on the other hand, is made to do this sort of thing because each component on a page is self-contained in a frame, so you can layer, resize, and move frames independently.

Creating a Page Border

A page border is created by applying a border to a transparent picture frame that is the size of the printing area of your publication. You can use lines as borders, or you can use BorderArt to produce more creative borders.

The techniques used to create page borders are also used to apply borders to a single frame, or to surround a group of frames.

To convert any frame to transparent, click the frame to activate it and then hold down the Control key and press T (Ctrl+T). To return a frame to opaque, make sure it is selected, and press Ctrl+T again.

 You can leave the empty frame with a border opaque if it is at the bottom of a stack of layers. Click the bordered frame and choose Arrange, Send to Back.

Both Line Borders and BorderArt are accessed the same way. Click the frame you want to have a border and choose Format, Border to open the BorderArt dialog box. It has two tabs, Line Border and BorderArt.

Using Line Borders When you have the BorderArt dialog box open, click the Line Border tab (see Figure 29.11).

Figure 29.11
Click the selection arrows to apply or remove the Line Border from that side.

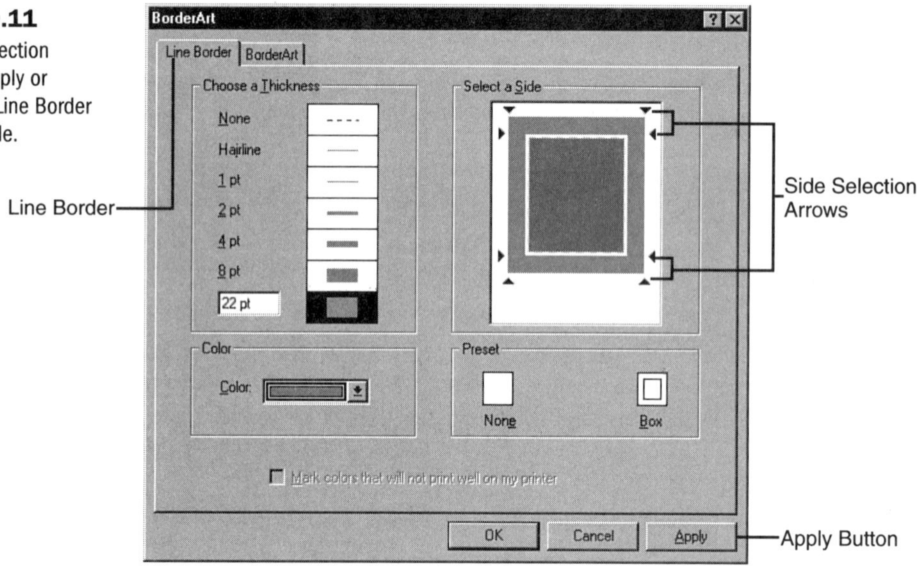

Click one of the icons under Choose a Thickness to select any of the predefined lines, or enter a custom line thickness in the text box beside the bottom line icon. To define a line color, click the drop-down menu beside Color and select the color you want. As you can see, you have the option to apply the border to any or all sides of a frame. If you want all sides to have a border, click the Box icon under Select a Side.

 Apply before you buy! You can click the Apply button in the Line Border or BorderArt tab but don't close the dialog box. Move the dialog box out of the way so that you can see your publication page that displays the border options you chose. If you like it, move the dialog box to a position where you can see and choose OK. If you don't like it, try, try again. Select other options and apply them until you are satisfied and then choose OK.

Using BorderArt   Publisher has 164 predesigned borders plus custom options in the BorderArt dialog box (see Figure 29.12).

Figure 29.12
There are classic borders for formal publications, holiday borders, food borders for menus, ethnic borders, and more.

Create Custom Border

Border Size

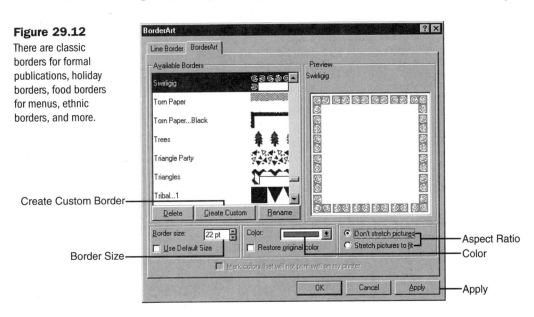

Aspect Ratio
Color
Apply

N O T E   Unlike Line Borders, you must use BorderArt on all four sides of a frame. You can, however, change the Border Size and Color as well as opt to Stretch Pictures to Fit, or not. ▪

When you apply BorderArt to a frame, the entire border is applied inside the frame. Text or graphics already inside the frame accommodate themselves to the width of the BorderArt so that nothing is covered by the border. The frame remains the same dimensions as when you created it. Remember to click Apply (see earlier Tip) and choose OK.

To Delete or Rename a border, click the border you want to remove or rename and click the appropriate button below the list of Available Borders.

Creating a Custom Border

To create a unique border, say for your Web Page, click the Create Custom button in the BorderArt tab. If you want to select ClipArt, click Use Clip Gallery to Choose the Picture, then click the Choose Picture button.

If you prefer to use a graphic file that you have on your computer, do not click Use Clip Gallery to Choose the Picture—just click the Choose Picture button. The Insert Picture File dialog box opens. Locate and click the file you want to use, then choose OK. Publisher uses the file you select to manufacture a border for you. The new border is added to the Available Borders with the generic name, BorderArt and a number (see Figure 29.13).

Figure 29.13
This Custom Border was created using a Photoshop graphic saved in GIF format and used on the Web. To see the original, visit **http://www.ebetts.com/**.

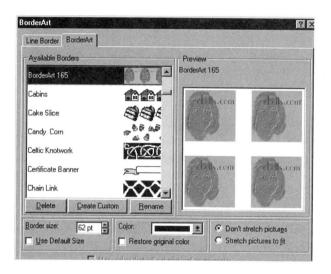

You can resize and recolor the custom border after it is created. Remember to click Apply (see earlier Tip) and, if you're satisfied, choose OK to close the BorderArt dialog box.

Because Custom Borders remain in your BorderArt collection until you delete them, you can reuse them at any time. To Delete or Rename a custom border, click the border that you want to remove or rename in the BorderArt dialog box and click the appropriate button below the list of Available Borders.

Inserting the Date and Time

In the business world, most things are time sensitive. Catalogs may have a seasonal reference, promotional give-aways often have expiration dates, business letters, of course, always need dates. To insert a Date or Time stamp, you must first create a frame to hold the information.

▶ **See** "Creating Frames for Content in a Publication," **page 622**

Once the frame is created, choose Insert, Date or Time. When the dialog box opens, select the format you prefer, one with date only, or one with date and time. You can also select the means of expressing these: a combination of text and numeric, or strictly numeric. If you click the Update Automatically option button, your publication displays the current date each time you open it, which is perfect for a letterhead. If you'd rather have today's date firmly fixed on your publication, click Insert as Plain Text. Choose OK, and the date/time stamp is inserted in the text frame.

Adding or Deleting Pages

Some things are so logical. You delete pages using the Edit menu, and you add pages using the Insert menu. The tricky part is being sure you delete the page or pages you mean to delete, and add pages where you want them to be. The trick for deleting is to be sure the page you want to delete is showing on-screen when you choose Edit, Delete Page. In multipage publications, it may be more convenient to choose View, Two Page Spread, to display side-by-side pages before you delete one or both. The dialog that appears differs, based upon whether you are viewing one or two pages on-screen. With one page on-screen, the Publisher query requests confirmation that you really do want to delete this page. If you are viewing a two page spread, the query asks if you want to delete Both Pages, the Left Page Only, or the Right Page Only. Click your choice and then choose OK.

Computer programs are smart, but not clairvoyant. If Publisher thinks you are about to make a gaffe by deleting only one page in a publication that requires an even number of pages, a query appears to explain the consequences of what you're about to do, and offer alternatives. You can follow the advice or proceed as you intended. Choose OK to continue, or Cancel to back out and revise your thinking.

CAUTION

The best advice before deleting pages is, "Play it safe." Save your publication before deleting pages.

▶ **See** "Understanding Publisher Basics," **page 611**

TROUBLESHOOTING

I've deleted the wrong page! Am I out of luck? That depends on whether you saved your publication immediately before you deleted the page, and did *not* save it immediately after you deleted the page. If that's the case, you have an out. Close the publication by choosing File, Close Publication. A query opens to ask if you want to save changes before closing. You DON'T! Choose No, then re-open your publication. Your deleted page is back again, exactly as it was before you deleted it. If you forgot to save your publication before deleting pages, you will lose all unsaved work by following the instruction, but it may be worth it. At least you have your pages back.

If you saved immediately after deleting pages, they're gone.

Formatting Frames

In Chapter 28, "Using Publisher to Market Your Business" we talked about making frames; now it's time to make the frames look different. Because everything in Publisher is held within the confines of a frame, things you do to a frame could pack that extra visual punch that your marketing materials need, like adding a shadow to make the frame appear to lift off the page, or adding a background color, or a pattern.

▶ **See** "Creating Frames for Content in a Publication," **page 622**

Adding a Shadow

Create the illusion of depth, that third dimension, by applying a shadow to a frame. The standard shadows created by Publisher are black and drop below and to the right of the frame.

Although you can add fill color or a pattern to the frame, you can't change the color of the shadow.

To apply a standard shadow, choose Format, Shadow. Because Publisher created the shadow, it automatically travels with the frame if you move it.

Creating a Custom Shadow   Creating your own shadow takes a few extra steps, but is especially effective if you want to increase the illusion of depth, change the light source's position, or coordinate the shadow's color with the scheme of your publication. Since everything in Publisher is contained within a frame, you can create a custom shadow for anything.

To create your own shadow, follow these steps:

1. Click the frame you want to have a shadow. Copy the frame to the Clipboard and then Paste the duplicate back on top of the original frame. For the time being, it's easier to work with the duplicate on top.

2. If the original frame has already been filled with text or a graphic, delete the contents from the duplicate, and choose Format, Fill Color. In the Colors dialog box that opens, click the color you want the shadow to be, then choose OK.

3. Choose Format, Border and click None in the Choose a Thickness section of the Border dialog box. This eliminates the hard edge around the duplicate.

4. Choose Arrange, Send Farther, to place the shadow behind the original frame.

5. Click the Pointer tool in the Publisher toolbar and drag a rectangle that encompasses both frames, the original and the duplicate, but nothing else. Immediately after you release the mouse button, the Group Objects icon appears at the bottom of the multiple selections. Click it. Notice that the two puzzle pieces in the icon join together. Your original and duplicate frames are now Grouped and can safely be moved as a single object.

 If it's not possible to use the rectangle selection technique (described in step 5) because of other nearby objects, hold down the Shift key and click both the original and the duplicate. Shift+click is a technique for selecting multiple objects of any sort, throughout your Microsoft Office Small Business suite.

To change the color of your custom shadow, you must Ungroup the two frames. Click the grouped frames and click the Group icon at the bottom. The puzzle pieces separate, indicating the frames are no longer functioning as a single Object. Click the frame you want to revise, do whatever you had in mind, and then re-Group them as described in step 5.

You can edit the contents of the original frame, recolor, or resize either the original or duplicate frame while it is grouped.

Adding Fill Color

Fill color on frames offers some interesting possibilities. You can use a dark tone fill color on a Text frame, then make the text inside the frame white, which creates the illusion that the words are stamped out of a colored block, the frame. A colored frame could be the foundation for a logo you design as part of your corporate identity.

To color a frame, click the one you want to color and choose Format, Fill Color. In the Colors dialog box, in the Color Model area, click Basic Colors option button, to use the swatches, or All Colors to access the color palette. You can test the look of any color on the frame by moving the dialog box so that you can see the frame you are coloring, then click Apply When you have the color you want, choose OK to close the Colors dialog box and apply the color to the frame.

You're not locked in to any color you apply. To change the color, click the frame, and repeat the previous instructions.

 TIP Right click the mouse to quickly access frequently used commands that apply to an object, such as the Border, Fill Color, Patterns and Shading commands used on frames.

If you are working on a Web page, be aware that many colors that look fine on your computer may look awful on another monitor.

▶ **See** "Adding Web Page Elements," **page 655**

▶ **See** "Converting a Publication to a Web Site," **page 703**

▶ **See** For Web safe color information, read Designing Web Graphics by Lynda Weinman, New Riders, ISBN 1-56205-532-1.

Adding Fill Patterns and Shading

The Fill Patterns and Shading dialog box has three options for enhancing a frame: Tints/ Shades, Patterns, and Gradients. Each works with color a little differently.

Tints/Shades allow you to select a single color, the Tint, and then decide how dark or light you want that color to print, from the lightest possible tint, white, to increasingly darker shades of that color. The darkest possibility is black.

Patterns work with two colors that you pick in the Color area of the Fill Patterns and Shading dialog box, a Basic Color and Color 2. In the Style area, you have a variety of stripes, bricks, basket weaves, cross hatches, and checkers made up of the two colors. Click the pattern you want to use, then choose OK to close the dialog box.

Gradients create the impression of movement, a third dimension. A Gradient is a transition from one color to another. That transition can be from left to right, corner to corner, center to edge, top to bottom. Publisher uses the two colors you indicate in the Color area of the Fill Patterns and Shading dialog box to create Gradients. Choose OK to apply your gradient.

Choose Format, Fill Patterns and Shading, and click the option button under Tint/Shades, Patterns, or Gradients, according to what you want applied to the active frame.

Note that you can avert disappointment at printing time by putting a check in the box beside Mark Color That Won't Print Well on My Printer. If you have only a black and white printer, this option is dimmed. You can still use colors in your design if you plan to send your publication out for printing. You get at least a hint of what things will look like if your printer does gray scale output.

▶ **See** "Working with Final Output," **page 691**

CAUTION

Don't use Gradients if you are designing a Web page. They are lost in the translation from your world to cyberspace.

Using Transparent Frames

By default, all frames are opaque. As you begin layering objects and text in frames, an opaque frame in the stack can hide objects farther down in the stack. It's easy to resolve this. Click the opaque frame and press Ctrl+T. Now the frame is transparent and reveals anything below it.

You can also use transparent frames with borders to surround an entire publication page, or several objects on a page.

If you decide to return the frame to its opaque state, you'll have to choose Format, Fill Color, and choose white or another color.

Note that you can make objects drawn with tools in the Publisher toolbar transparent. That tidbit should percolate some creative ideas.

▶ **See** "Creating a Page Border," **page 645**

▶ **See** "Creating Graphic Elements," **page 670**

Setting Frame Properties

Frame Properties are defaults that affect the way frames behave. For instance, the Text frame defaults determine the font attributes, the frame's color, whether it has a border, and so on. A frame uses its defaults unless you make specific editing adjustments.

Wouldn't it be faster if a frame automatically formatted text in the font you use as part of your corporate identity, or was the color you use most often? You could save a lot of time, and time is money in any small business!

You can change the factory defaults for many of the tools in the Publisher toolbar. With the proper tool selected, you can even change defaults for Tables.

Click the tool you want to have properties that you pick. Don't do anything with the tool just yet. Rather, select all the properties you want for that tool. These options are located in the Format menu. To test the new defaults, use the tool for what it was designed to do; create a frame and enter some text, or create a shape, and so on. Remember that you can revise defaults now or at any stage of a publication's production. Things already created with factory defaults, or your defaults, are unaffected by new defaults. New defaults apply only to newly created objects after the defaults are changed, and apply to this publication *only*.

▶ **See** "Inserting a Table," **page 687**

▶ **See** "Viewing Frame Properties," **page 653**

You can override your personal default properties at any time, exactly as you override factory defaults. Just choose the formatting options you want applied to a specific object. Your defaults are in tact, but the object's properties are changed.

Viewing Frame Properties

To view properties for anything in a publication, click it, and choose Format to drop down the menu. According to what you clicked, one of these will appear: Text Frame Properties, Picture Frame Properties, Table Cell Properties, Object Frame Properties, (not Lines, Ovals, or Boxes). The Properties dialog box shows all the specifications that apply. You can edit the properties, or leave them as they are, and close the Properties dialog box. This is also one way to set up your own defaults for Publisher tools.

Grouped objects confuse Publisher when you ask to see Properties. The program wonders, "Which one shall I show? Hmmm." So the menu choice is dimmed. To see Properties for any single thing in a group, you must Ungroup and select it.

▶ **See** "Setting Frame Properties," **page 652**

▶ **See** "Grouping and Ungrouping Objects," **page 683**

▶ **See** "Working with Frames," **page 622**

Copying a Frame

You copy a frame by selecting it and using the Copy and Paste buttons in the Standard toolbar. It's exactly the same technique used in all Windows applications. When you Paste the copy of the frame into your publication, it is positioned on top of the original, unless you change to view another page in a multipage publication. In that case, the copy is pasted in exactly the same position as the original, but on a different page.

If you plan to do a major repositioning on the same page, there is another way to make a copy. Hold down the Control key and drag the frame you want to copy. This is particularly convenient because you accomplish the copy and the move, all in one action.

 Would you like to experiment with page layouts, but are afraid you might spoil what you already have created? You can copy everything you have on a publication page and the Background and Foreground, to another page in the publication. Choose Insert, Page. Under the Options section of the dialog box, click Duplicate All Objects On Page Number X, and enter the number of the page to copy. Now you can safely fiddle with the duplicate page. Keep the page you prefer and delete the page you don't want. Make sure the page you are abandoning is in view on-screen and choose Edit, Delete Page.

Deleting a Frame

As you read in Chapter 28, sometimes you decide that you don't want a frame you've created. If the frame is still empty, and not selected, click it and use the Delete or Backspace key to remove it. If you have already filled the frame, some frames, like text frames, require you to click the Cut button in the Standard toolbar.

▶ **See** "Inserting a Frame," **page 623**

Working with Design Gallery

The Design Gallery has many designs you may need in publications. Categories of design elements already in the Design Gallery are: Attention Getters, Headlines, Ornaments, Pull Quote, Reply Forms, Sidebars, Table of Contents, Titles, and Web E-mail Buttons, Web Page buttons, and Web Page Dividers.

If you, or someone else, custom designed your corporate look, you can also store your personalized components in the Design Gallery. You can even create your own categories of Design Gallery objects and access only those related to a particular task or topic.

To access these options, click the Design Gallery button in the Publisher toolbar. In the dialog box that opens, click the name of things you want to view, listed under Choose a Category and scroll through the choices shown to the right of the list (see Figure 29.14).

Figure 29.14

Don't miss the More Designs button. Every category has additional designs from which to choose.

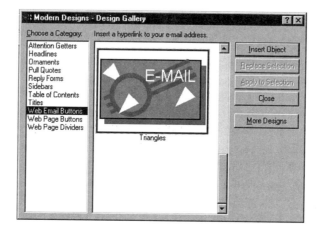

When you find something you want to use, click it and then click the Insert Object button.

As with any other inserted element in a publication, the inserted Design Gallery object is already inserted in a frame. That means you can reposition it, resize it, or even recolor it (if you Ungroup it first).

▶ **See** "Recoloring Pictures," **page 685**

Creating Sidebars and Pull Quotes

Though they serve different functions, sidebars and pull quotes are created exactly the same way. Sidebars and pull quotes are commonly used in newsletters and magazines. A *sidebar* holds information that expands or gives details about a topic mentioned in the main body of an article. A *pull quote* is a snippet of text drawn from the body of an article. Sidebars usually are placed on the same page with the topic mentioned in the article, but can appear on a later page, close enough to maintain the thought connection. Pull quotes always appear on the same page they are drawn from.

Publishing conventions dictate that sidebars appear along the outside edge of facing pages. On single page publications, or multiple page publications without facing pages, you can place a sidebar on either edge. Pull quotes always appear on the first page of an article. Now, let's be honest. Some of the most captivating graphic design throws those sorts of conventions out the window, and so can you, but only if you can justify your decision.

It is easiest to use one of the Design Gallery's sidebars or pull quotes, but you can design your own, and, perhaps, store it in the Design Gallery for use later. Creating your own sidebar or pull quote is as easy as creating a Text frame, sizing, positioning, and formatting the frame and then entering and formatting the text.

▶ **See** "Working with Design Gallery," **page 654**

▶ **See** "Adding to Design Gallery," **page 657**

▶ **See** "Creating Frames for Content in a Publication," **page 622**

▶ **See** "Formatting Text in Frames," **page 667**

Creating a Table of Contents

Unlike Word, Publisher does not automatically generate a Table of Contents, but it does help you with the layout. The Design Gallery has seven different styles suitable for almost any multipage publication.

▶ **See** "Working with Design Gallery," **page 654**

After you have selected and inserted a Design Gallery Table of Contents, drag to select and replace the Greek text (which is actually imitation Latin, used as a placeholder for your text). Enter the text and page numbers that apply to your publication.

Adding Web Page Elements

Even if you start the process of creating a Web site from a PageWizard, you will add elements to pages to make them meet your company's look and needs. As you design a web site with one or more pages, there are certain considerations specific to the way Publisher converts a publication to a web site. For instance, in the conversion process, many of the elements in the publication are converted to graphics. If you have text preceding a web page graphic element, such as an E-mail button, that text becomes part of the E-mail graphic. You may decide that your design is stronger with that placement of text, but you should be aware that sometimes web graphics don't load, in which case your text is not there, either. When they do load, it is always less briskly than loading only text.

▶ **See** "Converting a Publication to a Web Site," **page 703**

There are hundreds, thousands, probably millions of web sites full of graphics that load remarkably quickly, so don't hold back because of the rumor that *all* web graphics load slowly. As often as not, slow loading graphics, and graphics that don't show at all, are a result of heavy Internet traffic, a user's slow modem, or a glitch in the host of a site.

For thorough, in-depth explanations of web page design elements, visit: **http://ds.dial.pipex.com/pixelp/wpdesign/wpdintro.htm.**

▶ **See** Chapter 41, "Web Browsing with IE 4," **page 857**

The Design Gallery holds many things used on web pages; forms, e-mail buttons, clever navigation buttons, and decorative page dividers.

Web Page Buttons   Every business site on the World Wide Web includes an e-mail button somewhere on its site, and all Web sites use some method of getting from one page of the site to another, or to another site. Why not use buttons to guide your visitors?

The Design Gallery has a large collection of button designs, navigational buttons with placeholder text that you replace with your own words, and e-mail buttons that need no touch-up at all. Go through the collection and select the one you want, click it, and then click Insert Object.

After you have selected and inserted a Design Gallery button, drag to select and replace any greek text (that imitation Latin used as a placeholder for your text) with the words you want on your button. Because buttons are translated into graphic hyperlinks when Publisher converts a publication to a Web site, you can format the button text any way you like.

▶ **See** "Working with Design Gallery," **page 654**

▶ **See** "Converting a Publication to a Web Site," **page 703**

Web Page Dividers   On the World Wide Web, page dividers help your site visitors recognize when one topic is concluded and another begins. They also contribute visual impact, so pick any of the Design Gallery web page dividers that appeals to you and fits in with the overall design of your site. If the colors don't exactly suit you, you can always recolor a divider after it's inserted in your publication.

▶ **See** "Adding Fill Color," **page 650**

▶ **See** "Adding Fill Patterns and Shading," **page 651**

Position your dividers any place that is compatible with your page layout and identifies a logical break, like between the introductory header or after informational text about your company. As with all page layout designs, the choice is yours.

Reply Forms

Small businesses of all sorts use reply forms. If you sell products by mail, you may want an order form. Perhaps you need a reply form to assemble statistics that indicate how your clients found you. Maybe you want to take a poll of your customers, to see if there are things you can do to better serve them. Maybe you want to compile a mailing list for promotional materials. If you are using an outside printing service, check with them to see if they provide perforating. It's a good idea, and not costly if done in large batches.

The Design Gallery has two basic reply forms, but a number of designs you can apply to them. If the two basic forms don't quite meet your needs, pick the form that is closest to what you need, and a style that appeals to you. After it is inserted, you can Ungroup the form, and add or delete parts to fit your needs.

▶ **See** "Grouping and Ungrouping Objects," **page 683**

Adding to Design Gallery

There are already plenty of things to use in the Design Gallery, but, you may have things you want to add. The things you add can be reused, the same as those in Publisher sets. Don't worry about getting yours mixed up with Publisher's. You can't add things to Publisher sets. You create sets all your own.

Follow these steps to create a new set:

1. Click a component in the publication you have open. Go to the Publisher toolbar and click the Design Gallery tool.

2. Click the <u>M</u>ore Designs button at the right when the Design Gallery dialog box opens and click Add Selection to Design Gallery in the drop-down menu.

3. If it's the first time you have tried to add something, a query opens to remind you that you can't add to Publisher's design sets and asks if you want to start a new set. You do. Click <u>Y</u>es (see Figure 29.15).

Figure 29.15
Click Yes to begin a new design set.

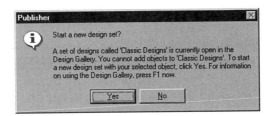

4. This opens the Adding an Object dialog box where you see the component you selected. It is displayed at the right, as well as text boxes to enter an <u>O</u>bject Name and a <u>C</u>ategory. Keep it short and informative. You can only enter a total of 17 characters, including spaces.

If you create other sets later, this name and the names of any new sets you create appear in the drop-down menu attached to the <u>C</u>ategory text box.

5. Choose OK to open the final dialog box, Create New Category. Type a brief description of the set and choose OK again. Your new Design Gallery set has now replaced Publisher's sets (see Figure 29.16).

> **CAUTION**
> Notice that the set has assumed the same name of the publication that is open when you create the set. This is a *very* important bit of information that you will need later, when you want to use things in this set, or add new things to it.

Figure 29.16

Store anything you have created in one publication and want to reuse in other publications.

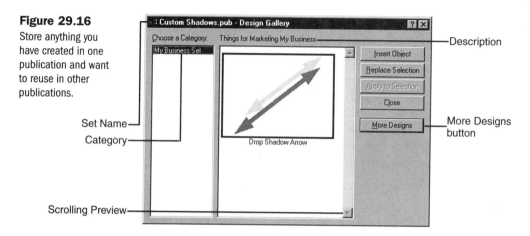

Set Name

Category

Scrolling Preview

Description

More Designs button

If you want to see what happened to the Publisher sets, click the More Designs button.

Choose Close to go back to your publication. If you have other objects in this publication that you want to store in your new Design Gallery set, repeat the steps just listed.

You can create other sets at any time, following the same steps with another publication open. You can add categories to this set whenever you like. You can add objects to this set from other publications.

Reopening Your Own Design Gallery Sets   It doesn't do much good to store your own set of design components if you can't find them again. *Your custom sets aren't listed with the Design Gallery sets!* What to do?

You don't have to be Sherlock Holmes. You just have to remember the publication that was open when you created the set. Newly created design sets assume the name of the publication that was open when you created the set.

With that in mind, while any publication is open, click the Design Gallery button in the Publisher toolbar. If you see only the list of Publisher sets, click the More Designs button, then click Other Designs in the drop-down menu.

The Other Designs dialog box opens, looking remarkably like a typical Open File dialog box. Navigate through your hard drive to locate the publication that was open when you originally created the set you want to use now. When you find it, highlight it, and choose OK. Your design set is now available to use in the publication you are working on.

TROUBLESHOOTING

What happens if I delete the publication that was open when I originally created a set of design components? You can't. If you try, your computer tells you, "Access is denied." That Microsoft—they think of everything.

What happens if I move that publication to a floppy? You just have a backup copy on a floppy, because you can't delete the original.

If I format my hard drive and obliterate publications that hold my custom design sets, what then? Well, as a wise business person, we have to assume you regularly back up your hard drive. At the very least, you should have a copy of publications that originate your design sets on a floppy. Reload the publication on your hard drive and all's well.

I travel a lot. How can I use my custom designs on the road? One way is to copy the original publication to a floppy and take it with you. That way you can use it with your laptop installation of Publisher, or on someone else's computer that also has Publisher 97 loaded.

Using Design Checker

Design Checker is both your sternest critic and your best friend. It combs your publication for empty frames, forgotten text overflow, pictures that look like reflections in Fun House mirrors, excessive special effects, too many fonts, and other things that can be pretty insulting if found. It's nothing personal, though. Design Checker just *suggests* that these are problems. You decide if Design Checker is right or not.

Choose Tools, Design Checker to open the dialog box. If you are working on a multipage publication, you can check the All option button or check only certain pages you indicate after clicking the Pages option button. You also can have the Background of your publication examined if you click Check Background Page(s) (see Figure 29.17).

Figure 29.17
If you don't have anything on the Background, remove the check mark to save Design Checker some needless searching.

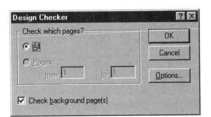

Before you set Design Checker loose with your ego in hand, perhaps you'd care to limit the areas where it looks for problems. Click the Options button to turn off things that don't apply to your publication, or that you are sure don't need changing (see Figure 29.18).

If you limit the things that Design Checker can investigate, Check Selected Features is automatically selected. After you've set the things in Options that you want checked, choose OK to return to the Design Checker dialog box. Choose OK again and another Design Checker dialog box opens (see Figure 29.19).

As Design Checker finds things that are problematic, a brief explanation of the problem appears in the dialog box and offers suggestions (as well as more complete details, if you click the Explain button). You can choose to Ignore this instance, or Ignore All occurrences of this problem. Click Continue.

Figure 29.18

If your publication is black and white, or has no special effects, obviously you want to deselect these, as well as any other things in the list that don't apply.

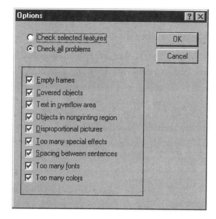

Figure 29.19

If Design Checker finds a problem, it displays the place in your publication where the problem is located.

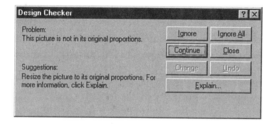

If you prefer to fix a problem Design Checker finds, you can work on your publication without closing Design Checker. When you have the situation rectified, click Continue to reactivate the design check.

TROUBLESHOOTING

Design Checker says I should use no more than three fonts in my publication and tells me to reformat. Is my publication a disaster if I don't? Far from it. Design Checker is setup on the conservative side of good design. There are plenty of instances where more than three fonts work very well. Run a test print, look at it from afar, show someone you trust what you've designed and trust your good taste. If it works, leave it alone. If not, change it.

Using Fonts to Improve Your Publications

Fonts can play a big role in whether or not your publications are noticed and read, or relegated to the permanently circulating file. There are three generic kinds of fonts—serif, sans serif, and display.

What are serifs? They're those little, tapering, angled strokes that finish off the ends of letters. These little strokes perform an important service. Let's take a moment to look at how humans read. In First Grade, or there about, we learned to identify letters, "c." Next came groups of letters, "cat." We learned that sometimes these groups of letters are syllables, "cat-a-log." In time, we learned to assemble syllables into words, "catalog." From there on, we read, for the most part, by identifying words as whole units.

What does this have to do with serifs? Well, the serifs visually join letters into units. Those tiny serif strokes reach out toward the next letter like children in a row holding hands. The space after a unit of letters signals a new word. The serifs and spaces lead your eye quickly across the lines of text. For that reason, it's always less taxing to read blocks of text, lots of words, set in a serif font.

Sans serif fonts offer no such assistance and cause your eye to hesitate, trying to assemble letters into words. Sans serif does have a useful function, though. Headlines, short, one-line bursts of text set in sans serif fonts, carry more impact *because* they slow the eye. That's what hooks you into reading the body of an article (set in a serif font).

Display fonts function as eye-catchers. They can be as simple as the one in the examples in Figure 29.20, or so fancy they're virtually unintelligible. Their job is not to improve the mind, or simply slow down reading, but to visually stop you in your tracks. Display fonts are used in logos, in signs, and any other place where it counts more that you *look at* it than read it.

 T I P Fonts are the most subtle of all the design components in a publication, but have a profound effect on communication. There is an almost endless array of each kind of font. The more you look at fonts, the more discriminating you become. The more discriminating you become, the more powerful your publication designs will be.

 ON THE WEB

Visit these Web sites for more about fonts:

http://www.microsoft.com/truetype/

http://www.agfahome.com/products/prodfam/type.html/

http://www.emigre.com/

http://www.slip.net/~graphion/style.html

http://www.dsiegel.com/type/eaglefeather.html

http://www.garagefonts.com/

http://www.philsfonts.com/

http://www.imageclub.com/

http://www.bearrock.com/

http://www.typeart.com/

http://www.fontbureau.com/

And then there's that problem of ALL CAPS, especially on the Web. In cyberspace there's nothing but the written word and graphics to convey your meaning and your image. All caps look like *screaming*! Besides that, they're hard to read, even in a serif font. Small doses of all caps can HELP. They're effective for emphasis. Beyond that, they have little use in good publication design.

Figure 29.20
Look closely at the differences in these A's.

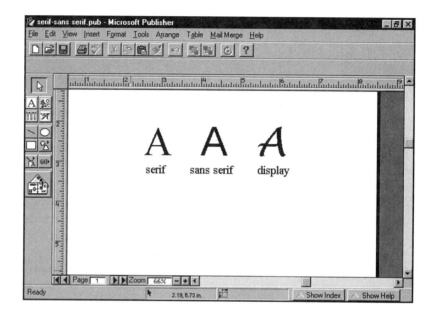

Spacing Between Characters

Extended spacing between letters is called tracking. Pulling pairs of letters closer together is called kerning. Tracking is a handy graphic device. Kerning improves readability and the visual unity of words. Most computer fonts are designed to kern certain pairs of letters, double f's and double l's, for example, but even these pairs can look too far apart in a very large point size. Double o's nearly always can use some tweaking. They have no serifs to unite them.

In Publisher, you can kern or track specific letters or whole paragraphs. Highlight the specific letters or multiple paragraphs you want to have adjusted spacing, or click your cursor anywhere in a single paragraph:

1. Choose Format, Spacing Between Characters. Under Set Spacing For, you can track or kern an Entire Paragraph, or Selected Characters Only. Depending on that choice, Spacing Options change.

2. If you select Entire Paragraph, your Spacing Options are Normal, Very Tight, Tight, Loose, and Very Loose. Test your choice by looking at the sample, or click Apply and move the dialog box to a position where you can see the words you highlighted in your publication. If you don't like the effect, try another choice.

3. When you click Selected Characters Only under Set Spacing For, the Spacing Options are, Normal, Squeeze Letters Together, and Move Letters Apart. Unless you choose

Normal, you need to enter a point increment for By this Amount. Again, the sample shows you how your choice will look. When you are satisfied, choose OK to close the dialog box.

If the preset choices available under Spacing Options for an Entire Paragraph don't quite accomplish the effect you want, you can highlight all the words and use Selected Characters Only. That allows you to set a more specific point increment.

Using Fancy First Letters

Fancy first letters are also called drop caps. You've probably seen them all your life. It's that big "O" at the beginning of fairy tales, "Once upon a time..." If fonts have a purpose in communications, so do drop caps. They signal the beginning of something important that's going to take a bit of reading. They function visually just like sans serif headlines.

Drop caps aren't restricted to first paragraphs of books and magazines. They can be used to signal a new topic in a flyer, or as a graphic element in an ad.

To create drop caps, click in the paragraph where you want to use drop caps, and choose Format, Fancy First Letters. The dialog box that opens has many preset drop caps. Scroll through them.

If you look closely at the predesigned drop caps, you'll see that you can use one or two letters as drop caps, and that some extend down one, two, three, or four lines. Some even extend upward from the first line of a paragraph rather than dropping into it (see Figure 29.21).

Figure 29.21

You can change the Fancy First Letter font after it's inserted, but you can't change its size.

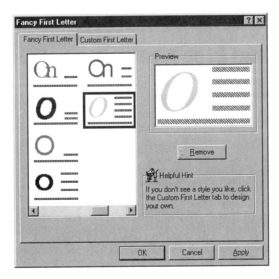

If none of these appeals to you, click the Custom First Letter tab, and design your own. Under Choose Letter Position, click Dropped or Up. Enter the Number of Letters you want to be fancy. The number of Lines can be adjusted, but is limited by the number you enter under Size, Lines High, below Choose Letter Size and Font. Pick a Font, a Color, and make it Bold or Italic. If you prefer, uncheck one or both of these (see Figure 29.22).

Figure 29.22

Experiment with font Size and Lines to see how these two are related.

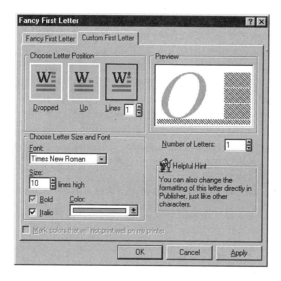

 Try a symbol font drop cap at the beginning of a paragraph! You may be delighted by the effect.

When you finish designing your Fancy First Letters, choose OK.

Setting Text Frame Properties

Here is the place where you establish visual design and continuity in text placed on pages. By setting properties for frames, you determine the distance text is away from the edge of the frame, the number of columns in a frame, how far apart they are, and if the text has permission to wrap around objects placed on top of the frame. For multipage publications, you have the invaluable Continued On and Continued From options (see Figure 29.23).

Choose Format, Text Frame Properties to open the dialog box and set your text frame specifications. Use the spinners under Margins to determine how far from the edges of the frame your text is inset. Under Columns, set the Number of columns and their Spacing. If you want only one column, Spacing is not relevant. In the Options area of the dialog box, click to place a check beside the choices you want to apply, Wrap Text Around Objects, Include "Continued On Page," and Include "Continued From Page." After your properties are set, choose OK.

Figure 29.23

Frame Properties can be changed even after the frame is full of text.

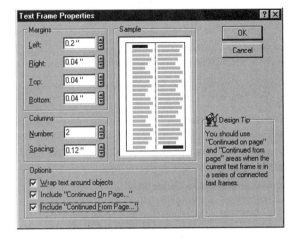

Connecting Text Frames

Connecting frames is a simple as clicking a button. At the bottom of every text frame you create, there is a Connect Frame button. You need at least two frames to flow text, one to start in, and one to pour into. If there is more text inside a frame than can be displayed, the button has three black squares (see Figure 29.24).

Figure 29.24

If this frame were not overflowing, the Connect Frame button at the bottom would have a white diamond.

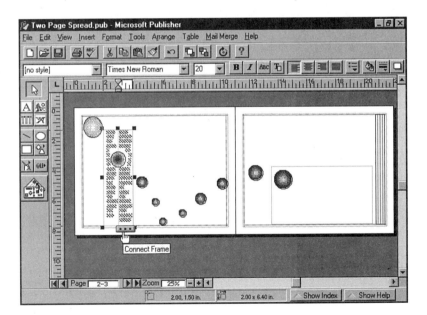

You must identify the frame of origin every time you flow text to another frame. It's a two click process. Click the Connect Frame button of the first frame, and the Pointer changes to a pitcher. The destination text frame must be in view on-screen, so, you may have to change pages, or do some scrolling. With the pitcher full of text from the frame of origin, click in the destination frame. The pitcher tilts, pours the text not visible in the frame of origin, and flows into the frame that you click. If you still have an overflow, read on.

One of the handiest features in Publisher's text flowing is its AutoFlow capability. Start with one text frame and import or type text into it. If you exceed the capacity of the frame, a query appears asking if you want to activate the AutoFlow feature (see Figure 29.25). You can choose Yes or No. Why No? Maybe your page design is planned to have text only in one text frame, not in two or more. The query tips you off that you'd better edit your copy or revise your font size or the frame properties, to make it all fit.

▶ **See** "Setting Text Frame Properties," **page 664**

Figure 29.25

It's nice when Publisher helps you with your text flow.

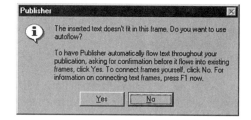

TROUBLESHOOTING

I clicked on the Connect Frame button and have the pitcher, but when I click the destination frame, nothing happens. As you try to flow text, is there a Connect Frame button at the bottom of the destination frame? Chances are, you are clicking a frame that is a picture frame.

Disconnecting Frames

You don't lose any of your text when you disconnect frames. Remember, there are really only two frames connected, although the two may be part of a longer chain of connected frames. Text flows back into the frame of origin when you disconnect two frames. You can create or locate another text frame and pour the overflow into it.

To disconnect text frames, click the frame of origin. Notice the Connect Frame button, which now has a chain, and the Go to Next Frame icons at the bottom of the frame. This is your clue that you have selected a frame of origin. The arrow in the Go to Next Frame icon indicates the direction of the text flow.

Click the Connect Frames button that now has a chain. Text in the destination frame flows back into the frame of origin. This is a boon when you have made a mistake and poured text into the wrong text box. You can reflow excess text into another frame, or edit the text to fit.

Formatting Text in Frames

You have a small business. You understand that saving time and resources is important, so let's save some here. This is an area where Publisher works much like Word.

You can also copy text formatting with the Format Painter, exactly as in Word.

Inserting Text in a Frame

Sometimes you may decide to assemble your thoughts and publication copy in Word and then import the file into Publisher. Or, maybe you have a "staff copywriter" who gives you a file on a floppy disk. You can very simply import the file.

Create the text frame for your file. Choose Insert, Text File. Locate the document you want to import in the Insert Text File dialog box, and Choose OK. You can reformat the text after it's imported.

Setting Line Spacing

In Publisher, you set line spacing by choosing Format, Line Spacing. It is slightly different from the way Word does it (see Figure 29.26).

Figure 29.26
Line Spacing is also called "leading" in the publishing world.

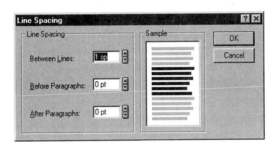

Click in the paragraph you want to revise, or highlight multiple paragraphs to format all at once. Choose Format, Line Spacing, and set your specifications in the dialog box. Look at the Sample to decide if you like your choices, and choose OK when you're satisfied.

Setting Tabs

Here again, we have something that operates so close to the way that Word does, you may already know it. Click in the paragraph that you want tabs in. To access the Tab dialog box, choose Format, Tabs. Select an Alignment, the kind of Leader you want, position your tabs by entering numbers in the Tab Position box, click Set, and you have your tabs.

Adding Bullets and Numbering

Publisher's bullets and numbering are a bit different from Word's. Publisher has more bullets immediately available when you click the Bulleted or Numbered List button in the Formatting toolbar. When you click More at the bottom of the drop-down menu, your options have that familiar Word look.

Inserting Symbols

Inserting symbols in Publisher is exactly the same as in Word. You choose Insert, Symbol. In the dialog box, click the drop-down menu beside Show Symbols From, to select a font from those you have already used in your publication. Click the symbol you want to use and choose OK.

Checking Hyphenation and Spelling

To establish a hyphenation pattern, choose Tools, Hyphenation. The first time you apply hyphenation to a text frame, the dialog box offers options to Turn Off Automatic Hyphenation, Confirm Every Automatic Hyphen, and set the a hyphenation zone in the spinner beside Change Hyphenation Zone To. Smaller numbers maintain a more even right edge by using more hyphens. Larger numbers allow fewer hyphens. If you return to the dialog box, your Options are to revise the original settings for the text box. You can click Automatically Hyphenate This Story, Suggest Hyphens For This Story, or change the Hyphenation Zone.

When you have finished a publication, you *always* check your spelling. Even the most meticulous of spellers has occasional lapses.

Choose Tools, Check Spelling. In the dialog box, if you click Check All Stories, every word throughout your publication is checked. Left unchecked, only the text frame, or connected frames that comprise a story, are spell checked. You can scroll through a list of Suggestions for words that Publisher identifies as either misspelled or not in its dictionary. You can click Ignore Words in UPPERCASE.

The buttons at the right of the dialog box allow you to Ignore a particular word, Ignore All occurrences of it, Change the word to the suggested word, Change All occurrences of this word, Add the word to the dictionary, and to Close the dialog box.

 You never can clearly see a publication you have created. Have at least one other person proof your publication. You may be surprised at the little things they discover. Those "fresh eyes" could spare you a bit of embarrassment.

CHAPTER 30

Adding and Formatting Objects

by Elaine Betts

In this chapter

Inserting Graphic Objects

The function of Publisher is to combine text and graphics in a way that no other application in your Microsoft Office 97 Small Business suite can accomplish. The graphics in your publications convey an image of your company and establish the tone of their content, the text. Some publications are meant to catch your clients' attention. Others are informational. The graphics and their placement play a large part in the overall effect and effectiveness of publications. Your business letterhead may use a formal layout design with few graphics—perhaps your logo and a watermark. Other publications, such as flyers or ads, may be loaded with graphics.

Because your other Small Business applications are compatible with Publisher, things you have created in the other applications, such as Word Pictures and Word documents, can easily be inserted in publications. You also can insert clip art, scanned photographs, picture files, WordArt, and Design Gallery components.

In earlier chapters, we discussed the concept of frames and how they contribute to your publication's graphic design. Now, let's investigate the power of graphics.

- ▶ **See** "Working with Design Gallery," **page 654**
- ▶ **See** "Creating Frames for Content in a Publication," **page 622**
- ▶ **See** "Formatting Frames," **page 649**
- ▶ **See** "Setting Text Frame Properties," **page 664**

Creating Graphic Elements

It would be nice to have the artistic talent and training of Leonardo DaVinci, but computers make it possible for anyone to draw, even those who swear they can't. Create a straight line, an oval, or a rectangle. These are the foundation of all drawing. There's very little you can't "draw" by compiling these shapes (see Figure 30.1).

Figure 30.1

A combination of layered and grouped rectangles and ovals, with a pattern and gradients applied, create the illusion of a 3-D column.

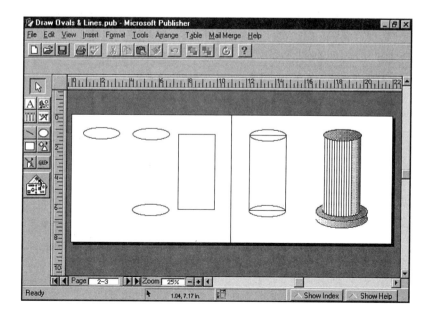

The impression of a third dimension is accomplished by assembling shapes as shown in the previous figure, or by using Custom Shapes. If you want, you can add a shadow to simulate light from a directional source. This lifts objects off the two dimensional plane and creates the illusion of depth.

▶ **See** "Creating Custom Shapes," **page 672**

▶ **See** "Adding a Shadow," **page 649**

▶ **See** "Creating a Custom Shadow," **page 650**

Part **V** Ch **30**

Drawing Shapes   The technique for creating any of the shapes in Publisher is exactly the same. Click the tool in the Publisher toolbar, move the tool onto the page of your publication, hold down the mouse button and drag the size shape you want.

 The Scratch Area is the area that surrounds your publication when you view it at a small magnification. The Scratch Area is a handy space for creating and temporarily storing objects you've already made. (Notice the color. At last, we know where "the gray area" really is.) Objects on the Drawing Board don't print, but they do add to your file size, so it's a good idea to clean them off the Scratch Area before your final output.

Hold down the Shift key before you depress the mouse button to begin dragging out your shape. The shape is perfectly symmetrical, that is, a square, a circle, or a custom shape of equal height and width.

You can create shapes to specific dimensions. Just look at the dimensions at the bottom of your publication screen as you drag out the shape. The left set of dimensions is the exact location on the page, and the right set is the exact height and width of the shape you are drawing. Release the mouse when you have achieved the size you want. You can always resize or reposition the shape (see Figure 30.2).

Both ovals and boxes are drawn by using the appropriate tool and dragging out the shape. After you have drawn an oval or a box, you can revise the default border and change the fill.

To adjust the border thickness and color, choose Format, Border. In the dialog box that appears, under Choose a Thickness, click one of the predefined border thickness icons, or set your own border weight by entering the thickness in the text box at the bottom of the column of icons. To set the color, use the drop-down menu beside Color to open the color swatches.

To change the inside of your shape, choose Format, Fill Color, or Fill Patterns and Shading, as you prefer.

▶ **See** "Using Fill Color, Patterns, and Gradients," **page 673**

Creating Lines   When you use the Line tool to create a line, the line can be at any angle. After the line is drawn, you can set how thick it is and its color. To constrain any line you draw to a perfectly straight line, positioned at 90° or 45°, hold down the Shift key as you drag out the line.

Figure 30.2

Shapes, by default, are drawn with a black border and a white fill, either or both of which can be changed.

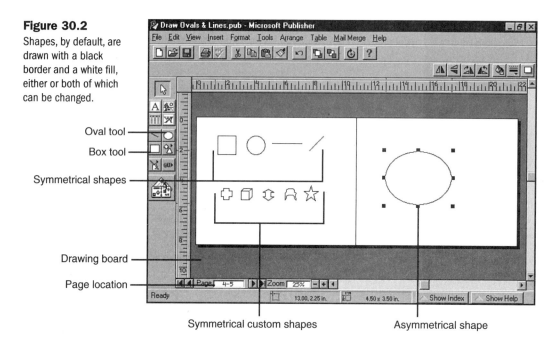

Oval tool

Box tool

Symmetrical shapes

Drawing board

Page location

Symmetrical custom shapes

Asymmetrical shape

To set the line width and color, choose F<u>o</u>rmat, Li<u>n</u>e. In the Line dialog box, click one of the predefined border thickness icons, or set your own line weight by entering the thickness in the text box at the bottom of the column of icons. To set the color, use the drop-down menu beside <u>C</u>olor to open and select from the color swatches. After your color is set, the Sample and all the lines in the dialog box assume that color. For endcaps placement, use any of the predesigned Arrowheads, <u>R</u>ight, <u>L</u>eft, <u>B</u>oth, or <u>N</u>one. After selecting a placement, you can determine the shape of the Arrowheads using the Type drop-down menu (see Figure 30.3).

N O T E   As many things as you *can* do in Publisher, there are a few you can't. You can't apply a pattern or gradient to lines. █

Creating Custom Shapes   Publisher has 36 predesigned custom shapes available in the Publisher toolbar. Click the Custom Shape tool, and the 36 shape options appear. Click the one you want to draw, move the cursor to your publication page, hold down the mouse, and drag the shape to the size you want. After it's drawn, you can revise the border and fill of your custom shape, as well as reposition it (see Figure 30.4).

Figure 30.3

Lines work well in Web page publications.

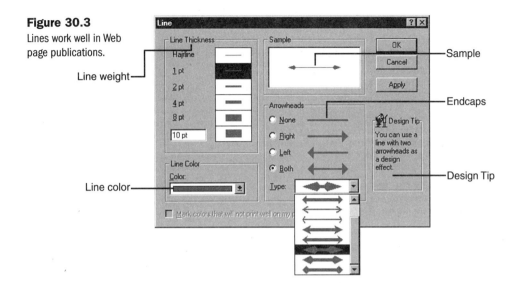

Line weight

Line color

Sample

Endcaps

Design Tip

Figure 30.4

Custom shapes are convenient and readily available.

TIP You can duplicate any Object by holding down both the Alt and Control keys (ALT+CTRL) as you drag the object to a new location.

Using Fill Color, Patterns, and Gradients

Before you make a decision to apply fill color, patterns, or gradients, a word about printing in color. Spot color and color separations are two ways of printing color when your business publications are to be sent out for professional printing. Spot colors are premixed inks that are applied in one pass through the printing press. Separated colors are run through the printing press four times, once for cyan, once for magenta, once for yellow, and once for black. These four colors are used to create any color you choose for your publication. Spot color costs more than black and white printing, since it requires a second pass through the press. Four-color processing costs more than spot colors because it requires four passes, so consider your budget before choosing which to use.

> **CAUTION**
>
> Call your print house to get an estimate and advice *before you begin creating* a color publication that they will print.

If you plan to use a color desktop printer, your color choices are controlled by its ability to produce color. Be aware that the color you see onscreen may print out entirely differently. It's all based upon correlating (calibrating) your printer and your monitor. Check the computer mail-order catalogs for calibration software or ask a professional printer for advice. They work with electronic files for a living. They know what to suggest that will assure that you get what you design.

Fill color is a single color applied evenly. Patterns are a combination of two colors that create a design. Gradients are two colors that gradually blend together in any one of various possible directions, such as, horizontally, vertically, diagonally, or a circular transition.

Selecting a Fill Color   You can fill drawn objects with any of Publisher's premixed colors, shown in the color swatches of the Colors dialog box. Choose Format, Fill Color to open the dialog box. By default, the Basic Colors option button is selected as the Color Model. That's exactly what you want for selecting a color swatch. Changing to All Colors opens the More Colors dialog box described in the next section.

There are color swatches displaying 12 variations of each: Purple, Blue, Green, Yellow, Orange, Red, and Black. The Clear swatch removes any fill, making your object transparent, which leaves only the border color.

There is one particularly helpful thing to notice in the Colors dialog box: The warning for colors that won't print on your specific color desktop printer. This produces an X in colors that won't print. To take advantage of this, you must have a color printer designated for your output, and click in the box beside Mark Colors That Will Not Print on My Printer. If you inadvertently select a color that doesn't work on your printer, black or gray is substituted for the color when you run a test print.

Click the color swatch you want to use and choose OK (see Figure 30.5).

Figure 30.5
Even if you have no color printer, you can use colors for publications that will be sent out for printing and run test prints in grayscale on a desktop printer.

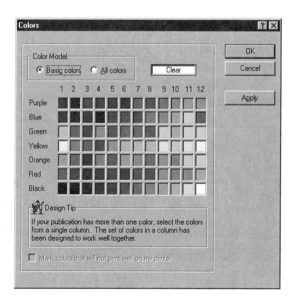

Part
V

Ch
30

Creating More Colors   The More Colors dialog box is where you select most of the colors used in Web Page publications because you can set specific values for Red, Green, and Blue (see Figure 30.6).

> **CAUTION**
>
> As beautiful as they are, there are many colors that just don't work on the Web. Before applying colors in publications bound for the Web, you may want to visit Lynda Weinman's Web site:
>
> **http://www.lynda.com/**
>
> She explains all you need to know about setting Red, Green, and Blue values to create colors for Web graphics. She also has several books about Web graphics design, published by New Riders, each with a CD enclosed. These are full of samples and have color swatches for "safe Web colors."

Figure 30.6
Your color printer may not handle every color you select here.

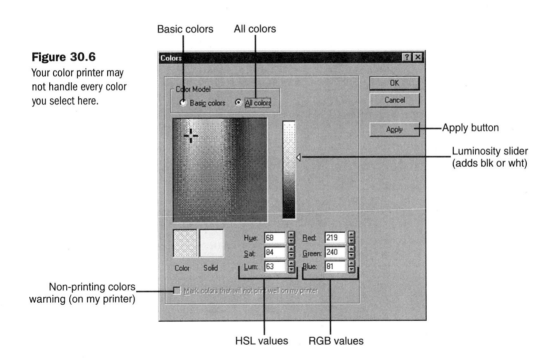

Using a Pattern or a Gradient   Be sure the object you want to have a pattern or a gradient is active. Click it, if it is not already selected. Choose Format, Fill Patterns and Shading and then click the option button under Tint/Shades, Patterns, or Gradients.

The Fill Patterns and Shading dialog box has three options for enhancing an object: Tints/Shades, Patterns, and Gradients. Each works with color a little differently.

Begin in Tints/Shades and choose a single color, the tint and decide how dark or light you want that color to print, from the lightest possible tint, white, to increasingly darker shades of that color, to the darkest possible shade, black.

Patterns work with two colors. You pick both colors in the Color area of the Fill Patterns and Sḥading dialog box, a Basic Color and Color 2. In the Style area, you see a variety of patterns made up of the two colors. Click the pattern you want to use, and choose OK to close the dialog box.

To create a gradient, click the Gradient option button. Next, in the Color area of the Fill Patterns and Sḥading dialog box, choose the two colors you want to use. Finally, scroll through and select a direction you want the two colors to blend. Choose OK to apply your Gradient.

CAUTION

Gradients do not convert to Web pages in Publisher; so, if that's where you are planning to display your publication, avoid them.

Making Objects Transparent   All drawn objects are filled with white, by default. To remove any fill in a drawn object, press Control+T. To remove the transparent property and return the object to the default white fill, click the object to select it, and press Control+T again.

▶ **See** "Creating a Page Border," **page 645**

Using transparent objects, you can assemble a stack of things without hiding anything in the stack. In the next figure, there are three stacked ovals, created by holding the Shift key to make perfect circles (see Figure 30.7). The two outer circles have wide, colored borders and are transparent. The center circle has a fill color and no border. The arrow is a custom shadow design component that is stored in a custom Design Gallery set for re-use.

After drawing and positioning all the components, they are Grouped.

Figure 30.7

The lighter color applied to the circles, and the custom drop shadow applied to the arrow, help create a 3-D effect.

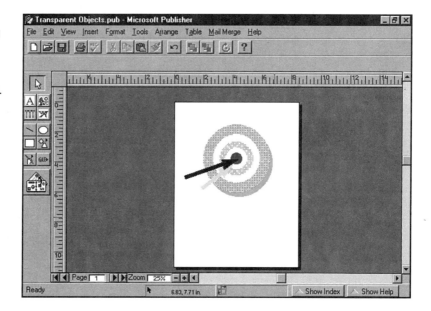

▶ **See** "Working with Design Gallery," **page 654**

▶ **See** "Grouping and Ungrouping Objects," **page 683**

Using Format Painter

Deciding on, and setting your formatting options for, an object frequently requires trying several different options, opening and closing several dialog boxes, and assessing the results in the page. When you finally have it just the way you want it, and want to use the same formatting for another object, do you have to repeat all those steps? No.

After you have formatted a drawn object with a fill color, pattern, or gradient, and a border that suits your overall design, you can apply exactly the same formatting properties to other drawn objects by using the Format Painter. To pick up the formatting properties of an object you have drawn, click first on the formatted object, then click the Format Painter button in the Standard toolbar. Now click the object you want to have the same formatting. Your second click instantly changes the object to formatting that matches the first object you clicked.

TROUBLESHOOTING

I don't like the color I used to fill an object. Must I delete it and start over? Absolutely not. You can click that object, then return to the F̲ormat menu, and choose F̲ill Color to reopen the dialog box and change colors.

Why do my gradients look "raggedy" onscreen? Monitors are pixel-based and can only display color transitions in little square chunks, pixel by pixel. Don't worry. Gradients print beautifully, if professionally printed.

When I print gradients on my color desktop printer, they have bands instead of smooth transitions of color. Was it the colors I chose? No, it's a function of your printer's ability to handle color and the resolution it can achieve. Lower resolution printers, such as color HP inkjet printers, try, but the best they can do is print successive bands of color to simulate a true, blending gradient. If your printer supports Error Diffusion, or has a Graphics tab in its Properties dialog box, you can set Error Diffusion under Dithering.

Using the PageWizards Button

Creating a logo, ad, coupon, or calendar in a publication is as close as the Publisher toolbar and as convenient as all Publisher's PageWizards. The process for creating an ad, a coupon, or a calendar is exactly the same as for a Logo, so we'll use that to explain PageWizards.

A logo projects the image and tone of your company in a single graphic. Every letter, every ad, every small business publication of any sort that you produce, has a logo somewhere. If you already have a logo, you probably have scanned it and stored it in your custom set of the Design Gallery.

▶ **See** "Working with Design Gallery," **page 654**

If you don't have a logo, you can design one yourself. The simplest and quickest way is to use the PageWizards button in the Publisher toolbar. The PageWizards button doesn't create a new publication. Anything you create with the button, an ad, a coupon, or your logo, is inserted in the publication you are working on at the moment.

Click the PageWizards button, then, in the drop-down menu, click Logo, and move the pointer onto the publication page. Drag a rectangle to indicate the approximate size and position on the page where you want to insert the logo. The exact size isn't too important because you can resize it later. When you release the mouse, the Logo PageWizard Design Assistant dialog box opens (see Figure 30.8).

Figure 30.8

Logo is but one of four PageWizard Design Assistant templates available.

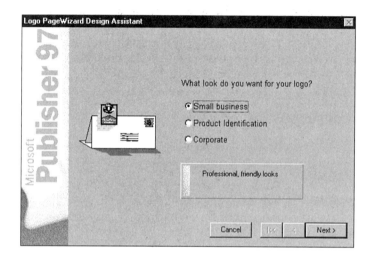

▶ **See** "Resizing Objects," **page 683**

If your curiosity gets the better of you, you can click through all the screens for each type of logo, just to see what's there. Notice that several of the screens have buttons to display More design options. In the Create It! Screen, use the button at the bottom of the screen to go back and cruise through each of the different types until you've seen them all.

▶ **See** "Using Design Assistant to Create Envelopes," **page 639**

Now that you've seen the depth of logo choices and have settled on the one you like best, go through the PageWizard Design Assistant screens, entering text and clicking the option buttons to create your logo. In the final screen, click Create It!, and the logo is inserted where you indicated in the open publication.

Inserting Clip Art, Pictures, and Objects

Throughout all your Microsoft Small Business suite of applications, you find that you insert clip art and picture files in exactly the same way. Choose Insert, ClipArt, or Insert, Picture File, and locate the ClipArt or Picture File on your computer that you want to use. Choose OK, and the job is done.

As with the other Microsoft Office applications, you can also insert objects. Click the Insert Object button in the Publisher toolbar. The Insert Object dialog box opens. A scrolling list, under Object Type, shows objects you can insert. Included in the list are Microsoft Graph 97 Chart, Microsoft Scan, Microsoft Word Documents, and Paintbrush Picture. Select the type of object you want in your publication, and click either the Create New or Create From File option button. What happens next depends on the kind of object you chose. Create New opens another application, Create From File lets you locate and insert a file already created.

Using Picture Display Options

The way inserted pictures are shown on-screen makes a significant difference in the time it takes for your computer to redraw them each time you change views or resize a picture. If you want to see all the details of your pictures, or have very large images, it may take more time than you care to wait. You can display a low resolution version, or hide the pictures all together. Nothing is lost in the printing with low resolution or hidden pictures. Hiding images, or displaying a low resolution version, is merely a way to speed up your publication production.

Choose View, Picture Display to open the dialog box. Click the option button beside Detailed Display, Fast Resize and Zoom, or Hide Pictures, then choose OK (see Figure 30.9). You can change these options at any time as you work on a publication.

Figure 30.9
If your publication has many pictures, and your concentration is on text at the moment, try temporarily hiding the pictures.

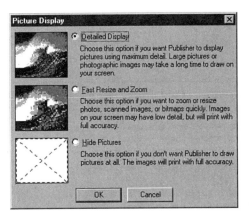

Arranging Frames in Layers

Layering frames in Publisher has many advantages. You can place a text frame on top of an image and make the text frame transparent in order to have text inside it run across an image, like a watermark. You can place a graphic on top of a text frame and have the text run around the image. You can place several graphics on top of one another. (Refer to Figure 30.7, earlier in this chapter.) The combinations are limited only by your imagination.

▶ **See** "Positioning Graphics on Text Frames," **page 686**
▶ **See** "Making Objects Transparent," **page 676**

Each frame in a stack is considered a layer. You may have as many layers in a stack as you like. As you work with layers, you will surely need to rearrange them. There are four menu commands to use. Two move a frame up or down, one layer at a time. Another command moves a layer to the top of a stack, and another moves a frame to the bottom of a stack.

N O T E   If the download speed of your Web page is paramount, avoid layering text and graphics because layered objects *all* become graphics in the conversion process and graphics do take longer to download than text alone.

Although the Bring to Front, and Send to Back buttons in the Standard toolbar work well with only two objects, they don't always offer the layering option you want when you have several objects in a stack. You may want to reposition an object only one layer up or down, not all the way at the top or bottom of the stack. Then the menu choices serve better. In either case, you must click the frame you want to reposition in the stack.

Use the appropriate button, or choose Arrange, Bring to Front. This puts the frame on the very top of the layers. Send to Back moves a frame to the bottom of a stack of layers. Bring Closer moves a frame up one level, whereas Send Farther takes the frame down one level in the stack.

After you have positioned the frames in a stack, Group the layers to prevent accidentally pulling the layers apart as you move or resize them. Yes, you can do both, when layers are grouped.

▶ **See** "Resizing Objects," **page 683**
▶ **See** "Grouping and Ungrouping Objects," **page 683**
▶ **See** "Using the Move Pointer," **page 681**

You can create stacks of stacks. If you have several layered stacks, and each is grouped, you can layer and group these stacks. This is not at all uncommon if you have, say, a layered graphic and a text frame that is layered with a graphic so that the text runs around it.

Using Snap To

When you choose Tools, Snap to Guides, page elements that you move close to a layout guide line automatically snap to the guide line. In the Tools menu, you can also activate Snap to Ruler Marks, as well as have objects snap to other objects on a page by choosing Snap to Objects. This last choice causes objects you move near to other objects to snap to the edge of the object you are approaching.

Turning Off Snap To   Although it's often helpful to use Snap To, there may be occasions when it gets in your way. Things snap when you really want them close, but not right next to a grid line, a guide line, or an object. To de-activate Snap To, again choose Tools, Snap to Guides, or Snap to Objects, or Snap to Ruler Marks. With no check mark beside these, the Snap To instruction is no longer in effect.

Aligning Objects

Publisher uses the term *line up* when referring to aligning objects on a page. If you want to precisely position several frames in relation to one another, this is for you.

You can align objects on the horizontal plane by using Top To Bottom, and on the vertical plane using Left To Right. It's probably easier to grasp these concepts by looking at the Line Up dialog box, which, fortunately, has a preview area labeled, Sample. Below that sample is a description of your choices (see Figure 30.10).

Part

V

Ch

30

Figure 30.10

The Sample area visually reflects your choices.

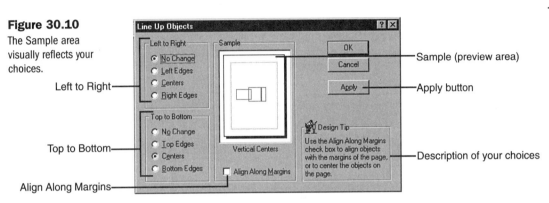

Left to Right

Top to Bottom

Align Along Margins

Sample (preview area)

Apply button

Description of your choices

First, Shift click all the objects you want to align. Next, choose Arrange, Line Up Objects to open the dialog box. In the dialog box, click the option button beside the various choices until you achieve the alignment you want. You can align objects on the horizontal plane by clicking No Change, Left Edges, Centers, or Right Edges, below Left to Right. Vertical options are below Top to Bottom. Again, you click No Change, Left Edges, Centers, or Right Edges. Finally, there is an option to Align Along Margins. As you make choices, observe the relationship of the object icons in the Sample area. You can also test your choices by clicking the Apply button, moving the dialog box out of the way, so you can see the results before you close the dialog box. When you have the alignment you want, choose OK.

Using the Move Pointer   Each object in Publisher, be it text or graphic, is held within a frame. Every time you want to reposition a frame manually, use the move pointer. It's not shown on any toolbar but appears when you click a frame and position the pointer along the perimeter, but not on a handle of the frame (see Figure 30.11).

When the pointer changes to the moving van shape, hold down the mouse and drag the frame into position. Release the mouse when the object is located where you want it.

Nudging Objects   If you move a frame almost to the position you want, but not right on the spot, you can choose Arrange, Nudge Objects to open a dialog box where you have nudge controls (see Figure 30.12).

Figure 30.11

If you choose Tools, Options, you can change the shape of this moving van pointer to a simple crosshair by deselecting Use Helpful Pointers.

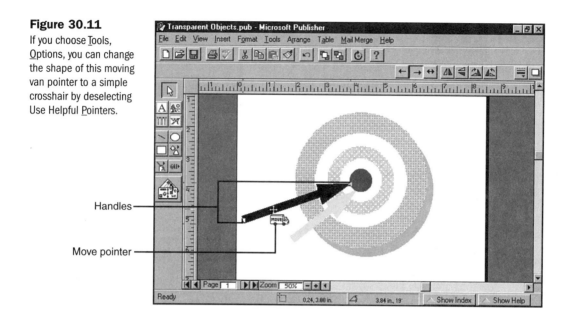

Handles —

Move pointer —

Figure 30.12

The Nudge shortcut key, Alt + arrow keys, is shown in the Design Tip.

Nudge Control buttons —

Nudge a specific distance

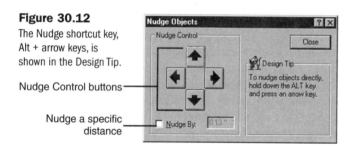

After the Nudge Objects dialog box opens, move it to a place on-screen where you can see the object you are nudging and still click the arrow buttons. Use the directional arrow buttons to nudge up, down, left, or right. If you prefer, you can use specific dimensions (stated in inches) for nudging, which sometimes isn't a nudge at all. You can type in any number, a part of an inch, an inch, or several inches. When you click the arrow buttons, your object hops that distance in whatever direction the arrow you click points. Choose Close, to exit the dialog box.

N O T E Nudging can produce some surprising results if you set a dimension number for Nudge By. That dimension remains in effect until you change it, or deselect Nudge By in the dialog box. In other words, if you enter "1" for Nudge By, everything you Nudge thereafter, using either the shortcut key or the dialog box, is nudged in one inch increments. ▪

Rotating Objects

You can rotate grouped or single objects. The most controlled way to rotate things in Publisher is by using the Rotate Objects dialog box that appears when you click the Rotate button in the Standard toolbar. In this dialog box, you set the degrees of rotation in the spinner beside Angle, or click the rotation arrow buttons below Click a Button to Rotate. Naturally, an object must be clicked to select it before it can be rotated (see Figure 30.13).

Part
V
Ch
30

Figure 30.13
A negative number rotates clockwise and a positive number rotates counterclockwise.

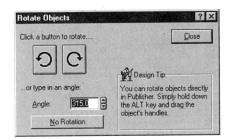

If you need only a 90° rotation, the Rotate Right and Rotate Left buttons in the Formatting toolbar are faster. Click the object you want rotated, then click one of the buttons. If you click rotate buttons repeatedly, the object continues to rotate in 90° increments.

Grouping and Ungrouping Objects

Click the Pointer tool in the Publisher toolbar and drag a rectangle with it that completely surrounds all the objects you want kept together. Immediately after you release the mouse button, the Group Objects icon appears at the bottom of the multiple selections. Click it. The two puzzle pieces in the icon join together. Your objects are now grouped and function as a single object.

Resizing Objects

Every object in all publications is held within its own frame. You can resize any frame, thus any object, using one of the eight handles that appear on the perimeter of a frame you have clicked.

To maintain the proportions of a frame you are resizing, use a corner handle. Press the Shift key before you click the mouse on the frame's corner handle and continue holding down the Shift key until you have dragged the frame to the size you want. Release the mouse button first, then the Shift key.

To resize a frame from its center, press the Control key before you click the mouse button and continue holding the key as you drag. Release the mouse button first, then the Control key. The frame is resized, but the center of the frame remains in its original position.

If you press both Shift and Control before dragging, you maintain the frame's proportions and resize it from the center.

Scaling Pictures

In almost every instance, when you insert a picture, it is too small. On the other hand, sometimes objects you create are too large. You will use your logo often in small business publications and it will need to be scaled up or down to suit the particular publication you are designing.

To scale an object, choose Format, Scale Object, to open the Scale Object dialog box (see Figure 30.14).

Figure 30.14

To maintain the same proportions vertically and horizontally, be sure that both percentage numbers are the same.

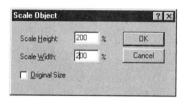

Because the new scale is not applied until you choose OK, occasionally, you will set a scale that doesn't work. If the scale you set proves to be something other than what you want, you can re-open the Scale Object dialog box and return the object to its original size by clicking Original Size in the bottom part of the dialog box.

Cropping a Picture

Cropping, cropping. What can it mean? In the graphic world, it means cutting off a part of an image. If the image is perfect, except for that part over on the right, or at the top, or on any edge, crop it. In Publisher, you can crop Picture and ClipArt files. Choose Format, Crop Picture to open the Format toolbar. In the toolbar is the Crop Picture button. Click the button and move out onto your publication. At first, the pointer is the Move tool, but as soon as you position the Move tool over a handle, the pointer becomes the crossed scissors Crop Picture pointer. Hold down the mouse button and drag the handle to eliminate as much of the image as you like. Release the mouse when your are satisfied (see Figure 30.15).

As long as the image is selected, you can crop along any edge. If you want to crop more after the image is deselected, click it and crop anything on any edge.

> **CAUTION**
>
> Cropping is irreversible. Once you have removed part of an image, you can't restore the cropped part. If you made a mistake, you must reinsert the image and try again.

Figure 30.15
Crop along one or more sides of an image.

Recoloring Pictures

Clip art and pictures are the spice of your publications, but what if you find the perfect image but your budget doesn't allow for full color reproduction? Go ahead and use the image. You can recolor it. Insert the image. Then choose Format, Recolor Object to open the Recolor Object dialog box (see Figure 30.16).

▶ **See** "Inserting Clip Art, Pictures, and Objects," **page 678**

Figure 30.16
Recoloring reduces the color information in a picture or clip art image to two colors.

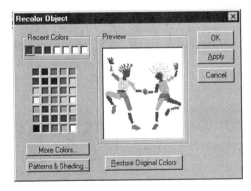

The Recolor Object dialog box is the same color dialog box available in so many places throughout Publisher. To select a color, click one of the color swatches, or choose More Colors, to create your own custom color. You can't apply a pattern or a gradient to the contents of an image frame, only to the frame holding your image.

The effect of recoloring an image is to create a duotone, that is, a two color image; white and another color. That "other color" can be a shade of black if you are restricted to black and white reproduction.

▶ **See** "Using Fill Color, Patterns, and Gradients," **page 673**

Click the right mouse button on any object for quick access to many commands applicable to the object, but located in several menus. It's a real time saver.

TROUBLESHOOTING

Why can't I recolor clip art by ungrouping it? I can't answer that one, but I can tell you how to recolor that clip art. Copy your image to the Clipboard. Open Microsoft Draw and paste it there. Edit the image and choose Exit and Return to reinsert your recolored image in Publisher.

Positioning Graphics on Text Frames

Wrapping text around graphics layered on top of a text frame involves setting properties for the text frame and for the object frame. It doesn't matter which order you work with these frame properties, just that you give the proper instructions to both.

You need to set options in the Text Frame Properties dialog box to Wrap Text Around Objects.

▶ **See** "Setting Text Frame Properties," **page 664**

You also must instruct the graphic how you want the text to wrap around it. Click the object, then click one of the buttons in the Formatting toolbar, Edit Irregular Wrap, Wrap Text to Frame, or Wrap Text to Picture. The effect is different for each button. Edit Irregular Wrap adds handles around the image. You can drag these handles to establish a shape that does not conform to either the rectangular object frame or the outline of the graphic inside the frame. Wrap Text to Frame runs text right up to the perimeter of the graphic's frame, and Wrap Text to Picture wraps text to a shape created by Publisher that surrounds the contents of the frame (see Figure 30.17).

Figure 30.17

This example shows the result of first setting Wrap Text Around Objects in the Text Frame Properties dialog box, and then clicking the Wrap Text to Picture button in the Formatting toolbar.

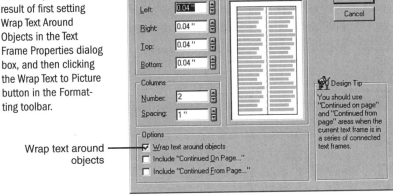

Wrap text around objects

Wrap text to picture

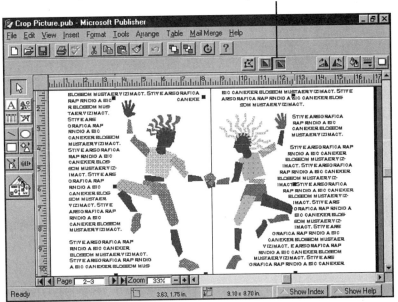

Part V

Ch 30

Inserting a Table

If you have worked with tables in Word, this is familiar territory in Publisher. Many of the things you want to do in a table are done in exactly the same way in Word as in Publisher, so the concentration here is on those things Publisher does differently.

The Table button in the Publisher toolbar looks like the button in Word; however, Publisher's Table button has no drop-down menu for setting the number of rows and columns. Instead, you move the pointer out on to your publication page and draw a rectangle the approximate size and position you want your Publisher table to be. This sets the frame to hold your table and opens the Create Table dialog box (see Figure 30.18).

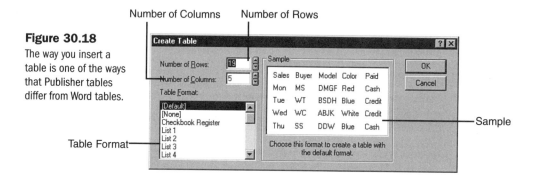

Figure 30.18
The way you insert a table is one of the ways that Publisher tables differ from Word tables.

Number of Columns   Number of Rows

Table Format

Sample

N O T E   Tables appear in Web pages on almost every site. They are about the only way you can control text flow on the Web. You should know, though, that Publisher tables are converted to graphic objects, so use them sparingly for faster download of your pages. ■

Formatting Tables

Publisher tables can have grid lines or none, cell fill colors, or transparent cells. The text in a table can be formatted in the same way any text is formatted throughout Publisher. You can also place a picture underneath a table to enhance its visual impact.

Highlighting an Entire Table

To apply formatting to all of your table at once, you need to select (highlight) all of the table. To do this, click at the intersection of the table row and column markers, at the upper leftmost corner of the table.

N O T E   To delete a table frame with its contents, you must highlight the entire table and hold down the Control key and then press the Delete key. ■

Using AutoFormat

Once a table is inserted, the formatting you chose may not work as well as you thought it would. All is not lost. You can revise the formatting with AutoFormat. When you choose Table, AutoFormat, the identical selection of table formats appears in a dialog box titled Auto Format, that appeared when you first created the frame to hold your table Scroll through the list of formatting choices under Table Format and when you see something interesting, click the name. A preview of your choice shows on the Sample area in the right side of the dialog box.

Try clicking the Options button to use Formats to Apply choices. These refer to the predesigned components of the various table formats. You can use them or click to remove the check mark and not use them. Observe changes in the Sample area as you check or uncheck options under Formats To Apply.

 TIP If you decided against using the Design Gallery to create a Table of Contents for your publication, use AutoFormat as the foundation to create your own. There are three basic varieties of AutoFormat Table of Contents.

Adding Fill Color to Table Cells

To add fill color to one or more cells, you must drag to select the cell and use the Object Color button in the Formatting Toolbar. Click the button to access the color swatches and click the color to apply to the background of the selected cell.

Using Grow to Fit Text

If the text in some or all of your cells is truncated (cut off), select the entire table and choose Table, Grow to Fit. Now all your text is revealed.

▶ **See** "Highlighting an Entire Table," **page 688**

Adding Pictures to Tables

Pictures used with tables don't live inside table cells. They are actually a graphic frame stacked with your table. Because the graphic is typically below the table, you need to make the table frame transparent. Select the entire table and press Ctrl+T to make the table transparent. Your graphic now shows through the table.

▶ **See** "Inserting Graphic Objects," **page 670**

 TROUBLESHOOTING

Why do some cells in my table obscure part of the graphic I have below the table? When cells are filled, they are opaque, so nothing layered below those filled cells shows through.

Why can't I merge two or more cells in the same column? You can't merge vertical cells. It's just one of those things.

Text in my table cells just doesn't fit. Must I edit the cells' contents? No, you can highlight the entire table and reduce the font size, or change the cell margins in the Table Cell Properties dialog box. Choose Format, Table Cell Properties.

CHAPTER 31

Working with Final Output

by Elaine Betts

In this chapter

Print Troubleshooting

In Chapter 28, "Using Publisher to Market Your Business," I admonished you to plan every phase of your publication *before* you begin working on it. Well, this is one of the reasons I said that. If you plan in advance, you dramatically reduce the chances of unexpected results during final output.

▶ **See** "Planning a Publication," **page 608**

Some common printing problems you might encounter include: gradients that look banded, book fold publications that don't print pages in the proper order, slow printing, and pages that print with part on one piece of paper, part on another. This is far from a complete list, but of these four, three are a function of the printer itself, and only one is a problem within the publication—the book fold.

▶ For more information on book folds, **See** "Using Special Papers," **page 634**

As you can see, printing problems involve more than just your printer and the publication. Desktop printing relies on printer drivers, printer capabilities, the amount of memory your printer has, the fonts you have installed, correct setup of the publication, the kind of paper you use, and, so some say, the phase of the moon.

If the problem is with something you have or haven't done in Publisher, chances are the solution is in the Print Troubleshooter. Print Troubleshooter is a giant step in the right direction toward resolving problems you're bound to encounter while working with publication output.

To activate Print Troubleshooter, choose Tools, Options, and click Print with Print Troubleshooter (see Figure 31.1).

Figure 31.1
This one click can save you hours of aggravation when printing publications.

Print with Print Troubleshooter

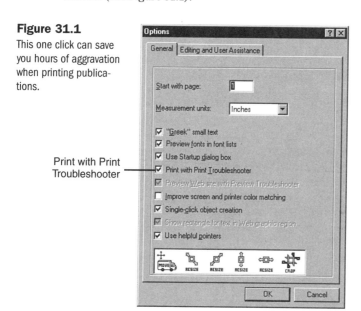

When you have worked for a while with publications, and get a handle on the way your printer operates, you may want to deactivate the Print Troubleshooter. Simply return to Tools, Options, and click Print with Print Troubleshooter to remove the check mark. You can always reactivate it when something unexpected arises. Choose Help, Print Troubleshooter, to open the same Help files opened by having Print with Print Troubleshooter checked in the Options dialog box.

Printing Test Prints

Throughout the development phase of a publication, you will run a test print at least once, and possibly much more often, to get a sense of what your work looks like on paper. If your final output is to be done on your desktop printer, you'll have a very good idea of how the publication looks. If you plan to send your publication out to a professional print house, or to duplicate an original you print yourself, you'll have an approximate idea of what the publication looks like. Even a black and white print of a color publication is helpful. At the very least, you'll be able to assess your overall layout, if not the colors or specific paper.

Choose File, Print. Deselect Print Crop Marks and click Use Print Troubleshooter if you need help. If you want to print only the page you are viewing onscreen, click Current Page. You may also choose a range of pages to print. Run off one copy to test your design and proofread the text. (See Figure 31.2 for a sample of the Print dialog box.)

Figure 31.2
You can run a test print of specific pages in a multipage publication.

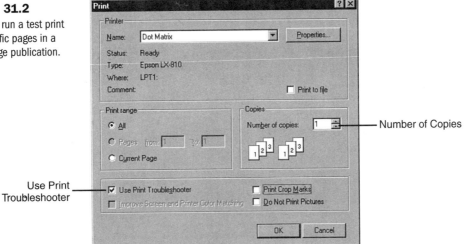

Number of Copies

Use Print Troubleshooter

T I P If you just want to proof the text in your publication, you can speed up your printing by clicking Do Not Print Pictures. Later, when you do want to print everything, you can remove the check mark.

Tiling Large Publications

Banners and posters are large publications that can't be printed on standard letter-size paper. Well, not without Tiling, that is. When you Tile a large publication, the publication is sectioned off, like graph paper, and each section is printed on one sheet of paper.

Notice that when you choose File, Print, for a large publication, the dialog box has a new Tile Printing Options button in the lower-left corner. Click this button to open the Poster and Banner Printing Options dialog box (see Figure 31.3).

After the sections are printed, you need to trim off the inescapable margin required by all desktop printers, and then assemble the Tiles. You can, however, set the slimmest margin your printer can produce. Check your printer's documentation for printing specifications. For instance, a Hewlett-Packard DeskWriter C can print an area 8 inches by 10.15 inches, indicating that the side margins may be .25 inch, while the top margin needs to be .5 inch, and the bottom margin as little as .35 inch. Enter the margin dimension beside Overlap Tiles By, and choose OK (see Figures 31.3 and 31.4).

Figure 31.3

This banner is actually 5 feet long.

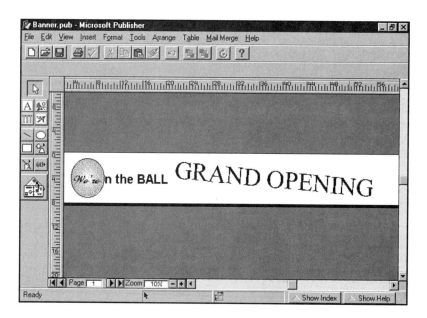

When the Tile Printing Options dialog closes, you return to the Print dialog, set the number of copies you want to print, and choose OK.

Figure 31.4

To save paper and time, you can print one tile to test how the entire banner will look.

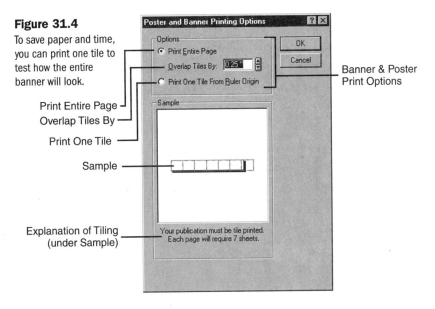

Print Entire Page
Overlap Tiles By
Print One Tile
Sample
Explanation of Tiling (under Sample)

Banner & Poster Print Options

Printing Small Publications

The Print dialog box in Publisher is a very smart dialog box. It recognizes when your publication is small enough to print more than one copy per page. When you choose File, Print, and then click the Page Options button, it has already selected Print Multiple Copies Per Sheet and determined the number of copies per page (refer to Figure 31.2). Look at the Sample to see how many copies per sheet of paper your printer can handle (see Figures 31.5 and 31.6).

Figure 31.5

This is a postcard, measuring 2.75 inches by 4.75 inches.

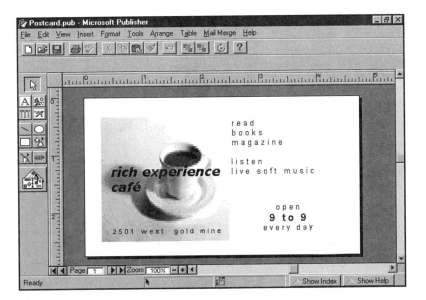

Figure 31.6

Publisher decides how many of these postcards you can print on each 8.5- by 11-inch sheet of paper.

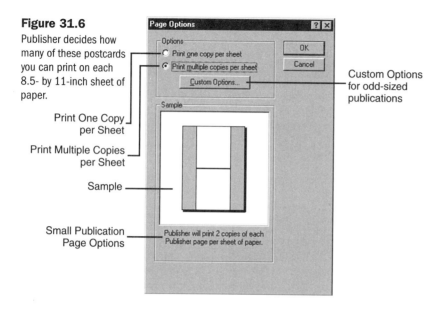

Print One Copy per Sheet

Print Multiple Copies per Sheet

Sample

Small Publication Page Options

Custom Options for odd-sized publications

Custom Options in the Page Options dialog box allow you to establish margins for other size publications.

Printing in Color

Color is the biggest variable you encounter in printing publications. Colors that were perfect on screen may print completely differently.

▶ **See** "Using Fill Color, Patterns, and Gradients," **page 673**

Fortunately, there is a way to come closer to what you expect, but your desktop printer *must* support Image Color Matching.

First, choose Tools, Options, and click Improve Screen and Printer Color Matching. Now, when you open the Colors dialog box, an "X" appears through colors that won't print on your printer. To take advantage of this, you must have a color printer designated for your output, and then click in the box beside Mark Colors That Will Not Print on My Printer, in the Colors dialog box.

Preparing an Outside Print Job

It never hurts to call your print house representative again to ask what settings you should use for your publication. This makes their job easier and saves you time, both of which save you money. If your print house supplies a printer driver, or recommends a specific one, be sure to use it. Publisher only refers to the driver in order to set your publication's print specifications to match the output printer's capabilities. You do not have to actually own that printer.

▶ **See** "Using Fill Color, Patterns, and Gradients," **page 673**

Installing a Generic Print Driver

A generic printer driver is available for Outside Printer publications. This driver is part of your Windows 95 installation. If you do not have the generic driver loaded on your system, you can load it from your system CD or disks (see Figure 31.7).

Figure 31.7
Press F1 while this Reminder dialog box and the Publisher Help files are open to step you through installing a generic outside printer driver.

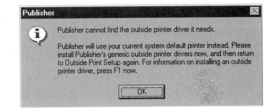

With a printer driver designated, you choose File, Outside Printer Setup, to access the Outside Printer Setup dialog box (see Figure 31.8). The Outside Printer Setup is a series of screens, much like any wizard. Click through the screens to set up your printing configuration.

Figure 31.8
Full color is also called Process printing, or CMYK (cyan, magenta, yellow, and black), whereas Spot Color is a premixed ink.

Black and White, or Gray Scale

Spot Color and Duotones

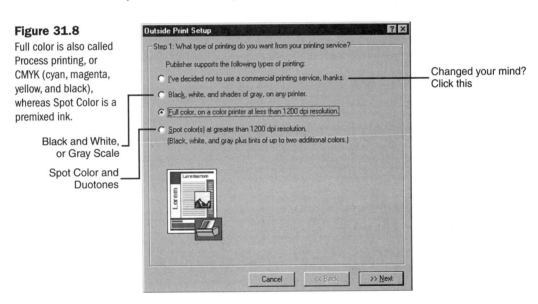

Changed your mind? Click this

Printing a Proof

With an Outside Printer designated, you can still use your desktop printer to make proof prints. Choose File, Print Proof. This opens the familiar Print dialog box, with a new name, Print Proof. Select the printer you want to use for proofing your publication, the page range, and number of copies you want. If you want to see the crop marks, click Show All Print Marks. When your options are set, choose OK.

Understanding Crop Marks

Crop marks indicate where you want the print house to trim (cut off) the excess paper required to run paper through any printing mechanism. Crop marks indicate the final size of your publication. Publishers' crop marks look like a capital letter "L," rotated at each corner of your publication to indicate the intersection of vertical and horizontal trim lines.

Full color and Spot Color publications require that each piece of paper be run through the printing press at least twice, and possibly more. To keep the paper from shifting position each time it goes through the printing press, registration marks are also used to align the paper in exactly the same position as each color is applied.

N O T E   If your publication is very close to the print size limitations of your printer, the crop marks may not show in your proof prints, even though you requested them in the Print Proof dialog box. Crop marks do show when your print house runs the publication. ▧

Printing a Print InfoSheet

Choose File, Print InfoSheet for a hard copy of all the specifications a print house needs to assure that they produce your publication the way you designed it. The Print InfoSheet includes the fonts, colors, print resolution, kind of proof printer you used, and other specification information that helps during the final phase of your Outside Print job.

> **CAUTION**
>
> No matter how thoroughly you prepare an outside print job, there is no guarantee of a perfect output *unless* you request a professional proof print to preview and attend the print run. Professional proof prints cost, but every cent spent for one is money saved in the final print run.

Using Mail Merge

Your publication is finished. Your design is great, Test prints look good, and now, it's time to get it in the mail. There is an entire chapter in this book that discusses Mail Merge: Chapter 15. As you read through Chapter 15, you need only perform a bit of mental gymnastics, changing Main Document to publication, and Data Source to Address List. The process for creating and editing a mail merge follows in exactly the same manner in Publisher.

You must have both a publication with mail merge fields and an address list (a data source). Each publication is linked to *only one* data source.

N O T E   The PageWizard has a ready-made set of address labels correlated to Avery label sizes. ▧

▶ **See** "Merging Documents," **page 302**

▶ **See** "Using the PageWizard," **page 615**

Creating an Address List

If there is no address list, you need to create one. Enter the name and address information, or create custom fields by clicking the Customize button. To access this screen, choose Mail Merge, Create Publisher Address List (see Figure 31.9).

Enter Address Information

Figure 31.9
Although this looks different, it functions the same as the Create Data Source screen in Word.

Customize Fields

Filter or Sort Entries

New Entry

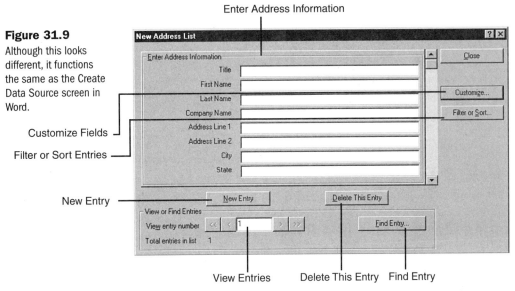

View Entries   Delete This Entry   Find Entry

Each person, even those working for the same company, needs a separate record in your Address List. Enter the name, address, and any of the other information you might use in a merge publication or on labels. To start a new record, click the New Entry button.

 T I P When you want to insert customer specific references in your Mail Merge publications, such as the name of a product they bought from you, when you last worked for them, or the amount and terms of a discount you arranged with them, click Add New Field in the Customize Address List dialog box. Then click Mail Merge, Insert Field, to create a field that holds the personalized data.

When your new Address List is complete, the Save As dialog box opens. Give your Address List any name that suits you. The extension .mdb is automatically appended.

Opening a Data Source

To tap into those data resources you've already created, perhaps in Word or Outlook, choose Mail Merge, Open Data Source (see Figure 31.10).

Part
V

Ch
31

N O T E Publisher does not *directly* support Outlook 97. You can, however, export an Outlook
Contacts list in .mdb or .dbf format, and use that file as your Data Source. ▪

Figure 31.10

The Open Data Source
dialog box has buttons
to Merge Information
from a File, or to Create
an Address List.

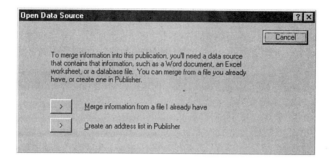

When you click <u>M</u>erge Information from a File I Already Have, the Open Data Source dialog
box opens for you to locate and use an existing data source. Navigate to find the one you want,
highlight it, and choose <u>O</u>pen.

▶ **See** "Maintaining a Contact List," **page 789**

Creating Merge Fields in a Publication

It's all well and good to have Data Sources, but you must have someplace for that data to go.
You can have a completely separate text frame for the data, such as an address label, or you
can insert field codes in the body of existing text to personalize one publication for many
recipients.

Follow these steps to insert merge code:

1. Create a new text frame to hold the mail merge data. Position the frame anywhere you
   like. If you are inserting a merge field in an existing text frame, position the cursor
   where you want the merge field information inserted.

2. The data source information must be in existence to actually perform a mail merge.
   Choose <u>M</u>ail Merge, <u>O</u>pen Data Source. Click <u>M</u>erge Information from a File I Already
   Have. If you forgot to create one, click <u>C</u>reate an Address List, save it, and then go on to
   the next step.

3. Locate the data source file, and choose Open.

4. In the Insert Fields dialog box, highlight the name of a field you want to include in your
   publication, and choose <u>I</u>nsert. The dialog box remains open for you to continue
   inserting fields. When you are finished, choose <u>C</u>lose.

   If you discover, after closing the dialog box, that you have omitted a field, choose <u>M</u>ail
   Merge, <u>I</u>nsert Field, and highlight the field, then choose <u>I</u>nsert, and choose <u>C</u>lose again
   (see Figure 31.11).

Figure 31.11

Field codes are inserted with no spaces.

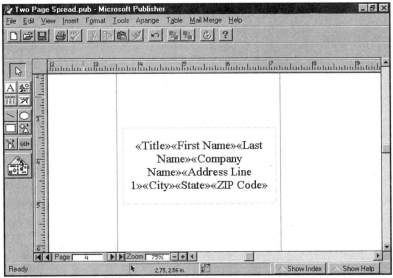

The field codes in your publication will probably differ from this illustration, but all field codes are inserted in a single string with no spaces. When you have concluded the selection of fields, and returned to your publication, it's time to insert spaces, commas, and paragraph returns between fields. This is a *must*. Otherwise, all your merge field data runs into a single, incomprehensible line of letters. When the spacing, line breaks, and punctuation are done, you can format the text so that it is compatible with your overall publication design.

▶ **See** "Formatting Frames," **page 649**

▶ **See** "Formatting Text in Frames," **page 667**

Outputting the Merge

The big moment is here. It's time to merge and print your publication. The field codes are replaced by real data that you can preview before actually setting your printer to the task.

Choose Mail Merge, Merge, and the Preview Data dialog box appears (see Figure 31.12). A new copy of your publication is created for each Data Source Record you included in the merge. These records are all held within the open publication window. Click the arrow buttons to check for errors in each copy of the merge publication.

Figure 31.12

You can merge as few as one or hundreds of Data Source records into one publication.

—Click here to preview

CAUTION

Click through every entry in the list to be certain the merged data is accurate and correctly spaced. A simple misplaced comma or period in a mail merge can ruin the professional impact of your publication.

After you have gone through each of the merged publication copies, choose Close. The publication displayed in your window returns to showing only field codes, but the information you want merged is still there and ready to be printed. From here, choose, File, Print Merge (see Figure 31.13).

The most important task you have, after previewing each merged publication copy, is to run off a test print of your merge. Click the Test button, and the first of your merged publications is printed. If the test goes well, you again choose File, Print Merge, and under Print Range, select All Entries or the range of Entries you want to print.

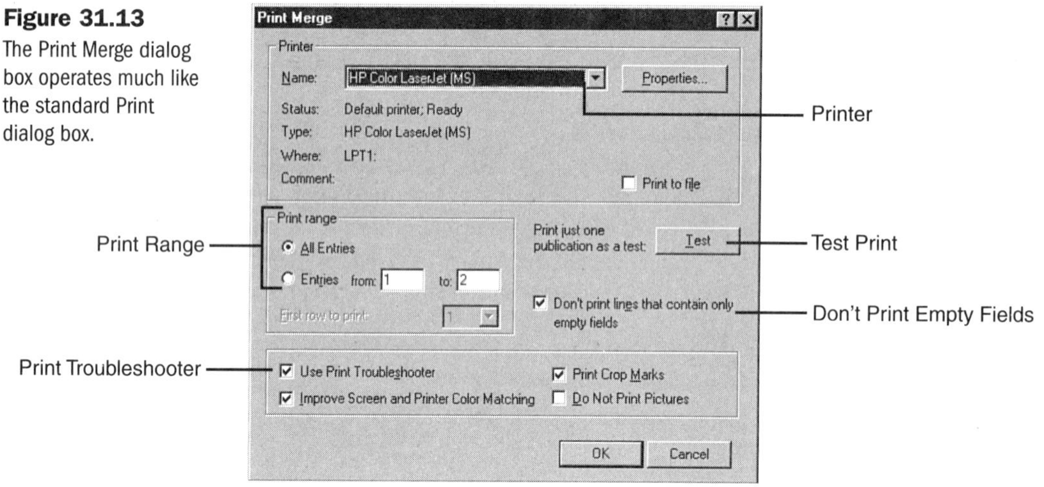

Figure 31.13

The Print Merge dialog box operates much like the standard Print dialog box.

Printer

Test Print

Don't Print Empty Fields

Print Range

Print Troubleshooter

TROUBLESHOOTING

Why can't I do a merge after I drag and drop my mail merge fields from one publication to another publication? Notice, there are no double brackets around your field codes. There is a lot of information underlying what looks like a simple process. Each mail merge publication has a link to its data source and that link does not travel to a new publication when you drag and drop, or even when you cut and paste. The selection arrives in your second publication as text, not as merge field codes.

Delivering a Publication via E-mail

A very economical way of delivering your marketing materials is via e-mail. You can bulk mail as many copies as you like, and it costs no more than your online time charges. To send your publication via e-mail, you must have a mail system that works with Publisher, such as Microsoft Exchange Client or Outlook.

Choose File, Send. A Publisher Reminder appears, prompting you to save before sending out your publication. Click Yes and your mail system opens. Finish by selecting those persons in your e-mail address list that you want to receive your publication.

Converting a Publication to a Web Site

Until now, we have concentrated most of our attention on printed publications because most people create and upload Web pages less frequently than they produce hard copy publications. Web sites, however, are the way of the '90s, and almost any business can profit from reaching the huge numbers of people who use the Internet. If you sell a product or provide a service, you can create a Web Site publication that tells viewers about your business and lists your clients, as evidence of your business history.

▶ **See** "Creating and Publishing Web Documents," **page 925**

You can convert publications you've already designed into a Web page. Perhaps you have a postcard, brochure, or catalogue you originally created for mailing, and now you want to use it on the Web. If your publication has multiple pages, it can become your whole Web site.

Choose File, Create Web Site from Current Publication. A Reminder dialog box appears to help you decide if the publication you've chosen will work as a Web site (see Figure 31.14).

Part
V

Ch
31

Figure 31.14
Take advantage of Publisher's Design Checker to help decide if a publication will work well on the Web.

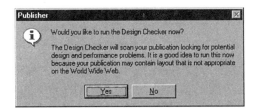

When you click Yes, the Design Checker opens and requests instructions as to how many of the current publication's pages you want to convert. You can convert All or a range of sequential Pages. Be sure to click the Options button to select the things Design Checker examines (see Figure 31.15).

Figure 31.15
Long Download is not a
time estimate, merely a
notation that it will
require extra time to
download.

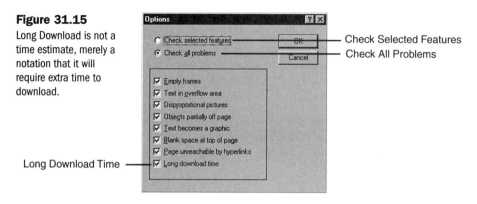

Check Selected Features
Check All Problems

Long Download Time

T I P If you want to convert pages that are not sequential in your publication, you can do multiple conver-
sions, a page at a time, and save them all to the same folder.

When you close the Options dialog box by choosing OK, you return to the Design Checker
dialog box. Choose OK here, and another Design Checker dialog box opens. This dialog box
states problems as they are found and offers suggestions to resolve the situation.

▶ **See** "Using Design Checker," **page 659**

N O T E The name of your publication becomes the name in the title bar of your Web site visitor's
browser. If you have been designing your Web publication under a filename that doesn't
say what you want to appear in every Web visitor's browser title bar, be sure to rename the publication.
Choose File, Save As, and enter a new name for the publication.

Adding Hyperlinks to a Web Publication

Hyperlinks are the device used on Web pages to move you from one page to another or from
your site to another site on the Web. Because the Hyperlink is actually code embedded beneath the surface of what appears on screen, you can use anything as the mechanism for a
hyperlink, including text, a button, a graphic, or even a section of a graphic. Hyperlinks can be
internal, that is, link to another page on your Web site, or external, linking to another Web site.

> **CAUTION**
>
> If your Web site publication has more than one page, you *must* have hyperlinks from page to page;
> otherwise, your site viewer has no way of navigating from the home page to the rest of your pages. Don't
> leave your Web visitors lost in the maze, either. Give them an option to return to your home page, no matter
> which page they are viewing.

To add hyperlinks to your Web pages, click an object or highlight the text you want for a
hyperlink. Next, click the Hyperlink button in the Standard toolbar to open the Hyperlink dialog box. Under Create a Hyperlink To, click the type of hyperlink you want. Your options are

A Document Already on the Internet, Another Page in Your Web Site, An Internet E-Mail Address, or A File on Your Hard Drive. (See Figure 31.16 for your hyperlink options.)

Figure 31.16
Notice that one of the hyperlink choices, A File on Your Hard Drive, can be used on pages viewed via an intranet, as opposed to the Internet.

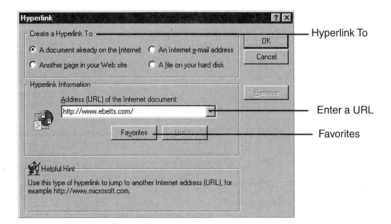

Hyperlink To

Enter a URL

Favorites

Below Hyperlink Information, specify an existing Web address (external hyperlink) and its URL (Uniform Resource Locator, aka: Address), or the page in your publication (internal hyperlink). If your pages are to be viewed on an intranet, a set of pages available only to networked computers, rather than the entire world, you can link to A File on Your Hard Drive, or to one somewhere on that network of computers. It's interesting to note that, if you are planning to upload your publication to the Internet, you can still use the link to A File on Your Hard Drive. The file you indicate becomes an integral part of your Web site when you upload your pages.

Adding In-line Text Hyperlinks   An inline text hyperlink is one that appears within the body of text on your Web page. It's not necessary to state the obvious in the text by entering, "Link to the Microsoft Publisher Home Page," or "Jump to Garage Fonts Virtual Garage," or equally explicit references. You can use any words to indicate the hyperlink because the URL is actually buried inside the Hypertext Markup Language (HTML) that your page is translated into when you convert a publication to a Web site. After it's defined, text that is hyperlinked changes color. The text you highlight is the visible cue that it is a link, so make the words interesting enough to coax your viewer into clicking the link. The curiosity your wording arouses is resolved when the link is clicked and your visitor arrives at the new destination.

N O T E   Don't forget that the combination of graphics within a text frame, or text frames that wrap around another text frame in your publication, become one large graphic when the publication is converted to a Web site. This means that inline hyperlinks cannot be created within that text.

Highlight the text you want to use for the hyperlink and click the Hyperlink button in the Standard toolbar to open the Hyperlink dialog box.

▶ **See** "Adding Hyperlinks to a Web Publication," **page 704**

After your Hyperlink dialog box choices are made, choose OK to return to your Web Site publication. Text within a frame that is designated as a hyperlink changes color to tip off your site visitors that it is a hyperlink. Its color coding says, "Click to leave this page and go elsewhere." After your visitor has followed that hyperlink, and returned to the page, the color changes again to indicate that the link was visited.

N O T E   In multipage Web Sites, it's easy to miss "connecting all the dots." Be sure your visitor sees all your wonderful work. Preview your Web site at least once before uploading it.

▶ **See** "Previewing Your Web Site," **page 709**

Adding Graphic Hyperlinks   Graphic hyperlinks technically are anything that isn't text on a Web page. The graphic may be a Clip Art button or an icon. It may be a picture. It may be a combination of text layered with another text frame or a graphic, because this combination becomes a graphic when you convert a publication to a Web site.

A graphic hyperlink requires that an Object already be inserted in your Web publication. Click the graphic object in your publication before you click the hyperlink button in the Standard toolbar. In the Hyperlink dialog box, select the kind of hyperlink you want, enter any hyperlink information required, and choose OK. The entire graphic object is now a hyperlink.

▶ **See** "Adding Hyperlinks to a Web Publication," **page 704**

Adding Image Map Hyperlinks   An image map, in Web speak, is any graphic you divide into sections, with each section being used for a different hyperlink. By sectioning off one portion of the graphic, and making it a hyperlink, you enter an instruction that determines where your visitor goes when the section is clicked. Image maps are typically used for internal links to other pages on your site.

Each section is called a Hot Spot. Graphic image maps have at least two, and often more, Hot Spots, leading to different internal links (see Figure 31.17). There is a special tool for creating Hot Spots in images. This button appears below the Design Gallery button in the Publisher toolbar *only* when you have a Web Page publication open onscreen.

The first thing you need to create your own image map is an Object inserted in your Web Page publication. Any sort of Object will work, since you use the Picture Hot Spot tool to define the sections that are Hyperlinks, and these Hot Spots lie invisibly on top of the Graphic Object.

CAUTION

As you are creating or removing Hot Spot or graphic hyperlinks, activate Show Boundaries and Guides under the View menu. If these are hidden, it's impossible to know where the edges of your Hot Spots are located and, thus, very difficult to position or select them.

Figure 31.17

The sections indicated in this image are Hot Spots used to navigate to other pages in the first Westword site (**http://www.westword.com**).

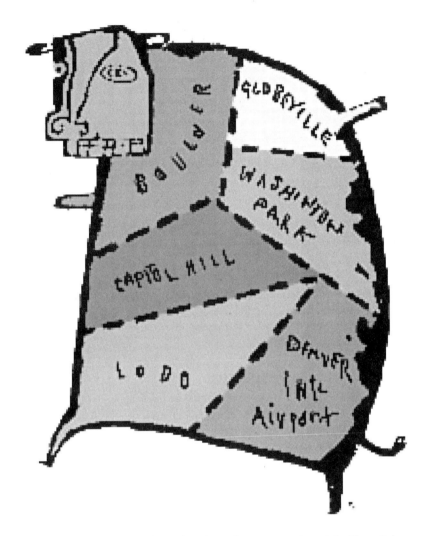

Each Hot Spot must be created individually, rather than all at one opening of the Hyperlink dialog box. To define a Hot Spot:

1. Click the Picture Hot Spot button in the Publisher toolbar.

2. Draw a rectangle on the part of the object you want to be a Hot Spot hyperlink. When you release the mouse, the Hyperlink dialog box opens.

3. Select the type of link you want, A Document Already on the Internet, Another Page in Your Web Site, An Internet E-Mail Address, or A File on Your Hard Drive.

4. Enter the hyperlink address. This may be a URL or the name and path to a document. Choose OK to close the dialog box.

5. Continue defining as many Hot Spots as you want by repeating the preceding steps.

T I P Hot spots should not overlap. When a viewer clicks a Hot Spot, it should refer to only one address. You can draw your Hot Spots a bit farther apart than you want them, since after the image map hyperlink is set up, you can accurately position it by pressing Alt+ the arrow keys to nudge the Hot Spot into place.

Changing a Hyperlink

If you want to change an existing hyperlink's destination, highlight the text hyperlink, or click the graphic, or the edge of a Hot Spot hyperlink, and then click the Hyperlink button in the Standard toolbar to open the Hyperlink dialog box. Change the kind of hyperlink, or revise the hyperlink information. Choose OK to close the dialog box.

If you want only to edit the words you used on the page to indicate a hyperlink, highlight the text and retype the words. The hyperlink information and the hyperlink color indication remain unchanged.

Removing a Hyperlink

Highlight the text, graphic, or Hot Spot hyperlink and click the Hyperlink button in the Standard toolbar. In the Hyperlink dialog box, click the Remove button. Text hyperlinks lose their color indicator, but graphic or Hot Spot hyperlinks show no visible change when a hyperlink is removed.

Viewing Web Site Properties

No matter what the name of your Web site publication, if it is a multipage Web site, the name of the first page defaults to "index.html" when you convert it to a Web site. Your particular Web service provider may require a different first page name or extension. You should call them to confirm their requirements. If the default "index.html" needs revision, choose File, Web Site Properties to make the changes (see Figure 31.18).

Figure 31.18
You can type in whatever your Web service provider requires, or select from the drop-down menus.

In the Web Site Properties dialog box, type in the changes, or select from the drop-down menus beside Home Page File Name and File Name Extension, and then choose OK.

Previewing Your Web Site

You're well on the way to completing your Web site, aglow with the prospects of the business it will generate; but, it might be a good idea to see what the site will look like on the Web before it gets there. It's a good way to test your links and catch any mistakes. This is the only instance in Publisher that you have a need to preview your work, since the technology and specifications applied to Web Site publications differ from printed materials. Choose File, Preview Web Site to open the Preview Web Pages dialog box shown in Figure 31.19.

Figure 31.19
After the first time you preview pages, this dialog box changes its title to Preview Web Site.

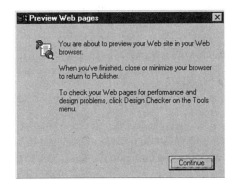

It takes a moment to make the transition, but shortly, Microsoft Internet Explorer opens with your home page displayed at 100%.

If, by chance, you don't have the Preview Troubleshooter onscreen, you can activate it by choosing Tools, Options. Click in the box beside Preview Web Site with Preview Trouble-shooter, and choose OK.

Click through your internal hyperlinks, looking at each page. Of course, because you're not online, you can't verify your external links. That happens after you upload. You can minimize Internet Explorer and make any revisions you feel are required, and then maximize it again for another look. When all your corrections are made and you're finished previewing, exit Microsoft Internet Explorer.

Publishing Your Web Site to Folder

If you're not quite ready to upload your site to the Internet, or you haven't yet made arrangements for an Internet Service Provider and *can't* publish to the Web, choose File, Publish Web Site to Folder to store your converted pages until you are ready for uploading. If this is your first Web Site publication, there is a folder already made and waiting to hold your pages (see Figure 31.20).

Figure 31.20
If you prefer, you can create a new folder to hold your Web site files.

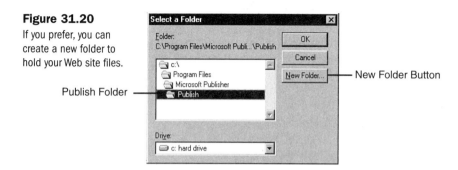

Publish Folder

New Folder Button

After you choose OK, your Web Site publication is converted to HTML (Hypertext Markup Language) and stored in the folder you indicated. Now you're done and the files are ready for immediate uploading when the time comes.

Publishing to the Web

If, after choosing File, Publish to the Web, you get a Reminder dialog box saying that you don't have Web Publishing Wizard, click the Yes button in the Reminder to go online and download it (see Figure 31.21).

Figure 31.21
You encounter this reminder in Publisher only if you haven't installed the Microsoft Web Publishing Wizard.

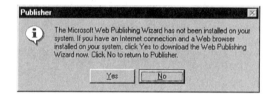

In the Microsoft Internet Explorer Help menu, click Microsoft Publisher Web Site, or point your browser to **http://microsoft.com/publisher/**. Locate and download the Microsoft Web Publishing Wizard, and try again.

When the Web Publishing Wizard appears, as with all wizards, answer the questions, read and follow the instructions, and you have a presence on the Web!

TROUBLESHOOTING

When I preview my Web site, I can't get to my second and third pages. That's because you forgot to put Hyperlinks from the first page to those other pages. You and your Web site visitors can only navigate to another page by using a hyperlink, so give them all sorts of directions to jump. Link sequentially, if that's what you want visitors to see, but give them a chance to go back or forward, or to the home page.

My site is uploaded, but when I go there, none of the pictures show. What's happening? If the problem is in the upload, it probably is something your Internet service provider can explain and even fix. Sometimes, if traffic on the Net is heavy, graphics lag way behind text in arriving at your browser. Patience cures that, or use the command that reloads graphics in your browser. Check also to see if you set your browser preferences to show no graphics, only text.

Why do my fonts look different on my best customer's browser than on mine? Odds are your best customer has been fiddling with the settings in his or her browser. Viewers have a lot of control over what they see on the Web. They can specify a font, the size of the font, whether graphics load or don't, the color for hyperlinks, and other things completely out of your control. It's the bane of every Web developer's existence, but that's what the Internet is all about—freedom of choice.

Outlook 98

CHAPTER 32

Outlook Quick Start Guide

by George Lynch

In this chapter

Understanding What Outlook Can Do

Outlook is a powerful tool for organizing the various types of information that you work with throughout the typical workday. Outlook can be used to:

- Manage your calendar, contact lists, and task lists
- Record events such as telephone calls in a journal as they occur throughout the day
- Send and receive electronic mail
- Schedule meetings
- Record freeform notes

The preceding tasks require managing all kinds of different data and storing and displaying them in a variety of ways. The type of information which Outlook manages (for example, schedules, task lists and contacts) can vary greatly from person to person.

Even the way you use a single tool such as the Contact List might vary, depending on whether you are using a personal phone list or a business contact list. With a personal list you may decide not to record the company name and work telephone number of someone, while those items would be crucial to a business contact list.

One of the great strengths of Outlook is its flexibility. You can adapt Outlook to work the way you want it to, and have it match the needs of your work environment and your preferences.

Understanding Outlook Modes

When you installed Outlook, it set itself up in one of three modes, depending on your system.

- *Corporate/Workgroup (CW) Mode.* If you are connected to a network, Outlook sets itself up in this mode, so you can take advantage of Outlook's workgroup features such as group scheduling.
- *Internet Mail Only (IMO) Mode.* If you are not connected to a network but you have a Dial-Up Networking connection to the Internet, Outlook operates in this mode. It allows you to use Outlook to send and receive e-mail.
- *PIM Mode.* If you have no means of communicating with the outside world (no modem or network), Outlook runs in this mode. It provides no messaging capabilities at all.

Most of Outlook's features work the same in all modes (or at least the first two modes; PIM mode is more limited). You may find subtle differences between the modes, such as some menu commands being present or missing. We will try to point the important differences out to you along the way in these chapters.

Using the Outlook Interface

Because Outlook combines several tools in one, it is important to understand how to select tools and how the menus, toolbars, and keyboard functions change when different tools are selected. Like most programs, Outlook has a menu at the top of its window and a toolbar below it. In addition to these standard features, Outlook also has another toolbar located on the left side of the window, called the Outlook Bar. Figure 32.1 shows the Outlook Bar.

Figure 32.1

The Outlook Bar allows you to quickly switch between tools.

Outlook Bar ———

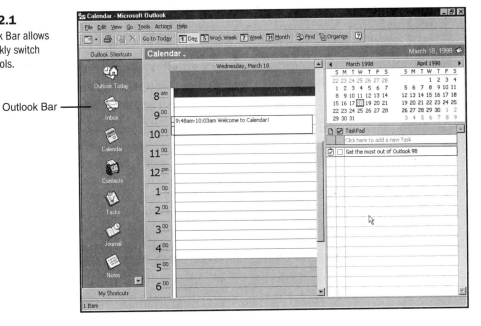

The Outlook Bar is used for selecting the Inbox, Calendar, Contact List, and other tools that are combined into Outlook. To the right of the Outlook bar is the Information viewer. When the Calendar is selected in the Outlook Bar, the Information viewer shows the list of events on the Calendar, as in Figure 32.1. When the Inbox tool is selected in the Outlook Bar, the Information viewer displays the list of incoming electronic mail. You can switch between tools by clicking on the icons in the Outlook Bar.

N O T E You can also switch tools by clicking on the Go menu and selecting the Outlook component you want. ▩

When you change between components in the Outlook Bar, the menus and toolbar at the top of the window change to match what you have selected. Also, note that the leftmost button on the toolbar also changes, depending on which component you select. If you select Calendar, for example, the button changes to New Appointment; if you select Contacts, the button changes to New Contacts. In other words, the leftmost toolbar button always creates a new item for whatever component you currently have selected.

N O T E The Ctrl+N keyboard combination always creates a new item for the tool that you are currently using. ▩

Part
VI

Ch
32

Views

Each Outlook component has a default "View" associated with it, but you can easily change this view to suit the way you work. A view is the particular display of data for the selected Outlook component. With the Inbox, for instance, you can use the default Messages view which gives you a list of message headers, or you can choose other views, such as "Messages with AutoPreview", which shows message headers and the first few lines of unread messages.

You can switch between views by choosing View, Current View from the menu and clicking another view (See Figure 32.2). The views available in the list vary depending on the component you have selected.

N O T E   In Outlook 98 there is an Advanced toolbar you can display with View, Toolbars, Advanced. It provides a drop-down list from which you can choose among the available views for the tool you are using. (This drop-down list was on the default toolbar in Outlook 97.)

In Outlook 98's Inbox, you can also choose whether to see a Preview pane below the list of messages, in which the currently selected message appears. To toggle its display on or off, choose View, Preview Pane.

Figure 32.2

Change views to find information more easily.

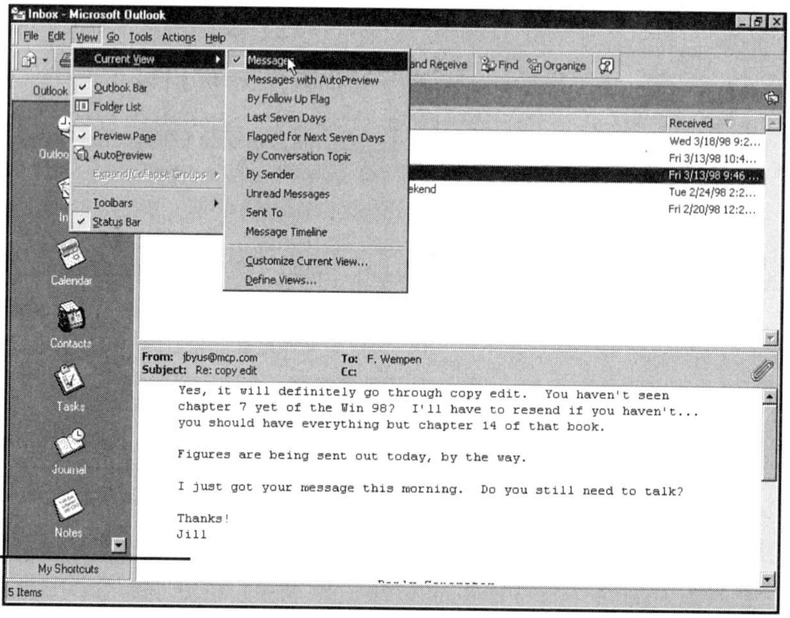

Preview pane

Different Views of Outlook Components

The Calendar views vary between the traditional grid and day planner views, and various types of tables which filter different groups of schedule items together in lists that can be sorted. You can choose to view Active Appointments, Events, Annual Events, Recurring Appointments or list items By Category.

In the list views, the lists can be sorted in ascending or descending order on any of the fields displayed in the column heading simply by clicking on the field heading (click once to sort in ascending order, click again to sort in descending order).

Contacts can be viewed as brief Address Cards, showing only partial information and as Detailed Address Cards showing more information. You can also view a Phone List that displays the name and various telephone numbers in a list format that can be sorted, or views for Category, Company, and Location.

The Task List offers a number of different views:

- Simple List
- Detailed List
- Active Tasks
- Tasks for Next Seven Days
- Overdue Tasks
- Tasks by Category
- Only those tasks you have assigned to people (Assignment)
- By Person Responsible
- Completed tasks
- A Task Timeline displaying a listing of tasks arranged on a horizontal timeline showing Start and Due date

In the Journal the Default view is a timeline showing Journal entries By Type. This view groups Phone calls, conversations, e-mail, meeting requests, and other types of Journal entries together. In addition, you can select between different views such as grouping By Contact, By Category, Entry List (which is a chronological list of Journal entries), entries made in the Last Seven Days, or Phone Calls.

Notes are displayed as Icons by default, but you can choose to view them in a list showing Subject, Time Created, Content, and Category. You can also view only those from the last seven days, or those organized by Category or Color.

Part VI

Ch 32

Creating Your Own Views

In each of the Outlook components you can create your own views in addition to using the built-in views. The simplest way to do this is to start with an existing view and modify it.

In the Calendar you could select the Active Appointments view, which is sorted by Start Time in ascending order, and change it to sort by subject. To save the current view, choose View, Current View, Define Views. In the Define Views for "Calendar" dialog box, select the <Current view settings> and click on the Copy button.

This opens a Copy View dialog box which prompts for a view name and offers choices of whether the view can be used on other folders or only the current folder, and whether it is visible to other users (in a network environment with shared folders). After you name and save the view, it is added to the list of views available for that folder. When defining a view you can specify the following:

- Fields displayed
- How items are grouped
- The sort order used
- The view filter (the criteria which displayed items must match)
- The format of the fonts of columns or rows

Introducing the Outlook Tools

Outlook offers a full complement of management tools, including e-mail, a calendar, a task list, a Notes area, and a contact management database.

E-mail

With electronic mail you can send and receive messages and files over the Internet or a local network. Incoming messages are delivered to your "Inbox," which is shown in Figure 32.3. They are listed in a table which indicates who the message is from, the subject of the message, when it was received, if there are any files attached, and if the message has been read. To read a message, double-click on it to open it in its own window.

▶ **See** "Receiving New E-mail," **page 732**

The Calendar

Use the Calendar, shown in Figure 32.4, to organize information about appointments, events, and meetings. Appointments have Location, Start, and End dates and times. When you enter an Appointment, any information on the Subject line is also displayed in the Calendar.

N O T E   If your computer is connected to a network using Microsoft Exchange Server, Outlook can display the free/busy time of the people you want to invite to the meeting, as well as send meeting requests directly to the invited participants. IMO mode users can view Free/Busy information for users who have provided their "Internet Free-Busy" address. ▪

Figure 32.3

The Inbox displays the messages that you have received.

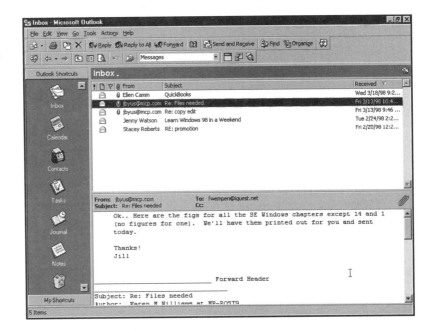

Figure 32.4

The Outlook Calendar organizes your appointments in a format you are probably already familiar with.

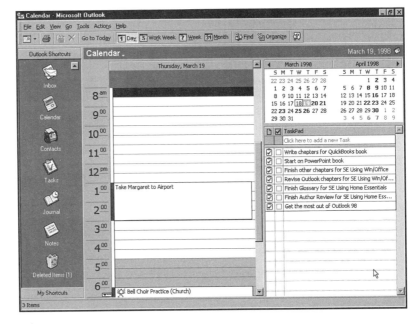

You can view the Calendar in a traditional Day/Week/Month format or by lists of appointments, events or categories of events, appointments, and meetings. In the Day/Week/Month view you can choose to see one day, a full week, or a full month at a time.

▶ **See** Chapter 36, "Scheduling with the Calendar," **page 779**

Contact List

Outlook's Contact List can be used to record names, telephone numbers, and addresses, as well as e-mail addresses, fax numbers, pager numbers, World Wide Web home page URL, and a huge variety of other types of contact information. You can also define your own fields of information if the built-in fields aren't adequate for you.

The Address Cards view is the default view for the Contact list. It resembles a personal telephone book, as shown in Figure 32.5. This view includes an alphabetic tab column on the right side to navigate quickly through a large list.

Figure 32.5
The Contact list has several views, with the Address Cards view being the default.

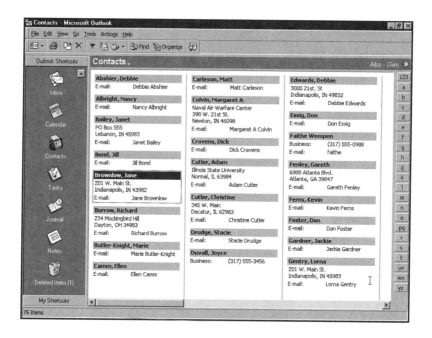

N O T E The contact list can easily be used as the data source in a mail merge with Microsoft Word 97. See Chapter 15, "Merging Documents." ■

▶ For more information, **see** Chapter 37, "Maintaining a Contact List."

Task List

Outlook's Task List, shown in Figure 32.6, allows you to record, sort, prioritize, and track tasks that you need to accomplish. You can also assign tasks to others and track their progress. The task list can show you which tasks are overdue, which are complete, and which are partially complete. The task list can be viewed by itself or in the default Calendar view, integrated with the view of the current day.

Figure 32.6

The Task List keeps track of items that need to completed.

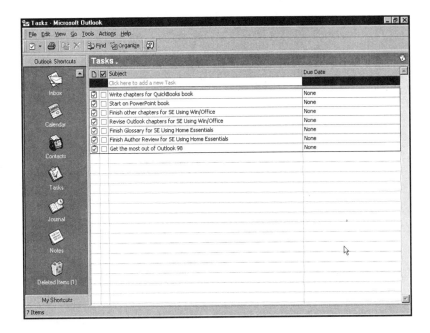

The default view of the Task list is a simple list of tasks, shown in Figure 32.6. You can change the view to include more detailed information with Detailed List view.

▶ **See** "Creating and Modifying Tasks," **page 799**

Journal

Outlook's Journal (see Figure 32.7) allows you to record events as they occur, such as telephone calls. You can also set the journal to automatically record events, such as the use of other Office 97 programs and the documents opened, or e-mail sent to or received from individuals in your address book.

Journal entries can include text and even have files of any type embedded in them. As with the other Outlook components, you can select from a number of different views.

▶ **See** "Creating and Editing Journal Entries," **page 814**

Part
VI
Ch
32

Figure 32.7

Events can be recorded in the Journal to record your actions and track your time.

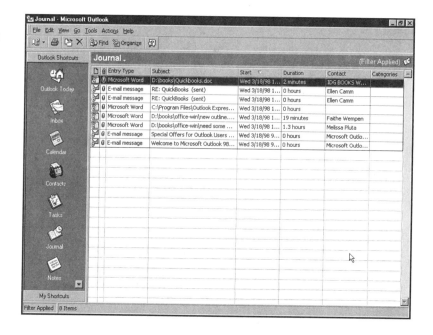

Notes

MS Outlook also has a tool for recording random scraps of information in a freeform manner similar to the yellow paper sticky notes that proliferate on computer monitors in many offices. As shown in Figure 32.8, Outlook Notes are not quite like their paper counterpart. However, like their paper equivalent, these notes can be useful for recording bits of information, but their organization is up to you.

Outlook gives you various ways of organizing the notes that you want to save (by color, by category, or by date). You also can search through the notes for a particular word, and you can drag a note to your desktop so you can see it when you start your computer.

▶ **See** "Working with Notes," **page 820**

Outlook Today

A great new feature in Outlook 98 is a summary tool called Outlook Today. It shows your current schedule and the tasks you need to be working on, sort of a summary of several different Outlook tools. Refer to it at any time during your busy day for an at-a-glance look at your responsibilities (see Figure 32.9).

From the Outlook Today screen, you can:

■ Double-click any Calendar item for a closer look at it.

■ Look up a contact by typing the name in the Find a Contact box and clicking Go.

■ Mark a task as completed by selecting its check box.

■ Read your new e-mail by selecting it from the list.

Figure 32.8
Notes record information that is not easily categorized.

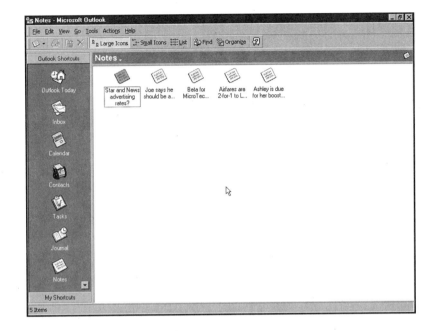

Figure 32.9
Use Outlook Today to make sure you are on track throughout the day.

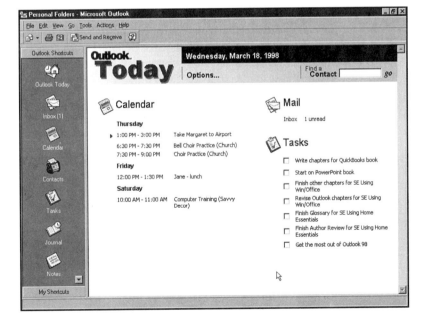

Creating and Modifying a Messaging Profile

If more than one person uses the same computer, you can keep separate Outlook configurations for each user by creating separate messaging profiles. Messaging profiles store the configuration settings for Outlook, so by creating a profile for each user, the computer can be shared without users changing each other's settings. A default profile is created when Outlook is installed, but you can add other profiles at any time.

It is most commonly the case that only one profile is used for Outlook. The default setting in Outlook is to use the default profile setting from the Mail Control Panel program.

Within Outlook you have two other alternatives:

- You can choose to use a different profile as the default.
- You can be prompted for which profile to select each time you start Outlook.

Overriding the default with another default is useful if you have another e-mail program that uses the default settings but is not compatible with the settings needed for Outlook. Prompting the user on startup would be useful if more than one person uses the same system. By asking the user to choose a profile, personal settings can be kept separate from other users.

Creating a New Messaging Profile

The first step is to select the services which the new profile will provide. Specifically, this means the type of e-mail connections that will be supported. One of the main functions of Outlook is to act as an interface to e-mail systems. Outlook can connect to different types of e-mail services, and the information about those connections is stored in the Messaging Profile.

To create a new Messaging Profile, click on the Start button, then select Settings, Control Panel and double-click the Mail (or Mail and Fax) Icon. Choose Show Profiles, and then Add, and the Inbox Setup Wizard (or Internet Connection Wizard, depending on your setup) will begin to guide you through the process of creating a new profile.

On a computer connected directly to a network, you may be able to use the Microsoft Exchange service (if your network has a Microsoft Exchange Server available). With this service you can use the advanced features of Outlook and Exchange to share certain information, such as Free/Busy time or schedule details, with other designated users on your system.

Once you have selected the services that comprise the Profile, you will be prompted for a Profile Name. You should provide a name which will allow you to distinguish the profiles based on functionality, or based on user name if you are using profiles to keep individuals services separate.

N O T E   Check with your network administrator for any configuration information that you are unsure of.

Modifying a Messaging Profile

You can add, remove or reconfigure services for a Messaging Profile by selecting the profile you want to modify and clicking on the Properties button. You may then modify settings for any of the existing services or add new ones. For example, you may need to modify your profile if your mail server is changed.

Setting General Outlook Properties

Customizing and configuring Outlook to match the way you work is the key to getting the most out of Outlook. Each of the tools can be configured separately, as we saw in the views. In addition, you can set general options for each component and for Outlook as a whole through the Options dialog box. Choose Tools, Options to open the Options dialog box, which is shown in Figure 32.10. This is a complex dialog box with 7 tabs. It allows you to configure, among other things:

- The way Outlook handles Messaging Profiles
- The services it checks for e-mail
- How it notifies you when new messages arrive
- Default settings for messages you send
- The days and times which Outlook should display as part of the work week
- The events which are automatically recorded in the Journal

Part
VI

Ch
32

Figure 32.10
Customize Outlook using the Options dialog box

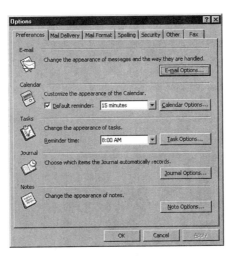

On the Preferences tab, you'll find buttons for each tool type (e-mail, tasks, journal, and so on). Click the respective button to open a dialog box of controls specific to that type. For example, you can specify how you want e-mails composed and replied to by clicking the E-mail Options button.

The Mail Delivery tab (if you have one, depending on your setup) contains controls for specifying how e-mail is sent and delivered. From the Mail Delivery tab, you can change the default settings for "Importance" and "Sensitivity" which you assign to the messages you send. You can also choose whether you want to receive notification when messages are delivered and when they are opened. (Some of these options only work on a local network mail system, and may not work with your Internet service provider's system.) You can also set these on individual messages for which this information might be useful.

You can specify e-mail formatting options on the Mail Format tab. For example, you can choose whether by default you will send plain-text messages (which all e-mail programs can accept) or formatted ones (which only MIME-compliant programs can accept.)

The Spelling tab provides controls for the built-in spelling checker. You can specify spelling rules, choose a dictionary to use, and add words to your custom dictionary.

On the Security tab, you'll find controls that keep your system safe from any potentially damaging Internet content.

The Other tab contains an assortment of miscellaneous options. For example, on the Other tab, click Advanced Options, and then click the Reminder Options button to open a dialog box where you can select a sound to play when Outlook reminds you of an appointment or overdue task by choosing the Reminders tab and browsing for an appropriate sound file.

Finally, the Fax tab (if you have installed fax support, see Chapter 35, "Advanced Messaging") contains settings that control how Outlook sends and receives faxes through your fax modem. You can tell Outlook to automatically answer the phone or to wait for your confirmation; you can specify a default cover page design; and you can enter identification that will be sent on outgoing faxes, such as your company name and fax number. If you are using Outlook in Workgroup mode, you can set fax properties from Tools, Services, Microsoft Fax, Properties.

Customizing the Interface

Outlook provides the tools that enable you to customize its appearance to fit a variety of different personal preferences and work styles.

Viewing the Folder List

You can customize the way you navigate through the tools in Outlook by having the Folder list displayed in a split window instead of a drop-down list. To display it, as shown in Figure 32.11, open the View menu and choose Folder List. Do the same thing again to hide it, or click the × in the corner of the Folder List window.

Figure 32.11
Outlook with the Folder
List displayed.

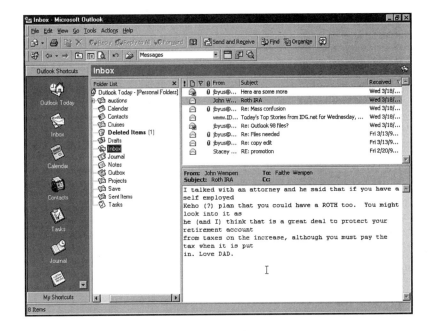

The Folder list is useful for navigating with the keyboard instead of the mouse. This can be useful on a laptop or for those who prefer to keep their hands on the keyboard for speed.

When the Folder list is displayed, you can tab between the Folder list and the messages in the Inbox, for instance, and use the cursor arrow keys to change to the Calendar or any other Outlook component.

Hiding the Outlook Bar

You can even hide the Outlook Bar completely. To hide the Outlook Bar, select View, Outlook Bar. This toggles off the view of the Outlook Bar, as shown in Figure 32.12. To bring it back, select the same menu item to toggle the view back on. Hiding the Outlook Bar can be useful if you are working on a laptop with limited screen real estate.

You can hide the status bar to squeeze out a couple of extra pixels by selecting the View, Status Bar. This toggles the status bar.

Part
VI

Ch
32

Figure 32.12

Outlook with Outlook Bar hidden.

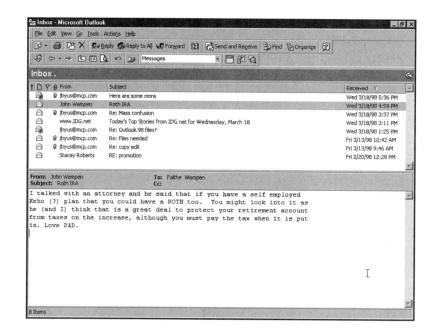

CHAPTER 33

Using Message Providers

*by George Lynch, Jesse Cassell,
and Faithe Wempen*

In this chapter

The Outlook Inbox

E-mail is the Outlook feature that many people use most often. You can receive e-mail from other people in your company (through your Local Area Network), and also from the Internet.

Click the Inbox icon in the Outlook bar to view your Inbox, which is where all incoming messages arrive. (You can move them to other folders later for storage, as you'll learn later in this chapter.)

E-mail messages appear in a table that shows the sender, the subject, the receipt date, and whether any files are attached. Messages that appear in boldface are new (that is, you have not read them yet).

As you learned in Chapter 32, "Outlook Quick Start Guide," Outlook's Inbox provides a Preview pane that previews the selected message (see Figure 33.1). By default the first message on the list is selected. You can select a different message by clicking on it.

Figure 33.1

The Inbox displays the messages that you have received.

New messages are bold

Attachment indicator

Preview pane

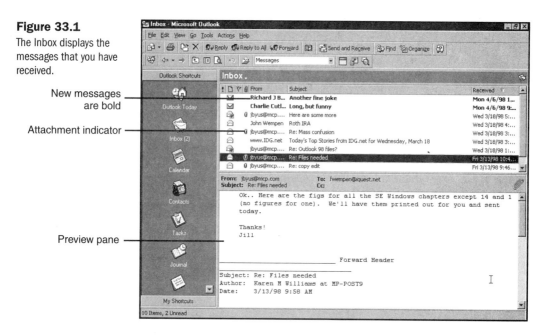

Receiving New E-mail

If you are on a computer connected directly to a network, your e-mail will be delivered to your Inbox automatically, provided your e-mail account has been configured correctly in Outlook. Your Network Administrator should handle this for you.

▶ **See** "Setting Up E-mail Accounts," **page 733**

If you are using Outlook on a computer with a modem, your e-mail will be sent and delivered whenever you ask for it. You can check for your e-mail by clicking the Send and Receive button on the toolbar. If you have more than one e-mail account and you want to check them all, choose Tools, Send and Receive, All Accounts

Setting Up E-mail Accounts

When you first used Outlook, the Internet Connection Wizard may have walked you through the process of creating an e-mail account (if you are using outlook in Internet Mail Only mode). If so, and you have only one e-mail address, then you're all set. (If a system administrator or other computer professional set up your system for you, he or she may have done this setup.) If you are currently using Outlook successfully to send and receive e-mail, you don't have to do anything else.

▶ **See** "Understanding Outlook Modes," **page 716**

However, if you need to add other e-mail accounts that you may have, you can do so by following these steps. (These steps are only for people working with Internet Mail Only mode, not those using Outlook on a network.)

N O T E Before going through these steps, read through them and make a note of the information you will need (such as incoming and outgoing mail server addresses). Then contact your service provider and get the information ▪

1. Choose Tools, Accounts. The Internet Accounts dialog box opens (see Figure 33.2).

Figure 33.2
Set up new accounts here.

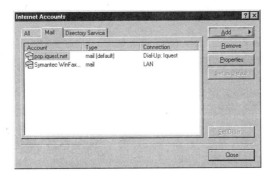

2. Click the Add button and choose Mail from the submenu. The Internet Connection Wizard appears.

3. In the Display Name field, type the name that you want to appear on your e-mail messages (for example, your first and last name, or first initial and last name). Then click Next.

4. In the E-mail Address field, type your full e-mail address for this account. For example, bobsmith@isp.com. Then click Next.

5. Next, the E-mail Server Names controls appear (see Figure 33.3). Choose the type of server from the drop-down list. POP3 is by far the most common for Internet mail.

Figure 33.3

It's important to enter the correct server addresses so you can send and receive your mail.

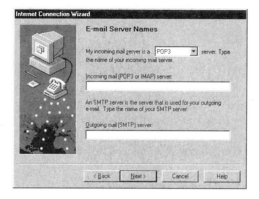

6. Enter the incoming and outgoing mail server addresses in the fields provided (see Figure 33.3). Then click Next.

N O T E   Depending on your service provider, the incoming and outgoing mail servers might be the same, or they might be different. For example, the provider joeinternet.com might use mail.joeinternet.com as both the incoming and outgoing server. A different provider, let's say maryinternet.com, might use pop.maryinternet.com as the incoming and smtp.maryinternet.com as the outgoing. This information should be provided by your service provider or network administrator.

7. In the Internet Mail Logon controls, enter your user ID for the service in the POP Account Name field. For example, joeblow@isp.com might enter joeblow.

8. Enter your password in the Password field. Then click Next.

9. Enter a "friendly name" for the mail account. This name will appear on the list of accounts in the Accounts dialog box. Then click Next.

10. In the Choose a Connection Type list, click on the button for the connection type (see Figure 33.4). Then click Next. If you choose anything other than Connect Using My Phone Line, skip to step 13.

Figure 33.4

Choose how Outlook should establish a connection with that account.

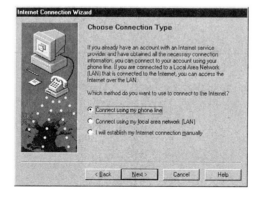

11. If you choose Connect Using My Phone Line in step 10, a drop-down list of the modems set up on the computer appear. Choose the one you want to use for this account, and then click Next.

12. Next, a list of the dial-up connections set up in Dial-Up Networking appears. Click on the connection you want to use, or click Create New Dial-Up Connection to set up a new one. Then click Next.

13. If you chose to set up a new dial-up connection, the wizard walks you through additional screens, prompting for information about that connection. Otherwise, the Congratulations screen appears.

▶ **See** "Adding a New DUN Connection," **page 843**

14. Click Finish to complete the setup. The new account now appears on the list.

15. Close the Internet Accounts dialog box.

Configuring E-mail Accounts

You can configure your various e-mail accounts to specify when and how messages are retrieved from them. For example, suppose you wanted Outlook to automatically check your Internet mail accounts every 15 minutes throughout the day, but you want to check your CompuServe mail only when you specifically ask for it.

To set this up, you create two classes of e-mail accounts: those that are included in a full Send/ Receive, and those that are not. By default, all e-mail accounts are included. To exclude one, follow these steps:

1. Choose Tools, Accounts to open the Internet Accounts dialog box.

2. Click on the account you want to exclude.

3. Click the Properties button. The Properties dialog box appears.

4. Deselect the Include this account when doing a full Send/Receive check box (see Figure 33.5).

5. Click OK.

6. Close the Internet Accounts dialog box.

Part
VI

Ch
33

Next, you need to tell Outlook how often to check the accounts that are *not* excluded. Follow these steps to do so:

1. Choose Tools, Options. The Options dialog box opens.

2. Click the Mail Delivery tab to select it (see Figure 33.6).

3. Select or deselect the Send messages immediately check box. If you deselect it, messages will wait in your Outbox folder until you issue the Send/Receive command.

4. Select or deselect the Check for new messages every check box. If you select it, enter an interval in the text box that follows, such as 10 or 15.

5. In the Dial-Up Options section, select or deselect any check boxes as desired to set special mail sending and receiving options.

Choose Warn before switching dial-up connection if you want Outlook to present a confirmation box before hanging up one connection and connecting to another, for example, if you have several different numbers you modem has to dial to connect to all your accounts.

Select Automatically dial when checking for new messages to let Outlook automatically dial your modem each time. If this is not selected, whenever it is time to check for mail, a dialing box will appear and you will have to click the Connect button to make the connection.

Select Hang up when finished sending, receiving, or updating to let Outlook hang up the modem when it is finished checking your mail. If you don't do this, a dialog box appears each time Outlook is done, asking whether you want to disconnect, and you must click OK in it before Outlook will hang up the modem.

Figure 33.5

Exclude an account from normal sending and receiving by deselecting its Include this account... check box.

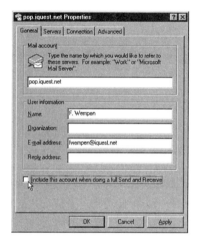

Figure 33.6

Set Outlook options for sending and receiving mail from the non-excluded accounts.

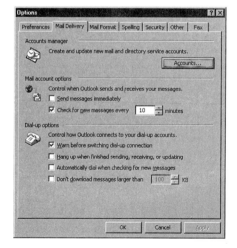

6. Click OK to close the Options dialog box.

Reading E-mail

You can read your messages directly from the Preview Pane if you want to. Just click on a message to select it, and then use the Preview Pane's scroll bar to scroll through it. However, most people prefer to open a message in its own window, as shown in Figure 33.7, by double-clicking it. When you do so, you have access to a fuller range of message-control features, as you will shortly see. Once you've read the message, you can close the window.

Figure 33.7

When you double-click a message, it appears in its own window.

Attachments

From the message window you have many options. You can simply close the message window, or you can choose to respond to the message, forward it to someone else, print the message, and extract a file if one is attached to the message.

N O T E A paper clip in the corner of the Preview pane (refer to Figure 33.1) indicates that the message has attachments. When you open the message (refer to Figure 33.7), the attachments appear in a separate pane below the message. Double-click an attachment icon to open it, or right-click it for a menu of other options (including saving it to your hard disk without opening it). ■

Another way of browsing your e-mail is to open a message, such as the oldest unread message, and using the Previous Item button on the message's toolbar (the Up arrow button) or Ctrl+< to "catch up" by reading your e-mail in the order in which it arrived. (alternatively, you can start with the newest one and use the Next Item button or Ctrl+>.) Note that the behavior of the Previous Item and Next Item toolbar buttons are consistent with the sort order currently selected in the Inbox. In other words, if the Received field of your Inbox is sorted in descending order (most recent messages at top), Ctrl + < moves to the next most recent message. So, if something unexpected happens when using the Next and Previous Item buttons remember to check the sort order of your Inbox.

N O T E   You can sort the Inbox by clicking on the Field headers at the top of the Inbox view. The field headers act like buttons and sort the contents of the Inbox when clicked. Clicking a field header once will sort the Inbox in descending order on that field, and clicking the same field header again will sort the list in the opposite order. This is handy, for example, when you want to see all the e-mail from a particular recipient grouped together. ▪

Saving Attachments

In addition to simple messages, files of any type can be attached to a message and sent or received. When you receive a message with an attachment it will indicate the attachment with a small paper clip icon next to the "From" field. When you read the message you will see icons at the bottom indicating the type of file that was sent, as shown in Figure 33.7.

You can save an attachment to the disk by choosing File, Save Attachments, and then picking the attachment to save from the submenu, or by right-clicking an attachment and choosing Save As. A dialog box opens (see Figure 33.8) prompting you to choose a location for the saved file. Choose it and click Save to save the attachment there.

Figure 33.8
Save each attachment before you delete the e-mail.

You can open an attachment directly if you prefer, without having first saved it. Just double-click the icon itself. The file opens in its native application, provided the application is installed on your computer.

> **CAUTION**
> When you delete the e-mail, the attachments are deleted too. Make sure you save all attachments to a safe location on your hard drive before deleting the e-mail message. You can either save them as described above, or you can use the Save As command from the application you open them in.

Replying to a Message

Outlook allows you to respond to a message while you are reading it. By clicking on the "Reply" button on the toolbar at the top of the message window you can create a new e-mail message. Outlook automatically fills in the "To:" field with the address of the person who sent you the original message, and enters "Re:" plus the subject of the original message in the "Subject:" field.

N O T E To send a message that you have received to someone else, click the "Forward" button. A new message is prepared that contains the message that you were viewing. You can then edit the message and enter recipients as you normally would, but without having to retype an entire message.

Your cursor will be in the body of the message, ready for you to begin typing, and the original text will be included at the bottom of your message. Figure 33.9 shows my reply to a message I received.

Figure 33.9

When replying to a message, you don't have to reenter the subject and the recipient.

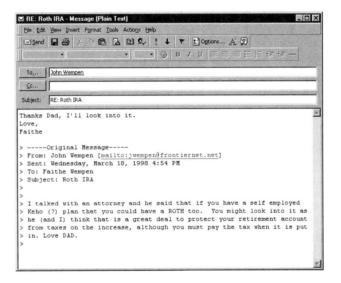

If you receive a message which was sent to a list of recipients, you can respond to the same list by using the "Reply to All" button, which does the same thing as the "Reply" button, except the "To:" field includes the entire list of the original message. You can also manually add to the "To:" field, or to the "Cc:" or "Bcc" field if you want to include other addressees.

Outlook provides an easy way to remember which e-mail you have replied to and which you haven't. Take a close look at the Inbox. Messages that you have replied to have a special icon next to them with an arrow "swoop," as shown in Figure 33.10. Forwarded messages have a different kind of arrow swoop on their icon.

Part

VI

Ch

33

Figure 33.10

Icons in the Inbox distinguish messages that you have replied to.

Replied icon ———

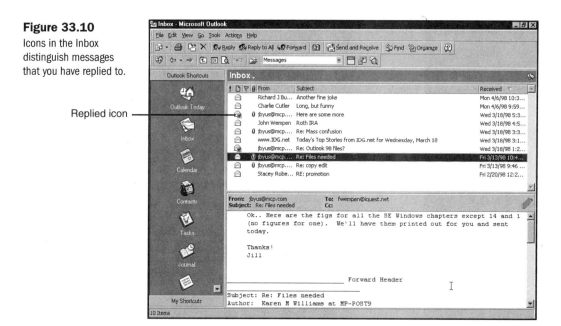

Composing E-mail

To create a new e-mail message, select the Inbox (or any other mail folder) from the Outlook bar and click the New Message button on the toolbar. This opens a new message window.

First, fill in the recipients in the To text box. You can type them manually if you know their e-mail addresses, but a better way is to click the To: button to open your Address Book, and select a name (or multiple names) from there. Add any additional recipients to the Cc: and Bcc: lines as well. Cc stands for "carbon copy", which is traditionally sent to people who are getting the message for information purposes only and need not take action on it. Bcc stands for "blind carbon copy," which sends a carbon copy without making any of the other recipients aware of it.

▶ **See** "Using the Address Book," **page 741**

 You can also add people to the list of recipients of a "cc" or "carbon copy" or "bcc", a "blind carbon copy." (Recipients on the "bcc" list will receive a copy of the message including the list of recipients except for those on the "bcc" list.)

You can then fill in a subject and then compose the text of your message. When you are done composing the message you can click on the Send button on the toolbar. Depending on your settings you specified in the Options dialog box earlier in this chapter, the message will either be sent immediately or placed in the Outbox folder until the next scheduled Send/Receive.

Using the Address Book

The Address Book works in conjunction with your Contacts list in Outlook. When you create a new contact in Outlook that includes an e-mail address, that address is automatically set up in your Address Book. This keeps your Address Book and your Contacts list in sync.

If you use Outlook primarily for e-mail, and do not make use of the Contacts feature to store names and addresses, you'll find it easiest to add recipients directly to the Address Book, as described in the section "Creating a New Address Book Entry" that follows.

On the other hand, if you do use Outlook's Contacts feature, and rely on it for current information about people, you should add the person's e-mail address to the Address Book through the Contacts feature, as described in "Adding an Outlook Contact to the Address Book."

Creating a New Address Book Entry   The quickest way to get an address into your Address Book is to add it directly there. Follow these steps:

1. While creating a message, click the To: button. Or, if you're not working on a message right now, select Tools, Address Book.

N O T E   The two alternatives in step 1 open two different dialog boxes, but each of them has the New Contact button that you need in step 2, so it doesn't matter. ■

2. Click the New Contact button. A Properties dialog box for a new contact appears (see Figure 33.11).

Part
VI

Ch
33

Figure 33.11
Fill in at least the fields for the name and the e-mail address; all other fields are optional.

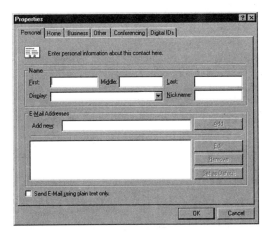

3. Fill in the person's first and last name in the First and Last fields. The name automatically appears in the Display field. The Middle field (for the middle initial) is optional.

4. Enter the person's e-mail address in the Add new text box, and then click Add.

5. (Optional) If the person has alternate e-mail addresses that you may sometimes need to use, repeat step 4 for each of them.

6. Make sure that the address you are going to use most frequently has Default next to it. If it doesn't, click on it and then click the Set As Default button.

7. (Optional) If you do not know what kind of mail system the recipient uses, or you are sure that the system does not support text formatting, select the Send E-Mail using plain text only check box.

8. (Optional) Fill in any other information for the person on any of the tabs in the dialog box. If you are just going to send them e-mail, this is not really necessary.

9. Click OK to add the person to your address book.

Now that the person is in your address book, you can choose his or her name from it when you want to send an e-mail. Refer to "Addressing a Message with the Address Book" later in this chapter for help.

Adding an Outlook Contact to the Address Book   If you want to add contacts to the address book via Outlook's Contacts feature, follow these steps:

1. In Outlook, click the Contacts button on the Outlook bar to display your contacts list.

2. Locate the person's entry on your contacts list and double-click on it to open it, or start a new contact for the person if they are not there already. Refer to Chapter 37, "Maintaining a Contact List" for help as needed (see Figure 33.12).

Figure 33.12

Add an e-mail address from your Address Book while setting up a contact.

Click here to
open the
Address Book.

3. Do one of the following:

If the person is not already in your Address Book, type the person's e-mail address directly into the E-mail field. The name will be added to your Address Book when you save this contact's new information.

If the person is already in the Address Book, and you want to link that entry to this contact, click the Address Book button (looks like a book) to the right of the E-Mail field. This opens your Address Book. Choose the recipient from your current address book. Then click OK.

4. Continue setting up the contact normally.

▶ **See** "Creating and Modifying Contacts," **page 799**

Addressing a Message with the Address Book   To choose a message recipient from your Address Book, follow these steps:

1. When creating a message, click the To, Cc, or Bcc button.

2. In the Select Names box that appears, locate the recipient's name and click on it (see Figure 33.13).

3. Click the To, Cc, or Bcc button to move that person's name to the appropriate list. (Use To: for the main recipient(s), and Cc and Bcc for people who are receiving copies for informational purposes only.)

4. Repeat steps 2 and 3 to select more recipients if needed.

5. Click OK to return to creating the message.

Figure 33.13
Address messages by choosing them from your Address Book.

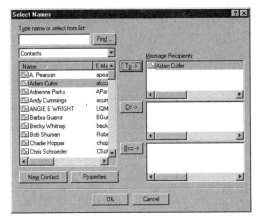

Part
VI

Ch
33

N O T E   On some corporate e-mail systems, with Outlook running in Corporate/Workgroup mode, there may be more than one address book set up. For example, there might be an address book on your network that lists all the employees at your company, separate from your personal address book of business contacts. If that's the case on your system, the drop-down list at the top of the Select Names dialog box will show multiple address books. (The default one is called Contacts.) Choose the address book that contains the recipients you're interested in. ■

Attaching a File

You can attach a file to a message you are sending by choosing Insert, File when you are composing the message. An Insert File dialog box opens. Choose the file you want to attach (changing folders and drives as needed) and then click the OK button to attach it. You can attach as many files as you want to a single e-mail, but you must attach them one at a time.

> **CAUTION**
>
> Sending a message with an attachment using a modem can take a long time, depending on the speed of your modem and the size of the file. A large scanned image, for example, can take well over 10 minutes to send.

Setting Message Options

Outlook enables you to set various options on a message that affect the way the message is displayed when it is delivered. (These options will be effective only on a network using an e-mail system like Microsoft Exchange, or when the addressee is also using Outlook).

To display the Options dialog box for the message (see Figure 33.14), click the Options button on the toolbar or choose View, Options. Here, you can set the "Importance" to "High," "Normal," or "Low," which will display an icon in the list of mail in the recipient's Inbox. You can also set the "Sensitivity" to "Normal," "Personal," "Private," or "Confidential."

Figure 33.14
Message options.

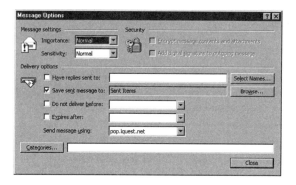

▶ **See** "Using Categories," **page 767**

Filing Your E-mail

You can file your e-mail in different folders to keep it organized. When you have a message open, you can choose to file it in another folder by selecting File, Move to Folder (Ctrl + Shift + V). This displays a list of available folders, as shown in Figure 33.15. Select a folder to move the message to and click on the OK button, or you can create a new folder by clicking on the "New..." button.

You can also move e-mail from one folder to another with drag-and-drop. Just turn on the Folder List display by choosing View, Folder List. Then drag an e-mail message out of the Inbox and onto one of the folders on the list.

▶ **See** "Archiving" on **page 770**

Figure 33.15
The Move Items dialog box lets you place messages into folders other than the Inbox.

Creating Your Own E-mail Folders

You can use subfolders as one method of organizing your e-mail. For example, you might want to create a folder for a project on which you are working. You could store all messages you receive regarding the project in the folder, or you could create folders for the most common types of e-mail you receive, or for the people who frequently send you e-mail which you want to receive, such as your boss or your spouse.

To create a subfolder, start at the Inbox choose File, Folder, New Folder. Figure 33.16 shows the Create New Folder dialog box that appears. Type a name for the folder and choose a location within the hierarchy. Select the default Mail Items from the list marked Folder Contains to create a folder into which you can file your e-mail.

Figure 33.16
Use the New Folder dialog box to name and choose a location for new folders.

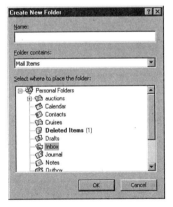

Part
VI

Ch
33

After you have created all the folders you need, you can move messages into them to keep your Inbox and all your e-mail messages organized. ●

CHAPTER 34

Managing MS Fax with Outlook

by George Lynch

In this chapter

Introducing WinFax

Outlook 98 contains a "lite" version of the very popular WinFax program by Symantec. It is fully integrated into Outlook and is much easier to use than the somewhat cumbersome fax feature in Outlook 97.

Faxes are treated just like e-mail in Outlook. The only difference is the method of transport. Most people have a fax/modem; that is, their modem has built-in fax capabilities. When you send a fax with Outlook, it taps into the fax capabilities of your modem and sends the fax directly from your PC.

Setting Up Outlook for Faxing

When you install Outlook, if you already have Microsoft Fax set up on your computer, Outlook may install faxing features automatically. If it does, you're all set. To see whether faxing is installed in Outlook 98 or not, choose Tools, Options to open the Options dialog box. If you see a Fax tab in that dialog box, faxing is installed.

Installing Fax Support

To set up Outlook for faxing, you must add the Symantec WinFax Starter Edition service to your list of Accounts. Follow these steps to do so:

1. Exit from Outlook, and open the Windows 95 control panel (Start, Settings, Control Panel).
2. Double-click the Add/Remove Programs icon. The Add/Remove Programs Properties dialog box appears.
3. On the Install/Uninstall tab, locate and double-click on Microsoft Outlook 98. The Outlook 98 Maintenance Wizard appears.
4. Click the Add New Components button, and then the Install from CD button. Internet Explorer opens to an Outlook 98 Component Install page.
5. A message appears asking whether it is okay to determine your current setup. Click Yes. A status report for each listed component appears, as shown in Figure 34.1.
6. Scroll down to the Mail Components section, and check Symantec WinFax Starter Edition.
7. Click the Next button at the bottom of the screen.

N O T E Depending on your setup, Outlook may want to connect to the Internet at some point in the setup process. This is not necessary, since the program is coming from the CD, so just close the dialog box by clicking its Close (X) button. ▓

8. On the Component Install screen, confirm that CD Installation is chosen in the drop-down list (see Figure 34.2), and click the Install Now button.

Figure 34.1

Components are either Already Installed or Not Installed.

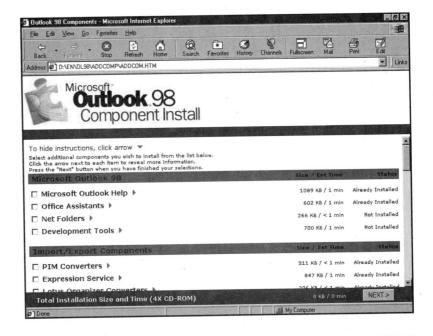

Figure 34.2

Choose the CD as the installation source, and then click Install Now.

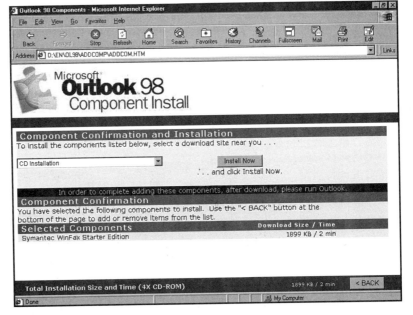

Part
VI

Ch
34

9. Wait for the fax support to be installed. You can monitor the progress with the Download Progress and Install Progress bars onscreen.

10. When you see a message that Fax Support installation has succeeded, click OK.

11. A message appears that you must restart Windows to finish the installation. Click Yes.

12. When Windows 95 restarts, it returns to the Outlook 98 Component Install screen. When asked again if you want it to determine your installed components, click No. Then close the Internet Explorer window.

When you're done and back in Windows 95, open Outlook 98.

The first time you start Outlook 98 after installing fax support, the Symantec WinFax Starter Edition Setup Wizard appears. It's self-explanatory. Fill in the information requested, such as your name, your phone number, and your fax number. Click Next to move from one screen to the next. When the wizard is finished, it dumps you into Outlook 98 and you can begin faxing.

N O T E   If you do not want to configure WinFax right now, you can click Cancel when presented with the Symantec WinFax Starter Edition Setup Wizard. You can enter the same settings later, as explained in the following section.

Reconfiguring Fax Settings

If the Symantec WinFax Starter Edition Setup Wizard did not appear when you started Outlook 98, or if you need to change the fax settings, you can do so at any time from within Outlook 98. To do so, choose Tools, Options, and click the Fax tab (see Figure 34.3).

Figure 34.3
Set or change fax options here.

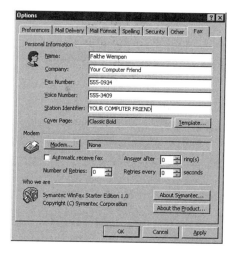

N O T E   If there is no Fax tab in your Options dialog box, you have not yet installed fax support. Refer to the preceding section for help.

On the Fax tab, you'll find the following settings:

■ *Personal Information.* Fill in your name, company fax number, voice number, and station identifier (the identifier that will print on sent fax pages) in the blanks provided.

■ *Cover Page.* Click the Template button to open the Cover Page Properties dialog box. Choose a different template from the Template drop-down list if you want. The Preview area shows a sample (see Figure 34.4). You can also turn off cover pages entirely by deselecting the Send Cover Page check box.

Figure 34.4

Select the default cover page to use for outgoing faxes.

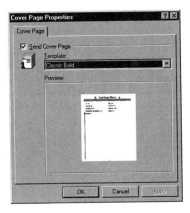

■ *Modem.* If your modem's name does not appear next to the Modem button, click the button to open a Modem Properties dialog box where you can select which modem to use. Choose it from the Active Modem drop-down list, and then click OK.

N O T E   If you choose a modem that you have not set up for faxing, you'll see a dialog box asking whether you want to run the WinFax Modem Configuration Wizard. Click Yes and then follow the prompts that appear to test and configure the modem. ■

■ *Automatic Receive Fax.* Select this check box if you want WinFax to answer the phone for you. Don't do this if you share the line with your voice telephone.

■ *Answer after.* If you chose Automatic Receive Fax, enter the number of rings it should wait before picking up.

■ *Number of Retries.* Enter the number of times it should try to resend a fax if it can't make it the first time (for example, if the receiving line is busy).

■ *Retries Every.* Enter the number of seconds between retries.

After making your selections, click Close to close the Options dialog box and accept your changes.

Part
VI

Ch
34

Sending a Fax

Sending a fax is a lot like sending an e-mail. The main difference is that Outlook delivers it via fax/modem rather than via a network or Internet connection.

To compose a new fax, follow these steps:

1. Choose Actio<u>n</u>s, New Fa<u>x</u> Message. An Untitled - FAX dialog box appears. It looks almost exactly like a new e-mail composition window (see Figure 34.5).

Figure 34.5

Compose a new fax as you would an e-mail.

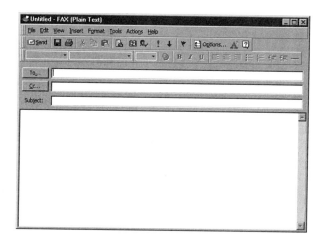

2. Click the To button and select a recipient (or multiple recipients) from your Address Book.

> **N O T E** If you are not sure whether a recipient has a fax number on file in your Address Book, click the potential recipient and then the Properties button to open that recipient's information. Add a fax number in the Fax field on the Home or Business tab if needed. ▪

▶ **See** "Using the Address Book," **page 741**

3. Enter a subject in the Subject field.

4. Enter your message in the message area, just like you would an e-mail. This message will appear on the fax cover sheet.

5. (Optional) If you want to fax a file along with the cover sheet (for example, a Word document), choose <u>I</u>nsert, <u>F</u>ile. The Insert File dialog box opens. Choose the file you want to send, and click OK.

6. (Optional) If you want to send an Outlook item (such as a task or some contact information) with the fax, choose <u>I</u>nsert, It<u>e</u>m. The Insert Item dialog box appears. Choose a folder from the Look In list, and its items appear on the Items list below (see Figure 34.6). Click the item you want, and then click OK.

Figure 34.6
You can attach Outlook
items to faxes.

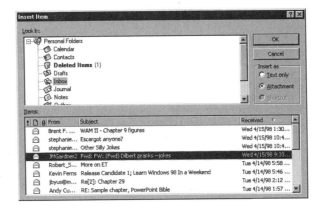

7. Set any other options, as you would for an e-mail. (Refer to Chapter 33, "Using Message Providers" as needed.)

8. Click the Send button. Outlook attempts to send the fax. If it cannot, it retries the number of times and at the interval you specified when you set up faxing. If it cannot send after exhausting all its retries, a message appears in your Inbox reporting that the fax could not be sent.

Receiving a Fax

To receive a fax, Outlook must be open, and you must have it set up in the Options dialog box to receive faxes automatically. If you share your voice telephone line with your fax/modem, you may want to set up Outlook to receive faxes only when you are expecting a specific fax, or set it to answer only after 4 or 5 rings, so you will have plenty of time to answer it by voice as needed.

N O T E In some fax programs, such as Microsoft Fax, when the phone rings, a box pops up asking you whether you want to answer it with your fax modem. Outlook doesn't have this capability; it either receives faxes automatically or not at all. ▪

To set up Outlook to receive faxes automatically, follow these steps:

1. Choose Tools, Options and click the Fax tab.

2. Select the Automatically receive fax check box.

3. In the Answer after field, enter the number of rings to wait.

4. Click OK.

After that setup has been done, you don't have to take any action to receive a fax. When a phone call comes in, the fax/modem answers it and receives the fax.

Reading a Fax

Incoming faxes appear in your Inbox, just like e-mails. To read a fax, double-click on it to open its status message, as shown in Figure 34.7. Notice that the message has an attachment; that's the actual fax.

Figure 34.7

Each fax arrives in your Inbox as a status message, with the actual fax as an attachment.

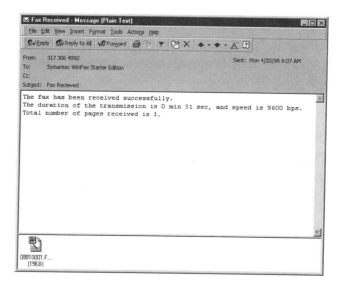

To open the fax itself, double-click its icon. A box pops up asking whether you want to save it to disk or open it. Choose Open It and then click OK. The fax appears in a viewing window, as shown in Figure 34.8.

Figure 34.8

The fax itself appears in a Fax Viewer window.

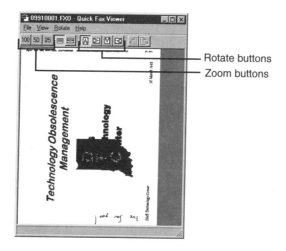

Rotate buttons
Zoom buttons

You can use the menus and buttons in the Fax Viewer window to view the fax differently and perform a number of actions on it:

- *Print.* To print the fax, choose File, Print.
- *Zoom in or out.* Use the Zoom buttons, or choose zoom commands from the View menu.
- *See the next or previous page.* Use the Next Page and Previous Page buttons, or choose those commands from the View menu.
- *Rotate the fax.* Use the Rotate buttons, or choose rotation commands from the Rotate menu.

After closing the Fax Viewer window, you can work with the fax normally, as you would any other message. You can file it, delete it, save it—anything you can do to a regular e-mail.

▶ **See** "Receiving New E-mail," **page 732**

CHAPTER 35

Advanced Messaging

*by George Lynch, Jesse Cassell,
and Faithe Wempen*

In this chapter

Overview: Customizing the Inbox Display

In Outlook 97, there were menu commands on the View menu for the various modifications you could make to the Inbox's view. In Outlook 98, the commands that make these modifications are most easily accessible through various toolbar buttons and shortcut menus.

However, there is still a central location from which you can access dialog boxes for all these commands. Choose View, Current View, Customize Current View to open the View Summary dialog box (see Figure 35.1). From here, you can click a button to open a dialog box.

Each of the buttons in Figure 35.1 points to a feature that is covered in great detail later in this chapter. For now, just know that this dialog box is here, available for you to access the many viewing options that you'll be learning about.

Figure 35.1

Each of these buttons takes you to a dialog box that helps you customize your view.

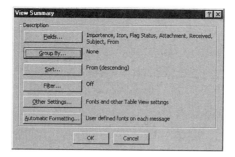

Sorting Messages

Perhaps the best way to organize your e-mail is to file it immediately. Most of us are not so organized, or we receive so much e-mail that it quickly piles up. Fortunately, Outlook provides many tools for organizing your Inbox and other e-mail folders.

Sorting Within a Folder

The default Messages view uses the Windows List control to display the list of e-mail messages in the Inbox. This control enables you to sort the messages in a variety of ways. Each column heading acts as a button which, when clicked, sorts the messages into order based on the data in that column. Clicking the Column Heading button once sorts the list in the default order for that column; this may be ascending or descending based on the data. Clicking the Column Heading button again reverses the sort order, and each time you click the Column Heading button it again reverses the order.

Virtually all of the columns can be used to sort a list of items in a view in any of the Outlook tools. This is an amazingly powerful, useful, and intuitive tool for quickly organizing your messages. Figure 35.2 shows an Inbox that has been sorted by sender.

The Messages view contains columns indicating the following:

- Who sent the message ("From:")
- The subject of the message
- The time and date you received the message
- The urgency level the sender assigned (the "!" icon column heading)
- A Flag column
- An Attachment column indicating messages that have files attached
- An Icon column indicating the type and status of the message

Figure 35.2

The faint triangle to the right of the word From in the column heading shows that the messages are sorted by sender.

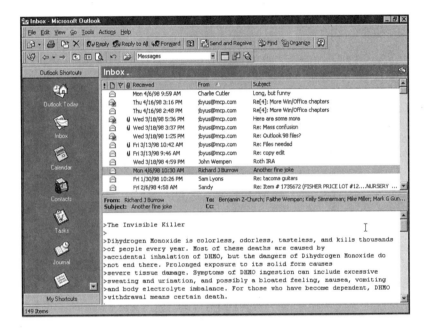

The normal sort order for this list view is in descending order, by time and date received. Incoming messages are added to the top of the list in the Inbox and older messages are pushed down. This is perfectly useful for reading messages as they arrive because new messages will be grouped together and can be quickly browsed or read in order of arrival. It can also be good for finding a message sent on a particular day.

This is not the only way of viewing new mail, however. Your personal preference may be to see new messages added to the bottom of the list. To achieve this, simply click the Received: Column Heading button.

When you click a column header, a triangle appears next to the column header text (if there is room to display it) indicating that sorting is applied to this field, and the order of the sort. A triangle with the point down indicates Descending sort order, that is Reverse Alphabetic (Z's first, A's last) for text fields and Most Recent to Oldest for date-type fields such as Received. An up-pointing triangle indicates Ascending sort order which reverses the order of the sorting.

For iconic columns, such as Flagged or Attachments, the sort order simply groups similar messages together. All messages with attachments will appear at the top of the list when sorted by Attachment in Descending order (right-click the paper clip icon; select Descending Order from the pop-up menu). You can sort on other fields to find, for example, all the messages in the Inbox flagged as completed.

N O T E You can also use all of the sorting techniques described in this chapter on other mail folders, such as the Sent folder, or any other custom folders you have created. ▓

Sorting Using the Sort Dialog Box

You can sort by up to four fields, each with its own ascending or descending order by using the Sort dialog box (see Figure 35.3). To open it, choose View, Current View, Customize Current View to open the View Summary dialog box, and then click the Sort button.

Figure 35.3
The Sort dialog box is used to sort Outlook data.

The items in the Sort Items By list box and Then By list boxes are controlled by the Select Available Fields From list box at the bottom of the dialog box. By default, the available items are shown in each of these list boxes from the Frequently-Used Fields list. You can select an item in the Sort Items By list box, choose Ascending or Descending, and sort the list or add additional sorting criteria. As you select a field to sort by at each level, the next level in the list is activated. If you wish to sort by fields that don't appear in the list, select a different set of fields in the Select Available Fields From list box.

You can remove the sorting criteria by selecting the Clear All button, which sets all the Sorting list boxes back to (none).

Finding Messages

When you accumulate a large quantity of e-mail, finding a particular message can be a real chore. Outlook's searching capabilities can make the process easier with its flexible and power-ful Find tool. (In fact, it may take a little time and practice to become fully familiar with all the searching tools Outlook provides. Fortunately, they are mostly intuitive and even fun to use.)

To find a particular message, follow these steps:

1. Click Find on the toolbar (or choose <u>T</u>ools, <u>F</u>ind Items). A Find pane appears above the Inbox, as shown in Figure 35.4.

Figure 35.4

Use Find to locate data in an e-mail quickly.

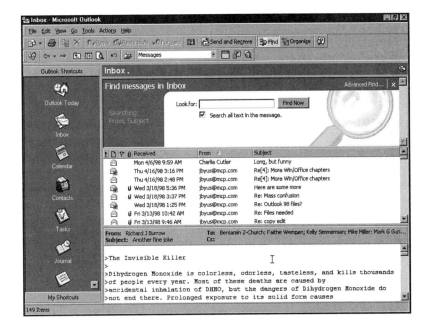

2. Enter the text string that you wish to find.

3. To look in the entire text of each message, leave the Search All Text in the Message check box marked. To search only in the Subject and From fields, deselect it.

4. Click Find Now. All messages disappear except ones that match your criteria.

5. Locate and read the message. When you are finished finding, click the X in the corner of the Find pane to close it and return to displaying the full list of messages.

If you have more sophisticated searching needs than can be accomplished with the preceding steps, consider Advanced Find. Click the Advanced Find button in the top right corner of the Find pane (see Figure 35.4), or choose <u>T</u>ools, A<u>d</u>vanced Find to display the Advanced Find dialog box (see Figure 35.5).

The Advanced Find dialog box has three tabs:

■ *Messages.* You can enter a text string to search for here, and choose which field to look for it in. You can also narrow down the list to show only messages where you are the only recipient, or where you were CC'ed. You can also narrow down messages with certain date and time stamps.

Part

VI

Ch

35

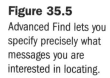

Figure 35.5
Advanced Find lets you
specify precisely what
messages you are
interested in locating.

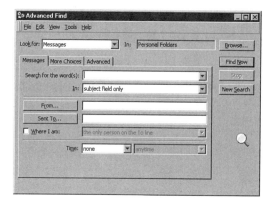

N O T E   The Messages tab appears in Advanced Find because we are working with a message
folder right now (the Inbox). If you use Advanced Find when working with other Outlook
tools (contacts, tasks, and so on), the tab in the dialog box changes to match that feature. ■

- *More Choices.* On this tab you can set up searches by Category (if you use those), search by importance, look for messages that either have or do not have attachments, and find messages that are read or unread.

- *Advanced.* On this tab you can create your own free-form criteria by specifying a field and then entering a value or range of values for it. For example, you might set up a filter to show only the messages that were from a certain recipient AND within a certain date range AND had a certain word in the subject line.

The controls in the Advanced Find dialog box are fairly self-explanatory, with the exception of the Advanced tab. To build an advanced search, click the Advanced tab; click the Field button and select a field from the list. Next, select a criteria in the Condition field based on the data type you have selected, and finally enter a value if applicable.

For example, to find messages which were due yesterday, select the Due By field from the Date/Time list. In the Condition list, scroll until the word Yesterday appears. Then click the Add to List button. The new search criteria will be copied to the box at the top of the dialog box. Then click the Find Now button.

You can also add additional criteria. One example is Incomplete Status. This one is more applicable when finding tasks than e-mails, but it is available no matter what you are searching for. To do this, select the All Task Fields list and choose %Complete from the top of that list. In the Condition list choose Is at Most and in the Value field enter 50. Click the Add button to save. This will add the condition to the query. Click Find Now to see a list of messages that meet the criteria you specified.

Grouping Messages

You can group messages by right-clicking a Column Heading button and choosing Group By This Field from the pop-up menu. This displays the Group By box at the top of the list of messages, with the selected field above the other fields. Figure 35.6 shows the Inbox grouped by the From field.

Figure 35.6

Messages have been grouped by the From field.

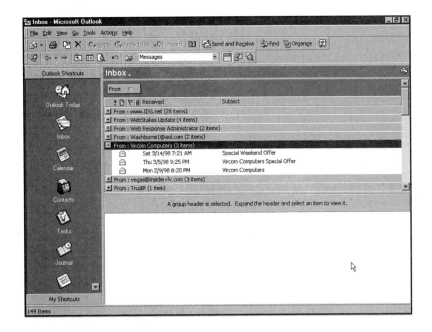

 T I P You can also create a grouping by dragging a column heading into the Group By box. To display the Group By box if it is not already displayed, click the Group By button on the toolbar.

By default, when you group by a column, all the messages collapse under headings for the column. For example, in Figure 35.6, the messages are hidden under headings for each From entry. Click on the plus sign next to an entry to expand its list. Figure 35.6 shows one grouping expanded. You can expand or collapse all groups at once by choosing View, Expand/Collapse Groups.

To return to a normal view of the Inbox, ungroup the messages. To do so, right-click on the column name that appears in the Group By box and choose Don't Group By This Field.

Using the Group By Dialog Box

If you want to group your messages by a category that isn't currently displayed in the Inbox, double-click the Group By box to open the Group By dialog box. Choose the fields you want to group by from the drop-down lists, in the order in which you want them grouped (see Figure 35.7).

N O T E Don't forget the View Summary dialog box you learned about at the beginning of this chapter. You can click its Group button to open the Group By dialog box. ■

Part
VI

Ch
35

Figure 35.7

Use the Group By dialog box to group data.

In the Group By dialog box, you can nest groupings up to four fields, with each grouping sorted independently, either ascending or descending within the group. Grouping creates an indented list with the Group By box at the top of the list and a sort order indicator for each grouping field. Figure 35.8 shows the results of the multi-level grouping set up in Figure 35.7.

Figure 35.8

Here is an example of 3-level Grouping of messages.

Group By box shows the grouping levels

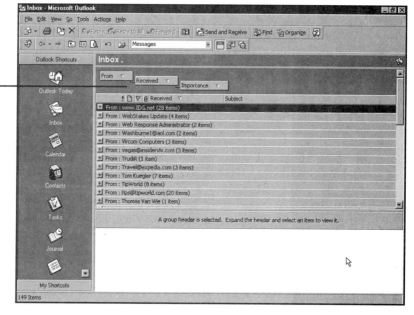

Adding Column Headings

When you group your messages, you may find that the column headings Outlook uses don't provide enough information for you. In this case, you can add more column headings, which in turn will provide more information about each message. For example, you might not have a column heading named Sent. This column will display the date and time the message was sent to you. In this case you can simply add the new column heading by using the Field Chooser window.

Open the Field Chooser window by right-clicking any existing column heading and then selecting Field Chooser from the pop-up menu. Alternatively, you can click the Field Chooser button on the toolbar. In either case, the Field Chooser window appears (see Figure 35.9).

Figure 35.9
Customize columns using the Field Chooser.

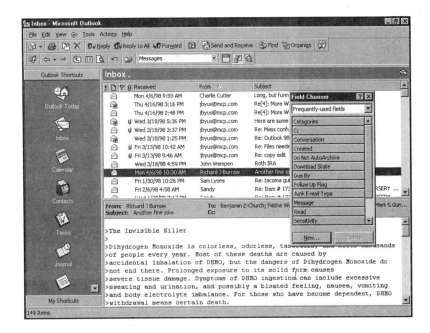

To add a field to the existing columns, simply click and drag the field you want out of the Field Chooser dialog box to the column headings. The new field will immediately appear. Be careful, however, to drop the field where you want it.

Deleting Column Headings

To delete a column heading for grouped messages, simply click and drag the heading you want to remove until you see an "X" appear over the heading. When you release the mouse button, the column heading will disappear. Remember, however, to click and drag *down*. If you drag up, you will add the column heading to the grouping area. If you drag left or right, you will reposition the column heading instead of deleting it.

Filtering Messages

Filtering messages is similar to querying a database. You specify criteria based on fields, and Outlook displays only the messages that satisfy the criteria. To create a filter, open the View Summary dialog box (View, Current View, Customize Current View) and click the Filter button. The Filter dialog box appears (see Figure 35.10).

Figure 35.10

Messages are filtered using the Filter dialog box.

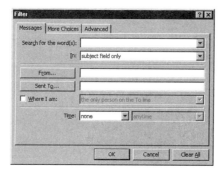

For example, you can specify a text string to search for in the subject field, such as "Financial" to display messages that contain that text in their subjects. Other sample filters you can create might include the following:

- An expanded filter to include messages with the specified text in the body of the message by changing the selection in the In list
- A filter displaying the messages from a particular sender by entering the sender's name in the From box
- A filter to display only recent messages by selecting Received in the Time list box and Today in the next list box

You can filter any combination of Categories by selecting the More Choices tab (see Figure 35.11) and entering categories, or selecting categories from the list displayed when the Categories button is clicked (see Figure 35.12). If you are diligent in assigning categories to messages, you can create filters that will be more useful and flexible than a hierarchical folder structure. Other basic filtering features include *importance*, *attachments*, and *size*.

▶ **See** "Using Categories," **page 767**

Figure 35.11

The Filter dialog box's More Choices tab offers access to the Categories button as well as some other options.

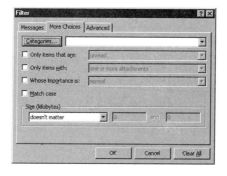

The Advanced tab enables you to create complex criteria based on any field defined in Outlook (see Figure 35.13). The list of possible choices under Conditions depends on the type of data in the selected filter field, whether it is a date, text, or status field. To enter criteria here, click the Field button and select a field. Next, select one of the listed conditions in the Condition list.

Finally, enter a value in the Value text box. For example, you might select Subject as the field to filter, Contains as the condition, and then you might type text that would be in the Subject field of some messages.

Figure 35.12
The Categories dialog box can be used to help filter messages by category.

Figure 35.13
The Filter dialog box has Advanced options that let you customize your own filters.

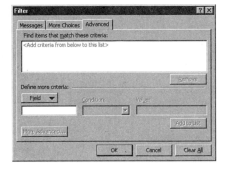

Using Categories

You can put messages in categories that you can later use to find and group messages. You can use categories on messages you send as well as marking messages you receive with the categories you choose. In effect, categories in Outlook provide you with a more powerful method of organizing your messages, tasks, and other items.

Adding Items to a Category

You have to select what you want to add to a category. For example, if you want to add several messages to a category, first select the messages. As in many Windows 95 programs, you can select contiguous messages by clicking the first one, pressing the Shift key, then clicking the last one in the list. That selects all the messages between the first one you selected and the last one you clicked. You can select noncontiguous messages by selecting the first one, then pressing the Ctrl key and clicking each other message you want to add to the selection.

Part
VI

Ch

35

When you've selected the messages, click the Edit menu and select Categories to open the Categories dialog box (see Figure 35.14). Alternatively, you can right-click any of the selected messages and select Categories from the pop-up menu.

> **CAUTION**
>
> Be sure you right-click a selected message. If you right-click elsewhere, you will lose your selection, and you won't get the appropriate menu.

Figure 35.14

Items are placed into categories using the Categories dialog box.

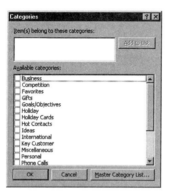

Select the category you want and click OK. The selected messages will now be in that category.

Removing Items from a Category

To remove an item from a category, first select the messages, and then open the Categories dialog box. If all the messages you selected were assigned to a category, that category will show a check mark. Simply clear the check mark to remove the message from that category.

N O T E If you select several messages you might find that when you open the Categories dialog box that one or more categories have shading in the check box instead of a check mark or being completely clear. This is because some of the messages you selected, but not all, have been assigned to that category. You can click each shaded check box to add or clear the check mark so that the entire selection will be assigned to or removed from that category.

Creating Categories

If Outlook's built-in categories are not sufficient for your needs, you can create your own. Click the Edit menu and then select Categories to open the Categories dialog box. Then type the new category name in the text box above the list of currently available categories. Finally, click the OK button to add the new category to the Master Category list.

Deleting Categories

You can delete any category, including the built-in ones that come with Outlook. In order to delete a category, you need to open the Master Category list. Begin by clicking the Edit menu and then selecting Categories to open the Categories dialog box. Next, click the Master Category List button at the bottom of the dialog box. When the Master Category List window opens, you can select any category and click the Delete button on the right (see Figure 35.15). This removes the category from the Master Category list, but leaves it in the Available Categories list.

Figure 35.15

All categories are in the Master Category list

When you delete categories, however, you need to remember that any messages that were assigned to those categories will still be assigned. You will have to take an extra step to remove the category assignment from those messages. To do this, select the appropriate messages, open the Categories dialog box and remove the check mark from the appropriate category.

Note that there is a Reset button in the Master Category List dialog box. You can use this to restore categories that you deleted, but only if they were originally part of Outlook's built-in categories. If you delete a category that you added previously, the Reset button will not restore that category for you.

Finding Messages by Category

One of the major benefits of assigning messages to categories is that you can find them when you want them. If you are diligent about assigning categories, you should find that you have little trouble finding important messages, regardless of who sent them, the subject, or the dates.

Begin by clicking the Tools menu and selecting Advanced Find. Then click the More Choices tab to display the options shown in Figure 35.16.

Click the Categories button, and the Categories dialog box appears (as you saw in Figure 35.14). Choose the category by which you want to search, and then click OK to transfer its name to the More Choices tab. Finally, click Find to perform the search.

Figure 35.16

Use the Advanced Find's dialog box to locate messages by category.

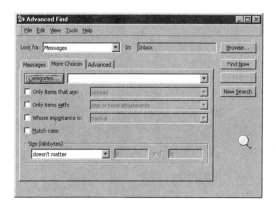

NOTE   If the category you want isn't available in the Available categories box, click Master Category list, type a name for the category, click Add, and then click OK. ▒

Filtering Messages by Category

As with finding messages by category, you can filter your messages by category so that only those you have in a particular category will be displayed by Outlook. You learned about filtering earlier in this chapter, but let's review filtering by category now.

Begin by selecting the folder you want to filter. Then open the View Summary dialog box (View, Current View, Customize Current View) and click the Filter button. The Filter dialog box appears. Click the more Choices tab, and then the Categories button to open the Categories dialog box. Choose the category you want to use for a filter, and then click OK. Complete the filter normally.

▶ **See** "Filtering Messages," **page 765**

Archiving

Archiving is the process of moving data from the Inbox and other folders into other storage (for example, older data might be saved on a CD or tape backup). You may have messages that are no longer current but you want to keep them for your records. Archiving is the process of moving those important, but older, messages off-line and out of your way without losing them forever. Archiving can be done either manually or automatically.

Manually Archiving

To manually archive a folder, choose File, Archive. This opens the Archive dialog box (see Figure 35.17).

If the option is not already chosen, select Archive This Folder and All Its Subfolders. (The option above it, Archive All Folders According to the AutoArchive Settings, is for use only when you have set up an AutoArchive system.)

Figure 35.17

Archive dialog box.

Type a name and a location for the archived items in the Archive File box, or click Browse to scroll through a list of folders. Enter a date in the Archive Items Older Than box, or click the down arrow to see a calendar to select the date. Messages older than the date you enter will be archived. Finally, click OK to perform the archiving.

If there are many messages to archive, the process may take a minute or so. You'll see an Archiving indicator in the bottom right corner of the Outlook window. It changes to Archiving Complete when the process is finished.

AutoArchiving

AutoArchiving means that you set the conditions for Outlook to automatically move messages and other items to another folder (or permanently delete them, if that's what you want). There are two elements to setting up AutoArchiving:

- Setting AutoArchive options in the Options dialog box (this is where AutoArchiving is turned on or off)
- Setting AutoArchive options for each folder you want AutoArchived

Begin by clicking the Tools menu and selecting Options. In the Options dialog box, click the Other tab. On it, there is an AutoArchive button. Click on it to open the AutoArchive dialog box shown in Figure 35.18.

Figure 35.18

Set your AutoArchiving preferences here.

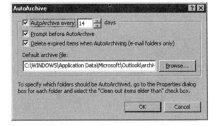

Part
VI

Ch
35

Here you enable and disable AutoArchive and set the basic AutoArchive options (how often, whether or not you are prompted, where the files are stored, and so on). The options you set in this dialog box will apply to all AutoArchived items in Outlook.

After you've set the basic options, you need to apply AutoArchiving to the specific Outlook folders you want automatically archived. AutoArchiving does not apply to individual messages or subfolders, but only to entire folders.

Begin by right-clicking the folder you want to AutoArchive (such as Inbox or Calendar). Then click Properties on the shortcut menu. This opens the Properties dialog box for that Outlook folder. Click the AutoArchive tab (see Figure 35.19).

Figure 35.19

Right-click the icon and choose Properties, then click the AutoArchive tab.

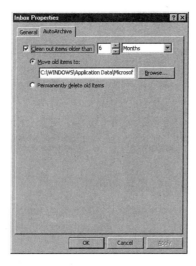

Set the AutoArchive properties as you desire. Note that you can opt to permanently delete the items rather than save them to another folder. When you have selected the options you want, click OK.

Retrieving Archived Items

To bring messages back into your Inbox or other active folders, follow these steps:

1. Choose File, Import and Export to start the Import and Export Wizard (see Figure 35.20). The Wizard will step through the process of importing a file and will enable you to control the way in which the items are restored.

2. Select Import from Another Program or File from the list of actions to perform. Then click Next.

3. When prompted for a file type to import from, choose Personal Folder File (*.pst). Then click next.

4. In the File to Import text box, type the name of your archived file, or click Browse to locate it. (It is probably archive.pst.)

Figure 35.20

The Import and Export Wizard walks you through the steps.

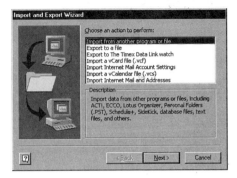

5. In the Options area (see Figure 35.21), choose an option button to describe how you want to handle duplicate entries. Then click Next.

Figure 35.21

Choose the archive file, and specify how you will handle duplicates.

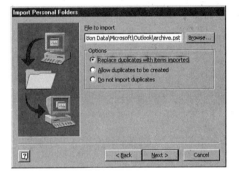

6. Next, a folder tree appears. It is a representation of the folders that have been archived in your archive file. Click on the folder that you want to import, or click on the top-level one to import them all.

7. Choose Import Items Into the Same Folder In and leave its drop-down list set to Personal Folders.

8. Leave the other settings at their defaults, and click Finish. Outlook imports the specified archived items.

Using Rules for Automated Processing of Messages

Often the best way to deal with large quantities of e-mail is to have an assistant deal with it for you. Outlook provides a Rules Wizard to manage rules for automatically handling messages.

Rules in Outlook are instructions for handling events. An event is typically the delivery of a message to the Inbox. When a message arrives in the Inbox, the rules provide the instructions on how it should be handled. The rules are applied in order from top to bottom as they appear in the list of rules that the Rules Wizard maintains. The wizard uses the conditions you define to determine whether a rule applies to a particular message. If it does, then the action you define for the rule is performed on the message. Typical actions include moving the message to a special folder or sending a "Thank you for your message" message back to the sender.

To set up rules, follow these steps:

1. Choose Tools, Rules Wizard. The Rules Wizard dialog box appears.

2. Click the New button to open a list of new rules you might want to create.

3. Click on a phrase to add it to your new rule. It appears in the Rule Description area (see Figure 35.22).

Figure 35.22

Set up rules and conditions in the Rules Wizard.

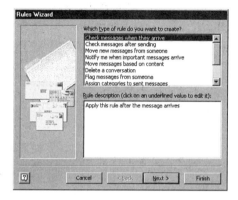

4. If the rule in the Rule Description contains an underlined word, click on it to open a dialog box where you can define the parameters. For example, in Figure 35.22, click on people or distribution list to open your address book and choose the people the rule applies to. Do this for each underlined word or phrase in the rule.

5. When you have finished working with all underlined words and phrases, the information you specified replaces the names of the parameters. Click Next to continue.

6. Next, a list of conditions to check appears. Click to place a check mark next to the conditions you want it to check. For example, you could choose Sent Only To Me to include only messages where you are the only recipient. Some of these check box lines have their own underlined text; click on it to set parameters.

7. When you are finished with the check boxes, click Next.

8. A list of actions to perform on the messages appears. Click to place a check mark next to each one that you want to happen, just as you did with the items in step 6. Then click Next.

9. A list of exceptions to the rule appears. Place a check mark next to each one that applies, as you have done with the preceding lists. Then click Next.

10. Type a name for the rule in the Please Specify a Name for This Rule text box.

11. Click the Finish button. The new rule appears in the Rules Wizard dialog box (see Figure 35.23).

12. Click OK to close the dialog box. Your new rule is now in effect.

Figure 35.23
Turn a rule on or off
with the check box next
to its name.

To turn a rule on or off, reopen the Rules Wizard dialog box at any time (Tools, Rules Wizard) and click to remove the check mark next to the rule. To edit the rule, click on underlined text in its description, or click the Modify button to reopen the series of screens you worked with in the preceding steps.

If it is important that the rules be applied in a particular order, sort them on the list in Figure 35.23 by clicking the Move Up or Move Down button to move a rule on the list.

Using Recipient Groups

If you frequently send messages to a group of people you can create a Personal Distribution list that will simplify addressing and help you avoid forgetting to send the message to all of the people who should receive a particular message.

N O T E The following steps apply to Internet Mail Only mode. If you want to create a distribution list in Corporate/Workgroup mode, create it in your Personal Address Book.

To create a Distribution list, follow these steps.

1. Choose Tools, Address Book. Your Address Book opens.
2. In the Address Book window, click the New Group button. A Properties dialog box appears for the new group (see Figure 35.24).
3. Type a name in the Group Name box (for example, Meeting Minutes or Funny Jokes).
4. Click the Select Members button. A list of the people in your address book appears.
5. Click on each name you want to select, and then click the Select button to move the name to the Members list. To move more than one at a time, hold down the Ctrl key as you click on the names you want (see Figure 35.25).
6. Click OK to return to the Properties dialog box. The recipient names now appear.
7. Click OK. Your group has been created. You can now send messages to the entire group by choosing the group name as the recipient in the messages you send.

Part
VI

Ch
35

Figure 35.24

Build a new group from this dialog box.

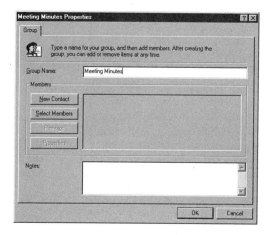

Figure 35.25

Select the people to belong to this group.

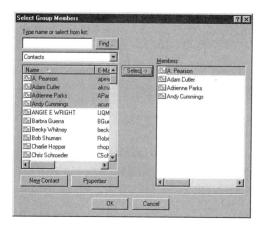

Using Signatures

Signatures are text that is automatically inserted at the end of messages you compose. They can contain any text you want, but remember they are attached to each message you send. The readers of your e-mail messages will see the signature on each message they receive from you. A signature of this type can be a great way to personalize your messages and to express yourself or to convey some important information, but you should be cautious of abusing the possibility. A long signature text can quickly become stale.

To create a signature and attach it to all sent messages:

1. Choose Tools, Options, and click the Mail Format tab.

2. Click the Signature Picker button. This opens the Signature Picker dialog box.

3. Click the New button to create a new signature. The Create New Signature dialog box opens.

4. Type a name for the signature. Keep in mind that you may someday want to have more than one signature, so don't just name it "Signature." Then click Next. The Edit Signature dialog box appears.

5. Type the text to use for your signature.

 TIP Try to keep it to between 3 and 6 lines; any longer than that is considered piggish because it wastes Internet bandwidth. Some people add a row of asterisks or equal signs at the top or bottom to make a sort of "box"; keep in mind that if you do this, you've used up two of your lines.

6. Click Finish. The new signature appears on the list in the Signature Picker dialog box.

7. If you want to create another signature to use for other occasions, return to step 3.

8. Click OK to return to the Options dialog box.

9. Select the signature to use as the default from the Use This Signature By Default drop-down list.

10. Click OK to close the dialog box.

CHAPTER 36

Scheduling with the Calendar

by Liz Tasker and Faithe Wempen

In this chapter

Overview of Calendar

Outlook's Calendar is an appointment book that helps you schedule and manage your time. The Calendar folder contains three types of appointment items: appointments, meetings, and events. Although they are similar, each type of item has its own special attributes.

By default, Outlook presents these items in a graphical Day\Week\Month view, which is where you are likely to spend most of your time. Figure 36.1 shows the Day format of the Day\Week\Month view.

Figure 36.1
The Day\Week\Month View in Day format.

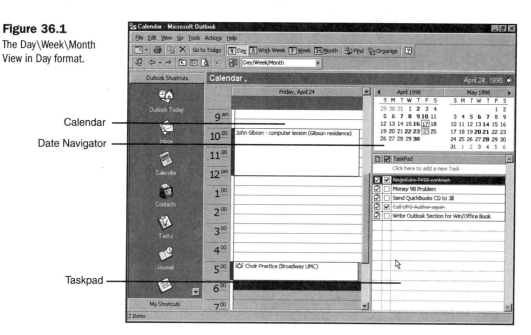

The Day\Week\Month view consists of these three main areas.

- *Calendar.* You can display this area in three formats: day, week, and month. The month format hides the Date Navigator and Taskpad areas of the view.
- *Date Navigator.* This is the small calendar next to the appointment area in Calendar. It provides a quick and easy way to navigate to different dates.
- *Taskpad.* This area displays a daily To-Do list of tasks, which you can add to and monitor.

Viewing the Calendar

Like all Outlook folders, the Calendar folder has a set of predefined views. In addition to the Day\Week\Month view, Outlook also provides several other predefined, table-type views, which you may also want to use from time to time.

To select a different view for the calendar, follow these steps:

1. Click the Calendar icon in the Outlook Bar.
2. Select View, Current View, and then the view you want. Table 36.1 lists the predefined views for the Outlook Calendar.

Table 36.1   Views for the Outlook Calendar

View	Description
Day\Week\Month	The default view, which provides three screen areas: the calendar, Date Navigator, and Taskpad
Day\Week\Month with AutoPreview	Same as Day\Week\Month except you see a Preview Pane at the bottom of the screen if you have the Preview Pane turned on (View, Preview Pane)
Active Appointments	Displays chronologically sorted list of appointments
Events	Spreadsheet style table with one line per event, sorted alphabetically
Annual Events	Same as Events except it shows events that recur annually, such as birthdays
Recurring Appointments	A list of all appointments set up as recurring events
By Category	Expandable table of events, grouped by category

If you choose one of the Day\Week\Month views, you have access to special toolbar buttons that let you switch between Day, Work Week, Week, and Month. The default is Day, but you may find one of the other choices helpful for your planning. For example, Figure 36.2 shows Day\Week\Month view in Week mode.

Use these buttons to switch among Day, Month, and Week.

Figure 36.2
You can change Day\Week\Month view to show the entire week, like this, rather than the default single day.

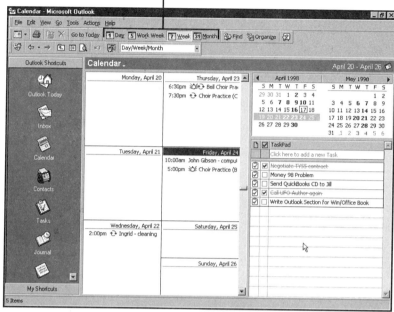

Creating Appointments

You can create new appointments either with the New Appointment dialog box or by typing directly into the calendar. The former is more powerful and flexible, but the latter is quicker.

Creating a New Appointment with the Dialog Box

1. Select File, New, Appointment or press Ctrl+Shift+A. An untitled Appointment window appears (see Figure 36.3).

Figure 36.3
Enter a new appointment from this dialog box.

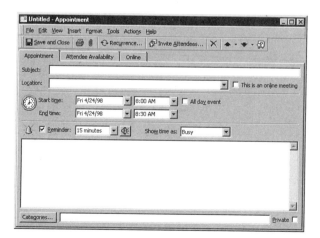

TIP Alternatively, if you have the Calendar folder open, you can use one of these methods to display an untitled Appointment window:

- Click the New Appointment icon in the toolbar.
- Select Actions, New Appointment.
- Press Ctrl+N.
- Double-click in a blank area of the Calendar.

2. Type a subject for the Appointment in the Subject field.

3. Type a location, or select a location from the list. All locations that exist in your calendar will appear in the location list.

4. Select or type a start and end date.

5. Enter any additional information that you want on Appointment tab as follows:

   - Reminder   Turn on Reminder check box, specify how long prior to the appointment you want to be reminded, and click the bell icon to select the .WAV file to use as the reminder sound.

   - Show Time As   Select how the time will appear on your published calendar—busy, free, tentative, or Out of Office.

   - Comments   In the large white text box, type any information you might want to remember for the appointment.

   - Categories   Select or type one or multiple categories under which you want to file this appointment.

   - Private   Specify that subject and location of this appointment should not appear on your public calendar.

6. Click the Save and Close button; select File, Save; or press Ctl+S.

Entering an Appointment Directly on the Calendar

If you want to quickly enter many appointments, you can type them directly into the calendar in the time slots provided in the Day format of the Day\Week\Month view. While you might eventually want to open each appointment item to adjust the duration and specify a location, this direct typing approach is very efficient when you have many appointments and little time to enter them.

Editing an Appointment

To edit an appointment, follow these steps:

1. Click the Calendar icon on the Outlook Bar. The Calendar folder opens, displaying the appointments for the day.

2. Use the Date Navigator to locate the day of the appointment.

3. Double-click the appointment you want to edit.

4. Make any changes to the appointment.

5. Click Save and Close.

 TIP If you only want to edit the subject of an appointment, you can do so directly on the calendar without opening the appointment item. You must be viewing the calendar in the Day format. Then you can find the appointment, insert your cursor on the text line next to the time slot, and type your changes directly on the line.

Scheduling Events

An event is a special type of appointment item that lasts at least one full day. When you schedule an event, you can still schedule appointments and meetings during the time of the event, unless you specify otherwise when you set up the event.

To enter a new event, follow these steps:

1. Click the Calendar icon on the Outlook Bar.

2. Select Actions, New All Day Event. An untitled Event window appears.

NOTE The Event window is identical to the Appointment window except that the All Day Event check box is selected and there are no fields for entering start and end times. If you deselect the All Day Event check box, the title bar changes to Untitled – Appointment and the date fields appear. ▪

3. Type a subject for the Event in the Subject field.

4. If desired, type a location, or select a location from the list. All locations that exist in your calendar will appear in the location list.

5. Select or type a start and end date.

6. Enter any additional information that you want on the Appointment tab, including reminders, comments, and categories.

7. Click the Save and Close button; select File, Save; or press Ctl+S.

 TIP If you want to quickly enter one or multiple events, you can type them directly into the calendar in the slots provided in the Week and Month formats of the Day\Week\Month view. This direct typing approach is very efficient for entering events on your calendar, especially if the events do not require additional detailed information.

Scheduling Meetings

In Outlook, a meeting is a special type of appointment item in which you select attendees, view their schedules, and then create the appointment. Outlook automatically sends invitations to the attendees by generating a mail message. Attendees can respond to a meeting invitation message by accepting or rejecting the meeting.

In addition to people, attendees can also include resources, such as rooms and equipment. Resources must be set up with an Outlook profile and an e-mail ID. For example, your system might have two resources established: Conference Room A, and Conference Room B. Each conference room would have its own schedule, but both conference room profiles would link to the e-mail ID of the department's administrative assistant.

To set up a meeting, follow these steps:

1. Click the Calendar icon on the Outlook Bar.

2. Select Actions, Plan a Meeting. The Plan a Meeting dialog box appears (see Figure 36.4). This dialog box enables you to check the availability of the people and resources required for your meeting before you send out invitations.

Figure 36.4

Plan a meeting and invite participants from here.

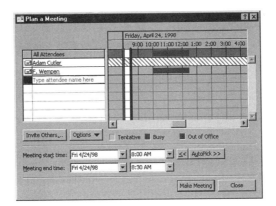

3. Invite attendees. If you know the contact names or e-mail addresses of the people and resources you want to invite, you can type them directly into the All Attendees list. If you are not sure, click Invite Others and use the Select Attendees and Resources dialog box to look them up.

N O T E   If you click Invite Others in step 3, you can place invitees into three categories: Required, Optional, and Resources. People on the Optional list are not required to attend, so AutoPick (step 4) will not take their schedules into consideration when picking a meeting time. ▨

4. Select AutoPick to determine a meeting time that is available for all required attendees. (This works only if the attendees use Outlook on your company network to schedule their appointments, or if you have Internet Free/Busy information available.)

5. Click Make Meeting. The Plan a Meeting dialog box closes to reveal an Untitled Meeting window that is partially filled. The To field contains all the attendees that you have selected, and the date and time are filled in as you have specified (see Figure 36.5).

Figure 36.5

Outlook generates an e-mail inviting participants.

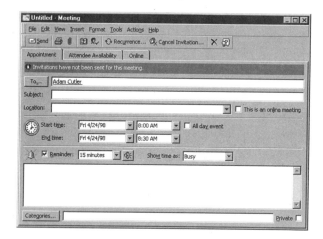

6. Type a subject for the meeting in the Subject field.

7. If you did not schedule a room, type a location or select a location from the list.

8. Enter any additional information that you want on the Appointment tab, including reminders, comments, and categories.

 If you want to send an agenda or a document for the attendees to read in preparation for the meeting, you can insert an item or a file into the comments box by selecting either the Insert, Item or Insert, File menu option.

9. If you decide to add attendees, change the meeting time, or want to check attendee status, select the Meeting Planner tab, and edit the meeting information as needed.

10. Click the Save and Close button; select File, Save; or press Ctl+S.

Creating Recurring Appointments, Meetings, and Events

Outlook provides the ability to create recurring appointments, meetings, and events. This feature can be handy for scheduling regular business activities, such as filling out expense reports, coordinating weekly staff meetings, or scheduling an annual conference for a team of people to attend. This feature can also help you schedule recurring personal activities, such as paying monthly bills or holding an annual picnic.

There are several ways to create recurring appointment items:

■ You can create a new recurring appointment or meeting by using those options provided on the Actions menu.

■ You can create a new nonrecurring appointment, meeting, or event and then optionally add recurrence information to it by selecting the Actions, Recurrence menu option.

■ You can turn an already existing, nonrecurring appointment, meeting, or event into a recurring appointment at any time by opening the item and selecting the Actions, Recurrence menu option.

Whatever method you choose to make an item recurring, all methods eventually lead you to the Appointment Recurrence dialog box, as shown in Figure 36.6.

Figure 36.6

The Appointment Recurrence dialog box.

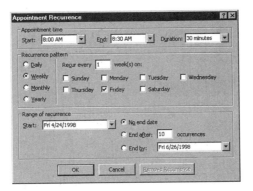

The Appointment Recurrence dialog box enables you to specify the following information about an appointment, meeting, or event:

■ *Appointment time.* Including start time, end time, and duration. End time and duration are mutually dependent on each other. That is, if you change the end time, it affects the duration; and if you change the duration, it affects the end time. Outlook will not let you create recurring events less than 24 hours long. Any event less than 24 hours gets converted into an appointment.

■ *Recurrence pattern.* The four main choices are daily, weekly, monthly, yearly. Within each of those choices, you can specify particular days or dates.

■ *Range of recurrence.* Including the start date and a milestone for ending the recurrence, which can be based on number of occurrences, an end date, or never ending.

CHAPTER 37

Maintaining a Contact List

by Liz Tasker and Faithe Wempen

In this chapter

Working with the Contacts Folder

The Contacts folder helps you keep track of contact information for the people you deal with for business or pleasure. For each contact, you can store e-mail, address, telephone information, and other information (such as birthdays and spouse names). Figure 37.1 shows a typical list of contacts. As you can see, not all entries have to use every field; some entries contain only e-mail addresses, while others contain more complete information.

Figure 37.1

The Contacts folder.

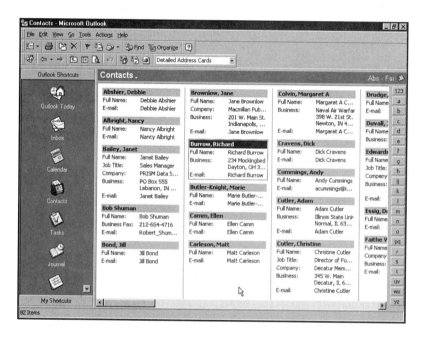

You may eventually want to separate your contacts into folders (for example, for business or personal use). By default, Outlook provides one Contacts folder, which you cannot delete. But you can create additional contacts folders if you want to keep separate lists of contacts for different purposes. You may want to keep business-related contacts in the Contacts folder provided with Outlook, create a separate contacts folder for friends and relatives, and create yet another contacts folder for people who belong to a club or organization in which you are active. If possible, however, you should keep all contacts in the predefined Contacts folder supplied by Outlook, both for simplicity and to take advantage of all Outlooks automation features.

N O T E Some of the automated features for contacts, such as automated journal entries, work only for the default Contacts folder supplied by Outlook. ▪

When you install Outlook, the Contacts folder is available for your immediate use. You can create contacts by typing them directly in Microsoft Outlook or by importing contact information from another source, such as Microsoft Schedule+ or Outlook Express, or a file downloaded from a mail server. You can start adding or importing contacts immediately. Before you begin, however, you may want to take look at how your Contacts properties are configured.

Viewing the Contact List

Like all Outlook folders, the Contacts folder has a set of predefined views for contacts. The default view for the Contacts folders is Address Cards, as shown in Figure 37.1.

To select a different view for the contact list, follow these steps:

1. Click the Contacts icon in the Outlook Bar to open the Contacts folder.
2. Choose View, Current View, and then the view you want.

Table 37.1 lists the predefined views for the Contact List.

Table 37.1   Views for the Contact List

View	Description
Address Cards	Small cards that list the following general information for each contact: name, mailing address, all e-mail addresses, and most phone numbers
Detailed Address Cards	Larger cards that list all general information for each contact
Phone List	Spreadsheet-style table with one line per contact, sorted alphabetically
By Category	List of contacts grouped by category
By Company	List of contacts grouped by company
By Location	List of contacts grouped by country
By Follow-Up Flag	List of contacts grouped by flag status

Creating New Contacts

To create a new contact, open a new Contact dialog box (see Figure 37.2) with any of the following methods:

- Click the New Contact button on the toolbar.
- Choose File, New, Contact.
- Press Ctrl+N.
- Right-click the area where the current contacts appear, and choose New Contact from the shortcut menu.

Figure 37.2

A new Contact window.

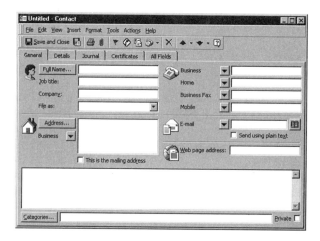

The Contact window provides five tabs of fields for the new contact: General, Details, Journal, and All Fields. Click on each tab and fill in the information in the fields. It's okay to skip any fields that are not applicable or for which you do not have information. You can always come back later and fill in more information. When you are finished, click the Save and Close button.

General Tab

The fields on the General tab (refer to Figure 37.2) are very straightforward. They ask for name, address, phone number, e-mail address, and other information about the contact. Just click in the field you want and type the information.

Details Tab

The Details tab contains less frequently used fields, such as Spouse's Name and Department. Again, just click in the field you want to use and type the information. Nothing tricky here.

Journal Tab

On the Journal tab, select or deselect the Automatically Record Journal Entries for This Contact check box. If you mark this check box, all meetings and events you schedule with this contact and e-mails you exchange with him/her will appear in your Journal.

Certificates Tab

If you use digital certificates to ensure authenticity when communicating with this contact via e-mail, set them up on this tab. Begin by clicking Import and following the prompts to set up the certificate. Then manage the certificate by clicking on it and then clicking the Properties button.

All Fields Tab

Some people find it frustrating that the various fields of information for a contact are spread out over multiple tabs. You can overcome this, and work with all fields at once, on the All Fields tab. Just open the Select From drop-down list and choose the subset of fields to show (for example, Frequently-Used Fields). Then type in the text box next to each field's name to record information (see Figure 37.3).

Figure 37.3
You can work with all the fields at once on this tab, in a spreadsheet-like format.

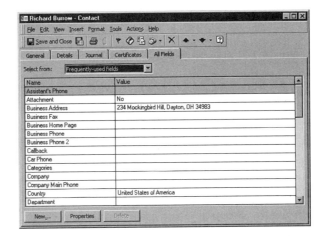

Editing Contacts

Outlook provides two main methods for making changes in contacts. You can type changes directly into one of the Contacts views, or you can redisplay the Contacts dialog box for a single contact. The former is faster, but you do not have access to all fields. The latter is slower, but provides more flexibility.

The easiest way to edit contacts depends on the changes that you want to make. If you want to edit one particular field (such as the address) for one or multiple contacts, editing directly in a view of the Contacts folder probably is easier. If the field that you want to edit does not appear in any view that you have, however, or if you want to review and modify many details about a particular contact, you need to use the Contacts window.

Editing in the Contacts Window

The Contacts window provides a multiple-panel form that allows you to view and edit all contact information.

To edit a contact in the Contacts window, follow these steps:

1. Display the contact list, and choose the view that you want to work in. Each view has its own pros and cons. For editing a single contact, Address Cards works well; for editing the same field in a list of contacts, try one of the spreadsheet-like views such as By Company.

2. Click where you want to begin editing, to place the flashing cursor there.

3. Use Backspace or Delete to remove any old information, and type new information.

 TIP   If you want to add a field to a view, choose View, Define Views. In the Define Views dialog box, click the Fields button. Then, in the Show Fields dialog box, click the New Field button.

Editing in the Contact Dialog Box

To reopen a contact's dialog box, so you again have access to the five tabs of fields that you saw earlier, double-click on the contact name (in Address Cards or Detailed Address Cards view) or click on the index card icon next to the name in one of the other views.

> **N O T E**   You can design your own forms in Outlook, not only for contacts but for any other Outlook tool. You might want to include an additional field in the Contact dialog box, for example, to keep track of some special information about clients (perhaps their favorite drinks or restaurants). To modify a form, display the form, and then choose Tools, Forms, Design This Form. ■

Importing and Exporting Contacts

If you already have a list of contacts stored in another file on your computer, you can use the Import and Export Wizard to load them into Outlook. The Import and Export Wizard makes it easy to import contacts and even easier to export them.

Importing Contacts

You can import names, addresses, and other contact information from any of these sources: Eudora Light, Eudora Pro, Internet Mail and News, Outlook Express, and Netscape Mail and Messenger. You can also import information from contact management programs like Schedule+, Act!, ECCO, Lotus Organizer, and SideKick.

To import a contact list, follow these steps:

1. Choose File, Import and Export. The Import and Export Wizard appears, as shown in Figure 37.4.

Figure 37.4
The Import and Export Wizard.

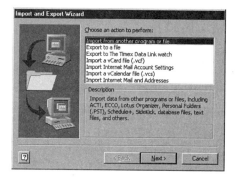

2. If importing from an e-mail program, choose Import Internet Mail and Addresses. If importing from a contact management program, choose Import From Another Program or File.

3. Click Next.

4. If asked to choose which program to import from (if importing from another program), choose it and click Next.

5. In the File to Import box, enter the name and path to the file, or click Browse to locate it. Then click Next.

6. Perform any additional steps as prompted. You may see additional prompts depending on the file type you chose in step 2.

7. When you see a message that the following actions will be performed, click Finish.

Part
VI

Ch
37

 TIP If you import from a file used in Microsoft Word or PowerPoint, the file should be formatted with tab-separated values or comma-separated values.

Exporting Contacts

You can export contact information to an ASCII file for use in other external programs, to a personal folder file (.pst) to share with other Outlook applications, or to the Timex DataLink.

To export contacts, follow these steps:

1. Choose File, Import and Export. The Import and Export Wizard appears.

2. Choose an action. If exporting to a Timex DataLink, choose Export to The Timex DataLink Watch; otherwise choose Export to a File. Then click Next.

3. When prompted for a file type, choose a type that the program you are exporting for will understand. If your program is not listed, choose a generic format like Comma Separated Values (DOS). Then click Next.

4. When prompted to select a folder to export from, click the Contacts folder. Then click Next.

5. When prompted for a name, type a file name for the export. Then click Next.

6. When you see a message that the following actions will be performed, click Finish.

Telephoning Contacts

Before Outlook can make phone calls for you, you must set up your computer and a modem for automatic phone dialing. Then Outlook can dial phone numbers, including numbers for your contacts in the Outlook contact list.

You can automatically create a journal entry to record the duration of your phone call and add notes from your conversation to the journal entry. You can also create a speed-dial list of phone numbers that you call frequently.

To use Outlook to make new phone call, follow these steps:

1. Click on the contact that you want to call.

2. Choose Actions, Call Contact. On a submenu, all the phone numbers for that person appear. Click on the one you want to call. The New Call dialog box appears, with the information already filled in, as shown in Figure 37.5.

Figure 37.5

Use your modem to dial your telephone using this dialog box.

3. To keep a record of the call in a Journal, click Create New Journal Entry. ·

   If you select this check box, after you start the call, a journal entry opens with the timer running. You can type notes in the text box of the journal entry while you talk.

4. Click Start Call. You hear your phone dialing and ringing through your modem.

5. Pick up the receiver and click Talk.

6. If you created a journal entry for the call, when you finish, click Pause Timer to stop the clock and then click Save and Close.

7. Click End Call, and then hang up the phone.

CHAPTER 38

Managing Tasks and Your Time

by Liz Tasker

In this chapter

Viewing the Task List

Outlook's Tasks folder acts as an online to-do list that you can use to keep track of any task that needs to get done, whether it's a business task or a personal chore.

By default, Outlook presents the Tasks List in the Simple List view, as shown in Figure 38.1. To display the Tasks list, click the Tasks icon on the Outlook Bar.

Figure 38.1

The Simple List view.

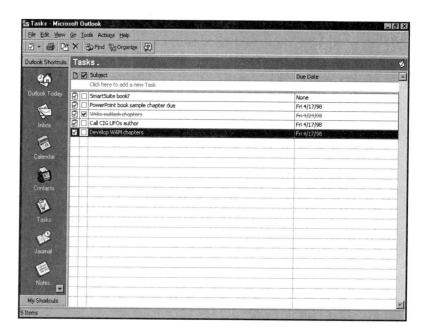

Tasks that are finished have a line drawn through them, and appear in gray rather than black print. Figure 38.1 has one completed task. You can mark a task as completed by clicking the check box to its left.

The Simple List view provides only the most basic information about each task. Different views provide more information about the tasks.

To select a different view for the tasks list, follow these steps:

1. Click the Tasks icon in the Outlook Bar.
2. Choose View, Current View, and then the view you want. Table 38.1 lists the predefined views for the Tasks list.

Table 38.1   Views for the Tasks List

View	Description
Simple List	The default view, which provides a list of all tasks with their due dates. Useful for viewing a list of all tasks, along with their due dates.

View	Description
Detailed List	A list of all tasks, with more detailed information, including status, due dates, percent complete, and category.
Active Tasks	A detailed list of all tasks except those that are completed or deferred.
Next Seven Days	A detailed list of all tasks due within the next seven days.
Overdue Tasks	A detailed list of all overdue, uncompleted tasks. This is useful when you have a long, outdated task list that you need to update. You can quickly view overdue tasks and determine whether to mark them complete, defer them, extend the due date, or take some other action.
By Category	A detailed list of all tasks grouped by category. Useful for viewing only tasks that are for business, or only personal tasks.
Assignment	A list of all tasks assigned to others. If you use Outlook to share task assignments, you can use this to manage that process.
By Person Responsible	A detailed list of all tasks, grouped by owner. This view is useful for assessing the workloads of multiple users and for separating your own tasks from other people's tasks.
Completed Tasks	A detailed list of all completed tasks, so you can assess what work has been finished.
Task Timeline	Provides a graphical picture of task durations and simultaneously occurring tasks. This pictorial representation can be useful to assess peak workload occurrences.

Part VI
Ch
38

Creating and Modifying Tasks

You can create and modify tasks in the Task window, which provides a form-based interface for entering and editing task items. The Task window, as shown in Figure 38.2, is one of the predefined forms supplied with Microsoft Outlook.

Within this window you can create new tasks and task requests and then edit and track them as their status changes. You can also specify options for task recurrence.

Entering New Tasks

You can create new tasks whenever you like. When you create a new task, Outlook automatically adds it to your task list.

To enter a new task, follow these steps:

1. Choose File, New, Task or press Ctrl+Shift+K. An untitled task window appears.

Figure 38.2

The Task window.

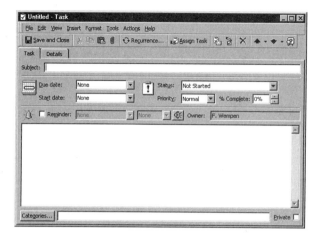

Alternatively, if you have the Tasks folder open, you can use one of these methods to display an untitled Task window:

- Click the New Task icon in the toolbar.

- Press Ctrl+N.

- Double-click in a blank area of the task list.

- Right-click a blank area of the task list and choose New Task.

2. Type a subject for the Task in the Subject field.

3. Enter any additional information that you want on the Task tab as follows:

- *Status*. Select from the following predefined choices to provide a general indication of how the task is progressing: Not Started, In Progress, Waiting On Someone Else, Deferred. This field can be useful when viewing the task list, both as a column to display and as a field to sort by.

- *Due Date*. Choose the date by which the task should be finished.

- *Start Date*. Choose the date by which the task should be started.

- *Priority*. Select High, Medium, or Low. This field can also be useful when viewing the task list, both as a column to display and as a field to sort by.

- *% Complete*. Select or type a number that represents the percentage of the task you think is complete.

- *Reminder*. Select the Reminder check box, specify the date and time you want to be reminded, and click the speaker icon to select .WAV file to use as the reminder sound.

- *Comments*. In the large white text box, type any information you might want to remember for the task or insert another Outlook item, such as a note, to reference.

- *Categories*. Select or type one or multiple categories under which you want to file this task.

- *Private*. Specify that subject and location of this appointment should not appear to others who have access to this folder.

4. Select the Details tab (Figure 38.3) and enter any additional information that you want as follows:

- *Date Completed*. Enter the date if you have completed the task.

- *Total Work*. Enter the number of hours you think it will take to complete the task.

- *Actual Work*. Enter the number of hours that have been spent working on the task.

- *Mileage*. If applicable, enter the number of miles you traveled to perform the task.

- *Billing Information*. If applicable, enter billing information, such as an account number or an hourly billing rate.

- *Contacts:*. If applicable, enter the names of contacts associated with this task.

- *Companies*. If applicable, enter the names of companies associated with this task.

Part
VI

Ch
38

Figure 38.3

The Details tab's fields are optional; they provide extra information.

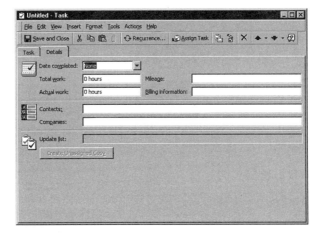

5. Click the Save and Close button, choose File, Save, or press Ctrl+S.

 TIP If you want to quickly enter many tasks, you can type them directly into the task list by clicking the first line of the task list, typing the task subject, and pressing Enter. While you might eventually want to open each task item to edit the due date or assign it to someone else, this direct typing approach is very efficient for quickly creating a to-do list.

Editing or Updating a Task

To edit a task, follow these steps:

1. Click the Task icon on the Outlook Bar. The Tasks folder opens, displaying the tasks.

2. Double-click the task you want to edit.

3. Make any changes to the task, such as updating the status, percentage complete, or actual hours.

4. Click Save and Close.

 You can also edit any information that appears in a view by typing directly on the task list. For example, in the Detailed List view, you could edit the % Complete field for each task just by clicking the % Complete cell in the row of each task you want to edit, and then typing the new percentage directly into the cell.

Task Assignments and Requests

If you use e-mail with Outlook, you have the ability to assign tasks and send task requests to other Outlook users. You also can receive task requests and status reports from them. The person who receives the task request can accept the task, decline the task, or assign the task to someone else.

When you send a task request, the person who receives the task request becomes the owner of the task. Although you can keep an updated copy of a task in your task list and receive status reports on it, you cannot make changes to a task once you've assigned it to someone else. Only the owner of the task can make changes to it.

If you own a task that was assigned to other people before you accepted it, every time you make a change your change is automatically made to the copies of the task in their task lists. And when you complete the task, Outlook sends automatic status reports to the other people who were assigned the task and requested status reports.

Assigning a Task

If you have a task in mind for someone else, you assign it to him or her by creating a new task request. You can also assign one of your existing tasks to someone else, which will also create a new task request. Either way, Outlook will send your task request to that person. The task request will appear in the recipient's Inbox and on his or her task list.

To enter a task request, follow these steps:

1. Choose File, New, Task Request or press Ctrl+Shift+U. An untitled Task window appears. Unlike the regular Task window, this screen looks more like an e-mail, with blanks for entering recipients as well as task information (see Figure 38.4).

 Alternatively, if you have the Tasks folder open, you can use one of these methods to start a new task request:

- Double-click an existing task that you want to assign to someone else and then choose Task, Assign Task.

- Double-click in a blank area of the task list and then choose Task, Assign Task.

- Right-click in a blank area and then choose New Task Request.

Figure 38.4

Assign a task to someone else with a Task Request.

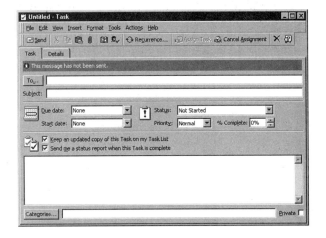

Part **VI**

Ch **38**

2. Type the name of the person you want to receive the task request or click the To button to look up the name in an address book.

3. If this is a new task, type the Subject.

4. Specify Due date, Start date, Status, Priority, and % Complete as desired.

5. If you want to track the task you are assigning, select the Keep an Updated Copy of This Task on My Task List check box.

6. If you want to receive a copy of the status report on task completion, select Send Me a Status Report When This Task Is Complete.

7. Select the Details tab and fill in or update any pertinent information.

8. Click Send. Outlook sends the task request to the person you specified. Based on the options you selected, the task will either disappear from your task list or be viewable in the Assignment view.

N O T E Normally, you can assign tasks only in Corporate/Workgroup mode. However, you can assign tasks over the Internet for another Outlook user, with Outlook in Internet Mail Only mode, if you send the items in RTF (Rich Text Format). ■

Responding to a Task Request

When you receive a task request, you can accept the task, decline the task, or assign the task to someone else. Based on your actions, the task workflow will continue as follows:

■ If you accept the task, you become the new owner of the task and are the only person who can edit it.

■ If you decline the task, it is returned to the person who sent you the task request.

■ If you assign the task to someone else, you can keep an updated copy in your task list and receive status reports, but ownership is transferred to the person who receives the assignment.

To respond to a task request, follow these steps:

1. From your Inbox, double-click the message that contains the task request.

2. Accept, decline, or reassign the task by selecting the appropriate option.

3. If you want to add a comment, click Edit the Response Before Sending and type your comment in the text box.

4. Click Send. Your response will be delivered to the person who sent you the task request.

Recurring Tasks

Outlook provides the ability to create recurring tasks. This feature can be handy for reminding yourself and others to do things like prepare for a weekly meeting, take out the garbage, or get your hair cut. Once you set up a recurring task, Outlook provides options for skipping an occurrence or removing recurrence altogether.

Creating Recurring Tasks

When you create a new task or a task request, you can specify that it is recurring, or you can turn a nonrecurring task into a recurring task at any time.

To make a task or task request recurring, follow these steps:

1. Click the Task icon on the Outlook Bar.

2. Start a new task or task request, or double-click an existing task to open it.

3. Click the Recurrence button on the toolbar inside the task's window. The Task Recurrence dialog box appears, as shown in Figure 38.5.

Figure 38.5
The Task Recurrence dialog box.

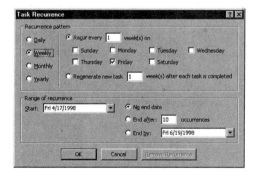

4. Click Daily, Weekly, Monthly, or Yearly. This selection determines your choices for specifying exactly when the task recurs. For example, if you select Monthly, you have three options for specifying recurrence:

- Task recurs on a specific day within an interval of months. For example, you can set up a task to recur monthly, such as the 15th day of every month, or you can set up a task to recur quarterly, such as the 1st day of every 3rd month.

- Task recurs on a specific day of a specific week within an interval of months. For example, you can set up a task to recur monthly, such as the first Monday of every month, or you can set up a task to recur quarterly, such as the first Monday of every third month.

- Task recurs on a number of months after the current task is complete. For example, you can specify that the system regenerate a new task one month after the current task is complete.

5. Specify a Range of recurrence, including the Start date and a milestone for ending the recurrence. You can set up a recurring task with No End Date, or you can end task recurrence based on a specified number of occurrences or on a particular date.

6. Click OK when you are finished entering recurrence information.

7. Click Save and Close.

Part
VI

Ch

38

Skipping an Occurrence

Occasionally, you may want to skip a recurring task. For example, if you set up a task to remind you to send a status report to your boss every week, you can skip a week when your boss is on vacation. Or, maybe you are taking the summer off from a weekly activity that you do the rest of the year, such as attending a dance class.

When Outlook generates the next occurrence of a recurring task, you can skip the occurrence and remove it from your task list. To skip an occurrence, follow these steps:

1. Double-click the row containing the occurrence of the task you want to skip.

2. Choose Actions, Skip Occurrence.

CAUTION

Do not delete the task if you just want to skip an occurrence. Deleting the task will delete all future occurrences.

Removing Recurrence

You can easily change a recurring task into a one-time task by following these steps:

1. Double-click the row containing the recurring task you want to change.

2. Choose Actions, Recurrence.

3. Click Remove Recurrence.

4. Click Save and Close.

Sending Status Reports

You can send a status report on any task to any other e-mail user whenever you like. Additionally, when you complete a task assigned to you by another user, Outlook automatically sends the user a status report upon task completion.

To send a status report for a task, follow these steps:

1. From the task list, double-click the task you want.
2. Choose Actions, Send Status Report.
3. Type recipient names or click the To and CC buttons to select them from an address list.

N O T E If the task was assigned to you, names of people on the update list are already filled in. ▣

4. Click Send. Outlook generates and sends an e-mail message to the recipients.

Configuring the Tasks Folder

You can set a variety of options for your task list that make it work exactly the way you want it. Although most people will be happy with the default settings, let's take a quick look at the choices you have, in case you someday want to make a change.

Setting Task Options

The most basic option you can set for tasks is to change the default reminder time. To do so, choose Tools, Options to open the Options dialog box. In the Reminder Time text box, change the default (8:00 a.m.) to some other time.

You can also change the colors used for overdue and completed tasks. From the Options dialog box, click the Task Options button. The Task Options dialog box appears. See Figure 38.6.

Figure 38.6
The Task Options dialog box.

Choose different colors from either of the two drop-down lists, and then click OK.

Setting Task Properties

The Tasks Properties dialog box is where you define configuration properties for the Tasks folder. To access this dialog box, right-click the Tasks icon on the Outlook Bar and choose Properties from the shortcut menu.

The properties are grouped on four panels as listed:

- *General panel*, which allows you to edit the folder description and set general processing properties for the folder.
- *Automatic Archiving panel*, which allows to specify properties for backing up and purging items in the folder.
- *Administration panel*, which allows you to define access and processing properties for public folders. (Appears in Corporate/Workgroup mode only.)
- *Forms panel*, which allows you to define the forms associated with the folder. (Appears in Corporate/Workgroup mode only.)

Typically, you set task properties when you install your system and change them infrequently. Figure 38.7 shows the Tasks Properties dialog box.

Figure 38.7
The Tasks Properties dialog box.

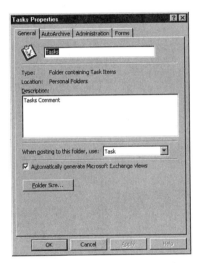

The three fields on the General tab are described in Table 38.2.

Table 38.2 Tasks Properties: General

Property	Description
Description	Optional comment about the folder.
When Posting to This Folder, Use:	The form and item type used to create and store items in the current folder (default value is Task).
Automatically Generate Microsoft Exchange Views	An option for public folders that allows views created in Outlook to be available in Microsoft Exchange.

There is also a Folder Size button on the General tab. It opens an informational box that tells the amount of space each of your task folders is taking up on your hard disk.

The AutoArchive tab sets options for how Outlook handles old Task items (that is, appointments, events, and meetings) during the automatic archiving process. The fields on this tab are described in Table 38.3.

Table 38.3   Tasks Properties: AutoArchive

Property	Description
Clean Out Items Older Than	Enables automatic archiving of items in the Tasks folder, based on the age you enter.
Move Old Documents To	Specifies that aged items should be archived and allows you to select the location and name of the archive file.
Permanently Delete Old Documents	Removes old items from the system; select this option if you do not want to archive items in your Tasks folder.

T I P   To activate automatic archiving, choose Tools, Options and then go to the AutoArchive tab and fill in the information.

▶ **See** "Archiving," **page 770**

Most of the properties on the Administrative tab are options for configuring access and processes for public folders, as described in Table 38.4.

Table 38.4   Tasks Properties: Administrative

Property	Description
Initial View on Folder	The default view for the selected Tasks folder.
Drag/Drop Posting Is A	Determines which user appears as the owner of tasks copied to public folders. The Forward option specifies that the task is posted by the user who copied it. The Move/Copy option specifies that the task appears exactly as it was in its original location. The user who copied the task to the public folder is not indicated.
Add Folder Address To	Adds the folder address to your Personal Address Book so you can send mail directly to the folder.
This Folder Is Available To	Allows access to all users who have the appropriate permission, or Owners Only.
Folder Assistant	Edits the processing rules for posting items in Exchange public folders. This button is not available if you are working offline.
Folder Path	Shows the folder location.

The Forms tab contains options for managing the forms associated with the folder. Unless you need to use customized forms to view your task items, you won't need to change any properties on this tab. Table 38.5 describes the properties.

Table 38.5   Tasks Properties: Forms

Property	Description
Forms Associated with This Folder	Lists the forms copied or installed in the folder; these forms are located in the Folder Forms Library.
Manage	Copies a form from a different forms library to the Folder Forms Library, or installs a new form in the Folder Forms Library.
Allow These Forms in This Folder	Specifies which forms can be stored in the Tasks folder.

Part
VI

Ch
38

CHAPTER 39

Using Journals and Notes

by Liz Tasker

In this chapter

Overview of Journals and Notes

Journals and notes are two additional items that Outlook provides to help you track information, activities, and ideas happening in your business and personal life. Outlook organizes all of your journal entries into a folder, which is called your Journal, and all notes into a Notes folder.

Journal enables you to keep a personal audit trail of your communications and other activities. Communications can include phone calls, e-mail messages, meeting and task requests, faxes, and even offline conversations. Other activities can include changes to any Microsoft Office document. Journal is useful in that it lets you chronologically organize and view Outlook items, Microsoft Office documents, and other miscellaneous communications in one place.

Notes enables you to quickly jot down any miscellaneous facts or ideas that you might have, which could include anything from a grocery list to an idea for improving your business. Like the other Outlook items, journal entries and notes are both kept in their own Outlook folders, which appear in the Outlook bar.

Displaying Your Journal

To display your Journal, click the Journal icon on the Outlook bar. The first time you do so, a box appears asking whether you want to turn the Journal on. Click Yes. A box then appears asking which items you want to track in the Journal (see Figure 39.1).

Figure 39.1
Set up your Journal once, and Outlook will remember your preferences.

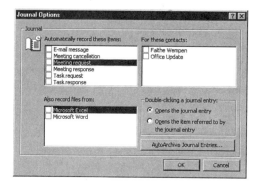

Click to place a check mark next to each item that you want to record in the journal. These fall into three categories:

- *Automatically Record These Items* Here you can choose the various activities that Outlook performs, such as sending e-mail, scheduling a meeting, and completing a task.

- *For These Contacts* Select each person for whom you want to record the activities you chose in the above.

- *Also Record Files From* Choose any additional Microsoft Office programs that you have installed for which you want to maintain journal entries. For example, if you choose Word, your Journal will show every Word document that you open.

You can also choose what happens when you double-click a journal entry. The default is to open the journal entry in a dialog box, but you can choose the Opens the Item Referred to By the Journal Entry option button to make that happen instead.

Click OK when finished. The Journal appears. (Of course, there won't be any entries in it yet; you'll have to do some work in Outlook or one of the chosen Office programs to get some Journal entries.)

From then on, to display the journal, just click the Journal icon on the Outlook bar to make it display immediately.

Understanding the Journal Screen

When you first look at the Journal, there many not be much there. But after it has been turned on for a while (see the preceding section), you will accumulate many activities there. Entries appear on a timeline, so you can see when a particular activity happened. Figure 39.2 shows a busy Journal.

Figure 39.2

This journal has recorded quite a bit of activity.

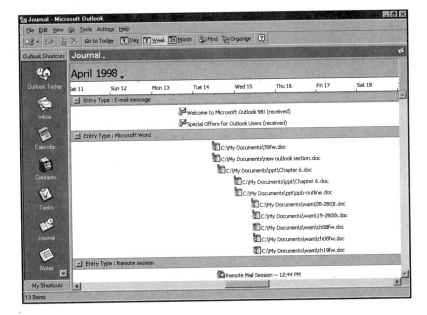

The Journal groups activities by type, with each type being a gray heading bar. You can open the entries under each heading by clicking the plus sign next to it, or collapse the list by clicking the minus sign. Figure 39.2 shows all types expanded.

You can open a journal item by double-clicking on it. What happens then depends on how you answered when you set up the journal—it either opens a journal entry or it opens the item that the entry refers to.

N O T E If you want to change the settings for the Journal, go to Tools, Options and click Journal Options to reopen the Journal Options dialog box from Figure 39.1. ▦

Changing the Journal View

The default Journal view, shown in Figure 39.2, is a timeline, which is very useful in giving you a complete chronological picture of the various activities in which you are involved. This can be a valuable tool in assessing whether you are spending your time effectively and really doing the things you want and need to do.

In addition to the By Type view, Outlook also provides several other predefined views, which you may also want to use from time to time.

To select a different view for your Journal, follow these steps:

1. Click the Journal icon in the Outlook bar.
2. Select View, Current View, and the view you want.

Table 39.1 lists the predefined views for Journal.

Table 39.1 Views for Journal

View	Description
By Type	The default view, which provides a chronological timeline of all journal entries grouped by entry type.
By Contact	A chronological timeline of all journal entries grouped by contact.
By Category	A chronological timeline of all journal entries grouped by category.
Entry List	A detailed list of all journal entries.
Last Seven Days	A detailed list of all journal entries for the last seven days.
Phone Calls	A detailed list of phone call entries, indicating subject, time, duration, and contact information.

▶ **See** "Using Categories," **page 767**

▶ **See** "Creating and Modifying Contacts," **page 799**

Creating and Editing Journal Entries

Outlook generates automatic Journal entries when you perform certain activities. You can also enter Journal entries manually, to track activities that you want to be part of your permanent records but that Outlook does not automatically add.

Creating Manual Journal Entries

Although Outlook provides options to generate automatic journal entries for some Outlook items, you must manually record journal entries for other items, including your own tasks and appointments. Additionally, you might want to create manual journal entries to make note of documents that you receive, such as letters and faxes, and conversations you have in person or on the phone.

To enter a new journal entry, follow these steps:

1. Select File, New, Journal Entry or press Ctl+Shift+J. An untitled Journal Entry window appears (see Figure 39.3).

Figure 39.3

Create your own manual Journal entries.

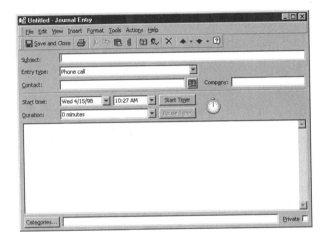

Part
VI

Ch

39

Alternatively, if you have your Journal open, you can use one of these methods to display an untitled Journal Entry window:

- Click the New Journal icon in the toolbar.
- Select Actions, New Journal Entry.
- Press Ctrl+N.
- Double-click in a blank area of the Journal.

2. Type a subject for the Journal entry in the Subject field.

3. Select the appropriate entry type from the drop-down list.

4. Optionally, enter any other information for the journal entry as follows:

- Type or select one or multiple contact names to associate with the journal entry.
- Type a company name.
- If the entry type is a phone call or meeting, record the exact length by clicking the Start Timer and Pause Timer buttons, or enter an approximate length by typing or selecting a value in the Duration field.

- Type a text entry in the big white comment box, or attach a note, Outlook document, or other object using the Insert menu.
- Select one or multiple Categories for the journal entry.
- Select Private to keep others from viewing this journal entry in a public folder.

5. Click the Save and Close button; select File, Save; or press Ctl+S.

Editing a Journal Entry

You can edit a journal entry if you want to modify any of the information about the journal. For example, you might edit a journal entry for a meeting request to add a document describing the results of the meeting.

To edit a journal entry, follow these steps:

1. Click the Journal icon on the Outlook bar. The Journal opens, displaying a list of journal entries.

2. Double-click the journal entry you want to edit.

3. Make any changes to the journal entry, such as updating the date or duration, or adding a contact, category, or document.

4. Click Save and Close.

N O T E If you have set up Outlook so that double-clicking a Journal entry opens the referenced item rather than the Edit Journal Entry dialog box, you can edit the entry instead by right-clicking on it and choosing Open Journal Entry. ▪

Tracking Phone Calls

Outlook's automatic phone dialing capabilities can create journal entries. If you want to automatically time a call and type notes in Outlook while you talk, you can set an option before you start the call to create a journal entry for the call. For example, you might want to use this option if you bill clients for your time spent on phone conversations.

To track a phone call, follow these steps:

1. Click the Contacts icon on the Outlook bar.

2. Click the AutoDialer button on the toolbar to open the New Call dialog box (see Figure 39.4).

Figure 39.4

You can create a journal entry while placing a call.

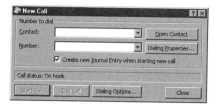

3. To have Outlook look for a number in the contact list, type a name in the Contact text box.

4. If the name you type in the Contact text box is in the Outlook contact list and you already entered phone numbers for that contact, click the phone number you want in the Number text box.

5. If the name is not in the Outlook contact list or does not have a phone number already, type the phone number in the Number text box.

6. Select the Create New Journal Entry When Starting New Call check box if it is not already marked.

   If you select this check box, after you start the call, a journal entry opens with the timer running. You can type notes in the text box of the journal entry while you talk.

7. Click Start Call.

8. Pick up the phone handset, and then click Talk.

9. When you are finished, click Pause Timer to stop the clock.

10. Click Save and Close.

Setting Journal Properties

The Journal is fully customizable. With a little setup, you can make it perform to your exact specifications. The following sections explain the various options you can set. These are not really necessary to work with, but power-users may find them helpful.

AutoArchiving Journal Entries

You may have noticed in the Journal Options dialog box (refer to Figure 39.1) an AutoArchive Journal Entries button. We didn't set it upfront because it wasn't an issue at that point. But eventually you will want to specify how you want your journal entries archived.

Archiving is a way of keeping your journal uncluttered by events that occurred in the past. It moves old entries to a backup file. You can specify how often this occurs, and where the old entries are sent. Follow these steps:

1. Choose Tools, Options, and click the Journal Options button top open the Journal Options dialog box (refer to Figure 39.1).

2. Click the AutoArchive Journal Entries button to display the AutoArchive tab in the Journal Properties dialog box (see Figure 39.5).

3. Enter a number in the Clean Out Items Older Than box. Six is the default.

4. Specify a path in the Move Items To box (or leave the default), or click the Permanently Delete Old Items option button.

5. When you are finished setting Journal properties, click OK three times to return to the Journal.

Figure 39.5
Specify how old a journal entry must be before it is archived.

The Journal Properties Dialog Box

The Journal Properties dialog box is where you define configuration properties for the Journal. Journal properties include general options, automatic archiving options (which you saw in the preceding section), folder access options, and forms associated with the Journal. Typically, you set Journal properties when you install your system and change them infrequently.

To access the Journal Properties dialog box, follow these steps:

1. On the Outlook bar, click the Journal icon. The Journal opens.
2. Select File, Folder, Properties for Journal. The Journal Properties dialog box appears (see Figure 39.6).

TIP   Another way to access the Journal Properties dialog box is to right-click the Journal icon in the Outlook bar and choose Properties from the shortcut menu.

The Journal Properties dialog box provides these four tabs of options for configuring your Journal: General, AutoArchive, Administration, and Forms. (The latter two are available only if you are using Outlook in Corporate/Workgroup mode.)

The three fields on the General tab are described in Table 39.2.

Table 39.2   Journal Properties: General

Property	Description
Description	Optional comment about the folder.
When Posting to This Folder, Use:	The form and item type used to create and store items in the current folder. The default value is Journal.

Property	Description
Automatically Generate Microsoft Exchange Views	An option for public folders that allows views created in Outlook to be available in Microsoft Exchange.

Figure 39.6
The General tab describes the Journal properties.

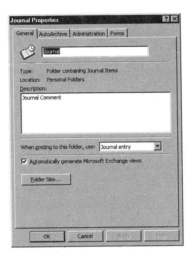

The AutoArchive tab sets options for how Outlook handles old Journal entry items during the automatic archiving process. (You have already seen how this works.)

Most of the fields on the Administration tab involve options for configuring access and processes for public folders, as described in Table 39.3.

Table 39.3 Journal Properties: Administration

Property	Description
Initial View on Folder	The default view for the Journal.
Drag/Drop Posting Is A	Determines which user appears as the owner of journal entries copied to public folders. The Forward option specifies that the journal entry is posted by the user who copied it. The Move/Copy option specifies that the journal entry appears exactly as it was in its original location. The user who copied the journal entry to the public folder is not indicated.
Add Folder Address To	Adds the folder address to your Personal Address Book so that you can send mail directly to the folder.
This Folder Is Available To	Allows access to all users who have the appropriate permission, or to owners only.

continues

Table 39.3 continued	
Property	**Description**
Folder Assistant	Edits the processing rules for posting items in Exchange public folders. This button is not available if you are working offline.
Folder Path	Shows the folder location.

The Forms tab contains options for managing the forms associated with the folder. Unless you need to use customized forms to view your journal items, you won't need to change any properties on this tab. Table 39.4 describes the properties.

Table 39.4 Journal Properties: Forms	
Property	**Description**
Forms Associated with This Folder	Lists the forms copied or installed in the folder. These forms are located in the Folder Forms Library.
Manage	Copies a form from a different forms library to the Folder Forms Library, or installs a new form in the Folder Forms Library.
Allow These Forms in This Folder	Specifies which forms can be stored in your Journal.

Working with Notes

Outlook provides a Notes folder where you can keep online notes about anything that you want to jot down. Notes can be useful to record a miscellaneous thought or idea that you can later insert into a mail message, task, appointment, or other Outlook item.

CAUTION

Don't overuse notes at the expense of other program features, like tasks. Outlook is much more adept at tracking tasks and calendar commitments than it is with notes. You will be better off in the long run if you use notes only for those items that do not fit in any of the other Outlook sections.

Viewing Notes

By default, Outlook presents the Notes folder in the Icons view, as shown in Figure 39.7.

In addition to the Icons view, Outlook also provides several other predefined views, which you may also want to use from time to time.

Figure 39.7

The Notes Folder in Icons view.

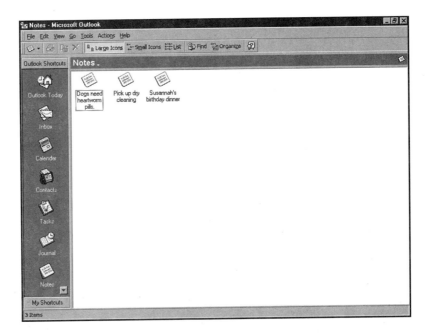

To select a different view for the Notes folder, follow these steps:

1. Click the Notes icon in the Outlook bar.

2. Select View, Current View, and the view you want.

Table 39.5 lists the predefined views for the Notes folder.

Table 39.5   Views for Notes

View	Description
Icons	The default view, which provides an icon and title for each note. You can arrange the icons by dragging and dropping.
Notes List	A detailed list of all notes that displays the first three lines of each note.
Last Seven Days	A detailed list of all notes for the last seven days.
By Category	A detailed list of all notes grouped by category.
By Color	A detailed list of all notes grouped by color.

Creating and Editing Notes

When you create a note, it's like typing on a little slip of paper. There aren't any fancy controls; just a Close button and a Note icon (see Figure 39.8).

Figure 39.8

The Note window is like an online sticky note.

The Note window does not contain a menu bar, as other forms for other Outlook items do. Instead, the Note icon drops down to reveal a few menu items, as shown in Figure 39.9.

Figure 39.9

The drop-down menu in the Notes window.

Creating Notes

To create a new note, follow these steps:

1. Select File, New, Note or press Ctl+Shift+N. An untitled Note window appears.

Alternatively, if you have the Notes folder open, you can use one of these methods to display an untitled Note window:

- Click the New Note icon in the toolbar.
- Select Actions, New Note.
- Press Ctrl+N.
- Double-click in a blank area of the Notes folder.
- Right-click the notes area and choose New Note.

2. Type the text for your note.
3. If you want to change the color of your note, select a category for it, or print it, click the Note icon and select the appropriate menu option.
4. Click the Close icon.

If you have different types of notes (for example, business and personal), you may want to use different colors to differentiate them. You can also use categories that you have set up in Outlook to organize your notes.

▶ **See** "Using Categories," **page 767**

Editing a Note

To edit a note, follow these steps:

1. Click the Note icon on the Outlook bar. The Note folder opens.

2. Double-click the note you want to edit.

3. Type your changes to the note text.

4. Click the Close icon.

Configuring Notes

You configure the Notes folder through Notes Options and Notes Properties. When you install Outlook, the system provides default setting for both so that you can use Outlook without ever changing your configuration.

> **N O T E** Note properties are identical to the properties for journals and all other Outlook items. For a description of these properties, see "Setting Journal Properties" earlier in this chapter. ▓

To set note options, follow these steps:

1. Select Tools, Options.

2. Click the Note Options button. The Notes Options dialog box appears (see Figure 39.10).

Figure 39.10
The Notes Options dialog box is where you define the default appearance of notes.

3. Select a default color and size for your notes.

4. Click the Font button to change the default font type, size, and style for your notes.

5. When you are finished setting Notes options, click OK.

Internet Explorer 4

CHAPTER 40

Establishing a Dial-Up Connection

by Ed Bott

In this chapter

Using the Internet Connection Wizard

If you can't access the Internet through an office network, there are literally thousands of independent service providers and online services scattered throughout the world who will gladly give you a dial-up account—for the right price, of course. Windows 98 supplies all the software you need to make a fast, reliable Internet connection. All you need to add is a modem or other connecting device.

The first time you open the Internet icon on the desktop, you'll launch the Internet Connection Wizard (see Figure 40.1); after you run through this initial setup routine, the Internet icon starts Internet Explorer.

Figure 40.1

These three options are just a small sampling of what you can do with the Internet Connection Wizard.

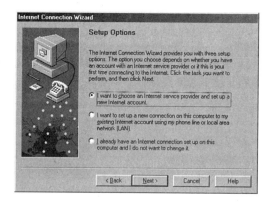

The Internet Connection Wizard is a remarkably versatile piece of software. After you get past the initial explanatory screen, you have three choices:

- You can sign up for a new Internet account; the Internet Connection Wizard will offer a referral list of Internet service providers in your area.
- You can set up an existing Internet account for access through Windows 98, either over the phone or through a network.
- You can tell the Internet Connection Wizard to use your existing Internet connection. If you're comfortable with TCP/IP and networking, this is a reasonable choice.

The Internet Connection Wizard isn't just a one-time deal either. You can make the wizard reappear at any time by following these steps:

1. Right-click the Internet icon on the desktop.
2. Choose Properties and click the Connection tab. The dialog box shown in Figure 40.2 appears.
3. Click Connect.

Figure 40.2

Want to use the Internet Connection Wizard again? Click the Connect button on this dialog box.

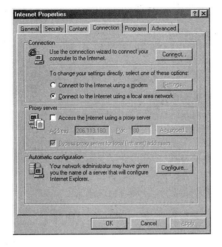

Don't underestimate the Internet Connection Wizard. Although it's easy to stereotype it as a tool for beginners, this wizard is useful for experts as well, and it handles nearly every imaginable task when it comes to setting up and managing Internet connections.

Because of the sheer number of choices available when you run the Internet Connection Wizard, it's pointless (and probably impossible) to try to explain or illustrate every step in order. But this is a partial list of what you can use it for:

- Install and configure a modem (or set up a LAN connection for Internet access instead).
- Adjust the dialing settings you use, including the local area code and the prefixes you use to access outside lines.
- Create and edit Dial-Up Networking connection icons for one-button access to the Internet.
- Adjust advanced Internet settings.
- Enter and edit account information you use to connect with an Internet service provider.

Part

VII

Ch

40

N O T E If you have not yet installed Dial-Up Networking, the Internet Connection Wizard will install these system services automatically. You will need your original Windows 98 CD-ROM or disks, and you will need to restart the computer to complete the installation.

Installing and Configuring a Modem

There are two obvious prerequisites to any dial-up connection—you need a modem (or another type of connecting device, such as an ISDN adapter) and you need a phone line. If you haven't previously set up a modem, the Internet Connection Wizard includes a series of steps that automatically installs the correct drivers and configures your modem. You can also use the Modems option in Control Panel to add a new modem or to configure an existing one.

Although most dial-up connections will use only one modem at a time, you can install multiple communication devices. The system depicted in Figure 40.3, for example, includes an analog modem and an ISDN adapter—you can assign only one device to each Dial-Up Networking connection.

Figure 40.3

This system includes two communication devices—a 3Com ISDN adapter and a Microcom analog modem. Both are available for dial-up connections.

Adding a New Analog Modem

Windows 98 does a super job of identifying and configuring the correct modem type from a list of hundreds of choices. If your modem is Plug and Play compatible, Windows should detect it automatically, install the correct drivers, and configure all relevant settings. For modems that don't take advantage of Plug and Play detection, you may have to do the installation and configuration duties manually.

To add a new modem, follow these steps:

1. Open the Modems option in Control Panel.

2. If you have not previously set up a modem on this system, the Install New Modem wizard appears. If you are adding a new modem, click the Add button.

3. In the Install New Modem dialog box, click the Next button to allow Windows to detect your modem. If you've downloaded a driver or the manufacturer supplied a driver on disk, and you're certain that this driver is more up-to-date than the built-in Windows drivers, select the option to skip detection, click Next, and skip to step 5.

4. If Windows detected your modem properly, click Finish to install the driver. Skip over all additional steps.

5. If you bypassed the detection process, you'll see a list of available modem drivers. If Windows did not correctly detect your modem, click the Change button to display this same list. Choose the modem manufacturer from the list on the left and the model name from the list of modems on the right. If you have an updated Windows 95 or Windows 98 driver, click the Have Disk button and specify the location of the driver.

6. Select the port to which the modem is attached. Most desktop PCs have two serial ports (COM1 and COM2), and a mouse is often attached to one; Windows will not list a serial port if the mouse is attached to it. If you have multiple free serial ports, Windows should detect the correct one. You may need to check the system documentation or the label on the physical port to verify which port the modem is using.

7. Click Finish to install the driver and configure the modem.

 TIP If you can't find a compatible Windows 95 or Windows 98 driver for your modem, select Standard Modem Types from the top of the Manufacturers list and choose the generic model that most closely matches your modem's speed. You will lose any advanced features included with your modem, but this procedure will usually allow you to send and receive data at the modem's rated speed.

Configuring an Analog Modem

After you've installed drivers for an analog modem, it should be configured correctly. Still, it can't hurt to double-check settings to guarantee that the device is properly set up for maximum performance. A series of nested dialog boxes include options for adjusting drivers, connection speeds, port assignments, and hardware-specific connection settings, including control over the volume of the modem's built-in speaker.

To set basic modem options, open the Modems option in Control Panel, select the modem whose settings you want to adjust, and click Properties. A dialog box like the one shown in Figure 40.4 appears; click the General tab.

Figure 40.4
Use this properties sheet to adjust the volume of the modem's internal speaker; confusingly, the Maximum Speed setting does not control modem-to-modem speeds.

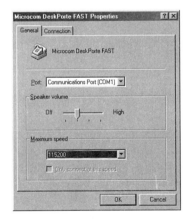

Three basic options are available here:

■ Note that this dialog box displays the port the modem is configured to use. To switch the modem to another port, use the drop-down Port list.

■ This is also the place to adjust the modem's speaker. The slider control uses four positions—from left to right, they are Off, Low, Medium, and High. For most circumstances, the Low setting is the best, because it allows you to hear the dialtone and handshaking sounds and retry a connection when your modem and the one at the other end are not communicating correctly.

■ Don't be confused by the Maximum Speed control at the bottom of this dialog box. This setting controls the internal speed at which your computer communicates with the modem, and on most Pentium-class computers that speed is invariably faster than the transmission speed of the modem itself. Previous versions of Windows typically set this value too low. On most Pentium PCs, you can safely set the port speed to 115,200bps. Reduce this setting only if you experience persistent data errors when sending and receiving. Avoid the check box labeled Only Connect at This Speed.

To set general connection options, click the Connection tab. You'll see a dialog box like the one in Figure 40.5.

Figure 40.5

Avoid the temptation to tinker with these connection settings; for the majority of circumstances, the default settings will work best.

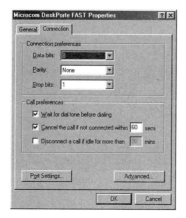

You can adjust four settings here:

■ The Connection Preferences section at the top of the dialog box specifies settings for data bits, parity, and stop bits. These settings are typically used for direct modem-to-modem communications rather than TCP/IP connections that use the Internet-standard Point-to-Point Protocol (PPP) or Serial Line Interface Protocol (SLIP). It should not be necessary to adjust these settings for Internet access.

■ Under the heading Call Preferences, note the check mark in front of the box labeled Wait for Dial Tone Before Dialing. If your phone system uses a dial tone that differs from the standard U.S. dial tone, Windows mistakenly believes the line is dead and refuses to dial until you clear this box. Likewise, voice-mail systems that alter the normal dial tone to a "stutter" signal can confuse Windows unless you clear this box.

■ The 60-second Timeout is sufficient for most domestic calls. If some of your dial-up connections routinely require lengthy connect times, you should increase this value to avoid timeout errors.

- The Disconnect option at the bottom of the dialog box lets you specify the amount of time that the connection can be idle before Windows disconnects automatically. This setting is appropriate only for modem-to-modem connections; for Internet connections, use the timeout settings defined by the Internet Explorer Connection Manager.

Finally, you can set hardware-specific options that control the basic functioning of your modem. Click the Advanced button to see the dialog box shown in Figure 40.6.

Figure 40.6

Adjust these advanced connection settings only if you understand the consequences of your actions. Unnecessary tinkering here can actually reduce data transmission speeds.

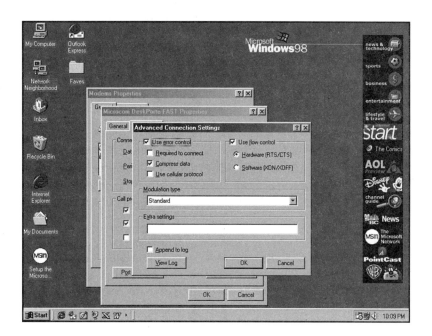

Four advanced options are available in this dialog box:

- Error control options reduce the risk that noisy phone lines will cause data corruption. Most modern modems support both data compression and error control. The modem information file should set these options for your specific modem. The Use Cellular Protocol box enables the MNP10 error control protocol for use with some (but not all) cellular modems.

- Flow control governs the integrity of the connection. By default, Windows 98 enables hardware flow control, and most modern modems support this mode for best performance. Software flow control should never be used for an Internet connection.

- Do not change modulation types unless specifically recommended by the manufacturer of your modem.

- If necessary, click in the Extra Settings box and add AT commands that enable or disable a particular feature of your modem or adapter. For example, S0=5 tells your modem to answer automatically after 5 rings. Check your modem documentation for AT commands applicable to your hardware.

N O T E   Zoom Telephonics offers a comprehensive source of information about modem technology
and the AT command set; browse its listings at

http://www.modems.com

Configuring an ISDN Adapter

Most home and small-office dial-up connections use conventional analog lines. In some areas,
you can use the Integrated Services Digital Network (ISDN) to establish high-speed digital
connections. Compared with analog lines, ISDN circuits offer significant advantages: Connection times are practically instantaneous, for example, unlike analog lines that require 20 seconds or more to establish a connection. Speeds are typically 2-5 times faster than most analog
modems. The connection is digital from end to end, which means you won't lose data because
of noise on the line—something that can't be said for the typical analog connection. A typical
ISDN configuration includes two digital data channels and one analog data port, allowing you
to plug in a conventional telephone or modem and talk or send data over an analog connection
while simultaneously sending and receiving data on a digital channel.

ISDN technology has its share of disadvantages as well. Generally, these lines cost more—
sometimes many times more than an analog line. Not all ISPs support ISDN, and those that do
often charge a premium as well. Configuring an ISDN connection can be a nightmare as well,
and the technology is difficult and filled with jargon.

ISDN hardware comes in all shapes and sizes, and every piece of hardware uses a different
setup routine. Some devices install as network adapters, others as modems, and still others as
routers on a network. When you choose an ISDN device using the Add Hardware option in
Control Panel, Windows installs the ISDN Wizard. This tool allows you to configure the technical details of your ISDN line, as we've done in Figure 40.7.

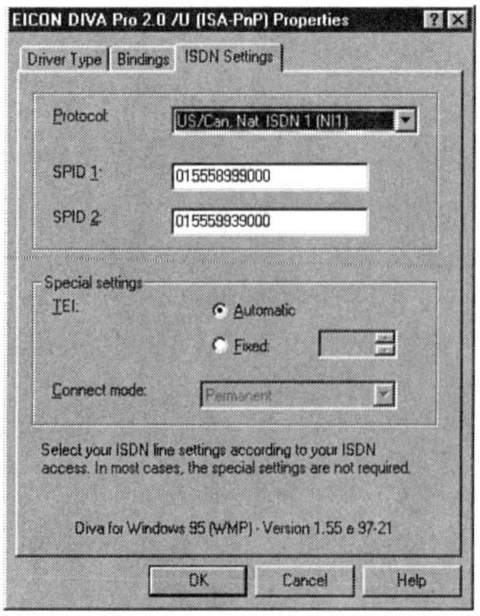

Figure 40.7
Although some ISDN
adapters emulate
modems, this device
from Eicon Systems
looks like a network
card to Windows 98.

NOTE For more information about ISDN technology, check out Dan Kegel's detailed page at

http://www.alumni.caltech.edu/~dank/isdn/

For details on how to order ISDN service, plus links to updates of the ISDN software for Windows 98, try Microsoft's Get ISDN page at

http://www.microsoft.com/windows/getisdn/about.htm

Although the ISDN Configuration wizard makes setup somewhat easier than it used to be, the process is still complex. When connecting an ISDN line, get detailed instructions from the manufacturer of the adapter and from the phone company—and follow those instructions to the letter. At a minimum, you'll need to know the Service Provider IDs (SPIDs) and telephone numbers for each channel, as well as the switch type used in the telephone company office. Some ISDN hardware includes a utility that allows you to upload this information to the adapter itself.

When you've successfully installed your ISDN adapter, it will appear as a choice in the Internet Connection and Dial-Up Networking wizards.

 TIP Most ISDN adapters sold today come with their own setup software, and certain features of the adapter may not work if you don't run it. The setup software may or may not be written for Windows 98; if you have trouble running it, see the manufacturer's Web site for a more recent version.

Other High-Speed Access Options

Telephone companies are no longer the only sources of access to the Internet. There are an increasing number of high-speed alternatives to traditional dial-up access that use different types of wires—and in some cases no wires at all.

Hughes Network systems sells a small satellite dish called DirecDuo, which allows Internet access at speeds of up to 400Kbps as well as several hundred channels of TV programming.

Not to be outdone, many phone companies are rolling out systems that use Digital Subscriber Line (DSL) technology to provide Internet access at speeds in excess of 1MB per second, while allowing you to use the same line for voice calls.

Some cable TV companies now offer Internet access over the same cable you use to receive television signals. Depending on the system configuration, these solutions can deliver data at speeds of up to 10MB per second, roughly on a par with local area network performance.

Windows 98 does not offer built-in support for any of these cutting-edge technologies, but third parties offer hardware and Windows drivers that work well. If you plan to use any of these services, be sure to ask the provider for detailed instructions on how to access the service from Windows 98.

Part
VII

Ch
40

Configuring a Connection to an Existing Internet Account

Windows 98 uses a service called Dial-Up Networking (DUN) to connect your system to the Internet over telephone lines. The Internet Connection Wizard automatically installs DUN if necessary. Individual connection icons within the Dial-Up Networking folder contain all the information you need to connect with the Internet. You'll find the Dial-Up Networking folder in the My Computer window; to open this system folder from the Start menu, choose Programs, Accessories, Dial-Up Networking.

If you already have an account with an Internet service provider, the wizard's step-by-step procedures can create a Dial-Up Networking connection with a minimum of clicking and typing. The default settings assume you're making a standard PPP connection, with IP address and DNS settings assigned dynamically.

1. Start the Internet Connection Wizard and choose the option to set up a new connection to an existing account. Click Next to continue.

2. Choose the option to connect using your phone line and click Next.

3. Choose the modem you want to use with this connection and click Next. (If you haven't set up a modem, you'll be able to do so here.)

4. You can choose an existing connection icon if there are any in your Dial-Up Networking folder. In this case, select the option to create a new icon and click Next to continue.

5. Enter the dial-in phone number of your Internet service provider and click Next.

6. Enter your username and password and click Next.

7. The wizard asks whether you want to adjust advanced settings for the connection. For standard PPP connections where you don't need to specify an IP address or DNS servers, select No and click Next.

8. Give the connection a descriptive name, as in Figure 40.8, and click Next.

Figure 40.8
The default connection icon uses a generic name. Add location information, as we've done here, to make the icon's purpose easier to identify.

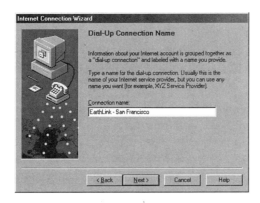

9. If you need to set up mail and news accounts or a directory server, the wizard includes separate steps to help with each of these tasks. When you reach the end of the wizard, click Finish to create the Dial-Up Networking connection icon.

Adjusting Advanced Settings

The Internet Connection Wizard includes an option to adjust advanced connection settings. If your Internet service provider uses a SLIP connection or requires scripting, or if you need to enter a fixed IP address and specify addresses for DNS servers, select Yes in the Advanced Settings dialog box (see Figure 40.9) and fill in the four boxes that follow.

Figure 40.9
When you select Yes in the dialog box, the Internet Connection Wizard takes a brief detour into advanced configuration options.

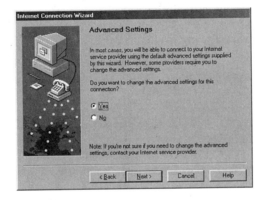

Advanced settings include the following:

- *Connection Type.* Choose PPP or SLIP connection.
- *Logon Procedure.* Select the manual option to bring up a terminal window when connecting, or specify a logon script.
- *IP Address.* If your ISP provides a fixed IP address, enter it here.
- *DNS Server Address.* If your ISP requires you to specify primary and backup name servers, enter their IP addresses here.

 TIP These Advanced settings are useful if you have multiple dial-up accounts—a corporate dial-up server and a personal account with an ISP, for example. Create separate Dial-Up Networking icons for each account, and then adjust the IP address and other settings for each connection icon individually.

Using Multilink Options for Faster Connections

Most dial-up Internet connections are a simple one-modem, one-line proposition, and transmission speed is limited by the slower of the two modems on either end of the connection. Under specialized circumstances, though, you can use two or more connecting devices to increase the speed of a dial-up connection. These so-called multilink connections require the following conditions:

Part
VII

Ch
40

- You must have multiple devices to bind together into a single virtual connection.
- Each device requires its own driver software.
- Each device needs access to a separate analog phone line or a channel on an ISDN line.
- The dial-up server at the other end of the connection must support multilink PPP connections.

The most common use of multilink connections is to join two 56K or 64KB channels on an ISDN line to create a 112K or 128K connection.

To enable multilink options on an existing connection, follow these steps:

1. Open the Dial-Up Networking folder, right-click the connection icon you want to modify, and choose Properties from the shortcut menu.
2. Click the Multilink tab. The dialog box shown in Figure 40.10 appears.

Figure 40.10

If your Internet service provider supports multilink PPP, use these settings to combine two modems to create a faster virtual connection.

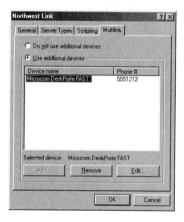

3. Select the option labeled Use Additional Devices. The grayed-out buttons at the bottom of the dialog box will become available.
4. Click the Add button and choose a modem or ISDN adapter from the drop-down list. If no choices are available, click Cancel and set up your additional hardware, and then continue.
5. Enter a separate phone number for the additional device, if required. The hardware documentation and service provider can supply more details about your specific configuration.
6. Select any entry and use the Remove or Edit buttons to modify entries in the list.
7. Click OK to save your changes.

CAUTION

If you are enabling multilink for an ISDN adapter, make sure you disable any multilink capabilities in any adapter-specific software you have installed. For example, the U.S. Robotics IDSN adapters have a feature called TurboPPP that is functionally equivalent to Windows 98's multilink, and must be turned off.

Creating and Editing Logon Scripts

Today, most commercial Internet service providers use logon servers that communicate easily with Windows Dial-Up Networking connections. Some older providers, however, or noncommercial dial-up sites may require additional keyboard input that the Windows connection can't provide. In these cases, you will need to create a logon script for use with the Dial-Up Networking connection; when you open a connection icon whose configuration details include a script, Windows opens a terminal window and sends the additional commands. The script may operate unattended in the background, or it may stop and require that you make an entry in the terminal window.

Script files are simple text files that end in the extension SCP. You'll find these four general-purpose scripts in the Program Files\Accessories folder:

- Cis.scp establishes a PPP connection with CompuServe.
- Pppmenu.scp logs on to a server that uses text menus.
- Slip.scp establishes a SLIP connection with a remote host machine.
- Slipmenu.scp establishes a SLIP connection on a menu-based host.

 TIP Some scripts require editing before use; in that case, it's prudent to back up the script file you plan to modify before you make any change.

To assign a script to a connection icon, follow these steps:

1. Open the Dial-Up Networking folder, right-click the icon, and choose Properties from the shortcut menu.
2. Click the Scripting tab. The dialog box shown in Figure 40.11 appears.
3. Click the Browse button and navigate to the Accessories folder. Select a script from the list and click Open.
4. If you need to modify the script, click the Edit button. The script will open in Notepad; be sure to save your changes before closing the editing window.
5. To avoid being distracted by the script as it runs, check the box labeled Start Terminal Screen Minimized.
6. To tell Windows that you want the script to pause after each step so you can see where modifications are needed, check the box labeled Step Through Script.
7. Click OK to save your changes.

Part
VII

Ch
40

Figure 40.11

Choose a logon script from this dialog box. Click the Edit button to open Notepad and edit the script.

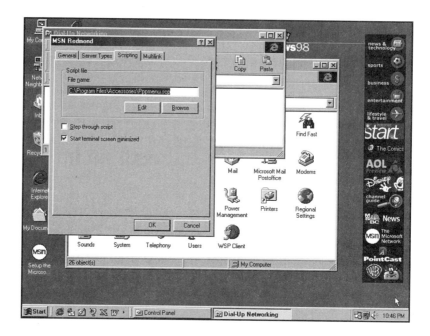

When you open a Dial-Up Networking connection with a script attached, the terminal window shown in Figure 40.12 appears. If you've selected the Step Through Script option, you'll also see the Automated Script Test window.

Figure 40.12

Use the step option to walk through a logon script one step at a time for debugging purposes.

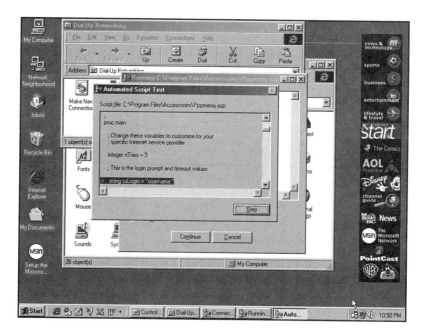

Normally, the terminal window doesn't accept keyboard input. If you need to respond to a prompt, check the box labeled Allow Keyboard Input. When the script has finished processing, you may need to click Continue to complete the connection.

N O T E For detailed documentation of the dial-up scripting language, look in the Windows folder for a file named Script.doc. ■

Setting Up a New Account with an Internet Service Provider

The top option on the Internet Connection Wizard lets you choose an Internet service provider and set up a new Internet account. Although you can research available ISPs and sign up for an account on your own, this wizard offers a quick, hassle-free way to change service providers or set up a new account.

Using the wizard is a straightforward process. You specify the country you live in, the area (or city) code, and any necessary dialing instructions. The wizard installs a handful of required software components, including support for TCP/IP and Dial-Up Networking. During the setup and configuration process, the wizard may restart your system one or more times. Although the wizard manages the details of shutting down and restarting, you'll have to respond to dialog boxes like the one in Figure 40.13 to move the installation process along.

Figure 40.13

The Internet Connection Wizard's automatic signup option requires almost no intervention except for input in this dialog box.

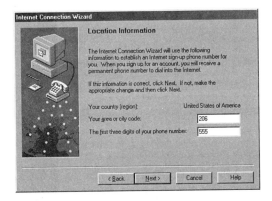

Eventually, the wizard makes two phone calls. The first is to Microsoft's Internet Referral Server, which uses your area (or city) code and the first three digits of your phone number to identify Windows 98-compatible Internet service providers available in your area and language. Because Microsoft regularly updates the roster of eligible service providers, the exact choices you see will vary; the list should resemble the one shown in Figure 40.14.

Figure 40.14

The Microsoft Referral Server generates this list of available Internet service providers just for you, based on your location and operating system.

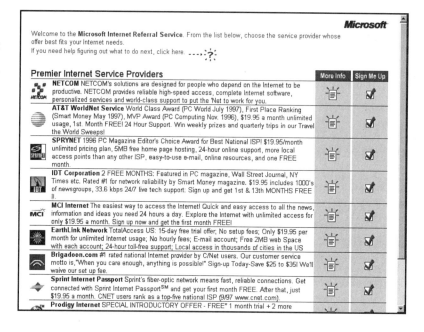

If the summary information isn't enough to help you decide, click the More Info icon to the right of a listing for extra details about that company's services. When you're ready to choose, click the Sign Me Up icon to the right of the entry you've selected. The Internet Connection Wizard makes a second phone call, this one to the provider you've chosen. Each provider's signup procedure varies, but in general you'll have to supply your name, address, and credit card info. The wizard takes care of remaining details, including setting up Dial-Up Networking connection icons and installing any necessary access software.

Managing Dial-Up Networking Connections

Windows stores every connection icon you create in the Dial-Up Networking folder. Although you can make copies and shortcuts for use elsewhere, the only way to create or manage these icons is to open the Dial-Up Networking folder (see Figure 40.15). You'll find it in the My Computer folder, or inside the Accessories folder on the Start menu.

N O T E   Believe it or not, some Microsoft documentation calls these icons *connectoids*. ▨

Like the Desktop, Control Panel, and Printers folders, the Dial-Up Networking folder is a special system folder and doesn't have a corresponding MS-DOS-style directory. You can make this folder more accessible, however; open the My Computer window and drag the Dial-Up Networking icon onto the Quick Launch bar, or drag the icon onto the Start button to create a shortcut at the top of the Start menu.

Figure 40.15

Open the Dial-Up Networking folder to create or manage your connection icons. Note the additional Create and Dial icons in the toolbar.

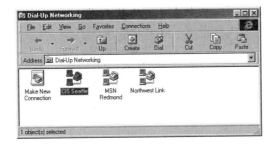

Adding a New DUN Connection

As we've seen, the Internet Connection Wizard creates connection icons as part of the process of configuring your Internet connection. If you're comfortable working directly with connection icons, you can create them from scratch using a two-step wizard in the Dial-Up Networking folder. Follow these steps:

1. Open the Dial-Up Networking folder and open the Make New Connection icon.
2. In the Make New Connection wizard, give the connection a name and select a modem or other communication device. Click Next.
3. Enter the area (or city) code, country code, and phone number of the server you want to dial. Click Next.
4. Click Finish to save the connection in the Dial-Up Networking folder, where you can edit it later.

CAUTION

Although this is a quick way to create a Dial-Up Networking icon, the default settings will almost always require editing. For example, by default these connections use three different protocols; for most Internet connections, only TCP/IP is needed.

Part
VII

Ch
40

Adjusting Properties of an Existing Connection Icon

Regardless of how you create a Dial-Up Networking connection icon, you can change its properties at any time. Open the Dial-Up Networking folder, select an icon, right-click, and choose Properties. You'll see a multi-tabbed dialog box like the one in Figure 40.16.

On the General tab, you can adjust the area code, country code, and phone number for any connection. You can also change the modem or other connecting device you use with the connection.

Click the Server Types tab to adjust properties specific to the server with which you plan to connect. Figure 40.17 shows the choices available.

Figure 40.16

Use this dialog box to change the phone number or modem associated with a connection.

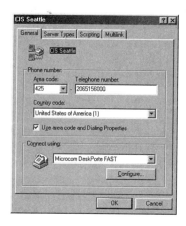

Figure 40.17

If your ISP uses any nonstandard settings, you'll need to adjust them here.

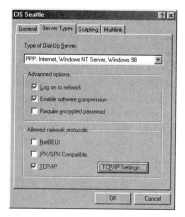

In the drop-down list labeled Type of Dial-Up Server, you'll find five choices. Select PPP for the overwhelming majority of cases. If you're dialing in to a UNIX server with a shell account, you may need to choose SLIP or CSLIP.

NOTE PPP stands for Point-to-Point Protocol. SLIP is short for Serial Line Interface Protocol. PPP has largely replaced SLIP as the standard way to remotely access Internet service providers, thanks to its better error checking and its ability to handle automatic logons.

Unless your ISP recommends that you change settings in the Advanced options area, leave them alone. The defaults are correct for standard PPP connections. For example, most ISPs support Password Authentication Protocol (PAP) or the Challenge-Handshake Authentication Protocol (CHAP) ; if you check the box labeled Require Encrypted Password, you won't be able to log on.

For Internet access, improve performance by clearing the check marks in front of NetBEUI and IPX/SPX in the list of Allowed Network Protocols. TCP/IP is all you need, unless you're dialing in to a Windows NT server.

Finally, click the TCP/IP Settings button to check the configuration details of your connection. You'll see a dialog box like the one in Figure 40.18.

Figure 40.18

If your ISP has assigned you a static IP address, enter it here, along with the addresses of DNS servers.

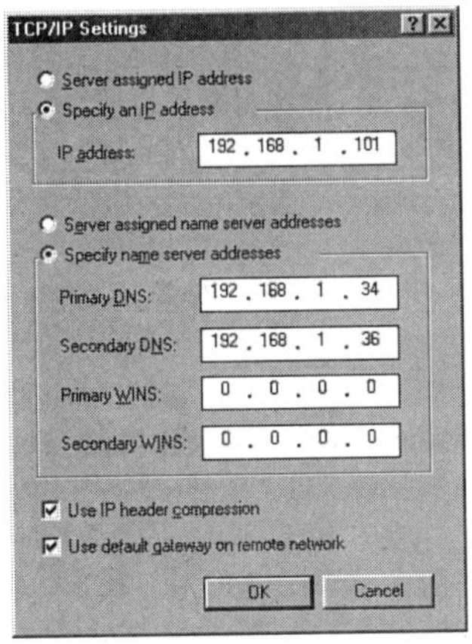

The default settings for a Dial-Up Networking connection assume you're dialing into a network that assigns you an IP address automatically each time you connect, without requiring that you specify DNS servers. On networks that use static IP addresses, these options let you fill in your IP address and the addresses of DNS servers. For access to an ISP, leave the WINS server entries blank, and don't change the default gateway or IP header compression unless your ISP specifically recommends it.

Creating a Shortcut to a Dial-Up Connection Icon

Although connection icons can exist only in the Dial-Up Networking folder, you can create shortcuts to those icons and use them anywhere you like. To place a shortcut on the desktop, open the Dial-Up Networking folder, select an icon, right-click, and choose Create Shortcut. You can also right-drag a connection icon to any folder or onto the Start menu and choose Create Shortcut(s) Here from the menu that appears when you release the icon.

> **N O T E** If you need to change the properties of a dial-up connection, you must change them in the Dial-Up Networking folder; you cannot change the properties of a shortcut to change the original. ■

▶ **See** "Using Shortcuts," **page 45**

Moving or Copying Connection Icons

When you right-click a connection icon, there are no Cut, Copy, or Paste menus. But you can share these icons with other users or copy them to other machines, if you know the undocumented technique. When you drag a connection icon out of the Dial-Up Networking folder and drop it in any legal location, including the desktop or a mail message, Windows creates a special Dial-Up Networking Exported File, with the DUN extension.

Although these exported files resemble shortcuts, they behave differently. There's no shortcut arrow, for example; when you right-click a Dial-Up Networking Exported File and choose Properties, you see an abbreviated properties sheet in place of the normal shortcut information. But if you drop one of these files in the Dial-Up Networking folder of another machine running Windows 95 (with Dial-Up Networking version 1.1 or later) or Windows 98, it works just as though you'd created the connection from scratch. This is an excellent technique for quickly giving other users access to Dial-Up Networking without forcing them to go through the process of creating a connection icon from scratch.

▶ **See** "Moving and Copying Files and Folders," **page 38**

Renaming and Deleting Connection Icons

To rename a connection icon, open the Dial-Up Networking folder, select the icon, right-click, and choose Rename. To delete a connection icon, select the icon, right-click, and choose Delete.

Using Locations to Control Dial-Up Connections

Each time you use a Dial-Up Networking connection icon, you have the option to specify what location you're dialing from. Settings for each location include the area (or city) code for that location, as well as prefixes required to reach an outside line or to dial long distance, calling card information, and much more. Locations are especially useful for owners of portable PCs; by doing nothing more than selecting a location entry from a list, you can tell Windows to simply dial the access number for your ISP's server when you're at home, but to use a dialing prefix, area code, and calling card number when you're on a business trip in another city.

Even if you always dial in from your home or office, though, you can still take advantage of multiple "locations." This is especially true if your Dial-Up Networking calls sometimes incur long-distance or toll charges, or if your telephone company requires special dialing procedures for nearby area codes.

To set up dialing locations for the first time, use the Telephony option in Control Panel. To adjust dialing options on-the-fly each time you make a dial-up connection, click the Dial Properties button to the right of the phone number in the Connect to dialog box. If you've opened the Modems option in Control Panel, click the Dialing Properties button on the bottom of the General tab. Regardless of which technique you use, you'll see a dialog box like the one in Figure 40.19.

N O T E Why are dialing settings collected under the Telephony icon? All 32-bit Windows communications programs use a common feature set called the Telephony Application Programming Interface, or TAPI for short. Programs that use TAPI can detect when another TAPI-aware program wants to use a phone line, making it easier to share a single line gracefully. A simple TAPI function lets them use centrally defined dialing settings as well. ▨

Figure 40.19

Don't be fooled by the name—you can use dialing locations to define dialing prefixes and area code preferences, or to bill your calls to a telephone credit card.

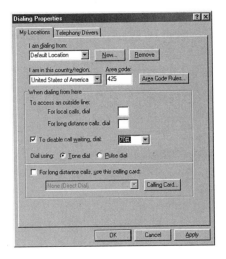

If your ISP has multiple access numbers and you sometimes get a busy signal on your local number, you may want to call a number outside your area code. Follow these steps to set up a "location" that lets you charge the daytime calls to a less expensive long-distance provider using a telephone credit card.

Follow these steps to set up a new location called Credit Card call from Home:

1. Use the Telephony option in Control Panel to open the Dialing Properties dialog box.
2. Click the New button and click OK to the message box that confirms you've created a new location.
3. Note that the text in the box labeled I Am Dialing From is selected. Start typing to replace the default location name with a descriptive entry, such as **Credit Card from Home**.
4. Check the box labeled For Long Distance Calls, Use This Calling Card.
5. Select your calling card from the drop-down list; if you're using a prepaid card or your telephone card isn't in the list, select None (Direct Dial).
6. Click the Calling Card button. The dialog box in Figure 40.20 appears.

Part

VII

Ch

40

Figure 40.20

Use this dialog box to set up access options for a telephone calling card.

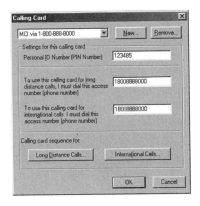

7. If you're creating a new card type, click the <u>N</u>ew button and give the entry a name. Enter your PIN (if required) and enter or verify access numbers for long distance and international calls.

8. Click the Long <u>D</u>istance Calls button. The dialog box shown in Figure 40.21 appears, with suggested default settings for your call. Make a note of the sequence of steps your long distance company requires for you to make a call with your calling card, and use the drop-down lists to add or edit those steps here.

Figure 40.21

Although this dialog box looks daunting, it's remarkably effective in scripting calls you make with a calling card.

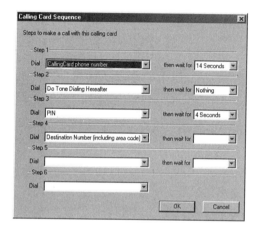

9. Click OK to save the sequence, and repeat the process for international calls if necessary.

10. Click OK to save your dialing settings.

Now, whenever you want to call a Dial-Up Networking connection using a telephone calling card, select the appropriate location in the Connect To box and Windows will automatically punch in the correct sequence of tones.

Because Telephony locations work with all TAPI applications, you can reuse calling card settings with the Windows 98 Phone Dialer (found in the Accessories group) and other communication programs as well.

Another good use of dialing options, at least for residents of the United States, is to help cope with the explosion of new area codes over the past few years. There was a time when you dialed all local calls direct and dialed 1 plus the area code and number for long distance. No more. Today, most large metropolitan areas have already been partitioned into smaller zones, each with its own area code. Some local calls demand an area code, others don't, and there's no firm set of rules that dictate when you dial 1.

The version of Dial-Up Networking that debuted in Windows 95 worked well enough, but it fell down completely on this job. Windows 98 vastly improves your ability to deal with nonstandard area codes and dialing configurations. To adjust these options, open the Dialing Properties dialog box and click the Area Code Rules button. You'll see the dialog box shown in Figure 40.22.

Figure 40.22
Have local dialing rules changed for you? Use these advanced area code options to tell Windows exactly how to dial.

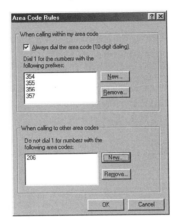

Use the options at the top of the dialog box to specify dialing rules for prefixes within your own area. The bottom options specify how to handle nearby area codes.

 TIP Would you prefer not to use dialing properties at all? When you create a Dial-Up Networking connection icon, clear the check mark from the box labeled Use Area Code and Dialing Properties. Then enter the phone number exactly as you'd like Windows to dial it, complete with any prefixes, area and city or country codes, and calling card numbers.

Using the Microsoft Network for Internet Access

Although it started out with the launch of Windows 95 as on online service competing with America Online and CompuServe, today The Microsoft Network (MSN) is a curious hybrid. Partly an entertainment medium, with "channels" of content ranging from the Disney Blast to Microsoft Investor, it's also a low-cost Internet service provider with worldwide coverage and a variety of access plans.

Naturally, Microsoft makes it easy to install the MSN access software and sign up for a trial account. Look on the Windows desktop for an icon called Set Up the Microsoft Network. If you choose this option, it will load nearly 4MB of software and call a Microsoft server to establish your account. Although MSN uses many of the same components as Windows 98, most notably Internet Explorer 4.0, it also adds its own distinctive touches, including a custom Connection Manager.

A typical MSN setup makes these changes to your system:

- MSN's Connection Manager replaces the Internet Explorer dialer.
- MSN automatically configures e-mail and news accounts with the username you chose at startup.

- The icon in Outlook Express and Internet Explorer changes from the stylized Explorer logo to MSN's logo.

- When you connect to MSN, you'll see an additional icon in the taskbar's notification area. Right-click that icon to pop up a cascading menu with access to all of MSN's services.

- MSN makes other subtle changes throughout the operating system, including installing and configuring a handful of multimedia players.

 TIP If you use MSN to access the Internet but aren't fond of its interface, you can have the best of both worlds. When you install MSN, it adds a connection icon to the Dial-Up Networking folder. Use that icon to connect, and you'll bypass all of the MSN interface changes. Even if you uninstall the MSN software completely, you can still access your MSN account with this connection icon; for your username, enter MSN/*username* (include the slash, but substitute your username), and dial your local MSN access number.

Using Other Online Services

Increasingly, online services are resembling Internet service providers, both in the services they offer and the rates they charge. When you open the Online Services folder on the Windows desktop, you have access to shortcuts that allow you to connect with America Online (AOL), AT&T WorldNet, CompuServe (which is now owned by AOL), and Prodigy Internet.

The icons in the desktop folder are shortcuts to much larger setup files stored on the Windows 98 CD-ROM. You can use these icons to open a new account or to enable access to an existing account with one of these services.

For more details about each of the online services, including technical support numbers, see the text file in the Online Services folder.

Connecting to the Internet

After you've created a Dial-Up Networking icon that contains your connection settings, Windows 98 gives you three choices for establishing a connection:

- Open the Dial-Up Networking folder and use that icon to manually connect to the Internet. This option gives you maximum control over when and how you connect to the Internet.

- Set up Internet Explorer to automatically open a Dial-Up Networking connection whenever you attempt to access a Web page. By default, this option requires you to respond to a confirmation dialog box before actually dialing. This is your best choice when you share a single line for voice and data calls.

■ Use advanced settings in the Dial-Up Networking folder to make a hands free connection, without requiring confirmation from you, whenever you attempt to access any Internet resource. This option is best if you have a dedicated data line and don't want any interruptions from Windows.

Making a Manual Connection

To connect to the Internet manually, follow these steps:

1. Select the connection icon and open it. A dialog box like the one in Figure 40.23 appears.

Figure 40.23

Regardless of the settings you defined in the connection icon, this dialog box lets you temporarily change phone number, username, location, and other settings.

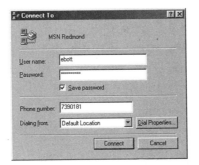

2. Check your username and enter a password if necessary. To store the password for reuse, check the box labeled Save Password.

3. Check the entry in the Phone Number box; if the format is incorrect, choose a new location or edit the number to include the required prefixes.

4. Click the Connect button.

After you complete those steps, Windows opens a modem connection and attempts to dial the number. You'll see a series of status messages, like the one in Figure 40.24, as the connection proceeds.

Figure 40.24

Status messages like this can help you identify problems when making an Internet connection.

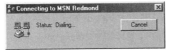

After you successfully complete the connection, you'll see an informational dialog box, like the one in Figure 40.25. At the same time, a Dial-Up Networking icon appears in the notification area to the right of the taskbar.

Part
VII

Ch
40

Figure 40.25

If you'd prefer not to see this dialog box after every completed connection, check the option just above the Close button.

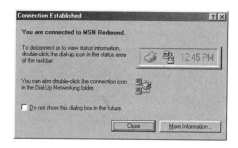

Monitoring Connection Status

Whenever you have an open connection to the Internet, Windows 98 offers you a variety of ways to check its status. Double-click the icon in the notification area, for example (or right-click and choose Status) to see a display showing the total time this connection has been open, as well as the total number of bytes you've received and sent, as in Figure 40.26.

Figure 40.26

To eliminate the display of connection information in the bottom of this status window, click the No Details button.

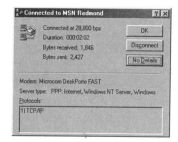

 TIP To see status information at a glance without opening a dialog box, point to the icon in the notification area; after a few seconds, a ScreenTip will appear.

Closing Your Internet Connection

When you've finished working with your Internet connection, you have three options to close it:

- Right-click the icon in the notification area and choose Disconnect.
- Right-click the connection icon in the Dial-Up Networking folder and choose Disconnect (note that the same menu is available if you right-click a shortcut to a connection icon). This technique is useful if the taskbar icon is not available for any reason.
- If the connection status dialog box is open, click the Disconnect button.

Connecting (and Disconnecting) Automatically

Internet Explorer includes a component called Connection Manager, which can automatically establish an Internet connection whenever you attempt to access a Web page. You can configure Connection Manager to pause for confirmation or to dial automatically.

NOTE Connection Manager does not work with other Internet programs. If you want Outlook Express to dial automatically each time you check your mail, you'll have to set up separate dialing options using that program. ▪

To set up Connection Manager, open the Internet Options dialog box and click the Connection tab. Choose the option labeled Connect to the Internet Using a Modem, then click the Settings button. The dialog box shown in Figure 40.27 appears.

Figure 40.27

Internet Explorer can handle the dialing duties, but you'll have to specify these options first.

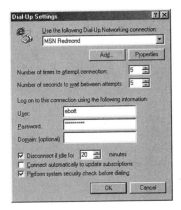

After you've configured all Connection Manager options, click OK to close the Dial-Up Settings dialog box, and click OK again to close the Internet Options dialog box. Open Internet Explorer and try to access a Web page. If you don't have an open Internet connection, you'll see a Connect To dialog box like the one in Figure 40.28.

Part

VII

Ch

40

Figure 40.28

By default, Connection Manager prompts you before trying to make a dial-up connection.

Here are some tips for getting maximum benefit out of Connection Manager:

- Check the <u>S</u>ave Password box to store your password in the Windows cache. Uncheck this box if you don't want other users to be able to access your Internet account.
- If you see the Connection Manager dialog box but you're not ready to connect, click the Work <u>O</u>ffline button.
- Check the box labeled <u>C</u>onnect Automatically if you have a dedicated data line and you don't need to confirm your action each time you dial.

The Disconnect If <u>I</u>dle option automatically closes your dial-up connection if there's been no activity for the amount of time you specify. The default value is 20 minutes, but you can reset the idle time to any value between 3 and 59 minutes.

If you're working with a Web page when the idle timer expires, Internet Explorer won't suddenly close the connection. Instead, you'll see a warning dialog box like the one in Figure 40.29. You have 30 seconds to respond before Connection Manager shuts down access to the Internet.

Figure 40.29

You'll receive fair warning before Connection Manager shuts down an open connection.

The Auto Disconnect dialog box gives you these options:

- Click the Disconnect <u>N</u>ow button to close the connection immediately.
- Click the <u>S</u>tay Connected button to reset the timer and continue working with Internet Explorer.
- Check the Don't Use <u>A</u>uto Disconnect box to disable this feature until you reset it. This has the same effect as clearing the check box in the Dial-Up Settings dialog box.

CAUTION

Some sites can keep an Internet connection open indefinitely. For example, stock tickers that automatically refresh every few minutes will keep your connection from hanging up, as will sites that deliver streaming data such as RealAudio. Don't expect Internet Explorer to disconnect automatically if you leave one of these pages open and then walk away from your computer.

Making a Hands-Free Manual Connection

If you prefer not to use the Connection Manager, open the Internet Options dialog box and configure Internet Explorer to connect using a local area network. You'll have to connect manually using a Dial-Up Networking connection icon before attempting to access a Web page. To turn this into a single-click process, follow these steps:

1. Open the Dial-Up Networking folder.

2. Open the connection icon you want to automate, and enter your username and password. Check the Save password box.

3. Click Connect. When the status dialog box appears, click Cancel to abort the connection and return to the DUN folder.

4. Choose Connections, Settings.

5. Clear the check marks in front of the box labeled Prompt for Information Before Dialing and Show a Confirmation Dialog After Connected, as shown in Figure 40.30.

Figure 40.30

Use these settings to bypass all dialog boxes when you click a connection icon.

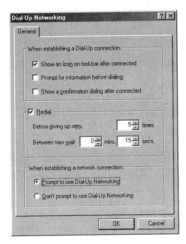

6. Check the Redial box and set automatic retry options if desired.

7. Click OK to save your changes.

CHAPTER 41

Web Browsing with IE 4

by Ed Bott

In this chapter

What Is Internet Explorer 4.0?

Internet Explorer 4.0 delivers all the basic functionality you've come to expect from a Web browser. It lets you gather information from servers located on your company's intranet or on the World Wide Web. It displays text and graphics in richly formatted pages, runs scripts, accesses databases, and downloads files. With the help of Internet Explorer 4.0, you can establish secure, encrypted sessions with distant servers, so that you can safely exchange confidential information like your credit-card number, without fear that it will be intercepted by a third party.

Internet Explorer 4.0 also makes it easier for you to protect your computer. It uses the concept of security zones, for example, to tightly restrict the ability of unknown Web servers to interact with local computers and network resources. With one set of security settings for your local intranet, another for trusted sites, and another for the Internet at large, you can automatically download files from local servers but control downloads from external sites.

Using subscriptions, you can transfer Web-based information automatically to a desktop or notebook PC, then view those pages even when you're not connected to the Internet.

It looks different, too. You can use the versatile Explorer bar—a simple frame that locks in place along the left edge of the browser window—to organize your Favorites list, search for information on the Web, or browse pages stored in your local cache. Because the browser shares code with the Windows Explorer, you can display the contents of a folder on your local PC or network, then jump to a Web site in the same window. And there are dozens of configuration options to make the interface more comfortable.

To open Internet Explorer and display your home page, click the Internet icon on the desktop or the Quick Launch bar. Figure 41.1 shows the default browser window.

Decoding URLs

Before you can open a Web page, you have to specify its location, either by clicking on a shortcut or link that points to the file, or by entering its full name and path in the Address bar. For an HTML document stored on your local PC or a network server, use the familiar [drive]:\filename or \\servername\sharename\filename syntax. For Web pages stored on a Web server on the Internet, you'll need to specify a Uniform Resource Locator, or URL.

> **N O T E** Some otherwise credible sources insist that URL actually stands for Universal Resource Locator, but the organizations that set Internet standards agree that U is for Uniform. Opinion is evenly divided on whether to pronounce the term earl or spell out the letters U-R-L. ▪

As Figure 41.2 shows, each URL contains three essential pieces of information that helps Internet Explorer find and retrieve information from the Internet. (Some optional types of information, including port numbers and query parameters, may also be part of a URL.)

Figure 41.1

The Internet Explorer interface includes these basic navigational elements.

The Standard toolbar gives you one-click access to frequently used tasks.

Explorer bars help you find information and revisit favorite Web pages.

Check this status bar for useful information about the current page, especially as it loads.

The Uniform Resource Locator for the current page appears in this Address bar.

You can hide the Quick Links bar or move it to another location at the top of the browser window.

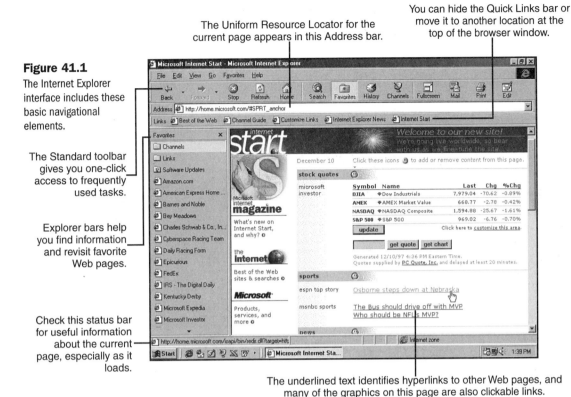

The underlined text identifies hyperlinks to other Web pages, and many of the graphics on this page are also clickable links.

Figure 41.2

Every URL is different, but these basic components help define the location of all sorts of Web resources.

Prefix (protocol or retrieval scheme)

Port number (optional)

Parameters (optional)

Network location

Resource path

Part

VII

Ch

41

- The prefix tells Internet Explorer which protocol or retrieval scheme to use when transferring the document. The prefix is always followed by a colon. Standard Web pages use the http: prefix, while secure Web pages use https:. The URL for a file stored on an FTP server uses the prefix ftp:. Internet Explorer will automatically add the http: and ftp: prefixes if you type an otherwise valid Web or FTP address.

- The network location, which appears immediately to the right of the prefix, identifies the Internet host or network server where the document is stored: www.microsoft.com, for example. Note that you must separate the prefix from network location in URLs with two forward slashes. This part of an URL may also include a username and password for connecting with resources on servers that require you to log on. If the server requires connection over a nonstandard TCP port number, you can add a colon and the port information at the end of this entry.

■ The resource path defines the exact location of the Web page or other resource on the specified server, including path, file name, and extension. This entry begins with the first forward slash after the network location. If the URL doesn't include the name of a page in the resource path, most Web servers will load a page called default.htm or index.htm. Two special characters define parameters that appear after the path: ? indicates query information to be passed to a Web server, while # identifies a specific location on the page.

 T I P To display a blank page in your Web browser, use the URL about:blank.

There are a surprising number of prefixes you can type in the Address bar. Each uses its own protocol or retrieval method to gather information. For a detailed listing of most generally used URL prefixes, see Table 41.1.

Table 41.1   Legal URL Prefixes

Prefix	Description
about:	Displays internal information about the browser. IE 4 uses this prefix to display some error messages, including about:NavigationCanceled
file:	Opens a local or network file. Used in other browsers but not required with IE 4 because the Windows Desktop Update is installed.
ftp:	Connects with a server running the File Transfer Protocol
gopher:	Connects with a server running the Gopher or Gopher+ Protocol
http:	Retrieves information from Web servers using Hypertext Transfer Protocol
https:	Creates a connection with a secure Web server, then encrypts all page requests and retrieved information over Secure Hypertext Transfer Protocol
mailto:	Launches the default e-mail client and begins composing a message to the address named in the URL
news:	Connects with a Usenet news server using the default news reader
nntp:	Connects with a Usenet news server using the NNTP access
res:	Resource within a binary file; IE4 uses information with DLL files to display some help information
telnet:	Launches the system's default Telnet client to create an interactive session with a remote host computer
wais:	Connects with Wide Area Information Servers that contain large databases

Working with Web Pages

The basic building blocks of the World Wide Web are simple text documents written in Hypertext Markup Language, or HTML. To communicate with the Web server where a given page is stored, your browser uses Hypertext Transfer Protocol, or HTTP.

Every time you open an HTML document, Internet Explorer interprets the formatting tags and other coded instructions in that document and displays the fully formatted results in your browser window. A single Web page may contain text, graphics, links to other pages and to downloadable files, and embedded objects, such as ActiveX controls and Java applets. When you load that Web page, it may in turn load dozens of additional linked files, especially graphic images.

HTML pages can incorporate scripts that cause specific actions to take place in response to a trigger event—for example, clicking a button to submit data from a Web-based form for processing by a Web server. Dynamic HTML instructions let the contents of the browser window change as you work with the page.

To see the underlying HTML code for the current Web page, choose View, Source. Internet Explorer uses its basic text editor, Notepad, to display HTML source, as shown in Figure 41.3.

Figure 41.3

Because HTML documents are strictly text, you can view the underlying source code in the bare-bones Notepad editor.

```
index - Notepad
File  Edit  Search  Help
<CENTER><IMG SRC="/graphics/index/gifs/headsup.gif" WIDTH=241 HEIGHT=66
ALT="Heads Up"></CENTER>

<!-- <IMG ALIGN=LEFT SRC="/graphics/index/gifs/spacer.gif" WIDTH=10
HEIGHT=280>
<IMG ALIGN=RIGHT SRC="/graphics/index/gifs/spacer.gif" WIDTH=10
HEIGHT=280> -->
<BLOCKQUOTE>
<FONT SIZE=2>
<P>
<FONT SIZE=5><B>B</B></FONT>ack by popular demand...
<BR>    
If you are looking for a reliable, high-capacity removable storage
solution for your Mac or PC, the <A
HREF="/cgi-bin/auth/docroot/iomega.html?nonce=guest">Iomega Jaz</A>
drive should top your list.  Fast, quiet and priced-to-move, these 1Gig
drives may well be the last storage device you will <I>ever</I> have to
buy.
<BR>    
And to sweeten the deal, we are giving away 3-packs of Jaz media
($269.95 value) to ten more lucky winners during December.  Just
think...three more gigs of space for all of your stuff...<B>for
FREE!</B>  <I>(No purchase necessary.  See contest rules for your <A
```

Part
VII

Ch
41

 T I P FrontPage Express adds an Edit button to the Internet Explorer toolbar. When you install Microsoft's full-strength Web page editor, FrontPage, it takes over this function. Click this button to begin editing the current Web page.

Working with Hyperlinks

Hyperlinks are HTML shortcuts that activate with a single click. Clicking a link has the same effect as typing its URL into the browser's Address bar. The specific action depends on the prefix: a link with the http: prefix, for example, allows you to jump from page to page. Other prefixes typically found in links carry out specific actions: a link can allow you to begin executing a script (javascript:), download a file (ftp:), begin composing a mail message (mailto:), or open Outlook Express to read a linked newsgroup message (news:).

On a Web page, the clickable portion of a hyperlink can take several forms. Text links appear in color (blue, by default) and are underlined. A Web page designer can change the look of a text link and can also attach a link to a picture or button on the screen. Internet Explorer changes the shape of the pointer when it passes over a link. To see additional information about a link, look in the status bar or inspect its properties. Some Web pages, such as the one in Figure 41.4, include pop-up help text for the image under the pointer; the status bar shows where the link will take you.

Figure 41.4
The pop-up ScreenTip and the status bar offer helpful information about this link; you can also right-click to inspect its properties.

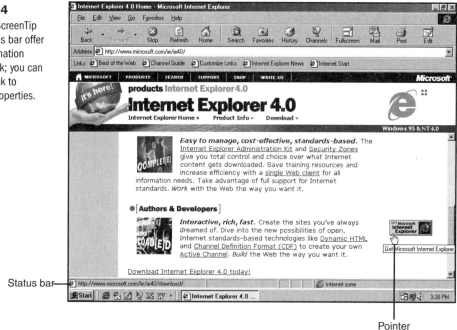

Status bar

Pointer

TROUBLESHOOTING

You click a link, but the linked page doesn't open properly.   Clicking a link most often fails because the specified page has been moved or no longer exists on that server. It's also possible that the author left out a crucial portion of the Web address or simply mistyped it. You can sometimes open the link (or its parent) anyway, although it may take several extra steps: Right-click on the link and choose Copy Shortcut. Select the entire contents of the Address bar, right-click, and choose Paste. Edit the URL as needed and press Enter.

To copy the underlying URL in text format from a link to the Windows Clipboard, right-click on the link and choose Copy Shortcut. For a link that's attached to a graphic, choose Copy only if you wish to copy the image itself to the Clipboard.

Normally, clicking on a link replaces the page displayed in the current window. To open the linked page in its own window without affecting the current page, right-click on the link and choose Open in New Window.

Starting Internet Explorer

The browser window opens automatically when you click on a hyperlink or an Internet short-cut. To open Internet Explorer and go directly to your home page, use the Internet Explorer icon on the desktop or on the Quick Launch bar.

 You can have two or more browser windows open at one time—a technique that's handy when you're gathering and comparing information from multiple sources.

 To open a new browser window, use any of these three techniques:

- Choose File, New, Window. The new window will display the same contents as the current browser window.

- Press Ctrl+N. This keyboard shortcut has the same effect as using the File menu. In both cases, the new browser window "remembers" previously visited sites, so you can use the Back button just as you would in the original window.

- Click the Launch Internet Explorer Browser button in the Quick Launch toolbar. The new window will open to your home page.

Navigating Internet Explorer

There are at least six ways to display a Web page in the current browser window:

Part
VII
Ch
41

- Type a URL in the Address bar, or choose a previously entered URL from the drop-down list, and press Enter.
- Type a URL in the Run box on the Start menu.
- Click a link on an HTML page.
- Open an Internet shortcut on the desktop, in a folder, in the Favorites list, or in a mail message.
- Click a shortcut on the Links bar.
- Use the Back and Forward buttons, the File menu, or the History list to return to previously viewed pages.

Using the Address Bar

You can click in the Address bar and painstakingly type a full URL to jump to a particular Web page, but Internet Explorer 4.0 includes several shortcut features that reduce the amount of typing required for most Web addresses.

There's no need to start with a prefix when you enter the address of a valid Internet host. For example, when you type

www.microsoft.com

the browser automatically adds the http:// prefix. If the address you enter begins with ftp, it adds the ftp:// prefix.

CAUTION

There's an important distinction between the forward slashes used in URLs and the backslashes used in local files and in UNC names that refer to network resources. If you enter \\servername in the Address bar, you'll see a list of all the shared resources available on a network server, while //servername jumps to the default HTML page on the Web server with that name.

If you type a single word that doesn't match the name of a local Web server, Internet Explorer automatically tries other addresses based on that name, using the common Web prefix www and standard top-level domains—.com, .edu, and .org. To tell Internet Explorer to automatically add www to the beginning and com to the end of the name you typed, press Ctrl+Enter.

Using AutoComplete to Fill in the Blanks

As you move from page to page, Internet Explorer keeps track of the URL for every page you've visited. Each time you begin to type in the Address bar, Internet Explorer checks the History list and attempts to complete the entry for you, suggesting the first address that matches the characters you've typed. You can see the results of this AutoComplete feature in Figure 41.5. Note that the characters you type appear on a plain white background, while the suggested completion is highlighted.

Figure 41.5

The AutoComplete feature suggests the first address that begins with the characters you've typed.

Address   http://www.microsoft.com/ie/ie40/main.htm

When it makes an AutoComplete suggestion, Internet Explorer scans the list of addresses you've entered previously, in alphabetical order, then chooses the first matching address. If you type **www.m**, for example, www.matrox.com might be the first suggestion. To accept the completed address, just press Enter.

If the suggested address isn't the one you want, you have two alternatives: If you continue typing, Internet Explorer will revise its suggestion based on the new text you type. In the previous example, if you type **i** so that the contents of the Address bar read **www.mi**, Internet Explorer might suggest **www.microsoft.com**.

What do you do if there are dozens of pages in your History list that begin with the same domain name? After AutoComplete makes its first suggestion, use the down arrow to cycle through every entry in your history list that begins with that string of text. When you reach the right address, press Enter to load that page.

You can simply ignore AutoComplete suggestions and continue typing the address. If you find the feature more confusing than helpful, follow these steps to turn AutoComplete off:

1. Choose View, Internet Options.
2. Click the Advanced tab.
3. Clear the check mark from the box labeled Use AutoComplete.
4. Click OK to close the dialog box and save your changes.

Navigating with the Mouse

Click the Back button to jump to pages you previously visited, then click the Forward button to return. When you right-click on either button (or use the arrow at right), a list of the nine most recent pages appears, as seen in Figure 41.6. (The same list of up to nine pages also appears at the bottom of the File menu.)

Figure 41.6
Right-click or use this drop-down arrow for a faster alternative to repeatedly clicking the Back or Forward button.

If you own a Microsoft IntelliMouse, use the wheel (located between the buttons) to take advantage of four navigational shortcuts:

- Hold down the Shift key and roll the wheel downward to return to the previously viewed page; hold down Shift and move the wheel up to go forward again.

- Roll the wheel up or down to scroll three lines at a time through a Web page (the Advanced tab of the Internet Options dialog box lets you adjust this setting).

- Hold down the wheel button and move the mouse in any direction to scroll. Release the wheel button to stop scrolling.

- Click the wheel to turn on continuous scrolling. When you see the indicator in Figure 41.7, move the pointer and the page will scroll automatically in that direction, like a Teleprompter. The further you move the pointer, the faster the page will scroll. To resume normal scrolling, click the wheel again or press Esc.

Figure 41.7
Use your IntelliMouse to automatically scroll at a controlled speed; in this example, moving the pointer down makes the page scroll more quickly.

 Virtually every object on a Web page is accessible via shortcut menus. Right-click to inspect properties, copy or print an image, or add a page to your Favorites list, for example.

▶ **See** "Using the Favorites Folder to Organize Your Favorite Web Sites," **page 885**

Working with Frame-Based Pages

Frames are an effective way for clever designers to make Web pages more usable. Unlike ordinary pages, which fill the browser window from border to border, frame-based pages split the window into two or more zones, each with its own underlying HTML code and navigation controls. The most common use of frames is to add a table of links along one side of the browser window, with pages displayed in the frame on the other side; because the frame containing the list of links is always visible, it's easy to quickly move through the site without constantly hitting the Back button. Not surprisingly, Microsoft's developer pages (see Figure 41.8) make good use of frames.

Figure 41.8

Look carefully and you'll see four frames in this page. In addition to the obvious navigation area at left, there are two frames along the top. The main browser window is a frame with its own scroll bar.

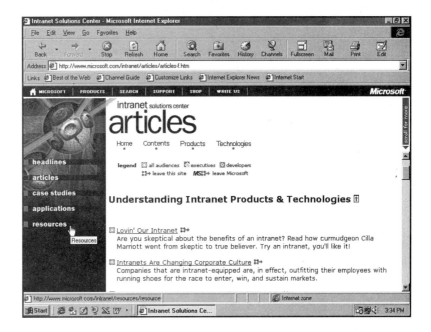

Working with frames takes practice. The Back and Forward buttons, for example, won't let you navigate within a frame. To move back and forth within a frame, you have to select the frame itself, right-click, and then click the Back or Forward menu choices. Likewise, to view the source code for a frame, you'll need to right-click in the area of interest and choose View Source from the shortcut menu. When you save or copy a frame-based page, make sure you've selected the portion of the document you want and not just the small master document that contains pointers to the frames.

▶ **See** "Arranging Frames on the Printed Page," **page 897**

Navigating with the Keyboard

For most people, most of the time, the mouse is the best way to navigate using Internet Explorer. But the Web browser also offers superb keyboard support, which is important for users who have physical disabilities that make it difficult or impossible to use a mouse. Keyboard shortcuts are also a useful way to accelerate Web access for skilled typists who prefer to keep their hands on the keyboard while they work.

Most of the movement keys in Internet Explorer 4.0 work as they do elsewhere in Windows. Home and End go to the top and bottom of the current page, for example. The Up and Down arrow keys move through the page, and the Page Up and Page Down keys move up and down in bigger jumps.

Part
VII

Ch
41

You can use shortcut keys to choose commands and view documents. Many of the pull-down menus include pointers to keyboard alternatives. The following table lists the most useful keyboard shortcuts in Internet Explorer.

To do this...	Press this
Go to the next page	Alt+Right Arrow
Go to the previous page	Alt+Left Arrow, Backspace
Display a shortcut menu for a link or object	Shift+F10
Move forward between frames	Ctrl+Tab
Move back between frames	Shift+Ctrl+Tab
Move to the next link on a page	Tab
Move to the previous link on a page	Shift+Tab
Activate the currently selected link	Enter
Refresh the current page	F5
Stop downloading a page	Esc
Open a new location	Ctrl+O
Open a new browser window	Ctrl+N
Save the current page	Ctrl+S
Print the current page or active frame	Ctrl+P

Using Image Maps

One popular navigational aid on some Web pages is the image map. Instead of assigning links to a series of graphic objects or buttons, a Web designer can create links to specific coordinates of a single large image. The image map in Figure 41.9, for example, lets you jump to linked pages using a map of Houston, Texas. How do you know when you're working with an image map? Watch the status bar at the bottom of the browser window as the mouse passes over the image—if you see coordinates, as in this figure, there's an image map under the pointer.

Image maps are clever and useful jumping-off points on Web sites. Their only drawback is that they require the use of the mouse—there's no way to use an image map with the keyboard.

Gathering Information from the Status Bar

Each time your browser makes a connection with a Web server, valuable information appears on the status bar along the bottom of the screen. The status bar (see Figure 41.10) shows the following:

■ The status of the current download—look for an hourglass over a globe as a page loads, and a full-page icon when the download is complete.

■ The status of objects currently loading, including linked graphics, ActiveX components, and Java applets. This area also counts down the number of items that have not yet been downloaded.

Figure 41.9

The coordinates at the end of the URL in the status bar are your tip-off that this site is using an image map for navigation.

Figure 41.10

You'll find important information about the status of the current page here.

Status bar ———

■ Point to a link to see its associated URL in the status bar; use the Advanced tab of the Internet Options dialog box to switch between full URLs (**http://www.microsoft.com/ default.asp**) and friendly names (shortcut to default.asp at **www.microsoft.com**).

■ A blue progress bar shows what percentage of the entire page has been loaded.

■ Look for a padlock icon to indicate when you're viewing a page over a secure connection or using international language support; when you print a page, you'll see a printer icon here.

■ The security zone for the current page appears at the far right of the status bar.

 T I P   Want to quickly adjust Internet Explorer options? Double-click the status bar; that shortcut has the same effect as choosing View, Internet Options from the pull-down menus.

Stopping Downloads and Reloading Pages

There are many reasons why a Web page doesn't load properly, but the most common is too much traffic on the server you're trying to reach or on one leg of the connection between your browser and the remote server. Click the Stop button (or press Esc) to immediately stop a download. Take this step if you're certain the page you requested has stalled or is unavailable and you don't want to wait for the browser to time out. It can also be a time-saving tactic if there are many bulky graphic elements on the page and you can already see the link you want to follow or the section you want to read.

The Refresh button is especially valuable when viewing frequently updated pages, such as weather information, traffic maps, or stock quotes, to guarantee that the version you see is the most recent and not a stale copy from the Internet Explorer cache. You should also click the Refresh button when a download fails in the middle of a page or when one or more objects on a page fail to load, as in the example in Figure 41.11.

Figure 41.11
The icon in each empty box means that a graphic file failed to load. Click the Refresh button to reload the entire page, or right-click to download just one image.

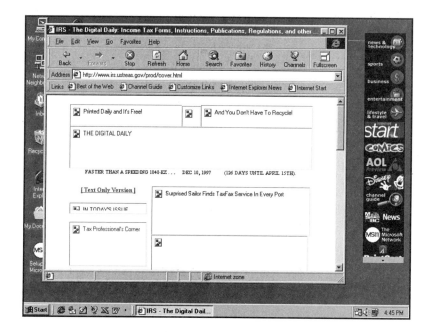

You don't have to refresh the entire page if a small portion of the page failed to load. Look for a red X or broken image icon, indicating a linked file that failed to load. To refresh just that portion of the page, right-click and choose S<u>h</u>ow Picture.

Setting Your Home Page

Every time you start Internet Explorer, it loads the page you designate as your home page. By default, Microsoft takes you to home.microsoft.com, where you can follow links to assemble a home page based on your own interests. You can designate any Web page as your home page; if you're connected to a company intranet, you may prefer to set a local page to load automatically at startup.

To reset your home page, load the page you wish to use, then choose <u>V</u>iew, Internet <u>O</u>ptions and click on the General tab (see Figure 41.12). Click Use <u>C</u>urrent to set the current page as your home page. Click Use <u>D</u>efault to restore the default Microsoft home page. Click Use <u>B</u>lank to replace the home page with a blank page that loads instantly.

Figure 41.12

Choose your preferred home page, then navigate to this dialog box to designate that page to run every time you start Internet Explorer.

 When choosing a home page, make sure it's readily accessible, to avoid delays when you start your browser. Better yet, use FrontPage Express to construct your own home page, with links to favorite sites inside your intranet and on the World Wide Web. See Chapter 44, "Creating and Publishing Web Documents," for more details on how to use FrontPage Express.

Increasing the Size of the Browser Window

Pieces of the Internet Explorer interface can get in the way of data, especially on displays running at low resolutions. There are several ways to make more space available for data in the browser window. Most involve hiding, rearranging, or reconfiguring these optional interface elements.

The simplest way to reclaim space for data is to hide the toolbars and status bar. To hide the status bar, choose View and click Status Bar; to eliminate one or more of the three built-in toolbars, right-click on the menu bar and remove the check marks from Standard Buttons, Address Bar, or Links.

You can also rearrange the three toolbars, placing them side by side or one on top of the other. You can even position any toolbar alongside the menu bar. To move a toolbar, click on the raised handle at the left, then drag the toolbar to its new position. Drag the same handle from right to left to adjust the width of the toolbar.

Want to cut the oversize buttons on the browser window down to size? Choose View, Internet Options, click on the Advanced tab, and check the option to use the smaller Microsoft Office-style buttons instead; next, choose View, Toolbars, and clear the check mark from Text Labels. The results should resemble what you see in Figure 41.13.

Figure 41.13

These smaller buttons, without labels, fit comfortably alongside the Address bar to make room for more data in the browser window.

To configure Internet Explorer for the absolute maximum viewing area, load any page, then click the Full Screen button. This view, shown in Figure 41.14, hides the title bar, menu bar, Address bar, and Links bar. The Standard buttons toolbar shrinks to its smallest setting, and even the minimize and close buttons in the upper-right corner adjust their size and position.

Figure 41.14

Click the Full Screen button to expand the Internet Explorer browser window to its maximum size.

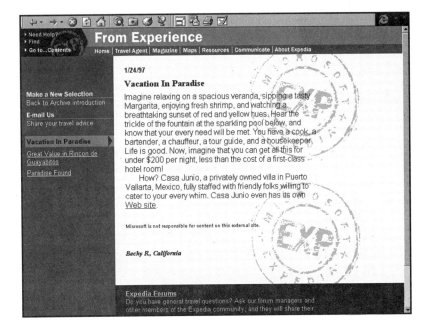

 TIP If you prefer the extra screen real estate you get with Full Screen view, you can configure IE4 to automatically open all Web pages this way. You can also configure IE4's Channels to appear by default in Full Screen view. To set up either option, choose View, Internet Options, click the Advanced tab, and check the boxes labeled Launch browser in full screen window or Launch Channels in full screen window.

In Full Screen view, right-clicking on the toolbar lets you add the menu bar, Address bar, or Links bar to the same row. The Auto Hide choice on the same shortcut menu lets every last piece of the interface slide out of the way; to make the toolbar reappear, move the mouse pointer to the top edge of the screen.

To switch back to normal view, click the Full Screen button again.

Adjusting Fonts and Colors to Make Web Pages More Readable

Can you change the look of a Web page? That depends on decisions the designer of the page made when creating it. Some Web pages use only generic settings to place text on the page. Sophisticated designers, on the other hand, use Web templates called cascading style sheets to specify fonts, colors, spacing, and other design elements that control the look and feel of the page. You can specify fonts and colors you prefer when viewing basic Web pages; advanced settings let you ignore style sheets as well.

The primary benefit is for people with physical disabilities that make it difficult or impossible to read the screen. To adjust any of these settings, choose View, Internet Options, then click the General tab.

 TIP If you're curious about how a Web designer created the specific look of a page, use the View Source option to inspect the HTML code. If you like a particular look, you may be able to copy and paste the code to adapt the design for use in your own Web page.

To adjust the default fonts, click the Fonts button. Besides selecting from a limited assortment of options for proportional and fixed fonts, you can also change the size that Internet Explorer uses for basic Web pages from its default Medium. Choose smaller settings to pack more information onto the screen; use larger values to make text easier to read.

Click the Colors button to change the default values for text and backgrounds on basic Web pages. By default, Internet Explorer uses the Window colors you defined using the Windows Display; with the Standard Windows settings, that means black text on a white page. To change the defaults, you must change that system-wide setting or click the clear the Use Windows Colors check box and specify different Text and Background colors, as shown in Figure 41.15. Internet Explorer also allows you to reset the colors for links here.

Figure 41.15

Setting alternate font choices will affect only basic Web pages—those that don't use style sheets.

Changes you make to default fonts and colors will not apply to pages that use style sheets, unless you make one final adjustment. Click the Accessibility button and check the appropriate boxes to tell the browser to ignore colors, font styles, and font sizes specified in style sheets.

You can increase or decrease default font sizes exclusively for pages you open in the current session. Choose View, Fonts, and select one of the five relative sizes from that menu. This change will apply only when viewing pages that use standard fonts, and Internet Explorer will return to normal settings if you close and then reopen the browser window. When you adjust font sizes, be aware that pages can look odd and, in some cases, can even become unreadable. If you find yourself using this feature regularly, go to the Advanced tab on the Internet Options dialog box and check the option to add a Fonts button to the Standard toolbar.

Viewing Web Pages in Other Languages

Do you frequently find yourself browsing pages created by designers using an alphabet that's not the same one used in your Windows language settings? Before Internet Explorer can display foreign-language pages, you must use the IE 4 setup program to install Multi-Language Support for the appropriate languages. You'll find a Pan-European add-on that allows most Western European languages to display correctly. There are Japanese, Korean, and Chinese add-ins as well.

Once you've installed the additional font support, you should be able to see pages in any of those alphabets, as shown in Figure 41.16.

Figure 41.16

If you try to view foreign-language Web pages, you may see only a garbled mess (left); you'll need to add fonts for the extra languages to see them correctly (right).

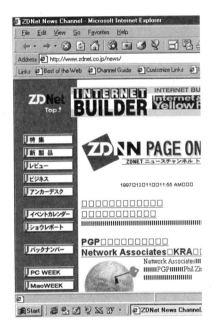

 TIP If you regularly view Web pages that are designed to display in your choice of languages, tell IE 4 which one you prefer. Choose View, Internet Options and click the Languages button on the General tab. Add support for the appropriate languages, and place your preferred language at the top of the list.

Part
VII

Ch
41

Configuring IE to Work with Other Programs

When you first install Internet Explorer, it includes most of the capabilities you need for browsing basic Web pages and handling other types of data, such as streaming audio and video. IE 4 allows you to dramatically expand its capabilities using a variety of add-in programs. Some install themselves automatically, with your permission, while others require that you run a separate setup program.

Installing and Using Add-ins and Plug-ins

Core components of Internet Explorer let you view text formatted with HTML as well as graphics created in supported formats, including JPEG and GIF images. To view other types of data, you must install add-in programs that extend the capabilities of the basic browser. Add-ins can take several forms:

- ActiveX controls offer to install themselves automatically when needed. Depending on your security settings, Internet Explorer may refuse to install ActiveX add-ins, or you may have to click a confirming dialog box. ActiveX controls can perform a practically unlimited variety of functions; examples range from simple data-viewing panels to sophisticated analytical engines for tracking stock quotes. MSNBC's home page, shown in Figure 41.17, includes an ActiveX control that automatically turns current headlines into entries on a cascading menu, making it easier for you to navigate through the day's news.

Figure 41.17

This ActiveX control on MSNBC's home page allows you to browse news headlines and jump to linked pages using cascading menus.

Commerce Front Page
More U.S. firms catch the Asian flu
Another day, another stock warning
OTC market scrutinized; Net next?
Seagate, Quantum issue warnings
Hashimoto faces no-confidence vote ove...
Microsoft shutting down adventure travel W...
FRONTIER: The trains that could, but didn't
'War for eyeballs' isn't over yet
Justice urges FCC to nix BellSouth bid
AOL to enter navigation market
Sun Microsystems circumvents Microsoft Ja...
Publicis ordered to withdraw tender for True...
News from Internet World
CNBC business news
AUDIO REPORT: Hear top Commerce headlines
NEWS BY INDUSTRY ▶
HOLIDAY SHOPPING OUTLOOK ▶
MARKETS & ECONOMY ▶
INTERNATIONAL ▶
INVESTOR TOOLKIT/QUOTE LOOKUP ▶
CHRIS BYRON ▶
BUSINESS VIDEO ▶
MICROSOFT INVESTOR ▶
MSNBC INVESTMENT CHALLENGE ▶
INTERACTIVES, FEEDBACK, MASTHEAD ▶

T I P   There's no need to seek out ActiveX controls. Pages that require add-ins will offer to install the control when you need it, and most controls download in a matter of minutes, even over relatively slow connections.

- Java applets download and run each time you access the page containing the helper program. The security settings for Java applets prohibit them from interacting with local or network resources except on the machine where they originated, and you can't install them permanently, as you can ActiveX controls.

- Other add-in programs and plug-ins use standard installation routines and can often run on their own. Two must-have add-ins for Internet Explorer are RealNetworks' RealPlayer, which allows your browser to receive live audio and video broadcasts over the Internet, and Adobe's Acrobat Reader (Figure 41.18), which lets you display and print richly formatted documents, complete with graphics, columns, and other design elements that go far beyond HTML. Both are free (in fact, RealPlayer 4.0 is included with IE 4); upgrades to more powerful versions are available for a price.

Figure 41.18

When you view a formatted document using the Adobe Acrobat Reader, it takes over the browser window and adds its own toolbars.

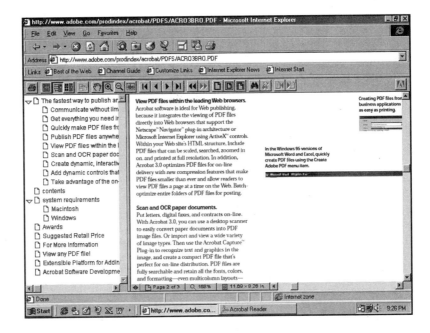

N O T E To download the most recent streaming audio and video player from RealNetworks, follow the links from

http://www.real.com. ■

N O T E To find the most recent version of Adobe's Acrobat reader, follow the links from

http://www.adobe.com. ■

Tuning In to the Internet with NetShow 2.0

One of the most intriguing uses of Internet bandwidth is to deliver so-called streaming media. Unlike conventional sound and video files, which require that you download the entire file before beginning to play it back, streaming media begins playing as soon as the first bits reach your browser. With streaming media, radio stations can "broadcast" their signals over the Internet, making it possible for sports fans, for example, to follow the exploits of their home-town heroes no matter how far they roam.

Streaming media can consist of audio, video, or both. On a normal dial-up connection at 28.8K, audio will typically work well, but video signals are unbearably choppy because the pipe between server and client simply can't deliver data fast enough. Video broadcasts are more practical on company intranets, where network cables can deliver data fast enough to handle broadcast-quality signals.

Internet Explorer includes two useful streaming-media players—RealPlayer and NetShow. For video broadcasts, the NetShow player can function as an ActiveX control, with the viewing screen embedded in the HTML page, or it can run as a stand-alone application with its own menus and VCR-style controls. (See Figure 41.19 for an example of the NetShow player in action.)

Figure 41.19

With its menu bar and VCR-style controls, the NetShow player looks like a standard Windows application. If only the video window is visible, right-click to set options.

NetShow includes several useful customization options. To access the NetShow properties sheet, right-click on the image window or on the player controls and choose Properties. You'll see a dialog box like the one in Figure 41.20.

Figure 41.20

Use the settings on the Advanced tab to configure NetShow to work through a proxy server.

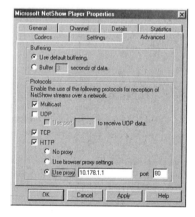

Click the Settings tab to shrink the video window to half-size or expand it to double the default size. Another drop-down list on this tab lets you choose full controls, simple controls, or none at all.

Use the options on the Advanced tab to configure NetShow on a network that uses a proxy server. You'll need to check the documentation from the server to see which TCP and/or UDP ports are required.

Basic title information appears on the General tab, while the Details and Statistics tabs display information about the current connection.

Setting Default Mail and News Clients

The Mail button on the Standard toolbar launches your default e-mail program. Links that begin with the news: prefix fire up your default news reader. If you have more than one program that can work with Internet Explorer, you can control which one starts up when it's needed. To switch between Outlook and Outlook Express as your default mail program, for example, choose View, Internet Options, click the Programs tab, and choose the preferred program from the drop-down lists shown in Figure 41.21.

Figure 41.21

To switch from one helper program to another, use these drop-down lists. Only programs specifically written to work with Internet Explorer will appear here.

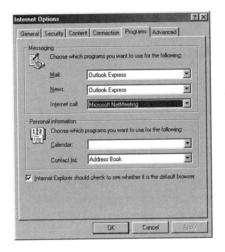

See Chapters 32 through 35 to learn more about managing e-mail with Outlook.

Speeding Up Web Connections

Tuning Internet Explorer for speed and responsiveness involves inevitable tradeoffs between rich content and quick results. Elaborate graphics, video clips, sound files, and other large elements add fun and extra dimensions to the Web, but waiting for those elements to download over a slow connection can quickly become frustrating.

Selectively filtering out some types of downloadable content can reduce the amount of time it takes to load a page the first time. Intelligently managing the browser's cache makes it much faster to access pages a second or subsequent time. Of course, even the most careful configurations can't overcome traffic jams on the Internet.

Browsing Without Graphics

When slow downloads are a problem, the most common culprit is a page that's overstuffed with graphics, sound, and video files, which take time to download. To turn Internet Explorer into a lightning fast text-only browser, follow these steps:

1. Choose View, Internet Options and click on the Advanced tab.
2. Scroll down to the Multimedia branch of the tree.

3. Remove the check marks from all boxes in this section, as shown in Figure 41.22.

4. Click OK to apply your changes.

Figure 41.22

Clear all the check boxes in the Multimedia section to transform Internet Explorer into a speedy text-only browser.

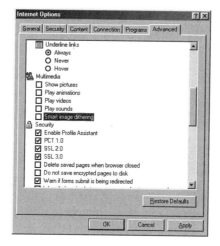

With multimedia options turned off, Internet Explorer will show generic icons, empty boxes, and simple text labels where you would normally see images. It will also ignore any sound files, animations, or video clips embedded in the page. Some sites work perfectly well without images; Fortune magazine, for example, offers an all-text page (see Figure 41.23) that loads quickly and doesn't require any graphic images. (You can always use right-click shortcut menus to manually request any content you've turned off.)

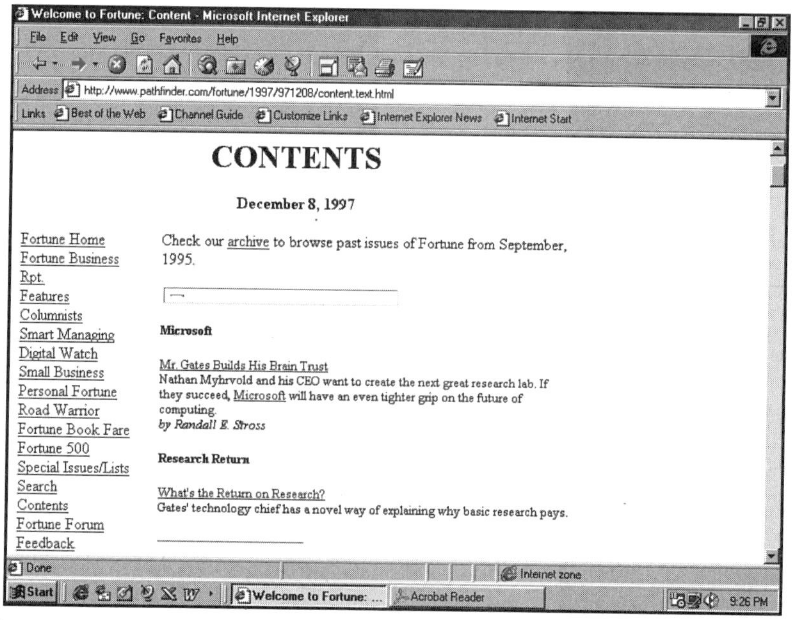

Figure 41.23

Who needs graphics? Even without images for its buttons, this all-text page is eminently readable, thanks to excellent labels.

Although turning off the browser's ability to load image and multimedia files can dramatically improve performance, it can also block important information. On sites that use image maps as their only navigation tool, for example, there's literally no way to get around without displaying that image. To selectively show a picture after downloading the text-only page, right-click and choose Show Picture from the shortcut menu.

 T I P One of the most useful Internet Explorer Power Toys adds a Toggle Images button to the Standard toolbar. If you want to speed up downloads by selectively turning off the display of images, without having to continually open and close dialog boxes, this add-in is essential. You'll find it at

http://www.microsoft.com/ie/ie4/powertoys

Managing the Browser's Cache

With or without graphics, the best way to improve performance is to make sure the browser's cache is correctly configured. Each time you retrieve a new Web page, Internet Explorer downloads every element and stores a copy of each one in a cache directory on your hard disk. The next time you request that page, the browser first checks the cache; if it finds a copy of the page, it loads the entire document from fast local storage, dramatically increasing performance.

When the cache fills up, Internet Explorer throws out the oldest files in the cache to make room for new ones. To increase the likelihood that you'll be able to load a cached copy of a page instead of having to wait for it to reload from the Internet, adjust the size of the cache. Choose View, Internet Options, and click the General tab (see Figure 41.24) to find all the controls you need to fine-tune the Web cache.

Figure 41.24
Give the browser cache extra working room and you'll increase Internet Explorer's performance.

Part
VII

Ch
41

> **CAUTION**
> If you tell Internet Explorer you never want to check for a more recent version of cached pages, your browser will seem remarkably faster. Beware, though—for pages that update frequently, such as news headlines or stock quotes, you'll have to work to see the most recent version. If you choose this setting, get in the habit of clicking the Refresh button to make sure the page is up-to-date.

When should you click the Delete Files button? This action completely empties the Temporary Internet Files folder and can have a noticeable negative impact on how fast your favorite pages load. Under ordinary circumstances, Internet Explorer will manage the size of the cache by itself. You might need to clear the cache manually, though, if a corrupt cached file is causing Internet Explorer to crash, or if you've run out of disk storage and you need to make room for crucial files, or if you plan to do a full system backup and you don't want to include all these cached Web files.

Viewing Cached Files and Objects

Normally, you'll use the History Explorer bar to browse full pages stored in the browser cache. But you can also view the individual objects in the cache—HTML pages, graphics, ActiveX controls, and even cookie files. Click the View Files button in the Settings dialog box to see a full listing, like the one shown in Figure 41.25.

Figure 41.25

The Temporary Internet Files folder holds a copy of every object you've viewed in the browser recently. Right-click to open, copy, or delete any file.

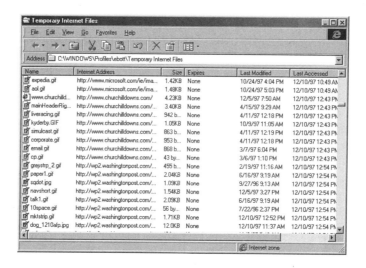

The Temporary Internet Files folder is unlike any other folder you'll see in Windows. Notice the column headings, for example, which track the time a file was last created. Double-click on column headings to re-sort the list—that's particularly useful for finding and deleting large files that are cluttering up the cache. Use right-click shortcut menus to inspect the properties of stored objects and open, copy, or delete them.

N O T E Where are cached pages really stored? Windows organizes all cached files using a maze of hidden folders inside the Temporary Internet Files folder. These folders have randomly generated cryptic names like 25NMCE84; shell extensions in Windows pull the contents of all these folders together into a single display in the Temporary Internet Files folder. Although you can use the DOS Attrib or Windows Find commands to see these files in their actual locations, avoid the temptation to move or delete these hidden objects. Use Internet Explorer's View Files button to manage them instead. ■

CHAPTER 42

Finding, Organizing, and Saving Web-Based Information

by Ed Bott

In this chapter

Using Internet Shortcuts

Regardless of where you find a Web page—on a corporate intranet or on a distant server—deep down inside it's nothing more than a document file. And just as you use conventional shortcuts to organize documents stored locally, Internet shortcuts are the most effective way to organize Web-based information. When you inspect the properties of an Internet shortcut, you'll see a page of settings like the one in Figure 42.1.

Figure 42.1

The target for an Internet shortcut is an URL rather than a local or UNC file specification.

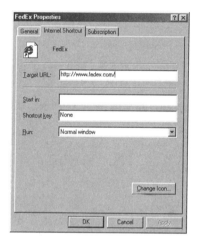

Internet shortcuts behave just like other shortcuts. You can add Internet shortcuts to the desktop or Start menu, move them between folders, send them to other people in mail messages, or rename the shortcut without affecting the target it points to.

▶ **See** "Using Shortcuts," **page 45**

If you start the Create Shortcut wizard and enter a valid URL in the Command line box, Windows creates an Internet shortcut. You can drag that shortcut into the browser window or the Address bar to open the target page, or drop it into the Favorites folder or Links bar to make the page more readily accessible.

 It's easy to create a shortcut that points to the Web page you're currently viewing in the browser window. Just choose File, Send, Shortcut to Desktop. Once the shortcut is on your desktop, you can rename it, modify its properties, move it to another folder, or send it to a friend or coworker in an e-mail message.

Using the Favorites Folder to Organize Your Favorite Web Sites

If you've used a Web browser before, you're already familiar with the concept of saving pointers to Web sites you visit frequently. Netscape Navigator calls them bookmarks, while prior versions of Internet Explorer saved shortcuts to Web pages in a Favorites folder. Internet Explorer 4.0 also lets you collect Internet shortcuts in a Favorites folder, but the user interface for working with Favorites is dramatically different.

 TIP If you had a copy of Netscape Navigator installed when you upgraded to Windows 98, all your Netscape bookmarks are available in the Favorites folder. This conversion is a one-time process; however, new Navigator bookmarks you create after installing Windows 98 are not saved in the Favorites folder.

Click the Favorites button to open the Favorites Explorer bar; this frame along the left border pushes the main browser window to the right. When you choose an entry from the Favorites list, the page you selected appears in the browser window, as in Figure 42.2.

Figure 42.2
Click on a shortcut in the Explorer bar at left and the target page appears in the browser window at right. Arrows at the top and bottom of the Favorites list let you scroll to additional entries.

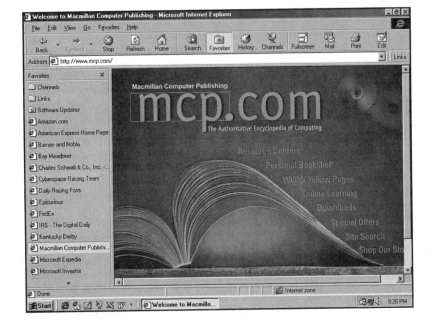

The Favorites folder is located within the Windows folder; if you've enabled multi-user settings, each user with a profile on the computer gets a personal Favorites folder. The contents of the Favorites list appear in alphabetical order on the pull-down F̲avorites menu and in the Explorer bar. To reorder the shortcuts in the Favorites menu, drag any entry to a new position by holding down the mouse button instead of clicking.

 T I P Although the Favorites folder is most useful with Internet shortcuts, you can move any object there, including files, folders, and shortcuts to documents or programs. Clicking on a document or program shortcut in the Explorer bar will usually launch the associated application in its own window.

Adding a Web Page to the Favorites Folder

To add the current page to the Favorites list, use one of these two techniques:

- Drag the page icon from the left of the Address bar and drop it into the Favorites Explorer bar.

- If the Explorer bar is not visible, choose F̲avorites, A̲dd to Favorites.

You can also use shortcut menus to create new entries in the Favorites folder. Follow this simple procedure:

1. Right-click on any blank space or text in the current page.

2. Choose Add to F̲avorites from the shortcut menu; you'll see a dialog box like the one in Figure 42.3.

3. Give the shortcut a descriptive name, if you want, or use the default page title.

4. Click the C̲reate in button and choose a subfolder in the Favorites list.

5. Click OK to create the new shortcut and close the dialog box.

Figure 42.3

When you create a new entry in the Favorites folder, give it a new name if necessary to help you identify the page later.

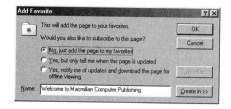

 T I P If the current page contains a link to a page you'd like to add to your Favorites folder, you can use the same technique without having to open the page. Point to the link and right-click, then follow the steps previously outlined.

When you add a Web page to your Favorites list, you also have the option to download pages automatically at scheduled intervals.

▶ **See** "Using Subscriptions to Download Web Pages," **page 909**

Deleting and Renaming Favorites

To delete an Internet shortcut in the Favorites folder, point to the shortcut, right-click, and choose Delete.

To rename an Internet shortcut, point to its entry in the list and choose Rename. Edit the name of the shortcut and press Enter to save your changes.

Using Subfolders to Organize Favorites

As you add items to the Favorites folder, the list can quickly become too long to work with comfortably. When you reach that point, use subfolders to help organize the Favorites list. You can create an unlimited number of subfolders in the Favorites folder, and you can even add new folders within those subfolders.

With the Favorites Explorer bar open, it's easy to move one item at a time from folder to folder. However, you can't use the Explorer bar to create new folders or to move more than one shortcut at a time. For these more serious organizing tasks, choose Favorites, Organize Favorites; that opens the dialog box shown in Figure 42.4, which includes the full set of tools you'll need.

Figure 42.4

Use the buttons along the bottom of this dialog box to organize your Favorites folder. Right-click or use ScreenTips like this one to gather more information about a shortcut.

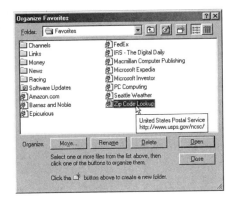

Moving shortcuts to a new folder is a simple process, as long as you perform the steps in the right order. Open the Organize Favorites dialog box and do the following:

1. Click the New Folder button; the new folder appears at the end of the current folder list, with a generic name selected for editing.
2. Type a name for the new folder and press Enter.
3. Select one or more shortcuts from the Favorites list and click the Move button.
4. In the Browse for Folder dialog box, click the name of the folder you just created.
5. Click OK to make the move, and click Close to return to Internet Explorer.

Part
VII

Ch
42

You can also drag and drop Internet shortcuts within the Organize Favorites dialog box. If your collection of Favorites is relatively small, you'll probably find it easier to rearrange them this way than by using the cumbersome procedure previously outlined.

Folders appear in alphabetical order at the top of the Favorites Explorer bar. To see the contents of a folder, click on its entry there—the list of shortcuts in the folder will appear just below the folder icon, also in alphabetical order. Click the folder icon again to close it.

 For fastest access to the Favorites folder, click the Start menu. The cascading Favorites menu appears between the Programs and Documents choices.

Changing or Adding Quick Links

Although the Favorites folder is a convenient way to organize Web pages, it still takes a couple of clicks and some scrolling to find a particular page. For the handful of sites you visit most frequently, use the Links toolbar instead. The shortcuts on this toolbar are never more than a click away, and you can easily arrange them for fast, convenient access.

To show or hide the Links bar, right-click on the menu bar and click Links. When you first start Internet Explorer, there are only five shortcuts on the Links bar, and they all point to pages at Microsoft. In less than five minutes, you can give the Links bar a complete makeover and give your productivity a dramatic boost in the process.

 Do you really need all those Microsoft pages on the default Links bar? Not likely. The Internet Start link, for example, is completely unnecessary; anytime you want to jump to **home.microsoft.com**, just click the spinning Explorer logo in the upper right corner of the browser window. And the Customize Links button leads to a simple Help screen that tells you how to change links; once you learn the technique, you can safely delete this link!

There's no limit to the number of shortcuts you can add to the Links bar. To keep navigation simple, though, you'll probably want to limit the number of links to no more than 10 or 12, depending on your screen resolution. On the Links bar in Figure 42.5, for example, there are nine shortcuts; adding even one more would push the last link off the screen. When that happens, arrows appear at either side of the Links bar to aid in scrolling.

To give your Links bar a makeover, follow these steps:

1. Right-click on any Links you don't plan to keep and choose Delete from the shortcut menu.

2. To add the current page to the Links bar, drag the icon from the left side of the Address bar and drop it alongside any existing link. The shortcut icon tells you when it's okay to drop.

3. Click the Favorites button and drag shortcuts from the Favorites folder to the Links bar.

4. To rearrange the order in which links appear, grab an icon and move it to its new location. Other links will shift left or right to make room for it.

5. To rename a link, open the Favorites Explorer bar, click on Links, right-click on the entry you want to change, and choose Rename.

Figure 42.5

To squeeze the maximum number of shortcuts onto the Links bar, change long page titles to shorter labels.

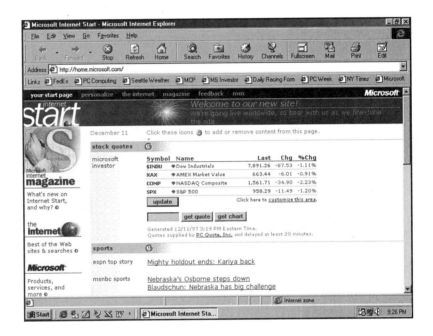

 TIP The width of each shortcut on the Links bar is defined by its label. The shorter the name, the more links you can use. "FedEx," for example, takes up much less space than "Federal Express Home Page," without sacrificing any meaning.

Using the Search Bar to Find Information on the World Wide Web

How many pages are there on the World Wide Web? No one can say for sure, but the number is at least 50 million, probably more than 100 million, and growing every day. How do you find specific information in the billions of words and hyperlinks on all those pages? That's where search engines come in.

Internet Explorer offers easy access to several popular search engines through an Explorer bar that works much like the Favorites bar. When you click the Search button, an Explorer bar like the one in Figure 42.6 takes over the left side of the screen.

Figure 42.6
Use the default search engine, or pick another one from the drop-down list in the Explorer bar, then enter the text you're looking for. Click links in the search results to view pages in the window at right.

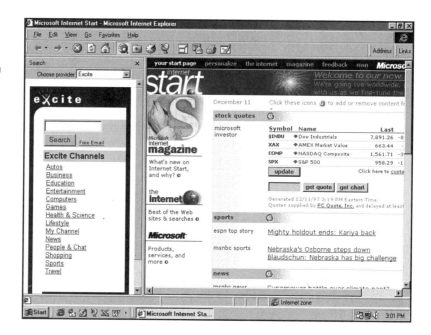

Finding information on the Web is a two-step process: First, you have to choose a search engine that's appropriate for the type of information you're looking for; then you have to construct your search so the pages you're looking for appear at the top of the list.

Choosing the Right Search Engine

In general, search engines can be divided into two types. Category-based sites like Yahoo! organize the Internet by classification. Indexed search engines, such as Excite and AltaVista, use Web robots to gather text and create searchable databases of information. Most popular search sites now combine both techniques on their home pages.

Category searches are ideal for broad, open-ended questions, while indexed sites are better for finding specific facts. In either case, getting the right results takes practice and some basic understanding of how the search engine works. To avoid playing favorites, Internet Explorer picks one of its featured search engines at random every day and spotlights that choice when you click the Search button. You can accept the default, or study Table 42.1 and make your own selection using the drop-down list.

Table 42.1   Popular Internet Search Engines

Name	URL	Description
AOL NetFind	**www.aol.com/netfind**	America Online calls on a huge database of reviews to help you find people, companies, places, and information. Powered by Excite technology, it's open to non-AOL members as well.

Name	URL	Description
Excite	**www.excite.com**	If you can't find it using Excite, it probably isn't on the Internet. Click on "Channels" to find information by topic, or use its massive database to search the entire Web.
Infoseek	**www.infoseek.com**	Enter text or click on topic links to find information. Jump to Infoseek's main page to try its impressive capability to process plain-English questions.
Lycos	**www.lycos.com**	One of the oldest search engines around, Lycos began as a research project at Carnegie Mellon University. Today it offers Yahoo!-style category lists and superb international support.
Yahoo!	**www.yahoo.com**	The original category-based search engine now uses AltaVista's indexing software to do keyword searches as well. Make sure you choose the correct search method before sending your request.

 Don't like any of the built-in search options? Then choose List of all providers from the drop-down list in the Search bar. That option opens Microsoft's all-in-one search page, with links to dozens of general-purpose and specialized search sites.

Performing the Search

After you've selected a search engine, follow these steps to carry out your search:

1. If you see a category that's relevant to your search, click that link. Otherwise, enter the text you're looking for in the search box.

2. If the search engine provides any options, check them carefully. For example, do you want to search the Web, Usenet newsgroups, or both?

3. Click the button that submits your request to the search engine.

4. A list of search results will appear in the Search bar, as in the example in Figure 42.7. Scroll through the list and click on any links that look promising. The page will appear in the browser window to the right of the Search bar.

Part
VII

Ch
42

Figure 42.7
This search produced a staggering 247,558 matches, but the most relevant pages appeared in the top 10. Use the Next button to move through the list ten links at a time.

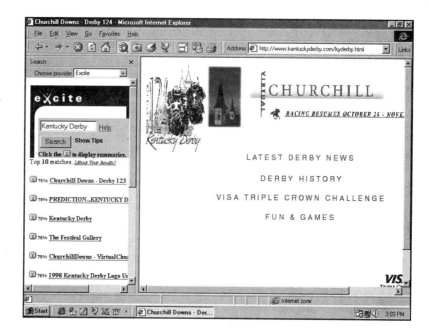

5. Use the Next button at the bottom of the results list to see more entries in the results list.

6. If the search request didn't produce the correct results, change your search or choose a different search engine and try again.

 There's no need to click the Search button if you simply want to look for a keyword or two. If you type **find, go** or **?** in the Address bar, followed by one or more words, Internet Explorer's AutoSearch feature submits your request to Yahoo! for processing, returning results in the main browser window.

If you've found a favorite search engine, you can tell Internet Explorer to take you to that site instead of Yahoo! each time you use AutoSearch. To make the change, you first have to download Microsoft's Tweak UI utility, one of the unofficial Power Toys for Windows 95 and Windows 98. You'll find all the Power Toys, with full instructions for their use, at

http://www.microsoft.com/windows95/info/powertoys.htm

After installing Tweak UI, open Control Panel and start the utility; click the General tab and use the drop-down list to change the default search engine.

Tips and Techniques for More Successful Searches

How can you guarantee better results when you search the Web? Try these techniques:

■ Visit the major search sites often. They regularly add new features and upgrade search interfaces. If you use only the Internet Explorer Search bar, you won't see those improvements.

■ Learn how to combine search terms using the logical operators AND, OR, and NOT to narrow the results list. Every search engine uses a slightly different syntax for these so-called Boolean queries; check the help pages at the search engine's site. The default operator is usually OR, which means if you enter two or more words you'll get back any page that contains any of the words; use an ampersand or AND or quotation marks to be more specific.

■ Don't stop at simple searches. Some search engines let you specify a range of dates to search, for example, to avoid being bombarded with stale links. Others let you specify or exclude a particular Web server. Still others let you progressively narrow down a list of results by searching only in those results. Read each search engine's online instructions to see what advanced features it offers.

Saving a Successful Search

When you find a search that you think you'll want to reuse, follow these steps to save it:

1. Right-click anywhere in the Search bar and choose Properties.

2. Select the entire URL that appears on the General tab, then right-click and choose Copy from the shortcut menu. Click OK to close the Properties dialog box.

3. Select the entire contents of the Address bar, right-click, and choose Paste.

4. Press Enter to load the page whose URL you just copied.

5. Create a shortcut to the current page, either on the desktop or in the Favorites folder, and give it a descriptive name.

Searching for Information on the Current Page

A Web page can consist of a single paragraph, or it can run on for tens of thousands of words. Internet Explorer's Find feature lets you search for words or phrases on the current page or within a selected frame. This feature can be extremely helpful when a search engine turned up a list of pages and you're trying to find the matching word or phrase in a specific page. To begin, press Ctrl+F and enter your text in the Find dialog box shown in Figure 42.8.

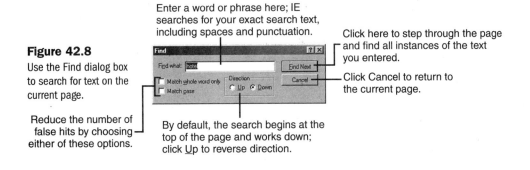

Figure 42.8
Use the Find dialog box to search for text on the current page.

Reduce the number of false hits by choosing either of these options.

Enter a word or phrase here; IE searches for your exact search text, including spaces and punctuation.

Click here to step through the page and find all instances of the text you entered.

Click Cancel to return to the current page.

By default, the search begins at the top of the page and works down; click Up to reverse direction.

Part
VII

Ch
42

Note that the Find dialog box searches only text that actually appears on the page; it won't look at hidden text or HTML tags in the source for the page. To search for hidden text or tags, choose View, Source and use Notepad's Search menu.

TROUBLESHOOTING

Your search for text turned up no matches, but you're certain the word you're looking for is on the page. Looking for text on frame-based pages can produce unexpected results if you're not careful. On these pages, the Find feature searches only in the current frame, not in all frames visible in the browser window. Before you open the Find dialog box and enter your search text, make sure you click in the frame in which you want to search.

Using the History Bar to Revisit Web Sites

In addition to the cache in the Temporary Internet Files folder, Internet Explorer keeps a record of every URL you load. This History list is indispensable when you want to return to a page you visited recently but can't remember its address. If you've enabled multiple user settings on your Windows 98 PC, each user who logs in gets a private History folder.

▶ **See** "Managing the Browser's Cache," **page 881**

Click the History button to open an Explorer bar similar to the one in Figure 42.9. The History bar looks and acts just like the Favorites bar, snapping into position along the left edge of the browser window and pushing the main viewing window to the right.

Figure 42.9
Every time you visit a Web page, it gets an entry in this History list. If you can remember when you saw the page, you can find it here.

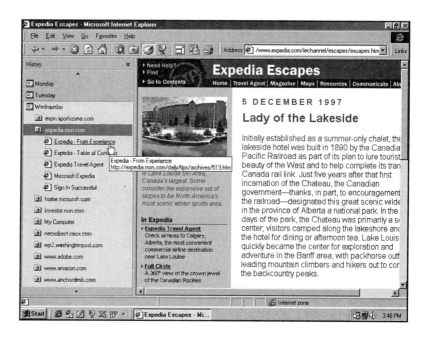

N O T E From the Windows Explorer, you can examine the History list by double-clicking the History icon. Individual shortcuts are not actually stored in the History folder, however; instead, Internet Explorer uses an internal database to manage the collection of shortcuts, with a single data file for each day. The entire collection is organized in one or more hidden folders. Although it's possible to view these hidden files from a DOS prompt, there's no way to see their contents without using Explorer's system extensions. ▨

Navigating Through the History Folder

By default, the History folder keeps a pointer to every page you've accessed for the past 20 days. When you click the History button to open the Explorer bar, you'll see the list of short-cuts organized by day, with the most recent day's collection at the bottom of the list. Click on the entry for any day to see the list of shortcuts for that day, with a single entry for each re-source location. Click again on any of these entries to see a shortcut for each page within that domain. When you click on an Internet shortcut in the History list, Internet Explorer loads the page in the browser window at the right.

 T I P To increase or decrease the size of the History list, choose View, Internet Options and change the number of days to keep pages in history. Use the spinner control on the General tab to select a number between 0 and 999. Choosing 0 clears the History list every day, although you can still recall any page you visited earlier in the same day.

Although you cannot directly add an Internet shortcut to the History list, you can copy an entry from the History list to a variety of places—the desktop, the Start menu, the Favorites folder, or an e-mail message, for example. Drag a shortcut from the History list to any legal destination, or use the right-click menu to copy the shortcut to the Windows Clipboard.

Clearing Out the History

Internet Explorer allows you to empty the History folder completely, or to delete entries one at a time. Clearing out the History folder can reclaim a modest amount of disk space, and it can also make the list easier to navigate. But a more practical reason to remove items from this list is for privacy reasons, to keep another user from seeing the list of sites you've visited recently.

- To clear a single shortcut from the list, point to the shortcut, right-click, and choose Delete.
- To remove a group of shortcuts, point to the entry for a given Web location or day, right-click, and choose Delete.
- To empty all entries from the History folder, choose View, Internet Options, click the General tab, and click the button labeled Clear History.

Browsing the Web Offline

Internet Explorer's cache and History folders work together exceptionally well when you choose to work offline. With the History folder visible in the Explorer bar, you can choose File, Work Offline, and view any files stored in the cache, even if you have no current connection to the Internet.

When you work with Internet Explorer offline, a network icon with a red X appears in the status bar along the bottom of the browser window. Except for that indicator, you can browse pages in the History cache just as if you were working with a live Internet connection. When you point to a link that isn't cached locally, the pointer changes shape and you'll see the dialog box shown in Figure 42.10. Before you can view the selected page, you must open an Internet connection.

Figure 42.10

The X in the status bar means you're working offline. You'll see this pointer when you attempt to access a page that isn't stored in the Web cache.

Offline icon —

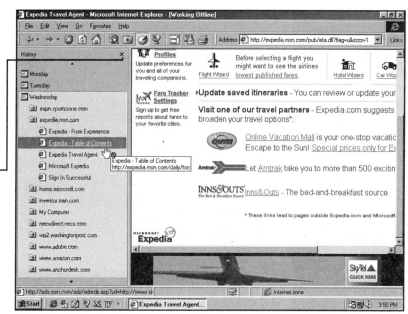

▶ **See** "Using Subscriptions to Download Web Pages," **page 909**

Printing Web Pages

Successfully transferring a Web page to paper can be as simple as clicking a button, although complex page designs require some preparation for best results.

To print a full Web page that doesn't include frames, click the Print button on the Standard toolbar. This action sends the current page to the printer without displaying any additional dialog boxes. Internet Explorer scales the page to fit on the standard paper size for the default printer. The entire Web document will print, complete with graphics, even if only a portion of the page is visible in the browser window.

 T I P By default, Internet Explorer ignores any background images or colors when printing. That behavior is by design, because most of these decorations simply make printed text harder to read. To add background images or colors to printed pages, choose View, Internet Options, click the Advanced tab, and check the appropriate box in the Printing section. Be sure to reverse the process after printing.

Arranging Frames on the Printed Page

For more complex pages, especially those that include frames, choose File, Print (or press Ctrl+P). That opens the Print dialog box shown in Figure 42.11 and lets you specify how you want to arrange the page on paper.

Figure 42.11

Watch the display at the left of the Print Frames box to see how a frame-based page will appear when printed.

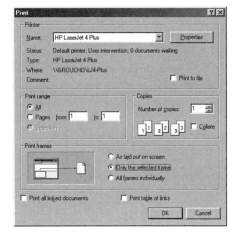

Follow these steps for maximum control over any printed page:

1. Choose the area to be printed. The Selection option is grayed out unless you've selected a portion of the page.

2. Choose the number of copies to print. The default is 1.

3. Tell Internet Explorer how to deal with frames—print a single frame, print the page as it appears onscreen, or print each frame on a separate page.

4. Choose either of the two options at the bottom of the dialog box to specify whether and how linked pages will print.

5. Click OK to send the page to the printer. An icon on the status bar confirms that the page has gone to the printer.

Part
VII

Ch
42

> **CAUTION**
>
> An option at the bottom of the Print dialog box lets you print all linked documents along with the current page. Exercise this option with extreme care, because printing indiscriminately in this fashion can consume a ream of paper with a single click.

Adding Headers and Footers to a Printed Web Page

To control most options that Internet Explorer applies before printing a Web page, choose File, Page Setup. Using this dialog box (shown in Figure 42.12) you can change the orientation, margins, and paper specifications for the current page. More importantly, though, you can specify a header and footer to print on each page.

Figure 42.12

Use these formatting codes to specify a header and footer to appear on each page you print. Internet Explorer saves the format you enter here as your default.

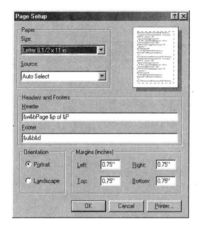

You can enter any text as part of the header or footer; in addition, Internet Explorer uses a set of arcane codes, each prefixed by an ampersand, to add information about the current page to the header or footer. Table 42.2 lists each of these codes:

Table 42.2 Custom Header/Footer Variables

To Print This	Enter This Code
Window title	&w
Page address (URL)	&u
Date (short format)	&d
Date (long format)	&D
Time (default format)	&t
Time (24-hour format)	&T
Single ampersand	&&

To Print This	Enter This Code
Current page number	&p
Total number of pages	&P
Right-align following text	&b*text*
Center *Text1*, right-align *Text2*	&b*text1*&b*text2*

N O T E   If you can't remember the codes for headers and footers, click the question mark icon in the title bar of the Page Setup dialog box and point to the <u>H</u>eader or <u>F</u>ooter box. Watch out for a bug in the documentation, though: Any text you add after the characters &b will be right-aligned, not centered, in the header or footer. ▨

Saving and Editing Web Pages

Only the simplest Web pages consist of a single, simple document. More often, the page you see in your browser consists of one or more HTML documents and several linked images. There's no way to save all the elements on the entire page in one smooth operation. Instead, when you choose <u>F</u>ile, Save <u>A</u>s, Internet Explorer saves the underlying HTML document and ignores any images or pages that are linked to that page. (You can also choose to save the current page as a plain-text document instead of an HTML-formatted page.)

To save graphics, frames, and other files linked to the current page, you must right-click on each one and choose Save Target <u>A</u>s from the shortcut menu. Right-click on any link and use the same menu choice to save a linked page without opening it.

 T I P   With the help of a handy Internet Explorer keyboard shortcut, you can turn any Web graphic into wallpaper for your desktop. When you find an image you'd like to install on the desktop, right-click and choose Set As <u>W</u>allpaper.

▶ **See** "Customizing the Windows Desktop," **page 135**

You can also edit any Web page, by loading it directly from your browser into FrontPage Express. Using the Web browser, open the page you want to edit, and then click the Edit button on the Standard toolbar. You can also create a shortcut to the current page, then right-click on that shortcut icon and choose <u>E</u>dit.

▶ **See** "Creating Web Pages Instantly," **page 929**

Downloading Files from FTP Sites

One of the most common ways to distribute files of all types over the Internet is with FTP servers. Unlike Web servers, which are designed primarily to assemble hypertext documents

Part
VII

Ch
42

for viewing in a browser window, FTP servers use File Transfer Protocol (FTP) to move files between computers. Internet Explorer is capable of acting as a basic FTP client.

To connect directly to an FTP site using your Web browser, enter the name of the site in the Address bar. Because FTP servers don't include graphic support, the display you'll see in the browser window will be as austere as the one in Figure 42.13.

Figure 42.13

Don't expect fancy graphics or menus when you connect to an FTP site. Although this listing is plain, it's easy to find your way around.

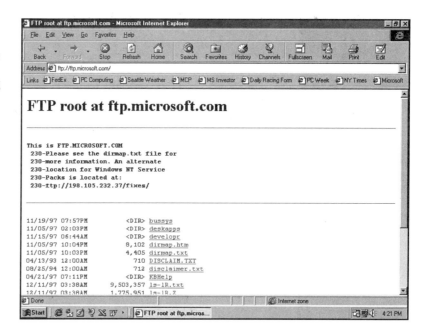

Click on any link in the FTP window to begin downloading that file. When you click on a link to a file stored on an FTP server, Internet Explorer handles the details of logging on to that server and negotiating the details of how to transfer the file. If Internet Explorer succeeds in connecting to the FTP server, you'll typically see the dialog box shown in Figure 42.14. Choose the option labeled Save This Program to Disk, then designate a name and destination for the downloaded file to begin the transfer.

Figure 42.14

Under most circumstances, you'll want to save a file rather than run it directly from an FTP server.

Based on the size of the file and the speed of your current connection, Internet Explorer will attempt to estimate the time remaining on your download. This process isn't always successful; in particular, it fails when the FTP server at the other end of the connection fails to report crucial information about the file you've chosen to download. In those cases, the dialog box you see will tell you how much of the file has been downloaded so far.

When downloading a file of any sort using IE4, you'll see a dialog box like the one in Figure 42.15, which may include an estimate of the amount of time remaining for the file to download.

Figure 42.15

You'll see this progress dialog box whenever Internet Explorer downloads a file to your computer.

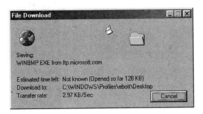

 T I P If you minimize the Download dialog box, you'll see the progress of your download in the label and ScreenTip of the Taskbar button. You can close the browser window or switch to another page without interrupting the download.

Logging On to Password-Protected FTP Servers

Many FTP servers allow anonymous access without a designated user name and password. Microsoft, for example, uses its FTP server to freely distribute patches and updates for Windows and other products. Internet Explorer handles anonymous logons easily. Other FTP servers, however, may refuse to allow logon unless you enter valid account information; this is especially true of corporate sites intended for use only by employees and other authorized users. Because Internet Explorer does not properly respond to password prompts from FTP servers, you'll have to construct a custom URL to connect to a password-protected FTP server. Click in the Address bar and enter the URL in the following format:

ftp://<username>:<password>@<ftp_server>/<url-path>

Substitute the proper username, password, and FTP server address in the preceding example.

Using Windows 98's FTP Client

Because Internet Explorer offers only the most basic FTP capabilities, it is incapable of connecting properly with some FTP servers. If you encounter such a server, use the Windows 98 command-line FTP client instead. Follow these steps to download a file from **ftp.microsoft.com**; the same techniques should work with any site:

1. Click Start, and choose Run.

2. In the Open box, type **ftp** and press Enter.

3. At the ftp> prompt, type **open ftp.microsoft.com**.

Part

VII

Ch

42

4. Enter **anonymous** as the username; although any password will do on an anonymous FTP server, the widely accepted custom is for you to enter your e-mail address as the password.

5. Use the **cd** command to navigate to the proper directory, and **ls** or **dir** to list the contents of the current directory.

6. If the file you want to download is a binary (non-text) file, enter **bin** and press Enter.

7. Type **get filename** to begin the download (substitute the name of the file for *filename*). To retrieve multiple files, type **mget filespec** (*filespec* can include wildcards, such as *.zip).

8. When your FTP session is finished, enter **close** to disconnect from the server and **quit** to close the FTP window.

For rudimentary help with FTP commands, type **help** at the FTP> prompt.

If you use FTP regularly, invest in a full-featured FTP client such as FTP Explorer. You'll find this shareware product at

http://www.ftpx.com

CHAPTER 43

Web Subscriptions and the Active Desktop

by Ed Bott

In this chapter

Adding Web Content to the Active Desktop

The Active Desktop represents a key change to the Windows interface. While the classic Windows 95 interface uses the desktop simply as a holding area for icons, the Active Desktop treats the entire Windows desktop as if it were a Web page. You can still store icons there, but you can also add live Web pages, components written in HTML, ActiveX controls, and Java applets. To see the Active Desktop in operation, look at Figure 43.1.

Figure 43.1
Add live Web content, including the headline and stock tickers shown here, to the Active Desktop.

N O T E Don't confuse the Active Desktop with the Windows Desktop Update. The Windows Desktop Update, standard in Windows 98, makes sweeping changes to the Start menu, taskbar, Explorer, and other parts of the Windows interface. The Windows Desktop Update offers a number of options, including the choice of Web-style single-click navigation or the traditional double-click style. The Active Desktop is one choice in the Windows Desktop Update, but even if you choose to disable Web-based content on the desktop, the other changes in the Windows Desktop Update remain in place. ▪

When you choose Web style as your preferred interface, the Active Desktop is automatically enabled. If you choose Classic style, on the other hand, the Active Desktop is automatically disabled, and your desktop looks and acts like Windows 95.

▶ **See** "Choosing a Browsing Style," **page 16**

You can enable or disable the Active Desktop at any time, regardless of which navigation style you've chosen. Follow these steps:

1. Right-click on any empty space on the desktop and choose <u>A</u>ctive Desktop from the shortcut menu.

2. To enable or disable the Active Desktop, select the View As <u>W</u>eb Page option. A check mark appears in front of this menu choice when the Active Desktop is enabled.

3. To hide or show individual Web items, select <u>A</u>ctive Desktop, <u>C</u>ustomize my Desktop. Uncheck items on the Web tab of the Display Properties dialog box to prevent them from displaying on the Active Desktop. Restore an item's check mark to once again show it on the Active Desktop.

 T I P What good is information on the Active Desktop if your application windows cover it up? To quickly clear away all windows, use the Show Desktop button on the Quick Launch toolbar.

Using an HTML Page as Your Desktop

If you're a skilled Web page designer, it's a trivial task to create a custom page that organizes essential information and links. In corporate settings, using a standard HTML-based background page can be an excellent way to ensure that every user has access to the same crucial information on the Intranet. Windows 98 allows you to specify an HTML page as the desktop background, just as previous versions of Windows allowed you to use a graphic image as wallpaper.

You can use any HTML editor, including FrontPage Express, to create your background page. Think of this page as the base layer of the Active Desktop: Standard desktop icons sit on top of this layer, and you can add other Web elements as well. The HTML page you use as your Windows background can include hyperlinks, graphics (including a company logo), tables, HTML components, and ActiveX controls.

▶ **See** "Introducing FrontPage Express," **page 926**

After you've created the background page, save it to local or network storage. To begin using the page as your desktop background, follow these steps:

1. Right-click on any empty space on the desktop and choose P<u>r</u>operties.

2. In the Display Properties dialog box, click the Background tab (see Figure 43.2).

3. Click the <u>B</u>rowse button to display the Browse dialog box. Select the HTML file you want to use as the desktop, then click <u>O</u>pen.

4. Click <u>A</u>pply to see your new background immediately.

5. Click OK to close the Display Properties dialog box.

Figure 43.2

Create a custom Web page and use it in place of wallpaper to make a truly custom interface.

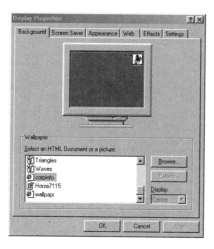

 If you prefer to see only your custom background when you view the Active Desktop, open the Display Properties dialog box, click the Effects tab, and choose <u>H</u>ide icons when the desktop is viewed as a Web page. To switch between the Active Desktop and the desktop icons, right-click any empty space on the desktop, choose <u>A</u>ctive Desktop from the shortcut menu, and enable or disable the View As <u>W</u>eb Page choice.

Displaying Objects on the Active Desktop

Enabling the Active Desktop lets you use the Windows desktop to display a wide variety of content. You can add:

- An HTML page as the Windows background; unlike wallpaper, this background can contain text, hyperlinks, images, and HTML code.
- One or more Web pages, each in its own self-contained region.
- Web components, including ActiveX controls and Java applets.
- Active Channels, which let you download prepackaged collections of Web content for offline browsing.
- Pictures, stored locally or from a Web server.

Adding a New Web Page to the Active Desktop

Before adding a new Web page to the Active Desktop, create an Internet shortcut to the page. Then follow these steps:

1. Right-click any empty space on the desktop and choose P<u>r</u>operties from the shortcut menu. The Display Properties dialog box appears. Select the Web tab to display the dialog box shown in Figure 43.3.

Figure 43.3

Enter a filename or Web address to add pictures or entire Web pages to your Active Desktop.

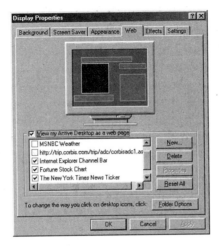

2. Click the New button. (Choose No if you're prompted to connect to Microsoft's gallery of Active Desktop components.)

3. If you know the exact filename or URL of the item you wish to add, enter it. Otherwise, click the Browse button.

4. The Browse dialog box displays only files you can add to the Active Desktop—typically images and Internet shortcuts. Select the item you wish to add and click Open.

5. Click OK. If you entered an Internet shortcut, you'll see the dialog box shown in Figure 43.4. Click the Customize Subscription option if you need to enter a password or reschedule updates. Click OK to continue.

Figure 43.4

Use this button to customize login and update options for Web pages on the Active Desktop.

6. The new object appears in the list at the bottom of the Web tab. Note that the screen display at the top of the dialog box shows the approximate position of each desktop item. Click Apply to display the new item and add another. Click OK to save your changes and close the dialog box.

 There's a far easier way to add a new element to the Active Desktop. First, view the Web page or open the graphic file in the browser window; size the window so you can see a portion of the desktop. To add a Web page, hold down the right mouse button and drag the icon from the left of the address bar onto the desktop. To add a picture to the Active Desktop, right-drag the image onto the desktop. Choose Create Active Desktop Item (or Image) Here.

To move or resize objects on the Active Desktop, let the mouse pointer hover over the object until a gray border appears around the object. Click on the thick bar at the top of the object and drag it to a new location. Use the borders to resize the windows itself. Scroll bars will appear if the object is larger than the window you've created.

Placing a Picture on the Active Desktop

The Classic Windows 95 interface lets you add one graphic, centered or tiled, as wallpaper on the Windows desktop. Using the Active Desktop, you can add multiple pictures to the desktop and rearrange them as you see fit. You can use saved image files, such as a family picture or a postcard of your favorite tropical resort. Or you can select a Web-based image that is regularly updated, such as a weather or traffic map.

> **N O T E**   The Active Desktop supports three standard graphic file formats: Windows Bitmap (BMP), GIF, and JPEG File Interchange Format (JPEG). GIF and JPEG are the most common graphic formats on the Internet. ▪

For photographs and other images that remain static, your best strategy is to create the Active Desktop item from a file stored on your local drive. Linking to a graphic file on a Web site forces the browser to try to update the file for no good reason. To save an image you find on a Web page, right-click on the image and choose Save Picture As from the shortcut menu. Give the picture a meaningful name, and store it where you can find it later.

▶ **See** "Saving and Editing Web Pages," **page 899**

> **CAUTION**
>
> Images and other original elements on most Web sites are protected by copyright. Displaying an image file on your personal desktop is generally considered acceptable, but reusing a copyrighted graphic on a commercial Web site without permission could land you in court.

Adding a Component to the Active Desktop

Unlike Web pages, which sometimes have to be forced into service as an Active Desktop object, components are made for this very purpose. A component can be a simple scrap of HTML, or it can include an ActiveX control or a Java applet. Some components are actually mini-programs that you can customize to match your own preferences.

 Microsoft's Active Desktop Gallery includes an assortment of interesting desktop components, including a useful search box, stock tickers, and several clocks. Browse the entire collection at:

> **http://www.microsoft.com/ie/ie40/gallery**

Adding a new component to your Active Desktop is simple. In most cases, the Web page designer will include an Add to Active Desktop button, like the example shown in Figure 43.5. Click this button to download and install the component.

Figure 43.5

Choose a component like this weather map from Microsoft's gallery, then click the button to add it to your desktop.

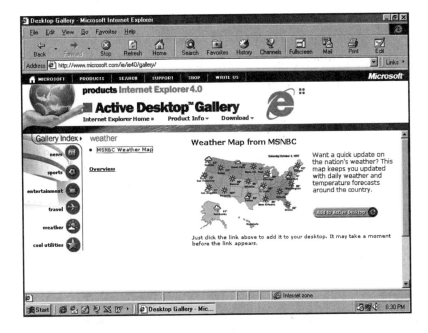

Hiding, Removing, and Editing Objects

You don't have to display every installed component, picture, and Web site on your Active Desktop. Hide objects you use infrequently so that they remain available when you need them. To display, hide, remove, or edit objects on the Active Desktop, right-click the desktop, then choose Properties. Select the Web tab in the Display Properties dialog box.

- ■ To hide an object, clear the check box next to its entry. The object remains in your list of installed objects.
- ■ To remove an object from the list, select the object and click Delete. The object will be permanently removed from your system.
- ■ To adjust the subscription settings for the object, click the Properties button.

Click OK to accept your changes.

Using Subscriptions to Download Web Pages

When you subscribe to a Web site, you instruct IE4 to regularly visit the site in search of new content. Don't let the term *subscription* mislead you; there's no fee associated with the process. Subscriptions are simply a way for you to automatically search for and download content from your favorite sites.

If you can load a Web page into the browser window, you can subscribe to it. You can specify the amount of information to download from the site, although this capability is limited and might not produce the results you're expecting.

You can also subscribe to Active Channels—prepackaged collections of Web content that include a site map and a recommended schedule for updates. With the help of Channel Definition Format (CDF) files, a Webmaster can assemble just the information you need, and not a page more.

> **CAUTION**
>
> With an IE4 subscription, you can instruct the browser to retrieve a given page and all pages linked to it, to a depth of as many as three pages. On Web sites that contain large collections of files, this "Web crawling" can cause an unacceptable performance hit. For this reason, some sites ban Web crawlers, and you'll find that your subscriptions to these sites won't update correctly.

Subscribing to Web Sites

To subscribe to a Web site, you start by adding it to your Favorites list. Follow these steps:

1. Open the Web page in the browser window.
2. Choose Favorites, Add to Favorites. Rename the shortcut, if you wish, and choose a folder. Note that the Add Favorite dialog box includes two subscription options, as shown in Figure 43.6.

Figure 43.6
Choose one of these options to add a Web page to your Subscriptions list.

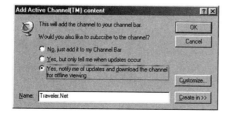

T I P When you subscribe to a Web site, IE4 adds a shortcut in your Favorites folder and in the Subscriptions folder. Deleting the shortcut in the Favorites folder does not delete your subscription, nor does deleting a subscription remove the entry from your Favorites list. The property sheet for an Internet shortcut includes extra tabs when you've subscribed to that site.

3. If you simply want IE4 to notify you when new content is available on this page, choose Yes, but only tell me when this page is updated. Click OK to accept these settings and skip all remaining steps.
4. To set up a subscription that automatically downloads content from the specified Web site, choose Yes, notify me of updates, and download the page for offline viewing.
5. Default subscription settings download only the specified page; the update is scheduled daily at 1:00 a.m. To accept these settings, click OK and skip all remaining steps.
6. If the Web site to which you're subscribing requires a password for access, or if you want to adjust any other subscription properties, click the Customize button. That launches the Subscription Wizard, shown in Figure 43.7.

Figure 43.7

To customize subscription options, follow the wizard's prompts.

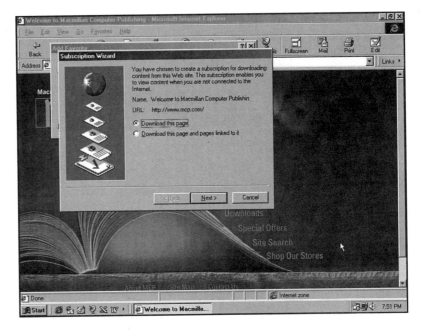

The wizard includes four options (for further details on each of these options, see the following section):

- Download pages linked to the specified page. Choose a number between 1 and 3.
- Ask IE4 to send you an e-mail message when the page is updated.
- Adjust the schedule IE4 uses to update this subscription. Choose daily, weekly, monthly, or custom options.
- Enter a username and password if the site requires it.

7. When you've finished the Subscription Wizard, click OK to add the entry to your Subscriptions list.

Managing Subscriptions

Internet Explorer maintains your list of subscribed sites in the \Windows\Subscriptions folder. Special extensions to the Windows Explorer let you view subscription details, edit update schedules, and delete sites when you no longer want to subscribe.

To open the Subscriptions folder, choose Favorites, Manage Subscriptions. You'll see a window like the one in Figure 43.8.

Select one or more sites from the list and use the right-click shortcut menus to open, copy, delete, or update the selection. Select a single site and choose Properties to adjust the subscription's settings.

Figure 43.8

Switch to Details view to see information about each entry in the list, including error messages from the last update attempt.

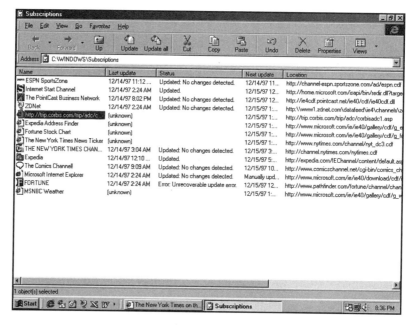

Customizing Subscriptions

By default, each subscription downloads one page, once a day, around 1:00 a.m. For most subscriptions, you'll probably want to change those defaults. Most often, you'll want to increase the amount of content that IE4 downloads as well as the update schedule.

You can adjust all the following options when you first create a subscription, using the Subscription Wizard. To change a subscription's properties, open the Subscriptions folder, right-click the entry for the site, and choose Properties from the shortcut menu. Select the Subscription, Receiving, or Schedule tabs and make any of the following changes.

Controlling the Size and Depth of Subscriptions   Chances are you'll want to see more than one page for your favorite Web sites. On the front page of a newspaper like the *Los Angeles Times*, for example, you'll usually find links to the day's top stories. When you go to those pages, you'll find links to still more stories.

As part of the settings for each subscription, you can tell IE4 to follow all the links on the subscribed page. For subscriptions you plan to read offline, it's crucial that you enter a number large enough to gather the information you need. But it's also important to monitor the amount of material that IE4 will have to download. The number of pages needing updating can increase dramatically with each additional layer. If you don't set the right limits when setting up a subscription, the downloaded content may consume all the space in your Temporary Internet Files folder.

TIP If you typically read only one portion of a Web site, don't start at the site's home page; instead, pick the site that contains the links you plan to follow. On highly structured sites, this page may be deep within the site. You may not be able to do this with an active server page or a page that was created in response to your query.

To define exactly which pages IE4 will download with each update, follow these steps:

1. Right-click the site's entry in the Subscriptions folder, then choose Properties.
2. Select the Receiving tab. You'll see a dialog box like the one in Figure 43.9, with the lower option selected in the Subscription type box.

Figure 43.9
If you've opted to download a subscription for offline viewing, click the Advanced button to adjust how much content to retrieve.

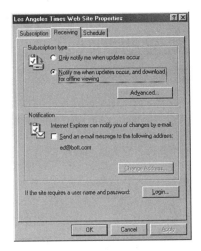

3. Click the Advanced button. The Advanced Download Options dialog box appears (see Figure 43.10).

Figure 43.10
Balance these options to download the right amount of content without consuming too much disk space.

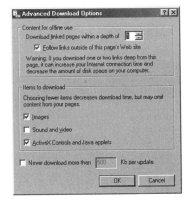

4. To download pages linked to the main page in your subscription, adjust the Download linked pages option. Enter a number between 1 and 3. To restrict the download to pages on the main site, clear the check box labeled <u>F</u>ollow links outside of this page's Web site.

5. To restrict the total amount of content downloaded with each update, check the box labeled Never download more than *x* Kb per update. Enter a limit in kilobytes (the default is 500 K).

6. To further limit downloads, review the list of options in the center of the dialog box. By default, IE4 gathers image files, ActiveX controls and Java applets, while not retrieving sound and video files.

CAUTION

Many Web pages use images to help with navigation and to supply information. Don't restrict image downloads unless you're certain a site will be useful in text-only mode.

---

7. Click OK or select another tab to further customize the subscription.

Specifying a Format for Update Notifications   How do you know when there's been a change in a Web site to which you subscribe? Look at any Internet shortcut, on the desktop, in the Favorites bar, in the Channel Bar, or in the Subscriptions window: A red gleam in the upper left corner of an icon means there's new content, as in Figure 43.11.

Figure 43.11

The star in the upper left corner of two icons means the latest update turned up new material.

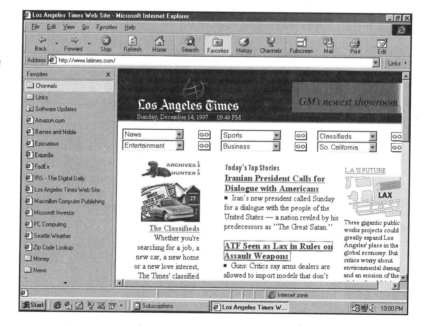

If you prefer a more emphatic notice, ask IE4 to send you an e-mail message every time it notices a change in a Web site to which you subscribe. The e-mail message can be a simple notice with a hyperlink, or it can contain a copy of the updated HTML page.

To set up e-mail updates, follow these steps:

1. Select an entry in the Subscriptions folder, right-click, and choose Properties.

2. Click the Receiving tab.

3. Choose one of the two Subscription types at the top of the dialog box. If you select the option to download content for offline viewing, IE4 will send you the page via e-mail.

4. Check the box labeled Send an e-mail message to the following address. If necessary, click the Change Address button and enter or change the address and server information.

5. Click OK to close the dialog box and save your changes.

Scheduling Automatic Updates   By default, IE4 updates your subscriptions once a day, at 1:00 a.m. You can adjust the update interval, if you wish, or set the subscription for manual updates only. You can also specify whether IE4 will dial your Internet connection automatically.

To adjust a subscription's update schedule, open the Subscriptions folder and select the Schedule tab. You'll see a dialog box like the one in Figure 43.12.

Figure 43.12

Use these options to control how and when IE4 updates your subscriptions.

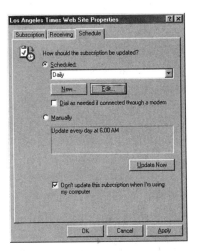

To use a regularly scheduled interval, choose the Scheduled option and select Daily, Weekly, or Monthly from the drop-down list. Click the Edit button to adjust the details of this schedule. For example, if you subscribe to an online magazine that appears every Friday at midnight, you can tell IE4 to update your subscription each Friday morning at 5:00 a.m., before you arrive at work.

Network administrators might be horrified at the thought of thousands of users requesting Web updates on the hour. IE4 attempts to minimize that problem by randomly varying the exact time for each update by a few minutes in either direction. To take maximum control over how users work with Internet Explorer 4.0, make sure you check the Internet Explorer Administrator's Kit, available from Microsoft. For more information about the most current release of IEAK, look here:

http://ieak.microsoft.com/

You can also create a custom schedule, using a dizzying variety of options. For example, if you have a favorite business-oriented site, you can set a subscription to update once an hour, from 8:00 a.m. through 5:00 p.m., every weekday. You can update a subscription every Monday, Wednesday, and Friday. You can even specify that a site update at 9:00 a.m. on the second Tuesday of every other month. When you save a custom schedule, you can reuse the schedule with other subscriptions as well.

To create a custom schedule for updates, follow these steps:

1. Select an entry in the Subscriptions folder, right-click, and choose Properties.
2. Click the Schedule tab and click the New button. The Custom Schedule dialog box (see Figure 43.13) opens.

Figure 43.13
Be sure to give each custom schedule a descriptive name, so you can reuse the schedule with other subscriptions.

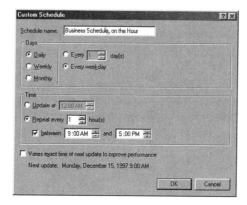

3. Choose the day or days to update. Select Daily, Weekly, or Monthly and adjust the available options that appear to the right.
4. Choose the time or times to perform the update. Options lets you repeat the update throughout the day; if the exact time of each update is not important, check the option to vary the exact time of each update to avoid causing network congestion.
5. Give the schedule a descriptive name and click OK.
6. Set two final options to tell Internet Explorer whether it should automatically dial up your Internet connection or update a subscription when you're working with your computer.
7. Click OK to save your changes.

Updating Subscriptions Manually　IE4 lets you manually update all your subscriptions with the click of one button. This capability is especially useful if you are about to leave on a trip and you want to make sure your notebook computer contains the most current versions of all your Web subscriptions. You can also update an individual site if you know there's new content and you don't want to wait for the next scheduled update.

To manually update all subscriptions, follow these steps:

1. Verify that you have a working Internet connection. If necessary, open a Dial-Up Networking connection.
2. If the Subscriptions folder is open, click the Update all button.
3. If the Subscriptions folder is not open or the toolbar is not visible, choose Favorites, Update All Subscriptions.
4. If you have a lengthy list of subscriptions to update, the process can take a long time. The Downloading Subscriptions dialog box (see Figure 43.14) displays the status of the operation, including any error messages that may appear. To cancel all further updates, click Stop. To skip over one site's update and proceed with the next site, click Skip. Click the Hide button to move this dialog box out of the way and continue working. You can close the browser window or view other sites while the update process continues.

Figure 43.14

If you don't see this full status window, click the Details button.

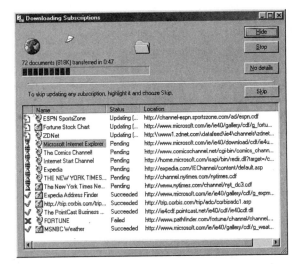

To update an individual subscription, follow these steps:

1. If the Subscriptions folder is open, click the Update button.
2. If the Subscriptions folder is not open or the toolbar is not visible, choose Favorites, Manage Subscriptions.
3. Right-click the name of the site you want to update and choose Update Now.

If you subscribe to a site that rarely changes or one you rarely visit, you can tell IE4 to update that subscription only when you manually choose to do so. Right-click on the subscription icon and choose Properties. Click the Schedule tab and choose the option labeled Manually. The Update Now button at the bottom of this dialog box also lets you refresh the subscription with the most current content.

Subscribing to Password-Protected Sites   Sites like the Wall Street Journal **(http://www.wsj.com)** require that you enter a username and password before browsing their site. If you're using IE4 interactively, you can type the information directly into a login box. When you subscribe to a password-protected site, IE4 lets you include the login information so that you can get the information you're looking for automatically.

You do not have to subscribe to the specific page that includes the login screen. You can subscribe to a page above the login screen and specify a depth of delivery that reaches below the login screen. When IE4 reaches the page that requests your user ID and password, it supplies them and continues updating the subscription.

To enter a username and password for use with a Web subscription, follow these steps:

1. If you are initially creating the subscription, click the Login button. If you are editing an existing subscription, right-click its entry in the Subscriptions folder, then click Properties. Click the Schedule tab and click the Login button to display the Login Options dialog box (see Figure 43.15).

Figure 43.15

Enter login information here for IE4 to gain access to password-protected sites when updating a subscription.

2. Enter the user name and password you use to gain access to the site. Make sure both entries are spelled correctly and that the case (the mix of capital and lower-case letters) is correct.

3. Click OK to return to the Schedule tab. Click OK again to close the dialog box and save your changes.

After setting up a subscription to a password-protected site, it's always a good idea to verify that it works. Update the subscription manually; if the update fails because of an incorrect username or password, try logging in manually to make sure the site is working and the information you enter is correct. Then edit the subscription's username and password to match those you've tested.

Speeding Up Subscription Updates

If you're about to hit the road and you're running short on time, two shortcuts can dramatically reduce the time it takes to update all the subscriptions on your notebook. First, cut the update list to the bare minimum. Choose Favorites, Manage Subscriptions, and hold down the Ctrl key as you select the sites you want to update. When you're finished, right-click and choose Update Now from the shortcut menu.

To speed the update process even more (and save precious disk space), tell IE4 to concentrate on text and ignore large graphics and media files. Note that some sites use images for navigation, and at other sites images may contain important information; as a result, the pages you end up with when you use this technique may be of limited use. Still, when time is short, you can follow these steps:

1. Open the Subscriptions dialog box.
2. Right-click on each site you plan to update, choose Properties, and click the Delivery tab.
3. Click the Advanced button to open the Advanced Download Options dialog box.
4. In the Items to download box, clear the check mark next to the options labeled Images, Sound and video, and ActiveX Controls and Java applets.
5. Repeat steps 2–4 for each subscription you plan to update.
6. Select the group of icons to update, right-click, and choose Update.

Subscribing to Active Channels

Channels are prepackaged subscriptions. Instead of indiscriminately delivering Web pages to your hard disk, a Webmaster can put together a collection of pages, just as a newspaper publisher assembles a daily paper. When you subscribe to an Active Channel, you download a single file, created using the Channel Definition Format (CDF). Channel files typically include multiple HTML files, graphics, a map of the Web site (including links to pages not included in the CDF file), and a publisher's recommended schedule for updates.

By default, Windows 98 adds a Channel Bar to your desktop, with shortcuts to dozens of brand-name channels. Note that you don't have to subscribe to view the content in a channel.

The Channel Bar contains an Internet shortcut that takes you to Microsoft's Active Channel Guide. Browse through this lengthy list by category, or search for keywords using the built-in search button. The Active Channel Guide, shown in Figure 43.16, is updated frequently.

 ON THE WEB

If you inadvertently delete the Channel Guide shortcut from the Channel Bar, don't worry. You'll find the latest list of Active Channels at

http://www.iechannelguide.com

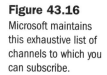

Figure 43.16
Microsoft maintains
this exhaustive list of
channels to which you
can subscribe.

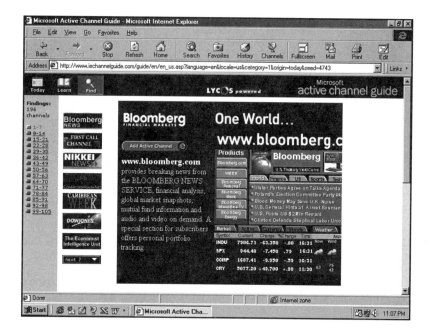

Adding a Channel to the Channel Bar

Most channels include an Add Active Channel button that allows you to add its shortcut to
the Channel bar. When you add a channel to the Channel bar, you typically have the option to
subscribe to the channel, using the publisher's recommended schedule or a custom schedule
of your choosing; if there's no Add This Channel button on the preview pane in the Channel
Guide, right-click and choose Subscribe from the site icon at left.

Viewing Channels

When you click on a shortcut in the Channel Bar on the Windows desktop, Internet Explorer
opens in full-screen mode, with the Channel Bar visible along the left side of the browser
window.

Although the Channel Bar in the browser window includes the same sites as its desktop counterpart, the two bars behave differently. In the browser's bar, for example, the icon for each
channel is black and white until the mouse pointer passes over it. When you click on a shortcut, the channel's home page opens in the pane to the right. If the CDF file for that channel
includes a site map, clicking the channel button will open the list of available pages.

 TIP   You can view channels as ordinary Web pages, as desktop components, or in full-screen mode. To
specify whether IE4 should use full-screen mode for all channels, choose View, Internet Options, click
the Advanced tab, and check the option labeled Launch Channels in full-screen window.

Some channels include a screen-saver view as well. You may see this option during the initial Channel setup. To enable, disable, or adjust the Channel screen saver at any time, right-click on the desktop, choose Properties, click the Screen Saver tab, and choose the Channel Screen Saver option.

▶ **See** "Using the Screen Saver," **page 138**

When you view a channel in full-screen mode, the Channel bar slides off the screen when you read the page; it reappears when you move the pointer to the left edge of the screen. If you're running at a high screen resolution, use the pushpin icon to lock the Channel bar in place, as we've done in Figure 43.17.

Figure 43.17
Watch the colorful logo appear when the mouse pointer passes over each entry in the Channel Bar.

Pushpin icon —

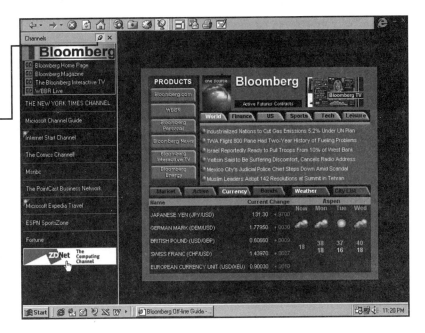

Browsing Channels Offline

To view Channels and other subscriptions without making an active Internet connection, choose File, Work Offline. Like all subscriptions, Active Channels share the Temporary Internet Files with pages you browse interactively. When the cache fills up, IE4 pitches the oldest pages to make way for the newest ones.

▶ **See** "Browsing the Web Offline," **page 896**

If you encounter frequent error messages when you attempt to update or view subscriptions, you may have used all the available space in your Temporary Internet Files folder. To make room for more content, increase the size of the Web cache.

▶ **See** "Managing the Browser's Cache," **page 881**

N O T E   Don't be surprised when you discover that some channels actually provide only a table of contents and links. Although these sites can give you a good idea of what's available when you go back online, you won't find enough information to justify keeping a subscription to this sort of channel. ▨

Managing the Channel Bar

The Channel Bar appears on the Desktop when you install Windows 98. It also appears as an Explorer bar within the browser window when you click the Channels button.

By default, the Channel Bar includes built-in shortcuts to channels delivered by some well-known companies, including Disney, America Online, and MSNBC (see Figure 43.18). There are also shortcuts to categories—news, entertainment, and business, for example—which include shortcuts to additional channels.

Figure 43.18
Out of the box, the Channel Bar includes these preset selections. You can change the collection of shortcuts and rearrange the Channel Bar itself.

Although the Channel Bar initially gets a place of honor on the Windows desktop, it's really just another HTML component on the Active Desktop. That means you can customize its look and feel to suit your computing style. After you've sampled the selection of built-in channels and subscribed to a handful, give your Channel Bar a makeover, as we've done in Figure 43.19.

Figure 43.19
After deleting unnecessary channels and changing its size and orientation, this Channel Bar looks vastly different from its default settings.

- To move the Channel Bar to a different location on the desktop, click on any empty desktop space, then let the mouse pointer hover over the top of the bar until the gray sizing handle pops up (see Figure 43.19). Click and drag to a new location.

- To resize the Channel Bar, aim the mouse pointer at the bar and wait for a thin gray border to appear. Click on any border and drag to change the size and orientation. Note that as the size of the bar changes, shortcuts on the bar reorder themselves automatically.

- To add or delete channels from the bar, right-click on any channel icon and choose <u>D</u>elete from the shortcut menu.

CAUTION
Be careful before deleting any of the category icons on the Channel bar. If you've subscribed to a channel within that category, you'll lose easy access to the channel.

- To rearrange channels on the bar, simply drag them to the location you prefer. Other shortcuts on the bar will rearrange themselves automatically.

- To remove the Channel Bar from the desktop, let the mouse pointer hover over the top of the bar until the gray sizing handle pops up. Click the X in the top-right corner.

 The Channel Bar on the desktop is identical to the one that appears in the browser window. When you add or remove channels from one, the other changes accordingly. If you'd rather use the Windows desktop for other items, close the Channel Bar there and use the Channels button on the Internet Explorer toolbar when you want to work with channels.

CHAPTER 44

Creating and Publishing Web Documents

by Paul Sanna

Introducing FrontPage Express

The best way to introduce a product is state exactly what the product is. FrontPage Express is a WYSIWYG HTML page editor. Given that definition, you may be confused, having thought that FrontPage Express was a tool used for building Web pages, something like Microsoft Word for the Internet. Both descriptions are accurate. FrontPage Express' sole purpose is to build pages to be viewed in a web browser either over the Internet or local corporate intranets. Lets take a quick look at what HTML and WYSIWYG mean.

Like most design products today, FrontPage is WYSIWYG, which stands for *what you see is what you get*. This means that you see exactly how your page will appear in a browser *as* you build it. This allows you to build web pages quickly and accurately, without having to worry *later* about how your design decisions will appear in a browser.

HTML stands for *hypertext markup language*. This means that in HTML, special character codes are inserted into text to generate particular effects, such as bold face or the appearance of a graphic, hyperlink or a table. When a browser opens a page, the browser reads and then translates the HTML into to the text and images you see on the screen.

▶ **See** Chapter 41, "Web Browsing with IE 4," **page 857**

You will see a few examples of HTML in this chapter, but fortunately, you will not have to write any HTML. The reason for this is that FrontPage Express develops the HTML for you. As you lay out your pages in FrontPage Express, the HTML is automatically being written behind the scenes. When you save your work, FrontPage Express saves the HTML required to present the page you have developed.

So, now that you have an introduction to FrontPage Express and its capabilities, lets look next and how to use it.

Launching FrontPage Express

You can launch FrontPage Express either from the Start menu or from Internet Explorer browser. When you launch Front Page Express from the browser, the page you were viewing is loaded directly into FrontPage Express. By using this technique, FrontPage Express gives you the capability to edit any pages you see on the World Wide Web directly at your desktop with FrontPage Express. Naturally, you won't be able to change the Web pages you're viewing (unless you are working on a web to which you have rights), but this gives you a great way to see first-hand how real-life web pages are built. In addition, if you are working on an existing web, say for your company or organization, this method makes it easy to select the page you want to work without having to attach or access the server where the pages are stored.

Here are the two methods you can use to launch FrontPage Express:

■ To launch FrontPage Express from the Start menu, open the Start menu, choose <u>P</u>rograms, Internet Explorer, and then FrontPage Express. a new blank web page is displayed.

To launch FrontPage Express from Internet Explorer, choose Edit, Page from the menu, or click the Edit button on the Standard Buttons toolbar. The page you are viewing in the browser is opened in FrontPage Express (see Figure 44.1).

A blank page is displayed when you launch FrontPage Express from the menu.

Figure 44.1

The page you were viewing in Internet Explorer opens in FrontPage Express when you choose Edit from the browser.

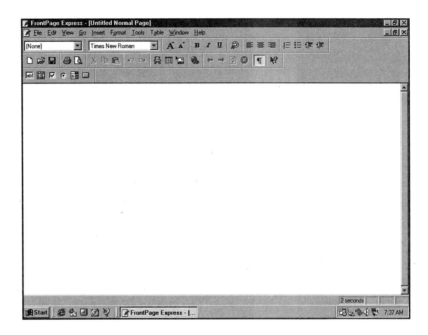

Opening Page

You can open existing pages stored locally or on an existing web. Follow these steps to open a page.

1. Choose File, Open from the menu.
2. If you are opening a page that has not yet been published to a web, or if it is stored locally, then choose the From File option. Enter the name of the file in the edit box. Use the Browse button if you need help locating the file and/or entering its name and location. Choose OK.
3. If you are opening a page that already has been published to a web, even a page that you have not developed, choose the From Location option. Next, enter the URL and the name of the page in the edit box, and choose OK.

Hiding and Displaying Toolbars

FrontPage Express includes three toolbars. Like toolbars in other applications, the toolbar in FrontPage Express show buttons for common tasks, such as changing text size, indenting, inserting an image, and more. Unlike many applications, however, you cannot modify the buttons on any of the toolbars, nor where any toolbar appears in the FrontPage Express window.

Here is a description of each of the toolbars:

- *Standard.* The Standard toolbar provides many buttons you see on toolbars in other applications, such as New, Open, and Save. In addition, it provides access to the Insert WebBot, Insert Table, and Image buttons.

- *Format.* The Format toolbar gives you access to most of the choices that appear on the Format Menu, such as the style, font, and color selections. You will use the Format toolbar when you are formatting text you have entered onto your page.

- *Forms.* You will use the Forms toolbar when you are creating a web page that contains standard Windows controls, such as a push button or drop-down list. The Forms toolbar provides you access to the buttons that add these control to the page.

You can hide or display any of the four toolbars. To display or hide a toolbar, just choose <u>V</u>iew from the menu and choose the appropriate toolbar from the menu. If a check appears beside the toolbar name, then the toolbar is already displayed. If a check does appear beside a toolbar name and you select the toolbar, it becomes hidden. Figure 44.2 shows each of the three toolbars.

Standard

Figure 44.2
You can display all three of the FrontPage Express toolbars at one time.

Forms   Format

Saving Your Work

At some point, you will want to save the work you have completed on your web page. You have two choices for saving Web pages. You can save your work to a file or to an existing Web. How you originally opened the page and whether you have started a Web will determine which choice you make. Here are your options:

- *If your Web has not yet been started*, save your page to a file (instructions below). You will publish your pages to a web later.

- *If your Web has been started and you are adding a new page*, save your page to the Web, and be sure you provide the hyperlinks to the page. To do so, choose <u>F</u>ile, Save <u>A</u>s, choose Location, and then supply the URL and the name of the file.

- *If you are editing page on your Web*, just choose <u>F</u>ile, <u>S</u>ave, and you will update the Web with your new changes.

- *If you are editing a page from a Web you don't control*, you probably will not be able to save to someone else's web, so you can save the page to a file or save it to your own Web.

To save a page you are working on to a file, follow these steps:

1. Choose File, Save As from the menu.
2. From the Save As dialog box, choose As File.
3. Select a directory from the Save As File dialog box, enter a name for the file, and then choose Save.

Creating Web Pages Instantly

Almost all of the information presented in this chapter that helps you build Web pages uses FrontPage Express' long list of features. FrontPage Express provides, however, templates and wizards that remove much of the manual work that normally is involved with developing a page, such as positioning and formatting text. The list of templates and wizards are displayed when you choose File, New from the menu (see Figure 44.3).

Figure 44.3
You see the list of templates and page wizards available when you choose File, New.

The following sections explain how to use the templates and wizards.

Using the Personal Home Page Wizard

Many Internet Service Providers (ISPs) and on-line services host web pages and even web sites for their subscribers, sometimes at no additional cost. Many universities and colleges also provide this service to their students. This means that even persons without access to the hardware required to run a web server can establish a presence on the Web. Many times, this presence is nothing more than a personal home page with a number of links that provides an update on the life and activities of the person who posted the page.

The only requirement for this type of presence is for the user to supply the content. FrontPage Express makes it easy to develop these types of pages with the Personal Home Page Wizard. This wizard walks the user through the steps required to create a personal page. When you have answered all of the questions posed by the wizard, an attractive page is created that you may then submit to the service that is hosting your web page. Your only work is to supply the details into the preformatted sections, which are created based on your responses to the wizard.

Here is the type of information you can supply using the Personal Home Page Wizard:

- Your employment
- Projects you're working on
- Your favorite web sites
- Biographical information
- Your interests
- Information on how to contact you
- A form to send information or comments to you

To use the Personal Home Page Wizard, follow these steps:

1. Choose File, New from the menu. The New Page dialog box appears.

2. Select Personal Home Page Wizard from the Template or Wizard list box, and then choose OK. The Personal Home Page Wizard dialog appears.

3. From the Personal Home Page Wizard, select what type of content you would like included on your home page. Keep in mind that the Wizard will create just one page rather than a web of linked page. This means that the more items you select from the Personal Home Page Wizard, the longer your home page would be. After making your selections, choose Next.

4. In the next dialog, specify the name of the page as it will be stored on the Web in the Page URL box. In the Page Title edit box, enter the name of the page as it will appear in the browser.

5. Depending on the choices you made in step 3, you will next be presented with a series of dialogs where you supply personal information that the Wizard uses to build your page. For example, if you chose to include biographical information, you would be prompted to select whether to include academic information, such as the institution, date, or degree, professional, such as company and title, or personal, such as date and important milestone. Obviously, the content and number of dialogs will vary based on the types of information you want to provide. Choose Next to move to the next dialog box, or choose Back to change information already provided.

6. When the wizard has collected all of the information it needs to build your page, you are prompted with a dialog box similar to the one shown in Figure 44.4.

   The dialog includes a list box that shows each of the major sections of your personal home page wizard. This is your opportunity to choose the order in which the sections appear on the page. Choose a section and then click either the Up or Down button to specify the order of the sections.

7. Choose Finish from the final dialog box. Next, the almost-completed page appears in a window in FrontPage Express. Review the page, and replace any of the instructions with the information required, as shown in Figure 44.5.

Figure 44.4

You can choose the order of sections on your personal home page.

Figure 44.5

When the wizard has completed building your page, you supply some of the detailed information yourself.

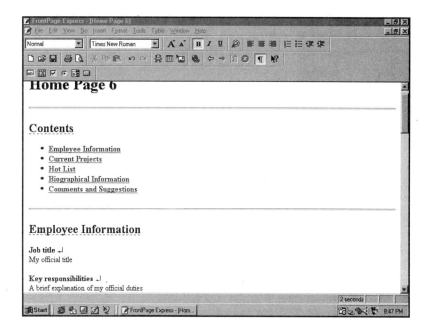

Using the Form Page Wizard

The Form Page Wizard is used to create a web page that collects different types of information from the person viewing the page in a browser. Examples of form pages you might create are order forms if you were selling over the Internet or a list of questions of you were conducting a survey. Form pages can contain many of the controls used today in Windows applications (see Figure 44.6). Controls are the on-screen elements used in Windows and in Windows application to operate the system, such as list boxes, buttons, check boxes, and more. The Form Page Wizard automatically creates controls on the page necessary to collect the information you require from the user.

Figure 44.6

Web pages can use many of the controls used in non-Web applications.

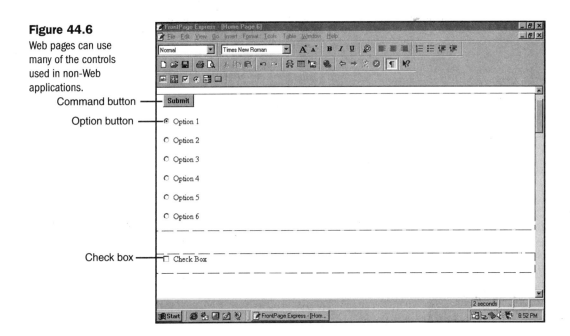

There is an important point you should understand about the Form Page Wizard. Your work is not close to complete after the wizard has created your page. The wizard will build many of the controls your page requires based on your responses. Most of the logic required to put your page to work, such as validating that a zip code supplied does not contain non-numeric values or calculating the total amount of an order, must be completed without the help of the wizard. This warning is not meant to discourage you from using the wizard, though, only to inform you that the wizard alone will not build a fully-functioning form.

The steps below will get you started with the Form Page Wizard.

1. Choose File, New from the menu. The New Page dialog box appears.

2. Select Form Page Wizard from the Template or Wizard list box, and then choose OK. The Form Page Wizard dialog appears.

3. Choose Next.

4. Specify the name of the page as it will be stored on the Web in the Page URL box. In the Page Title edit box, enter the name of the page as it will appear in the browser.

5. Choose Next. If the file you specified in step 4 already exists, the wizard will scan the page you specified for any content it believes to be form-related. This makes it easy for you to take an existing form page and modify it, or to continue work on a page you've already started.

   If the wizard finds any questions, they will appear in the list shown in the dialog box. To add new a question to the form, or to add the first question to your form if the page is new or the existing page was not a form, choose Add. A list of possible types of information your form can collect appears (see Figure 44.7).

Figure 44.7

The Form Page Wizard can collect different types of information.

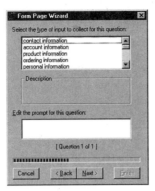

6. Scroll through the list presented and select the first of the types of information you want to collect on your form. Notice that when you select a particular type from the list, a note about the type appears in the Description frame beneath the list. Also notice that the prompt for the information, as it will appear to the person viewing your page, appears in the edit box at the bottom of the dialog box. If you like, you can customize the prompt by editing the text in the box. When you have selected the information type to collect, and perhaps edited the prompt, choose the Add button.

7. Depending on the type of information you selected, you may be presented with another dialog box requesting more detailed information about your prompt. For example, if you specified "contact information" in step 6, the Wizard will ask you if your form should request information form the user like Name, Title, Organization, Address, Phone. Answer the prompts in the dialog and choose Next.

8. The dialog box described in step 6 appears again. Choose the next type of information your form will request, and follow the instructions in step 7. Repeat steps 6–8 until the all of the information your form will request is reflected in the list box. If the list of prompts is complete, choose Finish. FrontPage Express builds the page and presents it on the screen.

9. Review the page, and replace any of the instructions with the information required. You can also customize many of the fields, such as by specifying the default value. The options available to any of the fields are displayed by double-clicking on the field.

Using Templates

Templates can also be used to quickly create content for the Web with FrontPage Express. The templates provided with FrontPage Express work differently than the wizards. As you learned in the previous section, the wizards collect information and then build the page for you based on your answers. Templates do not prompt you for information. Rather, you choose the type of page you want to build from the list of templates, and then FrontPage presents a preformatted page with a series of placeholders that you replace with your information. For example, if you create a page based on the Survey Form template, you would need to replace the sample questions provided by the template, such as "What is your favorite color," with the questions you want to include in your survey. Figure 44.8 shows a new page created from the Survey Form template.

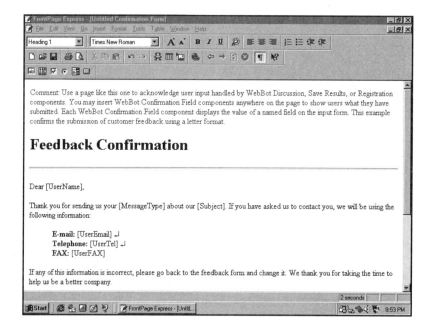

Follow these steps to create a page using a template:

1. Choose File, New from the menu. The New Page dialog box appears.
2. Select one of the templates from the list, and then choose OK.
3. The page appears on the screen. Review the page, and replace any of the instructions with the information required.

Formatting and Positioning Text

Entering text in FrontPage Express is very similar to entering text in any word processor. You click anywhere on the page and start entering text. You can also copy text from some other application and then paste it into your web page open in FrontPage Express. Once you have started entering text, you can begin formatting it, such as by specifying text and color for the text, special effects, breaking text into sections with lines.

▶ **See** "Using and Formatting Sections," **page 233**

You also specify where on the page text should appear. You can specify the position and alignment text on a line-by-line basis, or you can use built-in styles, which make it easy to apply groups of formatting commands in just one click. Here are the formatting topics covered in this section:

- Typeface, color, size, effects of text
- Alignment and indent/outdent of text
- Horizontal line effects
- Adding bullets and number to lists

Formatting Text

You format text in FrontPage Express much as you do with other Windows applications. You select the text to be formatted, and then make selections from either the toolbar or from choices on the Format menu.

To format text in FrontPage Express, follow these steps:

1. Select the text to be formatted.
2. Choose Format, Font from the menu.
3. To specify the typeface for the text, choose the font from the Font list.
4. To specify the style for the text, make a selection from the Font Style list. Keep in mind that the choices in the Style list will vary based on the Font selected.
5. To specify the size of the text, make a selection from the Size list box. Keep in mind that the choices in the Size list will vary based on the font selected.
6. Specify the text to be underlined, with a strikethrough effect, or with a typewriter font by selecting the appropriate check box(es) in the Effects group.
7. To select a color for the text, click on the arrow in the Color list and then select a color from the list displayed. To create a color, choose Custom from the list of colors.
8. To create a subscript or superscript effect, choose the Special Styles tab. Select the appropriate effect from the Vertical Position drop-down list, and then choose the amount of vertical offset from the By list.
9. Choose OK.

Positioning Text

To position text in FrontPage Express, you have two sets of options: 1) Use a combination of built-in styles, and indent/outdent and alignment commands, and 2) Use a table to layout your page and then position text within cells. The difference between the two is that the table option allows you more precision in locating text on the page, but adds an extra layer of work and complexity. The basic rule of thumb is to use a table to help you layout a page or a section of a page where graphics and text appear on the same line, such as in columns. Otherwise, the built-in styles and menu commands should suit your work.

▶ **See** "Creating and Editing Tables," **page 944**

To use one FrontPage Express' built-in paragraph styles and/or menu commands to position text, follow these steps:

1. Click anywhere in the paragraph to be formatted. You may also select all of the paragraphs that will be positioned the same way.

2. To indent the selected paragraphs, choose the Indent button from the Format toolbar.

   To outdent the selected paragraph(s), choose the Outdent button from the Format Toolbar.

   To choose a built-in style, choose one from the drop-down list on the Format toolbar. Table 44.1 provides a short description of each FrontPage Express built-in styles.

Table 44.1 FrontPage Express Built-In Styles

Style Name	Format
Address	Italics, no indent, double space
Bulleted List	Bullet and indented, single spaced
Defined Term	Single spaced, first line left align, subsequent lines indented
Definition	Single spaced, first line indented, subsequent lines further indented from first
Directory List	Same as bullet
Formatted	Bullet and single spaced
Heading 1	Bold face and left aligned
Heading 2	Bold face and left aligned
Heading 3	Bold face and left aligned
Heading 4	Bold face and left aligned
Heading 5	Bold face and left aligned
Heading 6	Bold face and left aligned
Menu List	Indented, bullet, and double-spaced
Numbered List	Same as standard numbered list

Creating Bullet and Numbered Lists

You can easily add a bullet or numbered list to your web pages. FrontPage Express provides a few styles of each, so you can customize your lists to a certain extent. You can quickly format a list as a bullet or numbered list from the Format toolbar, or you can make more specific choices form the Bullets and Numbering dialog box.

1. Enter the list of items to be bulleted on the page. Be sure to press Enter at the end of each line.

2. Select all the rows in the list.

3. To create a bullet list, click on the bullet list button the Format Toolbar. To create a numbered list, click the number list button on the Format toolbar.

To exert a bit more control on the appearance of the bullet or numbers, choose Format, Bullets and Numbering from the menu. Select either the Bulleted or Numbered tab, and then select the format. Choose OK.

Adding Horizontal Lines

You can add horizontal lines anywhere on your web page. These lines are useful for breaking your page into sections. You can specify the color, weight, alignment, and size of the line.

Part VII
Ch 44

To add a horizontal like, follow these steps:

1. Click on the page in the location where you want the horizontal line to appear.
2. Choose Insert, Horizontal Line from the menu. A line appears on the page. If you are content with the appearance of the line on the page, then your work is done. If you would like to customize the line, move to step 3.
3. Double-click anywhere on the line. The Horizontal Line Properties dialog box appears (see Figure 44.9).

Figure 44.9

You can customize the appearance of a horizontal line on your page.

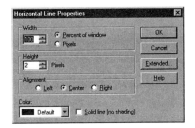

4. You can specify whether your line is a fixed length (in pixels) or whether it occupies a specific percentage of the width of your page. To do so, select either Percent of window or Pixels from the Width frame, and then enter the appropriate value in the scrolling list box.
5. Specify the height of the line (in pixels) in the height scrolling list.
6. Specify whether the line is left, center, or right-aligned by selecting the appropriate option from the Alignment group.
7. Select a color from the color drop-down list.
8. To create a solid line with no shadow effect, select the Solid line (no shading) check box.
9. Choose OK.

Creating Bookmarks

A bookmark is a label that points to a specific location on your page. Users don't see bookmarks. A bookmark is used with hyperlinks when you want to provide a link on a page to another location on the same page. As an example, if you want to provide a link from the table of contents which might appear on the top of the page to the relevant section later in the page, you would need to create a bookmark. The next section, "Inserting and Managing Hyperlinks," discusses hyperlinks.

Here is how you create a bookmark on your page:

1. Select the text for which to create a bookmark.

2. Choose Edit, Bookmark from the menu. The Bookmark dialog box appears (see Figure 44.10).

Figure 44.10

Creating a bookmark makes it easy to create a hyperlink to a specific position on a page.

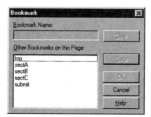

3. By default, the text you selected to bookmark will appear as the name of the bookmark. If this acceptable, choose OK. If you would like to specify other text as the bookmark, enter the text in the Bookmark Name edit box, and then choose OK.

Inserting and Managing Hyperlinks

The capabilities of HTML allow page developers to provide links to other web sites, and links on those web sites to others, and so on. Hyperlinks help the user navigate through the Web (or just through your site) through relevant, related information. This network of links creates the Web portion of the name World Wide Web. You will most likely want to provide hyperlinks on your pages to other locations on the Web.

To add a hyperlink, follow these steps:

1. Enter the text that will be used as a link. The text might be a word, or phrase, or a name that brings the user to a specific spot on the Web, or the link might be the actual URL for the location that will be linked. Keep in mind, the text that you want to use as a hyperlink may already have been entered. For example, you might provide a link from a word in a paragraph you entered when you first began developing the page.

N O T E You may choose to add hyperlinks when you have completed almost all of the other work on your page as compared to worrying about the links as you develop your page. You can add hyperlinks at any time, so you might choose to focus on the content of your page first, and then add hyperlinks at the end.

2. Select the text you entered in step 1.

3. Choose Insert, Hyperlink from the menu. The Create Hyperlink dialog box appears.

4. You can create a hyperlink to a page you already have open in FrontPage Express, to a page that already exists on the Web, or to a page that has not yet been created. The next three steps explain how to create each.

5. To create a link to a page already opened, including the current page, choose the Open Pages tab (see Figure 44.11). Each of the pages presently open in FrontPage Express appears in the Open Pages list. Click the name of the page and then OK to create the link. Keep in mind that this procedure will create a link to a specific file in a specific location in a directory. If the target file is moved to another directory, then the link will be come invalid.

To create a link to a bookmark on the same page, choose the page you are working on in the Open Pages list, and then choose the appropriate bookmark from the Bookmark drop-down list.

Part
VII

Ch
44

Figure 44.11
You can create a link to a page you already have open.

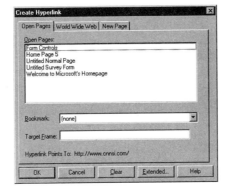

6. To create a link to an existing page on the World Wide Web, choose the World Wide Web tab (see Figure 44.12). Select the appropriate protocol from the Hyperlink Type drop-down list (more than likely, http: will be the type), and then specify the URL in the URL edit box. Choose OK.

Figure 44.12
You can create a link to any page on the Web.

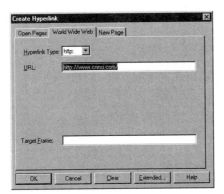

An easy way to specify a hyperlink to a World Wide Web target is to open that page in your browser when you define the link. The URL address of the page currently open in your browser automatically appears in the URL edit box when the Create Hyperlink dialog box is opened. This eliminates any chance of mis-typing the address when you create the link.

7. To create a link to a new page, choose the New Page tab. Enter the title of the page that should be created in the Page Title edit box and the filename of the page in the Page URL edit box. Choose OK. Next, the New age dialog box appears (as described earlier in the "Creating Web Pages Instantly" section).

   Select the type of page that should be created. Keep in mind that if you choose a page type based on a wizard, the appropriate wizard will be launched.

8. Choose OK.

Adding Graphics

It's rare to find a web page without at least one graphic element. You can certainly add an aesthetically-pleasing element to your page by adding some sort of graphics. Don't worry, you needn't create the graphic yourself using a drawing package. Many applications today ship with dozens of clipart images you can borrow for inclusion on your page. For example, Microsoft Word provides a wide selection of clipart, and you can borrow an image for use with FrontPage Express. Also, your local software store will probably have in stock a selection of graphics libraries available on CD, each storing thousands of different images.

Your challenge as a web page developer, then, is not in creating the graphics, but rather in deciding how to integrate one or more into your page. In the next two sections, we'll take a look at how to integrate a graphic onto your page, and also how to manage its size on your page. The first order of business, however, is to introduce the different types of graphics you can integrate onto your page.

Understanding Graphics Types

Many software applications are available today that let you draw anything from the most basic to the most complicated drawings. Some of these applications save the drawings in a specific format, which means only applications capable of reading the format can use the graphics. While many applications can read, as well as write, for different formats, graphics for the Web usually are found in two formats: GIF and JPEG.

GIF (pronounced *jiff*) is a graphics format developed by the online service Compuserve. While a number of versions of the GIF file exist, the most common one supports 256 colors. GIF is probably the most widely used format on the Web, and almost every browser and image editor support this format.

The GIF format also supports a process known as interlacing. An interlaced image is displayed in the browser in stages, so that the user can begin to view the image much sooner than if the graphic were not interlaced. You can specify any GIF image you've included on a FrontPage

Express page to be interlaced simply checking the Interlaced option when you select the image to be loaded.

Another option that FrontPage Express supports for GIF files is transparent images. When an image is created, a transparent color index is selected. This color blends with the background color of the browser when the image is displayed (only if the browser supports the display of transparent images). This effect, then, blends the focal part of the graphic, such as a picture of the author of this chapter, with the background of the browser, giving the appearance of a borderless image on the page.

JPEG images are sturdier than GIF images. JPEG (pronounced *jay-peg*) was developed by the Joint Photographic Experts Group. The standard JPEG may contain up to 16 million colors. The most interesting, colorful, and detailed images you see on the Internet are, most likely, JPEG graphics. Considering the great resolution JPEG images provide, you may be wondering why all graphics are not JPEG format. One of the problems with JPEG images is that the detail supported in a JPEG image means the file must usually be compressed when it is downloaded. The compression process sometimes results in a loss of detail. In addition, a loss of detail sometime results when a JPEG image is reduced from the size when it was drawn to a size to accommodate a specific space defined by the individual building the page.

Inserting the Graphic

You can insert a graphics from two different sources: a file on your computer or network, or from another site on the Web. When you insert a graphic from the Web, you are actually creating a pointer to the Web site where the graphic is located. The graphic will not be copied to your web site. With that in mind, you should be sure that any graphic you are referencing on another web site will not be moved.

TIP The best method for including a graphic from another Web site into yours is to copy the image. To do so, right-click on the target graphic, and then select the menu choice that saves the graphic locally. This way, you have your own copy of the graphic file. Be sure to respect any legal issues related to using a graphic from another web site, especially if that graphic was created by the host of the site.

To insert a graphic onto your web page, follow these steps:

1. From the menu, choose Insert, Image. The Image dialog box appears (see Figure 44.13).

2. To insert an image stored on your computer or a network resource to which your computer is attached, choose the From File option and then enter the name of the file in the edit box. Use the Browse button if you need help locating the file and/or entering its name and location.

   To insert an image stored on a web site, choose the From Location option. Next, enter the URL for the site and the name of the image in the edit box.

3. Choose OK. The image appears on the screen.

Figure 44.13

You add graphics to your page from the Image dialog box.

Managing the Size of Your Graphic

When you insert and image into your web page, the image will occupy an area on your page matching its size. That means if the image is 100 pixels wide by 100 pixels tall, it will occupy a 100×100 pixel area of your page at the location where you inserted the image. You may want to increase or decrease the size of the graphics. You can increase or decrease the size of any graphics inserted on your page. You can use two techniques to do so:

- Click and drag the handles that appear around the image when the image is selected. If you drag one of the handles at the corner of the image, you maintain the aspect ratio of the image. If you drag either horizontally or vertically, you change the horizontal and vertical aspect ratios.

- Double-click on the image to display the Image Properties dialog box. Choose the Appearance tab, and modify the image's size by clicking up or down in the Width and Height scroll boxes. You can specify the image's size by percent of the page occupied by choosing the in Percent option for either the Width or Height, or both.

Adding a Hyperlink to Your Graphics

You may want to provide a hyperlink with a graphic on your Web page. This gives the user the capability to link to another site via a graphics rather than a word or phrase.

To add a hyperlink to a graphics, follow these steps:

1. Double-click on the image to receive the hyperlink. The Image Properties dialog box appears.
2. Choose the General tab.
3. Enter the URL that the image will provide a link to in the Location edit box in the Default Hyperlink frame.
4. Choose OK.

Specifying Options for Your Graphics

As described earlier, depending on the format of your graphic, you may be able to specify a number of options, such as whether your GIF graphics is interlaced.

To specify options for your graphics, right-click the graphic, and then choose Image Properties from the menu. Options appropriate to the image type you selected will be available.

Using Backgrounds

You can add character to your Web pages by adding a background image or colors. When you add a background image to your page, any text or graphics you enter on your page appear against that background. The size of the graphic will determine how your background appears. FrontPage Express will tile the graphic across your page, which means it copies the graphic across the page and down to the bottom. Therefore, if you require a broad background, such as the sky and clouds, be sure your graphic is at least 640×480 pixels. If you prefer a tiled effect, such as displaying a company logo, than almost any size is suitable.

 TIP An attractive effect is to present a border down the left side of the page. To create this effect, the graphic you use should be 640 pixels wide, but the illustration or picture to use as the border should occupy the leftmost area of the graphic. By using a graphic that is wide as the screen, FrontPage Express cannot wrap the image. Instead, it repeats the image down the page.

To specify a background image or color for your page, follow these steps:

1. Select File, Page Properties from the menu. The Page Properties dialog box appears. Choose the Background tab (see Figure 44.14).

Figure 44.14
You can specify a background image and color for your page.

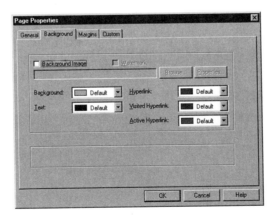

2. To add a background image, choose the Background Image check box in the edit box. Use the Browse button if you need help locating the file and/or entering its name and location.

To specify a background color for the page, select the color from the Background drop-down list.

3. Choose OK.

Creating and Editing Tables

Tables are a critical component of all but the most basic of web page designs, and it is likely you will create a table on a web page you are building soon. The application of tables in Web pages isn't strictly to handle columns and rows. Tables make it easy to position graphics and text at any location required. By merging and splitting rows and columns, tables can be used to place graphics and text in locations that would be difficult to access with indenting and alignment commands.

Adding a Table to Your Page

You can add a table to your Web page from either the Standard Toolbar or from the menu. Using the menu gives you the capability to specify a number of options for your table when it is created, such as cell padding and border size. Your choices are limited to number of columns and rows when you use the toolbar to create the table. Of course, if you have created the table with the toolbar, you can always select the entire table and then choose Table, Table Properties from the menu to customize it.

The following two bullets explain each method for creating a table.

- *Toolbar.* To create a table from the toolbar, click the Insert Table button on the Standard toolbar. Drag down to select the number of rows for your table and, *without releasing the mouse button*, drag across to select the number of columns. Then, release the mouse button (see Figure 44.15).

- *Menu.* To create a menu from the menu, choose Table, Insert Table from the menu. The Insert Table dialog box appears (see Figure 44.16). Enter the number of rows and columns in the respective controls in the Size frame. Use the up and down buttons in each of the controls to increment or decrement the current value.

Selecting with Your Table

After you created your table, it is likely you will need to customize it, such as by modifying its size, changing column layout, etc. In order to customize a table in FrontPage Express, you must first select either the table or the component of the table you want to work with. The following list shows you how to customize the different components of the table.

- *Table.* Click and drag over the table until all of the rows and columns are selected.

  -or-

  Click anywhere on the table and then select Table, Select Table from the menu.

- *One Cell.* Move the mouse pointer toward the leftmost edge of the table until the pointer becomes an arrow pointing to the right and then double-click.

  -or-

Click anywhere in the cell and then choose T<u>a</u>ble, Select C<u>e</u>ll from the menu

■ *One Column.* Move the mouse pointer above the top border of the first row in the column. The mouse pointer will change shape to a darkened, downward-pointing arrow. Click now.

-or-

Click anywhere in the column and then choose T<u>a</u>ble, Select Col<u>u</u>mn from the menu.

Figure 44.15
You can add a table to your page quickly by using the toolbar.

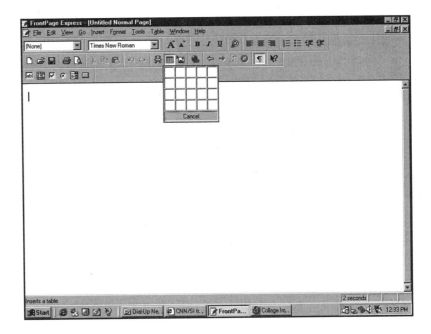

Figure 44.16
The Insert Table dialog box provides you with more options than by creating a table from the toolbar.

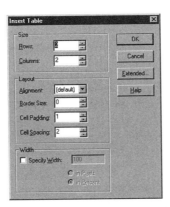

■ *Range of Columns.* Move the mouse pointer above the top border of the first row in the first column. The mouse pointer will change shape to a darkened, downward-pointing arrow. Holding down the Shift key, click and then drag to select additional columns.

■ *One Row.* Move the mouse pointer to the left of the table adjacent to the row to be selected. The mouse pointer will change shape to a darkened arrow. Click now.

-or-

Click anywhere in the row and then select Table, Select Row from the menu.

■ *Range of Rows.* Move the mouse pointer to the left of the table adjacent to the first row to be selected. The mouse pointer will change shape to a darkened arrow. Holding down the Shift key, click and drag to select additional rows.

Splitting and Merging Rows, Columns, and Cells

You can use a few techniques to further define the layout of the rows and columns in your table. These techniques are useful when you want to vary either the row or height of cells with respect to other cells in the same column or row. You can merge columns, rows, and cells together to achieve this type of effect. Figure 44.17 shows an example of a table in which a combination of splitting and merging is used to accommodate the different types of content in the table.

Figure 44.17
You can use merged and split cells to put information precisely where you want it.

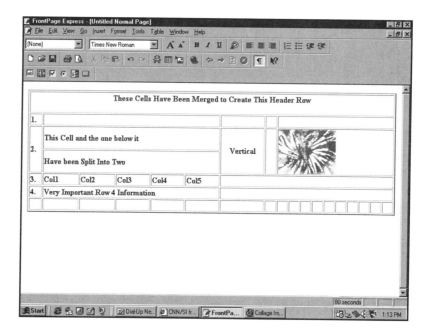

The following list shows the techniques for splitting and merging columns, rows, and cells.

■ *Split a Cell.* Select the cell to be split and then choose Table, Split Cells from the menu. The Split Cells dialog box appears (see Figure 44.18). Choose either the Split into Columns or Split into Cells option, and then specify the number of columns or rows the cell should be split into in the Number of Columns scroll box. Then choose OK.

Figure 44.18
You split cells into columns or rows, as many of each as you need.

- *Split All the Cells in a Column.* Select the column, and then choose T<u>a</u>ble, Split C<u>e</u>lls from the menu. The Split Cells dialog box appears. Choose the Split into <u>R</u>ows option, and specify the number of rows each of the cells in the column should be split into in the Number of <u>R</u>ows scroll box. Then choose OK.

- *Split All of the Cells in a Row.* Select the row, and then choose T<u>a</u>ble, Split C<u>e</u>lls from the menu. The Split Cells dialog box appears. Choose the Split into Columns option, and specify the number of columns each of the cells in the row should be split into in the Number of <u>C</u>olumns scroll box. Then choose OK.

- *Merge Cells.* Click and drag through the cells to be merged and then choose T<u>a</u>ble, <u>M</u>erge Cells from the menu.

Inserting a Table Within a Cell

Another method for customizing the layout of information in a table is to insert a table within a table. This gives you the capability to group and lay out one set of data or content within the context of a larger table. Figure 44.19 shows an example of table within a table layout.

Figure 44.19
You can insert a table within another table.

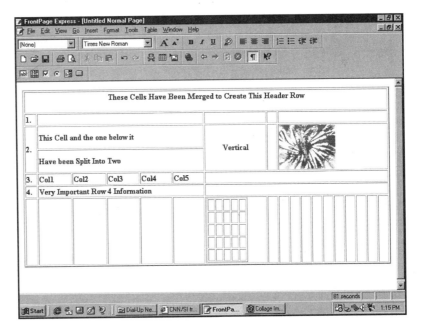

To insert a table within a cell in a table, select the cell and then repeat steps in the "Adding a Table to Your Page" section earlier in this chapter.

Customizing Your Table

In addition to merging and splitting rows, columns, and cells in your table, a number of other options are available in FrontPage Express to help customize your table. The following list explains the options and techniques for customizing your table:

- *Caption.* You can add a caption to your table that provides a quick description of the table's contents for the user. The caption appears centered, above the table, and whenever the table is resized or moved, the caption is automatically moved, too.

  To add a caption to your table, click anywhere in the table and then choose Table, Insert Caption from the menu. The cursor moves over the table. Enter the caption.

- *Borders.* You can specify a border for the cells in your table. To do so, first select the table, and then choose Table, Table Properties from the menu. Select a width for the border from the Border Size scroll box. You can also select a color for both the light portion of the shading and the heavy portion of the border shading, as well as for the border itself. Make these selections from the Custom Colors frame at the bottom of the dialog box, and then choose OK.

  It is possible to override border settings for the entire table for specific cells, columns, or rows. To do so, select the cells whose borders will be customized and then choose Table, Cell Properties from the menu. Make selections from the Custom Colors frame, and then choose OK.

- *Background Image/Color.* You can specify a cell-specific background or image. In the case of the background image, the cell must be large enough to accommodate a graphic if you want the user to see all of the graphic.

  To specify either a background image or color for a cell, select the cell, choose Table, Cell Properties from the menu, and then select either a color or image from the Custom Background Frame.

- *Alignment.* You can specify the alignment for the content of any or all of the cells in the table. To do so, select the components of the table for which to specify alignment. Next, choose Table, Cell Properties from the menu. Specify the Horizontal and Vertical alignments for the cells selected in the Layout frame.

- *Column Width/Table Width.* You can specify the width of either a column or the entire table easily. You specify the width either in pixels or percentage of the entire page occupied. To specify the width for the table, select the table and then choose Table, Table Properties from the menu. Choose the Specify Width option, and then select either the in Pixels or in Percent option. Lastly, enter the value and then choose OK. To do the same for a column(s), choose the column and instead choose Table, Cell Properties from the menu.

Adding Content to a Table

Now that you have learned how to format and structure a table, here is a quick word on how to enter content for the table. Text and other content are entered into a table in the fashion as entered directly onto the page. You click on the cell to receive the content, and then either enter text, or choose one of the options from the Insert menu to add other content, such as an image.

Adding Sound and Video

Part

VII

Ch

44

The appeal of a Web page can be significantly enhanced by the inclusion of multimedia content, such as sound and video. Many web pages you can browse through today include video clips that you can view online, such as excerpts for upcoming films. Other Web sites provide background music as you browse through its pages. Integrating sound and video are simple exercises in FrontPage Express. In this section, you will learn how to integrate video, as well as background music, to your web pages.

Adding Video to Your Page

Video is an attractive option for a web page, and the development of video for the Web, as well as it inclusion into your web pages, is not a difficult issue (especially as it once was). Specifically, the availability of new video production hardware and software tools makes it easy to develop video at the desktop. Even the objections to the time it takes to download video clips has been addressed. New technologies, such as *streaming*, in which the video clip (as well as other multimedia content) is played *as* it is downloaded, to the increased modem speeds, remove almost all protestations about complicated multimedia content on the Web.

To add video to your web page, follow these steps:

1. From the menu, choose Insert, Video from the menu. The Video dialog appears (see Figure 44.20).

Figure 44.20

You specify the video to add to the page from the Insert Video dialog box.

2. Enter the name of the file containing the video content in the From File edit box. Use the Browse button if you need help locating the file and/or entering its name and location. Choose OK.

3. A block will appear on the page. This corresponds to the position on the page where the video will be played when the page is opened.

4. To customize how the video will be displayed, right-click the block and then choose Image Properties from the menu. Choose the Video tab (see Figure 44.22).

Figure 44.21

You can control how often the video runs from the Image properties dialog box.

To specify the video start when the page is opened, choose the On File Open check box. Alternatively, to launch the video when the mouse passes over the video, choose the On Mouse Over option. Continuing, you choose the number of times the video should repeat by entering the number in the Loop control. To repeat the video as long as the page is opened, choose the Forever check box.

Adding a Background Sound to Your Page

You can add a sound to your page that is played automatically when the page is opened. The sound can be played once, or you can specify how many times it is played, even as long as the page is open.

To specify a background sound for your page, follow these steps:

1. Select File, Page Properties from the menu. The Page Properties dialog box appears. Choose the Background tab.

2. Enter the name of the file with the background sound in the Location edit box. Use the Browse button if you need help locating the file and/or entering its name and location.

3. Specify the number of times the sound should repeat by entering the number in the Loop control. To increment or decrement the value shown in the control, click on either the up or down button beside the edit portion of the control. To repeat the sound as long as the page is opened, choose the Forever check box.

4. Choose OK.

Advanced Web Editing Techniques

As the Web has grown in popularity and complexity, so has the technology surrounding it. This section of the chapter provides a brief overview of some of the most important Web technologies and how each relates to FrontPage Express:

- Java
- ActiveX
- Active Server Pages
- WebBots
- ISAPI

Understanding Java

Java is a programming language for the Web developed by Sun Microsystems and now released in modified form by Sun, Microsoft, Borland, and a few other companies. Java is useful for enhancing web functionality in that the language is operating system and hardware independent. This means that separate versions of a Java needn't be produced for each operating system or type of hardware on which the program could be run. This is significant considering the number of different types of computers connecting to the Internet. Many of the interesting functionality you see at different web sites is developed with Java.

Understanding WebBots

WebBots are packaged functionality you can add to your web pages. Rather than developing functionality from scratch, such as a feature allowing your user to search your web page or site for a specific word or phrase, you can use a WebBot to add that type of feature with just a few clicks of the mouse. FrontPage Express comes with three WebBots, Timestamp, Search, and Include. Descriptions of each WebBot follow:

- *Search.* Provides a box that the user can enter a word or phrase to search for on the current page, as well as a button to start the search and another button to clear the box.
- *Include.* Automatically merges another page on the Web into the current page at the position where the WebBot was run. The merged page is updated whenever the page is opened.
- *Timestamp.* Automatically updates on the page the last time and date the page was modified.

Considering that WebBots are designed to save the user work, you would expect that it would be easy to integrate one or more on a Web page. Fortunately, this happens to be the case.

To add a WebBot, follow these steps:

1. Click on the location on the page where the WebBot component should be installed
2. Choose Insert, WebBot Component from the menu. The Insert WebBot Component dialog appears.

3. Select the WebBot Component to integrate from the list, then choose OK.

4. Depending on the WebBot selected, you may need to specify additional options, such as the format of the date and time presented with the Timestamp WebBot. Proceed through the dialog boxes, choosing Finish at the end.

Understanding ISAPI

ISAPI stands for *Internet Server Application Programming Interface*. As you may be able to guess, ISAPI is concerned with the server side of web processing, meaning the computer where web pages are stored and processed when a browser requests one. Web technology has progressed to the point where it provides more than pictures and text. Web applications can be used to query databases, such as checking the status of your account if your bank happens to be on-line, or placing an order for some merchandise. In these types of applications, the server must execute work on its side, such as querying the bank central computer for the information. Before ISAPI, a separate miniature programming script was required for every task a web server was expected to perform. The number of scripts on a server, then, could become quite large, and poor performance could become an issue. ISAPI addressed these issues by collecting tasks and functionality in a small number of files, hence providing service to the server that a browser could call more efficiently. This is the model Windows and Windows applications use.

Publishing Pages to a Web Site

When you have created all of the pages for your Web, you probably will want to publish the pages to a Web where uses can access the pages. Simply saving the pages you've created in FrontPage Express isn't enough, however. You must publish the pages to a specific Web so that Web server software (which is different from both FrontPage Express and your browser and must be installed separately) can process requests from users for the pages. This Web server software (on which a Web is created) must reside on a computer that browsers can access. There are two general steps that must be followed in order to publish your pages to the Web:

1. Establishing or locating a Web site on which to publish your web and pages

2. Publish the pages

We will look at these two steps in this section.

Establishing or Creating a Web Site

As described earlier in the section, "Using the Personal Home Page Wizard," many Internet Service Providers will host home pages for subscribers. If you plan to provide more than a single page of information, you may want to consider a host site with greater capabilities. A search of the Web will turn up dozens of companies interested in hosting your web site for a nominal amount per month, usually less than $50. If you have access to the server and are interested in learning the technology, Windows NT Server includes the software to host a Web site. In addition, Windows NT Workstation and Windows 98 both provide web hosting software perfect for local Webs, such as via Intranets.

Publishing Your Pages

Windows 98 provides the tools to publish your Web page via the Web Publishing Wizard. The Wizard is available from the Internet Explorer menu, which is accessed from the Programs menu. If you do not see the Web Publishing Wizard on the menu, then it probably has not been installed. You can install the wizard from either the Windows 98 or Internet Explorer CD, or you can download it from Microsoft's site on the Internet. The Wizard walks you through the steps of publishing your pages as well as creating a starting home page. The steps are easy to follow, and there is no requirement for in-depth web server knowledge.

When Should You Upgrade to FrontPage?

As you become more adept at Web page development, or when your Web site development projects grow in complexity, you might consider upgrading to the full version of Microsoft FrontPage. FrontPage Express is very similar to FrontPage, especially considering that FrontPage Express is based on FrontPage, so you should run into little difficulty during the transition. Here are the main differences:

- FrontPage provides many more WebBots than the four provided with the Express version.
- The fill version includes FrontPage Explorer, which helps to develop and manage entire web sites made up of the pages developed with FrontPage editor.
- The full FrontPage provides clip art samples, including video and animated samples.
- FrontPage gives you a direct link to your web browser allowing you to view your pages in the browser as you develop them, rather than having to save and load them individually.

PART VIII

Advanced Topics

Internet Security

by Ed Bott

Setting a Security Policy

By its very nature, the Internet is an insecure place. Packets of data move from machine to machine across connections that anyone with a little technical knowledge can tap into. On the Internet, simply clicking a link can download and run a program written by someone you've never met, whose motives you can't even begin to guess. When you transmit sensitive data over the Internet, it can be intercepted by complete strangers. If you run a server program, a stranger can connect directly to your computer, with consequences you might not be aware of. There's no need for paranoia, but everyone who accesses the Internet should have a healthy respect for its risks.

Windows 98 and Internet Explorer 4.0 include a broad set of security tools. Before you can properly configure these options, however, you need to establish a security policy. This policy should balance the need to protect sensitive data against the undeniable value of open access to information and the wealth of information available on the world's largest network. Different environments have different security requirements as well: With a dial-up Internet connection at home, you might not worry about the risk of break-ins, but on a corporate network, firewalls and other sophisticated security precautions are a must.

These elements should be central to any security policy:

- *Authentication.* When you connect to a Web site, how do you know who's really running that server? When you download and run a program, how do you know that it hasn't been tampered with or infected with a virus? When extremely sensitive information is involved, you might want to insist on secure connections guaranteed by digital certificates.

- *Encryption.* Certain types of data—usernames and passwords, credit card numbers, and confidential banking information, for example—are too sensitive to be sent "in the clear," where they can be read by anyone who can intercept the packets. For these transactions, only secure, encrypted connections are acceptable.

- *Control over executable content.* The Internet is filled with programs and add-ins that can expand the capabilities of your browser. Unfortunately, poorly written or malicious add-ins can carry viruses, corrupt valuable data, and even expose your network to unauthorized break-ins. On most networks, administrators try to limit the potential for damage by restricting the types of files that users can download and run.

N O T E Microsoft publishes regular security news, advisories, and updates for Windows and Internet Explorer users; find the latest announcements at this address:

http://www.microsoft.com/security

Configuring Internet Explorer to Use a Proxy Server

With ordinary dial-up Internet connections, client machines connect directly to Web or FTP servers, making it possible for a would-be hacker to break into the network. To minimize that risk, most corporate networks include a *firewall*, a secure gateway made up of one or more systems that sit between the network and the Internet at large. Firewalls restrict the ability of outsiders to connect with machines inside the network, while allowing legitimate users to access resources on the Internet. This combination of hardware and software is designed to intercept and filter packets of information, letting through only those that meet strict standards of security.

Carefully isolated machines called *proxy servers* are crucial components of most corporate firewalls. When a client computer inside the firewall requests a service from the Internet—a Web page, for example, or a file on an FTP server—the proxy server intercepts the request and handles the transaction. To the server on the other end of the connection, the request looks as though it came from the proxy server; there's no possibility of a direct (and possibly compromised) connection between it and the host machine inside the firewall.

N O T E　Want more information about firewalls? You can find links to the definitive Firewalls FAQ and mailing list at

http://www.greatcircle.com ■

Before Internet Explorer 4.0 can use a proxy server, you must specify its name or IP address. Some proxies (Microsoft Proxy Server 2.0 or later, for example) can automatically configure client machines; in that case, you need to enter the name of the machine that contains the configuration files.

TROUBLESHOOTING

You're connected to a corporate network, and some or all of the options described in this chapter are unavailable. That's usually a sign that the network administrator has used Microsoft's Internet Explorer Administration Kit to enforce security policies from a central server. In that case, most security settings (and many other options, for that matter) are grayed out and inaccessible. See your network administrator if you need to change one of these settings.

Follow these steps to set up Internet Explorer for use with a proxy server:

1. Choose View, Internet Options and click the Connection tab. A dialog box like the one in Figure 45.1 appears.

Figure 45.1

Check this box and enter the name or IP address of your proxy server; port 80 is the standard setting for virtually all Web proxies.

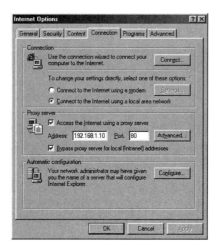

2. Check the box labeled Access the Internet Using a Proxy Server.

3. If your network includes a server that can automatically configure Internet Explorer, click the Configure button, enter the full URL of the server, and click OK. No additional configuration is necessary.

4. If your network does not include an auto-configuring proxy server, click in the Address box and enter the name or IP address of the proxy machine.

N O T E When configuring a proxy server, you can use either the server's name or its IP address. The effect is identical no matter which technique you use. The administrator in charge of the proxy server can supply information about your network's configuration.

5. Click in the Port box and enter the name of the TCP port that the proxy server uses. In the overwhelming majority of cases, this will be port 80, the standard for Web traffic.

6. If your network uses separate proxy servers to handle other protocols, click the Advanced button to open the dialog box shown in Figure 45.2. Enter those settings here.

Figure 45.2

Click in the Exceptions box and specify URLs that you want to access directly, without using the proxy server.

7. Your network administrator might provide direct access to some sites and block access through the proxy server. If instructed to do so, click in the Exceptions box and enter the names of any domains that do not require access through the proxy server. Be sure to enter a protocol prefix (typically http:// or https://) for each address. Use semicolons to separate entries in this list.

8. Click OK to close the Advanced dialog box.

9. Click OK to close the Internet Options dialog box and begin using the proxy server.

TIP On most corporate networks, you should check the box labeled Bypass Proxy Server for local (intranet) addresses. The proxy's safety features shouldn't be necessary inside the firewall, and routing intranet requests through the proxy hurts performance without improving security.

Establishing and Maintaining Internet Security Zones

Internet Explorer 4.0 includes dozens of security settings. Applying each of those options to individual Web sites would be impractical; instead, the system lets you group sites into four security zones, each with its own high, medium, or low security settings. Initially, as Table 45.1 shows, all sites are divided into two groups: those inside your company's intranet and those on the Internet. As part of a comprehensive security policy, you can designate specific Web sites as trusted or restricted, giving them greater or less access to machines inside your network.

Table 45.1   Security Zones at a Glance

Security Zone	Default Locations Included in Zone	Default Security Settings
Local intranet zone	Local intranet servers not included in other zones; all network paths; all sites that bypass proxy server	Medium
Trusted sites zone	None	Low
Internet zone	All Web sites not included in other zones	Medium
Restricted sites zone	None	High

As you move from one address to another using Internet Explorer, the system checks to see what zone the address has been assigned to and then applies the security settings that belong to that zone. If you open a Web page on a server inside your corporate intranet, for example, you can freely download files and work with ActiveX controls or Java applets. When you switch to a page on the Internet, however, your security settings may prevent you from using any kind of active content or downloading any files.

There are three built-in security levels, plus a Custom option that lets you pick and choose security settings for a zone. Table 45.2 summarizes the security options available when you first start Internet Explorer 4.0.

Table 45.2   Default Security Levels

Security Level	Default Settings
High	ActiveX controls and JavaScript disabled; Java set to highest safety level; file downloads prohibited through browser; prompt before downloading fonts or logging on to secure site.
Medium	ActiveX enabled for signed controls only, with prompt before downloading; file and font downloads permitted; Java set to medium safety level; all scripting permitted; automatic logon to secure sites.
Low	Enable all ActiveX controls but prompt before using unsigned code; Java set to low safety; desktop items install automatically; file and font downloads permitted; all scripting permitted; automatic logon to secure sites.
Custom	Allows user or administrator to select security settings individually.

Adding an Internet Domain to a Security Zone

Initially, Internet Explorer includes every external Web site in the Internet zone. Over time, you'll identify some sites that are extremely trustworthy, such as a secure server maintained by your bank or stockbroker; on these sites, you might want to relax security settings to allow maximum access to information and resources available from that domain. Other sites, however, might earn a reputation for transferring unsafe content, including untested software or virus-infected documents. On a network, in particular, you might want to tightly restrict access to these unsafe sites.

To add the addresses for specific Web sites to a given security zone, open the Internet Options dialog box and click the Security tab; the dialog box shown in Figure 45.3 appears.

Figure 45.3

Adding a Web site to the Restricted Sites zone lets you tightly control the site's ability to interact with your PC and network.

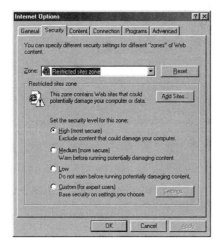

By definition, the Internet zone includes all sites not assigned to other zones; as a result, you can't add sites to that zone. Follow these steps to assign specific sites to the Trusted Sites or Restricted Sites zones:

1. Open the Internet Options dialog box and click on the Security tab.
2. Choose a zone from the drop-down list at the top of the dialog box.
3. Click the Add Sites button.
4. Enter the full network address of the server you want to restrict in the text box and click the Add button.

   Be sure to include the prefix (http://, for example) but don't add any address information after the host name; Internet Explorer applies security settings to all pages on that server.
5. Repeat steps 3 and 4 to add more server names to the selected zone.
6. Click OK to close the dialog box.

 To remove a Web server from either the Trusted Sites or Restricted Sites zone, click the Add Sites button, select the address from the list, and click the Remove button. Any addresses you remove from a zone will once again belong to the default Internet zone.

Some special considerations apply when adding sites to the Trusted sites or Local Intranet zone:

- By default, only secure sites (those with the https:// prefix) may be added to the Trusted sites group. To add other sites, clear the check box that reads Require server Verification (https:) for All Sites in This Zone.
- To add sites to the Local Intranet zone, you have to go through one extra dialog box, shown in Figure 45.4. Clear the middle check box if you want resources that you access without using the proxy server to fall into this group by default. Click the Advanced button to add sites to the Local Intranet zone.

Figure 45.4
Clear one or more of
these check boxes to
move sites from the
Local Intranet zone to
the default Internet
zone.

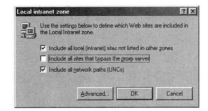

 TIP   The status bar always displays the security zone for the current page. After you add a site to a security
zone, load the page to confirm that the change is effective.

Changing Security Settings by Zone

When you first run Internet Explorer 4.0, all Web pages use the same Medium security settings, but it doesn't have to stay that way. If your intranet is protected by a reliable firewall and
you use ActiveX components developed within your company, you might want to reset security
in the Local Intranet zone to Low. Likewise, if you're concerned about the potential for damage
from files and programs on the Internet, you can reset security for the Internet zone to High.

To assign a different security level to any of the four built-in zones, follow these steps:

1. Open the Internet Options dialog box and click the Security tab.
2. Choose the appropriate zone from the drop-down list.
3. Click the High, Medium, or Low radio button.
4. Click OK to save your new security settings.

When you choose the High option for the Internet zone (or use custom options to choose
similar security settings), don't be surprised if many pages don't work properly. Because
ActiveX controls are disabled by default, for example, you're likely to see a dialog box like the
one in Figure 45.5 when you load an ActiveX-enabled page or attempt to download and play a
streaming audio file.

Figure 45.5
With the security level
set to High, many forms
of rich content simply
won't work. Instead of
hearing multimedia files,
for example, you'll see a
dialog box like this one.

Setting Custom Security Options

If none of the built-in security levels is quite right for the policy you've established, you can
create your own collection of security settings and apply it to any of the four security zones.
Instead of choosing High, Medium, or Low, use Internet Explorer's Custom option to step

through all the security options, choosing the ones that best suit your needs. Follow these steps:

1. Open the Internet Options dialog box and click the Security tab.

2. Choose the appropriate zone from the drop-down list.

3. Click the Custom radio button.

4. The Settings button, which is normally grayed out, should now be available. Click it, and the Security Settings dialog box shown in Figure 45.6 appears.

Figure 45.6

Internet Explorer includes a long list of security settings for each zone. Use context-sensitive help for a concise explanation of what each one does.

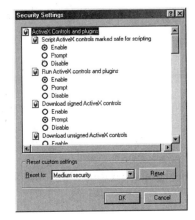

Part
VIII

Ch
45

5. Scroll through the list and choose the options that best apply to your security needs. If you're not sure what an option means, right-click its entry and choose What's This? for context-sensitive help.

6. After you've finished adjusting all security settings, click OK to apply the changes to the selected zone.

 Have you experimented with security settings to the point where you're afraid you've done more harm than good? Just start over. Open the Security Settings dialog box, choose a security level in the Reset To box, and click the Reset button. That restores the custom settings to the default security settings for that level and lets you begin fresh.

Restricting ActiveX Controls

The single most controversial feature of Internet Explorer 4.0 is its support for ActiveX controls. ActiveX technology, an extension of what was known in previous versions of Windows as Object Linking and Embedding (OLE), commonly refers to component software used across networks, including the Internet. Internet Explorer 4.0 uses ActiveX components in the browser window to display content that ordinary HTML can't handle, such as stock tickers, cascading menus, or Adobe Acrobat documents. An ActiveX chart control, for example, can take a few bits of data from a distant server and draw a chart at the speed of the local PC, instead of forcing you to wait while downloading a huge image file. The Microsoft Investor page (see Figure 45.7) offers a particularly rich example of this capability to quickly gather and manipulate data.

Figure 45.7
An ActiveX control on this page makes it possible to quickly analyze and display complex data such as stock prices.

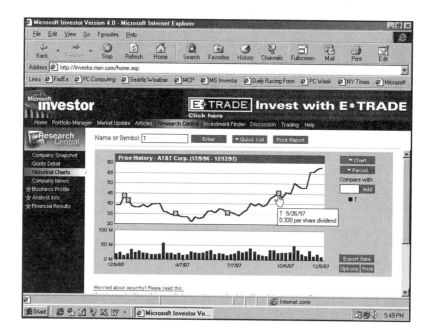

When you view a page that includes an ActiveX control, you don't need to run a setup program and restart your browser; the program simply begins downloading, and then offers to install itself on your computer. That's convenient, but automatic installation also allows poorly written or malicious applets free access to your computer and network. Internet Explorer security options let you take control of ActiveX components and apply security settings by zone: You can completely disable all such downloads, or you can rely on digital certificates to decide which components are safe to install.

Customizing ActiveX Security Settings

Whenever Internet Explorer encounters an ActiveX control on a Web page, it checks the current security zone and applies the security settings for that zone:

■ The default Medium security settings disable any unsigned ActiveX controls and prompt you before downloading and installing those that have a valid certificate.

■ The most drastic ActiveX security option completely disables any components you encounter in a given security zone, signed or not. To enable this setting in the Internet zone, set the security level to High.

- When security is set to Low, the browser runs any ActiveX control. Signed controls download and install automatically; Internet Explorer prompts you before using an unsigned control.

> **CAUTION**
>
> Low security settings put your computer and network at risk. The only circumstance in which we recommend this setting is in the Local Intranet zone, to allow access to trusted but unsigned ActiveX controls developed by other members of your organization.

In zones where some or all ActiveX controls are disabled, Internet Explorer downloads the prohibited control but refuses to install it. Instead, you see an error message like the one in Figure 45.8.

Figure 45.8

Unless you set security options to Low, you see this dialog box anytime you encounter an unsigned ActiveX control. With High security, all ActiveX components are disabled.

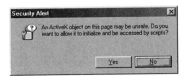

Table 45.3 shows default ActiveX settings for each security zone. If you don't see a mix of options appropriate for your security policy, choose a zone and use Custom settings to redefine security levels.

Table 45.3 ActiveX Security Settings by Zone

Security Setting	Option	High	Medium	Low
Download unsigned ActiveX controls	Prompt			X
	Disable	X	X	
	Enable			
Script ActiveX controls marked safe for scripting	Prompt			
	Disable			
	Enable	X	X	X

continues

Table 45.3   Continued

Security Setting	Option	High	Medium	Low
Initialize and script ActiveX controls not marked as safe	Prompt		X	X
	Disable	X		
	Enable			
Download signed ActiveX controls	Prompt		X	
	Disable	X		
	Enable			X
Run ActiveX controls and plugins	Prompt			
	Disable	X		
	Enable		X	X

Custom security settings offer a way to take advantage of only the ActiveX controls you specifically approve, while prohibiting all others. Choose the Custom security level for the Internet
zone, click Settings, and enable two options: Run ActiveX Controls and Plugins, and Script
ActiveX Controls Marked Safe for Scripting. Disable all other ActiveX security settings. With
these security settings, currently installed ActiveX controls function normally. When you encounter a new page that uses an ActiveX control, it refuses to install; you can choose to install it
by temporarily resetting the security options for that zone.

Using Certificates to Identify People, Sites, and Publishers

Internet Explorer uses digital certificates to verify the publisher of an ActiveX control before
determining how to handle it. This feature, called Authenticode, checks the ActiveX control for
the existence of an encrypted digital signature; IE4 then compares the signature against an
original copy stored on a secure Web site to verify that the code has not been tampered with.
Software publishers register with certifying authorities such as VeriSign, Inc., who in turn act
as escrow agents to verify that the signature you're viewing is valid.

N O T E   For more information about how Authenticode uses digital signatures and certifying
authorities, see

http://www.verisign.com/developers/authenticodefaq.html

If Internet Explorer cannot verify that the signature on the ActiveX control is valid, you see a Security Warning dialog box like the one in Figure 45.9. Depending on your security settings for the current zone, you might be able to choose to install the control anyway.

Figure 45.9

You see this warning when Internet Explorer can't verify that a certificate is valid. Click Yes to install the software anyway or No to check again later.

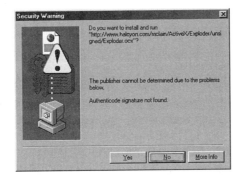

If the Certifying Authority verifies that the signature attached to the control is valid, and the current security zone is set to use Medium settings, you see a dialog box like the one in Figure 45.10.

Figure 45.10

Use the links on this certificate to see additional information about the publisher of ActiveX controls you download.

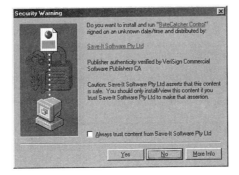

Part
VIII

Ch
45

The Security Warning dialog box confirms that the signature is valid. In addition, it offers links you can follow for more information about the publisher and gives you the option to add that publisher to a list of trusted sites:

- Click here for detailed information about the publisher gathered from its certificate. If the applet or control is requesting permission to access system resources, an additional link appears. Detailed Help is available.

- Click here to see additional information about the applet or control. This link typically points to a Web site run by the software publisher.

- Choose Yes to install the software and No to abort the installation.

- Check this box to add the certificate to your list of trusted publishers. Future downloads accompanied by certificates on your trusted publishers list install automatically, without requiring your approval.

N O T E To view and edit the full list of trusted publishers and certifying authorities, choose View, Internet Options, click the Content tab, and look in the Certificates box. ■

■ Click here for general information about certificates and ActiveX security.

CAUTION

A valid certificate provides no guarantee that a signed ActiveX control is either bug free or safe. The certificate simply identifies the publisher with reasonable certainty. Based on that identification and the publisher's reputation, you can decide whether to install the software; and in the event something goes wrong, you know whom to call for support.

Managing ActiveX Components on Your Computer

Every time Internet Explorer adds an ActiveX control, it downloads files to the local computer and makes adjustments to the Windows Registry. Unlike conventional programs, you can't use the Control Panel's Add/Remove Programs applet to remove or update components; but there is a way to manage this collection. Follow these steps:

1. Choose View, Internet Options and click the General tab.

2. In the box labeled Temporary Internet files, click the Settings button. The Settings dialog box appears.

3. Click the View Objects button to open the Downloaded Program Files folder. You see a list of all installed ActiveX controls and Java class libraries, as in Figure 45.11. If you're not sure what a control does, right-click and choose Properties to see additional information.

Figure 45.11

All installed ActiveX controls appear in this folder. Use the right-click shortcut menus to inspect the file's properties, update it, or remove it.

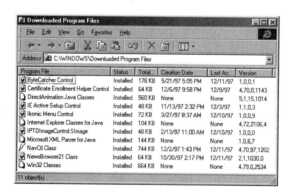

4. To delete one or more components, right-click the entry or entries and choose Remove from the shortcut menu. This step deletes each component's executable file and clears out any registry settings as well.

5. To update one or more components with the most recent versions, right-click on the entry or entries and choose Update from the shortcut menu. This step checks the original source for each file (usually an Internet address), replaces the component with new versions, and updates applicable registry settings as needed.

6. Close the Downloaded Program Files window and click OK to close the Settings dialog box.

Limiting Java Applets

Like ActiveX controls, Java applets extend the capabilities of Internet Explorer by displaying and manipulating data and images in ways that HTML can't. There's a significant difference between ActiveX and Java, though. Java applets run in a virtual machine with strict security rules. The Java Security Manager (sometimes referred to as the "sandbox") prevents applets from interacting with resources on your machine, whereas ActiveX controls are specifically designed to work with files and other applications.

Unlike ActiveX controls, Java applets are not stored on your machine. Instead, every time you access a Java-enabled page, your browser downloads the applet and runs the program in the Java virtual machine. When you've finished with the applet, it disappears from memory, and the next time you access the page you have to repeat the download. Over slow links, large Java applets can take excruciatingly long times to load, although the results can be impressive, as the example in Figure 45.12 shows.

Part
VIII

Ch
45

Figure 45.12
This stock-charting page is an excellent illustration of the rich capabilities of Java applets.

Internet Explorer's Security Settings dialog box lets you control specific aspects of the Java interface. Like the security settings for ActiveX controls, you can assign ready-made Low, Medium, or High options to Java applets, or disable Java completely. There's even a Custom option, although most of its settings are meaningful only to Java developers. To adjust Java security, follow these steps:

1. Choose View, Internet Options and click the Security tab.

2. Choose a zone from the drop-down list and click the Custom radio button.

3. Click the Settings button.

4. Scroll through the Security Settings dialog box until you reach the Java section.

5. Choose one of the five safety options.

6. If you select the Custom option, a new Java Custom Settings button appears at the bottom of the dialog box. Click this button, and the Custom Permissions dialog box appears (see Figure 45.13).

Figure 45.13

Concerned about security with Java applets? Internet Explorer lets you tightly control the Java virtual machine, but only an experienced Java developer will be able to work comfortably with these options.

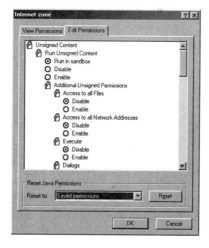

7. To change permissions in this dialog box, click the Edit Permissions tab. Select individual security options from the top of the dialog box, or use the drop-down list at the bottom of the box to select High, Medium, or Low security settings.

8. Close all three dialog boxes to apply the changes you've made.

N O T E   Earthweb's Gamelan site is the best place on the Internet to look for Java applets and detailed information about the Java language. You can find a link to these pages at

http://www.developer.com/directories/directories.html ▪

Blocking Dangerous Scripts and Unsafe File Downloads

In addition to its capability to host embedded controls and applets, Internet Explorer supports simple scripting, using JavaScript and VBScript. With the help of scripts, Web designers can create pages that calculate expressions, ask and answer questions, check data that users enter in forms, and link to other programs, including ActiveX controls and Java applets.

Although the security risks posed by most scripts are slight, Internet Explorer gives you the option to disable Active scripting as well as scripting of Java applets. You find both options in the Security Settings dialog box when you choose Custom settings.

A far more serious security risk is the browser's capability to download and run files. Although the risk of executing untrusted executable files is obvious, even document files can be dangerous. Any Microsoft Office document, for example, can include Visual Basic macros that are as powerful as any standalone program. To completely disable all file downloads, select the built-in High security level. With this setting turned on, you see a dialog box like the one in Figure 45.14 whenever you attempt to download a file from a Web page.

Figure 45.14
With the security level set to High, no file downloads are allowed. When you attempt to download any file, including programs and documents, you see this dialog box instead.

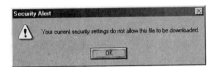

Part
VIII
Ch
45

Working with Secure Web Sites

When is it safe to send confidential information over the Internet? The only time you should transmit private information, such as credit card numbers and banking information, is when you can establish a secure connection using a standard security protocol called Secure Sockets Layer (SSL) over HTTP.

To make an SSL connection with Internet Explorer 4.0, the Web server must include credentials from a designated Certification Authority. The URL for a secure connection uses a different prefix (https://), and Internet Explorer includes two important indications that you're about to connect securely: You see a warning dialog box each time you begin or end a secure connection, as well as a padlock icon in the status bar, as in Figure 45.15.

Figure 45.15
The padlock icon and the https:// prefix tell you that the data you just sent was encrypted for safety's sake. Internet Explorer also warns you when you switch between secure and insecure connections.

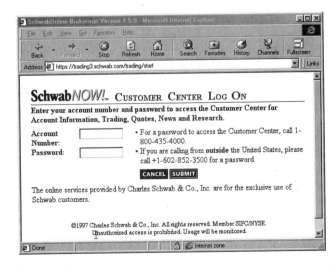

After you negotiate a secure connection, every bit of data is encrypted before sending and decrypted at the receiving end; only your machine and the secure server have the keys required to decode the encrypted packets. Because of the extra processing time on each end, loading HTML pages over an SSL connection takes longer.

NOTE For more information on certificates for commercial Web servers, visit

http://www.verisign.com/microsoft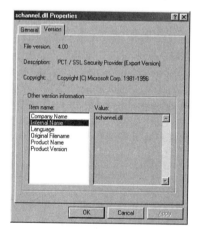

Although the built-in encryption capabilities of Internet Explorer 4.0 are powerful, one option can help you ensure even greater security. Because of United States Government export restrictions, the default encryption software uses 40-bit keys to scramble data before transmission. That makes it difficult to decode, but a determined hacker can break 40-bit encryption in relatively short order. A much more powerful version of the encryption engine uses 128-bit keys that are nearly impossible to crack; some banks and brokerage firms require the stronger encryption capabilities before you can access personal financial information online.

At this writing, the 128-bit security software is available only in the United States and Canada, although Microsoft has won permission to make this code available through banks and financial institutions overseas as well. To check which version you have, find a file called Schannel.dll, normally stored in the \Windows\System folder. Right-click on the file icon and choose Properties, and then inspect the Version tab, as in Figure 45.16.

Figure 45.16

If your copy of Internet Explorer includes the Export version of this security code, your commercial transactions are not as safe as they could be.

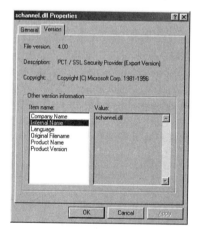

The weaker 40-bit encryption code includes the words "Export version" on the Properties tab. The stronger 128-bit security engine includes the label "US and Canada use only." You can download the 128-bit upgrade, as long as you do so from a machine that is physically located within the United States or Canada. You can find complete download instructions for the 128-bit upgrade at

http://www.microsoft.com/ie/ie40

How Safe Are "Cookies"?

When you view a page in your Web browser, some servers give you more than you asked for; quietly, without your knowledge, they record information about you and your actions in a hidden file called a *cookie*. In more formal terms, these data stores are called *client-side persistent data*, and they offer a simple way for a Web server to keep track of your actions. There are dozens of legitimate uses for cookies: Commercial Web sites use them to keep track of items as you add them to your online shopping basket; the *New York Times* Web site stores your username and password so you can log in automatically; still other sites deliver pages tailored to your interests, based on information you've entered in a Web-based form.

The first time you access a cookie-enabled server, the server creates a new cookie file in the Temporary Internet Files folder. That record contains the server's domain name, an expiration date, some security information, and any information the Webmaster chooses to store about the current page request. When you revisit that page (or access another page on the same site), the server can read and update information in the cookie record. Although information stored in each cookie is in plain text format, most sites use codes, making it nearly impossible to decipher exactly what's stored there.

If you're troubled at the thought of inadvertently sharing personal information with a Web site, you can disable cookies completely, or you can direct Internet Explorer to ask your permission before setting a cookie. To control your cookie collection, follow these steps:

1. Choose <u>V</u>iew, Internet <u>O</u>ptions and click the Advanced tab.
2. Scroll to the Security heading and find the section labeled Cookies (see Figure 45.17).

Figure 45.17

If you prefer not to share personal information with Web sites using hidden "cookie" files, change this default option.

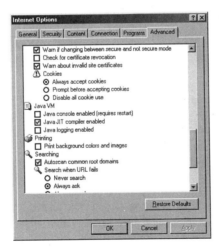

3. Choose the option you prefer: Disable All Cookie Use, or Prompt Before Accepting Cookies.
4. Click OK to record the new security settings.

Should you be overly concerned about cookies? The privacy risks are minimal, thanks to strict security controls built into your Web browser that limit what the server can and cannot do with cookies. They can't be used to retrieve information from your hard disk or your network; in fact, a server can retrieve information only from a cookie that it or another server in its domain created. A cookie can track only your movements within a given site; it can't tell a server where you came from or where you're going next.

Many Web designers set cookies simply because that's the default for the server software they use; the information they collect gathers dust, digitally speaking. So when you ask Internet Explorer to prompt you before accepting a cookie, be prepared for a barrage of dialog boxes like the one in Figure 45.18. Try saying no; the majority of Web sites work properly without cookies.

Figure 45.18

You can ask Internet Explorer to warn you before it accepts a cookie; click the More Info button to see the contents of the proposed cookie file, as shown here.

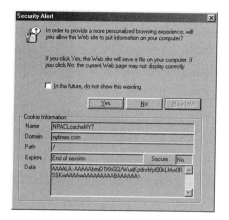

Simplifying Online Purchases with Microsoft Wallet

A new feature in Internet Explorer 4.0 makes it possible to conduct safe transactions over the Internet without having to continually re-enter your credit card and address information. The Microsoft Wallet lets you store address and credit card information in encrypted form on your hard disk. When you encounter a Web site that allows payments from the Microsoft Wallet, you select a credit card and address from the lists you created earlier, and then complete the transaction.

You can add multiple addresses and credit card entries to the Address Selector and Payment Selector lists. By entering separate home and work addresses, for example, as in Figure 45.19, you're free to order products and services for shipment to either address.

Figure 45.19

With multiple entries in the Microsoft Wallet Address Selector, you can easily tell a merchant where you want to receive goods you order over the Internet.

To add credit card information to the Payment Selector, follow these steps:

1. Choose View, Internet Options. Click the Content tab.
2. Click the Payments button to open the Payment Options dialog box.
3. Click the Add button and choose a payment method—Visa, MasterCard, American Express, or Discover—from the drop-down list.
4. Use the wizard (see Figure 45.20) to enter credit card information, select a billing address (or create a new address entry), and protect the information with a password.

Part

VIII

Ch

45

Figure 45.20

The display name you enter here identifies this card when you use the Microsoft Wallet. The following screen lets you protect this information with a password.

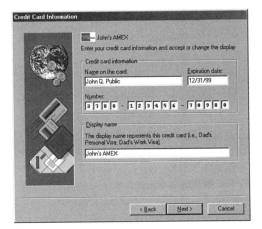

5. To add another credit card, repeat steps 3 and 4.
6. Click Close to exit the Payment Options dialog box.

Note that address information is not encrypted; anyone with access to your computer can view, edit, or delete this information. Credit card details, on the other hand, are password protected; if you forget your password, you have to delete the entry from the Payment Selector and re-enter it.

Controlling Access to Undesirable Content

Not every site on the Internet is worth visiting. Some, in fact, are downright offensive. That can present a problem at home, where children run the risk of accidentally stumbling across depictions of sex, violence, and other inappropriate content. It's also potentially a problem at the office, where offensive or inappropriate content can drain productivity and expose a corporation to legal liability in the form of sexual harassment suits.

Internet Explorer includes a feature called the Content Advisor, which uses an industrywide rating system to restrict the types of content that can be displayed within the borders of your browser. Before you can use the Content Advisor, you have to enable it: Choose View, Internet Options, click the Content tab, and click the Enable button. You have to enter a supervisor's password before continuing. After you've handled those housekeeping chores, you see the main Content Advisor window, shown in Figure 45.21.

Figure 45.21

Use the Content Advisor's ratings system to restrict access to Web sites that contain unacceptable content.

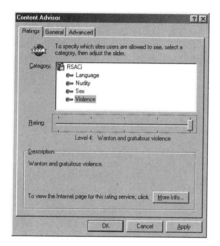

The Content Advisor interface is self-explanatory: You use slider controls to define acceptable levels of sex, violence, language, and nudity. After you click OK, only sites whose ratings match your settings are allowed in the browser window.

Surprisingly, many adult sites adhere to the rating system, and an increasing number of mainstream business sites have added the necessary HTML tags to their sites as well. Unfortunately, many mainstream business sites don't use these ratings; as a result, you want to avoid setting the option to restrict unrated sites. ●

CHAPTER 46

Building Compound Documents

by Joe Kraynak

In this chapter

Sharing Office Data Between Applications

Each Microsoft office application offers specialized tools. Word excels in text editing and layout; Excel specializes in numbers, calculations, and charts; PowerPoint provides superior tools for creating presentations; and Access is best for database management.

As separate components, these applications are very powerful. However, if you want to tap the full power of the Office synergy, you need to use the applications together.

As you create reports, slideshows, brochures, and other documents, you will start to see a need to share data between documents. For example, you may need to insert a chart from Excel into a PowerPoint presentation or insert a portion of an Excel worksheet into a report.

Overview of Compound Documents

Compound documents are documents that contain data from two or more applications that support OLE (object linking and embedding, pronounced oh-LAY). With OLE, applications and documents can share data dynamically. If you copy and paste data from an Excel worksheet into a Word document, for example, the pasted worksheet data is inserted as an OLE object in the Word document.

If you paste the object as a link, whenever you edit the worksheet in Excel the changes automatically appear in the Word document. If you paste the data as an embedded object, the link to the source document is broken but the object still retains a relationship with the application used to create it. You can edit the embedded object in its source application by double-clicking it.

When you copy and paste data as OLE objects, one document acts as the destination (container) and the other as the source (server). The document that receives the pasted data is called the destination document. The contributing document is called the source document. By copying objects from a source document and pasting them into a destination document, you create a compound document.

Copying and Pasting Between Applications

Simple copy/paste or drag-and-drop operations typically use the Windows Clipboard to transfer the copied object to the destination document. This terminates the relationship between the source and its copy and between the copy and the application that was used to create it. In many cases this is just what you want to do; you can then edit the copy without changing the source.

In other cases you may want to preserve the relationship between the source and the copy so that when you change the source its copy is automatically updated. For example, if you paste a portion of an Excel worksheet into a Word document, you may want the pasted worksheet data automatically updated whenever you edit the worksheet in Excel. This prevents you from having to enter your changes in two documents. It also saves storage space because you do not have to store the same data in two files.

Linking and Embedding

As you copy and paste data between Office documents, you need to be aware of the available options and question how you want the source and the copy related. You can share data in any of the following four ways:

- *Link*. If you're using Office 97 applications or any other applications that support OLE, you can share data between documents by creating a link. With a link, the file into which you pasted the data does not actually contain the linked data; the linked data is stored in a separate (source) file. Whenever you edit the linked file (the source), any changes you make to it appear in all other documents that contain links to the source. For example, if you insert an Excel chart into a Word document as a link, whenever you change the chart in Excel, the modified chart appears in the Word document.

- *Embed*. With OLE, you can also embed data from one file into another file. With embedding, the pasted data becomes a part of the file into which you paste it. If you edit the source, the changes do not show up in the copy. Likewise, if you edit the copy, the changes are not made to the source. In short, embedding breaks the link between the copy and the source. However, the pasted data retains a connection with the program that you used to create it. So if you double-click the embedded object, Windows automatically runs the associated application and you can edit the data.

- *Paste*. You can paste data in any number of ways (including pasting the data as an embedded or linked object). However, not all applications support OLE. For those applications that do not support OLE, you can still share data between documents by copying and pasting the data, assuming the application supports the file format of the pasted data. However, the pasted data will have no connection with the source document or with the application that you used to create it.

- *Hyperlink*. If you work on an intranet, you can create online documents with hyperlinks that point to other documents on your computer or on the intranet. To view a document with the most up-to-date information, the user clicks the hyperlink. Although hyperlinks do not display data from a source file in the destination file, they do make it easy to access related information and they are very easy to manage.

Part VIII
Ch
46

In-Place Editing

One of the major advantages of OLE in Office 97 is that you can edit objects in place. When you choose to edit an embedded or linked object in an Office document, the Office application does not kick you out to another application. Instead, the application used to create the source data takes over the current application window, displaying its own toolbars and menus (see Figure 46.1). You can then edit the object right inside the same window that displays the destination document.

Format Options for Links and Embedded Objects

When you choose to paste data as a link or as an embedded object (using Edit, Paste Special), the Paste Special dialog box (see Figure 46.2) displays several formats from which to choose. For example, if you paste Excel worksheet data into a Word document, you can choose to paste it as an Excel Worksheet Object, as Formatted Text (as a Rich Text File), or as a picture. Use the following list to help you decide which format to choose:

Figure 46.1

With in-place editing, you can edit the source document right inside the destination document's application window.

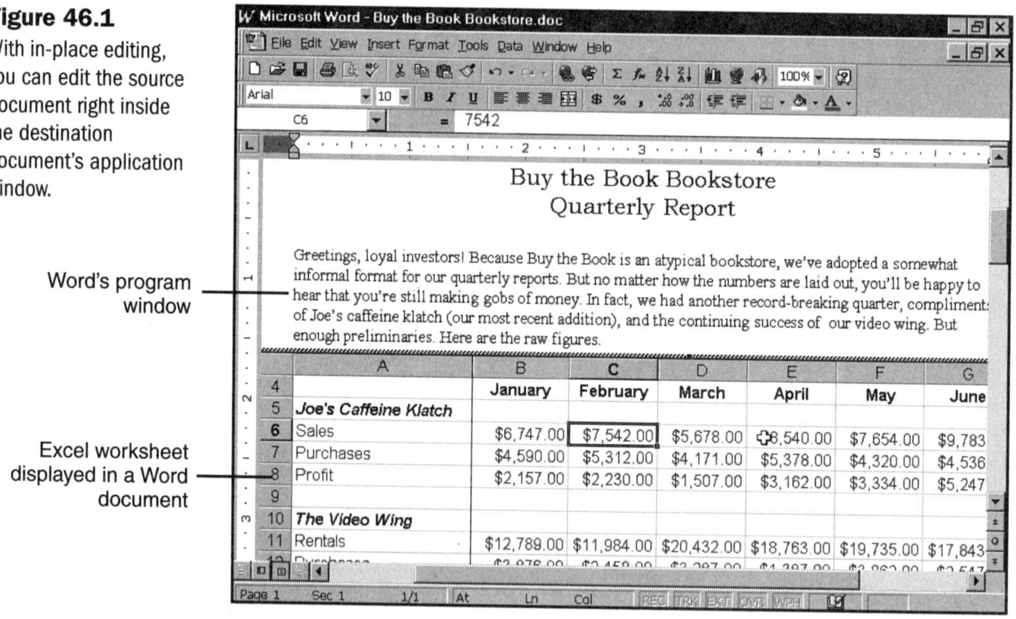

Word's program window

Excel worksheet displayed in a Word document

- **Object.** In most cases you should choose the option with "Object" in its name (for example, Microsoft Excel Worksheet Object or Microsoft PowerPoint Slide Object). This inserts the object as a Windows Meta File (WMF), which displays a graphic representation of the source data. You can edit the object by double-clicking it.

- **Formatted Text (RTF).** This option inserts the object as formatted text. For example, if you paste data from a spreadsheet into a Word document or a PowerPoint slide, the text is formatted using the Tables feature. With RTF, you can edit individual entries in the linked or embedded object. However, if you edit a linked object and then close and reopen the document that contains the link, any edited entries revert back to the entries used in the source document.

- **Unformatted Text.** Select this option to insert text without formatting. This is not a very practical option, especially for pasting Excel worksheet data, because the data no longer appears in columns. However, if you are pasting data from a document that contains incompatible formatting codes, this may be your only option.

- **Picture.** This option inserts the data as a high-quality graphic image that requires relatively little storage space and displays quickly in the destination document. If you choose to embed pasted data and share the destination document with other users, this option is best in terms of speed, storage, and quality.

Figure 46.2

The Paste Special dialog box lets you specify how you want the object inserted.

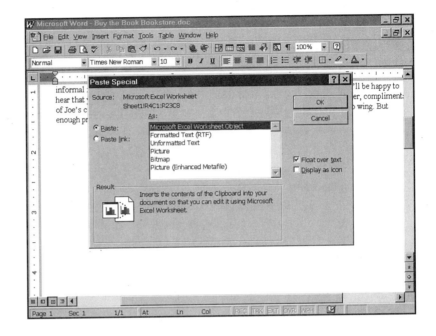

Embedding Objects in a Document

When you want to share data between documents but keep the source file from being altered, you can copy and paste the data as an embedded object. The copy becomes the sole possession of the destination document. If you edit the source data, the copy does not reflect the changes.

Another consideration with embedded objects is file size. When you embed objects in a document, those objects contain the copied data. As you embed objects, the file size of the destination document grows. If you are concerned about file size, you may want to paste the copied data as a link. See "Inserting Linked Objects in Documents," later in this chapter.

To insert data as an embedded object, choose one of the following:

- You can copy existing data from a document and paste it as an embedded object.
- You can create a new embedded object, using the Insert, Object command. You use Insert, Object if the object you want to insert does not yet exist. The following sections provide instructions on how to copy and paste embedded objects and create new embedded objects.

Copying and Pasting Data as an Embedded Object

All of the Microsoft Office 97 applications support OLE, so you can paste data as embedded objects from a document you created in any of your Office applications into any document created in another Office application. In addition, you can share data with any other Windows application that supports OLE, such as WordPerfect, Lotus, Windows Paint, or CorelDraw! To insert data as an embedded object, complete the following steps:

1. Open the document that contains the data you want to copy and select the data. For example, you might drag over the cells you want to copy in an Excel worksheet or select PowerPoint slides in Slide Sorter view.

2. Choose Edit, Copy or click the Copy button.

3. Open the document in which you want to embed the copied data. Move the insertion point to the location where you want to paste the copied data.

4. Choose Edit, Paste Special. The Paste Special dialog box appears, as shown in Figure 46.2.

5. Make sure Paste (not Paste Link) is selected.

6. In the As list, select the desired format for the pasted object. See "Format Options for Links and Embedded Objects," earlier in this chapter, for details.

7. By default, Float Over Text is on (checked). This places the object on the drawing layer so that you can position it over existing text or other objects in the document. If you want to treat the object as text, choose the Float Over Text check box to turn it off (clear the check).

8. To display the inserted object as an icon that people can click to view the object, select Display As Icon.

9. Click OK. The object is inserted. The preferences you entered control the object's appearance and position.

TROUBLESHOOTING

Embedded object appears cropped. If the embedded object is too large to fit inside its frame, it may appear cropped. To make the object fit inside the margins, reformat the data in the source application to make it smaller, for example, reduce the font size. Or, paste the data as Formatted or Unformatted Text and then change the formatting in the destination document.

When you insert data from an Excel worksheet into a Word document, Word can display data from only one worksheet at a time.

Creating a New Embedded Object

The most convenient way to insert an embedded object is to copy data from an existing document. If you have not yet created the document, you can create and paste the embedded object on the fly, using another OLE compatible application, such as one of the Office applications.

In addition, Office comes with several OLE applets, such as MSGraph, that act as mini-server applications. You cannot execute these applets as stand-alone applications; they run only from within a destination document. To use them to create embedded objects, you must create the embedded object as a new object.

To create a new embedded object, complete the following steps:

1. Open the document in which you want to embed the object and position the insertion point where you want the object inserted.

2. Choose Insert, Object. (In some non-Office applications, you may have to select Edit, Insert Object.) The Object dialog box appears, displaying the Create New tab in front.

3. Select the type of object you want to insert and click OK. The application for the type of object you selected starts. If you look at the toolbar and menu commands, you can see that you are in a different application.

4. Create the object using the commands and features of that application.

5. When you complete the object, click anywhere inside the document. This closes the application you used to create the embedded object. You cannot open the embedded object as a separate file, but you can edit the object by double-clicking it.

Working with Embedded Objects

When you insert cut or copied data as an embedded object (by selecting the Object or Picture option from the As list), the data appears as part of the document. When you select an embedded object (usually by clicking it), selection handles appear around the object, as shown in Figure 46.3.

Figure 46.3
You can select an embedded object to move or resize it.

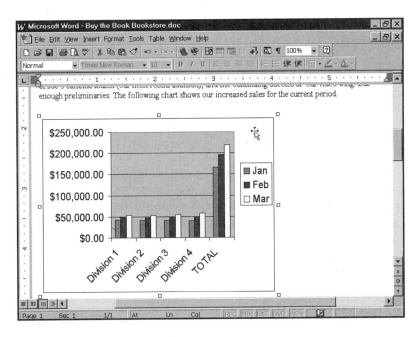

You can then do any of the following to modify the object:

■ To move the object, move the mouse pointer to a border (but not a selection handle) and drag the object to where you want it.

- To resize an object, move the tip of the mouse pointer over a selection handle and drag the handle to change the object's size or dimensions. Drag a corner handle to resize the object proportionally.

- To edit the object, double-click it. Windows runs the application associated with the object, allowing you to use the application's tools to modify the object.

- To delete an object, select the object and then press the Delete key.

- To convert an object from an icon to content or vice versa, select Edit, ObjectName Object, Convert. Select Display As Icon to turn it off or on, and click OK. If you turn Display As Icon off, the pasted object appears instead of the icon.

If you pasted Word text or Excel worksheet data as Formatted Text (RTF), no selection handles appear around the object when you click it. Also, you cannot double-click the object to edit it in its source application.

TIP When you're working with the Office 97 applications, don't forget one of the data sharing features built right into Windows 95—scraps. If you select data in a document and then drag it to a blank area on the Windows desktop, Windows creates a shortcut for the data and marks it as a scrap. You can then drag this scrap into another document to insert it.

Inserting Linked Objects in a Document

Links are excellent if you need to share data on a network, or if you must use data from the same source document in several documents. You simply edit the source document and the updated data automatically appears in all of the documents in which you have inserted its data as links. However, links do have a couple of drawbacks:

- When you link data, you have two separate documents stored in two separate files: the destination and source documents. If you send someone the destination document, you must also send the source document. And, because the link specifies the location of the source document, that document must be stored on the same drive and in the same folder where your system stored the document.

- A link extracts data from a source document stored in a specific folder. If someone renames or moves the file, the link will no longer work. This can be a problem if someone else is in charge of maintaining the source document.

Despite these drawbacks, links are a very valuable tool, especially if you work on a network and need to share files with other departments or coworkers. The following sections provide instructions on inserting links, working with linked data, and using hyperlinks as an alternative to links.

Inserting Links

Before you can insert data from one document as a link in another document, you must make sure you have access to both documents. If you work on a network and you need to link to a document on the network, you must know the location of the file and have permission to open and modify it. You can then complete the following steps to create the link:

1. Open the document that contains the data you want to copy and select the data. For example, you may select one or two slides of a PowerPoint presentation or select a range of cells or a chart in Excel.

2. Select Edit, Copy or click the Copy button.

3. Open the document in which you want to paste the data. Move the insertion point to the location where you want the data pasted.

4. Select Edit, Paste Special. The Paste Special dialog box appears.

5. Select Paste Link, as shown in Figure 46.4. If you do not select this option, the data will be pasted as an embedded object.

6. In the As list, select the desired format for the pasted object. See "Format Options for Links and Embedded Objects," earlier in this chapter, for details.

7. By default, Float Over Text is on. This places the object on the drawing layer so that you can position it over existing text or other objects in the document. If you want to treat the object as text, select Float Over Text to turn it off.

8. To display the inserted object as an icon that people can click to view the object, select Display As Icon.

9. Click OK. The object is inserted. The preferences you entered control the object's appearance and position.

Part
VIII

Ch
46

Figure 46.4

The Paste Special dialog box lets you determine how the data will be pasted.

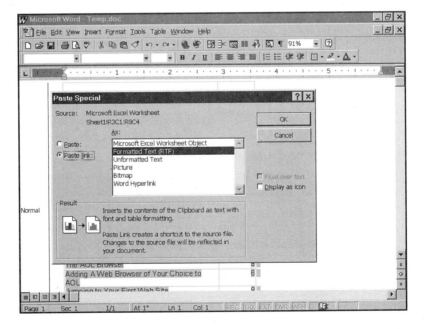

Editing Links

If you inserted data as a linked object or picture, you can select it by clicking it and then move or resize it, just as if you were working with an embedded object. To edit the object in the source application, double-click the object.

However, if you inserted the link as Formatted Text, you cannot select the object or double-click the object to edit it. To format or edit the data, you must first open the link in the source application by performing the following steps:

1. Choose Edit, Links. A list of links in the current document appears, as shown in Figure 46.5.

2. Click the link you want to edit or format and select Open Source. This displays the source document in the application used to create it.

3. Enter your changes to the source document.

4. Choose File, Exit (or File, Close if you want to continue working in Excel).

Figure 46.5

You can view a list of links in the current document.

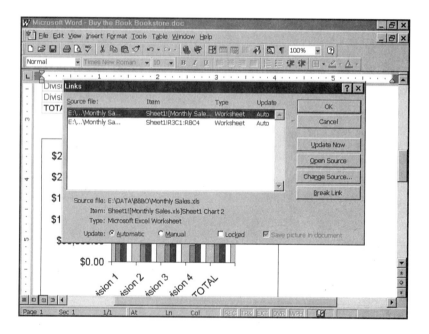

TROUBLESHOOTING

Cannot edit the link. If you receive an error message indicating that you cannot edit the link, check the following:

- If you are working on a network, make sure no one else has the source document open.

- Make sure the source document has not been moved or renamed. If it has, see "Relinking When Files Move," later in this chapter, to learn how to redirect the link.

- In order to edit the link, you must have a copy of the source application and your system must have sufficient memory to run both applications.

- Make sure no dialog boxes are open in the source application.

 You can quickly edit a linked object in any format by right-clicking the linked object, choosing Linked Object, and selecting Edit Link. If the linked object is an Excel table pasted as RTF, first make sure the insertion point is inside the table but that nothing in the table is highlighted.

Using Hyperlinks

If you are working on an intranet, you may want to insert hyperlinks rather than pasting data as embedded or linked objects. The user can then click a hyperlink in your document to view updated data. This keeps the size of the destination document small. It also makes it easy to maintain the links; you simply need to make sure that the link always points to the correct location of the file.

N O T E Do not confuse hyperlinks with links. Hyperlinks are used in Web documents to link one document to another. They point to a specific file stored on another drive, Web server, or other Internet server. Links are used in Office documents to pull data from one document into another document. ▨

Part

VIII

Ch

46

There are two ways you can insert hyperlinks. The easiest way is to insert a hyperlink as if you were linking to a Web page. Complete the following steps:

1. Type the text or insert an image that you want the user to click to view the linked data and select the image or text.

2. Select Insert, Hyperlink (Ctrl+K) or click the Insert Hyperlink button on the Web toolbar. This opens the Insert Hyperlink dialog box, as shown in Figure 46.6.

3. In the Link To File Or URL text box, type the path to the file you want the link to point to or click Browse to select the file from a list.

4. In the Named Location In File text box, enter the bookmark name, range name, database object, or slide number you want the link to point to or click Browse to select the object from a list.

CAUTION

Do not type anything in the Named Location in File text box or use the Browse button next to it unless you have already inserted bookmarks in the document to which you are linking. Otherwise, you will receive an error message indicating that no bookmarks exist.

5. Click OK. Your application displays the link as blue text or places a blue border around the image.

Figure 46.6

You can create a hyperlink to a specific area in a document.

You can also insert copied data as a hyperlink by choosing Edit, Paste As Hyperlink. However, this inserts the entire object as a hyperlink. For example, if you paste a portion of an Excel worksheet as a hyperlink, all the cell entries in the pasted object appear blue and all point to the same Excel file.

Maintaining and Updating Links

Because links (not hyperlinks) allow you to share data dynamically, you must maintain them to ensure that they work properly and that your destination document always has the latest data from the source document. If you work on a network and someone moves the source document, you must edit the link's properties so it points to the document's new location.

In addition, links may be too automated for your purposes. When you open a document that contains links, the links automatically extract the latest data from the source document and insert it into the destination document. However, you might not always want the latest data. For example, if you are working on a quarterly report, you may want the link to insert last quarter's figures. To do this, you can lock the link to prevent the link from automatically updating itself.

Office provides several options for maintaining your links and for specifying how automated you want them to be. The following sections explain these options in detail.

Relinking When Files Move

If you work with Web documents, you know that a hyperlink works only as long as the file that the hyperlink points to does not move. The same is true with links. Links contain information about the location and name of the source document. If you or someone else moves the source document, you must redirect the link to point to the source document's new location. Complete the following steps to redirect the link:

1. Choose Edit, Links. The Links dialog box appears, displaying a list of links in the current document.

2. Click the link you want to redirect and click Change Source. The Change Source dialog box appears, allowing you to select the source document.

3. Change to the folder where the source document is stored, select the source document, and click OK. This returns you to the Links dialog box.

4. Click OK to save your changes.

Locking Links

To prevent links from automatically extracting updated data from the source document, you can lock the link. Locking the link is like turning it into a temporary embedded object. To lock one or more links in a document, complete the following steps:

1. Choose Edit, Links. The Links dialog box appears, as shown in Figure 46.7, displaying a list of links in the current document.

2. Click the link you want to lock. Ctrl+click to select additional links.

3. Select Locked to place a check in its check box.

4. Click OK to save your changes.

Figure 46.7
You can lock links to prevent them from showing updated data from the source document.

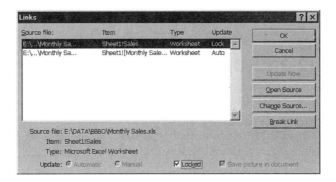

Part
VIII
Ch
46

When you lock a link, the data from the source document remains fixed and you cannot manually update the link. Perform the same steps to unlock the link.

Updating Links

By default, links are set to automatically update themselves. However, you can change the properties of the link so that the link updates itself only when you enter the update command. To set a link for manual updates, complete the following steps:

1. Choose Edit, Links. The Links dialog box appears, displaying a list of links in the current document.

2. Click the link you want to manually update. Ctrl+click to select additional links.

3. Next to the Update option, select Manual.

4. Click OK to save your changes.

When you set links for manual updates, you can pull updated data from the source document by performing one of the following steps:

- In the destination document, select Edit, Links. Select the links you want to update and click Update Now.
- You can update the links automatically when you print the container document. Select Tools, Options and click the Print tab. Under Printing Options, click Update Links. Click OK.

 T I P To quickly update a single link, select the link and press F9.

Unlinking Links

You can terminate the relationship between the link and the source document by breaking the link. This essentially transforms the link into an embedded object, preventing any changes to the source document from appearing in the container document.

To break a link, select Edit, Links. Select the link you want to break and click Break Link.

N O T E When you unlink a link, the link is broken. The only way to reestablish the link is to insert it again. ■

Using Data from Non-OLE Applications

Most new applications, such as CorelDraw! and WordPerfect, are OLE compatible, allowing you to paste data as a link or embedded object. However, some applications do not support the dynamic data-sharing capabilities of OLE. In such cases, you can still copy and paste data between documents by using the Windows Clipboard.

Copying and pasting via the Clipboard does not activate any dynamic data sharing capabilities. It simply pastes the copied data into your document. You can't double-click the copy to edit it in its source application, and the pasted data does not reflect changes made to the source document.

Complete the following steps to copy data from a non-OLE document into your Office document:

1. In the non-OLE application, open the document that contains the data you want to copy.
2. Select the data.
3. Use the application's Copy command to place the data on the Windows Clipboard.
4. Run your Office application and open the document into which you want to paste the Clipboard contents. Move the insertion point to where you want the data to be pasted.
5. Choose Edit, Paste or click the Paste button.

N O T E Although Office has several file format converters, you may run into problems if you try to paste data in a format that Office does not support. If you encounter problems with incompatible file formats, open the file in the program used to create it and save the file in a format that your Office application supports. ▨

Other Ways to Share Data in Office

Word, Access, PowerPoint, and Excel offer additional tools that allow you to share data and make the most of the specialized tools available in each application. For example, you can use an outline you created in Word to create a PowerPoint presentation or use Word's advanced page layout tools to format and print a report you created in Access. The following sections provide details on how to use the Office applications together.

Exporting a PowerPoint Presentation as a Word Outline

Not only does PowerPoint allow you to view and edit a presentation in Outline view but you can also export the presentation as a Word outline. You can then modify the outline in Word and add text and other objects to flesh out your document. To convert a PowerPoint presentation into a Word outline, complete the following steps:

1. Open the presentation in PowerPoint.
2. Choose File, Send To, Microsoft Word. The Write-Up dialog box appears, asking how you want the slides and text laid out on Word pages (see Figure 46.8).
3. Under Page Layout In Microsoft Word, select the desired slide and text layout. To export the presentation as an outline (without slides), select Outline Only.
4. If you chose to include slides in the Word document, you can select Paste Link to paste the slides as a links. (This option is unavailable if you selected Outline Only in step 3.)
5. Click OK. PowerPoint converts the presentation into a Word document and displays the document in Word, where you can start working on it.

You can also transform an outline you typed in Word into a PowerPoint presentation. Open the outline you created in Word. Select File, Send To, Microsoft PowerPoint. Select the desired slide layout and click OK.

Analyzing Access Data in Excel

Although Access is the best tool to use for storing and extracting data, Excel provides superior tools for performing calculations and for analyzing data. If you have tried entering formulas in your Access report, you know how difficult it can be to enter the correct formula using the correct field codes. It's much easier to enter formulas in Excel using cell addresses or the point-and-click method.

In addition, Excel offers scenarios that allow you to play "What if?" with a set of values. You can change one or more values to see how the changes will affect the net result. And you can create several scenarios to see how they compare.

Part
VIII

Ch
46

Figure 46.8

PowerPoint lets you export a presentation as a Word document.

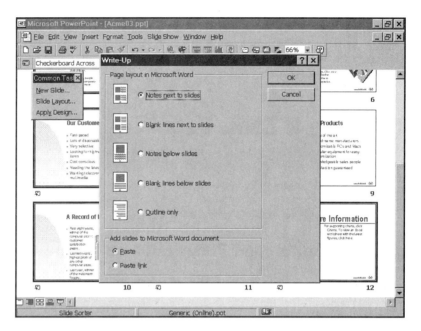

To send a table, form, query, or report to Excel, first open it in Access. Then, select Tools, Office Links, Analyze It With MS Excel (or click the OfficeLinks button and select Analyze It with MS Excel).

Publishing Access Reports with Word

Access provides excellent tools for storing and managing data, but its page layout features are inadequate and difficult to master. For more control over the look and layout of your reports, consider converting the report into a Word document.

To convert an Access report to Word format, first open the report in Access. Click the Office Links button and select Publish It With MS Word. Access exports the report to Word, creating a new document (see Figure 46.9). You can now format the document using Word's advanced formatting tools, and you can add graphics and other objects to enhance the document.

You can also use Access and Word together to merge your Word documents with an Access database. For example, you can merge a form letter created in Word with an address list stored in Access or automate the creation of mailing labels.

Figure 46.9

You can export an Access report to create a Word document.

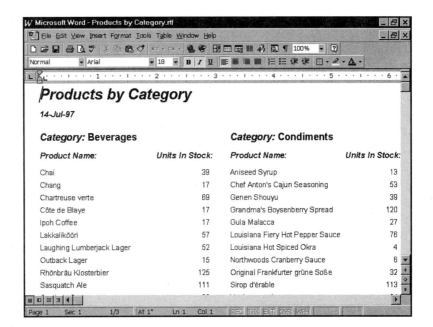

CHAPTER 47

Sharing and Securing Resources

by Nancy Warner

In this chapter

Using Resource Sharing and Security

Mainframe computers were the original networks, with their many workstations continually sending and receiving information. While a user was initiating the work from the workstation, the mainframe did all the work—and it had to, because it had all the resources. All the processing power, storage devices, and printers were connected to the mainframe. This arrangement made security easy to set up, because all requests to use resources had to go through a single location.

The growth of the PC resulted in a new type of network, in which workstations could perform tasks without making a request of a central computer. The PC has all the resources that the mainframe once had a monopoly on—namely, processing power and storage capability. Although the PC became a valuable tool, it could not replace the mainframe; it still had to use the mainframe's resources. Eventually, the PC was created with many of the same capabilities as the mainframe, which resulted in the creation of client/server networks.

In a client/server network, one or more PCs (or a mainframe) acts as a server that controls access to network resources. PCs that are being used as workstations are called *clients*. Clients request the use of resources from servers. The final step in the evolution of the network allowed workstations to use resources located on other workstations, which is called *peer-to-peer networking* or sharing peer resources. Although a server normally handles security, peer-to-peer networking also gives the client the capability to control access to its own resources. Figure 47.1 shows the different elements that a modern network can contain.

Figure 47.1

Modern networks must integrate the new technology with the old.

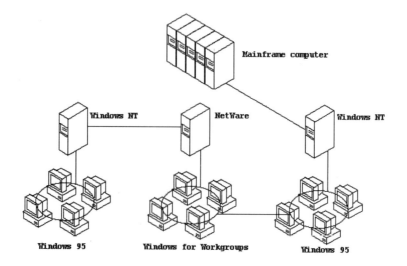

You can use peer-to-peer networking to share files created in any of the Office applications. The following two sections discuss how to share resources and which types of security you can use.

Sharing Peer Resources

A network is normally made up of many workstations and several servers. Files that many users need to use are usually stored on a server, but in some situations, files are stored on a workstation. Resources that are stored on a workstation instead of on a server are called *peer resources* because they are shared by means of peer-to-peer networking. Peer-resource sharing is a networking service that must be installed before you can take advantage of it. Open the Control Panel and open the Network settings to see whether peer-resource sharing is installed. Figure 47.2 shows a Network properties dialog box for a workstation with peer-resource sharing installed for Microsoft Networks—File and Print Sharing for Microsoft Networks.

Figure 47.2

You can share files and printers by using peer-resource sharing.

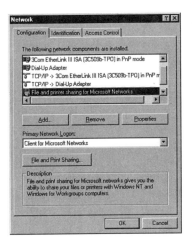

CAUTION

Peer resources can be shared for either Microsoft Networks or NetWare Networks, but they cannot be shared for both. Use the sharing method that gives more users access to your resources, using the desired security method.

If peer resource sharing isn't installed, you have to install it before you can give other users access to documents on your computer. To install peer-resource sharing, follow these steps:

N O T E For information about how to perform this procedure in Windows NT Workstation, see your Windows NT Workstation documentation. ▪

1. Open the Control Panel.
2. Open the Network properties.
3. Click the Add button in the Configuration page of the Network properties dialog box to open the Select Network Component Type dialog box, shown in Figure 47.3.

Part
VIII

Ch
47

Figure 47.3

Use Select Network Component Type dialog box to select network components.

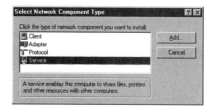

4. Choose the Service option.

5. Click the Add button to open the Select Network Service dialog box, shown in Figure 47.4.

Figure 47.4

Use the Select Network Service dialog box to install the proper services.

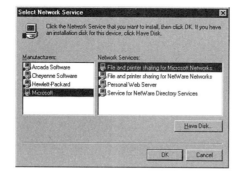

6. Select Microsoft in the Manufacturers list.

7. Select File and Print Sharing for Microsoft Networks in the Network Services list.

    If your computer is on a NetWare network, select File and Print Sharing for NetWare Networks instead.

    If prompted, insert the Windows 98 CD and click OK.

8. When you return to the Properties dialog box, click the OK button to apply your changes. If prompted to restart the PC, choose Yes.

N O T E   To use file and print sharing for Microsoft Networks, you must have the Client for Microsoft Network installed. To install that client, follow the steps that you use to install peer-resource sharing, but choose Client and Client for Microsoft Networks in place of Service and File and Print Sharing for Microsoft Networks. ▧

When peer-resource sharing is installed, you can share files and printers with other users on your network. If you want to, you can share only files or only printers by choosing the Network option in the Control Panel and then clicking the File and Print Sharing button. The File and Print Sharing dialog box, shown in Figure 47.5, opens, allowing you to specify which types of resources can be shared on your computer.

Figure 47.5

Use this dialog box to select the resources to be shared.

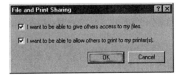

A consideration that you must make before sharing resources on your computer is how to protect them from unwelcome users. Two types of security are available to protect shared resources; the following section covers both of them.

Securing Shared Resources

You can use Windows 98 security to limit the availability of shared resources on a network. The type of network and the type of established security measures determine the type of security that you can use on your network. Depending on those factors, several elements become important in securing shared resources:

- Windows 98 logon
- Share-level security for peer-resource sharing
- User-level security for peer-resource sharing
- Password cache

The Windows 98 logon becomes a key security feature if computers on a network must be logged onto a Windows NT domain or NetWare server. Windows cannot be started if a proper logon does not occur. In this case, network resources are protected, because all access to the network is denied. Remember that this feature prevents a user from starting Windows only when your network is using a Windows NT domain or NetWare server.

Forcing a computer to log onto a network before it can access the resources of that network protects the network resources. However, a user could still access the files on a computer without logging on to the network. A user could access files by using one of two methods:

- Starting the computer in safe mode
- Using a boot disk to start the computer

If these security problems are unacceptable, you should look into installing Windows NT Workstation on your computer.

Users can connect to shared folders and printers on Windows 98 computers that are using file and printer sharing services. You can protect these shared peer resources by using either share-level or user-level security. Both types of security require a user to supply a password to use a shared resource.

Share-level security (which is discussed further in "Using Share-Level Security" later in this chapter) is the simpler of the two types of security for peer-resource sharing. All the security and password validation is done on the computer that has the shared resource. Figure 47.6 shows the communication that takes place if a computer accesses a shared resource that uses share-level security.

Part

VIII

Ch

47

Figure 47.6

For share-level security, each computer handles the security of its own resources.

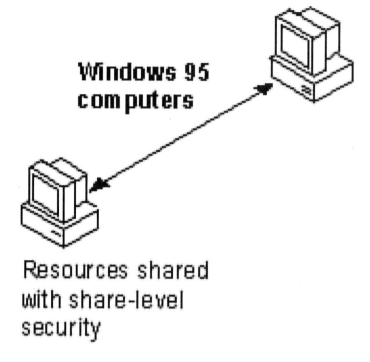

You can use share-level security to share resources as read-only, full access (read, write, or delete), or a combination. When using share-level security, you can specify how resources can be used when a password is supplied, but you cannot specify how specific users can use those resources. In other words, anyone who supplies the proper password can use the resource. You can supply a different password to be used for read-only and full access, however.

 A resource can be shared more than once. If you need some users to have access to a resource for only a week and other users to have access for a month, share the resource twice and use a different password each time.

User-level security is a more complex type of security that uses the power of your network's built-in security. Instead of the security mechanism that resides on the machine that has the shared resources, user-level security checks users and their passwords against the network server. This type of security is referred to as *pass-through security* because the user name and password are passed through to the network server for authentication. Figure 47.7 shows the communication that takes place if a computer accesses a shared resource that uses user-level security.

Figure 47.7

User-level security uses the network server to limit access to resources on other computers.

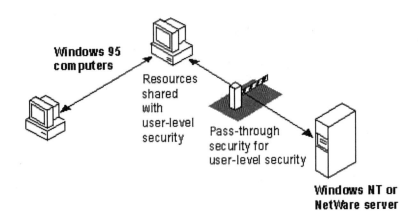

You can use user-level security to share resources as read-only, full access, or custom. (Custom sharing is discussed further in "Using User-Level Security" later in this chapter.) You don't have to supply any passwords—only users or groups of users. All user names and password information are maintained on the network server. Figure 47.8 shows the process that occurs when a user asks to use a resource shared with user-level security. The process goes as follows:

1. A computer requests a shared resource.
2. The computer with the shared resource asks the server if the user name and password supplied with the request are valid.
3. The server tells the computer with the shared resource if the user name and password are valid or invalid.
4. The computer with the shared resource either gives the requesting computer access to the resource that was requested or refuses it access, depending on the outcome of step 3.

When you designate which users can use the shared resource, you also designate how they can use it: read, write, delete, and so on.

CAUTION

Groups of users are designated on a network server. A group named Accounting, for example, might include all the users in the accounting department. If a shared resource is made available to a group, everyone in the group is added, so be sure that is what you want.

Using Share-Level Security

To use share-level security, you must specify in your network properties. To verify the security that your computer is using, open the Network properties dialog box by choosing the Network option in the Control Panel. Click the Access Control tab. Figure 47.9 shows the Network Properties dialog box for a computer that is using share-level access control.

Part
VIII
Ch
47

Figure 47.8

The network sever decides whether a user can use a shared resource.

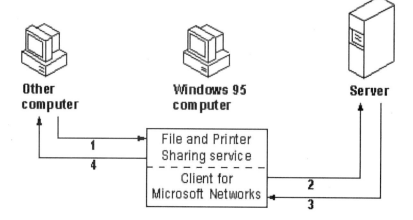

Figure 47.9

Access control security is specified in the Network Properties dialog box.

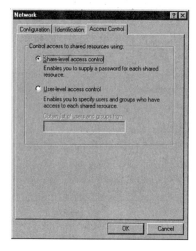

Share-level security puts the burden of limiting the access to shared resources on the computer that contains the shared resource. These resources can be folders or printers.

To share a folder by using share-level security, follow these steps:

N O T E Share-level security cannot be used on NetWare networks. ▪

1. Open a Windows Explorer window.
2. Right-click the Program Files folder.
3. Choose Sharing from the shortcut menu that appears. Figure 47.10 shows the Sharing dialog box that opens.

Figure 47.10

The Sharing dialog box indicates when a resource is not shared.

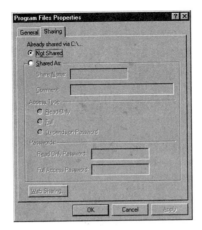

4. Click the Shared As button to share the folder.

   The shared resource is given a default share name: the first 12 letters of the folder's name. The share name is what other users see when they use Network Neighborhood to locate the resource on your computer.

5. Change the share name to **Share Test**.

6. Add the comment **This is a test**.

 You can hide a shared resource from users who are browsing the Network Neighborhood by placing a dollar sign (**$**) at the end of the share name (**INVISIBLE$**, for example). The resource is still shared; users just can't find it by using Network Neighborhood.

---

7. Choose Depends on Password Access Type. When you choose this option, the type of access that users have depends on the passwords that they provide.

8. Type **read** in the Read-Only Password text box.

9. Type **full** in the Full Access Password text box.

   Figure 47.11 shows what the Sharing dialog box should look like now. Users who enter **read** as the password have the capability only to read files in this folder, but users who enter **full** have full access to the folder. Entering passwords is covered in "Understanding the Password Cache" later in this chapter.

N O T E For security purposes, typed passwords appear onscreen as asterisks (*). ▉

 If you leave the password text box blank, users do not have to supply a password when they use that resource.

Figure 47.11

The share name can be different from the resource's actual name.

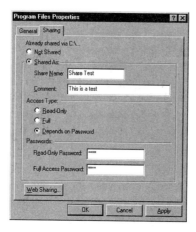

10. Click the OK or Apply button to force your changes to take effect.

11. Retype your password choice(s) and click the OK button.

N O T E   Click the Web Sharing button in the Sharing dialog box to share a resource by using the Internet's HTTP and/or FTP standards. ▪

Using User-Level Security

You must specify that you want to use user-level security. This property is listed in the Network properties dialog box, which you open by choosing the Network option in the Control Panel and clicking the Access Control tab. Figure 47.12 shows the Network properties dialog box for a computer that is using user-level access control.

Figure 47.12

You must specify the location of valid users and groups when you set up user-level security.

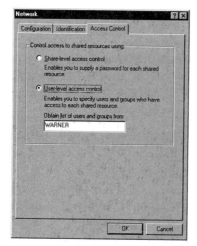

In addition to choosing user-level access control, you must provide the location of the users, groups of users, and their passwords. Those lists are used to enforce the security measures that you define for your shared resources. If you have to make this change in your network properties, you must restart the computer before the change takes effect.

N O T E If you are using file and print sharing for Microsoft Networks, a Windows NT domain or workstation must be your security provider. If you are using file and print sharing for NetWare, a NetWare server must be your security provider. ■

User-level security passes the job of limiting the access to shared resources to the computer that maintains security for the entire network. To share a folder by using user-level security, follow these steps:

1. Open a Windows Explorer window.
2. Right-click the Program Files folder.
3. Choose Sharing from the shortcut menu that appears. Figure 47.13 shows the Sharing dialog box that opens.

Figure 47.13
You use the Sharing dialog box to give users access to shared resources.

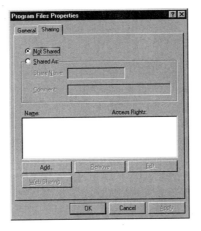

Part
VIII

Ch
47

N O T E If your screen looks like Figure 47.11 instead of 47.13, make sure you have chosen User-Level Access Control in the Network Properties dialog box, as explained in the text preceding these steps. ■

4. Click the Shared As button to share the folder.
   The shared resource is given a default share name: the first 12 letters of the folder's name. The share name is what other users see when they use Network Neighborhood to locate the resource on your computer.
5. Change the share name to **User** Test.
6. Add the comment **This is a test**.

N O T E To stop a resource from being shared, open the Sharing dialog box and click the Not Shared radio button. ▓

That's all there is to sharing a resource when you use user-level security, but you still need to specify which users or groups of users can use the shared resource. As mentioned earlier in this chapter, you can specify what rights each user has to the shared resource. Follow these steps to allow users to access a shared resource:

7. Click the **A**dd button to open the Add Users dialog box, which is shown in Figure 47.14. The list on the left is the list of users and groups obtained from the network server that will enforce security. On the right side is a list of the types of rights that can be given to a user: Read Only, Full Access, and Custom.

Figure 47.14

User lists are obtained from the network server.

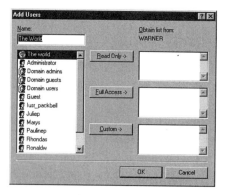

8. Choose The World (which basically means anyone) in the user list and click the Read Only button. Now anyone can have read-only access to the shared resource.

9. Choose the user Administrator and click the Full Access button to give that user full access to the shared resource. A single person in an icon represents a single user.

10. Select a group of users (indicated by an icon with two people) and click the Custom button.

11. Click the OK button and define the custom set of rights for the group you added in the previous step. Figure 47.15 shows the Change Access Rights dialog box that you use to customize users' access rights.

12. Select the rights that you want the user or group to have.

13. Click the OK button.

 T I P You can give custom rights to users or groups that need only a certain type of access. For example, you may want to give a user who performs backups or data entry more than read-only access but less than full access.

Figure 47.16 shows the Sharing dialog box after the preceding changes.

Figure 47.15

Use this dialog box to customize rights for users who need only particular types of access.

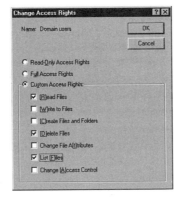

Figure 47.16

You can modify the user list for a shared resource in the Sharing dialog box.

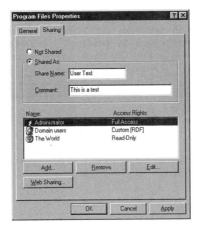

14. Click the OK or Apply button to force your changes to take effect.

 TIP Use Net Watcher to see who is accessing your shared resources. Start Net Watcher by choosing it in the System Tools subfolder of the Accessories folder.

Understanding the Password Cache

When a network has many resources, the number of passwords needed to use all of them can become overwhelming. You could write all the passwords on a piece of paper and keep them near your computer, but they would nearly defeat the purpose. The password cache solves the problem of remembering multiple passwords; it stores your passwords in a password-list file, which has the extension .PWL. Password list files are encrypted, and unencrypted passwords are never sent over a network. This file can store passwords for the following network resources:

■ Windows 98 shared resources that are protected by share-level security

- Password-protected applications that are written to the Master Password API
- Windows NT computers
- NetWare servers

> **CAUTION**
>
> You need to re-enter all your passwords if you delete the password-list file. Keep the passwords written down and stored somewhere safe, such as in your wallet or at home.

The password list is loaded when you log on to Windows 98. If the proper password isn't supplied to the Windows 98 logon or if you click the Cancel button, the password list is not loaded, and you have to enter a password for each password-protected resource.

When you try to access a password-protected resource, you see the Enter Network Password dialog box. You enter the password and click the OK button to use the resource. If the check box at the bottom of the dialog box is checked, the password is stored in the password cache.

 Use the password-list editor (PWLEDIT.EXE) to remove passwords from your password list. If the password-list editor is not in your Windows directory, you can locate it on your Windows 95 disk(s), in the ADMIN\APPTOOLS\PWLEDIT directory.

Now that you know how to share resources, you can apply that knowledge to sharing your Office documents. The following section discusses sharing Office documents.

Sharing Office Documents

Before you can share your documents, you need to know where they're saved. In Word, choose Tools, Options to open the Options dialog box. Then click the File Locations tab. Figure 47.17 shows the Options dialog box open to the File Locations page.

Figure 47.17
Different types of files can be saved in different locations.

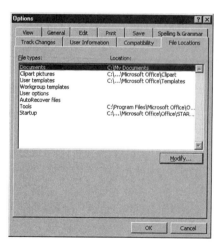

N O T E While Each Office application has a setting for file locations in the Options dialog box, the location of this option in the Options dialog box varies from one application to another. ■

File types are listed on the left side of the File types/Location list, and the location of those types of files is listed on the right. Clip art, for example, is saved in the C:\PROGRAM FILES\MICROSOFT OFFICE\CLIPART directory. Documents normally are saved in the C:\MY DOCUMENTS directory. If that is where you save most of your files, you may not want to share that directory. You can change the Documents location by clicking the Modify button and choosing a new folder as the new default location for saving documents.

 T I P Create different folders for different users or groups and share each folder for the user or group that it was created for. You can make the shared folders subfolders in the directory in which you save your documents by default. Then you just have to double-click a shared folder when you save a document that needs to be shared.

Place all the documents that you want to share in a folder that you also want to share. Then use the sharing method that matches the security being used on your network.

You may have also noticed the two types of templates that can be saved. *Templates* are skeleton documents that are used to create new documents; they use the .DOT file extension. Two factors determine which templates are available and which tab templates are displayed with when you choose File, New:

■ The file-location setting

■ The folder in which the template is stored

Figure 47.18 shows the New dialog box that opens when you create a new document.

Figure 47.18
Templates for new documents can be categorized.

Part
VIII
Ch
47

N O T E Any document (.DOC) file that you save in a Templates folder or one of its subfolders also acts as a template. ■

Templates are saved in the location specified in the File Locations section of the Options dialog box. Only templates in the specified folder(s) or its subfolders appear in the New dialog box. User templates appear in the General tab; templates in subfolders of the Templates folder appear in tabs that have the same names as the subfolders. Workgroup templates also appear in the General tab of the New dialog box.

Save any new templates that you create in the appropriate subfolder of your Templates folder, such as the Reports folder. Template (.DOT) files that you save in the Templates folder or any of its subfolders appear in the New dialog box.

 Generally, workgroup templates are those templates that all workgroups use. These templates should be stored in a folder that is shared by means of read-only access. Have your network administrator store workgroup templates on a network server for maximum protection, so that you or other users won't accidentally change them.

▶ **See** "Creating and Using Templates," **page 213**

Sharing Access Databases

Access databases are unique among files that can be created by Office applications. Most Office applications create files that are then distributed to users, although several users can create them in a collaborative effort. Access databases, however, change continually throughout their existence.

The continual change of Access databases occurs because users add and modify data. Also, other users periodically generate reports from that data. This interactive process makes Access databases valuable.

N O T E If you don't need any extra security for your Access database files, share them just as you would any other file. ▪

The type of security available through sharing isn't capable of handling Access files because of the unique nature of database files. Parts of a database file should be read-only; some parts should allow users to delete, add, and modify data; and other parts should allow users to add data but not delete or modify it. For these reasons, Access has its own system for securing data.

Applying Database Security in Access

The degree of security needed in an Access database can vary greatly. Access has several tools that allow you to customize the security of your database. The main security tools available to you in Access are the following:

- Passwords
- Encryption and decryption

- User accounts and groups
- Permissions

One of these security measures (or a combination) should fit your needs. These methods are discussed further in the following four sections.

Using Passwords   The simplest way to secure your database files is to set a password. Passwords are encrypted so that a user can't read them by reading the database file's contents. Each time that a password-protected Access file is opened, a dialog box requests a password from the user. If the user supplies the correct password, the file opens. Otherwise, the user is not allowed to open the file.

Passwords only limit who can open a database. Unless user-level security (described in "Using Accounts and Groups" and "Using Permissions") has been defined, a user can do anything to a database when it's open. If the database is being shared among a small group of users, setting a password is an ideal way to protect data without spending a great deal of time setting up a more advanced security scheme.

> **CAUTION**
> Replicated databases can't be synchronized if database passwords are defined.

▶ **See** "Using Replication in Access," **page 1018**

Before you can set a password for a database, all users (including you) must close the file. You should also make a backup copy and store it in a secure location. To protect a database by adding a password, follow these steps:

1. Choose File, Open Database to display the Open dialog box.
2. Click the Exclusive check box.
3. Select a database and click the Open button or double-click the database to open it. The database is opened for exclusive use, so no other users can open it.
4. Choose Tools, Security, Set Database Password to open the Set Database Password dialog box, shown in Figure 47.19.

Figure 47.19
Use this dialog box to set your database password.

5. Type the password (passwords are case-sensitive) in the Password and Verify text boxes.
6. Click the OK button.

   If you lose or forget your password, you cannot open the database.

Part
VIII

Ch
47

CAUTION

If a database links to a table in a password-protected database, the password is cached (unencrypted) when the link is established. This unencrypted cached password could compromise the security of your database.

The password is now set. The next time any user opens the database, he or she must supply the password. To remove the password from the database, open the database exclusively and choose Tools, Security, Unset Database Password. Enter the password in the Unset Database Password dialog box and click the OK button.

If a database password doesn't supply the right kind of security, you may want to look into user-level security for an Access database—not to be confused with user-level security for shared resources.

▶ **See** "Using User-Level Security," **page 1006**

N O T E   If user-level security is being used, you must have Administer permissions to set a database password. ▪

Encrypting and Decrypting Access Databases   Encrypting a database doesn't limit access by authorized users; it compacts the file so that a user can't view its data by using a word processing or utility program. For this reason, you should use encryption in conjunction with a password or user-level security. If you are using user-level security and want to encrypt or decrypt a database, you must have Modify Design permissions for all tables.

Decrypting a database simply reverses the action of the encryption process. To encrypt or decrypt a database, follow these steps:

1. Start Access without opening a database, or close the current database, if it is to be encrypted.

N O T E   A database can't be encrypted or decrypted if any user has it open. ▪

2. Choose Tools, Security, Encrypt/Decrypt Database to open the Encrypt/Decrypt Database dialog box, which is similar to an Open dialog box.
3. Select the database you want to encrypt or decrypt.
4. Click OK.
5. In the Encrypt/Decrypt Database As dialog box, specify the name and location of the encrypted or decrypted database.
6. Click the Save button.

   If you use the same name and location for the encrypted/decrypted file as the original file, the original file will only be overwritten if the entire operation is performed successfully.

CAUTION

You must have enough space on your hard drive to store both the original database and the encrypted/ decrypted database or the operation fails.

Using Accounts and Groups Accounts and groups are used for user-level security. User-level security is similar to the security used on a network. Users must supply an account name and password before they can use the database. Information about user accounts is maintained in the workgroup information file. These accounts are placed in groups. Although additional groups can be created, two groups are present by default:

- Admins (for administrators)
- Users (for users)

Permissions are granted to users and groups to control their use of the database. The Users group, for example, may be allowed to read and write data to a table used for recording customer orders but denied all access to a table that stores payroll information. The Admins group has full access to all objects in a database. You can create additional accounts and groups to customize security for your database.

Adding user-level security to a database is a complex procedure that involves many decisions. Review the procedure for adding user-level security before beginning your planning. To add user-level security to a database, follow these steps:

1. Join a secure workgroup or create a new workgroup information file. You must exit Access to change workgroups. If you are using Windows 95 or 98, create or join a new workgroup by running WRKGADM.EXE.

CAUTION

The default workgroup information file is created with the name and organization that you supplied while installing Office. This information is easy to find, and a user can use it to create a duplicate file easily. Then he or she can use the duplicate file to get around user-level security.

2. Open a database.
3. Choose Tools, Security, User and Group Accounts. Figure 47.20 shows the User and Group Accounts dialog box, which appears when you choose this command.

Figure 47.20

You use this dialog box to change user and group accounts.

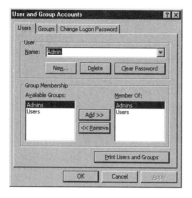

4. Verify that the Admin account is selected in the Users page.

5. Click the Change Logon Password tab.

6. Type the new password (which is case-sensitive) in the New Password and Verify text boxes, but don't type anything in the Old Password text box.

7. Click OK.

8. To create an administrator's user account, click the New button in the Users page to open the New User/Group dialog box, shown in Figure 47.21.

Figure 47.21

You use the user name and personal ID to create an encrypted account name.

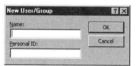

9. Type the user name in the Name text box.

10. Type a personal identification in the Personal ID text box. The personal ID is not a password; it is used to encrypt the user name.

11. Click OK to create the new account.

12. Choose Admins in the Available Groups list and click the Add button.

13. Click OK to create the new administrator account.

14. Exit Access and log on as the administrator, using the account that you just created.

15. Remove the Admin user from the Admins group by selecting the Admin user and clicking the Delete key in the User and Group Accounts dialog box.

N O T E If you want a user other than the administrator to own the database and all the objects in it, log on as that user. At minimum, the user must have Read Data and Read Design permissions in the database that is being secured. ▪

16. Open the database that you want to secure.

17. Choose Tools, Security, User-Level Security Wizard.

18. Follow the directions in the wizard dialog boxes.

The User-Level Security Wizard creates a new encrypted database and copies the objects from the database that is being secured. Object types that are selected in the first wizard dialog box are made secure by revoking all rights to those objects for the Users group. No changes are made in the original database that was being secured.

N O T E After you use the User-Level Security Wizard to secure a database, only members of the Admins group have access to secured objects. ▪

After securing a database, you want to establish users and assign them permissions for objects in the database. The following section, "Using Permissions," shows you how to assign permissions to users.

Using Permissions   Permissions are used to limit the user's capability to work with different database objects. A user must have an account before he or she can be assigned permissions. To assign permissions, follow these steps:

1. Open the database that contains the objects that you want to secure.

T I P   If you have only your groups created, you can assign permissions to groups and add the users later.

2. Choose Tools, Security, User and Group Permissions to open the User and Group Permissions dialog box, shown in Figure 47.22.

Figure 47.22
You can assign permissions to individual users or groups of users.

3. If you want to assign permissions to individual users, click the Users radio button in the Permissions tab.

   If you want to assign permissions to a group of users, click the Group radio button.

4. Click the name of the user or group to which you want to assign permissions.

5. Use the Object Type drop-down list box to select the type of objects to choose from.

6. Select the object you want to assign permissions for.

 T I P Select multiple objects to assign permissions for more than one object at a time.

7. Use the check boxes in the Permissions section to assign permissions to the selected user/group for the select object(s).

   A checked box means that the permission is assigned, and an unchecked box means that the permission is not assigned. Selecting some permissions automatically selects related permissions.

8. Repeat steps 3 through 7 for as many users and objects as necessary.

9. Click OK.

> **CAUTION**
>
> Permissions assigned to forms, reports, or modules do not take effect until the database is closed and opened again.

Using Replication in Access

Replication allows you to make a copy of a database that can be synchronized with the original database. Synchronization causes changes in data to be shared between the two databases and any design changes in the original database to be made in the replica. The original database is called the *design master*, and the copy is called the *replica*. You can create more than one replica. All the replicas and the design master together are called a *replica set*.

N O T E Any of the replicas in a replica set can be made the design master. Only one member of the replica set can be the design master at any time, however.

You can use replication to simplify many complex tasks, such as the following:

- *Distribute software written in Access.* Keep a design master that has the current version of the software and synchronize it with the replicas to make software updates.

- *Distribute data to users who must travel.* A salesperson could take a replica of a sales database to work with while traveling. Periodically, he or she could synchronize the database replica with the master.

- *Balance the load placed on database servers.* Load balancing can be accomplished by creating several replicas of a database to be placed on different servers. Users can then be distributed among the different servers to balance the load that each server has to handle.

■ *Back up databases.* Using Replication to perform backups allows the database to remain online. In other words, users can continue to make changes during the backup.

Creating a Replica Creating a replica makes a copy of a database design and the data contained in that database. You can use a replica for many purposes. To create a replica of a database, follow these steps:

1. Using the exclusive option, open the database that you want to make a replica of.

> **CAUTION**
>
> Make yourself aware of all the changes that are made in your database when it is replicated. AutoNumber fields, for example, generate unique random numbers instead of unique sequential numbers. The Access help file contains a complete list of the changes.

2. If the database is protected by a password, remove the password (as described in "Using Passwords" earlier in this chapter).

3. Choose Tools, Replication, Create Replica and click the Yes button in the dialog box that prompts you to close the database.

   If this replica is the first one that you are making for this database, you must first make it a design master. In this case, you are asked whether you want to make a backup copy of the database before making it a design master. You should always have a current backup.

4. Select the location for the replica in the Location Of New Replica dialog box.

5. Click OK.

After creating a replica, you eventually will want to synchronize the design master and its replica, as described in the following section.

Synchronizing an Access Database Members of a replica set are synchronized to exchange all updates that have been made in database objects and data. After two members are synchronized, their database design and the data that they contain are identical. To synchronize, follow these steps:

1. Open the member of a replica set that you want to synchronize.

2. Choose Tools, Replication, Synchronize Now.

3. Enter the name and location of the replica set member that you want to synchronize with the current database.

4. Click OK.

 T I P Click the Make "FILENAME" Design Master check box to make the replica the design master.

5. Click Yes when asked whether you want to close and reopen the database.

Part
VIII
Ch
47

CHAPTER 48

Document Collaboration

by Nancy Warner

In this chapter

Collaborating in Word

Microsoft Word lets you create documents that incorporate text and graphics. You can create letters, memos, faxes, newsletters, catalogs, and many other types of documents. Many times, Word is used in a business environment with groups of users that need to work together.

To accommodate the need for users to create documents as a team, Word has workgroup collaboration features that make it easier to protect and track changes in documents. These features can be broken into two distinct categories:

- Workgroup Review Features
- Security Features

Workgroup reviewing tools allow several users to work on a document either simultaneously or in succession and security features help limit the changes that can be made to a document in a workgroup environment. Both of these features are discussed in the next two sections of this chapter.

Reviewing Documents in a Workgroup

Documents created by more than one person have special requirements. There could be many parts to a document, each the responsibility of a different user. Someone could be in charge of creating the documents and need some control over the process, perhaps the final say on changes. Word has several tools to address the needs of documents being created in a workgroup. Those tools include:

- Master Documents
- Tracking Changes
- Comments
- Versions
- Routing

Each of these tools can help with creating documents in a workgroup, but they don't all have to be used. Review the following sections to determine which can best be used in your situation.

Using Master Documents

Only one person at a time can edit a regular Word document. This limitation can make creating a document with many authors very challenging. Either only one person can work on the document at a time, or the revisions must be compiled into a single document every time you want to see the results of everyone's work.

Word provides a tool to allow more than one author to work on a single document at one time. Any changes made to a part of the document are instantly reflected in the entire document. The tool that makes this possible is called a *master document*. Master documents consist of one or more subdocuments. Each subdocument is treated as if it were a regular Word document that is separate from the master document, but the contents of the subdocuments are combined to create the master document. To create a new master document, follow these steps:

1. Start a new document by clicking the New button.

2. Choose <u>M</u>aster Document from the <u>V</u>iew menu.

3. Create an outline of the master document using the Outlining toolbar.

4. Select the headings and text that you want to become subdocuments.

5. Click the Create Subdocument button on the Master Document toolbar, which is shown in Figure 48.1.

Figure 48.1

The Master Document toolbar can be docked or floating.

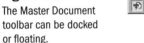

> **N O T E** The subdocument will be created with the heading style and outline level of the cursor's position when it is created.

6. Choose <u>F</u>ile, <u>S</u>ave to save the master document and its subdocuments.

7. After choosing a name and location for the master document, click the Save button.

> **N O T E** Word, based on the subdocuments' headings, automatically names them and saves them in the same location as the master document.

Now, each user can work on his or her section of the document by editing the subdocument assigned to that section. Changes saved to subdocuments are instantly displayed in the master document, even if someone is viewing or editing it. When the document is printed, Word combines the master document with all of the subdocuments and prints it as one large document. In addition, Word automatically numbers pages, lines, and footnotes in sequence.

 T I P Choose <u>V</u>iew, <u>D</u>ocument Map to quickly browse very large documents by seeing their structure and content at the same time.

▶ **See** "Using the Document Map," **page 196**

Tracking Changes

The Track Changes feature marks the revisions that are made to a document. Revision marks can be customized by specifying what color they are or how edited text is displayed—if displayed at all.

CAUTION

For the Track Changes feature to be effective, all users who edit a document must use it. If a user doesn't use the feature, other users will not know what edits were made to the document by that user.

Part

VIII

Ch

48

To begin using Track Changes, follow these steps:

1. Open the document that you want to edit.

2. Choose Tools, Track Changes, Highlight Changes to open the Highlight Changes dialog box shown in Figure 48.2.

Figure 48.2

Track Changes While
Editing activates the
Track Changes feature.

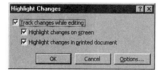

3. Click the Track Changes While Editing check box. This activates the Track Changes feature.

 N O T E When the Track Changes feature is inactive, the text TRK in the status bar is dimmed. The text TRK is not dimmed when the feature is tracking changes.

4. Select Highlight Changes on Screen to have the edits displayed onscreen.

5. Select Highlight Changes in Printed Document to have the edits printed when the document is printed.

6. Click the OK button after making your selections.

 T I P You can also activate the Track Changes feature by right-clicking the text TRK in the status bar and choosing Track Changes from the pop-up menu. This menu also gives you access to the other Track Changes dialog boxes.

After activating the Track Changes feature, edits that you make on the document will be indicated according to the options that you have chosen in the Track Changes page of the Options dialog box. In addition, the name and initials from the User Information page of the Options dialog box is recorded with the edits. Figure 48.3 shows the Track Changes page of the Options dialog box. Choose Tools, Options and click the Track Changes tab to view this information.

T I P Choose By Author as the color for edits and Word automatically chooses a different color for each different author who edits the document. An author is identified by the name contained on the User Information page of the Options dialog box.

Figure 48.3

Different types of edits can be marked differently.

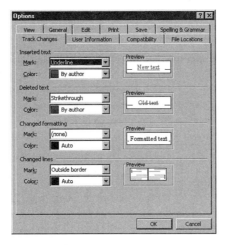

Eventually, you will want to review all of the edits and determine which to accept and which to reject. Changes are reversed if they are rejected and no longer tracked if they are accepted. To accept or reject changes follow these steps:

1. Open the document that you want to review.

2. Choose Tools, Track Changes, Accept or Reject Changes from the open dialog box shown in Figure 48.4.

Figure 48.4

Detailed information about the edit, including the user, is displayed in the Accept or Reject Changes dialog box.

3. Click either of the Find buttons to move to the next or previous edit.

4. Click the Accept button to accept a change or the Reject button to reject it.

 Click the Accept All or Reject All button to immediately accept or reject all changes in a document.

This process can go on until a document is complete. When the process of editing and reviewing is done, you will have your finished document. In addition to the methods for tracking changes outlined in this section, the Reviewing Toolbar has buttons that can be used in the process. Figure 48.5 shows the buttons and what their purposes are.

Part
VIII

Ch
48

Figure 48.5
The Reviewing toolbar.

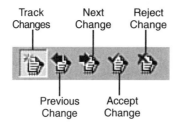

Track Changes   Next Change   Reject Change

Previous Change   Accept Change

Commenting on a Document   When reviewing a handwritten or printed document, you probably write notes in the margin or near the text you are commenting on. This very common task can also be done in Word using the Comments feature (previously referred to as Annotations).

Comments can be used to either encourage a change or to explain why a change was made. For example, you could track changes in a document and comment on the edits that you make. Track Changes indicates the edits and Comments explains them. To use the Comments feature, follow these steps:

1. Place the cursor within or at the start of the word that you want to comment on.

N O T E   You can also highlight selections of text containing more than one word.

2. Choose Insert, Comment. The text is highlighted and the Comments pane is opened, as shown in Figure 48.6.

Figure 48.6
The comments pane is contained within the document's window.

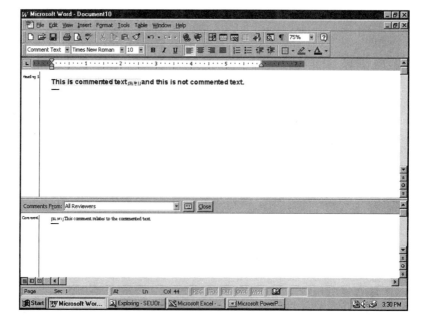

3. Type your comments, which will be identified by your initials and a unique number.

 TIP Click the Insert Sound Object button, which has a picture of a cassette tape on it, to record an audio message to be placed in the comment.

4. Click the Close button to close the Comments pane.

You or other users can view your comments by choosing Comments from the View menu. The Comments pane is displayed as in Figure 48.6. Select a user in the Comments From drop-down list to view only that user's comments.

As with the Track Changes feature, the Comments feature has command buttons on the Reviewing toolbar. Figure 48.7 shows the buttons and how they are used.

Figure 48.7
The Comments feature buttons appear on the Reviewing toolbar.

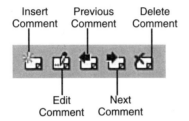

Insert Comment Previous Comment Delete Comment

Edit Comment Next Comment

 TIP Rest the mouse pointer over commented text to view the comments and the initials of the user that entered them in a pop-up window.

Saving and Comparing Versions of Documents   Word lets you create versions of a document. You can later compare versions of a document to determine if the changes made in it were necessary. There are two ways to save versions of a document:

- All versions in one file
- A separate file for each version

The next section discusses how to save versions of a document into a single file. After that, there are two sections on how to compare and merge documents.

Saving Document Versions

The ability to save multiple versions of a document in a single file is a new feature in Word 97. This feature, called *version control*, allows you to save a version of a document. After each edit, a new version can be saved until the document is completed. All of the versions are saved in the same file, but only one version of the document is active at a time. The user, the date and time, and any comments entered are saved with each version of a document. To save versions of a document, follow these steps:

1. After creating a new document, choose File, Versions.
2. Click the Save Now button in the Versions In Document dialog box shown in Figure 48.8.

Part
VIII

Ch
48

Figure 48.8
The Versions dialog box lists all the versions of a document.

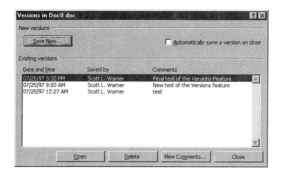

 TIP Select the Automatically Save a Version on Close check box to save a new version each time the file is closed.

3. Enter any comments you have in the Save Version dialog box shown in Figure 48.9.

Figure 48.9
Comments can help others understand the purpose of a document version.

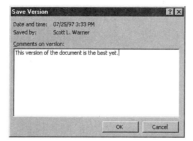

4. Click the OK button to save the document and the version.

5. Enter the name and location for the document in the Save As dialog box and click the Save button.

Use the Versions dialog box to save future versions of the document. You can also use the Versions dialog box to open or delete a version of the document or view comments. After opening an older version of a document, you can save it as a different document in its own file.

N O T E Word saves only the differences between the different versions to minimize the amount of storage space needed. ▪

Comparing Documents

After completing several versions of a document, it can become hard to remember what changes you have made. You also might have already accepted or rejected changes many times. In this case, you can use the Compare Documents tool to find the differences in the two documents. These are separate documents, not versions stored in a single file. To compare documents, follow these steps:

1. Open a document that you want to compare to another.

2. Choose Tools, Track Changes, Compare Documents.

3. Select the document that you want to compare to the current document and click the Open button.

 TIP If you want to use Compare Document on two versions of a document stored in the same file, use the Versions In Document dialog box to view the older version and save it as a separate document.

4. Accept or reject the changes that are indicated in the document.

The next section shows how to merge two different versions of a document when the versions are contained in different files.

Merging Documents

You can use the Merge Documents tool to combine the tracked changes from several different documents. The Merge Documents tool requires that the files used the Track Changes feature. If the files did not use this feature, you should use Compare Documents to review changes. To use Merge Documents, follow these steps:

1. Open the original copy of the document that you want to merge with the edited copies.

2. Choose Tools, Merge Documents.

3. Select the file to merge with current document and click the Open button.

4. Repeat steps 2 and 3 until you merge all of the edited copies.

5. Review the changes and accept or reject them.

Routing Documents with E-mail

Now that you know how to use the workgroup review features, you should learn how to use routing slips to move documents around. This feature lets you send documents to other users that have e-mail. They can then make their edits and return the document to you. To use routing slips, follow these steps:

1. Choose File, Send To, Routing Recipient.

2. Select the profile to use in the Profile Name dialog box if you are asked to.

3. Click the Address button on the Routing Slip dialog box and select the recipients from your address book. Figure 48.10 shows the Routing Slip dialog box.

Part **VIII**

Ch **48**

Figure 48.10

The routing slip determines who should receive the document and in what order.

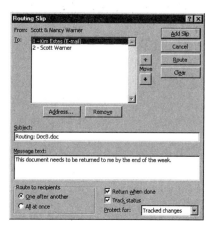

NOTE Use the up and down arrow buttons to change the order of the recipients. ▨

4. In the Route to Recipients section of the Routing Slip dialog box, select the One After Another radio button to have the document sent to each recipient in order. That way, each user reviewing the document can see the changes made by the previous recipient. Select the All at Once radio button to send the document to all recipients simultaneously.

5. In the Protect for drop-down list, the Tracked Changes option lets users make changes with the Track Changes feature activated. The Comments selection allows reviewers to enter comments, but they can't make any changes. Selecting Forms allows user to fill out a form, but they can't make changes to the form.

CAUTION

If you choose (None) in the Protect for drop-down list, no changes made by the reviewers are indicated in the document.

6. Select the Return When Done check box to have the document routed back to you after all of the recipients have reviewed it.

7. Type in any message text that you want and click the Add Slip button to save the routing slip information without sending the document. Click the Route button to save the routing slip information and send the document.

As each recipient receives the document, they can make their changes and send it on. After everyone has reviewed the document, it will be sent back to you and you can review the changes, accepting or rejecting them.

NOTE If you are sending the document to users with an older version of Word, be sure to save the document in a format that they can use. ▨

▶ **See** "File Compatibility and Conversion," **page 1039**

Securing Documents

As a document is passed around a workgroup, there are opportunities for users to view or edit documents that they shouldn't. The Windows operating system and network operating systems have security measures to help prevent this, but they aren't always reliable. Word supplies some added protection for your documents by allowing you to protect an entire document or specific elements of a document. These security features are in addition to any other security provided for the computers in your network or workgroup.

Protecting a Document Protecting a document is an option of the Save function. The author of the document controls this option. A document can be protected in three ways:

- The Read-Only Recommended feature displays a dialog box when the file is opened that suggests opening the document as read-only unless changes need to be made. This does not prevent the user from opening the file for editing. It is, as the title suggests, only a suggestion.

- The File Open Password feature requires the user to enter a password to open a document. If the correct password isn't supplied, the document cannot be opened.

- The File Modify Password requires that a user enter a password to make any changes to the document. When opening the document, you can choose to open it as read-only and you will not be prompted for the password.

Any of these methods can be used to protect a document or all three can be used at the same time. To use any of these protection features, follow these steps:

1. Choose File, Save As.

2. Click the Options button.

3. Select the Read-Only Recommended check box to activate that feature and enter the File Open password, the File Modify password, or both to activate those features. All of these fields are at the bottom of the Save dialog box shown in Figure 48.11.

Figure 48.11
Use the Save dialog box to assign password protection to your document.

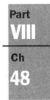

Part
VIII

Ch
48

CAUTION

If you forget a password, your document can no longer be used, including any links that other documents have to it.

4. If you entered any passwords, you will be prompted to confirm them. Type them again and click the OK button.

5. Click the Save button.

Protecting Specific Elements of a Document　In addition to protecting an entire document, you can protect specific elements, including Tracked Changes, Comments, and Forms. To protect a specific element of a document, follow these steps:

1. Choose Tools, Protect Document.

2. Click the radio button of the element that you want to protect. Figure 48.12 shows the Protect Document dialog box.

Figure 48.12

Use passwords to protect specific elements of a document.

3. Type a password and click the OK button.

4. Retype the password when you're prompted and click the OK button again.

Protecting the tracked changes prevents other users from turning the feature off or accepting or rejecting changes. Selecting Comments in the Protect Document dialog box only allows users to enter comments (no changes allowed). If the Forms option is selected, the user can fill out a form, but can't make any changes.

Collaborating in Excel

Excel workbooks can hold a variety of information coming from many different sources. Each source could submit information in a written or printed form for someone to consolidate the information into a single Excel workbook, but they would be very inefficient. Excel has two groups of features that allow workbooks to be shared by a workgroup:

- Workgroup Sharing Features
- Security Features

By using these features, Excel workbooks can edited directly by users who supply the information. There can still be a user who is in charge of overseeing the changes, but that user is now freed up to perform other tasks as well.

▶ **See** "Routing Documents with E-mail," **page 1029**

Sharing Workbooks in a Workgroup

Excel has a sharing feature that allows multiple users to edit a workbook simultaneously or for several workbooks to be combined into a single workbook. To share a workbook, follow these steps:

1. Choose Tools, Share Workbook.
2. Select the Allow Changes by More Than One User at the Same Time check box to activate the sharing feature. This check box is on the Editing page of the Share Workbook dialog box shown in Figure 48.13.

Figure 48.13
By activating this check box, you allow your Excel workbooks to be shared with other users.

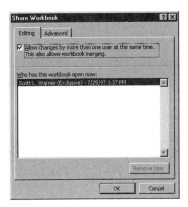

3. Click the Advanced tab.
4. In the Track Changes section, select how many days you want to keep a history of changes—if at all. You can also determine when to save changes and how conflicts should be resolved.
5. Click the OK button when you are finished.

Part
VIII

Ch

48

After sharing a workbook, you can place it on a shared drive or a network drive so that others can edit it. Then, you can periodically review everyone's changes. To review changes to a document, follow these steps:

1. Choose Tools, Track Changes, Accept or Reject Changes.
2. Choose which changes you want to review in the Select Changes to Accept or Reject dialog box shown in Figure 48.14, and then click the OK button.

Figure 48.14

By using the Accept or
Reject Changes dialog
box, you can limit the
changes that you review.

3. Accept or reject the changes in the Accept or Reject Changes dialog box shown in Figure 48.15.

Figure 48.15

The change and the user
who made it are listed
in this dialog box.

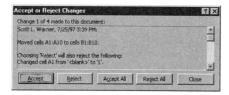

4. Click the Close button when you are finished.

NOTE Copies of shared workbooks can be merged, combining all changes for the two workbooks by choosing Tools, Merge Workbooks. Track Changes must be turned on for the workbooks and they must be versions of the same shared workbook. ▨

Using Comments in Workbooks

Comments can be used to explain the reason for a change or to explain the use of a cell in a workbook. Excel comments are denoted by a red triangle in the upper-right corner of a cell. To insert a comment, follow these steps:

1. Select the cell in which you want to place a comment.

2. Choose Insert, Comment.

TIP Right-click a cell and choose Insert Comment from the pop-up menu to add a comment to a cell.

3. Type your comments into the comment box that appears. Figure 48.16 shows the comment box.

4. Press the Esc key once to stop editing the comment.

5. Use the arrow keys on your keyboard or the mouse to position the note where you would like it to appear.

Figure 48.16

Comments look like sticky notes placed on the workbook.

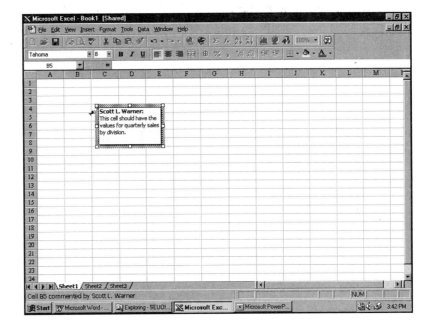

 TIP If you have several comments very close to one another, position them so that they do not overlap if viewed simultaneously.

6. Press the Esc key to close the comment.

Users can tell that a cell has a comment by the red triangle. They can choose Comments from the View menu or rest their mouse over the cell to view the comment. If they switch to the Comments view, they will see all of the comments on the current view of the workbook. Figure 48.17 shows a workbook with several comments in Comments view.

Comments can be used even if the workbook isn't being shared. They can make a workbook easier to read and understand, sometimes even to the author.

Part

VIII

Ch

48

Figure 48.17

Comments can be moved and edited in Comments view.

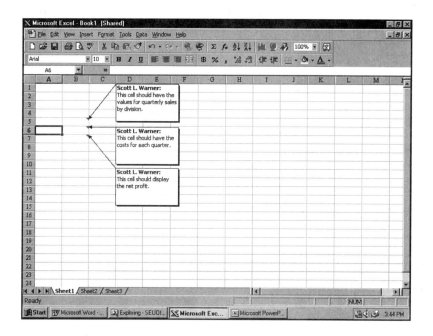

Consolidating Data

Data consolidation can be used to combine the data from workbooks or worksheets. It is not necessary to use Track Changes when using this tool. You can consolidate data in four ways:

- 3-D References
- By Category
- By Position
- PivotTable

Each of these methods has its advantages. For more information about each and how to decide which to use, consult the Excel help file for more information.

Securing Workbooks

Workbooks and individual worksheets can be secured. Choose Tools, Protection, Protect Sheet to open the Protect Sheet dialog box or choose Protect Workbook to open the Protect Workbook dialog box. Then, choose how you want to protect the workbook or worksheet and click the OK button.

▶ **See** "Protecting a Document," **page 1031**

To protect a workbook that you are going to share, choose Tools, Protection, Protect and Share Workbook. This is the only way that you can protect a shared workbook. After a workbook is shared, it can't be protected.

Collaborating in PowerPoint

PowerPoint has fewer collaboration features than other Office applications. There are no features that allow multiple users to work on presentations simultaneously, but there is a feature that lets many users participate in a PowerPoint presentation. To start a presentation conference, follow these steps:

> **NOTE** The Meeting Minder, which is on the Tools menu, can be used to record notes of a meeting. It can even add action items to individuals and schedule follow-up meetings using Outlook. ▨

1. Open a presentation.
2. Choose Presentation Conference from the Tools menu. Figure 48.18 shows the first dialog box in the Presentation Conference Wizard.

Figure 48.18

The first dialog box of the Presentation Conference Wizard outlines the process.

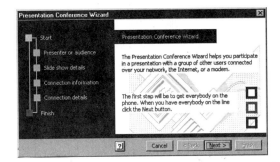

3. Click the Next button to continue.
4. Choose to be the Presenter in the dialog box shown in Figure 48.19 and click the Next button to continue.

Figure 48.19

The Presentation Conference Wizard makes joining a conference easy.

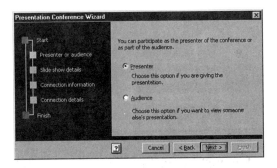

5. Click the Next button of the next wizard dialog box, which tells what slides will be shown.

N O T E Depending on your computer's configuration, your options might differ slightly. Click the question mark button at any time to receive help.

6. Click the Next button of the next wizard dialog box, which gives information about the connection to be used for the conference.

7. Enter the names of the computers to participate in the conference or their Internet addresses and click the Next button.

8. Click the Finish button on the last dialog box, but be sure that the audience members click their Finish buttons first.

If you wanted to view a conference as an audience member, you would choose Audience in the second dialog box of the wizard, shown in Figure 48.19.

T I P PowerPoint presentations can also be sent using a routing slip.

CAUTION

PowerPoint presentations can't be password protected using Save options.

Those are the ways that you can use your Office applications to collaborate on documents. While some features are common to all applications, each application has features that help take advantage of its strengths. ●

File Compatibility and Conversion

Understanding File Compatibility Issues

File compatibility is a very important issue. Your Office files are important and you want to be able to distribute them to others. However, other users may not have the same version of Office that you do or they may not have Office at all. To ensure that others can use the files that you create, you need to develop a strategy to make files compatible for as many users as possible. Some basic elements can be used as the basis for your strategy:

- Default Save
- File Viewers
- File Converters
- Dual File Formats

One of these features might resolve your compatibility issues, or you might have to use several of them in combination. The following sections discuss each.

Using Default Save

As you and other users upgrade your Office applications, there could be many different versions in use. The easiest way to share files in this situation is to always save files to the earliest version in use. This solution works very well for users who are outside of your company or location. However, this method has limitations, which are covered in the section "Understanding Backward Compatibility Issues in Office 97."

Default Save is a new feature in Office 97 that allows you to designate a particular format to use by default when saving a document. For example, you might always want to save documents in Word 2.0 format. Setting the Default Save option in each office application that uses it is covered in the following three sections.

N O T E The Default Save option can be used to save files in an earlier version of an Office application or to export the file to the file format for a different application.

Setting Default Save for Word

Before you can set the Default Save option in Word, you must have a document open. Otherwise, the menu choice used to set the option is unavailable. To set the Default Save option for Word, follow these steps:

1. Choose Options from the Tools menu.
2. Click the Save tab. Figure 49.1 shows the Options dialog box.
3. Select the file format you want to use in the Save Word Files As drop-down list box.

> **CAUTION**
>
> Make sure that you are aware of the limitations involved with saving your documents into an older or different format. Some features available in Word 97 are not present in other file formats.

4. Click OK to save your changes

Figure 49.1

Use the Save tab in the Options dialog box to set your Default Save options.

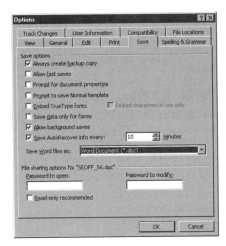

Now when you save a document in Word, it will use the file format that you chose by default. You can then distribute your documents with confidence that others will be able to use them.

Setting Default Save for Excel

You must have a workbook open before you can set the Default Save option in Excel. To set the Default Save option for Excel, follow these steps:

1. Choose Options from the Tools menu.

2. Click the Transition tab. Figure 49.2 shows the Options dialog box.

Figure 49.2

Using the Default Save option prevents you from saving Excel files in a format unusable by others.

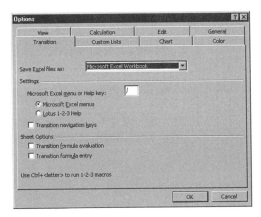

3. Select the file format you want to use in the Save Excel Files As drop-down list box.

 TIP Click the Transition navigation keys to use an alternate set of commands to perform tasks in Excel. This feature is for users who are new to Excel but proficient in another spreadsheet application, such as Lotus 1-2-3.

Part
VIII

Ch
49

4. Click OK to save your changes

Now when you save a workbook in Excel, it will use the file format that you chose by default. Others can then use the files even without the version of Excel that you are using.

Setting Default Save for PowerPoint

The Default Save option for PowerPoint can be set without opening a PowerPoint presentation. To set the Default Save option for PowerPoint, follow these steps:

1. Choose Options from the Tools menu.

2. Click the Save tab. Figure 49.3 shows the Options dialog box.

Figure 49.3

Use the Save tab in the Options dialog box to set your Save options in PowerPoint.

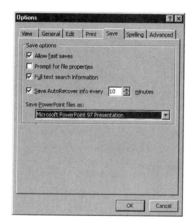

3. Select the file format you want to use in the Save PowerPoint Files As drop-down list box.

N O T E   PowerPoint's Default Save option only lets you choose PowerPoint file formats, from the latest version back to version 3.0. ■

4. Click OK to save your changes

After determining the best file format to use, this method makes it easy to share PowerPoint presentation files. The next section discusses the use of file converters.

Using File Converters

File converters change the format in which a file is saved. The conversion can be from one version's file format to another, or from one application's file format to a different application's file format. Two types of file converters exist:

■ Batch file converters
■ Installable file converters

Batch file converters change entire directories of files. This type of converter would be used after upgrading all users. *Installable file converters* give users the ability to open files saved in a different format. There is an installable file converter for Word and PowerPoint.

A converter can also work in the other direction. For instance, when Word 97 users save a file for someone using Word 6.0/95, they must convert the file to the other user's file format.

N O T E   Word 6.0 and Word for Windows 95 use the same file format, so documents saved in either are interchangeable. ■

Originally, the conversion to Word 6.0/95 format was accomplished by saving the file in Rich Text Format (RTF), but this caused some confusion. In response, Microsoft has released a converter that allows Word 97 to save files in native Word 6.0/95 format, or Word 6.0/95 binary format. The Word 97 binary converter is available from Microsoft's Web site. To download the converter, follow these steps:

1. Connect to the Internet using a dial-up connection or your network connection.

2. Open a Web browser and go to the address **http://www.microsoft.com/word/**. You should see a page similar to the one shown in Figure 49.4, but it could be different because Web pages are updated frequently.

T I P   Web pages for most Microsoft products can be viewed by adding a forward slash and the product name after Microsoft's Web address. For example, **http://www.microsoft.com/excel/** is the URL for the Excel Web page, while **http://www.microsoft.com/products/** will connect you to a page with hyperlinks to all Microsoft products.

Figure 49.4
Visit Microsoft's Word Web page to download the Word 6.0/95 Binary Converter for Word 97.

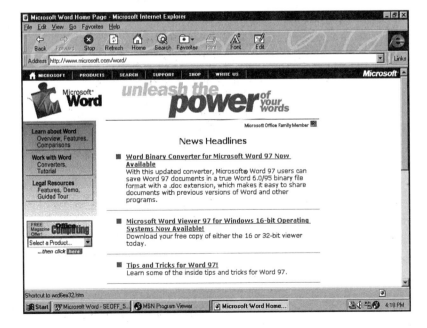

3. Find the Word 6.0/95 Binary Converter for Word 97 and download the file. If needed, you can click the Search graphic at the top of the page to find the file. After you find the file, download it to your desktop or another location and install it by running the program file.

N O T E The Word 97 binary converter is part of the Office 97 Service Release 1. If you have applied this service release, you already have the converter. ■

It is best to use converters when you have to share large documents that contain a lot of graphics or other embedded objects. The next section discusses the use of file viewers.

File Viewers

File viewers are programs that allow users to open and view files without having the software that created them. For example, the Word 97 viewer allows users to view Word 97 documents even if they don't have the full release of Word 97 installed on their computer. A PowerPoint viewer has been available since its original release. All Microsoft viewers are freely distributable. With viewers, user that don't have Office can view documents created in Office. Viewers are available on Microsoft's Web site for Word, Excel, and PowerPoint.

 WordPad is a word processor included with Windows 98. It is based on Microsoft Word and uses a file format very similar to Word 6.0/95. It can be used to view and edit Word 6.0/95 files, but some formatting might be lost in the process.

Dual File Formats

Dual file formats were created specifically for organizations that need to gradually upgrade their users to Office 97. It is available in Excel and PowerPoint. Files created in these applications can be saved as both the 97 version and the previous version (5.0/95 for both Excel and PowerPoint) using the Save As option of the File menu.

When a file is saved in a dual file format, a single file contains two sets of data. One set of data contains the file information that is common to both versions and the other contains the information specific to the new version.

N O T E When files saved using the dual file format are opened and edited by the previous version of the application, the formatting specific to the newer version is not affected. ■

Using Import/Export Filters

Users switching to Office 97 from other applications will be especially interested in the import and export filters. These filters allow Office applications to open files created in other applications and save files in the format of other applications. The filters available for the Office applications are covered in the next four sections.

N O T E Choosing a typical installation does not install all of the filters available for the Office Applications. ▉

Importing and Exporting Files in Word

Using an import filter is a fairly simple process. You save the file as you normally would, except that you choose a different format in the Save as type drop-down list box. Table 49.1 summarizes the filters that are included with Word.

Table 49.1   File Format Converters Supplied with Word

File Format	Description
HTML	Up to HTML 2.0
WordPerfect for MS-DOS	5.x and 6.0, can't save to 6.0
WordPerfect for Windows	5.x and 6.x, can't save to 6.0
Microsoft Excel	2.x, 3.0, 4.0, 5.0, 95, Excel 97 (open only, can't save)
Microsoft Word	2.x, 6.0, and Word 95
Word for the Macintosh	4.x, 5.x, Word 97
Microsoft Works	3.0, 4.0 (for Windows 95)
Lotus 1-2-3	2.x, 3.x, 4.0. (open only, can't save)
Recover Text from Any File	Recovers text from damaged documents
Text Only	Saves text in ANSI format
DOS Text Only	Saves text in ASCII format
Text Only w/ line breaks	Same as above with line breaks
DOS Text Only w/ line breaks	Same as above with line breaks
Text w/ Layout	Approximates formatting with spaces
DOS Text w/ Layout	Approximates formatting with spaces
Rich Text Format (RTF)	Saves all formatting using RTF standards

N O T E Unless you have installed the Word 97 binary converter discussed in "Using File Converters," documents saved as Word 6.0/95 are actually saved in Rich Text Format. However, these files are treated as Word 6.0/95 documents because they use the .DOC extension. ▉

Part
VIII

Ch
49

Chapter 49 File Compatibility and Conversion

The following steps are an example of saving (exporting) a Word document to WordPerfect 5.0 format:

1. Choose Save As from the File menu.

2. Select WordPerfect 5.0 in the Save as Type drop-down list box. Figure 49.5 shows the Save As dialog box ready to export a file.

CAUTION

Formatting can be lost or substituted when converting a file to a different format. You should make yourself aware of the consequences of exporting a file. Make backups of crucial documents before converting.

Figure 49.5

Choose the file type from the drop-down menu in the Save As dialog box.

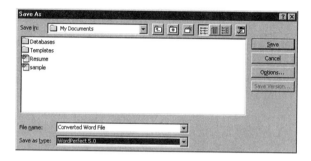

3. Click the Save button to complete the process.

To import a file of a different format into Word, simply select that file in the Open dialog box. Word performs the conversion automatically. The next section discusses the filters for Excel.

Importing and Exporting Files in Excel

By using the Open command in Excel, you can view files created in other programs or earlier versions of Excel. You can also save files to formats other than Excel 97 by using the Save As command. If files usually need to be saved in a format other than Excel 97, you can change the default save property as described in "Setting Default Save for Excel," on page 1041. Table 49.2 shows the import and export filters available for Excel.

Table 49.2   File Format Converters Supplied with Excel

File Format	Description
Microsoft Excel	2.x, 3.0, 4.0, 5.0/95, 5.0/95 and 97 (dual)
Lotus 1-2-3	1.x, 2.x, 3, 4
DBASE	DBF 2, DBF 3, DBF 4
SYLK	Symbolic Link
DIF	Data Interchange Format

File Format	Description
CSV	Comma delimited
Text	Tab delimited
Formatted Text	Space delimited
Template	Excel template

The File Conversion Wizard can be used to convert multiple files to Excel 97 format in one action. To use the File Conversion Wizard, follow these steps:

1. Choose File Conversion from the Wizard submenu of the Tools menu.

2. Supply the location of the files that you want to convert and what format they are currently in, as shown in Figure 49.6. Click the Next button to continue.

Figure 49.6

Use the Browse button to locate the files you want to convert.

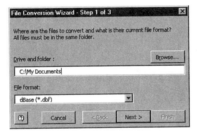

3. Select the files that you want to convert by clicking the box to the left of their name. A checked box means that the file will be converted. Figure 49.7 shows the second dialog box of the File Conversion Wizard. Click the Next button to continue.

Figure 49.7

Step 2 of the wizard allows you to choose the files to be converted.

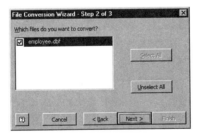

 TIP Click the Select All button to mark all of the files to be converted or the Unselect All button to make none of the files marked for conversion.

4. Select the location to save the converted files in by using the wizard dialog box shown in Figure 49.8. Click the Finish button to start the conversion.

Figure 49.8

Use the wizard's third step to select the destination to save your converted file(s).

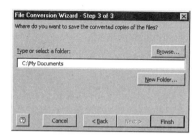

The formats that can be converted using this wizard translate well into Excel format. Other formats do not convert as easily.

Opening a delimited text file is a task that deserves some explaining. Delimited text files contain data that is separated by commas or some other character. To open a delimited text file, follow these steps:

1. Choose Open from the File menu.

2. Select the delimited text file in the Open dialog box and click the Open button.

3. The first dialog box of the Text Import Wizard, which is shown in Figure 49.9, opens. Select the options that describe your file. Usually, the default choices are correct. Click the Next button when you have finished.

Figure 49.9

Use the Text Import Wizard to open a delimited text file.

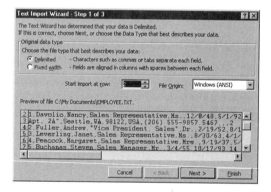

The first row of many delimited text files contains headers that describe the columns of data. Select 2 in the Start Import at Row spin box to avoid importing the row of headers.

4. Select the delimiter used in the text file as shown in Figure 49.10. You also need to identify the text qualifier, which indicates the beginning and end of a text field. Text qualifiers are used so text fields can contain the character being used as the delimiter. Click the Next button to continue. Use the Other edit box if your delimiter is not one of the choices.

Figure 49.10

Step 2 of the wizard allows you to select the delimiter.

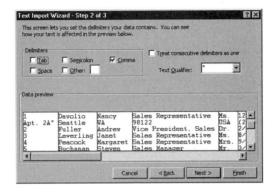

5. The final dialog box of the wizard, shown in Figure 49.11, allows you to specify the type of data that is contained in a column. Specifying a data type affects how the data is formatted after it is loaded into Excel. Click the Finish button when you are done.

Figure 49.11

Use the final step to specify the type of data contained in the column.

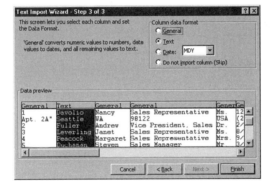

N O T E You can use the Back button to go back and change any of the choices that you made in the Table Import Wizard. ▦

The next section discusses PowerPoint's filters for importing and exporting.

Importing and Exporting Files in PowerPoint

PowerPoint has a limited ability to export files into the formats of other applications. It can only save presentations to PowerPoint formats, although it can save it to any version's format. In addition, a presentation can be saved in Rich Text Format or parts of a presentation can be saved as graphics files.

While PowerPoint can't save files into other applications' file format, it can import files created in other applications. Converters for Harvard Graphics and Lotus Freelance are included with PowerPoint.

Part

VIII

Ch

49

CAUTION

Most of the formatting in Harvard Graphics and Lotus Freelance files is preserved, but there may be some things that don't translate easily.

Using one of several text or graphics file formats, you can still use presentations created in programs for which PowerPoint doesn't have a converter. Text formats preserve the text of the presentation and slides can be saved as graphic images. These files can then be used by PowerPoint or Word. The next four sections briefly discuss using other file formats with PowerPoint 97.

Converting Harvard Graphics Presentations to PowerPoint PowerPoint's converter for Harvard Graphics automatically imports files for version 2.3 and DOS version 3.0. If the Harvard Graphics converter isn't installed, run the Office Setup program again, and choose to install it. To import a Harvard Graphics presentation, follow these steps:

1. Choose File, Open.
2. Select the version of Harvard Graphics files that you are searching for in the Files of Type drop-down list box.

 Saving newer Harvard Graphics files into an older version's file format allows you to use files from versions of Harvard Graphics that PowerPoint can't import.

3. Select the presentation that you want to convert.
4. Save the file to PowerPoint format after it's converted.

You can convert multiple files by opening them at the same time and then saving each one into PowerPoint format. The next section covers Lotus Freelance files.

Converting Lotus Freelance Presentations to PowerPoint Files from Lotus Freelance versions 1.0, 2.0, and 4.0 for DOS are automatically imported by the PowerPoint converter. Again, the converter must be installed using the Office Setup program if it isn't present. To convert a Lotus Freelance presentation, follow these steps:

1. Choose File, Open.
2. Select the version of Lotus Freelance files that you are searching for in the Files of Type drop-down list.
3. Select the presentation that you want to convert.
4. Save the file to PowerPoint format after it's converted.

Sometimes, a file format can't be converted. In such cases, the text and the graphics could be saved and used to create a presentation in PowerPoint. The next section discusses how graphics and text from a presentation can be used.

Converting Presentation Graphics and Text to PowerPoint   Graphics from presentations can be used even if the file format can't be converted into PowerPoint format. However, support for the specific graphic file format must be available. Table 49.3 shows the graphic file formats that are available in PowerPoint.

Table 49.3   Graphic File Formats Built into PowerPoint

File Format	Extension
JPEG	.JPG
Macintosh PICT	.PCT
Portable Network Graphics	.PNG
Windows Bitmap	.BMP
Windows Enhanced Metafile	.EMF
Windows Metafile	.WMF
AutoCAD	.DXF
CompuServe GIF	.GIF
Computer Graphics Metafile	.CGM
CorelDRAW! 3.0, 4.0, 5.0, and 6.0	.CDR
Encapsulated PostScript	.EPS
Kodak Photo CD	.PCD
Micrografx Designer/Draw	.DRW
PC Paintbrush	.PCX
Tagged Image File Format (TIFF)	.TIF
Truevision Targa	.TGA
WordPerfect Graphics/DrawPerfect	.WPG

These graphics filters can help you use the graphics from a presentation. If you want to use the text for a presentation that PowerPoint doesn't have a converter for, you can save the presentation in a text file format (using its native application). The graphic elements of the presentations won't be saved, but the text can be used in PowerPoint or Word.

N O T E   Graphics or text from a presentation can be used in any word processor or other application that can use the format that the text or graphics is saved in. ▪

The next section tells how to use the graphic design of a presentation that can't be converted.

Part
VIII

Ch
49

Converting Presentations Using Graphics File Formats   If you want to save the design of a presentation that can't be converted to PowerPoint, you can save the presentation into a graphic format. Saving a presentation in a graphics format converts each slide to a separate graphic image.

PowerPoint can then open the slides using the graphics filter. After all of the slides are imported, you can save the presentation into PowerPoint format. This or any of the previous methods can be used to import presentations into PowerPoint.

 Although PowerPoint can't save files directly into another application's format, you can save slides as graphics files and import them into other applications.

Importing and Exporting Files in Access

Access can work with data that comes from many different data sources. Some are specific file formats and others work with Open Database Connectivity (ODBC). Table 49.4 lists the data sources that Access can use.

Table 49.4   Data Sources Supported by Access

Data Source	Versions Supported
Microsoft FoxPro	2.x, 3.0 (import only)
dBASE	III, III+, IV, 5
Paradox	3.x, 4.x, 5.0
Excel	3.0, 4.0, 5.0, 7.0/95, 8.0/97
Lotus 1-2-3	1.x, 2.x, 3, 4 (link is read-only)
Delimited Text Files	N/A
Fixed-width Text Files	N/A
HTML	1.0, 2.0, 3.x
SQL Tables	ODBC-compliant data sources

NOTE   The availability of drivers for ODBC data sources depends upon the cooperation of the companies that distribute those products. Drivers for databases such as Oracle and SyBase are available, but may cost extra to obtain.

Information stored in one of these data sources can be imported and exported by Access. There are two different types of imports that can be performed.

The data can be imported; the table's design and data are copied into an Access database. Another way to use other data sources from within Access is to link to a table. Linking to a table allows you to view and edit a table that is stored in a different file format, as well as a different file. While you can change the data contained in a linked table, you cannot change the table's design. To link to a table using Access, follow these steps:

1. Choose Link Tables from the Get External Data submenu of the File menu. You would have chosen Import to copy the table into the current Access database.

2. Select the data source that the table is contained in from the Files of Type drop-down list box.

3. Select the table that you want linked.

N O T E You can import and link tables that are contained in other Access databases. ■

4. Click the Link button. A dialog box informs you when the process is completed.

 If you need data that is stored in a format that Access can't handle, save the data into one of the formats that it can handle and then import it.

The method for exporting data from an Access database is slightly different. Data can be exported to another Access database, as well as any of the data sources listed in Table 49.4. To export data from an Access database, follow these steps:

1. Select the table that you want to export.

2. Choose Save As/Export from the File menu.

 You can also right-click the table you want to export and choose Save As/Export from the pop-up menu. You can also copy the table to the current database

3. Choose the To an External File or Database option in the Save As dialog box, shown in Figure 49.12.

Figure 49.12
Use the Save As dialog box in Access to choose where the table should be saved.

4. Select the format to export the table into in the Save As Type drop-down list and then click the Export button.

The next section discusses some of the issues involved with saving files to an earlier version of the Office applications.

Part
VIII

Ch
49

Understanding Backward Compatibility Issues in Office 97

While the latest versions of the Office applications can save their files in the format of their previous versions, there are certain features that have changed or didn't exist in the previous version. If you are using any of the affected features, it is important for you to know the consequences of saving a file in the earlier version. These issues are addressed for Word, Excel, and PowerPoint in the following three sections.

Understanding Backward Compatibility Issues in Word

Table 49.5 shows the results of saving a Word file into an earlier version. These issues won't affect most people. If you are experiencing a problem with files saved to an earlier version, check this table.

Table 49.5   Word 97 Features with Issues in Word 6.0/95 Format

Word 97 Feature	Results in Word 6.0/95 Format
Embedded Fonts	The embedded fonts are lost, Word 6.0 or 95 assigns the closest font available.
Vertical text in table cells	Vertical text is reformatted as horizontal text.
Vertically aligned text in table cells	Vertically aligned text is reformatted to align at the top of the cell.
Vertically merged table cells	Merged table cells are exploded into unmerged cells.
EMF, PNG, and JPEG graphics	Graphics are converted to WMF (Windows Metafile) or PICT (Macintosh) format, which does not support graphics compression. This increases file size of documents that contain graphics.
Office Art objects	Office Art objects are converted to the nearest available shape and tool.
Animated text (Animation tab)	Animated text formatting is lost.
Embossed and engraved characters (Font tab)	Embossed and engraved character formatting is lost. The text becomes formatted as white text. To change the color of the text, select the text, click Font (Format menu), and then click Auto or Black in the Color box.

Word 97 Feature	Results in Word 6.0/95 Format
Outline and heading numbered list	Outline numbered lists and heading numbered lists are converted to regular text, but retain their appearance. In Word 6.0 and 95, you can use the Bullets and Numbering command (Format menu) to format the lists.
Multilevel bullets (Outline Numbered tab)	Multilevel bullets are converted to regular text, but retain their appearance. In Word 6.0 and 95, you can use the Bullets and Numbering command (Format menu) to format the lists.
Page borders (Page Border tab)	Page borders are not converted.
Character shading (Shading tab)	Character shading is lost.
Character borders (Borders tab)	Character borders are lost.
Paragraph borders (Borders tab)	New Word 97 paragraph borders are lost.
Floating pictures surrounded by wrapped text	Floating pictures are converted in frames to WMF (Windows Metafile)or PICT(Macintosh) format.
Floating OLE objects frames.	Floating OLE objects are converted to OLE objects in
Highlighting applied with the Highlight button (Formatting toolbar)	Highlighting is preserved in Word 95, but is lost in Word 6.0.
New document properties introduced in Word 95 (File menu)	New document properties are preserved in Word 95 but lost in Word 6.x. In Word, you can use the Properties command (File menu) to store information about the document, such as title, subject, author, manager, company, and so on.
HYPERLINK field (Insert menu)	The last value of the HYPERLINK field is retained as plain text, and the field itself is lost.
Password protection options in the Save As dialog box (File menu)	All document protection is lost. In Word 6.0 and 95, you can reapply document protection by clicking Save As (File menu), you clicking Options, and then selecting the options want on the Save tab.
Protect Document settings (Tools menu)	All document protection is lost. In Word 6.0 and 95, you can reapply document protection for tracked changes, comments, and forms by clicking Protect Document (Tools menu) and selecting the options you want.(In Word 6.0 and 95, tracked changes were called revisions, and comments were called annotations).

Part
VIII

Ch
49

continues

Table 49.5   Continued

Word 97 Feature	Results in Word 6.0/95 Format
Tracked changes to paragraph numbers and properties, display fields (Tools menu)	Tracked changes to properties, paragraph numbers, and display fields are lost, but other tracked changes are retained and shown with revision marks.
DOCPROPERTY field	The DOCPROPERTY field is retained in Word 95. In Word 6.x, the field appears as Error! Bookmark not defined.
ActiveX controls on forms	ActiveX Controls can be used, but not modified.
Unicode characters (2 bytes per character)	May result in potential data loss. Unicode characters are mapped to corresponding ANSI (Windows) or 1 byte per character (Macintosh), or are converted to question marks (?) if no equivalent character is available. Foreign language characters are most likely to be affected.
Visual Basic macros	All macros created in Word 97 Visual Basic are lost.
Embedded fonts	Embedded fonts are lost, and Word 95 or Word 6.x assigns the closest font available.

Understanding Backward Compatibility Issues in Excel

Table 49.6 shows the results of saving an Excel file into an earlier version. Consult this table if you are experiencing problems while trying to save Excel files into an earlier version.

Table 49.6   Excel 97 Features with Issues in Excel 5.0/95 Format

Excel 97 Feature	Results in Excel 5.0/95 Format
Angled text	Angled text is reformatted to horizontal orientation.
Conditional formatting	Conditional formatting is lost, and cells are reformatted as normal text.
Data validation	Lost in the conversion.
Indenting within cells	Indentation within a cell is lost, and data remains left aligned.
Merge cells option on the Alignment tab in the Cells dialog box (Format menu)	Merged cells are unmerged.

Excel 97 Feature	Results in Excel 5.0/95 Format
New border styles	New border styles are converted to the nearest border style available in Microsoft Excel 5.0 or 95.
Partial page breaks	Partial page breaks are converted to full-page breaks.
Shrink to fit option on the Alignment tab in the Cells dialog box (Format menu)	Text and data retain the same point size they had before Shrink to Fit was selected.
Defined labels	Lost in the conversion.
English language references in formulas	English language references are converted to A1 reference notations. However, names of named cells and ranges are preserved.
Calculated fields, calculated items, and formatting based on structure	These PivotTable features are preserved until the user makes changes to or refreshes the PivotTable data. Then they are lost.
PivotTable properties sheet	All new properties are lost. These include: Page field placement across column or down rows, Alternate strings for NA and error cell display, Server-based page fields, AutoSort and AutoShow on fields, Multiselect on page fields, Persistent grouping and sorting, Data fields displayed as numbers.
Preserved formatting	Formatting is saved, but structured behavior is lost as soon as the user makes changes to or refreshes the PivotTable data.
3-D bar shapes (cylinder, pyramid, and cone)	3-D shapes are converted to 3-D column charts.
Angled text on axis and data labels	The text is formatted straight (0 degrees).
Bubble chart format	Bubble charts are converted to type 1 XY scatter charts.
Data tables on charts	Lost in the conversion.
Gradient fills	Gradient fills are converted to the nearest color and pattern.
Office Art objects	Office Art objects are converted to the nearest available shape and tool.
Pie-of-pie and bar-of-pie chart types	These charts are converted to type 1 pie charts.

Part
VIII

Ch
49

continues

Table 49.6   Continued

Excel 97 Feature	Results in Excel 5.0/95 Format
Time series axis	Special scaling information is lost, and the axis is converted to a normal category axis.
Comments	Comments are converted to Cell Tips.
Hyperlink (Insert menu)	The HYPERLINK text and formatting is preserved, but the functionality is lost.
Multi-user workbooks	Sharing is disabled, and the change log is lost.
Revision marks and audit trail	Lost in the conversion; the change log is also lost.
Parameterized queries	Parameterized queries cannot be executed or edited.
Report templates	Lost in the conversion.
Shared queries (connections without a data source name, or DSN)	Files that contain connections without DSN are supported in Microsoft Excel 95 (with ODBC 2.0). In Microsoft Excel 5.0 (with ODBC 1.0), the user is prompted for connection information.
New Microsoft Excel objects, methods, and properties	Not all programming elements are 97 supported. For more information about compatibility, see Microsoft Office 97 Resource Kit and Microsoft Office Developer Web site.
ActiveX Controls (formerly OLE controls or OCX)	ActiveX Controls appear in the workbook but cannot be used.
User forms dialog controls	Lost in the conversion.
32,000 characters per cell	Characters beyond the 255th character are truncated.
65,536 rows per worksheet	Data in rows below row 16,384 is truncated.

Understanding Backward Compatibility Issues in PowerPoint

The look, or visual accuracy, of PowerPoint files is almost always preserved when saved to an earlier version. However, you may not be able to edit some objects that you otherwise could. Table 49.7 outlines the major issues for saving PowerPoint files to an earlier version's file format.

Table 49.7   PowerPoint 97 Features with Issues in PowerPoint 95 Format

PowerPoint 97 Feature	Results in PowerPoint 95 Format
Animated chart elements	Animated chart elements are displayed as static chart objects. PowerPoint 95 users must have Microsoft Graph to edit charts.
Custom shows	Slides appear in the presentation in the correct ordering, but Custom Show grouping information is lost.
Elevator effects	Elevator effects are converted to Wipe Up effects.
Native format movies and sounds	Movies and sounds are converted to Media Player and Sound Recorder objects.
Play options for CD tracking and movie looping	Play options are ignored.
Comments	Comments are converted to shapes with rich text format; cannot be turned on/off so hidden comments are displayed.
Hyperlinks that combine Play Sound with other action settings	Play Sound settings are lost.
Hyperlinks embedded within an object	The hyperlinks are lost.
Action settings embedded within an object.	The action settings are lost.
3-D effects	3-D effects are converted as pictures.
AutoShapes	If there is no matching shape, AutoShapes are converted to freeform shapes.
Composite shapes	Composite shapes are converted to separate shapes and lines, which are grouped together.
Connectors	Connectors are converted as freeform lines, and lose their automatic connecting behavior.
Curves	Curves are approximated with connected line segments.
Gradient fills	Semi-transparency is lost on gradient fills.
Joins and endcaps of lines	On AutoShapes, these become mitered joins and round endcaps. On freeform shapes, they become round joins and round endcaps.
Objects that are linked or embedded	Brightness, contrast, and color transformation settings are lost.

Part
VIII

Ch
49

continues

Table 49.7   Continued

PowerPoint 97 Feature	Results in PowerPoint 95 Format
Picture brightness, contrast, and color	These are rendered at current transformation PowerPoint 97 settings.
Picture fills	Picture fills are converted to picture objects.
Picture fills on shapes	The shape is converted as a picture object and is given a solid fill with the last applied foreground color.
Shadows, engraved	Engraved shadows take on embossed shadow effects.
Shadows, perspective	Perspective shadows are converted as shapes and grouped with the shape casting the shadow.
Shapes or arcs with attached text that are new in PowerPoint 97	These are converted to PowerPoint 95 freeform shapes or arcs and text boxes.
Text box margins block	Margins are averaged to center the text in the box.
Text effects	Text effects are converted as pictures.
Thick compound lines	Thick compound lines are converted as picture objects.
Charts	Users cannot edit charts unless they have Microsoft Graph.
Clip Gallery	The clip art is rendered as a picture object; double-clicking clip art does not launch ClipArt Gallery in PowerPoint 95.
PowerPoint macros	PowerPoint macros are not converted; there is no macro language in PowerPoint 95.
Unicode characters (2 bytes per character)	Unicode characters are mapped to corresponding ANSI. Foreign language characters are most likely to be affected.

Installing and Updating Windows 98

by Phil Callihan

In this chapter

Preparing to Install Windows 98

Windows 98's performance will hinge on the hardware of your computer. The minimum system requirements call for a 486DX processor with at least 4MB of RAM. If you choose to install Windows 98 on a system with these specifications, the following recommendations will speed up installation:

- Run setup from within Windows 95 or Windows 3.x. Try to avoid running the setup from MS-DOS.
- Remove any disk compression from your hard drive.
- If you are installing from floppy disks, extract the floppy disks to your hard drive and run setup from the hard drive rather than from the floppy disks.
- If during setup you notice that the busy light is flashing on an empty floppy disk drive, insert a blank formatted disk into the drive.

If you have problems during setup, increase the size of your permanent swap file.

No matter what system you are installing Windows 98 on, you should follow these steps as well:

1. Perform a thorough scan of your system for viruses. Ensure that the virus detection software that you use has the most current update of virus definitions available.
2. Disable any screensavers that your system may have configured.
3. Disable any antivirus detection software before proceeding with the Windows 98 installation.
4. Run ScanDisk and fix any problems that you may have on your hard drive.

You should also check to ensure that any components installed on your system are on the Windows 98 Hardware Compatibility List (HCL). The HCL contains components that have been tested to work with Window 98. The most current version of the HCL can be found on the Microsoft Web Site (**http://www.microsoft.com**).

While installation on a 386 is possible, performance will be poor. A computer running Windows 98 with this type of hardware configuration should only be considered for the most basic of operations, such as simple word processing or sending and receiving electronic mail. For users who plan on using their computer to run more than one application at a time or work with large documents, a machine with at least the following specifications is highly recommended:

- A Pentium computer
- At least 16MB of RAM
- At least 100MB of free disk space
- A doublespeed CD-ROM drive
- SVGA Video capability
- A mouse pointing device

NOTE Before beginning, check the Windows 98 installation CD for the setup.txt file. This file will have any last-minute setup information and warnings about possible problems that you may encounter during setup with specific pieces of hardware. ◾

Upgrading from Windows 3.x

Windows 3.x users will need to take the following additional steps before upgrading:

1. Backup your config.sys and autoexec.bat files.
2. Check to see if any of your system components (sound cards and so on) are not on the Windows 98 HCL.
3. Familiarize yourself with the new Windows 98 interface in Chapter 1, "What's New in Windows 98."

To begin installation, use File Manager to run setup.exe from the Windows 98 CD-ROM. The menu screens that display during installation will appear slightly different than when installing from Windows 95; most notably, the older full screen version of ScanDisk will run to check your hard drive for errors. Your program groups will be migrated to the Programs menu of Windows 98. You may need to manually edit your config.sys and autoexec.bat files to properly configure legacy devices that are not directly supported under Windows 98.

Upgrading from Windows 95

Upgrading from Windows 95 is fairly straightforward. Insert the Windows 98 CD-ROM into your computer and autorun will begin installation, or in Explorer, run setup.exe. All program groups will be migrated during the installation process. There have been three releases of Windows 98. Windows 98 will upgrade all three releases.

There are three releases of Windows 95:

- Windows 95 Build 950
- Windows 95 Build 950A
- Windows 95 Build 950B

The original release Build 950 is identical to product that has been sold on store shelves since August of 1995. While there have been service releases, no new full installations have been made available to the public. There have been two OEM releases (950A and 950B) that have been made available for preinstallation on new personal computers by original equipment manufacturers (OEMs). You can check your version by clicking on the My Computer icon with your left mouse button and selecting Properties, as shown in Figure A.1.

Figure A.1

The System Properties dialog box displays details of your system.

Checking the Version Number in Windows 95

These OEM releases include many bug fixes and patches to the original Windows 95. Some of these fixes have been made available to previous owners of Windows 95 through the Microsoft web site (**http://www.microsoft.com/windows95/info/updates.htm**) while others have only been available preinstalled on new computers. These releases also include various interface modifications in addition to bug fixes. All of these fixes are included in Windows 98. All your previous program groups will be migrated during the installation process, and most devices that have been supported under Windows 95 are also supported in Windows 98.

Installing Windows 98 on a Newly Formatted Hard Drive

If you want (or need) to install Windows 98 on a freshly formatted hard drive, follow these steps:

1. Create a new system disk by formatting a new disk and running sys.com from the command line, or using the Explorer and checking the Copy System Files check box.

2. Copy the Fixed Disk Utility (Fdisk.exe) and format.com and sys.com files over to the system disk.

3. Copy your config.sys and autoxec.bat utilities to your system disk and any files referenced in these files to your CD-ROM drive.

4. Boot your machine with the floppy disk. Make sure that you can access your CD-ROM Drive.

CAUTION

fdisk.exe will erase all the information on your hard drive. Make sure you have backed up any important data from your hard drive before using this utility.

1. Run fdisk.exe; remove your partition from your hard drive and re-create a new one.

2. Format your hard drive using format.com from the floppy disk and make it bootable by running sys.com on it.

3. Copy your config.sys files, autoexec. files, and your CD-ROM support files to your hard drive.

4. Remove the floppy disk and reboot your machine from your hard drive. Change the directories to your CD Drive. Insert the Windows 98 CD and run setup.exe to continue with the installation. If you are installing onto a newly formatted hard drive, you also need to choose an installation option during Windows 98 Setup.

Typical, Portable, Compact, or Custom

Windows 98 Setup will allow you to choose among these setup options only during an installation on a new system. During upgrades it will automatically upgrade previous versions of any Windows components that it finds.

> *Typical.* Components that most users will find useful (186MB).
>
> *Portable.* Option that is intended for laptop users (175MB).
>
> *Compact.* No extra components (159MB).
>
> *Custom.* Allows you to pick and choose among components (up to 285MB).

Common Installation Steps

The following steps are common to the installation procedure whether you are upgrading or installing to an empty hard drive. The Windows 98 installation process is driven by an easy-to-use installation Wizard. The Wizard will guide you through the necessary steps for a successful upgrade.

To begin the installation of Windows 98 from a CD, follow these steps:

1. Run setup.exe from the Windows 98 CD-ROM.

2. The Windows 98 Installation Wizard (see Figure A.2) appears and will guide you through the process of installing Windows 98. Click Continue to proceed.

3. The Microsoft licensing agreement appears (see Figure A.3). After reading through the licensing agreement, select the radio button next to I Accept the Agreement and click Next to continue.

4. The Setup Wizard checks to ensure that you have enough hard drive space to complete the installation. If you don't have enough disk space, the setup wizard will let you know how much disk space you need to free up in order to continue with the installation (see Figure A.4).

App
A

Figure A.2

The Windows 98
Installation Wizard
screen.

Shows you the status
of the installation
process

Message window

Time left in the
installation
process

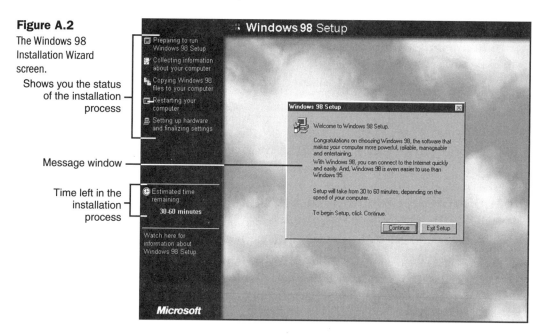

Figure A.3

The Microsoft License
Agreement screen.

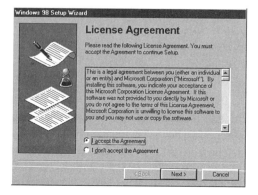

Figure A.4

The Not Enough Disk
Space notification
screen.

App
A

5. The Setup Wizard will ask if you want to save your old systems files (see Figure A.5). The system files are saved in compressed format that will take up approximately 50MB of disk space. You must choose Yes at this option if you want to uninstall Windows 98 in the future. These local files must be saved to a local hard drive (network drives and floppy drives won't work). When choosing to save system files, you will be prompted to select a disk drive where the files will be saved. At this point you will also need to choose your country for your Internet Channels to be configured correctly.

N O T E   You will not be given the option to save your system files if you are upgrading over an earlier beta version of Windows 98, are installing to a new directory, or are running a version of MS-DOS earlier than 5.0. ■

CAUTION

Whenever a new operating system is released, there are always some programs that will need to be updated in order to work properly. No matter how sure you are about not wanting to go back to Windows 95 or Windows 3.x, there may be a reason that you need to. You always have the option to remove the old system files after you're confident with Windows 98. Uninstalling Windows 98 is covered later on in this chapter.

Figure A.5
This is the point of no return if you choose to not save the previous version of your system files.

6. The Windows 98 Setup Wizard will now begin to automatically detect the hardware that is installed in your computer.

7. You'll next be prompted to create a Windows 98 startup disk (see Figure A.6). You can select Cancel to skip creating a backup disk, but this is not recommended. You can select "Next" and get the chance to skip Startup Disk creation.

8. Once it has collected the necessary information, the Setup Wizard will give you one last chance to change your mind. You can click Back to change your selections or Next to begin copying files to your hard drive (see Figure A.7).

As the file copy progresses, the installation Wizard will keep you updated on how long setup will take to finish.

Your system will now go through a cycle of hardware detection. Your computer will reboot a number of times until it has detected all legacy and plug-and-play components.

After the Setup Wizard has finished detecting the hardware on your computer, Windows 98 will boot and display the Welcome screen (see Figure A.8).

Figure A.6

The Emergency Startup Disk screen.

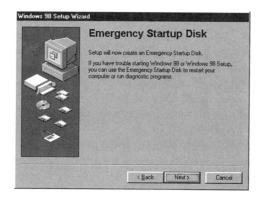

Figure A.7

This is your last chance to change your options before proceeding with the File Copy portion of the Windows 98 installation.

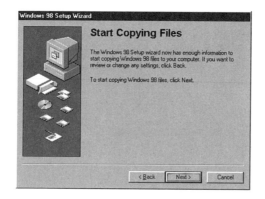

Figure A.8

After setup is complete, Windows 98 will boot and display the Welcome screen.

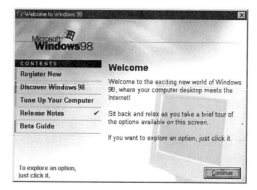

The Welcome screen will give you the opportunity to register Windows 98 with Microsoft, provide a tour of new features, help you configure the system scheduler to automatically fine-tune your Windows 98 system, and let you read the release notes.

> **CAUTION**
>
> The first time you run the system tuner after installation you will have the option of upgrading your hard disk to FAT32 format. FAT32 optimizes the way that Windows 98 stores data on your hard drive. If you choose to upgrade to FAT32, only Windows 98 and Windows NT 5.0 will be able to read the data on your hard drive.

Advanced Installation Techniques

Windows 98 includes some installation options that most home users will be able to ignore.

Using Custom Setup Mode

Custom setup mode allows you to pre-select options, making installation easier when rolling out Windows 98 to a large number of machines. This feature is most beneficial to companies that want to roll out Windows 98 to a large number of machines with a minimum of administrative intervention. By limiting choices, network administrators can automate installation by creating custom setup scripts. To create a custom setup, follow these steps:

1. Install Windows 98 on a test computer with the configuration you want to replicate.
2. Install the Batch Setup from the Windows 98 Resource Kit.
3. Run Microsoft Batch 98 from the Start menu.
4. Use the Batch Program to create an .inf file that will install Windows 98 with options you have selected (see Figure A.9).

Figure A.9
The Windows 98 Batch setup utility.

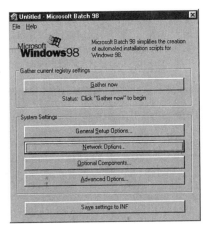

> **CAUTION**
>
> Microsoft Batch '98 is very involved. Refer to the Windows 98 Resource Kit for specific details regarding custom setup options.

Installing Windows 98 Network Features

Users who will be using Windows 98 in a network environment can install Windows 98 Network components by selecting Start/Settings/Control Panel/Network as shown in Figure A.10.

> **N O T E**   You'll also be prompted to install network features if Windows 98 detects a network
> adapter during setup. ▪

Figure A.10

The Network setup
screen in Control Panel.

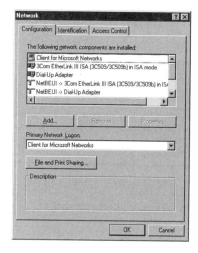

Here you can select options that will allow you to connect to Windows NT servers and NetWare servers. You can also configure network protocols like TCP/IP and IPX.

The specific options you will need to configure will vary depending on your network. Contact your Network Administrator for options particular to your corporate network.

Troubleshooting Windows 98 Installation

If you encounter problems during the installation process, you can take the following steps:

1. The main area you may experience trouble with is unsupported hardware. The best solution is to remove any problematic system devices in order to complete Windows 98 installation. After installation, reinstall components one by one, using the "Add New Hardware" icon in Control Panel.

2. Check the bootlog.txt, detlog.txt, and setuplog.txt files for clues to deciphering system problems. These files are created by Windows 98 during boot, setup, and device detection. By checking the final entry in this files, you can see what Windows 98 was doing if the system crashed during any of these processes.

N O T E You can also use Dr. Watson to diagnose system faults. Dr. Watson is a diagnostic tool that takes a snapshot of your system whenever a system fault occurs. Dr. Watson can sometimes identify problems and make recommendations to help you fix them.

Dr. Watson is not loaded by default. To launch Dr. Watson automatically, create a shortcut in your Startup group to \Windows\DrWatson.exe. ■

3. Try posting any installation problems to a Windows 98 newsgroup. Microsoft provides a NNTP news server (**msnews.microsoft.com**) for users to interact with each other. Netscape and Internet Explorer can easily be configured to attach to multiple news servers (consult your browser documentation). In addition, Microsoft employees monitor the newsgroups and provide limited feedback on problems. Downsides to using newsgroups are that there are usually many messages to wade through and you are not guaranteed of getting a timely (or any) response.

4. Consult the Knowledge Base on the Microsoft Web Site (**http://www.microsoft.com**).

5. If you have a Microsoft TechNet subscription, consult the knowledge base.

 T I P TechNet is a service available from Microsoft where every month you will be shipped a number of CDs containing information about a wide range of Microsoft products. A CD of updated drivers, a searchable knowledge base, and a number of white papers are included. TechNet subscriptions are expensive for an individual user, but any company that has Microsoft software deployed should consider purchasing a subscription. The subscription is especially important to companies who may not have web access to obtain the free support of Web pages or newsgroups.

6. Call Microsoft support. A card is included with the final product giving you an 800 number to call for support.

Using Safe Recovery

Use the safe recovery option if your initial installation of Windows 98 fails (as shown in Figure A.11). If regular installation fails, turn your computer off and on again. Run setup and Windows 98 will then use Safe Recovery to pass the point where the original installation failed.

Figure A.11
The Safe Recovery option screen.

Safe Recovery instructs the Setup Wizard to continue copying files from the point of failure rather than beginning again from the beginning. If you don't select Safe Recovery, your system may get caught in a loop, continuously failing at the same point during the installation over and over again.

 TIP If Windows setup fails repeatedly, even with the Safe Recovery option selected, you will need to begin removing hardware such as game cards, sound cards, and so on. After identifying the offending piece of equipment, complete the Windows 98 installation and then try to install the hardware.

Using Safe Detection

After the initial installation of the operating system, Windows 98 will go about detecting Plug and Play (PnP) devices. Windows 98 will prompt you for the installation drivers that have not been installed yet. During Safe Detection you will have the option of using a driver that is included with Windows or a third-party driver from a disk.

Performance Bottlenecks

It is important to recognize bottlenecks that may be hampering your system from running Windows 98 well. A definite consideration after installation is what component(s) you may want to upgrade to give you better performance. A lack of disk space is a major bottleneck for systems running either Windows 95 or Windows 98. Windows 9x uses disk space (swapfile) to simulate physical memory or RAM. By using the System Monitor (see Figure A.12) utility, you can see how this swapfile increases in size as you open additional programs. If your swapfile increases past the point of available contiguous disk space, you will get an out-of-memory error.

Figure A.12
The Windows 98 System Monitor.

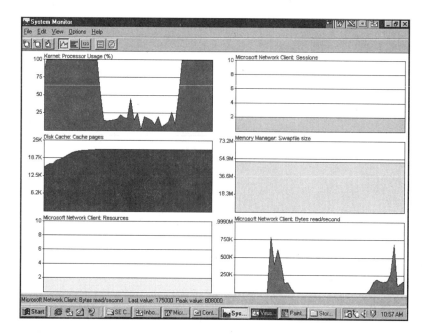

After disk space, the next major bottleneck is physical memory (RAM). In recent years, RAM prices have fallen steeply, and it is now relatively economical to upgrade. Other options to consider are 2D/3D video cards and faster CD-ROM drives.

If possible, only buy hardware devices and software with the Designed for Windows 98 emblem. This emblem signifies that this product is certified to work optimally with Windows 98. Be wary of devices that are marked as "works with" Windows 98. Sometimes these products use older real-mode drivers that don't perform as well as true native Windows 98 drivers.

Removing Windows 98

If you selected the "Save Old System Files" option during installation, you can remove Windows 98 by following these steps:

1. Click the Start button, select settings, and click the Control Panel icon.
2. Click Add/Remove Programs.
3. Select the Install/Uninstall tab, select Windows 98, and then click Remove. Windows 98 will uninstall itself, you will be prompted to reboot your machine, and your previous version of Windows or DOS will have been restored to your computer.

 If you have trouble uninstalling Windows 98 from the control panel, you can use your Windows 98 startup disk to perform the removal. Boot your computer using the startup disk, and run UNINSTALL from the command line.

The Windows Update Manager

In the past, tracking down system patches and updated drivers was difficult. Microsoft has streamlined the process in Windows 98 by including the Windows Update Manager directly on the Start menu. If you have Internet access, you will be able to update your installation of Windows 98 by using the Update Manager as shown in Figure A.13.

Figure A.13
The Windows 98
Update Manager.

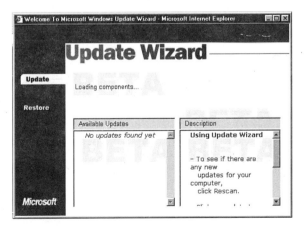

From the Start button, select Windows Update. After connecting to the Windows Update site, select Update Wizard. The Update Wizard will scan your Windows 98 installation and display any updates that are available from Microsoft (refer to Figure A.13). ●

Index